D1064779

Corinne Mandel

SIXTUS V AND THE LATERAN PALACE

ISTITUTO POLIGRAFICO E ZECCA DELLO STATO
LIBRERIA DELLO STATO

COMITATO NAZIONALE PER LE CELEBRAZIONI DEL IV CENTENARIO DEL PONTIFICATO DI SISTO V (1585–90)

Presidente: MINISTRO PER I BENI CULTURALI E AMBIENTALI
Presidente della Giunta esecutiva: PAOLO BREZZI
Coordinatore: MARCELLO FAGIOLO
Segretario Tesoriere: SANDRO BENEDETTI

Sede: Ministero per i Beni Culturali e Ambientali,
    Ufficio Centrale per i Beni Librari e gli Istituti Culturali
Direttore Generale: FRANCESCO SICILIA

SEGRETERIA GENERALE

Centro di Studi sulla cultura e l'immagine di Roma,
c/o Accademia Nazionale dei Lincei, via della Lungara 10, 00165 Roma

Segretario Scientifico: MARIA LUISA MADONNA
Redazione: MARIO BEVILACQUA
Segreteria: ANNA CAPUZZI

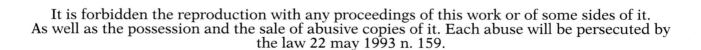

It is forbidden the reproduction with any proceedings of this work or of some sides of it.
As well as the possession and the sale of abusive copies of it. Each abuse will be persecuted by
the law 22 may 1993 n. 159.

© 1994 – ISTITUTO POLIGRAFICO E ZECCA DELLO STATO, ROMA

For My Parents

"Do you not know, Asclepius, that Egypt is an image of heaven, or to speak more exactly, in Egypt all the operations of the powers that rule and work in heaven have been transferred to earth below?"

Hermes Trismegistos, Asclepius, III, 24b.

CONTENTS

3

INTRODUCTION

INTRODUZIONE

As an art patron, Sixtus V has always been more talked about than really known or understood. Even after the important studies of L. von Pastor and J.A.F. Orbaan (among others), something was missing in the picture of his pontificate, namely a balance between the greatness of his intentions and the poverty of the results. We know he was an extraordinarily ambitious pope. In the short five years spent at the head of the Roman Church, he restored the economic stability of the papal states and strengthened the Catholic cause internationally. He changed the face of Rome by permanently altering its plan; completed St. Peter's; and built and decorated numerous churches, chapels and monuments of various importance and size including the imposing Lateran Palace, the chapel in S. Maria Maggiore that takes his name, as well as the Moses Fountain and the Scala Santa. But the odd thing was that so much ambition did not translate into a style of comparable breadth. This has usually been explained as a lack of tone: Sixtus was not Julius II or Leo X, he remained the simple, austere and somehow anti-intellectual Franciscan friar whose projects had limited cultural latitude. It has been stressed that he cared little about antiquities; his destruction of the Septizonium Severi and the Patriarchium Lateranense – the latter replaced by him with a mediocre architecture – is the example commonly given. Comparing the achievements of the two popes named Sixtus, Orbaan stated:

"[Sixtus IV] will always be noted as the founder of the Capitoline Museum. The reign of Sixtus V is marred by the razing of the Septizonium".[1]

The "Sixtine style" has been looked upon as unworthy in architecture as well as in painting: Domenico Fontana's buildings are uninspired, and the fresco decorations produced by the crowd of artists working mostly under Giovanni Guerra and Cesare Nebbia do not deserve any greater praise. The age of Sixtus does not fit into either the Renaissance or the Baroque, although it partakes of both. When histories of Baroque art start with his name, it is only because

Come mecenate delle arti, Sisto V è sempre stato più discusso che veramente conosciuto o capito; persino dopo importanti studi come quelli di Pastor e Orbaan, mancava qualcosa nella ricostruzione del suo pontificato, e cioè un equilibrio tra la grandiosità delle intenzioni e la povertà dei risultati. Sappiamo che fu un pontefice estremamente ambizioso: nei soli cinque anni del suo regno restaurò la stabilità economica dello Stato della Chiesa e rafforzò la causa cattolica nell'intera Europa; cambiò il volto di Roma modificandone stabilmente l'assetto urbanistico; completò la basilica di S. Pietro; costruì e decorò numerose chiese, cappelle e monumenti di varia importanza, compresi l'imponente Palazzo Lateranense, la Cappella in S. Maria Maggiore che da lui prese il nome, la Fontana del Mosè e la Scala Santa. Ma resta il fatto peculiare che tanta ambizione non si traduce in uno stile di comparabile ampiezza. Ciò è stato generalmente spiegato come una mancanza di 'tono': Sisto V non era Giulio II o Leone X, rimase il semplice, austero e in qualche modo anti-intellettuale frate francescano con progetti di ampiezza culturale limitata. E' stato sottolineato come egli si interessasse poco dei monumenti dell'antichità, decretando anzi la distruzione del Septizodium Severi e del Patriarchium Lateranense, quest'ultimo rimpiazzato con una mediocre architettura. Confrontando le realizzazioni dei due pontefici chiamati Sisto, Orbaan scrive: "[Sisto IV] verrà sempre ricordato come il fondatore dei Musei Capitolini. Il regno di Sisto V è sfigurato dalla distruzione del Settizodio"[1].

Lo "stile sistino" è stato disprezzato come indegno sia in architettura che in pittura: gli edifici di Domenico Fontana sarebbero banali, e le decorazioni pittoriche prodotte dalla folla di artisti che per lo più lavorarono sotto Giovanni Guerra e Cesare Nebbia non meritano molto maggiore interesse. L'età di Sisto V non rientra né nel Rinascimento né nel Barocco, pur partecipando dello spirito di entrambi: quando le storie dell'arte barocca cominciano dall'età di Sisto V, è perché nel suo pontificato assistiamo ad un massiccio incremento nell'attività artistica, la cui quan-

---

[1] Sixtine Rome, *p. 236*

[1] *Sixtine Rome*, p. 236.

with his reign we witness a massive increase in artistic activity whose quantity cannot be ignored, but whose quality remains crude and uninfluential.

In the last few years studies by Hans Ost (1978), Alexandra Herz (1981), René Schiffmann and Christopher Witcombe (1985), Helge Gamrath and Steven Ostrow (1987) have added a new dimension to the picture. These works – diverse in scope and covering different areas of artistic patronage – have changed the direction of the research. They demonstrate that everything Sixtus did in the domain of the arts was aimed to establish a new leading role for the See of Rome. They make clear that he is not to be seen as a Renaissance pope: his 'ambition' was the expression of an overpowering sense of his role as head of the Church in a new aggressive phase, the first example of a triumphant Catholicism. With the resumption of a systematic, extensive artistic patronage not seen since the times of the Renaissance, he was the first pope to translate the principles of Trent into the domain of the arts: his monuments express lucid doctrinal statements on all the controversial points of his age. Most important, it appears that Sixtus planned intelligently, and whatever he promoted embodied the doctrine in a sophisticated way. The new focus provided by these works allowed a better understanding of the art of Sixtus, connecting it more strictly with ideology and dispelling false or equivocal assumptions. Sixtine Rome (as the Milan of Carlo Borromeo before it) was found to express all the nuances of the spirit of Trent - its sense of pride and triumph as well as its reconquered faith in the dogma. The doctrinal and intellectual fervor of Sixtus and his collaborators gave a cultural dimension to what was once believed to be superficial and dry propaganda. The result of this new research is that late sixteenth century religious art in Rome has come into its own as an independent area of interest.

Corinne Mandel has now produced a study (which is the dissertation she defended at the University of Toronto) in keeping with those mentioned above and one which will occupy a place of distinction among them. She has selected the most important and least studied of the Sixtine monuments, the Lateran Palace, and gives us not only a thorough reading of its decoration including all the floors and all the rooms, the main subjects and the inscriptions (not a small task considering the size of the monument), but also an interpretation that provides us with a better understanding of the period as

tità non può essere ignorata, benché la qualità rimanga grezza e senza conseguenze.

Negli ultimi anni gli studi di Hans Ost (1978), Alexandra Herz (1981), René Schiffmann (1985) e Christopher Witcombe (1985), Helge Gamrath e Steven Ostrow (1987) hanno aggiunto una nuova dimensione a questo panorama; tali lavori - differenti nei fini e interessati ad aree diverse del mecenatismo artistico - hanno fatto mutare la direzione delle ricerche, dimostrando che qualunque cosa Sisto facesse nel campo delle arti era diretto a stabilire un nuovo ruolo protagonistico per la Chiesa di Roma, e chiarendo che egli non va visto come un pontefice rinascimentale: la sua "ambizione" era il segno di una potente percezione del proprio ruolo di capo della Chiesa in una nuova fase aggressiva, primo esempio di cattolicesimo trionfante. Con la ripresa di un mecenatismo artistico sistematico ed ampio, mai più visto dai tempi del pieno Rinascimento, fu il primo pontefice a tradurre i princìpi di Trento nel campo delle arti: i suoi monumenti esprimono lucide affermazioni dottrinali su tutti i punti controversi dell'epoca. Ancor più importante, sembra che Sisto fosse un intelligente pianificatore, e qualunque cosa promuovesse aveva sofisticate motivazioni dottrinarie. Il nuovo centro di attenzione fornito da queste opere ha consentito una migliore comprensione dell'arte sistina, ponendola in più stretta relazione con l'ideologia e dissipando prese di posizione false o equivoche. La Roma sistina (come già la Milano di Carlo Borromeo) esprime tutte le sfaccettature dello spirito di Trento, il suo senso di orgoglio e trionfo e di riconquistata fede nel dogma. Il fervore dottrinale e intellettuale di Sisto V e dei suoi collaboratori dà una dimensione culturale a ciò che un tempo si riteneva superficiale e vuota propaganda. Il risultato di questa nuova ricerca è che l'arte religiosa romana della fine del Cinquecento diviene di per se stessa un'area indipendente di interesse.

Corinne Mandel non ha prodotto uno studio (che è la dissertazione da lei discussa all'Università di Toronto) in sintonia con quelli sopra citati, occupando tra di essi un posto preminente; ha selezionato il più importante e meno studiato tra i monumenti sistini, il Palazzo Lateranense, dandone non solamente una lettura completa della decorazione di ogni ambiente, con i principali soggetti e iscrizioni (e non è poco se si considerano le dimensioni dell'edificio), ma anche un'interpretazione che consente una migliore comprensione dell'intero periodo storico. Corinne Mandel è stata capace di allargare la gamma di temi dottrinali che con-

a whole. Mandel has been able to broaden the spectrum of the doctrinal issues underlying the artistic production of Sixtus by starting with those decorative elements tied specifically to the personality of the pope and to his enterprises. These she calls the Good Works of Sixtus: all the deeds which made Sixtus a prominent pope, political as well as economic, ideological as well as artistic. These deeds, as we see them illustrated in every part of the Lateran decoration and most of all in the imprese of Sixtus, do not reflect mere personal ambition in Mandel's view. Rather they depict how to live by the Catholic doctrine of salvation through faith and works, a prominent point of dogma used to counteract the Protestant reliance on faith alone. These Good Works were especially relevant, Mandel shows, since they were tied to the responsibility of the chair of Peter and they were intended to discredit Protestant attacks on the merits of the ecclesiastical hierarchy, past and present. The Good Works also reflected the conviction that such actions were to be seen as a ring in a chain preordained by God and prefigured in the history of Christians, Jews, and pagans alike. In Mandel's novel way of reading tke Lateran frescoes, Sixtus' works were prefigured in the deeds of Augustus and Moses, Elijah and Francis. Thus, just as the doctrine of the two swords gave Sixtus both secular and spiritual supremacy, the symbolism connected to him was sacerdotal as well as imperial. Mandel demonstrates that Christian and Franciscan symbols in the Lateran decoration overlay the pagan symbols just as the cross crowns the pagan obelisks that the pope erected throughout the city. She also demonstrates that through a number of references to the decoration of the lost Patriarchium, Sixtus saw his Lateran Palace as a restoration of the original monument, again one step in an endless series of events through which the Church fulfills her role in history.

Sixtus' appearance with the symbols of Jupiter and Hercules conformed with the thinking of the time. We know from theology that reading history as a kind of prefiguration was still dominant in the sixteenth century Church, and that pagan gods were thought to have had real powers rightly usurped by Christ and the Christian Saints.[2] Nevertheless it is a revelation to

notano la produzione artistica sistina cominciando da quegli elementi legati specificamente alla personalità del pontefice e dei suoi collaboratori, e cioè le *Opere Buone* di Sisto V: tutte le realizzazioni che hanno fatto di Sisto V un pontefice di grande rilevanza, da un punto di vista politico ed economico, ideologico ed artistico. Queste realizzazioni, come le vediamo raffigurate in ogni parte della decorazione lateranense e soprattutto nelle *imprese* di Sisto, non riflettono, secondo l'opinione della Mandel, una mera ambizione personale, ma piuttosto una raffigurazione della vita secondo la dottrina cattolica della salvazione attraverso la fede e le opere, punto preminente del dogma utilizzato nella confutazione della fiducia protestante nella sola fede. Tali *Opere Buone* erano particolarmente rilevanti in quanto, come mostra la Mandel, erano legate alla responsabilità della Cattedra di Pietro e atte a gettare discredito sugli attacchi protestanti ai meriti della gerarchia ecclesiastica, passata e presente. Le *Opere Buone* riflettevano anche la convinzione che tali azioni andavano interpretate come l'anello di una catena prestabilita da Dio e prefigurata nella storia dei cristiani, dei giudei e anche dei pagani. Secondo questa nuova lettura degli affreschi del Laterano l'opera di Sisto sarebbe prefigurata dalle imprese di Augusto e Mosè, Elia e Francesco; in tal modo, così come la dottrina delle due spade diede a Sisto V la supremazia secolare e spirituale, il simbolismo a lui connesso era sia sacerdotale che imperiale. Corinne Mandel dimostra che simboli cristiani e francescani nella decorazione lateranense ricoprono i simboli pagani proprio come la croce che corona gli obelischi eretti dal pontefice nella città; dimostra inoltre che, attraverso i molteplici riferimenti alla decorazione del Patriarchio, Sisto V intendeva il suo Palazzo Lateranense come un restauro del monumento originario, un ulteriore passo avanti nell'infinita serie di eventi attraverso cui la Chiesa svolge il proprio ruolo nella storia.

La raffigurazione di Sisto V con i simboli di Giove e di Ercole si accorda con la mentalità dell'epoca: sappiamo che leggere la storia come una sorta di prefigurazione era un approccio ancora dominante nella teologia cattolica del XVI secolo, e che gli dei pagani venivano considerati come detentori di veri poteri poi giustamente usurpati da Cristo e dai santi cristiani[2]. Purtuttavia è una rive-

---

[2] *See for example G.A. Gilio,* Trattato de la emulazione che il demonio ha fatto a Dio, *Venice 1563, ff. 10v-11r and A. Possevino,* Apparato all'Historia di tutte le nazioni, *Venice 1598, p. 31 ff.*

---

[2] Vedi ad esempio G. A. Gilio, *Trattato de la emulatione che il demonio ha fatto a Dio*, Venezia 1563, ff. 10v-11r, e A. Possevino, *Apparato all'Historia di tutte le nazioni*, Venezia 1598, p. 31 e ss.

see the ideas debated by theologians surface in the artistic sphere: that Sixtus' Good Works are the fulfillment of events prefigured in distant history, and that the pope himself is prefigured in the secular and sacred authorities of the past. Moving with remarkable ease between historical sources from the classical period, Old and New Testaments and Christian history to Renaissance treatises of iconology, Corinne Mandel effectively reveals the many layers of meaning of the Lateran. She suggests, in fact, that Sixtine iconographers might even have used symbols in a radically free way, open to various levels of interpretation according to the understanding of the beholder. She convincingly shows that in the Sixtine imprese we have a unique example of a programme which is not ambivalent in its symbolism, like the manneristic decoration of Caprarola, but is a clear demonstration of the theological thinking which brought to the surface the Catholic version of the doctrine of predestination by uncovering the design of God in history. This degree of sophistication amply justifies her hypothesis that the programme was written by Pompeo Ugonio with the collaboration of Sixtus himself.

The other discovery made by Mandel is that the historical pattern evoked by the authors of the programme firmly established Sixtus' age as a new Golden Age. She is able to demonstrate that the Golden Age of Sixtus was a topos widely treated in the encomiastic literature of the period – something hitherto totally overlooked – and that it was in fact the leit-motif of his pontificate. Whether with their idea of the Golden Age Sixtus and his contemporaries might have envisaged the coming of Christ as foreseen in the millenarian tradition – Mandel seems to suggest this – is something that remains to be demonstrated. It seems to me that this Golden Age is different from that plenitude of grace to be brought only by Christ, and should be seen rather as the fulfillment of the Church Militant. Nonetheless the discovery of the motive is a very important addition to Sixtine iconography.

Having found the key to these crucial elements in the imprese, Mandel then traces this same chain of symbolism in other selected parts of the decoration of the Lateran Palace. She confirms the prominence of the topoi (the Good Works of Sixtus and the Golden Age) which, mixed with other subjects, appear in seven out of the sixteen decorated rooms of the palace. Then, moving from the particular to the general, she

lazione osservare come idee dibattute da teologi affiorino nella sfera artistica: le *Opere Buone* di Sisto V rappresentano il raggiungimento di eventi prefigurati nella storia antica, il pontefice stesso è prefigurato nelle autorità secolari e sacre del passato. Muovendosi con grande facilità tra fonti storiche classiche, antico e nuovo Testamento e storia cristiana fino ai trattati rinascimentali di iconologia, Corinne Mandel effettivamente rivela i molti livelli di significato del Laterano, suggerendo come gli iconografi sistini possano addirittura aver usato simboli in modo estremamente libero, aperto a vari livelli di interpretazione e a seconda delle possibilità di decodificazione dell'osservatore. L'autrice dimostra come nelle imprese sistine si abbia un esempio unico di programma che non è ambivalente nel suo simbolismo (come ad esempio la decorazione manierista di Caprarola), bensì una chiara dimostrazione del pensiero teologico che ha portato in superficie la versione cattolica della dottrina della predestinazione interpretando il disegno divino nella storia. Questo livello di raffinatezza giustifica ampiamente la sua ipotesi che il programma venisse redatto da Pompeo Ugonio con l'aiuto dello stesso Sisto V.

L'altra scoperta di Corinne Mandel è che il tema storico rievocato dagli estensori del programma caratterizza fermamente l'età di Sisto come nuova *Età dell'oro*; l'autrice può dimostrare che l'*Età dell'oro* di Sisto V era un topos ampiamente trattato nella letteratura encomiastica del periodo (e ciò era passato fino ad oggi completamente inosservato), costituendo un vero e proprio leit-motiv del suo pontificato. Se con la loro idea dell'*Età dell'oro* Sisto e i suoi contemporanei volessero prefigurare la venuta di Cristo conformemente alla tradizione millenaristica (come Corinne Mandel tende a credere), è qualcosa che rimane da dimostrare. A mio avviso questa *Età dell'oro* è diversa da quella pienezza della Grazia che può essere portata solo da Cristo, e dovrebbe essere vista piuttosto come una realizzazione della Chiesa Militante; ma nonostante tutto la scoperta del tema resta una importante acquisizione per l'iconografia sistina.

Avendo trovato la chiave per questi elementi fondamentali delle imprese, Corinne Mandel rintraccia lo stesso concatenamento di simboli in altre parti specifiche della decorazione del Palazzo Lateranense, confermando l'importanza dei topoi (*Opere Buone* di Sisto V e *Età dell'oro*) che, insieme ad altri soggetti, ritornano in sette dei sedici ambienti decorati del palazzo. Quindi, muovendo dal particolare al generale, getta luce sul "piano"

throws light on Sixtus' "master plan". This was, simply stated, to rewrite history according to the new historiography of Baronius which had begun to appear during Sixtus pontificate. As a result of Mandel's investigation Sixtus appears as a transformer rather than as a destroyer, and as an innovator in his own way. In short, Mandel makes it clear that in its unsuspected complexity the Lateran decorative cycle is the expression of a coherent, unique cultural climate still only partially known today. The Lateran cycle, moreover, is not simply tied in doctrinal way to the Counter-Reformation; it is a large historical fresco where the Church - all powerful once again - dictates the rules, and where the consciousness of its mission is rendered with immediacy. In summary, Mandel's study marks an important step in establishing Sixtus' age as the most faithful expression of the new Church emerging from Trent, a diverse independent phase of art history to be seen and studied not simply as late Renaissance or pre-Baroque but according to its own internal logic.

Giuseppe Scavizzi

sistino: riscrivere la storia seguendo la nuova storiografia del Baronio che aveva visto la nascita proprio negli anni del pontificato sistino. Come risultato delle ricerche di Corinne Mandel Sisto V appare un trasformatore piuttosto che un distruttore, e, a suo modo, un innovatore; in breve, Corinne Mandel chiarisce come nella sua insospettata complessità il ciclo decorativo del Laterano sia l'espressione di un clima culturale coerente e unico, a tutt'oggi ancora solo parzialmente conosciuto. Il ciclo lateranense, inoltre, non è semplicemente legato in modo dottrinale alla Controriforma; è un grande affresco storico in cui la Chiesa, nuovamente nel pieno della propria potenza, detta le sue regole, e in cui la consapevolezza della propria missione viene resa con immediatezza. In conclusione, lo studio di Corinne Mandel segna una tappa importante nel caratterizzare l'età di Sisto V come l'espressione più fedele della nuova Chiesa posttridentina, una fase diversa e indipendente della storia dell'arte, da osservare e studiare non solamente come fenomeno tardorinascimentale o prebarocco, ma secondo una sua logica interna.

Giuseppe Scavizzi

LIST OF FIGURES

11

87. *Samuel erects the "Stone of Help,"* Sala di Samuele, *piano nobile*, Lateran Palace.
   Samuele erige la "pietra del soccorso". Palazzo Lateranense, Sala di Samuele.

88. *Samuel anoints Saul*, Sala di Samuele, *piano nobile*, Lateran Palace.
   Samuele unge Saul. Palazzo Lateranense, Sala di Samuele.

89. *Genii* support the *stemma* of Sixtus V, Sala di Samuele, *piano nobile*, Lateran Palace.
   Genii reggenti lo stemma di Sisto V. Palazzo Lateranense, Sala di Samuele.

90. *Religion*, Sala di Samuele, *piano nobile*, Lateran Palace.
   Religione. Palazzo Lateranense, Sala di Samuele.

91. *Charity*, Sala di Samuele, *piano nobile*, Lateran Palace.
   Carità. Palazzo Lateranense, Sala di Samuele.

92. *Faith*, Sala di Samuele, *piano nobile*, Lateran Palace.
   Fede. Palazzo Lateranense, Sala di Samuele.

93. *Hope*, Sala di Samuele, *piano nobile*, Lateran Palace.
   Speranza. Palazzo Lateranense, Sala di Samuele.

94. *Good Work*, Sala di Samuele, *piano nobile*, Lateran Palace.
   Opera buona. Palazzo Lateranense, Sala di Samuele.

95. *Belief*, Sala di Samuele, *piano nobile*, Lateran Palace.
   Credo. Palazzo Lateranense, Sala di Samuele.

96. *Gratitude*, Sala di Samuele, *piano nobile*, Lateran Palace.
   Gratitudine. Palazzo Lateranense, Sala di Samuele.

97. *Law of Grace*, Sala di Samuele, *piano nobile*, Lateran Palace.
   Legge della Grazia. Palazzo Lateranense, Sala di Samuele.

98. Schematic diagram of the west wall of the Salone di Costantino, *piano nobile*, Lateran Palace.
   Schema della parete occidentale del Salone di Costantino.

99. Schematic diagram of the east wall of the Salone di Costantino, *piano nobile*, Lateran Palace.
   Schema della parete orientale del Salone di Costantino.

100. Schematic diagram of the north wall of the Salone di Costantino, *piano nobile*, Lateran Palace.
   Schema della parete settentrionale del Salone di Costantino.

101. Schematic diagram of the south wall of the Salone di Costantino, *piano nobile*, Lateran Palace.
   Schema della parete meridionale del Salone di Costantino.

102. "Single obelisk" device and *Religion*, Salone di Costantino, *piano nobile*, Lateran Palace.
   Impresa con obelisco singolo e *Religione.* Palazzo Lateranense, Salone di Costantino.

103. *Devotion* and "single obelisk" device, Salone di Costantino, *piano nobile*, Lateran Palace.
   Devozione e impresa con obelisco singolo. Palazzo Lateranense, Salone di Costantino.

104. "Single obelisk" device and *Knowledge of the True God*, Salone di Costantino, *piano nobile*, Lateran Palace.
   Impresa con obelisco singolo e *Conoscenza del Vero Dio.* Palazzo Lateranense, Salone di Costantino.

105. Personification with pear branch and "single obelisk" device, Salone di Costantino, *piano nobile*, Lateran Palace.
   Personificazione con ramo di pere e impresa con obelisco singolo. Palazzo Lateranense, Salone di Costantino.

106. *Constantine's Vision of the Cross*, Salone di Costantino, *piano nobile*, Lateran Palace.
   La visione di Costantino della Croce. Palazzo Lateranense, Salone di Costantino.

107. *Baptism of Constantine*, Salone di Costantino, *piano nobile*, Lateran Palace.
   Battesimo di Costantino. Palazzo Lateranense, Salone di Costantino.

108. *Donation of Constantine*, Salone di Costantino, *piano nobile*, Lateran Palace.
   Donazione di Costantino. Palazzo Lateranense, Salone di Costantino.

109. *Constantine acts as strator for Pope Sylvester I*, Salone di Costantino, *piano nobile*, Lateran Palace.
   Costantino strator di papa Silvestro. Palazzo Lateranense, Salone di Costantino.

110. *Moses*, Salone di Costantino, *piano nobile*, Lateran Palace.
Mosè. Palazzo Lateranense, Salone di Costantino.

111. *Aaron*, Salone di Costantino, *piano nobile*, Lateran Palace.
Aronne. Palazzo Lateranense, Salone di Costantino.

112. *David*, Salone di Costantino, *piano nobile*, Lateran Palace.
David. Palazzo Lateranense, Salone di Costantino.

113. *Solomon*, Salone di Costantino, *piano nobile*, Lateran Palace.
Salomone. Palazzo Lateranense, Salone di Costantino.

114. *Seascape*, Salone di Costantino, *piano nobile*, Lateran Palace.
Paesaggio marino. Palazzo Lateranense, Salone di Costantino.

115. *Landscape*, Salone di Costantino, *piano nobile*, Lateran Palace.
Paesaggio. Palazzo Lateranense, Salone di Costantino.

116. *Landscape*, Salone di Costantino, *piano nobile*, Lateran Palace.
Paesaggio. Palazzo Lateranense, Salone di Costantino.

117. *Landscape*, Salone di Costantino, *piano nobile*, Lateran Palace.
Paesaggio. Palazzo Lateranense, Salone di Costantino.

118. *Martyrdom, Immortality*, and *anima senza corpo*, lunette, juncture of eastern and southern logge, *piano nobile*, Lateran Palace.
Martirio, Immortalità, anima senza corpo. Palazzo Lateranense, volta tra le logge est e sud del piano nobile.

119. "Single obelisk" device, *Annunciation to Zacharias*, and *Sacrifice of Manaases*, eastern loggia, *piano nobile*, Lateran Palace.
Impresa con obelisco singolo, *Annunciazione a Zaccaria, Sacrificio di Manaases*. Palazzo Lateranense, volta della loggia est del piano nobile.

120. "Single obelisk" device, *Marriage of the Virgin*, and *Moses and the Burning Bush*, eastern loggia, *piano nobile*, Lateran Palace.
Impresa con obelisco singolo, *Sposalizio della Vergine, Mosè e il roveto ardente*. Palazzo Lateranense, volta della loggia est del piano nobile.

121. "Single obelisk" device, *Christ among the Doctors*, and Old Testament type, eastern loggia, *piano nobile*, Lateran Palace.
Impresa con obelisco singolo, *Cristo fra i Dottori, personaggio veterotestamentario*. Palazzo Lateranense, volta della loggia est del piano nobile.

122. "Single obelisk" device, *John the Baptist preaching in Judea*, and Old Testament type, eastern loggia, *piano nobile*, Lateran Palace.
Impresa con obelisco singolo, *Giovanni Battista predica in Giudea, personaggio veterotestamentario*. Palazzo Lateranense, volta della loggia est del piano nobile.

123. "Single column" device, *Adoration of the Shepherds*, and Old Testament type, eastern loggia, *piano nobile*, Lateran Palace. Photo: the author.
Impresa con colonna singola, *Adorazione dei pastori, personaggio veterotestamentario*. Palazzo Lateranense, volta della loggia est del piano nobile.

124. "Single column" device, *Circumcision*, and Old Testament type, eastern loggia, *piano nobile*, Lateran Palace.
Impresa con colonna singola, *Circoncisione, personaggio veterotestamentario*. Palazzo Lateranense, volta della loggia est del piano nobile.

125. "Single column" device, *Adoration of the Magi*, and Old Testament type, eastern loggia, *piano nobile*, Lateran Palace.
Impresa con colonna singola, *Adorazione dei Magi, personaggio veterotestamentario*. Palazzo Lateranense, volta della loggia est del piano nobile.

126. "Single column" device, *Presentation in the Temple*, and Old Testament type, eastern loggia, *piano nobile*, Lateran Palace.
Impresa con colonna singola, *Presentazione al Tempio, personaggio veterotestamentario*. Palazzo Lateranense, volta della loggia est del piano nobile.

COLOUR PLATES

I. *The Pope gives the Benediction (probable portrait of Sixtus V)*, S. Giovanni in Laterano, Loggia delle Benedizioni.
Il pontefice benedicente (probabile ritratto di Sisto V). S. Giovanni in Laterano, Loggia delle Benedizioni.

IIa. *Papal Benediction before the Patriarchium Lateranense*, Biblioteca Vaticana, Galleria.
Benedizione papale dall'antico Patriarchium. Biblioteca Vaticana, Galleria.

IIb. View of the New Lateran coplex, Biblioteca Vaticana, Salone Sistino.
Veduta del nuovo complesso lateranense. Biblioteca Vaticana, Salone Sistino.

III. Lateran Palace, detail of the vault of the grand staircase.
Palazzo Lateranense, particolare della volta dello scalone.

IV. Lateran Palace, detail of the vault of the eastern loggia on the piano nobile.
Palazzo Lateranense, particolare della volta della loggia est al primo piano.

V. Lateran Palace, vault of the Cappella Papale.
Palazzo Lateranense, volta della cappella pontificia.

VI. *The Quirinal and the via Pia*, Lateran Palace, Salone dei Papi.
Il Quirinale e la via Pia. Palazzo Lateranense, Salone dei Papi.

VII. *Christ's Investiture to Peter ("Tu es Petrus")*, Lateran Palace, Salone dei Papi.
Tu es Petrus. Palazzo Lateranense, Salone dei Papi.

VIII. *Sixtus V receives the medals found in 1587 and document listing them*, Lateran Palace, Salone degli Imperatori.
Sisto V riceve le medaglie trovate nel 1587. Palazzo Lateranense, Salone degli Imperatori.

IX. *The Church adored by Emperors*, Lateran Palace, Salone degli Imperatori.
Omaggio degli imperatori cristiani alla Chiesa. Palazzo Lateranense, Salone degli Imperatori.

X. Lateran Palace, vault of the Sala di Samuele.
Palazzo Lateranense, volta della Sala di Samuele.

XI. Lateran Palace, vault of the Sala di Davide.
Palazzo Lateranense, volta della Sala di Davide.

XII. Lateran Palace, vault of the Sala di Salomone.
Palazzo Lateranense, volta della Sala di Salomone.

XIII. Lateran Palace, vault of the Sala di Elia.
Palazzo Lateranense, volta della Sala di Elia.

XIVa. *Moses gathers the seventy elders of Israel*, Lateran Palace, Salone degli Apostoli.
Mosè raduna i settanta anziani. Palazzo Lateranense, Sala degli Apostoli.

XIVb. *The Holy Spirit descends on the Apostles on Pentecost*, Lateran Palace, Salone degli Apostoli.
Pentecoste. Palazzo Lateranense, Sala degli Apostoli.

XV. *Donation of Constantine* (detail), Lateran Palace, Salone di Costantino.
Donazione di Costantino (part.). Palazzo Lateranense, Sala di Costantino.

XVI. *Saint Sylvester baptizes Constantine* (detail), Lateran Palace, Salone di Costantino.
San Silvestro battezza Costantino (part.). Palazzo Lateranense, Sala di Costantino.

PREFACE AND ACKNOWLEDGEMENTS

This study tries to establish the main historical and iconological parameters of what has largely been an overlooked monument in the history of Cinquecento painting. It does not pretend to explain every facet of the Lateran Palace cycle, but rather takes the first steps to understand its meaning, and, in the process, to re-evaluate the art commissioned by its patron. The fundamental problem with a serious study of the Lateran Palace cycle is not the stylistic or aesthetic qualities of the art; it is the complexity of the underlying ideas that are projected by the art itself. The rather bland style of the individual frescoes, which nonetheless, in my view, combine to create a strikingly effective and aesthetically pleasing ambient for the dissemination of ideas, was necessary in order to convey what is ironically a very complex and straightforward message. This study focuses on the conservative side of the message delivered by the stern, Roman Catholic Reform Pope Sixtus V, "il papa tosto," as one modern historian has called him, and endeavours to shed light on the institutional meaning of the Lateran Palace cycle. Chapter II was published as "Golden Age and the Good Works of Sixtus V: Classical and Christian Typology in the Art of a Counter-Reformation Pope," in *Storia dell'arte* 62 (1988): 29-52, and is reprinted here, with corrections and additional information, as it is integral to the argument. In this regard, I should like to thank W. Chandler Kirwin for very kindly pointing out that "Roman Catholic Reform" is more correct than "Counter-Reformation."

I began research on the Lateran Palace fresco cycle during the summer of 1986, with the financial assistance of the Italian Government, the Associates of the University of Toronto, and the Department of History of Art, University of Toronto, for which I am very grateful. I was subsequently assisted by the Ontario Government, the York University Office of Research Administration, and the University of Western Ontario, for which I am equally grateful. Without the generous support of these institutions, this study would not have been completed.

While in Rome, my research was facilitated by the great kindness and assistance of Father Leonard Boyle, Prefect of the Biblioteca Apostolica Vaticana and his staff; Edith Cicerchia, her successor Guido Cornini, and the staff of the Archivio Fotografico Vaticano; Padre Salvatore Pandolfo, Rector of the Istituto Massimiliano Massimo; Donato Tamblé, of the Archivio di Stato di Roma and his staff; the staff of the Biblioteca Hertziana; and Antonella D'Agostino and her successor Marzia Basile of the Canadian Academic Center in Rome. I wish also to thank Signor Andrea Argenti, custodian of the Lateran Palace, and the Direzione Generale dei Musei Vaticani, who permitted me to enter the palace each time I was in Rome.

The genesis of my ideas was aided by Giuseppe Scavizzi, who first introduced me to Sixtine Rome in a graduate seminar on the Roman Catholic Reform in 1985, while I was in the Phil.M. programme at the University of Toronto. I wish also to thank Mario Bevilacqua, Clifford M. Brown, Liana Cheney, Elio Costa, Marcello Fagiolo, Philipp Fehl, Oreste Ferrari, Philip Jacks, W. Chandler Kirwin, Hans Lücke, Maria Luisa Madonna, Tod Marder, Michael McCarthy, Guy and Michelle Métraux, John Osborne, Jonathan Riess, Glenn Scott, Philip Sohm, Joaneath Spicer, Terence Tunberg, and Joyce Zemans, who all, in one way or another, supported my work and contributed to the maturity of my ideas on Sixtus V and the Lateran Palace programme. This is not to suggest that all necessarily agree with the ideas presented here, for which I must naturally, and quite happily, assume full responsibility.

Since this book was submitted in manuscript form in 1990, accepted for publication and translated into the galley stage in 1992, a number of studies on the art created for Sixtus V have appeared. I have endeavoured to incude those published prior to April 1992 in the text; those that have appeared after that date could not be included, the most important of which are Alessandro Zuccari's *I pittori di Sisto V* which contains attributions for paintings at the Lateran Palace, and the catalogue to the exhibition held at the Palazzo Venezia from 22 January – 31 May 1993 *Roma di Sisto V,* edited by M.L. Madonna. My own *"Felix Culpa* and *Felix Roma:* On the Program of the Sixtine Staircase at the Vatican" appeared in the March 1993 *Art Bulletin.* Since the Editors thought it best to exclude my research on the occult component of Sixtine Rome in this book, as in my essays for the catalogue to the exhibition, I refer the reader interested in alchemy, astrology, and white magic to this latter article, and to my forthcoming article in the journal of the Biblioteca Apostolica Vaticana entitled "Magic and Melancholy at the Vatican Library".

INTRODUCTION
THE LIFE AND GOOD WORKS OF POPE SIXTUS V

On 24 April 1585, after two weeks of deliberation, Cardinal Felice Peretti da Montalto was elected pope. He took the name of Sixtus V in particular remembrance of two of his predecessors: the great theologian Sixtus IV (della Rovere, 1471-84), also a Franciscan, and his saintly mentor, the grand inquisitor Pius V (Ghislieri, 1566-72), whose surname was likewise "The Fifth."[1] Sixtus V's reign was short-lived, yet in a mere five years he achieved a staggering amount and variety of works (fig. 1). In the temporal sphere, he took significant steps to reinforce the Catholic Church's position in France, thereby leaving open the way for that country to gain independence of the Spanish, while at the same time crushing the plans of the Huguenots for a Protestant Europe.[2] He quelled the Spanish forces under Philip II, who were envisioning a papacy subject to temporal authority, by assuring the position of the Church on Italian soil.[3] And he made plans not only to wage a final battle against the Turks, but also to retrieve the Holy Sepulchre from its pernicious captors, and, in the process, to annex Egypt![4]

With regard to the defense and well-being of Rome and the *respublica Christiana*, Sixtus V waged war against the bandits who had infested the countryside during the pontificate of Gregory XIII (Boncompagni, 1572-85) and finally extirpated them from the Italian frontier.[5] In the wake of a series of bad harvests, he brought to the Romans a plentiful and high grade supply of foodstuffs, in part made possible by his draining of the Pontine marshes which made them fit for agricultural production. He managed to accumulate so copious a supply of gold at Castel Sant'Angelo that the three million scudi remaining at his death would not be depleted until the French revolution. He created a papal fleet to deter pirates from preying on the coasts, and restored the ancient port of Terracina to accommodate trade. And he instated and indeed affected the death penalty for prostitution and the practice of abortion.

Within the Church herself, Sixtus V insisted that his bishops, archbishops, primates and patriarchs of both the Old and New worlds visit Rome regularly and submit reports on their dioceses so as to reinstate the ancient and venerable journeys *ad limina* of Saints Peter and Paul, and maintain the high level of devotion expected of Christ's ministers and their subjects.[6] For the maintenance of the faith in the highest echelons, Sixtus V instituted the Jubilee at the beginning of his tenure to invoke divine assistance in the leadership of the Church, and he reinstituted the *Cappelle papali*, whereby the pope himself celebrated High Mass in the principal basilicas of Rome.[7] To ensure that heresy not be allowed to impinge on the restored Catholic Church, he issued a bull against all types of witchcraft and divination, especially judicial astrology, a practice which had infiltrated the very Chair of Saint Peter, most recently that of his despised predecessor Gregory XIII.[8] Furthermore, Sixtus V ensured that anyone who was not ordained and had the

[1] Pietro Galesino, "Sanctissimo Patri Sixto Quinto ... ac rectori commentarium hoc de vita, rebusque ab eo in singulos annos diesq. publice et pontificie actis gestiq. distribute, ac luculente ...," B. A. V. Vat. Lat. 5438, 23. Ludwig von Pastor, *The History of the Popes from the Close of the Middle Ages*, trans., ed., Frederick Ignatius Antrobus, Ralph Francis Kerr, 40 vols. (London; St. Louis, 1891-1954), XXI, 22, note 4. During the 16th century, a pope's title was regarded as having both first and last names, witness, in addition to the above, the book devoted to popes with the same surname as Sixtus V by Giovanni Pinadello, *Invicti Quinarii Numeri Series Quae Summation a Superioribus Pontificabus et Maxime A Sisto Quinto ...* (Rome, 1589).

[2] von Pastor, *History*, XXI, 1-4, 262 ff; Baron von Hübner, *The Life and Times of Sixtus the Fifth*, trans. Herbert E. H. Jerningham, 2 vols. (London, 1872), II, 145-195; E. A. Segretain, *Sixte-Quint et Henri IV: Introduction du Protestantism en France* (Paris, 1864); P. M. Casimiro Tempesti, *Storia della vita e delle gesta di Sisto Quinto Sommo pontefice* (1754) revised ed., 2 vols. (Rome, 1866), II, 279-312.

[3] von Pastor, *History*, XXI, 349 ff.

[4] von Pastor, *History*, XXII, 145-146. His papal fleet was also designed to safeguard Italian shores from invaders, particularly the Turks. Just before his death, the fleet managed to catch three Turkish ships off the coast of Genoa, in *idem*, XXI, 97-98. On the Holy Sepulchre, consult Marcello Fagiolo, "Chiesa Celeste, Chiesa Umana, Chiesa di Pietra," in *Chiese e Cattedrali*, Italia meravigliosa (Milan, 1978), 45-46. On Sixtus V's wish to translate the Holy Sepulchre, see von Pastor, *History*, XXI, 160-161; and Roger Cushing Aikin, "The Capitoline Hill During the Reign of Sixtus V," diss., U of California, Berkeley, 1977, 14 ff, for the Turks in general and the tomb in particular. On the plans to annex Egypt, see Enrico Narducci, "Storia-Documenti storici relativi al taglio dell'istmo di Suez ed alla conquista dell'Egitto ideata da Sisto V," *Reale Accademia dei Lincei-Rendiconti* 1, Serie 4 (19 April 1885): 300-302.

[5] For this and the following, I am drawing on the Good Works of Sixtus V which were represented in the secular cycles the pope commissioned, in two of the portraits of Sixtus V executed during his pontificate (figs. 39-40), and in the medals issued by the pope, and commemorated in the postumous portrait illustrated in my fig. 1.

[6] *Bullarum Diplomatum et Privilegiorum Sanctorum Romanorum Pontificum Taurinensis Editio ...*, ed. Francisco Gaude, Aloysio Bilio, 25 vols. (n.p.; Naples, 1857-1872), VIII, 641-645; 991-992. Also consult von Pastor, *History*, XXI, 134-136.

[7] *Bullarum Romanorum*, VIII, 576-

temerity to say mass would be put to death.[9] He founded the Vatican Printing Press for the dissemination of Catholic literature, such as the works of Ambrose, Bonaventure, Gregory the Great and his own contemporary Cesare Baronio, the Septuagint edition of the Bible, as well as the Vulgate, which he himself revised.[10] He further contributed to the annals of Church history by canonizing both the Dominican Louis Bertrand and the Franciscan San Diego of Alcala, and he elevated Saint Bonaventure, already canonized by Sixtus IV, to the status of Doctor of the Church.[11] In keeping with his ardent desire to see the Roman Catholic Reform Church return to her original pristine order, he reorganized the Curia, fixing the size of the Sacred College of Cardinals to seventy and creating the fifteen congregations which govern the Roman Catholic Church.[12]

In addition to the above works, Sixtus V was also the last of the great Renaissance builders. Under this tireless pope the Eternal City was rationalized and made more coherent by means of a street plan which radiated from Santa Maria Maggiore to ideally encompass the six remaining pilgrimage churches of Rome as well as major pagan monuments of antiquity.[13] Thanks to the truly inspired engineering skills of his private architect and friend, Domenico Fontana, he erected Egyptian obelisks and de-paganized them with the "invincible cross." He also restored ancient Roman columns, exorcised and surmounted them with statues of the apostles Peter and Paul, to function as the *foci* of his street system.[14] Sixtus V built an aqueduct for Civitavecchia, and he also brought water to the city of Rome by restoring the Acqua Vergine of Severus and erecting the Moses Fountain in commemoration of the event. To further aid the Roman populace, he installed a public washbasin on the Esquiline, and planned other watering spots, likewise fed by the Acqua Felice, notably on the Capitol and the Quirinal, this latter in conjunction with the Dioscuri which he had restored and moved to the square before the favoured papal residence. With the help of both Giacomo della Porta and Fontana, Sixtus V constructed in less than two years all but the lantern of the dome of San Pietro in Vaticano as planned by Michelangelo. In collaboration with the architect Martino Longhi he rebuilt and in part decorated the Church of San Girolamo degli Schiavoni, in devotion to the author of the Vulgate. He also housed the Crib of Christ and erected tombs to himself and to his cherished predecessor Pius V at Santa Maria Maggiore, while at San Giovanni in Laterano he rebuilt and decorated the Benediction Loggia, thus restoring to the pope's titular Church one of her key monuments, and he moved the Scala Santa to a location facing the basilica and encased it within a lavishly decorated enclosure. He regirded the walls enclosing the city of Loreto, ensuring the safety of the Holy House of the Virgin; and he likewise made plans to fortify the city of Montalto and hence the bishopric which he had instituted there. In the secular sphere he made additions to his own Roman villa, the Villa Montalto, including the erection and decoration of the Palazzo delle Terme; he constructed and embellished a new library and papal residence at the Vatican, and restored the Sala di Costantino of Leo X (de'Medici, 1513-21) and Clement VII (de'Medici, 1523-34); and, as his greatest secular achievement, he rebuilt and refurbished the ancient residence of the popes at the Lateran, the Patriarchium Lateranense.

Acutely aware of his utterly supreme station as the spiritual head of Christ's earthly body, the Church, Sixtus V was dri-

578. On the Jubilee and *Cappelle papale*, see von Pastor, *History*, XXI, 138; and the recent discussion in Helge Gamrath, *Roma Sancta Renovata. Studi sull'urbanistica di Roma nella seconda metà del sec. XVI con particolare riferimento al pontificato di Sisto V (1585-1590)*, Analecta Romana Instituti Danici, Supplementum XII (Rome, 1987), 131 ff.

[8] *Bullarum Romanorum*, VIII, 646-650.

[9] *Bullarum Romanorum*, VIII, 951-960.

[10] *Bullarum Romanorum*, VIII, 841-847. Also consult von Pastor, *History*, XXII, 199-202.

[11] Louis Bertrand was canonized on 24 June 1586; San Diego on 2 July 1588; and St. Bonaventure raised to Dr. of the Church on 14 March 1588. Papal bulls were issued for the latter two, in *Bullarum Romanorum*, IX, 8-20; VIII, 1005-1012, respectively. For Louis Bertrand (as well as the Franciscans), see von Pastor, *History*, XXI, 138. Also consult Tempesti, *Storia*, II, 31-56.

[12] *Bullarum Romanorum*, VIII, 985-999. Also see von Pastor, *History*, XXI, 247-261.

[13] I treat this and the following in more detail in the following chapters.

[14] Aikin, "Capitoline," 51, notes that the "columns of Trajan and Marcus Aurelius ... were conceived of as a pair though they are blocks apart." This idea has been further elucidated in Philip Jacks, "A Sacred Meta for Pilgrims in the Holy Year 1575," *Architectura* 19, 2 (1989): 165, who notes that the columns were at the core of the street system; and recently in Giorgio Simoncini, *"Roma Restaurata." Rinnovamento urbano al tempo di Sisto V*, L'ambiente Storico, studi di storia urbana e del territorio (Florence, 1990), especially 98-99. I wish to thank Philip Jacks for kindly having sent me a copy of his article.

ven to complete these Good Works, and others, so that he might create a simulacrum of the Apostolic Age in his own time, and accordingly bring to the earth an age of peace and prosperity whereby mankind would be united in the Catholic faith. It was to this spiritual end that he not only endeavoured to inject new vigour into the faith of his subjects, extirpate heresy, and put the administration of the Church in order, but also to cohere the city of Rome, making it accessible to both prelate and pilgrim. Thus Sixtine Rome would be transformed into a grand reflection on earth of the Heavenly City. As a Franciscan, profoundly devoted to the founder of his Order and, like Saint Francis, to living a life in emulation of Christ, Sixtus V's actions were highly motivated by the justice and charity which the two main *exempla* of his life had embodied for the edification of mankind. His building works were likewise created in emulation of the structures which Saint Francis had erected to the glory of Christ and his Church. Sixtus V's work at the Lateran district, in particular, was in this sense a response to his Franciscan heritage: his Benediction Loggia recalled the dream of Pope Innocent III (de'Conti de'Segni, 1198-1216), in which Saint Francis was holding up the Lateran basilica, while his rebuilding and sumptuous decorating of the Lateran Palace recalled Francis' own dream of a magnificent palace adorned with costly furnishings, decorations and armaments, all marked with the sign of the cross and intended, as Christ himself revealed, for the use of his servants and their defense of the Church on earth.[15]

Sixtus V was also deeply and sincerely imbued with the conviction that he was the temporal head of Christ's earthly body and, in this sense, he believed that his office was also inherently imperial. The just and charitable natures of his achievements were accordingly perceived in another way as continuing the traditions established by the temporal rulers of the Roman empire, particularly the Emperors Augustus and Constantine, the greatest of those secular leaders who had followed Christ's word.[16] The grand scale in which he built was in this sense a direct response to the works of his imperial predecessors, while the propensity for self-glorification manifested itself in the prevalence of his *stemma* in all of his building and decorating works. Moreover, the representations of his Good Works in the cycles frescoed in secular buildings at the Esquiline, Vatican and Lateran districts attest to the pope's obsessive appropriation of imperial tradition. In total, sixty-three representations of Good Works were frescoed by the group of artists working at the Villa Montalto, Vatican Library and Lateran Palace and, with the exception of the four obelisks and two columns depicted in the Sala degli Obelischi of the Lateran Palace, all were accompanied by verses composed with the express purpose of glorifying the pope and his achievements. While the depictions of Sixtus V's Good Works have merited specific mention in the accounts of both Sixtine Rome and the city of Rome, since they have been used to document the complexion of Rome before, during, and after Sixtus V's renovations, their verses have never been studied from the point of view of form and content.[17] Consequently the Good Works have not been considered in and of themselves as viable means to elucidate the meaning of Sixtus V's pontificate, as pontiff and as person, and the programmes in which they are collectively so central a component. My purpose in the following chapters is to explore the meaning of the Later-

[15] Saint Bonaventure, *Legenda Maior*, III, 10; I, 3, in *St. Francis of Assisi. Writings and Early Biographies. English Omnibus of the Sources for the Life of St. Francis*, ed. Marion A. Habig, trans. Ralph Brown, *et al* (Chicago, Illinois, 1973), 637-638; 652-653, respectively for the dreams of Innocent III and Francis. I treat the context of Innocent III's dream in greater detail in Chapter I, 37, below.

[16] I am referring to Augustus' "secret" conversion to Christianity which Sixtus V commemorated on the base of the obelisk of S. Maria Maggiore. See Chapter IV, 147, below.

[17] The Good Works are used especially by historians of the Patriarchium Lateranense. See, for example, Philippe Lauer, *Le Palais du Latran: étude historique et archaeologique* (Paris, 1911). Also consult Enrico Stevenson, *Topografia e monumenti di Roma nelle pitture a fresco di Sisto V della Biblioteca Vaticana. Omaggio Giubilare della Biblioteca Vaticana al Sommo Pontefice Leone XIII* (Rome, 1888). The verses have, of course, been used to explain the subject matter represented in the accompanying frescoes. For a recent example, see René Schiffmann, *Roma Felix. Aspekte der städtebaulichen Gestaltung Roms unter Papst Sixtus V*, Europäische Hochschulschriften, Reihe XXVIII Kunstgeschichte, vol. 36 (Bern, Frankfurt am Main, New York, 1985), 61.

an Palace programme, since it is the most important cycle commissioned by Sixtus V and contains the greatest number of Good Works in a variety of different formats. In addition, as the one cycle created by a pope for himself and his successors, it relates in a fundamental way to the view which Sixtus V had of himself, and of his station as Christ's vicar. It will also be my task to attempt to explain the apparent contradiction between the seemingly pagan secular and Christian facets of the Good Works. But before turning to the Lateran Palace and the Good Works of Sixtus V, it is necessary to consider the life of Felice Peretti prior to his accession to the papacy because there is sufficient evidence to suggest that the key themes conveyed by the Good Works, and by the laudatory literature of Sixtine Rome, did not emerge phoenix-like in the wake of his election, but rather were inextricably bound with his early life.[18]

The history of the pope's birth and rise to the papacy is well known; it has been reported quite regularly by contemporaneous and modern scholars of Sixtine Rome, in most cases, with all the veneration accorded the gospels. Those who have questioned the veracity of certain parts of the story have neither endeavoured to explain why such incredible anecdotes were promulgated by the pope and his biographers, nor, as a result, has anyone considered the ramifications of this mythology for the pontificate of Sixtus V and the most visible carriers of Sixtine propaganda, the artistic programmes containing the pope's Good Works.

As documented in the many biographies written during his pontificate, the story of Pope Sixtus V opens even before his birth, with the dream of his parents that their future son would become very famous, rising from humble origins to achieve the "highest dignity."[19] The child was born soon after the good omen in Grottamare, on the Feast of Saint Lucy, Friday the 13th of December 1521 at 16 hours.[20] As the fourth of seven children, he was compared to the Sun in the middle of the planets, an analogy made the more appropriate since Saint Lucy was herself a symbol of light.[21] The parents, Piergentile "Peretto" di Giacomo and Marianna da Frontillo (di Camerino), baptised him "Felice," meaning "happy," or "fortunate" in order to seal, or at least prod, the future foretold for their auspicious son. The first sign of this exceptional nature occurred when, still a babe, the spark of a lamp caught his bed and by the time his mother found him, Felice was enveloped by flames.[22] Miraculously, he was not only untouched by the fire, like Moses before the burning bush, but actually smiled at his mother as she extinguished it. Having survived the inferno, Felice was next subjected to the pestilence which was ravaging the Italian peninsula following the Sack of Rome and to which his brother succumbed. Despite the fact that Felice had been in contact with his brother's clothes, he proved to be immune to the plague, just as Moses had been untouched by the Passover. Some years later, while playing with friends near the creek where his sister was washing clothes, Felice managed to fall into the water. He was saved from certain death by his sister, who ran to his aid, much as Moses had been rescued by the Pharaoh's daughter.[23] Aside from these rather dramatic events, Felice spent his youth quietly tending the fields and flocks of his father, as befitted a boy of humble circumstance. But at the same time he showed himself to have an unusually voracious appetite for things literary and, with the aid of an uncle,

[18] Marcello Fagiolo was the first to have explained in detail the relationship between Sixtus V's life and the street plan of Rome. See Marcello Fagiolo, "La Roma di Sisto V: le matrici del policentrismo," *Psicon* 3 (July-December 1976): 25-39; Marcello Fagiolo dell'Arco, "Il Pontificato Romano. Storia di una ideologia per una città sacra," in *L'Arte dei Papi. Come pontefici, architetti, pittori e scultori costruirono il Vaticano, monumento della cristianità*, ed. Maurizio Fagiolo dell'Arco (Milan, 1982), 24-26; *Roma 1300-1875. L'arte degli anni santi*, ed. Marcello Fagiolo and Maria Luisa Madonna (Milan, 1984), 33-34; and recently, Marcello Fagiolo, "Die Psycho-Ikonologie," in *Das architektonische Urteil. Annäherungen und Interpretationen von Architektur und Kunst* (Basel, Boston, Berlin, 1989), 148-162. I should like to thank Marcello Fagiolo and Maria Luisa Madonna for having graciously provided me with these studies.

[19] The most important biography of Sixtus V was written by his secretary Antonio Maria Graziani and annotated by the pope himself. It is transcribed in Francesco Pistolesi, *La Prima Biografia Autentica di Papa Sisto Quinto Scritta dell'anonimo della Biblioteca Ferraioli di Roma* (Montalto March, 1925), 69, 18, who provides extensive commentary on and quotations from the manuscript in question, including the assertion that Felice would rise to power, as indicated. I also consulted a colophon of this manuscript which was deposited in the Secret Archives of the Vatican in 1659 on order of Alexander VII: "De Vita Sixti Quinti ipsius manu emendata," B. A. V. Vat. Lat. 12141, 1v, 49v-52. It differs slightly on some points which are indicated below when appropriate. Other biographies consulted include "Vita," Vat. Lat. 9721, 1v; "Memorie del Ponteficato di Papa Sisto V[to]," B. A. V. Vat. Lat. 12142, 2; Galesino, 4; although not a biography *per se*, Pinadello, 27; and *Historia B. Platinae De Vitis Pontificum Romanorum …*, emended by Onophrio Panvinio and Antonio Ciccarelli (Cologne, 1600), 423. Although Ciccarelli's Life of Sixtus V was written after the pope's death, the information conveyed is useful as an indication of those aspects of the myth which were memorialized as fact. I also consulted Gaetano Moroni, *Dizionario di erudizione storico-ecclesiastica da S. Pietro fino ai nostri giorni*, 109 vols. (Venice, 1840-1879), LXVII, 89; and the excerpts from other biographies written during the pontificate of Sixtus V printed in Leopold von Ranke, *The History of the Popes during the last four centuries* (1874), trans. Mrs. Foster, revised G. R. Dennis, 3 vols. (London, 1908-1913), III, 123-146; and von Pastor, *History*, XXI, 407-438, in particular 432, n. 41, with regard to the future foretold for the child. Many more biographies are extant. A final note is in order: sometimes Felice's mother is accredited with the dream, sometimes his father, and sometimes both. To simplify matters, I have opted for the latter. On this problem, consult von Pastor, *History*, XXI, 417.

he was given an education in the rudiments of both a Classical and Christian education.

By the age of twelve, having been enrolled in the Conventual Franciscan convent in Montalto for three years, Felice wished to don the Franciscan habit. Owing to his profound devotion and erudition, he was allowed to become a full-fledged Franciscan in 1534, at the age of thirteen. When the friars wished to change Felice's name in honour of the event and in keeping with tradition, they met with opposition from the boy's parents, who were determined that their son, the future pope, maintain the name he had been given in anticipation of his future greatness.[24] At around this time, however, the teen-ager decided that he no longer wished to be known as Felice; he now wanted to be called "Crinitus," "the long-haired," so that he might compare himself to a comet.[25] The "long-haired" continued to further his education in numerous cities; he was ordained priest in Siena in 1547, and the following year, received his Doctor of Theology at Fermo.[26] In 1549, while he was participating in a disputation at Assisi, Felice was noticed by the protector of the Franciscan Order, Cardinal Carpi, who was much impressed by his eloquence and learning. From this time forward, Fra Felice would rise in the ranks of the Church with lightening speed. In 1552 Cardinal Carpi called Felice to Rome to deliver sermons at SS. Apostoli always, as it turned out, to a full house. The following year he became regent of the convent of San Lorenzo in Naples. In 1556, Paul IV (Carafa, 1555-59) made him Inquisitor for the Venetian Republic and, in 1557, "Ruler" of the Frari convent. Under Pius IV (de'Medici di Milano, 1559-65) he became Theologian to the Council of Trent, Consultor to the Roman Inquisition and, in 1561, Procurator-General of the Franciscans. In 1565, Cardinal Ghislieri (soon to become Pius V) helped him to secure a position as theological advisor to Cardinal Boncompagni (later Gregory XIII) on a mission to Spain, where Fra Felice also preached before King Philip II; in 1566 Pius V made him Vicar-General of the Conventual Franciscans as well as bishop of the diocese of Sant'Agata dei Goti in Naples; and on 17 May 1570, a Cardinal, with the title of San Girolamo degli Schiavoni and member of the Congregation of the Index. Pius V also made Cardinal Montalto his confessor, and bestowed on him a poor cardinal's pension. With the death of Pius V, Cardinal Montalto's speedy rise to power came to a sudden halt due to differences with Gregory XIII that have been traced back to their Spanish mission. He turned to his vast collection of books, began working on an edition of Saint Ambrose and, in 1576, purchased the Vigna Montalto in his sister's name. Seeing the magnificence of the cardinal's surroundings, Gregory XIII cut off his pension, but it was soon made up by the Grand Duke of Tuscany, Francesco de'Medici. Cardinal Montalto was accordingly given the wherewithal to complete the Villa Montalto and surrounding vineyards; to purchase more books; to build a monument to the Franciscan Pope Nicholas IV (Colonna, 1288-92) at Santa Maria Maggiore; and to begin his own chapel in the Liberian basilica, including provisions for the translation of the Crib of Christ to its center. In accord with the plan of Divine Providence, Cardinal Montalto at last attained the exalted chair of Saint Peter with the "incredible consensus of the cardinals" on 24 April 1585, the anniversary of the foundation of Rome, according, we are told, to the reckoning of the fourth century astrologer Firmicus Maternus.[27] That

[20] There has been some disagreement on the date of his birth as well as the place. See von Hübner, *Life and Times*, I, 240 note 1, who explains that Sixtus V's birth date was sometimes thought to have been the 12th, rather than the 13th of December. The question as to his birth place began as early as 1589 with Pinadello, *Invicti Quinarii*, 27, who states that Sixtus V was born in Montalto rather than Grottamare. The inscription on the tomb of Sixtus V at S. Maria Maggiore clearly states that he was born in Grottamare and reared in Montalto. Moreover, Sixtus V publicly stated that he was born in a *grotta*, a *double entendre* referring to both Grottamare and his similarity to Christ, as reported in an avviso of 27 April 1585, in von Pastor, *History*, XXI, 377, note 1; and recently mentioned in Gustavo Parisciani, *Sisto V e la sua Montalto*, Ricerche francescane (Padua, 1986), 20; and Steven F. Ostrow, "The Sistine Chapel at S. Maria Maggiore: Sixtus V and the art of the Counter Reformation," diss., Princeton U, 1987, 87. As Pistolesi, *Prima Biografia*, 8, explains, Graziani left a space for the pope to fill in his birthdate, place and time, which agrees with that presented here.

As for the time of the pope's birth, both the colophon of Graziani's "Vita," Vat. Lat. 12141, 1v; and Galesinus, 4, log in at "hora *circiter* decima sexta [emphasis mine]." However, Graziani in Pistolesi, *Prima Biografia*, 69, states that "hora XVI editus in lucem est" (whether this time is truly accurate or not is irrelevant in terms of the Sistine myth). Compare Moroni, *Dizionario*, LXVII, 77; and von Hübner, *Life and Times*, I, 213, 241, note 1.

[21] For the analogy to the Sun, see Graziani in Pistolesi, *Prima Biografia*, 69, 8; "Vita," Vat. Lat. 12141, 2v; "Vita," Vat. Lat. 9721, 1v; "Memorie," Vat. Lat. 12142, 2; and Galesino, "de vita," Vat. Lat. 5438, 7. The reference to the seven children actually regards Felice's extended family; he had one sister, one brother and four cousins. See the family tree in Parisciani, *Sisto V*, 260-261. The name Lucia, of course, means light.

[22] For this and the following potentially fatal incidents, consult "De Vita," Vat. Lat. 12141, 53; Galesino, "de vita," Vat. Lat. 5438, 7v-9v; and von Pastor, *History*, XXI, 25-26.

[23] The analogies to Moses are made in Galesino, "de vita," Vat. Lat. 5438, 9-9v. The spirit of the analogies may be gleaned from the following passage concerning the incident at the creek: "Quod Sixto Quinto tum à pueritia accidit, itidem alijs summis uiris euenit, qui ad celsissimos honoram gradus euetti sunt. Divina providentia Moses, ut omnem Israelis progeniem servaret, infans ex aquis / servatus est quem enim parentis crudelissimo Pharaonis edicto subacti, alueo inclusum, in profluentum, abiecerunt, inde divinitus liberatus, Moses nomen a voce hebrea accepit, quam sì latine reddimus, ex aqua servatum interpretamur. ..." Also consult the discussion in Tod Marder, "The

27

his election day fell on a Wednesday, finally, was regarded as confirmation of the extremely good fortune which this day had brought to Felice throughout his life, as Mercury had overseen every one of his major promotions, culminating in this greatest of them all.[28]

The history of the pope's rise to power, from his vows of 1534 to his elevation to the See of Peter in 1585, is not necessarily the chronicle of a meteoric career, especially by Renaissance standards. The accounts of omens and providential signs, therefore, can reasonably be categorized as hagiographical propaganda. It is equally important to stress that, in all probability, the pope and his parents believed the portent of his wondrous birth. Felice's wish to change his name to Crinitus, moreover, is particularly imaginative and lends a cryptic note to an already unusual course of events. While these anecdotes cannot be proven, or disproven, there are instances in which documentary evidence exists to indicate that the facts were stretched to suit the story. First, the idea that Felice is like the Sun in the middle of the planets, since he was the fourth of seven children, is borne out only when one considers his extended family, because Felice had only one brother and one sister.[29] Secondly, his brother Prospero did not die until 1561; if the plague story is actually based on reality (and there is really no reason to doubt that there is a modicum of truth in the story), then it probably refers to a cousin, possibly Pierantonino, whose dates, unfortunately, are not known. Thirdly, the idea that Felice became pope on the anniversary of Rome according to a fourth-century astrologer's computations conflicts with the generally accepted date of April 21st and indicates, therefore, that no small amount of erudition was involved in turning an ordinary day into an extraordinary one.[30] Finally, the idea that Wednesday was the day of all his major promotions is blown out of proportion, as Nicola Pansoni has shown; the first significant promotion that Mercury oversaw was Felice's donning of the purple in 1570 at the age of forty-nine, and there were no more auspicious Wednesdays until he was elected pope![31] Given these clear departures from fact, it must be possible to penetrate the hagiography of his life and to extract the significance which these alterations of the truth held for the man who tailored them. It is to this task that I shall now turn as a prelude to the discussion, in the chapters which follow, of how the story was harnessed by the "mythographers" of Sixtine Rome to create the glorious aura surrounding the pontiff.

The dream of his parents promising a "wonder child" recalls the son of Virgil's *Fourth Eclogue* and therefore serves to conjure the Golden Age, to assimilate Felice to the Emperor Augustus, and to cement his future station as Christ's vicar.[32] Moreover, it is not at all unlike the dream of Augustus' mother Atia, who likewise learned of the cosmological greatness of her future son, and it is certainly evocative of the portent circulating in Rome a few months before Augustus' birth that "nature was pregnant with a king for the Roman people."[33] The idea of a Golden Age ushered in at the birth of another Augustus and another Christ would be adopted at the accession of Cardinal Montalto to the papacy to become one of the key *topoi* of his pontificate not only in the panegyrics composed in his honour, and the sermons delivered *coram papa*, but also in the artistic cycles which he commissioned. The dream also has certain affinities to a dream of a century earlier, in which Sixtus IV's

Moses Fountain of Sixtus V," forthcoming in *Sisto V*, VI Corso Internazionale d'Alta Cultura. I should like to thank Tod Marder for kindly having sent me this article.

[24] von Pastor, *History*, XXI, 28.

[25] "De Vita," Vat. Lat. 12141, 47. Comets are stars with tails, or hairs of light (*comam*). Comets could be either good or bad portents, depending on the context. Consult Lynn Thorndike, *A History of Magic and Experimental Science during the first Thirteen Centuries of our Era*, 8 vols. (New York, 1923-1958), IV, 413 ff, esp. 428; and *idem*, *Michael Scot* (London and Edinburgh, 1965), 70-71. Also consult von Ranke, *Popes*, III, 134-135; and von Pastor, *History*, XXI, 431, note 41.

[26] For this and the following, I am following Moroni, *Dizionario*, LXVII, 76 ff; von Pastor, *History*, XXI, 28 ff; and Ostrow, "Sistine," 87 ff.

[27] Galesino, "de vita," Vat. Lat. 5438, 22; noted in Moroni, *Dizionario*, LXVII, 92; and von Ranke, *Popes*, III, 145.

[28] In their zeal to prove the good graces which Mercury bestowed on Felice, some biographers actually state that he was born on a Wednesday, rather than a Friday. See, for example, "Vita," Vat. Lat. 9721, 63v; and Ciccarelli, *Platinae De Vitis*, 422. Also consult note 31, below.

[29] See the family tree in Parisciani, *Sisto V*, 260.

[30] Varro's date was the generally accepted one, although this is not to imply that agreement was reached by all on the matter. For a different opinion, based on Plutarch's date of 9 April, see, for example, Mario Matasilani, *La Felicità del Serenissimo Cosimo Medici Granduca di Toscana ...* (Florence, 1572), 6-7. Also consult Jacks, "Meta," *Architectura*, 150-151.

[31] Wednesday became the subject of a heated debate at the turn of this century, in Nicola Pansoni, *Il Mercoledi di Sisto V e Gregorio XIII* (Cossignano, 1924). I have double-checked the most fundamental of the "auspicious Wednesdays" listed in "Vita," Vat. Lat. 9721, 63v, with the perpetual calendar in A. Cappelli, *Cronologia, Cronografia e Calendario Perpetuo dal principio dell'èra cristiana ai nostri giorni* (5th ed.; Milan, 1983), 44 ff, as follows: "Il Mercordì poi ... giorno a lui sempre Fortunato, perche di Mercordì nacque [13/12/1521, a Friday], di Mercordì si fece frate [Palm Sunday 1532], in tal giorno fù creato vescovo [15/11/1566, a Friday], in simil'giorno fu promosso al'Cardinalato [17/05/1570, a Wednesday!], et in Mercordì eletto Papa, e finalmente in tal giorno fu coronato l'ottavo giorno dopo la sua elezzione [1/05/1585, a Wednesday, indeed, to help to substantiate the myth]."

[32] Virgil, *Eclogue IV*, 17, in *Works*, trans., H. Rushton Fairclough, 2 vols., Loeb Classical Library (1916; Cambridge, Mass; London, 1935), I, 30, 31.

[33] Suetonius, *Divus Augustus*, XCIV, in *Suetonius*, trans. J. C. Rolfe, 2 vols.,

28

mother learned that she would give birth to a son to whom Saints Francis and Anthony would bestow the habit of their Order. It was on account of this dream that the della Rovere son was called Francesco,[34] much as another dream would spur the Perettis to name their child Felice.

The comparison of the youth to the Sun, recalling the syncretization of both the Emperor and Christ to the Sun-god Apollo, not to mention Saint Francis, reinforces the providentiality of his birth and future vocation, and echoes almost exactly the dream of Augustus' father that Atia would give birth to the Sun.[35] The idea that Felice is in the center of the planets affirms the Chaldean-Ptolemaic view of the universe, and conjures the Ciceronian and Macrobian appelation of the Sun in this context as the "leader, chief, and regulator of the other lights, mind and moderator of the universe."[36] It also, of course, brings to mind the creation of the Sun on the fourth day, and its interpretation by Christian exegetes as the first Mosaic prophecy of Christ's coming [Genesis: I, 16].[37] Felice's youthful wish to be called "Crinitus," moreover, was surely an allusion not only to a comet and the great political change he would bring to the *respublica Christiana* as pope, but also to the "crinitus Apollo" of Virgil's *Aeneid*, and, in this sense, designed to reinforce his solarian character.[38] The child's early brush with fire also has Apollonian, and hence Christological and Franciscan, resonances, owing to the god's assimilation to the Sun and accordingly his power over fire. His ability to overcome pestilence likewise suggests the Sun-god Apollo, in this sense as *medicus*, the healing god. It also finds parallels in the early life of Francesco della Rovere. Not only had Francesco's parents fled the plague-ridden area of Genoa prior to his birth, but he was a sickly child who was healed thanks to his mother's vow to Saint Francis and the Franciscan habit which he wore as testimony to this vow from an early age.[39] As pope, Sixtus IV would be celebrated as a vanquisher of pestilence in the form of heretics and the infidel Turk as another *pastor Apollo*, as would his successor Sixtus V.[40] To be sure, the youthful Felice's assimilation to the Sun would reverberate during the pontificate of Sixtus V from panegyrics to sermons, and obelisks to frescoed Good Works.

The symbolism of light, which is a corollary to the child's solarian nature, evokes Saint Lucy, on whose feast day Felice was born, and to whom he dedicated a side chapel at Santa Maria Maggiore. It also, of course, brings to mind the Virgin Mary as "stella maris," as the receptacle of light in the Incarnation, and as the woman of the Apocalypse crowned with twelve stars. Not incidentally, Felice would be profoundly devoted to the Virgin throughout his life, as had his namesake Sixtus IV, attributing his survival of the nearly fatal accidents of his youth to her divine intercession on his behalf, preaching on the Immaculate Conception as a renowned orator, and securing for himself and Pius V a burial chapel in her Roman basilica.[41]

Felice's rescue from a near watery death may also be attributed to his Apollonian nature, as shall become clear upon analyzing the Good Work of the *Acqua Felice* and its verse in the Salone dei Papi. It also has a counterpart in the life of Francesco della Rovere, who, as a babe, was left for dead in his mother's arms after having fainted while she bathed him. It was on this occasion that Lucchina della Rovere first gave her *poverino* the habit of Saint Francis, an act which saved her

Loeb Classical Library (Cambridge, Mass; London, 1964), I, 264, 265; 266, 267.

[34] This "dream" was first reported by Battista Platina, Sixtus IV's biographer and librarian. It is contained in all editions of Platina's *Lives*. I am quoting Battista Platina, *Historia delle vite de'sommi pontefici*, trans. and emended by Girolamo Beroardi (Venice, 1608), 261v, as follows: "Parve alla madre prima, che parturisse, di vedere in sogno, che ella havesse parturito un fanciullo, alquale san Francesco, e santo Antonio vestivano un loro habito con la cocolla, e li cingevano un lor cordo ne, come sogliono i frati di san Francesco usare. Il perche lo chiamarono nato, che fu, Francesco." I wish to thank John Osborne and Jonathan Riess for very kindly having suggested that I look into the parallels between Sixtus IV and Sixtus V, both biographical and artistic.

[35] For St. Francis as the Sun, consult, for example, Dante, *Paradiso*, XI, 49-54, in *Dante Alighieri. The Divine Comedy*, trans., commentary by Charles S. Singleton, Bollingen Series LXXX, 6 vols. (1970-1975; revised; Princeton, New Jersey, 1977), V, 120-123; *Legend of the Three Companions*, Prologue, in Habig, *St. Francis*, 889; and Pompeo Felici, *La prima delle Cinquanta Quattro Stationi di Roma* ... (Rimini, 1586), n.p.: "Et che il Sole, che l'adora [the star of the pope's heraldry], non sia il tuo buon Padre San Francesco, il quale se in tante cose fu à Christo conforme, ben potremo chiamarlo Sole?"

[36] Marcus Tullius Cicero, *Somnium Scipionis*, IV, 2, in Macrobius, *Commentary on the Dream of Scipio*, trans., intro & notes by William Harris Stahl (1952; New York & London, 1966), 73; and for Macrobius, *Commentary*, III, 3, *idem*, 194.

[37] Noted in Galesino, "de vita," Vat. Lat. 5438, 7. On the Sun, the middle and number four in Neoplatonic philosophy consult Raymond B. Waddington, "The Sun at the Center: structure as meaning in Pico della Mirandola's *Heptaplus*," *Journal of Medieval and Renaissance Studies* 3 (1973): 69-86, esp. 77-80. All references to the Bible are from *The Holy Bible translated from the Vulgate*, Douay Version, OT 1609; NT 1582 (Rockford, Illinois, 1971); and *Biblia Sacra iuxta Vulgatam Clementinam*, ed. Alberto Colunga and Laurentio Turrado, Biblioteca de Autores Cristianos, 14, 6th ed. (Madrid, 1982).

[38] Virgil, *Aeneid*, IX, 638, in *Works*, 156, 157. Compare the "intonsum Sminthea" in Ovid, *Metamorphoses*, XII, 585, trans. Frank Justus Miller, 2 vols., Loeb Classical Library (1916; Cambridge, Mass; London, 1958), II, 222, 223; and additional references to the "intonsum" cited in Natale Conti, *Mythologiae*, IV, s (1551; 1567; New York and London, 1976), 114-115.

[39] Platina, *Historia*, 261v: "Nel'qual luogo [Savona] erano e'l padre, e la madre andati, per fuggire la peste, che era all'hora grande nel Genovesato ... Di che [an illness to which I shall refer be-

3

frail son's life.[42] The incident at the creek also, as we are told, has affinities to the story of the youthful Moses, who had been left in a basket in the Nile and rescued by his future step-mother.[43] Other Mosaic incidents had also informed Felice's early life, the fire or burning bush, and the pestilence or Passover, being of paramount importance. The comparison of Felice to Moses serves to reinforce the Christian and particularly Franciscan way of life for which the youth was destined, since Moses is a type of Christ, as of Saint Francis, and, it must be added, of Sixtus IV. It also prefigures another fundamental *topos* of Sixtine Rome, as exemplified by the terminal Moses Fountain of the Acqua Felice, in which the central figure of Moses was to have struck water from the rock, just as Sixtus V would bring water to Rome by building aqueducts of "rock."[44] Even more telling is the time-line of Michele Mercati, the apostolic protonotary, appended to his 1589 treatise on the obelisk: Mercati places Moses' birth in 1589 B. C. so that it is related bilaterally to the pontificate of Sixtus V, with Christ as the central point in the earthly "trinity."[45] Sixtus V is accordingly given an historical *raison d'être* for his assimilation to Moses and, in this way, Mercati tacitly underscores the providentiality of his accession to the See of Peter in 1585 and, indeed, the waiting period forced upon the cardinal during Gregory XIII's pontificate. As I shall demonstrate in my analysis of the Lateran Palace cycle, Mercati's "trinitarian" method is also in keeping with the overwhelming organizational principal that informs this, as all artistic cycles of Sixtine Rome.

That Felice would later become pope on the anniversary of the foundation of Rome suggests that Sixtus V was to be aligned with the great founders of Rome, especially Romulus and the Emperor Augustus, and that during his pontificate he would re-establish and rule the Golden Age, thereby accomplishing anew the prophecies of Anchises in Virgil's *Aeneid*.[46] The incredible coincidences of his birth and rise to the papacy were therefore given a common basis in the Golden Age myth which was then applied to the city of Rome and the fated or, in Christian terms, providential mission of its ruler. The idea that Mercury oversaw the rise of Felice to power is suggestive of the god's traditional role as protector of Rome and its ruler. It also evokes the Christian Mercury, Saint Michael, protector of both the Hebraic and Roman nations; Michele Ghislieri (Pius V), the mentor of Bishop and later Cardinal Peretti da Montalto; as well as the Franciscan Mercury, Saint Francis, founder and protector of Sixtus V's Order.[47] Since Mercury is also a god of dreams, then it becomes clear that the youth was fated, even before his birth, to become the Franciscan vicar of Christ and, once again, an implicit connection is made between the birth of the "wonder child" and his accession to the papacy. That Felice's rise to power was due, in large part, to his superb skills as preacher and rhetorician only serves to underscore his affinities to this god of eloquence. To be sure, the sermons delivered by Fra Felice are replete with the syncretistic treatment of paganism and Christianity, antiquity and humanism, which characterize not only the mythology of his life story, but also the art and literature of Sixtine Rome, including the most significant carriers of this method, the representations of the pope's Good Works, in particular those located in the Salone dei Papi of the Lateran Palace.[48]

In the chapters that follow, my purpose will be to peel away the syncretistic layers of Sixtine iconography. In Chapter

low] ella [Francesco's mother] dell'insogno ricordandosi se voto di dovere vestirlo dell'habito di san Francesco, e di fargliele portare sei mesi. Passato poi questo tempo, e toltoli l'habito, di nuovo il fanciullo in una grave infermità ne venne, & era già d'un'anno, e piu. Rinovato il voto si rihebbe il fanciullo, e fu sano." Also consult von Pastor, *History*, IV, 205.

[40] For Sixtus IV, consult Elisabeth Schröter, "Der Vatikan als Hügel Apollons und der Musen. Kunst und Panegyrik von Nikolaus V. bis Julius II," *Römische Quartalschrift für Christliche Altertumskunde und Kirchengeschichte* 75 (1980): 219-220. I treat Sixtus V in this context in following chapters.

[41] See Ostrow, "Sistine Chapel," 226, for a concise list of other acts of the pope's which demonstrated his extreme devotion to the Virgin. On Sixtus IV's work on the Immaculate Conception, consult von Pastor, *History*, IV, 209; and Egmont Lee, *Sixtus IV and Men of Letters*, Temi e Testi 26, ed. Eugenio Massa (Rome, 1978), 19, note 41.

[42] Platina, *Historia*, 261v: "Mentre poi un di lo lavavano nel bagnò, come si fa a bambini, egli a tanto isuenimento ne venne, che lo posero fra le braccia della madre per morto. Di che ella dell'insogno ricordandosi se voto ... [as in note 39 above]."

[43] Significantly, the frieze in the gallery of the Villa Montalto contained a scene of *Moses saved from the water of the Nile*, in Vittorio Massimo, *Notizie istoriche della Villa Massimo alle Terme diocleziane, con un'appendice di documenti* (Rome, 1836), 46. This scene is also depicted at the Scala Santa, listed in Giuseppe Scavizzi, "Gli affreschi della Scala Santa - II," *Bollettino d'arte* XLV (1960): 334-335.

[44] There is some question as to whether the sculpted figure of Moses was actually given a rod in the final version of the fountain. See Philipp P. Fehl, "Hermeticism and Art: Emblem and Allegory in the Work of Bernini," *Artibus et historiae* 14, VII (1986): 156-159. I wish to thank Philipp Fehl for having told me about this article. I treat the Moses fountain in greater detail in Chapter III, 97-99, below.

[45] Michele Mercati, *Gli Obelischi di Roma* (1589), reprint ed., ed. Gianfranco Cantelli (Bologna, 1981), 329.

[46] Virgil, *Aeneid*, VI, 789-807. For Augustus' assimilation to Romulus, consult Suetonius, *Divus Augustus*, VII.

[47] On Mercury as protector of Rome in his Christian embodiment as St. Michael, consult Francesco Panigarola, *In Festo Sancti Michaelis Archang. Homilia vigesima septima* (Venice, 1604), cited and discussed in Frederick John McGinness, "Rhetoric and Counter-Reformation Rome: Sacred Oratory and the Construction of the Catholic World View, 1563-1621," diss., U of California, Berkeley, 1982, 321, 343-344. For St. Michael's protection of the Hebrews, consult Daniel X: 13, 21. Michele Ghislieri was baptised Antonio, after St.

I, I shall introduce the Lateran Palace fresco cycle, the most significant carrier of Sixtine propaganda, and indicate the main overlying messages conveyed by the narrative scenes of the logge and rooms of the *piano nobile*, as well as by the so-called *parerga* of the ground floor and grand stairway that provides access to all floors of the palace in terms of the Roman Catholic reformatory dogma against the Protestants. Since the Good Works are in my view the means to understanding the personal and institutional significance of the Lateran Palace programme, and to peeling away, layer by layer, the manifold meaning of the Sixtine pontificate, in Chapter II I shall focus on the one type of Good Work which best facilitates the reading of the Sixtine mythology, namely the four most important allegories of Sixtine Rome featuring the pope as the lion of his coat-of-arms. In Chapter III, I shall then turn to an analysis of the Salone dei Papi, the only hall of Sixtine Rome which contains all four of these allegories, together with topographical Good Works. In Chapter IV, I shall then treat the iconography of the Sala degli Obelischi, the one room of the many designed and decorated for Sixtus V in which his Good Works are unaccompanied by "explanatory" verses. Having determined the significance of this room, I shall then treat selected rooms of the *piano nobile* that contain Good Works of Sixtus V represented in "uncanonical" ways, whether as Old Testament narratives intended to be read as types for Sixtus V's achievements, as personifications holding Sixtine monuments, or as devices which likewise incorporate key Good Works and which notably echo those depicted in the *parerga* of the *piano terreno* and grand staircase.

Anthony, but changed his name to Michele when he became a Dominican, in Platina, *Historia*, 327v. On the traditional connection between St. Michael and the pope, consult Marcello Fagiolo and Maria Luisa Madonna, "La Roma di Pio IV: La 'Civitas Pia,' La 'Salus Medica,' La 'Custodia Angelica,'" *Arte Illustrata* V, 51 (November 1972): 387-388; and Marcello Fagiolo, "Preistoria dei Prati di Castello fino all'ottocento," in *Carlo Menotti e la sua dimora. Un esempio di stile per Roma Capitale* (Rome, 1988), 138-139. On St. Francis as Mercury, see Emile Mâle, *L'art religieux de la fin du XVIe siècle au XVIIe siècle: Étude sur l'iconographie après le Concile de Trente* (Paris, 1951), 491. Also consult Sergio Guarino, "Aspetti dell'iconografia di Michele Arcangelo tra XV e XVII secolo," and Marica Mercalli, "L'Angelo di Castello: la sua iconografia, il suo significato," in *L'Angelo e la Città*, exh. cat., Museo Nazionale di Castel Sant'Angelo, 29 September - 29 November 1987, (Rome, 1987), 83 ff; 95 ff.

[48] For a list of his published sermons, consult Enrico Narducci, *Intorno al alcune prediche stampate di Sisto Quinto. Notizie raccolte da E. N.* (Rome, 1870). I have used the following: Patre Fra Felice Peretti da Montalto, *Predica Sopra il non men difficil che misterioso Vangelo della Settuagesima ...* (Naples, 1554); *idem, Predica della Purissima Concettione della Gloriosa Madre de Dio Maria Vergine* (1554), reprint ed. (Naples, 1588); *idem, Predicata nella inclita citta di Perugia il di delle Cineri ... Predica della necessita della sacra scrittura à reformare l'huomo* (n.p., n.d.); and *idem, Prediche del R. Padre Fra Felice Peretti da Mont'alto Regente in S. Lorenzo di Napoli ...*, (n.p., n.d.), which contains four sermons, including those on the Mysteries and Immaculate Conception listed in the foregoing.

CHAPTER I

THE PAPAL RESIDENCE FROM CONSTANTINE
TO POPE SIXTUS V

1. HISTORY

During the pontificate of Melchiades (311-14), Emperor Constantine offered the Caelian Hill, known as the Lateran district, and the imperial residence of his wife Fausta, to the pope as the new home of the Bishop of Rome. By the end of Sylvester I's pontificate (314-35), the popes had embraced their new home, the Patriarchium Lateranense.[1] From this time until the beginning of the fourteenth century when the papacy removed itself to Avignon, the Lateran would be the most important site in Rome. Containing the papal residence and basilica dedicated to the Saviour, it would function as the center of Christian politics, religion and administration (figs. 2-3).[2]

The history of the ancient residence of the popes following Sylvester's pontificate is by no means clear. This is due not only to the rather sketchy descriptions offered in the *Liber Pontificalis*, the main literary source for the early development and decorations of the palace, but also to the fact that it no longer exists, having been torn down by Sixtus V between 1585 and 1587.[3] Only three vestiges of the ancient residence are now extant: the Sancta Sanctorum, the private chapel of the popes, also known as the Chapel of Saint Lawrence, which was believed to have been built by Pope Sylvester, and to have contained such venerable and truly incredible relics as the heads of Saints Peter and Paul, the tablets of the Law, the rods of Moses and of Aaron, the robes and sacerdotal ornaments of Aaron, a golden candelabrum of seven branches, and other items from the bounty brought to Rome from Israel by the Emperors Vespasian and Titus; the Scala Santa, the twenty-eight marble stairs believed to be those which Christ ascended to enter the house of Pilate and which legend tells were transported from Jerusalem to Rome by Constantine's mother Saint Helena; and the mosaic fragment, now in the Vatican Library, of an apostle's head issuing from one of the two *triclinia* built by Pope Leo III (795-816) around 798 or the beginning of 799, known variously as the triconch *triclinium*, Aula Leonina, or Basilica Leoniana maior, the whole of which is reflected in the eighteenth century copy attached to the niche on the side of the Scala Santa complex.[4] Thanks to the descriptions and sketches of the complex penned prior to its destruction during the sixteenth century by Onofrio Panvinio and Pompeo Ugonio, as well as the odd sketch or engraving of certain parts of the Lateran site executed by Renaissance artists and the Good Works of Sixtus V in the Vatican Library, scholars have been able to piece together the essential character of the Patriarchium Lateranense and surrounding monuments, but reconstructions which have been ongoing since the seventeenth century,

[1] Lauer, *Palais*, 5-6, 36; Schiavo, *Lateran*, n.p.

[2] Richard Krautheimer, *Rome: Profile of a City, 312-1308* (Princeton, New Jersey, 1980), 21; contrast Lauer, *Palais*, 32. The basilica had been part of the imperial residence and was transformed by Constantine into a Christian building.

[3] *Le Liber Pontificalis*, ed., intro. and commentary by L'Abbé L. Duchesne, 2 vols. (1886, 1892; Paris, 1955). See Krautheimer, *Rome*, 346, for a succinct list of the main sources available for the study of the ancient residence.

[4] The origins of the Sancta Sanctorum are unclear, although it has been determined that it was not built as early as Sylvester's pontificate. See Lauer, *Palais*, 69-70, who also discusses the many theories on the date of construction; Mario Cempanari, Tito Amodei, *La Scala Santa*, Le Chiese di Roma Illustrate, 72 (Rome, 1974), 20-37; *Guide Rionali di Roma. Rione I - Monti Parte I*, ed. Liliana Barroero, SPQR Assessorato alla Cultura (2nd ed; Rome, 1982), 74-77; and Krautheimer, *Rome*, 209. For the relics housed in the chapel, consult Lauer, *Palais*, 50; Giuseppe Maria Soresino, *De capitibus Sanctorum apostolorum Petri, et Pauli in Sacrosancta Lateranensi Ecclesia assernatis opusculum* (Rome, 1673); and *idem, Compendio istorico cronologico Delle cose più cospicue concernenti La Scala Santa e Le SS. teste delli Gloriosi Apostoli Pietro, e Paulo ... con un sommario Delle Reliquie ...*, trans. Giuseppe Pazzaglia (1673; Rome, 1674). On the Scala Santa, consult Cempanari, Amodei, *Scala Santa*, 37-51; and Barroero, *Guide*, 68-74. For the fragment with an apostle's head see Cäcilia Davis-Weyer, "Karolingisches und Nicht-Karolingisches in zwei Mosaikfragmenten der vatikanischen Bibliothek," *Zeitschrift für Kunstgeschichte* XXXVII (1974): 31-39; and for the triconch *triclinium*, see 62-64, below.

notably with G. Grimaldi, Nicola Alemanno and Cesare Raspono, are not always in accord with one another.[5] To be sure, research on the nature, location, and dates of the ancient residence of the popes is still underway, and will no doubt continue well into the future. The following outline of the history of the palace and its decorations, as well as other key structures in the vicinity, including the Constantinian basilica and Baptistry, which are still extant, accordingly makes no pretense to either originality or completeness.[6] Rather, it is designed to give the reader the fundamental information which, in my view, is vital to an understanding of the programme that Sixtus V and his iconographer devised for the new and improved residence.

The early history and development of the Patriarchium Lateranense are vague. With the Sack of Rome in 410, the basilica was raided and silver vessels donated by Constantine, as well as venerable objects which the Emperors Vespasian and Titus had brought back to Rome from Jerusalem, were stolen. The palace itself was apparently left unharmed and, by the end of Sixtus III's pontificate (432-44), its core had been built up considerably so that it extended southwards and eastwards. At the Basilica of the Saviour, Sixtus III apparently commissioned an extensive cycle of frescoes to cover the nave walls, and he completely gutted and rebuilt the interior of the Baptistry that Constantine had built to replace the Lateran family nymphaeum.[7] Soon after Sixtus III's renovations, Hilarius I (461-468) carried on work at the Baptistry, and dedicated two interior chapels to Saints John the Baptist and John the Evangelist. He also vaulted and restored an antique structure which was still standing adjacent to the Baptistry to serve as an enclosure for a relic of the True Cross, known thereafter as the Oratory of the Holy Cross. In addition, Hilarius apparently built two libraries at the palace.[8] The attention paid to the Lateran district by the fifth century papacy reflected their own view of themselves as Peter's successors and hence rulers of Rome, a view which would culminate with Hilarius I's predecessor, Pope Leo the Great (440-461).[9] Given this point of view, it can not be by chance that the *Legenda Sancti Silvestri* was written during the fifth century. The legend recounts how Constantine was converted to Christianity owing to his vision of Saints Peter and Paul, ultimately to be baptised by Sylvester I, hence stripping Eusebius of Nicomedia of his historical role, while stressing the spiritual aspect of the momentous event. It also lists the gifts bestowed by the emperor on the Church, including the Lateran palace, which is now given to Sylvester I, rather than Melchiades.[10]

During the next two centuries, filled as they were with invasions and wars, economic decline, natural disasters, and the influx of pilgrims in this time of need to Rome, building work focused on the shrines of the martyrs and the construction of new churches to honour them, rather than on the home of Rome's bishop. By the pontificate of John VII (705-707), plans were underway to either replace the papal residence altogether by transferring the seat of the papacy to the Palatine Hill, or to substantially add to it and, it is understood, to restore the existing structure.[11] These plans did not come to fruition, however, and it was not until some fifty years had passed that the palace, which was "found in great neglect" was at last restored by Zacharias (741-752), a restoration which included a cycle of saints in the Oratory of Saint Sylvester.[12] This pope also em-

[5] Renaissance sketches are reproduced quite frequently in modern studies on the ancient residence. The descriptions penned during the 16th century are as follows: Onophrio Panvinio, "De Sacrosancta Basilica et Patriarchio Lateranensi," in Lauer, *Palais*, 476-490; Pompeo Ugonio, "Schedario," B. A. V. Barb. Lat. 2160, reprinted in part in Lauer, *Palais*, 577-578. The works by three 17th century authors to whom I have referred are as follows: G. Grimaldo, B. A. V. Barb. Lat. XXXIV, in Lauer, *Palais*, 581-582; Nicola Alemanno, *De Lateranensibus parietinis ab illustriss. & Reverendiss. Domino D. Francisco Card. Barberino Restitutis Dissertatio Historica* (Rome, 1625); Cesare Raspono, *De Basilica et Patriarcho Lateranensi ... Ad Alexandrum VII Pont. Max.* (Rome, 1656). They are cited in most modern studies on the ancient residence of the popes.

[6] Until 1537, there had been an equestrian monument of Marcus Aurelius in the *piazza* which was thought to represent Constantine, hence its Medieval appellation of "caballus Constantini." Pope Paul III (Farnese, 1534-1549) moved it to the Capitol, where it now stands on the base made by Michelangelo.

[7] Krautheimer, *Rome*, 45; 49-51.

[8] Lauer, *Palais*, 54-65; Krautheimer, *Rome*, 50-51. Also consult Cäcilia Davis Weyer, *Early Medieval Art 300-1150*, Sources and Documents in the History of Art (1971; Toronto, Buffalo, London, 1986), 34-37.

[9] On Leo I and fifth century religio-political ideals, consult Walter Ullmann, "Leo I and the Theme of Papal Primacy," *Journal of Theological Studies* II (1960): 25-51; and *idem, The Growth of Papal Government in the Middle Ages. A Study in the ideological relation of classical to lay power* (1955; London, 1970), 2-13.

[10] On the *Legenda*, consult Wilhelm Levison, "Konstantinische Schenkung und Silvesterlegende," *Miscellanea Francesco Ehrle. Scritti di storia e paleografia ... Studi e testi*, 38, 2 vols (Rome, 1924), II, 159 ff; Christopher Bush Coleman, *Constantine the Great and Christianity. Three Phases: The Historical, The Legendary and The Spurious* (New York, 1914), 161-164; 217-277; Ullmann, *Growth*, 75ff; and Jorg Traeger, *Der reitende Papst* (Munich and Zurich, 1970), 12-15. Also consult Christopher Walter, "Papal Political Imagery in the Medieval Lateran Palace," *Cahiers archéologiques: fin de l'antiquité et moyen âge* XX (1970): 171-172.

[11] Lauer, *Palais*, 91; Krautheimer, *Rome*, 100.

[12] Lauer, *Palais*, 91-99; Krautheimer, *Rome*, 103.

bellished and enlarged the Patriarchium, in emulation of the imperial palace at Constantinople, with a great tower, known as the Torre degli Annibaldi; a new porch before the palace archives; and a new *triclinium* on the *piano nobile*, also known as the Basilica Zacharia, complete with a map of the world.[13]

The impetus begun by Zacharias to maintain and beautify the papal residence was carried on with Leo III, who built two more *triclinia*; restored the long corridor connecting the second *triclinium*, also known as the Sala del Concilio, to the basilica built by Constantine; and dedicated an oratory to the Archangel Michael, likewise in proximity to the council hall.[14] John VII's appropriation of imperial tradition, which almost produced a transfer of the Patriarchium to the ancient seat of the emperors on the Palatine, and Zacharias' adoption of imperial building types and iconography, reached a high point under Leo III. His imperial posturing was lent substance by the "discovery" of the *Constitutum Constantini*, a document actually composed during the eighth century, possibly during Leo III's pontificate, and much influenced by the fifth century *Legenda Sancti Silvestri*. The *Constitutum Constantini*, also known as the Donation of Constantine, was like the *Legenda* in that it stripped Melchiades of his historical role and gave the emperor's gift of the imperial residence to Sylvester I and his successors. The similarities ended here, however, since it also gave to Sylvester the city of Rome, all of Italy, and the West; the imperial prerogative, including insignia, regalia and pecuniary benefits; spiritual as well as temporal supremacy in the Western world; and authority over the patriarchates of the East.[15] In response to his newly-found, or newly legitimized status, the mosaics created for Leo III stressed the papal succession from Christ through Sylvester to the present pontiff; imperial succession from Constantine through King Charles, soon to be crowned the Emperor Charlemagne; papal primacy, which gave to the pope authority over earthly kings; the emperor's rightful duty as the pope's vassal; and, on a less political note, the mission of the apostles to spread the Word and to convert the world to the true faith in anticipation of the millenium - messages which still take visual form in the niche of the Scala Santa complex.[16] With the pope's imperial-temporal and spiritual claims now reinforced by law, the Patriarchium Lateranense became known as the Sacrum Palatium Lateranense, a name change which aptly realized John VII's wish to annex the Palatine, while maintaining the location which Constantine had sanctified to Christ's earthly representative on the Caelian hill.[17] So influential was the *Constitutum Constantini* that four centuries later it formed the subject for the comprehensive fresco cycle at the SS. Quattro Coronati, and this influence would continue well into the Renaissance.[18]

The eighth century also saw the production of manuals documenting traditional practices within the Church, notably including the pope's *possesso* to the Lateran basilica and palace. As Walter Ullmann has shown, this "ancient" rite looked not only to biblical sources but also to the *Constitutum Constantini*.[19] Among the highlights of the ceremony, the pope would first take possession of his titular basilica, now dedicated to Saint John the Baptist, by knocking three times at the locked door and identifying himself to the canons waiting inside. Having taken possession of the basilica, he would then proceed next door to the palace. In addition to being raised from the *sedes stercoraria* in emulation of I Kings II: 8, and be-

[13] Krautheimer, *Rome*, 103.

[14] A great deal has been written on the mosaics of Leo III in the two *triclinia*. See, for example, Lauer, *Palais*, 104-118; Davis-Weyer, *Early Medieval Art*, 88-92; *idem*, "Eine patristische Apologie des Imperium Romanum und die Mosaiken der Aula Leonina," *Munuscula Discipulorum. Kunsthistorische Studien H. Kaufmann zum 70 Geburtstag* (Berlin, 1968): 71-83; Hans Belting, "Die beiden Palastaulen Leos III. im Lateran und die Entstehung einer päpstlichen Programmkunst," *Frühmittelalterliche Studien XII* (1978): 55-83; *idem*, "I mosaici dell'Aula Leonina come testimonianza della prima 'Renovatio' nell'arte Medievale di Roma," *Roma e l'età Carolingia, atti delle giornate di studio 3-8 maggio 1976*, ed. Istituto di Storia dell'arte dell'Università di Roma, Istituto Nazionale di Archeologia e Storia dell'arte (Rome, 1976), 167-182; Walter, "Papal," *Cahiers*, 157-160; *idem*, XXI (1971): 170-177; and Krautheimer, *Rome*, 115-117. For a reference to the Oratory of S. Michele, consult Rodolfo Lanciani, *Storia degli Scavi di Roma e notizie intorno le collezioni Romane di Antichità*, 4 vols. (Rome, 1913), IV, 141-142.

[15] For the *Constitutum*, consult Levison, "Konstantinische," *Miscellanea*, II, 181 ff; and Coleman, *Constantine*, 175-183, 228-237. Also see Brian Tierney, *The Crisis of Church and State 1050-1300* (Princeton, New Jersey, 1964), 18-19; Walter, "Papal," *Cahiers*, 172; and Krautheimer, *Rome*, 114-117.

[16] The original decoration of the left side of the apse of the triconch *triclinium* has been questioned recently in Walter, "Papal," *Cahiers*, 170-177, who consequently denies any relationship between the *Constitutum Constantini* and the mosaics commissioned by Leo III. I have followed the general consensus in the above characterization, although the idea of Walter that an apolitical Paul should replace the political Peter is intriguing, especially in terms of the Sixtine programme. I treat this problem again below, 62-64.

[17] The Patriarchium Lateranense was known by its new name after c. 813. See Lauer, *Palais*, 124; and Ullmann, *Growth*, 148.

[18] See, for example, Traeger, *Papst*, 41-44.

[19] For this and the following, Walter Ullmann, *Law and Politics in the Middle Ages. An Introduction to the Sources of Medieval Political Ideas* (Ithaca, New York, 1975), 261-263; and Christopher L. C. Ewart Witcombe, "Sixtus V and the Scala Santa," *Journal of the Society of Architectural Historians* XLIV (December 1985): 368. Also consult Torgil Magnuson, *Rome in the Age of Bernini*, Kungl. Vitterhets Historie Och Antikvitets Akademiens Handlingar, 2 vols. (Stockholm, Sweden; New Jersey, 1982), I, 189-192.

35

ing seated on the two curule chairs, one dedicated to Saint Peter, and the other to Saint Paul, within the Oratory of Saint Sylvester, he would be given the staff and keys of the palace and basilica, as well as the *pallium*, objects which aptly symbolized the pope's dual authority in the spiritual and temporal realms.

Work continued on the palace during the pontificates of Leo IV (847-855) and Gregory IV (827-844), and with Sergius III (904-911) extensive restorations were carried out on both the palace and basilica, owing to the damage caused by the devastating earthquake of 896. But it was during the twelfth century, in the wake of the Investiture Struggle, that the victorious papacy lavished embellishments on their residence, both architecturally and with murals and, as one might imagine, these paintings glorified papal primacy and succession, as well as imperial subjection to the See of Peter and his city. Significantly, the twelfth century also saw the first three of five ecumenical councils held at the Lateran palace. The first council took place in 1123 and was convoked by Callistus II (Guy, 1119-1124) following the Concordat of Worms; the second, in 1139 by Innocent II (Papareschi, 1130-1143) had to resolve the present schism with antipope Anacletus II; and the third, in 1179 by Alexander III (Bandinelli, 1159-1181) had yet another schism with which to contend, this time with antipope Callistus III. Like the ninth century decorations of Leo III, the twelfth century decorations reflected contemporaneous history and the most recent papal political theories. Under Callistus II, a chapel dedicated to Saint Nicholas was built and decorated with the popes of the Investiture Struggle, from Alexander II (da Baggio, 1061-1073) through Callistus himself, together with earlier popes, including Leo the Great and Gregory the Great (590-604), as well as a second representation of Callistus II together with Anacletus II, the antipope who completed the cycle in the 1130s, in the traditional stance of donors at the feet of Mary as Queen of Heaven, flanked by Popes Anacletus I (79-91) and Sylvester I.[20] Callistus II also built an audience hall, known as the Camera pro Secretis Conciliis, and commissioned paintings which showed the Fathers of the Church trampling on schismatics, including a representation of Callistus himself stomping on the antipope Maurice Burdin, while holding, with King Henry V, the scroll containing the Concordat of Worms.[21] For his part, Innocent II also built and decorated two new rooms in the palace, one of which featured three scenes from the coronation of Lotharius III by the pope in 1133, including the emperor acting as strator to Innocent II, a position which he willingly accepted as successor to the Constantine of the *Constitutum Constantini*.[22] Near the close of the century, probably during the pontificate of Alexander III, the façade of the atrium of the basilica was also adorned with politically pregnant mosaics interspersed with those featuring traditional Christian subject matter.[23] Included in the programme was the Donation of Constantine, Baptism of Constantine, and Sylvester's expulsion of the dragon, all taken from the *Constitutum*; the Fleet of Vespasian before Jerusalem, and the attack on the Israelites by Titus, evidently referring to the treasure of the Sancta Sanctorum; as well as the martyrdoms of John the Baptist and Philomene, and Christ's descent into Limbo.[24]

The stress placed on the subservient role of the emperor in these twelfth century decorations drew not only on the *Consti-

[20] Gerhart B. Ladner, *Die Papstbildnisse des Altertum und des Mittelalters*, 2 vols. (Vatican City, 1941), I, 202-218; Walter, "Papal," *Cahiers*, 160-161; Krautheimer, *Rome*, 190. Contrast Lauer, *Palais*, 162-171. For the historical context, consult Tierney, *Crisis*, 25-86.

[21] Illustrations of this and other scenes from the Audience Hall were executed for Panvinio and are illustrated and discussed in G. Ladner, "I mosaici e gli affreschi ecclesiastico-politici nell'antico Palazzo Lateranense," *Rivista di Archeologia Cristiana* XII (1935): 265-292. Also consult *idem, Papstbildnisse*, I, 195-201; Traeger, *Papst*, 44-48; Walter, "Papal," *Cahiers*, 162-166, 109-133; Krautheimer, *Rome*, 190; and recently Ingo Herklotz, "Die Beratungsräume Calixtus' II. im Lateranpalast und ihre Fresken: Kunst und Propaganda am Ende des Investiturstreits," *Zeitschrift für Kunstgeschichte* 52, 2 (1989): 145-214.

[22] This scene of Lotharius III's submission greatly troubled the Emperor Frederick I less than twenty years later, when he came to Rome for his coronation. Consult Arsenio Frugoni, "'A pictura cepit'," *Bollettino dell'istituto storico italiano* (1967): 123-136; Walter, "Papal," *Cahiers*, 166-169; and Krautheimer, *Rome*, 190.

[23] Clement III (Scolari, 1187-1191) has also been accredited with the programme, see Walter, "Papal," *Cahiers*, 169, note 54.

[24] See Lauer, *Palais*, 181-184; Traeger, *Papst*, 58; and Walter, "Papal," *Cahiers*, 169-170, 109-133.

tutum Constantini and the fortuitous and willing servitude of Emperor Lotharius III, but also on a more recent political theory, as developed during the eleventh century and definitively enforced by Innocent III. Known as the Doctrine of the Two Swords, this theory deferred to the single most authoritative text in existence, the Bible, specifically Luke XXII: 35-38, in which the keys which Christ gave to Peter in the quintessential text of papal primacy (Matthew XXVI: 51) were explained in terms of swords: "But they said, 'Lord, behold, there are two swords.' And he said unto them, 'It is enough.'" Hence the pope (and not, contrary to imperial claims, the emperor) received both of the swords and although he had to relinquish the earthly one to the emperor, he nevertheless held the more powerful spiritual sword, and accordingly could exercise power over the earthly realm as well.[25] In keeping with the absolute authority which Innocent III had codified and enacted during his pontificate, it was only a short logical step to bestow on the papal residence the physical glory and beauty that reflected both the spiritual and political grandeur granted to Christ's vicar according to the scriptural sources. He accordingly restored the papal residence and added yet more rooms and an oratory to the complex, so that it became the most magnificent structure on earth; a place, in Dante's words, as wondrous to the barbarians as heaven was to his poetic imagination.[26] The pope was concerned with the Lateran for another reason as well: one day, during the spring of 1209, while Innocent III was walking on a terrace at the Lateran, he was approached by a stranger. Unamused by the invasion of his privacy, he immediately dismissed the man. That evening, Innocent III had a dream in which he saw a palm that grew into a great tree from between his own feet and realized thereafter that the palm tree was the stranger of that afternoon. Innocent accordingly sent for the man, who was Saint Francis, and heard Francis explain his desire to create a rule for the Order of Friars Minor. Soon after, the pope realized that the "poor beggarman" holding up the tottering Lateran basilica, whom he had seen in an earlier dream, was in fact Francis. As a result of these momentous dreams, Innocent III verbally approved Francis' rule for the Order of the Friars Minor, an act which he would repeat with the assembly of bishops at the fourth ecumenical Lateran Council in 1215, and which would be commemorated by Nicholas IV in an inscription within the Lateran basilica.[27]

In 1227 an earthquake struck Rome and wreaked havoc on the Lateran district and papal residence, especially the Sancta Sanctorum, which was debilitated to its foundations. Although Honorius III (Savelli, 1216-1227) restored the private chapel, fifty years later Nicholas III (Orsini, 1277-1280) found it necessary to have it rebuilt and decorated.[28] Under Boniface VIII (Caetani, 1294-1303), great building works were resumed at the Lateran; he built the Palazzo Nuovo, located at the northern end of Leo III's Sala del Concilio, and appended to this structure in 1299 the Benediction Loggia, also known as the *pulpitum Bonifacii*. In keeping with the spirit of the victorious Church, as embodied by his predecessor Innocent III, and ever cognizant of the venerable history of the papal residence, Boniface VIII commemorated his building undertakings in an inscription which recounted the Baptism and Donation of Constantine, as well as his own part in the restoration of the Lateran complex. To insure that the message of Boniface's his-

[25] The theory is succinctly explained in Alexandra Herz, "The Sixtine and Pauline Tombs: Documents of the Counter-Reformation," *Storia dell'arte* XLIII (September-December 1981): 250. Also consult Stanley Chodorow, *Christian Political Theory and Church Politics in the Mid-Twelfth Century. The Ecclesiology of Gratian's Decretum* (Berkeley, Los Angeles, London, 1972), 57 ff. And for the Roman Catholic Reformers' application of this doctrine in the sermons preached at the papal court, see McGinness, "Rhetoric," 346 ff.

[26] Dante, *Paradiso*, XXXI, 34.

[27] Bonaventure, *Legenda Maior*, III, 9, III, 10. Compare Thomas of Celano, *Second Life of St. Francis*, XI, 17 in Habig, *St. Fancis*, 377; and *Legend of the Three Companions*, XII, 50. There are a number of variations on the theme of the earlier dream, including one in which both Sts. Francis and Dominic uphold the Lateran. On the inscription of Nicholas IV, see Lauer, *Palais*, 193.

[28] Consult Lauer, *Palais*, 200-206; and, more recently, Julian Gardner, "Nicholas III's Oratory of the Sancta Sanctorum and its decorations," *Burlington Magazine* CXV, 842 (May 1973): 283-294.

torical role be grasped by all, the frescoes featured narrative scenes of the Baptism of Constantine, the founding of the Lateran basilica, and Boniface VIII himself blessing the people *urbi et orbi* from the loggia, while emblems of the Caetani family were interspersed around these narratives.[29]

A mere nine years after Boniface's improvements to the papal residence, a disastrous fire swept the complex and a year later, in 1309, the papacy definitively transferred its seat to Avignon (an exile already begun in 1305). Another earthquake in 1349, and a fire in 1361, while the popes were still in captivity in France, did extensive damage to the residence, as well as to the basilica, which had to be rebuilt again.[30] Following their return from Avignon in 1367, Gregory XI (Roger, 1370-1378) found it necessary to transfer the papal residence to the Vatican, since the Patriarchium had fallen into grave disrepair and, moreover, the district was virtually barren and considered unhealthy.[31]

During the Renaissance, popes lavished great expense on San Giovanni, but when it came to beautifying the papal residence, the Vatican took precedence.[32] Although Sixtus IV had considered restoring the ancient palace, nothing was done until the pontificate of his nephew Julius II (della Rovere, 1503-1513), who fixed up the great council hall of Leo III and possibly other parts of the Patriarchium in preparation for the fifth ecumenical Lateran Council which was convoked in 1512. The Council continued until 1517, well into Leo X's pontificate. Leo focused his attention on the Baptistry, as would Clement VII a few years later.[33] Whereas the historical context of earlier councils had been reflected in the iconographical programmes of the Patriarchium, no parallels were forthcoming under Julius II, Leo X and Clement VII; again, it was the papal residence at the Vatican which reflected recent Church history in the Stanze of Raphael, notably by drawing parallels to Biblical, Early Christian and Medieval Church history, as well as to the *Constitutum Constantini*.[34] Following the Sack of Rome in 1527, attention did not revert to the Lateran; even the Sancta Sanctorum, the sacrosanct chapel of the popes, had been forsaken and its contents virtually forgotten.[35] Aside from the grandiose restoration plans of Paul IV, very little work was done following that carried out under Julius II.[36] Pius V actually gave part of the eastern end of the residence to the Franciscans (near the large *triclinium* of Leo III which was turned into a garden). While this was certainly a generous act, and one which, of course, deferred to Innocent III, it also seems to have pre-empted any thought of restoring the compex.[37] The Lateran, once the most hallowed and glorious place in Rome, had become little more than a memory. This would all be changed with the ascendancy of Pope Sixtus V.

The order for the construction of a new Lateran Palace was one of the first items on the agenda of the newly elected Pope Sixtus V in 1585. At this time Sixtus V also ordered the building of a new Benediction Loggia for San Giovanni to replace that built by Boniface VIII for the Patriarchium.[38] One year later, he would order the erection of an enclosure for the Sancta Sanctorum and Scala Santa, which had been moved to a position before the private chapel. In 1588, he would erect the Obelisk of Constantius II, on the site once occupied by the Torre degli Annibaldi, and add to its base inscriptions referring to the Constantinian origins of the site as well as the new function of the obelisk as a monument to the "invincible cross."

[29] Charles Mitchell, "The Lateran Fresco of Boniface VIII," *Journal of the Warburg and Courtauld Institutes* XIV (1951): 1-6; Krautheimer, *Rome*, 21, 209.

[30] Witcombe, "Scala Santa," *JSAH*, 368.

[31] von Pastor, *History*, XXII, 270-271.

[32] Witcombe, "Scala Santa," *JSAH*, 368, provides a list of popes who worked on the basilica.

[33] Lauer, *Palais*, 305; von Pastor, *History*, XXII, 270-271.

[34] See I. L. Zupnick, "The Significance of the Stanza dell'Incendio. Leo X and François I," *Gazette des Beaux-Arts* LXXX, 1245 (October 1972): 195-204, who treats the Stanza della Segnatura, Stanza d'Eliodoro and Stanza dell'Incendio; and Rolf Quednau, *Die Sala di Costantino im Vatikanischen Palast. Zur Dekoration der beiden Medici-Päpste Leo X. und Clemens VII*, Studien zur Kunstgeschichte, vol. 13 (Hildesheim, New York, 1979), for the Sala di Costantino. Also consult Roger Jones, Nicholas Penny, *Raphael* (New Haven & London, 1983), 113 ff, 147 ff, 239 ff.

[35] von Pastor, *History*, XXII, 271.

[36] Lauer, *Palais*, 312; and for work done in the interim, 305-315.

[37] Lauer, *Palais*, 318.

[38] von Pastor, *History*, XXII, 270.

Two months after his election, the gradual process of taking down the Patriarchium Lateranense was begun.[39] By the following year, materials from the Patriarchate and other ancient monuments destroyed by Sixtus V were being used to construct a new Lateran Palace which, in the pope's view, was more worthy of his station (fig. 4).[40] Fontana's edifice was constructed consciously following the model of the Farnese Palace (1517-46), with a square plan, central courtyard and an elevation of three floors, each comprised of rooms around a loggia facing the courtyard. As the palace was connected to the basilica of St. John Lateran, it was given three façades rather than four, all of which were articulated with quoins and a great cornice; windows crowned with alternating canonical and segmental pediments on the *piano nobile* and *secondo piano*; and, at center, a grand portal of the Doric Rustic order, complete with Sixtine symbols (*monti* and stars) adorning the metopes. Above each portal Fontana built a balustrade; differentiated the central window on the *piano nobile* from the others by providing it with fluted herm-like pilasters and a broken segmental pediment; and surmounted the portal and window with the Sixtine coat-of-arms. The palace was also equipped with a corner belvedere, emulating Medieval precedent, at the north-west side.[41] Access to the belvedere was provided by a winding staircase that passed through the three floors of the palace. This staircase was placed adjacent to the pope's private chapel on the *piano nobile*. Air and sunlight were also provided by the central courtyard, which was built with seven arches on each of the four sides. The arcade on the *piano terreno* was given pilasters of the Doric order; that on the *piano nobile*, of the Ionic; and that on the *secondo piano*, transformed into very ornate female herms with fluted bases, in lieu of the canonical Corinthian, and echoing, in their bases, the fluted pilasters adorning the central window above each façade portal. The *piano terreno* was constructed with twenty-five rooms ranged around the central courtyard and logge; the *piano nobile*, with seventeen, as well as the ramp or "new staircase" connecting the palace to the basilica; and the *secondo piano*, with fourteen rooms. According to the documents of payments the decorations were begun in 1588, and by 30 May 1589 the palace was inaugurated.[42]

Although the Lateran Palace is the single most important monument commissioned by Sixtus V, a monument intended to house the pope and his cardinals, it has received the least attention of all Sixtine building and decorating campaigns. This has been due, in large part, to the fact that following its completion the palace was used for anything but a papal residence, ranging from a grain storage depot to a lodging for pilgrims, so that it hardly held a key place in the annals of Roman history.[43] In recent years, coinciding with the anniversary of Sixtus V's pontificate, interest has turned to Fontana's architecture, notably in the studies of Bettina Burkart and Matthias Quast.[44] Such is not the case with regard to the interior decoration. The general inaccessibility of the palace to the public over periods of time has not aided in the investigation of its contents, but, then, owing to the Late Mannerist style of the frescoes, few have been interested in looking at the paintings, much less considering their meaning. For the most part, those few authors who have written on the cycle have focused their attention on the *piano nobile*, specifically the narrative scenes and Good Works of Sixtus V, and for good reason, since it was to

[39] The Patriarchium Lateranense was already being torn down by 8 June 1585, as reported in an *avviso* quoted in von Pastor, *History*, XXII, 428. For further details on the building campaign, consult Witcombe, "Scala Santa," *JSAH*, 368-379, who utilizes this and other *avvisi* in his discussion.

[40] von Pastor, *History*, XXII, 236-239, 271; Schiavo, *Lateran*, n.p. Fontana, *Della trasportatione*, 59, explains that in the pope's (and his) view, the Patriarchium "era pieno di fabriche vecchie di poco valore, la maggior parte rouinate senza commodità alcuna, tal che più tosto erano d'ingombro oscure, e sordide da vedere, che altrimenti per essere vn luogo di tanta deuotione."

[41] C. Elling, "Function and Form of the Roman Belvedere," *Danske Videnskabernes selskab, Copenhagen Arkaeologisk-kunsthistorisken Meddelelser* III, 4 (1950): 23-32, especially 30.

[42] Lauer, *Palais*, 616, Folio 24; Schiavo, *Lateran*, n.p.

[43] For the intervening history of the Lateran Palace, see Filippo De Rossi, ed., *Descrizione di Roma Moderna formata nuovamente con le Autorità del Cardinal Baronio, Alfonso Ciaconio, D'Antonio Bosio, Ottavio Panciroli, E d'altri celebri Autori ...* (Rome, 1597), 592; P. Letarouilly, *Edifices de Rome Moderne ou Recueil des Palais, Maisons, Églises, Couvents et autres monuments publics et particuliers les plus remarquables* (Liège, 1849), 489-490; and J. A. F. Orbaan, *Documenti sul barocco in Roma* (Rome, 1920), 44-45, 210.

[44] Bettina Burkart, *Der Lateran Sixtus V und sein Architekt Domenico Fontana* (Bonn, 1987); Matthias Quast, "Le piazze di Santa Maria Maggiore, Termini e del Laterano nell'ambito della progettazione sistina," forthcoming in *Sisto V*, VI Corso Internazionale d'Alta Cultura. Alessandro Ippoliti, "L'architettura del Palazzo Lateranense", in *Il Palazzo Apostolico Lateranense*, ed. Carlo Pietrangeli (Florence, 1991), 193-199, appeared while this book was in press.

have been the main living and entertaining quarters of the pope as well as the place of business and, consequently, the most important floor of the complex. The utter neglect of the ground floor and grand staircase is understandable, since there are no narrative scenes depicted. This is not to suggest, however, that they are unimportant or that their neglect is justified, as I shall explain below.

2. HISTORIOGRAPHY OF THE LATERAN PALACE FRESCO CYCLE

A visitor to the Lateran Palace during the sixteenth century would have entered the portal located on the northern façade, on the eastern façade, or on the western façade facing the obelisk and adjacent to the Benediction Loggia (figs. 4-5).[45] The entrance chosen seems likely to have depended upon which of the main thoroughfares had been taken from Rome's center in order to approach the palace.[46] The visitor would then have been escorted through a vaulted entranceway to the northern, eastern, or western loggia. Next, one would in all likelihood have been taken through, or through to, the western loggia to the grand stairway to make an ascent to the *piano nobile*. Accordingly, a visitor would have caught no more than a glimpse of the decorations in one of the entrance vestibules and logge. Interestingly enough, the relatively brief span of time which one spends on the ground floor is directly proportionate to the decidedly pithy descriptions it has been allotted in the literature on the Lateran Palace. But these passing references are due not so much to the time spent in the logge as to the general consensus of opinion which dictates that the decorations were mere interludes, or fillers, and hence unworthy of description. With the notable exceptions of Domenico Fontana and Angelo Rocca, who described parts of the *parerga* in the Vatican Library (1588-1589) (but curiously, in the case of Fontana, not those in the palace), and Vittorio Massimo, those in the Palazzo delle Terme of the Villa Montalto (1589), without, it must be noted, regarding them as such, this opinion holds true not only for the Lateran Palace, but for all non-figurative decorations of Sixtine Rome.[47] Although not usually explicitly stated, the implication of this view is that the *parerga* were frescoed quite simply to please, or to appease, a pope who supposedly suffered from a severe case of *horror vacui*.[48] Consequently, the ground floor logge and entrance vestibules as well as the grand staircase of the Lateran Palace, which are completely covered with fresco painting, have never been described in detail. The decorations have been characterized by a number of authors who have written on the palace (see Appendix IV), but all follow Domenico Fontana, who is so concise that he actually speaks of the ground floor and all staircases in one breath, saying that they are "dipinte a grotteschi, e paesi con varie imprese."[49]

The *piano nobile* has fared much better in the literature (refer hereafter to fig. 6). The first to write on the decoration of the rooms of the *piano nobile* was Domenico Fontana, the pope's private architect. His treatment of their contents is by no means exhaustive, but it has served all subsequent commentators, including the present one, as an extremely useful model from which to proceed (for this and the following consult Appendix IV). He considers the four main halls, that is,

[45] von Pastor, *History*, XXII, 275, states that the "principal entrance [is] to the south [presumably the north, given the unusual orientation of the basilica of St. John Lateran]." Quast, "Le piazze," forthcoming in *Sisto V*, names the north entrance as the main one. However, in his poem celebrating the Lateran Palace, Vincenzo Robardo, *Sixti V. Pont. Max. Gesta Quinquennalia Ac. Ill.morum et Rev.morum S. R. E. Car.lium ...* (Rome, 1590), 7v, seems to refer to the lunette above the door of the western entrance (my fig. 13) as the main door: "Stat Leo vestibulis, vigilique interritus ore / Excubat, & tristes remouet e limine noxas. / Qualiter Hesperidum Flauentibus arbore ramis / Auricoma assistens hortis, & squalidus alui / Proluuie serpens piceo phaetonta veneno / Inficiens; numquam damnatus lumina somno / Robora seruabat croceo curuata metallo."

[46] Elling, "Roman Belvedere," *Danske Videnskabernes selskab*, 30.

[47] Fontana, *Della trasportatione*, 94, 96; Angelo Rocca, *Biblioteca Apostolica Vaticana A Sixto V. Pont. Max. in splendidiorem. Commodioremq. locum translata. et a Fratre Angelo Roccha a Camerino Ordinis Eremitarum S. Augustini... Ad. S. D. N. Gregorium XIV* (Rome, 1591), 193-196; Massimo, *Notizie*, 126-131. The Villa Montalto was torn down in the 19th century to make room for the train station. Happily, the Good Works of the Palazzo delle Terme were saved, and are now housed in the Istituto Massimiliano Massimo, Roma-Eur.

[48] This view has recently been enunciated in Gamrath, *Roma*, 75.

[49] Fontana, *Della trasportatione*, 59. Fontana does not mention the entrance vestibules, although one might suppose that they were to be included in his comprehensive characterization. See Appendix V, 255 ff, below. Compare later descriptions which draw on Fontana's in Appendix IV 245 ff, below.

The rooms of the ground floor and *secondo piano* are known to those who were fortunate enough to have visited the palace when it was still the Lateran Museums, and hence open to the public, or to those who, beginning in 1991, may be given access one Sunday a month. For the present author, they are shrouded in mystery, since they were strictly out of bounds during the 1980s and in 1990, and have not, to my knowledge, been characterized, much less discussed in terms of their decorations. The function of the ground floor as the main cooking quarters is explained in Armando Schiavo, *Restauri e Nuove opere nella Zona Extra-territoriale Lateranense (1961-1968)* (Vatican City, 1968), 59, who quotes an unidentified early 17th century source. This same source calls the rooms on the third floor (*secondo piano*) "brutte et sconciertate" and on this basis dismisses them as unworthy of discussion.

the Salone dei Papi, Salone degli Imperatori, Salone degli Apostoli (or dei Paramenti) and Salone di Costantino, the five Old Testament rooms dedicated respectively to Samuel, David, Solomon, Elijah and Daniel, and the papal chapel and antichapel, listing the inscriptions accompanying the narratives and *viri illustres* as well as the verses composed for the Good Works of Sixtus V. He skips over all "subsidiary" components such as personifications, *grotteschi*, and the like by speaking of "molti altri adornamenti di figure, fogliami, cornici, e compartimenti di stucco tutto dorato."[50] Also excluded from the discussion are the Sala degli Obelischi, the Sala della Gloria, and the four rooms of the private papal apartment. Of the eleven rooms which Fontana treats, the functions of four are elucidated: the antichapel enabled the pope to hear mass, presumably being held next door in the chapel, without being seen; the Salone degli Apostoli was intended as the pope's dressing room, where he would don his pontifical garb before entering San Giovanni (hence Salone dei Paramenti); and the Salone dei Papi was the main hall of the palace and, by implication, the locale of the most significant assemblies.[51] No attempt whatsoever is made to elucidate, much less interpret, the meaning of the programme since this was not Fontana's purpose. His descriptions were intended to document the basic contents of the palace which he had built for Sixtus V and formed part of a kind of appendix to his fundamental discourse on his engineering feats in the raising of the obelisks; as Fontana himself realizes, the palace could only be treated sufficiently in a book of its own.[52]

In 1663 Giovanni Battista Mola again treated the cycle of the *piano nobile*, this time as part of a guidebook on the "miglior opere" of Rome. The inclusion of the palace in this list is a clear statement of Mola's high regard for it, and this is attested to by his characterization of the frescoes as "superbissime," "finissime," and "bellissime."[53] Yet, when one reads his description of the subjects represented on the *piano nobile* one must wonder whether Mola had actually visited the palace, because the descriptions are culled almost verbatim from Fontana, including what must be a typographical error.[54] It is possible, of course, that Mola was simply a little lazy, and had actually viewed the *piano nobile*, but, in any case, he supplements the error of Fontana's treatise with more of his own! As per Fontana's method, Mola treats the four main halls of the *piano nobile*, but when he discusses the Old Testament rooms, he curiously omits the Sala di Daniele from his roster, and, moreover, he ignores altogether the papal chapel and antichapel. Needless to say, Mola also omits those rooms excluded from Fontana's description. Finally, Mola does not reproduce the inscriptions and verses accompanying the paintings, no doubt since he expected the reader of his guidebook to be standing in front of the frescoes and accordingly able to read them for himself.

Although the frescoes were restored during the pontificate of Innocent XI (Pignatelli, 1691-1700) in preparation for the conversion of the palace into the Apostolic Hospice of Saint Michael, this occasion does not seem to have spawned much interest in the art and pontificate of Sixtus V, much less in the Lateran Palace.[55] It was not until Luigi Biondi in the nineteenth century that the Lateran Palace of Sixtus V was again treated in the literature. Biondi's study corresponded to the restorations to the Lateran Palace carried out during the pon-

[50] Fontana, *Della trasportatione*, 62v, 63. But see the notebook in my Appendix V, 255 ff, below.

[51] Fontana, *Della trasportatione*, 62v, 63v, 59v, respectively for the antichapel and chapel, Salone dei Paramenti, and Salone dei Papi.

[52] Fontana, *Della trasportatione*, 64.

[53] Giovanni Battista Mola, *Breve Racconto delle miglior opere d'architettura scultura et pittura fatte in Roma et alcuni fuor di Roma* (1663), ed., intro., Karl Noehles, Quellen und Schriften zur bildenden Kunst, (Berlin, 1966), 64.

[54] Both Fontana and Mola speak of 16 popes depicted in the Salone dei Papi, and there are actually 19. Of course, Fontana then proceeds to list the 19 popes and their inscriptions; Mola does not!

[55] This is not to suggest, of course, that research did not continue on the Patriarchium Lateranense. See, for example, T. Reinesio, *De palatio Lateranense* (Jena, 1679); and Filippo Maria Renazzi, *Notizie storiche degli antichi Vicedomini del patriarchio Lateranense e dei moderni prefetti del sacro palazzo apostolico ...* (Rome, 1784).

tificate of Gregory XVI (Cappellari, 1831-1846) in preparation for the conversion of the ground floor into the Museo Gregoriano Profano.[56] While a restoration now prompted interest in the fresco cycle, Biondi still focused his attention on the programme of the *piano nobile*, rather than on that of the ground floor which was being transformed into the new gallery. Incorporating his discussion of the palace into the larger context of the Patriarchium Lateranense and the history of the papal residence, Biondi is quite taken with the style of the decorations, calling them "belle," "maravigliose," and "magnifiche."[57] Although, like Mola, he does not reproduce the inscriptions accompanying the narratives and historical figures, he does paraphrase the contents to give the reader an idea of their significance. The verses accompanying the Good Works in the Salone dei Papi are not described, however, probably owing to the difficulty inherent in providing a précis of their poetic content. Biondi adds to Fontana's identification of this hall as the main one by stating that it was intended for consistories and councils. He also discusses the same halls and rooms treated by Fontana and, in addition, mentions the existence of the Sala della Gloria (which he calls the sixth room) for the first time, suggesting that this may well have been the dining room. He then identifies the *quadri* of this room as depicting the four seasons, and mentions that there are also auxiliary figures and arabesques. In his descriptions of the subjects represented in other rooms of the *piano nobile* Biondi is also slightly more detailed than Fontana (and, of course, Mola): he identifies four personifications in the Sala di Samuele as *Faith, Hope, Charity* and *Religion*, and mentions the presence of four others; in the Chapel we are told that, in addition to the narratives listed by Fontana, there are representations of the four Evangelists and eight Doctors of the Church; in the antichapel, landscapes, arabesques and personifications; in the Sala di Davide, representations of the *stemma* of Sixtus V as well as eight virtues personified; in the Sala d'Elia, emblematic figures in addition to narrative scenes; in the Sala di Daniele, a virtue in each angle as well as arabesques and *imprese* accompanying narratives; and in the Salone di Costantino, four landscapes, four figures and four *imprese*, in addition to the scenes from the life of Constantine. In this way, Biondi not only adds to the breadth of knowledge concerning the actual layout of rooms on the *piano nobile*, and the *"parerga"* accompanying the narratives and *viri illustres*, but he also contributes to the depth of knowledge by actually identifying four personifications. Still, there are only minor attempts to synthesize the meaning of the odd room, so that by 1835 the message of the *piano nobile* is still essentially uncharted territory.

Dumesnil treated the Lateran Palace cycle soon after Biondi in his book on the life and pontificate of Sixtus V. It is probably no coincidence that Dumesnil's book was published not long after the *piano nobile* had been transformed into the Museo Pio Cristiano and the great ramp leading from the Salone di Costantino to the basilica apparently restored by Pius IX (Mastai-Ferretti, 1846-1878), as this new museum would have spawned a certain degree of interest in the pontificate of Sixtus V. Whereas Biondi made significant strides in the treatment of the *piano nobile*, Dumesnil reverted to the copy-cat method of Mola since both descriptions were in their own ways intended as guides to the palace. The gulf that separates their methods lies in the fact that Dumesnil actually states his

[56] On the Lateran Museum consult Touring Club Italiano, *Roma e Dintorni*, Guida d'Italia (1962; Milan, 1965), 361-369; and J. D. Breckenridge, "Lateranus Redivivus," *Art Bulletin* LIV, 1 (March 1972): 69.

[57] Luigi Biondi, *Intorno il Restauramento nel Palazzo Pontificio Lateranense* ... (Rome, 1835), 13. A year later, another study was published on Sixtus V, but this excluded the Lateran Palace, namely C. Fea, "Lavori di Sisto V," *Miscellanea Filologica* II (1836): 2-23.

method.[58] Dumesnil also avoids any aesthetic judgements as to the quality of the frescoes no doubt because his purpose was quite simply a documentary one. He accordingly lists the contents of the main hall, including the same error that Mola had taken from Fontana's treatise; he describes the narratives and personages represented in the Salone degli Imperatori; and mentions the existence of more rooms with subjects taken from the Old and New Testaments. Dumesnil's greatest contribution to the study of the *piano nobile* was his translation of the verses accompanying the Good Works of Sixtus V in the Salone dei Papi.

One of the most significant aids to the study of the cycle was finally published in 1882 by Bertolotti, whose main concern was not the Lateran Palace, but rather the North Italian artists working in Rome during the Renaissance and Baroque periods. For the first time Bertolotti located and published invaluable documents from the pontificate of Sixtus V concerning the payments made to artists for their work in four rooms of the palace, as well as in the Benediction Loggia of San Giovanni. Significantly, the documents mention the Sala degli Obelischi, a room which, until this time, had been completely ignored in the literature.[59] In addition, they note the existence of three *quadri* representing the Obelisks of San Pietro, San Giovanni, and Santa Maria Maggiore, as well as depictions of *grotteschi* and two lions on a red ground in this room. The documents also refer to the Sala di Samuele, and mention landscapes containing narrative scenes from the life of the prophet.[60] Although every author from Fontana forward had mentioned the presence of narrative scenes, most often listing the subjects represented, none had mentioned that each scene is set within a landscape. It becomes clear, therefore, that the landscape component of the narratives is actually quite significant (why else would it have merited mention in a record of payment?), and this has ramifications for the landscapes represented in the logge and private apartment of the pope (locales not yet mentioned in the sources). In addition, the documents mention that the coat-of-arms of Sixtus V was represented on the vault of the Sala di Samuele together with four *grotteschi* on a golden ground, each accompanied by a figure, and they confirm Biondi's identification of the four personifications in this room. With regard to the Sala di Davide, the documents first list the narrative scenes, as usual. They then mention eight virtues peculiar to Sixtus V, so that Biondi's notice of their existence is given a specific and very personal application, even though they are not identified by name. Also mentioned are images of the genius of Sixtus V which are represented on the vault of the room with crowns of flowers.[61] The last room to which the documents refer is the Sala di Salomone. Typically, the narratives are listed first. This is followed by a list of four devices located on the four corners of the vault concerning "gli atti et segni di N. S. di varia inventione."[62] One type of device is described as representing obelisks and columns together with the motto "RELIGIO MIRANDA TRIVMPHAT." This type is also mentioned with regard to the opposite corner, but with a different motto: "GLORIAM DEI EXALTAT." The remaining two corners also contain the same *corpo*, this time comprising mountains with a crown, star and keys, and both have diverse *anime*: the one reads "TERNA HAEC TRIPLICI," and the other, "BONITATIS SCIENTIAE DISCIPLINAE." From this characterization of the

[58] M.-A.-J. Dumesnil, *Histoire de Sixte-Quint: sa vie et son pontificat* (Paris, 1869), 425.

[59] A. Bertolotti, *Artisti Modenesi, Parmensi e Della Lunigiana in Roma nei secoli XV, XVI e XVII. Ricerche e studi negli archivi Romani* (1882; Bologna, n.d.), 28.

[60] Bertolotti, *Artisti Modenesi*, 29, for this and the following on the Sala di Samuele.

[61] Bertolotti, *Artisti Modenesi*, 29.

[62] Bertolotti, *Artisti Modenesi*, 29-30. Also consult Appendix V, 255 ff, below.

corners of the Sala di Salomone, the documents make clear to anyone who has not actually visited the palace that the programme of the *piano nobile* is not comprised simply of narratives, *viri illustres*, and Good Works of Sixtus V filled in with "*parerga*" devised of various supplementary and relatively insignificant components. However, the significance of the programme is not yet addressed.

Near the end of the century, Ludwig von Pastor embarked upon his monumental *History of the Popes* (1898-1953) treating the popes from the fourteenth century to his own time. In the second of his two volumes devoted to Sixtus V, he discusses the Lateran Palace in refreshing depth. Although von Pastor finds the frescoes to be, quite simply, "of no great importance artistically," and puts the onus for the poor quality on the pope who demanded that work be executed hastily, he is the first to try to understand the iconology of the art.[63] To this end, von Pastor provides a general description of the contents of the Salone dei Papi; he gives a brief indication of the narratives in the remaining three halls; and he mentions the existence of the Sala di Samuele, the private chapel, and "four other apartments" with scenes from the Old Testament, all of which, he tells the reader, have inscriptions.[64] He excludes the Sala degli Obelischi, antichapel, Sala della Gloria and private apartment of the pope from his outline. Significantly, he also mentions that at the time of writing, he was allowed access only to the Salone di Costantino. Although he does not explain why the palace was again *in clausura*, it may have been due to the preparations being carried out by Pius XI (Ratti, 1922-39) for the Museo Missionario Etnologico, which would open in 1926 on the third floor of the palace.[65] Clearly, then, von Pastor, like so many previous commentators, was forced, though not uncomfortably so, to rely on the fundamental treatise of Fontana. Unlike previous commentators, however, von Pastor's aims were not simply to document the contents of the palace. In keeping with his positivistic bent, he shifted the focus of discussion from the description of various components in the cycle to the first real synthesis of material from a cultural-historical point of view. As purveyor of a message of considerable relevance to the pontificate of Sixtus V, von Pastor pointed to the importance of the Lateran Palace cycle as a cultural document. He saw the cycle, like all programmes commissioned by Sixtus V, as a rebuttal aimed at the heretics and specifically the Protestants, since it shows the Apostolic and Roman origins of the Church and the dissemination of Christianity throughout the world.[66] His contribution was considered so significant, and probably so timely, given the project of Pius XI and the recent anniversary of the pope's birth, that the volume on Sixtus V's building works was actually translated and printed as a book quite separate from the series in 1922.[67] It was presented to Benito Mussolini, who became Prime Minister of Italy that very year.

While von Pastor was writing on the iconology of Sixtine Rome, scholars were also turning to the paintings executed for the pope, especially those by Paul Bril. Although unconcerned with the meaning of the frescoes which the Fleming created in the palace, A. Mayer was the first to draw attention to the existence of landscapes with Christian buildings and pagan ruins in the logge lunettes of the *piano nobile* by attributing six of them to the master.[68] He was followed by Maurice Vaes who, although giving all of the landscapes in the lunettes of the *piano nobile*, in the Salone di Costantino, in the private apart-

[63] von Pastor, *History*, XXII, 275, note 2. Similarly, on 295, von Pastor discusses the Sixtine Library decorations as "unequal in merit and to a great extent worthless [!]."

[64] von Pastor, *History*, XXII, 275-276.

[65] This may also have been due to restorations carried out under Pius X in 1908, as stated on an inscription above the representation of the Vatican Library in the Salone dei Papi. This has been noticed in Schiavo, *Lateran*, n.p.

[66] von Pastor, *History*, XXII, 275, 295.

[67] Ludwig von Pastor, *Sisto V. Il Creatore della nuova Roma* (Rome, 1922).

[68] A. Mayer, *Das Leben und die Werk der Brüder Matthäus und Paul Brill* (Leipzig, 1910), 27-29.

ment, where they are inhabited by hermits and saints, and on the ground floor to Bril (!), did draw attention to the fact that landscapes are found not only in the logge of the *piano nobile*, but also in the private apartment and on the staircase and, moreover, that at least some of these contain Christian subject matter.[69]

With the momentous signing of the Lateran Pact in the Salone dei Papi in 1929, interest in Sixtus V and the Lateran Palace naturally enjoyed renewed vigour. Following the signing of the pact, a number of studies appeared, some of which compared Sixtus V to Mussolini (not, interestingly enough, to Pius XI!),[70] and, almost inevitably, a study on the Salone dei Papi was published. Alberto Tulli, the author of this work, did not contribute anything new, however; he simply reverted to Fontana and copied, à la Mola, the architect's description, this time complete with verses and inscriptions.[71]

The momentum to study Sixtus V, which was spurred on at least in part by the anniversary of his birth and the signing of the Lateran Pact, was sustained during the following couple of decades, although interest in the Lateran Palace declined again. With the publication of the guidebook to the Lateran Museums by the Direzione Generale dei Musei e Gallerie Pontificie in 1950, the Sixtine frescoes were again treated, and for the first time described in a comprehensive manner.[72] As a guidebook concerned first and foremost with the pagan and Christian antiquities housed in the museum, the passages on the Sixtine frescoes are decidedly brief and, quite expectedly, no critical commentary is offered so that the meaning of the cycle is left to the visitor's imagination. Nonetheless, the anonymous author describes the main subjects represented in each of the rooms, save the Anticappella and Cappella Papale, and halls (which are not called by name, but rather by number, corresponding to the visitor's prescribed itinerary through the palace), including a listing of the "simboli della gloria" in Biondi's "sixth room" (called Sala VII), and of Vaes' hermits and saints in landscapes in the private papal apartment. Also included in the listing is the identification of the obelisk of Santa Maria del Popolo in the Sala degli Obelischi (called Sala XV). The fourth obelisk is now added to the list of three identified in the documents published by Bertolotti. This identification would be followed until 1985, when René Schiffmann recognized that the obelisk depicted was actually that projected for Santa Croce in Gerusalemme.[73] Returning to the 1950 guidebook, the main subjects represented in the logge vaults are also set forth for the first time. Hence, in the western loggia, we are told that the narratives are taken from the Old Testament, beginning with the creation of the world and ending with the birth of Esau and Jacob; in the southern loggia, scenes from the story of Judith and Holofernes; in the eastern loggia, episodes from the New Testament; and in the western loggia extension, scenes from the life of Saint Francis of Assisi. Finally, the author recognizes the significance of the so-called *parerga*, even though they are not explained; in the first room of the private apartment, the vault is characterized as containing "motivi araldici della famiglia del Pontefice," while that in the fourth room, "allegorie relative alla vita di Sisto V."

The guidebook was followed a decade later by a number of studies by Giuseppe Scavizzi on the artists of Sixtine Rome. Although concerned first and foremost with the style of these artists, and in assigning attributions, Scavizzi identified the

[69] Maurice Vaes, "Matthieu Bril 1550-1583," *Bulletin Institut Historique Belge de Rome* VIII (1928): 326. The Salone di Costantino is referred to as "la premiere grande salle." The landscapes of the grand staircase are actually located on the ground floor, in the western loggia which faces the stairs and acts as a landing. There is a possibility that Vaes was referring to the landscapes on the ramp-stairway connecting the basilica to the palace and the Salone di Costantino (he calls it the "grand escalier d'honneur").

[70] On Sixtus V and Mussolini, see, for example, Ugo Cuesta, *Un papa fascista* (Milan, 1929); and A. Zucconi, *Sisto Quinto e Benito Mussolini. Ritorni Storici* (Rome, 1934). Also consult Nicola Loy, *Cenni Biografici intorno a Felice Peretti indi Sisto V ...* (Grottamare, 1928); G. Amadio, "Come e perché Sisto V non nacque a Montalto," *Rassegna Marchegiana* VII (1929): 250-252; U. Donati, "Di alcune opere ignorate di Domanico Fontana a Roma," *L'Urbe* (December 1929): 15 ff; and Carlo Cecchelli, "Laterano e Vaticano," *Capitolium* V (1929): 63-78.

[71] Alberto Tulli, "La 'Sala del Concilio' nel Palazzo Laterano," *Per l'arte sacra* VII (March-April 1929): 30-55.

[72] *Il Palazzo del Laterano e i Musei Lateranensi Cristiano-Missionario, Etnologico e Profano: testo riveduto dalla Direzione Generale dei Musei e Gallerie Pontificie* (Rome, 1950).

[73] Schiffmann, *Roma felix*, 170, and fig. 45.

subject of one of the scenes from the life of Saint Francis in the western loggia extension, namely the *Birth of Saint Francis*, as well as three personifications in the Sala degli Obelischi, *Faith*, *Fortune* and *Fortitude*.[74] There followed the publication of Anna Maria Corbo on the sources available in the Roman State Archives for the study of the building works of Sixtine Rome, including Fontana's notebook on the construction and decoration of the Lateran Palace.[75] But it was not until 1969 that the programme of the palace was really treated in earnest, this time by Armando Schiavo.[76] As in the case of most of the studies considered thus far, his coincided with work on the palace, specifically, a restoration campaign carried out between 1963 and 1967 under the auspices of John XXIII (Roncalli, 1958-1963) and Paul VI (Montini, 1963-1978).[77] Like Fontana, Mola, Biondi, Dumesnil and Tulli, Schiavo lists the titles of the major scenes represented in the rooms and halls of the *piano nobile*, and, like Biondi, he mentions the existence of such aspects as personifications, historical figures and *parerga* which populate the decorations. However, he omits both the Anticappella and Cappella Papale from his discussion. Schiavo provides one new identification: the figure of Moses in the Salone di Costantino. He also explains that the "simboli della gloria" described in the 1950 guidebook are held by a personification. In addition, Schiavo gives Biondi's "sixth room" a name, the Salone delle Stagioni, or della Gloria, based on the identification of the personification at center vault; and he comments on the function of this room, suggesting that it was likely intended as the throne room. He finds this suggestion reinforced by the fact that it is currently (in 1969) used as such, but does not address Biondi's suggestion that it may have functioned as the dining room. Although critical commentary on the programme is brief, Schiavo does offer two extremely valuable observations based on the internal coherency of the cycle. First, he notes that the *quadratura* of the Salone dei Papi is echoed on the vault of the Sala della Gloria. Secondly, he realizes the importance of the patron in the iconographical scheme; in Schiavo's words: "The works accomplished by Sixtus V during the short but active period that he was Pope are illustrated, while his heraldic emblems, achievements with mottoes, the obelisks raised by him and the celebrative columns he restored appear as a constant theme of the figurative compositions." For the first time, finally, the character of the *piano nobile* is given visual explanation with colour reproductions.

The palace has been closed to the public since the restorations in the 1960s and the subsequent transfer of the Vicariato to the *secondo piano*. While interest has been mounting on Sixtus V, his pontificate and the works of art, architecture and city planning that he commissioned, particularly with the recent anniversary of his pontificate, no attempt has been made thus far to explore the over-all meaning of the Lateran Palace fresco cycle.[78] Indeed, even a full description of the contents of the *piano nobile* has never been published, and the ground floor and grand staircase, to which I shall turn shortly, have all but been ignored. As a result of the paucity of information on the decoration of the palace, only five of the rooms on the *piano nobile* have been mentioned with regard to their functions within the suite of rooms, and, notwithstanding the fact that Corbo has now drawn attention to Fontana's notebook on the palace in the Roman State Archives (see Appendix V), it is

[74] Giuseppe Scavizzi, "Gli affreschi della Scala Santa ed alcune aggiunte per il Tardo Manierismo Romano - I," *Bollettino d'Arte* (1960): 219-220; and "Sugli inizi del Lilio e su alcuni affreschi del Palazzo Lateranense," *Paragone* (May 1961): 46-47, for the St. Francis narrative and personifications, respectively.

[75] Anna Maria Corbo, "Appunti su una fonte per la storia urbanistica e edilizia di Roma: la serie "fabbriche" del Camerale I," *Rassegna degli Archivi di Stato* XXV, 1 (January-June 1965). I wish to thank Donato Tamble', of the Archivio di Stato di Roma, for very kindly drawing this work to my attention. The notebooks of Fontana are now being published, beginning in Enrico Guidoni, Angela Marino, Angela Lanconelli, "I 'Libri dei conti' di Domenico Fontana. Riepilogo generale delle spese e Libro I," *Storia della città. Rivista internazionale di storia urbana e territoriale* 40 (October-December 1986): 45-77. I should like to thank Mario Bevilacqua for this reference.

[76] Schiavo, *Lateran*, n.p.

[77] The work done under Paul VI unfortunately also destroyed the vestiges of decorations executed under Gregory XVI in the northernmost vault of the eastern loggia on the *piano nobile*, and added what can only be described as eyesores in 1969. See my Appendix I, 201, below, for a description of the vault and lunette decoration executed at this time; and consult my "Problems in the Study of the Lateran Palace," forthcoming in *La Roma di Sisto V. L'Arte, L'Architettura, La Città*, ed. Maria Luisa Madonna, exh. cat., Rome, Palazzo Venezia, 1992, for the decorations of Paul VI. Also consult F. Mancinelli, "Arte medioevale e moderna," *Bollettino dei Musei e Gallerie Pontificie* I (1959-1974): 123 ff, 128 ff, 130, 132, 133, for the notices of the restorations to the palace.

[78] Liliana Barroero, "Il Palazzo Lateranense: il ciclo pittorio sistino", in *Palazzo Apostolico*, 217-221, appeared while this book was in press. Also during this time the Lateran Palace was opened to the public, as I explain in note 49, above.

Ironically, given the bad press which late Mannerism has been given, more work has been done on the authorship and style of the Lateran Palace frescoes than on their meaning. The first to assign attributions to the frescoes painted by some 36 artists under the direction of Giovanni Guerra and Cesare Nebbia was Giovanni Baglione, *Vite de pittori, scultori, architetti ed intagliatai dal pontificato di Gregorio XIII dal 1572 a tempi di Papa Urbana VIII nel 1642* (1642) reprint ed. (Bologna, 1975), 38, 39, 103, 116, 119, 129, 139,148, 199, 299, 303, 401. Baglione, who worked on the frescoes at the Lateran Palace himself, is very general in his recollections and accordingly does not assign specific frescoes to specific artists. Baglione was followed by F. Titi, *Descrizione delle pitture, sculture e architetture esposte al pubblico in Roma* (1763), reprint ed.,

questionable whether the functions of more rooms will ever be known for certain. Of the 106 personifications frescoed in the rooms and halls of the main floor (that is, excluding the veritable overpopulation of personifications in the logge!), only twenty have been identified in the literature, a task made easier by the fact that twelve of these are still accompanied by inscriptions.[79] As for the landscapes, forty-one in all in the rooms and halls (again, excluding the veritable forest in the logge and the Old Testament narrative scenes), twenty, representing the Good Works of Sixtus V in the Salone dei Papi and housing Hebrew and Christian figures in the private apartment, have been identified; of the remaining twenty-one landscapes in the rooms, only eight have collectively merited mention in the context of the palace's iconography.[80] To compound the inherent difficulty in penetrating the meaning of the programme, the identity of the iconographer is not known for certain. Silvio Antoniano, once secretary to Charles Borromeo and, under Sixtus V, secretary of the Sacred College of Cardinals and Latinist *par excellence*, has been suggested as the iconographer of the Lateran Palace decorations, together with Sixtus V himself.[81] While this suggestion is certainly a reasonable one, I shall suggest an alternative possibility in Chapter III, as the analysis of the programme unfolds.

3. LAYOUT OF THE GROUND FLOOR LOGGE AND GRAND STAIRCASE AND PRELIMINARY ICONOGRAPHICAL ISSUES

The surfaces of the vaulted passageways of the entrance vestibules and logge on the *piano terreno*, as of the grand staircase, are completely covered with *grotteschi*, contrived in geometrical configurations of foliage and populated by a plethora of putti and angels holding aloft fiery urns, cornucopiae, garlanded and regal crowns, curtains, and the triple mountains, pears and star(s) of Sixtus V's personal heraldry. Sometimes angels crown the lion of the pope's *stemma* and sometimes they trumpet his fame; sometimes precocious putti play with the pope's keys and tiara, or with his baldachin; and at other times, lions hold up the triple mountains encircled with three crowns and surmounted by a star.[82] These compartments are punctuated with others featuring the coat-of-arms of the pope, in whole or in part. The complete *stemma* is represented, quite naturally, at the center of each entrance vestibule and loggia; it also holds center stage on the first and second arms of the grand staircase, while the third and fourth break with this symmetry, and feature the *stemma* at both top and bottom. Designed as a lion standing on his hind legs, holding a branch with three pears in his right forepaw, and crossed by a bar with three mountains and a star (or sometimes two), this coat-of-arms finds its way into every nook and cranny not only of the Lateran Palace, but of Sixtine Rome (fig. 7).[83] The lion, according to the pope himself, refers to his "magnanimity and beneficence;" the pears, to his surname, Peretti (small pear trees); the three mountains, to the town where he was schooled, Montalto; and the star, or stars, in one sense quite possibly to the Virgin.[84]

In keeping with the method used in all Sixtine monuments there are inscriptions on the vaults which state either the patron, or both the patron and year of execution: "SIXTVS V. P. M. AN. PONT. IIII," that is, 24 April 1588 - 23 April 1589,

ed. Hugh Honor (n.p., n.d.), 211, who simply adds to the roster of artists who worked on the frescoes. Likewise, Biondi, *il Restauramento*, 11; von Pastor, *History*, XXII, 275; and Orbaan, *Sixtine*, 172, list the various artists who painted at the palace, sometimes adding another artist to the list, but quite understandably shying away from specific attributions. The first to depart from this method was Mayer, *Leben*, 27-29, who, as I have explained above, gave six landscapes in the *piano nobile* logge lunettes to Paul Brill; and by Vaes,"Matthieu Bril," *Institut Historique Belge de Rome*, 326, who went so far as to attribute all of the loggia landscapes, the landscapes at the bottom of the papal staircase, the landscapes with hermits and saints situated in the pontifical rooms, and the four landscapes in the Salone di Costantino to Brill. Also consult Leo van Puyvelde, *La Peinture Flamande a Rome* (Brussels, 1950), 70. The next to assign specific attributions was Giuseppe Scavizzi, who looked at the narrative scenes and personifications from the point of view of style for the first time. He assigned attributions for two narratives in the Salone dei Papi, three personifications and the *stemma* with supporting angels in the Sala degli Obelischi, and one narrative in the western loggia extension, these latter, which I have discussed above; Scavizzi's attribution and identification of the St. Francis scene has recently been confirmed in Caterina Bon, "Una Proposta per la cronologia delle opere giovanili di Giovanni Baglione," *Paragone* XXXII, 373 (March 1980): 30; F. d'Amico, "Su Paolo Guidotti Borghese e su una congiuntura di tardo manierismo romano," *Ricerche di Storia dell'arte* 22 (1984): 83-84, assigned attributions for one narrative scene, one allegorical figure, and two angels (or genii) in the Sala di Davide. Recently, one of the popes in the Salone dei Papi has been attributed by Luciano Arcangeli, in *Andrea Lilli nella pittura delle Marche tra Cinquecento e Seicento*, exh. cat., ed. Luciano Arcangeli and Pietro Zampetti (Rome, 1985), 43.

[79] Those figures incorporated within the grotesques, which I have called "decorative figures" in Appendix I, have not been included in the count of personifications, although they certainly convey meaning. Similarly, the male *genii* in the Sala di Davide and the female *genii* in the last pontifical room have not been included in this count. The twelve personifications accompanied by inscriptions are in the Sala di Daniele and Sala della Gloria.

[80] The eight landscapes which have merited mention are those in the Anticappella and Salone di Costantino.

[81] A. Dupront, "Art et contre-reforme: les fresques de la bibliotheque de Sixte-Quint," *École française de Rome: Archéologie et histoire* (1931): 306, who cites Rocca, *Biblioteca*, with regard to the seminal role of Sixtus V, and Giuseppe Castiglione, the biographer of Antoniano; Erik Iversen, *Obelisks in Exile: Obelisks of Rome, I*

the fourth year of his pontificate. Inscriptions on ribbons also accompany elements of the Sixtine *stemma* and thereby transform them into devices (for this and the following see Appendix II). There are twenty-six *anime* attached to eight types of *corpi* on the *piano terreno* and grand staircase. In addition, there are solitary mottoes (*anime senza corpi*) attached to rondels at the north-west, east-west and south-east junctures of the logge.[85] There are also inscriptions accompanying personifications in lunettes on the landing of the first arm of the grand staircase. More personifications are housed in lunettes located on the ground floor, sometimes accompanying a plaque on which Sixtus V's name and the date of execution are, or were once, inscribed, and sometimes, like the personifications on the staircase, identified by inscriptions. Smaller personifications, without identifying inscriptions, are to be found on the vaults of the western loggia extension, of the northern entrance vestibule, and on the rondels at the junctures of landings on the grand staircase, while others, encased within surrounds of *grotteschi*, populate yet more lunettes on the ground floor. Finally, the three lunettes in the western loggia discussed by Vaes are given over to representations of landscapes with "genre" scenes, including wine-making, picnicking with conspicuosly eucharistic loaves of bread, and hunting (figs. 8-9).[86]

Fontana's "grotteschi, e paesi con varie imprese" also contain personifications, therefore, and three of these, located on the first landing of the staircase, were deemed so significant that they were also represented in window embrasures at the Vatican Library, albeit not in precisely the same manner. The smiling figure in the eastern lunette holds in outstretched arms what appear to be two hearts each with a lit and smoking candle. Her inscription is unfortunately no longer legible, but may be reconstructed on the basis of the decorations at the Vatican as "PROCREATIONIS EXPERS" so that, according to Rocca, she symbolizes fire (fig. 10).[87] Her counterpart in the southern lunette looks somewhat perturbed and outstretches her arms so that birds may perch comfortably (fig. 11). Unlike the former, this personification is seated beneath a baldachin and is accompanied by the words "INANITATIS IMPATIENS," signifying the element of air.[88] The third lunette, located on the western wall of the second domicile vault, features a female figure seated beneath a baldachin and holding an urn in each hand, with an outstretched net slung over both wrists (fig. 12). The water that she pours from the urns into the mesh net hardly escapes, suggesting the story of the vestal virgins who likewise could carry water through sieves without losing the contents.[89] Her inscription, "PROCREATIONVM ORIGO," repeats that in the Vatican Library which Rocca explains as signifying the element of water.[90] By virtue of the fact that each of these personifications is accompanied by female figures bearing elements of the Sixtine *stemma*, the inevitable conclusion is that Sixtus V holds sway over the elements of fire, air and water, and, by implication, the earth, this later to which he is assimilated in the programme of the main Vatican Library façade.[91] Far from insignificant fillers designed to assuage the pope's *horror vacui*, then, these components of the *parerga* are elements which must contribute to the overall meaning of the cycle.

Like the personifications, the devices were no doubt intended for the viewer's serious consideration. By definition, the device is an extremely personal and meaningful artifice - a fact which in and of itself indicates its significance for Sixtus V

(Copenhagen, 1968), 52, notes that Antoniano was "the acknowledged head of contemporary Latinity and master of a new orthodox style, heavily ornamented like the frame of a baroque altarpiece with Christian references and Biblical allusions, in direct opposition to his predecessors Bembo and Sodalito."

[82] The designs are repeated periodically throughout the logge, owing, quite clearly, to the use of a certain number of cartoons which were repeated respectively on the west and east, north and south logge vaults.

[83] Jacob Hess, "Some Notes on the Paintings in the Vatican Library," *L'illustrazione Vaticana* 15 (1938), reprinted in *Kunstgeschichtliche Studien zu Renaissance und Barock*, 2 vols. (Rome, 1967), I, 169, has observed that depictions of Sixtus V's heraldry are more plentiful than even those of Alexander VI (Borgia, 1492-1503).

[84] According to von Ranke, *History*, II, 135, "the pontiff himself told Paleotto that the pears in his arms were meant to signify his father (Peretti), and that the mountains designated his native land [Montalto]; the lion bearing the pears was meant to imply at once magnanimity and beneficence." von Ranke also states that the "strange story that Sixtus had desired in his youth to be called Crinitus (the long haired) ... is supposed to be [alluded to] in the star of his armorial bearings, but that is certainly not a comet." A slightly different explanation is provided by Francesco Pistolesi, *Sixtus Quintus. XI-II Decembris MDXXI - XIII Decembris MCMXXI. Album* (Rome, 1921), 43: "This coat of arms is the invention of Sixtus V, who representing himself by the lion alluded to his family name by the pears and his nation place by the three mountains and the star: heraldic signs that occur in all his works." See also J. A. F. Orbaan, *Sixtine Rome* (London, 1910), 30; Donald Lindsay Galbreath, *Papal Heraldry* (1930), 2nd rev. ed., Geoffrey Briggs, ed. (London, 1972); and, for another interpretation, Howard Hibbard, *Carlo Maderno and Roman Architecture 1580-1630*, ed. Anthony Blunt and Rudolph Wittkower, Studies in Architecture (London, 1971), 12. The star has been explained in connection with the pope's *stemma* by Felici, *Stationi di Roma*, n.p.: "La stella, chi dirà, che quella non sia, che fu mostrata in sogno al buon Giuseppe? ... Che le stelle siano tanti Prelati, che con tanto giubilo t'inchinano, & te adorano?" Compare *idem*, quoted in the Introduction, note 35, above. The *imprese* of *Justice* and of *Magnanimity* on Sixtus V's catafalque also included a star. In this context, it has been interpreted by Baldo Catani, *La Pompa Funerale fatti dall'Ill.mo & R.mo S.r Cardinale Montalto nella trasportatione dell'ossa di Papa Sisto Quinto* (Rome, 1591), 48, 64, respectively, as follows: "La stella, che chiaramente mostraua esser il Polo, che i nauiganti chiamano Tramontana, era messa quiui per la persona di Sisto, il quale à guisa di Tramontana nel torbido mare di questo mondo, nel quale

and the programme of his palace. This significance is under-scored by the sheer quantity depicted within the designs of the ground floor and grand staircase. Moreover, many of these devices are represented more than once, and, as further testimony to their significance, many were also depicted in the programmes of the Vatican Library and Villa Montalto, Sixtus V's other great secular monuments. For the moment, I shall identify as fully as possible the sources of the *anime* and indicate the thematic significance of those devices repesented more than once within the *grotteschi* of the ground floor and grand staircase; as it would be far too tedious to list each of the various devices in succession, the reader is asked to consult Appendices I and II.

One type of *corpo*, showing the Sixtine lion with facial features having a remarkable resemblance to the pope's, positioned in profile, holding a pear branch in his forepaw and surmounted by a ribbon bearing a motto, is represented more than once with five of the nine possible *anime* with which it is is enspirited. The mottoes are as follows: "NON DORMIT NEQ.[VE] DORMITABIT," a verse taken from Psalm CXX: 4 (fig. 13);[92] "SI RVGIET QVIS NON TIMEBIT," taken from Amos III: 8;[93] "IVSTVS VT LEO CONFIDENS," from the Proverbs of Solomon XXVIII: 1;[94] "DE COMEDENTI EXIVIT CIBVS," an intentionally cryptic verse taken from the first line of the riddle in Judges XIV: 14; and "DE FORTI EGRESSA EST DVLCEDO," appropriately enough, the second part of the riddle.[95] These latter *anime* are also inscribed on the ribbon enframing a *corpo* featuring the head of the Sixtine lion, and this device is likewise represented more than once in the decorative scheme. Also repeated are the solitary mottoes derived from these verses: "EXIVIT CIBVS" and "EGRES[S]A DVL-CEDO;" and two more verses whose sources have eluded this author: "TVTANDOS SVOS" and DEPEL[L]ENDOS NO-XIOS." Another type of device, the most prevalent of all on the ground floor and staircase, features the triple "Montalto" mountains of the pope's *stemma*, often actually equipped with eyes, one for each peak, encircled by three crowns, crossed by the keys of Peter and surmounted by a star with the phrase "CAELVM AEQVORA TERRAS" (fig. 14). This *corpo* also has another *anima*: "IN MONTIBVS ALTIS." Although depicted only once in the programme, a *corpo* of *monti*, which was described in Bertolotti's documents with regard to the Sala di Salomone and which differs only in that it is not endowed with visionary powers (i.e., the eyes), has the same motto, while another has the words: "FVNDAMENTA EIVS." Together, "FVN-DAMENTA EIVS" and "IN MONTIBVS ALTIS" represent a witty Sixtine paraphrase of the first verse of Psalm LXXXVI.[96] Finally, this unseeing triple mountain *corpo* has another motto which merits repetition, this time taken from Psalm LXVII: 17: "MONS IN QVO BENEPLACITVM EST DEO" (fig. 14).[97]

The one constant which unites each of these diverse devices is, of course, the Sixtine *stemma*. Not only are the *corpi* comprised of its elements, but the *anime* also relate in some fashion either to lions, mountains or pears (sweetness), characteristics which would no doubt have provided the pope and his entourage with the kind of enjoyment traditionally derived from the device. That the majority of the *anime* are taken from the Bible, either verbatim or altered slightly to imbue the passage with a particularly Sixtine flavour and relevance, attests to the didactic function, also traditionally associated with the

non pareua vi fusse alcuna strada, col suo lume ci haueua aperta sicurrissima via per arriuare alla bramata quiete del porto ... ", " ... nel piedestallo di questa figura [*Magnanimity*] vi fù posta vn'impresa, nella quale era quella stella, che d'intorno al piccol cerchio del Polo, siraggira, & che per ciò mai non tramonta: simile in questo al chiaro Sisto, il quale raggirandosi d'intorno à Dio suo fermo, & fido Polo, fece sì, che di lui veramente si dicesse quello ..." A *stemma* with two stars is extant in the foyer of the Istituto Massimiliano Massimo (my fig. 7); one with one star at the Campidoglio, this latter in Cecilia Pericoli Ridolfini, "Uno stemma di Sisto V da Villa Montalto al cortile del Palazzo dei Conservatori," *Bollettino dei musei comunali di Roma* XXV-XXVII (1978-1980): 102-110.

[85] These rondels are comparable to that illustrated in Hess, "Some Notes," *KSRB*, II, fig. 24. The artists seem to have used the same *modello* for these components of the Vatican Library and Lateran Palace decorations.

[86] The third landscape is in extremely poor condition. It seems to contain hunters and wolves as well as Christian buildings and pagan ruins.

[87] Rocca, *Biblioteca*, 196-197, concludes a long explanation about fire with the following: "Haec Aristoteles, qui vitalem in semine esse calorem, quem non ignem, neque ignis aliquam esse ait facultatem, ex qua gigni animal vllum, vt ipse inquit, / non posset. Huic doctrinae consonum videtur esse illud, quod idem Aristoteles ait de Vireone aue, quam igne procreari, fabulosum esse pro comperto habet. Haec de igne procreationis experte, vt a quattuor elementis ad quattuor anni tempora transeamus."

[88] Rocca, *Biblioteca*, 195: "Aer enim inanitas quodam modo dicitur multo plus raritatis quàm inferiora elementa admixtum habens. Hinc non solum Virgilius, verum etiam alij probatissimi scriptores per vacuum, & per inane aerem intellexerunt. Quamuis enim vacuum in rerum natura, vt Aristoteles recte docet, non reperiatur, vacuum tamen, vt aiunt, rusticale rudiores homines dari opinantur, dum aliquem locum re visibili, ac palbabili repleri non vident: sed vbi visibile corpus non extat, ibi statim aerem tanquam inanitatis impatientem adesse, locumq. ipsum replere dicas necesse est: natura enim vacuum nullo modo pati potest."

This personification also seems to evoke the Proverbs of Solomon VII: 11-23, in which the guiles of a harlot are analogized to a snare trapping a bird, especially given the expression on her face.

[89] The Vestal Virgin Tuccia, in particular, achieved this feat, as did Sixtus V's contemporary, Queen Elizabeth I. See Yates, *Astraea*, 113-120.

[90] Rocca, *Biblioteca*, 193-194: "... Quamuis autem terra primum, inferioremq. locum tanquam elementum ceteris grauius, ac ponderosius sibi vendicet, vt Aristoteli, alijsq. philosophis placet, & ratio ipsa suadet; Aqua tamen primo cernitur loco. Id quod vel picto-

device, since passages from the Scripture were hardly to be taken lightly, and were certainly never overlooked. These heretofore utterly ignored aspects of the cycle are therefore highly significant components, so much so that Sixtine devices also infiltrate the state rooms of the *piano nobile*, as the documents published by Bertolotti make clear. Just as Sixtus V early on in his pontificate added his own devices to those of his Medici predecessors in the Sala di Costantino at the Vatican residence of the popes, at the Lateran Palace the method was accelerated to such an extent that Sixtine devices in tandem with solitary mottoes, personifications, and landscapes are the sole means by which the visitor is given an inkling of the extensive cycle on the *piano nobile*.[98] In my view there can be no question that these Sixtine "decorations" were intended as amusing and instructive puzzles which, for an astute viewer well versed in Renaissance hieroglyphics, would ultimately yield a preliminary understanding of both the patron's ideals and the meaning of the programme, as set forth most elaborately in the state rooms of the *piano nobile*.[99]

4. LAYOUT OF THE *PIANO NOBILE* AND PRELIMINARY ICONOGRAPHICAL ISSUES

The *piano nobile* contains seventeen rooms, thirteen of which have frescoed ceilings and the remaining four, which are more properly halls, gilded and painted ceilings, and frescoed walls. Beginning with the room adjacent to the Benediction Loggia, in the south-west corner of the palace (fig. 6), they are: the Sala degli Obelischi, the main hall called the Salone dei Papi, the Salone degli Imperatori, the Sala di Samuele, the Anticappella and Cappella Papale, the Sala di Davide and, in the north-west corner, Sala di Salomone. Following along the northern side are the Sala d' Elia, Sala di Daniele, Sala della Gloria, Salone degli Apostoli, and, in the north-east corner, the Salone di Costantino. Also on the north side, but facing the courtyard, are the four rooms of the private pontifical apartment, and, on the remaining three sides, the logge containing biblical narratives.

In their descriptions of the halls and rooms of the *piano nobile*, Fontana and all subsequent commentators follow a particular sequence, which I have echoed above, beginning at the south-west corner and moving towards the north-east (see Appendix III). Since each author begins at the same corner (though not always the same room or hall), one must naturally ask whether they perceived an ideal order in which one was to procede through the *piano nobile*. Given that the Old Testament rooms follow each other in a chronological progression from Samuel to Daniel, this would appear to be a preordained order. It is most curious, however, that the Sala della Gloria was omitted from the lists until Biondi in the nineteenth century, since it is unavoidably located between one of the main halls and a room containing scenes from the Old Testament. In other words, it cannot be bypassed as one traverses the northern arm of the palace, unless one leaves the Sala di Daniele by way of the western loggia, enters the private apartment of the pope, and proceeds through three rooms to then enter the Salone degli Apostoli. Needless to say, this route is a rather bothersome one, and would, in any case, have been taken only by the pope or a close associate with access to his pri-

50

rum iudicio factum est, vel ad imitationem verborum Ouidij, qui elementis distribuit loca hunc in modum ... [*Metamorphoses*, Book I] ... Quibus verbis Ouidius quamuis aquae postremum locum tribuere videatur, si ea tamen perpendantur, nil aliud ex ijs-/dem verbis, quàm terrae superficiem circumfluentem ab aqua humectari, ac possedi colligi posse fatendum est. Hunc eundem fere sensum patitur illud Scripturae sacrae dictum: Qui firmauit terram super aquas, hoc est iuxta aquas terram ipsam humectantes, eo loquendi modo, quo dici solet: Haec ciuitas fundata est super mare, vt Venetiae: illa vero super Sequanam fluuium Galliae, Belgas a Celtis diuidentem. Hoc eodem fere modo intelligitur illud Psalmi dictum, quo super maria fundatum esse mundum legimus."

[91] The element of earth is included in the Vatican Library, in Rocca, *Biblioteca*, 194-195. On the Vatican Library façade see my forthcoming "Magic and Melancholy at the Vatican Library". At the palace, the architectural given of this landing dictates that only three lunettes exist, and hence three of the four personifications are depicted.

[92] This device is also located in the second room of the Libreria Segreta, in Fontana, *Della trasportatione*, 96, as well as in the vestibule of the Salone Sistino. It once adorned the center of the long courtyard façade of the Vatican Library, in Fontana, *Della trasportatione*, 96.

[93] This device was also present in the Palazzo delle Terme of the Villa Montalto, in Massimo, *Notizie*, 127. It is present in the first room of the Libreria Segreta as well.

[94] This device was also frescoed in the Sala di Costantino in the Vatican under Sixtus V's direction in 1585, in Quednau, *Sala di Costantino*, 928. It is also barely visible on the façade of the Gallery of the Geographic Maps frescoed for Sixtus V between ca. 1587-89.

[95] These devices were also represented in the Palazzo delle Terme, in Massimo, *Notizie*, 126, 131. In the second room of the Libreria Segreta of the Vatican Library, two rondels are inscribed with the second part of the riddle. Fontana, *Della trasportatione*, 94, indicates that both verses are present in this room.

[96] This device was also represented in the Palazzo delle Terme of the Villa Montalto, in Massimo, *Notizie*, 127, who characterizes the verse as "allusiva alla patria del Pontefice, ed alla situazione di questo palazzo."

[97] This device also appears more than once in the vestibule of the Salone Sistino of the Vatican Library and in the second room of the Libreria Segreta. Significantly, the device is also present in the Vatican Sala di Costantino, as commissioned by Sixtus V, in Quednau, *Sala di Costantino*, 929.

[98] On the Sala di Costantino and the significance of the Medici devices therein, consult Marilyn Perry, "'Candor Illaesvs': the 'Impresa' of Clement

vate living quarters. Nevertheless, given the fact that one could enter the *piano nobile* from no less than four stairways stationed on each side of the building; given that one could leave any room on the *piano nobile* in order to enter the logge, or stairways - save the Old Testament rooms of Samuel, David, Solomon and Elijah; and given that there is a relationship between the portal inscription one sees upon leaving the Salone dei Papi and the extension of the western loggia containing representations from the life of Saint Francis in the lunettes, then one must conclude that the overlying message of the programme could be gleaned as long as one viewed all of the rooms and halls regardless of the order.[100] This supposition is further validated when one considers the layout of the narrative scenes in the logge; rather than following each other in a progression, the logge have been decorated as separate entities and are not suggestive of any specific orientation.[101]

The Active and Contemplative Lives seem to be an important foundation on which the programme rests. In the official sense, these would not be the Neoplatonic Lives of so many Renaissance programmes, since this philosophy was not at all in keeping with the climate in Rome following Trent.[102] They would be respectively derived from and inspired by the traditional Medieval concepts of the *Liber Scripturae* and *Liber Naturae* - the two "bibles" on which Pope Sixtus V, the Franciscan friar, seems to have based his own existence.[103] In the artistic sphere, it seems likely that the almost contemporaneous programme at the Farnese Palace at Caprarola (1561/62-1583) also partook of this Medieval tradition in its representations of the deeds of the Farnese family and in the landscapes.[104] And just as the Farnese Palace is divided into a Summer and Winter apartment, respectively extolling the Active and Contemplative Lives, so the Lives of the Lateran Palace seem to correspond to the divisions inherent in the plan.[105] The outer area of the plan, containing rooms and halls whose function was necessarily of a public nature, seems to expound the Active Life primarily through the representations of historical figures complete with inscriptions describing their works, through narratives, and through the Good Works of Sixtus V, both image and text. The inner area of the plan, comprising logge and the private apartment of the pope, seems to expound the Contemplative Life primarily, and quite appropriately, by means of both landscapes with Christian content, including hermit saints and their Old Testament prototypes, and Good Works transformed from "active" carriers to "contemplative" ones in the form of Sixtine devices and personifications.

The scope of the subject matter on the *piano nobile* is, to say the least, vast. There are narratives, which span the beginnings of time, *ante legem*, to the period *sub gratia* (including the time of Sixtus V); verses and inscriptions, which evoke classical mythology, the Judaeo-Christian tradition, popes, emperors, saints and Sixtus V; personifications, which provide a host of Christian moral exemplars related to the character and pontificate of Sixtus V; and *stemmi*, devices and *imprese* of Sixtus V himself.[106] When read literally, the narratives contained in each room of the palace, including the Good Works, seem to relate to one another, as do the personifications, the inscriptions and/or verses, the devices and *imprese*, yet it is not always possible to grasp the connection between narrative and personification, *impresa* and narrative, inscription and *stemma* and so on within the rooms, nor is it always possible to see the inter-

VII and other Medici Devices in the Vatican Stanze," *Burlington Magazine* CXIX (October 1977): 676-686.

[99] I am drawing on an extremely important principle outlined by Frederick Hartt, "*Lignum Vitae in Medio Paradisi*: The Stanza d'Eliodoro and the Sistine Ceiling," *Art Bulletin* XXXII, 2-3 (June/September 1950): 135-136: "It will, I hope, eventually become axiomatic that in the interpretation of an apparently abstruse Renaissance picture the emblem, be it coat-of-arms, device, crest or *impresa*, is the first place to look / for a solution, particularly when it plays a conspicuous role in the visual articulation of the work of art." This principle is exemplified in Perry's study, cited in the previous note.

[100] See Appendix I, 215, n. 55 for the portal inscription. This view seems to be substantiated by the piece-meal way in which the decorations were carried out. For some indication, see Appendix V, below.

[101] The western loggia runs from south to north, culminating at the entrance to the Sala di Daniele (and to left and right, the circular stairway and the first room of the private apartment). The extension of the western loggia, conversely, runs from north to south and back up to the north, ending opposite the stairway, and beside the door to the main hall. The southern loggia runs from west to east. And the eastern loggia runs from south to north. The Genesis scenes of the western loggia thus run in the same direction as the scenes from the early life of Christ in the eastern loggia, while the southern loggia, containing representations of Judith and Holofernes, begins at the same corner as the first western loggia narrative and meets the first of the eastern loggia narratives.

[102] On this Neoplatonic conception, see Erwin Panofsky, *Studies in Iconology. Humanistic Themes in the Age of the Renaissance* (New York, 1967), 139 ff, 192 ff. On the move towards Aristotle, away from Plato, following the Council of Trent, see Chapter II, 84, below.

[103] For the two "bibles," see Ernst Robert Curtius, *Europäische Literatur und lateinisches Mittelalter* (Bern, 1948); trans. W. R. Trask, *European Literature and the Latin Middle Ages* (New York and Evanston, 1963), 319 ff. For a typical day in the life of Sixtus V, see von Pastor, *History*, XXI, 57-59.

[104] F. Baumgart, "La Caprarola di Ameto Orti," *Studj Romanzi* XXV (1935-37): 77-179. Also consult the recent study of Loren W. Partridge, *Caprarola, Palazzo Farnese* (Milan, 1988).

[105] Baumgart, "Caprarola," *SR*: 82; Jean Seznec, *The Survival of the Pagan Gods. The Mythological Tradition and its Place in Renaissance Humanism and Art*, Studies of the Warburg Institute, vol. XI , trans. Barbara F. Sessions , 1st ed. 1940 (Princeton, New Jersey, 1972), 286.

[106] For clarity's sake, I am making a distinction between the *impresa* and de-

connection between subjects represented in different rooms. This encyclopaedic type of programme, comprised of seemingly disparate parts, is typical of the late Cinquecento and must be read on a number of levels: the literal, typological, allegorical and symbolical.[107] Inherent in the programme, then, is a kind of *Stil des Werdens*; one cannot glean the whole on first reading, but rather has to put the pieces together so that, in the end, the message of seemingly diverse parts reconciles in the viewer's mind. It is only by reading the programme in this manner that the historical, religio-political, and religio-symbolical facets may be grasped.

With regard to the nature of the various elements within the programme, the historical figures (for example, the popes in the Salone dei Papi and the emperors in the Salone degli Imperatori) generally follow one another in chronological order as shown by their inscriptions. This is in keeping with the method used in other Sixtine monuments, most notably in the Salone Sistino of the Vatican Library in which figures and narratives are likewise positioned chronologically. It seems safe to assume that the narrative scenes, which are primarily taken from the Bible, would follow suit. The exceptions to this rule are in the Sala degli Obelischi, where column faces column, and obelisk, obelisk; in the Salone degli Apostoli, where biblical scenes are paired; and in the pontifical apartment where saints and Old Testament figures are similarly paired. However, there is a certain confusion in the literature regarding the order of both the historical figures and the narrative scenes. Since the components of the various rooms and halls do not always relate to one another on a literal level, this has only added to the confusion and, it would appear, to the reticence of earlier commentators on the cycle to actually attempt a synthesis and explanation of its meaning.[108]

The chronologies set forth by the narrative scenes and historical figures form a sequence from Moses to Christ, Peter to Sylvester, Constantine to Heraclius and all emperors thereafter, and end with Sixtus V. The gaps in the chronology are then filled in the inner area of the *piano nobile*. The western loggia completes the period *ante legem*; the eastern loggia explicates Christ's early life; the southern loggia presents the victorious Judith, the *typus Ecclesiae* and, one must add, *typus Sixti V*;[109] the western loggia extension presents Saint Francis, the *alter Christus* and founder of Sixtus V's Order; the private pontifical rooms, particularly the fourth room with representations of Christian saints and Old Testament prototypes, complete the lacuna between Sixtus V, a Franciscan friar, and his penitent predecessors; and, coming full circle, the saintly popes in the Salone dei Papi demonstrate the role of the saints in maintaining the Church's invulnerability and the unimpeachable succession of Christ's chosen vicars.

The place of Sixtus V in this overall scheme of things is essential. As patron of the construction and decoration of the palace, he stamps his imprint in good Renaissance fashion with his *stemma*. Just as his coat-of-arms occupies a central place in the decorative scheme of the ground floor and grand staircase, in four of the seventeen rooms of the *piano nobile*, namely the Sala degli Obelischi, Sala di Samuele, second and third rooms of the private apartment, the Sixtine *stemma* is borne aloft at center vault;[110] in the Sala di Davide, four coats-of-arms sustain the vault on its four corners; in the Salone degli Apostoli, they are embraced by angels at the mid-points of the short walls;

vice (the English translation) so that the one, also translated as emblem and comprised of *superscriptio, imago* and *subscriptio*, may be clearly differentiated from the other, comprised of *corpo* and *anima*.

[107] For encyclopaedic programmes of the late Cinquecento, consult Baumgart, "Caprarola" *SR*: 95; and Seznec, *Survival*, 286-287.

The literal, of course, refers to the actual *istoria* represented; the Old Testament scenes represented in so many of the rooms may be read typologically, in keeping with the well established exegetical tradition. For one of the authorities on this tradition, see Henri de Lubac, *Exégèse Médiévale. Les Quatre Sens de l'Ecriture* (Paris, 1959), 2 vols., 2 parts. John Shearman, *Raphael's Cartoons in the Collection of Her Majesty the Queen and the Tapestries for the Sistine Chapel* (London, 1972), 45-47, provides an excellent discussion on this issue. The typological method is naturally an allegorical method. For purposes of clarity, I refer to the allegorical level of the decorations when discussing the personifications and some of the pope's Good Works. Finally, the symbolical level here refers to the allusions to or actual *stemma* of Sixtus V.

[108] The discrepancies regarding order, and in some cases, the lack of data on any given room of the *piano nobile* are listed in Appendix III.

[109] That it was not unusual to compare a female saviour to a male figure and, moreover, that biblical incidents had contemporary relevance for Sixtus V, is amply demonstrated in a statement made by the pope himself regarding his joy over Jacques Clément's murder of Henry III of France, in which Clément is compared to Judith and, by implication, the Valois King to Holofernes, quoted in Robert H. Murray, *The Political Consequences of the Reformation. Studies in Sixteenth-Century Political Thought* (New York, 1960), 220. As head of Christ's earthly body, the Church, Sixtus V is readily assimilated to Judith.

[110] In the Sala degli Obelischi, angels appear to be lifting the pope's heraldry to place it beneath a baldachin (fig. 74). In the Sala di Samuele, acolytes resting on the supporting structure of the room and on the overhanging Sixtine cloth of honour hoist the *stemma* of the pope and balance crossed keys, papal tiara and cross, so that they too may be displayed beneath the overhanging baldachin (fig. 89). In the second pontifical room, the fruits and flowers of abundance hang from the *stemma* of Sixtus V at center vault, while a sunburst of divine light sets the tiara into relief, and embraces it. The third room of the private apartment contains a *stemma* borne aloft by angels at center vault.

while in the fourth room of the private apartment, an inscribed medallion encircled by putti commemorates the very name of Sixtus V. Many of the devices comprised of Sixtine heraldry manifest downstairs and on the grand staircase, as in the Villa Montalto and Vatican Library, also find their way into the rooms of the main floor, as I have already noted. The "lion in profile" device with the verse from the Psalms "NON DORMIT NEQVE DORMITABIT" is represented again in the Sala di Daniele; with the verse from Amos, "SI RVGIET QVIS NON TIMEBIT," both here and in the Sala degli Obelischi; with "IVSTVS VT LEO CONFIDENS" in the Sala degli Obelischi and eastern loggia; with an *anima* taken from Revelation V: 5, "VINCIT LEO DE TRIBV IVDA," a device which was represented only once on the grand staircase and hence not mentioned heretofore, in both the Sala di Daniele and eastern loggia;[111] and with "CVSTOS VIGILI," possibly taken from Psalms CXXVI: 1, on the vaults of the eastern logge of both the *piano terreno* and *piano nobile*. The "all-seeing triple mountain" *corpo* and the verse "SCIENTIAE BONITATIS DISCIPLINAE," taken from the words of King David in Psalm CXVIII: 66, is found on both the grand staircase leading to the *piano nobile* and, without eyes, in the Sala di Salomone, while this same *corpo* and the verse "LVX ORTA EST IVSTO," taken from Psalm XCVI: 11, is represented on the grand staircase leading to the *secondo piano* and, with the intriguing addition "LVX ORTA EST IVSTO TPΥ[Σ]ΜΕΓΙΣΤΟΣ," in the Sala della Gloria.[112] Finally, this "addition" becomes an *anima* of its own in the "triple mountain" device sprouting pear branches in lieu of keys located in the Northern entrance vestibule. The Sala della Gloria above and northern entrance vestibule below share other devices as well: a *corpo* comprised of a three-branched candelabrum upholding three open books sometimes inscribed with a circle, triangle and square is accompanied by the *anima*, part of which was also paired with the "triple mountain" device, "SCIENTIAE BONITATIS DISCIPLINAE," and the remainder, "TERNA HAEC TRIPLICI," found also in the Sala di Salomone with the "triple mountain" *corpo*;[113] while a seven-branched candelabrum supporting seven open books surmounted by seven stars has the verse, possibly taken from the Proverbs of Solomon XXIV: 16, and certainly alluding to Isaiah II: 2, "LVCEANT SEPTIES IVSTO."[114] Finally, the solitary mottoes on the junctures of the ground floor logge find a foil in the last room of the private apartment, with the often repeated inscription taken from Judges "DE FORTI EGRESSA EST DVLCEDO."

Elements of Sixtus V's *stemma* are also incorporated into the biblical narratives so that his place within the history of the Church is reinforced. The elements of his *stemma* that are used in the biblical narratives are the lions and mountains which apparently proved so inspiring for the creation of the devices and, as one would expect, these components are inherently related to the biblical histories. In the Sala di Daniele, the scenes of Daniel's incarceration in the lion's den and his concomitant rescue by God's messengers feature a veritable pack of lions (fig. 15); while the triple mountains of the pope's *stemma* find their way into the Cappella Papale, at center vault no less, and serve to relocate Christ's *Ascension* above the city of Montalto (fig. 16)![115]

The lion of the Sixtine heraldry also plays a starring role, together with the mountains and pears, in the allegorical representations of the pope's Good Works in the Salone dei Papi,

[111] This device was also included in the decorations of the Palazzo delle Terme, in Massimo, *Notizie*, 131. It is also found in the first room of the Libreria Segreta of the Vatican Library, and is still partly visible on the façade of the Gallery of Geographic Maps.

[112] Compare the "triple mountain" device with the abbreviated verse "LVX ORTA EST" in the Palazzo delle Terme of the Villa Montalto, in Massimo, *Notizie*, 127.

[113] This same device, featuring the candelabrum and double *anima*, is also present in the second room of the Libreria Segreta of the Vatican Library.

[114] This device is also represented in the second room of the Libreria Segreta of the Vatican Library. On the implications of the situation and contents of the Sala della Gloria and northern entrance vestibule, consult my forthcoming "Simbolismo ermetico negli obelischi e colonne della Roma Sistina," *Sisto V*, Atti del VI Corso Internazionale d'Alta Cultura, ed. Marcello Fagiolo, Maria Luisa Madonna.

[115] Massimo, *Notizie*, 53, notes the parallels between the subjects represented in the Villa Montalto featuring lions and Sixtus V's coat-of-arms. Schiavo, *Lateran*, n.p., notes that "the subjects of the principal paintings [in the Sala di Daniele] are an occasion for repeated representations of the lion, an heraldic emblem of Sixtus V."

to which I shall turn in the next chapter. Moreover, the pope's heraldry forms the attributes for key personifications which are strategically located to underscore his central place in the iconographical scheme. In the Anticappella and Sala della Gloria personifications, rendered *dal di sotto in su* and given the place of honour at center vault, hold the *monti* and star of Sixtus V's *stemma* (fig. 17); in the Salone di Costantino, a female holds the Peretti pears (fig. 105), as do others in the second room of the private apartment; and in the fourth room of the private apartment, another female personification holds a scale kept in perfect equilibrium by a single Peretti pear (fig. 129)![116] Just as certain devices are repeated both upstairs and down, the most significant personifications merit a double presence. The woman holding the "Peretti" scales of justice is found not only in the private apartment, but also in the lunette located at the juncture of the north and west logge on the *piano terreno*, and hence among the first components of the cycle which an interested visitor to the palace would notice (fig. 18).[117] She is accompanied here, as on the *piano nobile*, by a personification holding the Antonine and Trajanic columns flanking an obelisk (figs. 18, 128). As Schiavo first observed, the obelisks and columns, like the elements of the Sixtine heraldry, also find their way into other parts of the programme. As might be expected, devices with *corpi* comprised of Sixtus V's most celebrated Good Works play a prominent role: the northern entrance vestibule, western loggia extension of the *piano nobile*, and the Sala di Salomone, all host devices featuring the columns flanking an obelisk with the same motto: "RELIGIO MIRANDA TRIVMPHAT" [or "TRIVNPHAT"]; and the western loggia extension and Sala di Salomone also share this *corpo* with the verse "GLORIAM DEI EXALTAT";[118] while that on the grand staircase leading to the *secondo piano* is animated by the verse taken from the song of Christ's disciples in praise of God in Luke XIX: 38, and echoing Luke II: 14: "GLORIA IN EXCELSIS DEO,"[119] and finds counterparts in devices comprised of a single obelisk *corpo* in the eastern loggia of the *piano nobile*, and in the adjacent Salone di Costantino (fig. 105, for example). In keeping with the method by which the Sixtine *stemma* infiltrates the various components of the programme, the obelisks and columns are represented on a large scale, as feigned panel paintings in the Sala degli Obelischi, and respond to the feigned tapestries hosting allegorical and topographical Good Works in the adjacent Salone dei Papi. Finally, the Sixtine obelisk is found in a biblical narrative: in the Sala di Samuele one is shown that the "stone of help" was actually an obelisk raised in the manner described and illustrated in Fontana's treatise, and carried out in key *piazze* of Sixtine Rome (figs. 87, 83)!

Despite, or perhaps because of, this proliferation of the pope's personal heraldry, devices, personifications, Good Works, and inscriptions commemorating his name, Sixtus V's portrait is depicted only once in the palace, in a scene documenting contemporaneous history in the form of his receipt of the list of imperial medals found when excavations on the Patriarchium Lateranense were underway in 1587 (fig. 147). His presence in the history of the Church may accordingly be viewed as serving a double function. On the one hand, the emphasis on Old Testament prophets who foretold Christ's coming, and on Old Testament types of Christ, to the exclusion, it would seem on first consideration, of Sixtus V, reflects his es-

[116] In the Anticappella, the personification at center vault likely represents *Sixtine Prosperity* or *Triumphant Christianity under Sixtine Rule*. The sceptre which this figure holds refers to Sixtus V, since it is crowned with the star and *monti* of his heraldry. The cornucopia, according to Cesare Ripa, *Iconologia o vero descrittione di diverse imagini cavate dall'antichità, e di propria inventione* (1593; 1618) reprint ed., ed. Piero Buscaroli, preface Mario Praz, "La Torre d'avorio," 2 vols. (Turin, 1986), I, 30, is a symbol of abundance: "Hà la ghirlanda de'fiori percioche sono i fiori dei frutti che fanno l'Abbondanza messaggieri ..." The crown on the figure's head clearly refers to her royalty. Finally, the statuette may well represent *Roma*, such as that in Giulio Romano's *Donation of Constantine* in the Sala di Costantino at the Vatican. The manifest references to Sixtus V (sceptre, crown and cornucopia) seem to imply that this personification represents prosperity or abundance under his "kingly" pontificate, or the triumph of Christianity, by way of apotheosis, under his rule. The second personification who ascends to the heavens in the Sala della Gloria has been sensibly identified as *Glory*, or *Sixtine Glory* by Schiavo, as noted above.

[117] The scale of justice held by the figure on the *piano terreno* is not balanced by a pear, but I would explain this by pointing to the "faulty" brush of a restorer.

[118] These devices are also found in the first room of the Libreria Segreta at the Vatican Library.

[119] This *corpo* is also accompanied by the verse "MIRABILIA TVA CREDIBILIA," a conflation of the verses from Psalm XCII: 4-5, on the first arm of the grand staircase leading to the *terzo piano*. This verse, in slightly extended form ("MIRABILIA TVA DOMINE CREDIBILIA"), was also used to animate the body of a device comprised of "una corona i tre monti sui quali sono impressi quattro SSSS. [sic], ed incrociate una chiave ed una tromba, con la stella sopra," in the Palazzo delle Terme of the Villa Montalto, in Massimo, *Notizie*, 126.

sentially Medieval conception of the pope subsumed by his office *vis-à-vis* the Renaissance conception wherein the office is subordinate to the personality of the head. On the other hand, the almost overwhelming preponderance of Sixtine heraldry, devices, and personifications in both the state rooms and the logge, as well as the Good Works of Sixtus V in large scale format, particularly in the main hall of the palace, indicates the importance of the personality of this Franciscan pope.[120] Sixtus V may be said, therefore, to presage Urban VIII (Barberini, 1623-44), who would similarly acknowledge his function as the vehicle of a larger order, while at the same time glorifying his pontificate, and the Barberini clan, as providentially chosen to embody the spirit and age of the Triumphant Church.[121]

Much as Pietro da Cortona's visual panegyric in the Barberini Palace (1633-1639) would grant immortality to Urban VIII owing to the excellence of his Good Works on earth as Christ's vicar, visual panegyric in the Lateran Palace consistently celebrates the achievements of Sixtus V's triumphant pontificate on earth and its reverberation in heaven.[122] In four of the five Old Testament rooms there are narrative scenes on the vault showing spiritual occurrences portending a victory in heaven as on earth. Invariably a victory on earth is represented on the cove below, to literally underline the triumph at center vault.[123] When read typologically, the triumph is Christ's alone, but a symbolical reading, as amply demonstrated by the new location of the *Ascension* and the "stone of help," yields associations to Sixtus V so that the victory of Christ becomes the victory of his vicar. Since the frames are actually supported by elements of Sixtus V's *stemma*, a conceit likely attributable to the artists, but certainly agreed upon by the pope and his iconographer, then the decorations reinforce Sixtus V's essential role in maintaining Christ's victory. The western and southern logge, which convey this theme in a similar manner in the vaults, with the "heavenly" at summit, and the "earthly" at the sides, have the addition of landscapes in lunettes beneath the vault. The "action" of the narratives in the earthly sphere of the vault here, as once, in all likelihood, in the eastern loggia, is therefore calmed and presented in a natural and more contemplative-oriented context suggesting that the superiority of the Church can be derived from a God-given principle, but can also be found in nature herself. In the halls, "earthly" and "heavenly" divisions also apply, but since the soffits contain no imagery, save the *stemma* of the pope and elements therefrom, the divisions are made on the walls themselves both in terms of form, and the content and combination of narrative scenes and historical personages.[124] Thus, the message revealed by the synchronic narrative scenes is that the superiority of the Catholic religion is manifest in history. A diachronic reading, on the other hand, suggests Revelation. Finally, the landscapes with "genre" scenes are the permanent and natural contemplative way of discovering the Christian message in nature herself and parallel sacred history as manifested in those with scenes from the Scriptures. Indeed, the decision to include three landscapes at the base of the grand staircase was not a fortuitous one; like the devices, solitary mottoes and personifications, these deceptively simple representations of verdant locales spotted with antique ruins and Christian buildings, and featuring such "prosaic" activities as wine-making and hunting, prepare the viewer for the landscapes of the *piano nobile*, likewise containing "genre" scenes

[120] For the Medieval and Renaissance conceptions, see Walter Ullmann, *A Short History of the Papacy in the Middle Ages* (London, 1972), 317 ff. Also consult Hess, "Some Notes," *KSRB*, I, 169, note 1. Baumgart, "Caprarola," *SR*, 88-89, is insightful with regard to the position of the Roman Catholic Reform pope.

[121] Francis Haskell, *Patrons and Painters. Art and Society in Baroque Italy* (New York, 1963), 32 ff.

[122] A number of studies have been published on the Barberini Ceiling, consult Walter Vitzthum, "A comment on the iconography of Pietro da Cortona's Barberini Ceiling," *Burlington Magazine* (1961): 427-433; Dante Bernini, *et al*, *Il voltone di Pietro da Cortona in Palazzo Barberini*, Quaderni di Palazzo Venezia, 2 (Rome, 1983) and recently, John Beldon Scott, *Images of Nepotism. The Painted Ceilings of Palazzo Barberini* (Princeton, New Jersey, 1991), Part III, 125 ff.

[123] In the Sala di Davide, the scene at center vault represents *David killing Goliath* and therefore occurs on earth, rather than in heaven, or some otherworldly ambient. When read typologically, however, this scene is understood in similarly spiritual terms as Christ's victory over the Devil, a victory which is emphasized by the earthly triumph of David carrying Goliath's head as he enters Jerusalem, and equally of the future triumph of Christ who, having entered Jerusalem, will die for the salvation of mankind. See Louis Réau, *Iconographie de l'art Chrétien*, 2 vols., 2 pts., (Paris, 1955), II, I, 260, for this typological reading.

[124] Only the ceiling of the Salone dei Papi is original. The ceilings of the Salone degli Imperatori, Salone dei Paramenti, and Salone di Costantino were redone during the pontificate of Gregory XVI, according to the designs of Luigi Poletti, in Schiavo, *Lateran*, n.p.

replete with Christian content (fig. 20), as well as those of the state and private rooms containing scenes from sacred history.

5. HISTORICAL CONTEXT I: THE ROMAN CATHOLIC REFORM

The iconographical programme of the Lateran Palace is typical of post-Tridentine cycles. First and foremost, the aim of the ensemble as an official statement is more didactic than pleasure-giving and as such befits the tenets of the time when Mannerist ambiguity and titillating sacrilege had been outlawed by the Church, and clarity of Christian teaching embraced.[125] The main thrust of the programme, which extols the glory and triumph of the invulnerable Catholic Church and of her chief bishop, is a message which was being propagated at this time in history by a Church who liked to regard herself as triumphant. This is not to suggest that the Protestant and Turkish threats, which had been particularly vivid in the minds of such post-Tridentine popes as Pius IV and Pius V, had been altogether eradicated by the pontificate of Sixtus V, but the successive enactments of the dictates of the Council of Trent during the 1570s and early 1580s had effectively set the stage for a Church who could view herself as victorious.[126] Sixtus V's determination to enforce these enactments, both in words at the beginning of his pontificate, and in actions throughout his tenure as pope, in tandem with his victories in the temporal realm, notably his seminal role in the reconciliation between Poland and Austria, served to seal this jubilant "Baroque" spirit.[127] It was during the pontificate of Sixtus V that the transfer from a primarily defensive stance to a more confident Church Militant, and the celebratory spirit which accompanied such a change, found its first really grandiose manifestations.

In order to propagate this renewed sense of the Church's victory, Sixtus V embraced the ideas of Cesare Baronio, who had begun his voluminous work, the *Annales Ecclesiastici* (1588-1607), on command of Filippo Neri. Sixtus V took over patronage of his friend's work, and saw the completion of the first two volumes of what would become a twelve volume enterprise. When the first volume was published in 1588, both author and book were received with incredible enthusiasm; for the Catholic, it was "as if an enormous danger threatening the fatherland had been magically removed."[128] The main thrust of Baronio's argument was that sacred history was superior to secular history; it was, in effect, timeless, since the authority of the Church, and of her vicar, had been preordained by God and could be traced back to man's earliest beginnings in the Old Testament. In Baronio's words: "Just as successive links form a single chain, so years joined to years by many cycles of years compose one same work, and reveal to you that the Church has been always one and the same. Thus, certainly, nothing can seem more pleasing to a pious mind which desires only the truth, nothing more delightful than to consider the Christian faith in which it believes to have been the same since the beginning of the Church, as taught, spotlessly preserved, and guarded in sanctity through all the centuries".[129]

The Lateran Palace cycle is, in some ways, a visual parallel to Baronio's *Annales*. In each case, an annalistic, or chronological, method was harnessed to prove the continuous and victorious march of the Church through time.[130] To set the argu-

[125] Anthony Blunt, *Artistic Theory in Italy, 1450-1600* (Oxford, 1962), 103 ff; Maria Cali, *Da Michelangelo all'Escorial* (Turin, 1980), 3-35; Federico Zeri, *Pittura e Controriforma. L'arte senza tempo di Scipione Pulzone da Gaeta* (Turin, 1957), 23 ff; Baumgart, "Caprarola," *SR*: 86-88; Seznec, *Survival*, 263-278.

[126] M. R. O'Connell, *The Counter Reformation 1559-1610* (New York, Evanston, San Francisco, London, 1974), 103-118.

[127] This attitude was reflected early on in the spiritual writings of such men as Filippo Neri and Ignatius of Loyola; and in literature, Tasso's *Gerusalemme Liberata* (1575) may be regarded as exemplary. See Charles Dejob, *De l'influence du Concile de Trente sur la littérature et les beaux-arts chez les peuples catholiques. Essai d'introduction a l'histoire litteraire du siècle de Louis XIV* (Paris, 1884), 268 ff, who also devotes a chapter to Tasso, 286 ff.

[128] Cyriac K. Pullapilly, *Caesar Baronius. Counter Reformation Historian* (Notre Dame, London, 1975), 55, quotes A. G. Roncalli (Pope John XXIII), *Il Cardinale Cesare Baronio* (Rome, 1961), 40 ff. In this context it is interesting to note that it was Pope John XXIII who decided to restore the Lateran Palace.

[129] Cesare Baronio, *Annales ecclesiastici* (Rome, 1588-1607), 12 vols.; reprint ed., 37 vols., (Bar-le-Duc, 1864-83), III, trans., by W. J. Bouwsma, *Venice and the Defense of Republican Liberty: Renaissance Values in the Age of the Counter Reformation* (Berkeley and Los Angeles, 1968), 309. Also consult Pullapilly, *Baronius*, 153, who translates part of Baronio's preface along the same lines.

[130] The succession of historical personages emphasizing a lineage was a mode favoured in artistic cycles during the Renaissance and Roman Catholic Reform periods. In addition to this lineage of the popes, which derives ultimately from imperial traditions, the family history was also a favourite topic for such representation, as seen, for example, in the Sala dei Fasti Farnesiani at the Farnese Palace at Caprarola, where there are representations of Paul III's ancestors and of Paul III himself; and in the Room of Nobility at the Villa d'Este, Tivoli, where ancient philosophers and lawgivers are represented. See Baumgart, "Caprarola," *SR*: 82, 106-11; and David R. Coffin, *The Villa d'Este at Tivoli* (Princeton, New Jersey, 1960), 56-58. At the Sixtine Chapel, S. Maria Maggiore, there are representations of the ancestors of Christ. In the Salone Sistino of the Vatican Library there are representations of the nine great libraries, eight councils, and twenty-six principal inventors of the alphabet and of language. Similarly, in the vestibule to the west of the Salone Sistino, there are depicted more councils, continuing in chronological fashion from those represented in the library proper, culminating with the Council of Trent. Consult Fontana, *Della trasportatione*, 82r ff; Titi,

ment on solid foundations, a wealth of antique and Early Christian sources, including the literary, epigraphic and numismatic in the case of Baronio, were consulted so that rebuttal by unsympathetic or downright hostile readers would, it was believed, be rendered virtually impossible.

The impetus for Baronio, as for Sixtus V, was the appearance, almost thirty years prior, of the *Ecclesiastica Historia* (1559-1574), the monumental Protestant tract written by the Centurions of Magdeburg under the supervision of Matthias Flacius Illyricus, which had caused shock and dismay in Rome.[131] The most efficacious way for the Catholics to rebut this heretical and most contemptible work was not to take the defensive, but to prove beyond a shadow of a doubt that the doctrine and institution of the Roman Catholic Church, as recently defined at Trent, adhered to the pristine form set forth by Christ and followed during apostolic times. If the Centurions had used a wealth of antique and Christian sources to prove that the Church had undergone a steady decline, beginning with the events following Christ's death through the Middle Ages, and blaming the vicars of Christ in Rome as the chief culprits of the decline, then the Catholic response to this misinformed contention must use these and other sources, read properly, to prove that the Catholic Church "had always been one and the same in all times: one Faith, one Christ and one God."[132] Since he had been appointed by Pius V to the commission of cardinals instituted in 1571 with the express purpose of determining the best manner in which a reply should be made to the *Ecclesiastica Historia* (a commission which, unfortunately, had lasted but a couple of years to disintegrate with the accession of Gregory XIII), it was natural that Sixtus V use the programme at the Lateran Palace to refute the essential claim of the Centurions that the pope was to blame for the Church's present woes. After all, this was to be the new home of Christ's Roman vicar, and, at the time of its initiation, no appropriate Catholic response had appeared (the frescoed cycles of Gregory XIII would have been anathema to Sixtus V!).

As von Pastor noted long ago, the Lateran Palace was not the only monument of Sixtine Rome aimed against the Protestants; each in its own way was designed to prove that the Church and her vicar were functioning as they had been intended by Christ, in conformity with his words as documented in the Bible and as explained by the apostolic Fathers of the Church. The programme of the Villa Montalto seems also to have been a refutation in paint of the *Ecclesiastica Historia*; the conspicuous presence of pagan subject matter there, as in the Lateran Palace (albeit in a more subtle manner), was evidently intended, as I shall demonstrate by example later on, to prove that all earth history, be it pagan, Hebrew or Christian, was part of a divinely ordained plan instituted by God to culminate in the attainment of the Heavenly City, even though this divine purpose was unsuspected by pagan and Hebrew alike, because veiled beneath superstition and ignorance.[133] As the product of a cardinal forced into retirement by a pope who did not even have the good sense to perpetuate Pius V's commission, the programme of the Villa Montalto seems to have represented Cardinal Montalto's first "official" reply to the Protestants.[134] When the opportunity presented itself to Pope Sixtus V to expand upon his initial thesis, in a monument intended to house Christ's vicars, no less, he and his iconographer rose to the occasion and replied by covering the gamut of Church history.

Descrizione, 253-254; Dupront, "Art et contre-reforme," *EFR*: 282 ff; and J. W. Clark, *The Care of Books* (1901; London, 1975), 322 ff. At the Lateran Palace, this method is most clearly manifested in the succession of popes and emperors in the Salone dei Papi and Salone degli Imperatori respectively.

[131] For this and the following, I am drawing on the excellent discussion in Eric Cochrane, *Historians and Historiography in the Italian Renaissance* (1981; Chicago and London, 1985), 445-478; Morton C. Abromson, *Painting in Rome during the Papacy of Clement VIII (1592-1605): a documented study* (New York and London, 1981), 120-124; and the recent treatment of the issue in Ostrow, "Sistine," 51-58.

[132] For the use of antique and Christian sources by the respective sides, consult Enrico Norelli, "L'autorità della chiesa antica nelle Centurie di Magdeburgo e negli *Annales* del Baronio," *Baronio storico e la controriforma: atti del convegno internazionale di studi Sora 6-10 ottobre 1979*, ed. Romeo De Maio, Luigi Gulia, Aldo Mazzacane (Sora, 1982), 253-307. I am quoting Panigarola's précis of Baronio's thesis, in Cochrane, *Historians*, 461.

[133] In addition to Old Testament, New Testament, Franciscan and Constantinian subject matter, the programme at the Villa Montalto also featured such pagan gods as Apollo, Jupiter and Hercules, in Massimo, *Notizie*, 50, 53.

[134] Some twenty years prior, while preaching in Naples, Fra Felice had summed up the fundamental issues in *Predica*, n.p., as follows: "O Germania già muro, & ante murale de la Santa Chiesa, come sei sedutta, ingannata, et fascinata da falsi Propheti: par che non ti sappire soluer s'ì Sacramenti son dù, o tre, ò uer sette: Entri entri ne la benedetta Vigna del Signor che ne resterai resoluta: Se dubiti de la intercession de Santi, si Christo è realmente nel'Hostia, se si troua lo Purgatorio, se l'opre giustificano, sel nostro Arbitrio é libero, Quanta sia la podestà del Pontifice Romano, non star piu otiosa nella piazza de l'ignoranza, ma indrizzi, indrizzi il camino alla Vigna del Signor, alla Santa Catholica Chiesa, che di modo ne sarai instrutta, che non te resterà piu, che dubitare ..."

As was his method at the Villa Montalto, Sixtus V did not do this by refuting Protestant claims point by point; he and his iconographer asserted Catholic truths, much as Baronio was doing at that very moment under Sixtus V's aegis. Indeed, the encyclopaedic tradition on which the Lateran Palace and all Sixtine monumental artistic cycles draw was the only tradition available by which the global issues of Catholicism could be treated in as concise and clear a manner as possible.

Steven Ostrow has admirably discussed Sixtus V's reply to the Protestants in his private chapel at Santa Maria Maggiore, and has isolated four fundamental issues which are given precedence: the sacraments, and especially the Eucharist; the efficacy of religious images; the cult of saints; and, drawing on the earlier findings of Alexandra Herz, papal primacy and infallibility. He has described Protestant opposition to each of these issues, and has explained the Catholic stance and its manifestation in bronze and paint in the chapel.[135] As von Pastor realized as a matter of principle, and as I have intimated in my discussion of the key subjects and themes represented in the Lateran Palace (and in the mythology of his life), these issues are as central to Sixtus V's intended residence as to his private chapel. In addition to these basic concepts, I would add a fifth which is absolutely vital to an understanding of the Lateran Palace and all secular cycles commissioned by Sixtus V, and which also plays a significant role in the Sixtine Chapel, namely the Catholic "faith-works" formula, a formula most clearly and conspicuously manifested in his frescoed Good Works, and in the sculpted achievements of himself and Pius V adorning their tomb monuments. For purposes of clarity, I shall indicate briefly Ostrow's research on the aforementioned doctrines, supplementing them with the recent studies of Giuseppe Scavizzi and indicating their relevance to the Lateran Palace cycle, and shall then treat the fifth issue concerning the necessity of Good Works in the Catholic quest for justification.

Of all the sacraments, the Eucharist is at the very heart of the Catholic faith; it is the most venerable of the sacraments whereby the wine and bread are transformed during Mass into Christ's blood and body. By partaking of this wine and bread during Communion, the faithful become united with Christ, and hence bonded with his body, which is the Church. Not only did the Protestants question the magical properties of the sacrament, whereby the recitation of the Mass could affect so miraculous a transformation (known as transubstantiation), but some, notably Zwingli, had gone so far as to deny the sacramental ceremony of all powers. To venerate the Eucharist was tantamount to idolatry, and this was only aggravated by the insistence of the Catholics on using costly vessels of silver and gold to hold this object of their "stupid adoration."[136] After all, had Moses not smashed the tablets of the Law when he saw the Hebrews worshipping the Golden Calf, and, asks Flacius, had not Constantine destroyed pagan idols as a testimony to the practice of the apostolic Church?[137]

The Council of Trent responded to the early heresies of Zwingli and Calvin and others by reasserting the efficacy of the Eucharist, calling it the "most august" of the sacraments, and encouraging devotion to it by the faithful. Sixtus V himself was not only highly devoted to the sacrament, like his mentor Pius V, but he constructed a grandiose and sumptuous tabernacle to house the host and to act as the focal point of the bur-

[135] Ostrow, "Sistine," 33-51.

[136] Ostrow, "Sistine," 38-41, who cites Calvin, 39. On the use of costly vessels, consult Giuseppe Scavizzi, "Storia ecclesiastica e arte nel secondo Cinquecento", *Storia dell'arte* LIX (1987): 31-32.

[137] Scavizzi, "Storia ecclesiastica," *Storia dell'arte*, 31.

ial chapel at Santa Maria Maggiore, and made it the object of his devotion for all eternity, as his sculpted effigy kneels before it with hands folded in prayer.[138] As if in direct response to the likes of Flacius, in the Salone dei Papi one of his predecessors is accredited with the decree that vessels ought to be made of costly material for the worship of God. Moreover, Angelo Rocca calls many a Good Work of Sixtus V's a "eucharistic symbol," not just the cross-topped obelisks, but others, like the amassing of gold at Castel Sant'Angelo![139]

Related to the sacrament of the Eucharist is the cult of images. I have touched on this issue with regard to the Protestant perception of idolatry and the concomitant fashioning of objects of precious materials above. To be sure, the cross as another manifestation of Christ's body was among the most hotly debated issues. For the Catholic, the cross was not only a symbol of the crucifixion, but also of the human and divine natures of Christ. Moreover, it had been venerated by both Constantine and Helena.[140] Like the Eucharist, then, the cross was worthy of great devotion and prayer. In fact, all religious images, whether of Christ himself, of the Virgin, or of saints who had lived and died in emulation of Christ, were worthy of such veneration. As the Catholics reasoned, Constantine, like Gregory the Great after him, had smashed pagan idols, not Christian ones. While this stance ultimately drew on the argument forwarded by the champions of images during the Byzantine controversy of the eighth and ninth centuries, the Protestants quite naturally adopted the stance and arguments of the Byzantine iconoclasts. For them, the cross was a symbol of the Passion, but it was not a divine image. Taken to its ultimate extreme in the words and actions of Zwingli, all images, not just crucifixes, but statues, reliquaries and paintings with religious content, were confiscated from Churches and destroyed. Zwingli and, after him, Flacius, thus became the new Constantines, in their view, of the sixteenth century.[141]

Of course, in this sense and others, Rome had her own Constantine in the person of Pope Sixtus V, who sometimes resorted to hurling pagan statues into the Tiber as one way of expulsing the demons from the *respublica Christiana*![142] But these were pagan images and pagan daemons, and hence quite unrelated to the sacred images which the Council of Trent had deemed so essential to the instruction and piety of Christ's flock. Indeed, sacred images proliferated during the Sixtine pontificate, and not only in the religious monuments he commissioned: they crown his most visible Good Works, the obelisks and columns, and Constantine himself is victorious over Maxentius in the Lateran Palace due to the power of the cross (fig. 106).

The cult of saints, which is very much related to the cult of images, was also subjected to Protestant invective. As far as the most radical of the Protestants were concerned, the saints, foremost among them the Virgin Mary, had no intercessory powers so that prayers addressed to them were rendered wholly inconsequential. Moreover, the pope had no right, in their view, to create saints.[143] In response to the Council of Trent, Sixtus V translated, sheltered and venerated saints' relics; he dedicated a chapel to Saint Lucy, the patron saint of his birth, and one to Saint Jerome at Santa Maria Maggiore; he was extremely devoted to the Virgin, so much so that he was buried in her basilica; he was a devout Franciscan, and commemorated the founder of his Order in image and in text not only in the

[138] Ostrow, "Sistine," 40, 252-260.

[139] See Appendix I, 213-214, n. 45 for the decree of Saint Urbanus I; and 216, n. 60 for the *Treasure at Castel Sant'Angelo*.

[140] Scavizzi, "Storia ecclesiastica" *Storia dell'arte*, 35-36, 42-44; idem, *Arte e architettura sacra. Cronache e documenti sulla controversia tra riformati e cattolici (1500-1550)* (Rome, 1981), 246-248.

[141] Ostrow, "Sistine," 45-51; Scavizzi, "Storia ecclesiastica," *Storia dell'arte*, 32-37.

[142] Seznec, *Survival*, 264. Compare Ugonio's statement regarding the pope's removal of eight pagan statues from the Campidoglio in Scavizzi, "Storia ecclesiastica," *Storia dell'arte*, 41.

Aikin, "Capitoline," 131, suggests that Sixtus V "may also have seen himself as the imitator of Constantine."

[143] Ostrow, "Sistine," 42-45.

Lateran Palace, but also in the Vatican Library, Villa Montalto and Sixtine Chapel; and, what is more, he created the first new saint in sixty-three years, and followed this act with the creation of another, as well as a Doctor of the Church.

The power that enabled Sixtus V to create new saints was part of a much larger authority which extended from the spiritual to the temporal realm. It was this authority which Christ handed down to Peter and which all subsequent vicars consequently enjoyed - at least this was the Catholic stance, based, in large part, on the *Constitutum Constantini* and its full flowering in the Doctrine of the Two Swords, that Doctrine which was reflected in the twelfth century murals of the Patriarchium Lateranense, and which, as Alexandra Herz has shown, was subscribed to wholeheartedly by the popes of the Roman Catholic Reform in general, and by Sixtus V in particular.[144] For the Protestants, the *Constitutum* was wholly unacceptable since it was both spurious and extra-biblical, and the Doctrine, the result of faulty claims based on a profound misreading of the Scriptures. They saw the Roman pope as the Antichrist, wreaking havoc in both the temporal and spiritual realms, and generally reducing the once chaste and unblemished Church of Christ to a den of iniquity. Not only was the "popish" practice of creating saints a reprehensible activity, but the Roman vicar endeavoured to usurp the authority of Church councils and regularly trespassed on the temporal affairs of kings and emperors.[145] To be sure, Christ's vicars did all of these things, and more, but they did them, in their view, not only according to the Bible and Catholic tradition, but also according to Christ's unimpeachable wishes as reflected in that tradition. There can be little doubt that Sixtus V was well aware of the fact that the *Constitutum Constantini* was a forgery (Lorenzo Valla had conclusively demonstrated this already in the fifteenth century),[146] but this neither deterred his belief in the Doctrine which it spawned, nor his decision, like that of Leo X before him, to include a scene of the Donation in the frescoes depicting the life of Constantine in the Lateran Palace. If the reasoning of Baronio may be taken as indicative of Sixtus V's attitude, the fact that the *Constitutum* was a forgery was actually irrelevant. On the one hand, Constantine's Donation symbolized the end of Christian persecution under the empire and the investment of Christianity as the state religion, and accordingly stood as an "historical" event of signal importance. On the other hand, the pope's original authority to act in the capacity of emperor was given him by God, just as earlier such authority had been given also to Samuel. The authority given by the emperor was therefore redundant, since spiritually sanctioned authority wins out over that sanctioned in the temporal sphere every time.[147]

The Good Works of Sixtus V, as frescoed and sculpted, are in one very important sense testimonies to the pope's authority in the temporal and spiritual realms. In another fundamental sense they are inextricably bound with the Catholic doctrine of justification. As one of the most significant tenets of Catholicism, and one which had become increasingly open to attack and revision by the Protestants, justification was treated early on in the proceedings of Trent, having been made law on 13 January 1547 at the close of the sixth session.[148] It was determined that justification could be attained only through faith and good works. Right actions on earth, carried out in a state of grace achieved through belief in Christ's sacrifice on the

[144] Herz, "Sixtine," *Storia dell'arte*, 252-255.

[145] Ostrow, "Sistine," 35-38.

[146] Lorenzo Valla, *The Profession of the Religious and the principal arguments from the Falsely-Believed and Forged Donation of Constantine*, trans., ed. Olga Zorzi Pugliese, Renaissance and Reformation Texts in Translation 1 (Toronto, 1985), 63-74. Nicholas Cusanus and Reginald Peacock had also worked on de-mythologizing the Donation at the same time as Valla. The former's text is reprinted in Coleman, *Constantine*, 238-242, who also discusses the various criticisms, 188-202.

[147] Baronio, *Annales*, IV, 88-89, devotes little time (and space) to the Doctrine, and discusses Samuel's prefiguration of the eternal right of the pope in the context of the coronation of Charlemagne, in *idem*, XIII, 347-350. Consult Coleman, *Constantine*, 206-207; Pullapilly, *Baronius*, 146-147; and Miles L. Chappell and W. Chandler Kirwin, "A Petrine Triumph: The Decoration of the Navi Piccole in San Pietro under Clement VIII," *Storia dell'arte* XXI (1974): 124.

[148] This and the following are based on *Canons and Decrees of the Council of Trent: original text with English translation*, intro & notes H. J. Schroeder (1941; Rockford Illinois, 1978), 29-46, esp. 36, Ch. X., and 45, Can. 24; J. Pohle, "Merit," *The Catholic Encyclopedia*, ed. Charles G. Herbermann, et al, 15 vols., (New York, 1911), X, 202-208; O. M. T. Logan, "Grace and Justification: Some Italian Views of the Sixteenth and Early Seventeenth Centuries," *Journal of Ecclesiastical History* XX, 1 (April 1969), 67-78; and Catherine Wilkinson, "The Iconography of Bernini's Tomb of Urban VIII," *L'Arte* IV (1971): 57-58.

cross, would result in a God-given reward which could lead, ultimately, to eternal life.[149] The more good works carried out by the faithful, the greater would be the glory in the afterlife, although by no means was there a guaranty to man while alive that he would attain salvation and the "crown of justice" in heaven [II Timothy IV: 7]. Faith alone was insufficient for the receipt of God's final reward and likewise good works carried out without faith could not be considered "good." Like the Catholics, the Protestants relied in large part on the words of Saint Paul, but, as they interpreted them, determined that good works were by no means requisite to achieving eternal life. In fact, for Luther, good works were sinful, since they camouflaged man's inherently unchaste soul, while for Calvin, good works were "impurities and defilement," and served only for temporal satisfaction, not eternal life.[150] Only through faith, said the Protestants, could man attain salvation. Significantly, during his residence in Rome in 1552, Fra Felice expounded three times a week on the Epistle to the Romans, one of the key sources for Catholic and Protestant definitions of justification.[151] And while these sermons have not, to the best of my knowledge, survived, it is nonetheless possible to glean some idea of the friar's thoughts on justification by looking to later, published works. In his sermon on the conversion of the gentiles, delivered in Naples in 1554 (that is, three years prior to the Tridentine decree), Fra Felice follows Saint Augustine and points to essentially three good things in Christ's holy vineyard, the Church: "Anima sancti in bonis perseuerans, quae speciosiore est Sole: Sancti Angeli, qui eam suscipiunt: & Paradisus, in quem ducitur *L'anima del giusto perseuerante nelle bone opere*: l'Angeli santi, che la abracciano: & il santo Paradiso, ouè la locano meglior de queste tre cose, non se troua: e però con animo pronto, con spirito franco Ite, ite & uos in uineam meam [emphasis mine]".[152]

In his conclusion, he then refers to Christian exemplars who merited the greatest reward from God of the "corona iustitiae," notable among them being Saint Francis. Sixtus V's early views on justification, as conveyed in the context of this sermon, accordingly agree with those enforced at Trent, since both, of course, adhered to the Bible and tradition. More importantly for my purposes, the justice of Sixtus V, which was a leitmotif of panegyrics during his pontificate, and which has become equally prevalent in the modern characterizations of Sixtine rule in the temporal realm, in this sense takes on a much larger, and extremely significant meaning.[153] Indeed, the prevalence on the *piano nobile* in particular of devices with mottoes concerning justice, and especially those collocated with the "triple mountain" *corpo* and its conspicuous triple crowns, are most certainly in this sense the three good things in Christ's holy vineyard; the visible prayers of a pope desirous of attaining glory in the afterlife and of being crowned for his achievements.

6. HISTORICAL CONTEXT II: THE PATRIARCHIUM LATERANENSE

Perhaps the most unexpected of the sources used at the Lateran Palace was the programme of the Patriarchium Lateranense.[154] At a time when Christian archaeology was in its infancy and very much in vogue (the first discovery of a Christ-

[149] Justification was accordingly bound with the Eucharist as well, since Good Works could only be efficacious if carried out in emulation of Christ.

[150] Quoted in Pohle, "Merit," *Catholic Encyclopedia*, 204.

[151] von Pastor, *History*, XXI, 30-31.

[152] Fra Felice Peretti, *Predica* , n.p.

[153] It will, I hope, suffice to cite two works on Sixtus V and justice, one from each period, as follows: R. P. Frate Innocenzo Alberti da Pesaro, *Ragionamenti intorno alla giustitia di N. S. Papa Sisto Quinto ...* (Urbino, 1587); Fabrizio Sarazani, *La Roma di Sisto V "er papa tosto": Potere assoluto e grandezza irrazionale di un personaggio entrato nella fantasia popolare*, iconographical research by Giulio Fefé (Rome, 1979).

[154] Scholars have remarked on the fact that certain rooms of the Lateran Palace were constructed on the approximate sites of those of the Patriarchium, but few have drawn parallels between the iconographical programmes of the Patriarchium Lateranense and the Lateran Palace. However, see Traeger, *Papst*, 59; and recently, Sigrid Epp, *Konstantinszyklen in Rom. Die päpstliche Interpretation der Geschichte Konstantins des Großen bis zur Gegenreformation*, Schriften aus dem Institut für Kunstgeschichte der Universität München (Munich, 1988), esp. 96-97, both of whom focus on the Constantinian component of the cycle. I should like to thank Sigrid Epp for very kindly having given me a copy of her book.

ian catacomb on the Via Salaria had occurred only years earlier, in 1578), Sixtus V's decision to dismantle the ancient papal residence quite naturally met with an uproar in Rome - an uproar which may still be heard in certain "Early Christian" and "Medieval" quarters to this day.[155] Still, in what may be viewed as a paradoxical stance by some, Sixtus V partook of the same movement to investigate the past as Baronio; in the end, the necessity of conveying the invulnerability and triumph of Catholicism and of her head, by a monument which was physically splendid, won over the desire to save dilapidated testimony to her greatness - hence Sixtus V's explanation, as conveyed by Fontana, as to why the destruction was carried out.[156] This move to research Early Christian history with the primary purpose of proving that the present Church was like the Church under Peter's administration, as under Sylvester's, had a precedent in the Council of Trent and found a parallel under Sixtus V in the realization of its edicts, ranging from the renewal of such ancient practices as the visit *ad limina* and the *Cappelle papali*, to the reorganization of the College of Cardinals and of the Curia, so as to reflect ancient practice and bolster the absolute power of the pope in both the temporal and spiritual realms.[157]

An indication of Sixtus V's regard for the Patriarchium Lateranense is evident in the mere fact that he did not demolish *in toto* the structure. That he left the Sancta Sanctorum in its original location, moreover, attests to the veneration he gave to this chapel of his predecessors, and his decision to incorporate the Scala Santa in the complex, an indication of his desire to see the continuity of Church history at once maintained and glorified. Likewise, his preservation of the large *triclinium* of Leo III, notwithstanding that it had been in such ill-repair as to prompt Pius V to transform it into a garden, suggests that the apse and its decorations held more than a passing interest for Sixtus V. Further, his decision to save the Oratory of Saint Nicholas, which glorified the papal succession in tandem with the Queen of Heaven, to whom he was profoundly devoted all his life, suggests motives in keeping with those that spurred the pope to restore and embellish the Sancta Sanctorum and Scala Santa.[158] Far from being indifferent to the past, Sixtus V seems to have been ever cognizant of the Patriarchium's venerable history. If, therefore, certain parts of the complex had to be destroyed because of their irreparable condition, it was vital that certain others be preserved, because they were in reasonable condition, and, more importantly perhaps, because they were extremely pertinent to the message being propagated during the Sixtine pontificate. In this regard, I would go so far as to suggest that those parts of the ancient residence which were saved were intended to stand as reminders of those which were destroyed, and as guides to understanding the message of the new Lateran Palace. A particularly good case in point is the apse of the triconch *triclinium* of Leo III which was left standing as a mere shell and reflection of its past glory.

The precise content of Leo III's apse mosaic has been disputed, owing to the lack of clear descriptions of the entire mosaic prior to its restoration under Francesco Barberini in 1625 (the eighteenth century copy, now located in the niche behind the Scala Santa complex, only vaguely reflects the original). It is certain that the apse originally displayed Christ, standing on a hill with the four rivers of paradise flowing from its base,

[155] For the study of Christian archaeology in Roman Catholic Reform Rome, consult Silvia Grassi Fiorentino, "Note sull'antiquaria romana nella seconda metà del secolo XVI," *Baronio storico*, 197-211; Philip J. Jacks, "Baronius and the Antiquities of Rome," *Baronio e l'arte: atti del convegno internazionale di studi Sora 10-13 ottobre 1984*, ed. Romeo De Maio, Agostino Borromeo, Luigi Gulia, Georg Lutz, Aldo Mazzacane (Sora, 1985), 77-96; and recently, Scavizzi, "Storia ecclesiastica," *Storia dell'arte*, 38-42. For the uproar in Rome, see von Pastor, *History*, XXII, 272.

[156] See note 40, above.

[157] Since it actually gave to the pope greater power than was initially agreed upon at Trent, his bull concerning the reorganization of the College of Cardinals, quoted in part below, was not strictly in accord with the decrees. See John Butler Tomaro, "The Papacy and the Implementation of the Council of Trent: 1564-1588," diss., U of North Carolina at Chapel Hill, 1974, 294-300.

[158] von Pastor, *History*, XXII, 238, understood Sixtus V's regard for the monuments of both the pagan and Christian past. Aikin, "Capitoline," 46-47, 71-72, has recently reiterated and expanded upon this view.

holding an open book inscribed "PAX VOBIS" in his left hand while blessing with his right, and flanked by his eleven disciples. The apse was surmounted by an inscription taken from Luke II: 14: "GLORIA IN EXCELSIS DEO ET IN TERRA PAX HOMINIBVS BONAE BOLVNTATIS," and underscored by another taken from Matthew XXVIII: 16 ff, referring to the mission of the apostles to preach the Word and to baptize in the name of the Father, the Son and the Holy Ghost.[159] This central mosaic was flanked by at least one politically charged scene, featuring Saint Peter giving the *pallium* to Leo III and the *vexillum*, or battle standard, to King Charles. It is generally believed that flanking this triad was another group, located to the left of the central apse, comprised of Christ giving the keys to Sylvester I (or, according to some, Saint Peter) and the *labarum*, or Roman military standard, to Constantine, hence conveying the essential precepts of the *Constitutum Constantini*.[160]

The mission of the apostles, which is an integral part of the message of the triconch *triclinium*, as the inscription beneath the apse mosaic conveys, finds a much expanded parallel in Sixtus V's Salone degli Apostoli, where narratives show the apostles going out to preach the Word and to convert the world to the true faith (refer hereafter to Appendix I). So, too, the corresponding Lucan inscription in the Leonine *triclinium* is echoed in the adjacent Salone di Costantino and eastern loggia of the *piano nobile* (locales which face the site then occupied by the garden) and on the grand staircase leading to the third floor as the motto of a device (fig. 19). Whereas one might expect the *anima* to be collocated with a "triple mountain" *corpo*, so as to reflect Christ's position atop the mount of Paradise, such one-to-one correspondances are not always forthcoming. Rather, the Lucan verse accompanies a single obelisk *corpo* on the *piano nobile*, while on the stairway leading to the third floor it enspirits another device featuring the columns flanking an obelisk. The choice of the obelisks and columns in lieu of the obvious choice, in my view, of the Montalto mountains would seem to point to the apostolic origins of the papacy (columns) as well as to the imperial subjection to Christ's vicar (obelisk), messages which are contained in both the ninth and sixteenth century cycles. To be sure, the Salone di Costantino responds to the politicizing triads of the Leonine *triclinium*, as to the subsequent murals created for Innocent II and the mosaics of the twelfth century basilica, in its inclusion of narrative scenes representing Constantine's Donation and performance of the *officium stratoris*. The Salone degli Imperatori, its counterpart on the western arm of the *piano nobile*, commemorates Christian emperors who acted as the pope's fighting arm in extirpating heresy and maintaining the faith beginning, quite naturally, with Constantine himself (fig. 21). The marriage of the apostles' mission and the peaceful rulership of the *respublica Christiana* by the pope and emperor in the Leonine *triclinium* also finds a counterpart in the Salone di Costantino, where Sylvester baptizes Constantine in keeping with the *Legenda* and *Constitutum vis-à-vis* historical reality; in the Salone dei Papi, where Sylvester I is remembered in part as the converter of Constantine and extirpator of heresy; and in the prevalent theme of the Christian Golden Age which, as I shall explain in the following chapter, lies at the very core of the Lateran Palace programme, as of the pontificate of the pope-emperor Sixtus V.

[159] "DOCETE OMNES GENTES VAPTIZANTES EOS IN NOMINE PATRIS ET FILII ET SPIRITVS SCS ET ECCE EGO VOVISCVM SVM OMNIBVS DIEBVS VSQVE AD CONSVMATIONEM SECVLI"

[160] Christopher Walter has recently suggested that in lieu of Christ and the politically-charged duo of Sylvester and Constantine there was more likely a depiction of Saint Paul with two figures more appropriate to the iconograpy of his mission to the Gentiles. See note 16, above.

The most overwhelming influence of the monuments saved by Sixtus V, and one which is intimately bound with his papal and imperial natures, is the tripartite or "trinitarian" organizational scheme. This system not only informs the whole of the triconch *triclinium*, from its architectural given to the general layout of the apse, but it also extends to its parts in the form of Peter, Prince of the Apostles and vicar of Christ, flanked, though on an inferior level, by his latest successor and the earthly ruler, and, *pace* Walter, of Christ flanked by pope and emperor.[161] In one sense, the stance, size, and positioning of Peter and Christ within their respective groupings reveal the clear distinction between the spiritual above and the temporal below. In another sense, the lower, temporal tier, containing Sylvester and Constantine, Leo III and King Charles, yields to these very same distinctions on the horizontal or synchronic, rather than the vertical or diachronic, with the popes as the spiritual representatives on earth, and the emperor as the temporal ruler. Thanks to Matthew XXVI: 51 and the *Constitutum Constantini*, these triads yield yet a third level of interpretation, which gives to the pope, both in heaven in the form of Peter, and on earth in the form of Sylvester and Leo III, the dual powers of temporal and spiritual sovereignty so that the macrocosm of the image, as it were, is repeated in the microcosm of the pope. It is precisely such a complex of ideas, issuing from the most basic of "geometrical" schemes, that finds parallels in the Lateran Palace programme.

Owing to the Matthean passage, the *Constitutum*, and especially the later Doctrine of the Two Swords, the Sixtine triads are rarely as lucid as the fundamentally synchronic theme espoused by Leo III, whereby Christ is flanked by his spiritual and secular aids, the pope and emperor. More often than not, Sixtus V's programme draws on the diachronic scheme of typologies, and subsumes in the person of Sixtus V the temporal and spiritual, the Petrine and Pauline, the Old and New Dispensations, the pagan and the Christian. Hence, among the many permutations to which the Leonine theme was subjected in the narratives of the *piano nobile*, Sylvester and Peter flank Christ, Peter and Moses in the Salone dei Papi; in the Sala degli Obelischi, Peter and Paul on their respective columns flank a central Sixtine *stemma*; in the Sala d'Elia, Moses and Elijah flank Christ in the *Transfiguration*; and the list could be extended considerably also to include both Saint Francis and Constantine, as I shall explain in Chapter IV. It is not in the Lateran Palace, but rather on the last pier of the Salone Sistino, that the Leonine theme, in its most fundamental sense, is most clearly and succinctly demonstrated, with Christ flanked by Pope Sylvester I and Emperor Constantine.[162] As Philipp Fehl has recently shown, the triumphal Moses Fountain which terminates the aqueduct of the Acqua Felice also partakes of this scheme, with Moses in the central niche prefiguring Christ, Aaron symbolizing Sixtus V in the left niche, and Joshua, Emperor Rudolph II in the right, with these latter actually bearing portrait-likenesses to their contemporaneous counterparts.[163] In the more secular components of the primarily religious programme of the Sixtine Chapel at Santa Maria Maggiore, Alexandra Herz has shown that the tomb monuments of Sixtus V and his cherished predecessor and mentor Pius V demonstrate the pope's temporal and spiritual powers, in both form and content. Here, as at the palace, the distinctions between temporal-imperial, temporal-papal and

[161] These triads are often illustrated in the literature on the triclinium. See, for example, Davis-Weyer, "patristische Apologie," *Munuscula disciplorum*, figs. 68-70.

[162] Listed in Fontana, *Della trasportatione*, 91-91v; and discussed in Mutio Pansa, *Della Libraria Vaticana ...*, (Rome, 1590), 312-315; and Rocca, *Biblioteca*, 173-184.

[163] Fehl, "Hermeticism," *Artibus et historiae*, 156-159.

spiritual-papal are conflated, leaving only vestiges of the pope-Christ-emperor scheme as stated in the Vatican Library as, on one level, in the Leonine *triclinium*.[164] At the Villa Montalto, the thrust of the programme, which had much in common with that of the Lateran Palace, likewise concerned Christ, Moses and additional Old Testament types for the Saviour and the pope in the persons of Adam, Abraham, Noah, Samson, David, Solomon, Elijah and Daniel, as well as Saint Francis, with the Emperor Constantine as the strictly imperial and synchronic representative in this primarily diachronic scheme of world history.[165] And the decorations of the Palazzo delle Terme, carried out during Sixtus V's pontificate, explicitly added the papal-biographical and hence temporal and spiritual elements in the form of his Good Works.[166]

The idea of investiture, which is stated explicitly in the Leonine triads, as in the monuments created for Innocent II and Callistus II, also plays a seminal role in the cycle of the Lateran Palace. The thesis is stated in the main hall with narrative scenes representing Christ's double charge to Peter, the "rock" on which the Church will be built, and pastor of Christ's flock (figs. 63-64), alluding to the Matthean passage by which Christ gives to Peter the keys of heaven, as he does in the triconch *triclinium*. The theme of rightful papal succession, as conveyed in both the Oratory of Saint Nicholas and Camera pro Secretis Consiliis, is reflected in the Old Testament rooms of the *piano nobile*, beginning with Samuel anointing Saul in the Sala di Samuele (fig. 88), and progressing through the Sala di Davide, where Samuel anoints David (fig. 148); the Sala di Salomone, where David's son and rightful heir to the throne rides to Gihon where he will be anointed king (fig. 155); in the Sala d'Elia, where Elisha awaits Elijah's mantle as the prophet ascends in his fiery chariot (fig. 22); and in the Sala di Daniele, where Daniel emerges victorious over the dragon Bel while the statue of Nebuchadnezzar's dream, like the statue of Mercury in the Sala di Costantino in the Vatican (figs. 23-24), is smashed by the stone which would fill the earth as the Catholic Church led by the Peretti pope, identified as the "lion of the tribe of Judah" in the Sixtine devices in this room, as elsewhere in the palace.[167] Investiture also figures prominently in the remaining halls of the outer area of the *piano nobile*, with the creation of the Church on Pentecost in the Salone degli Apostoli; with Constantine translating his empire to Sylvester I in the Salone di Costantino; and with Constantine and his successors devoting their lives to the service of the cross in the pendant Salone degli Imperatori.

Divine unction, investiture and the *translatio imperii* find their ultimate focus in the person of the anointed one who will appear at the end of time, at once Christ and the *alter Christus*, Pope Sixtus V. They also, of course, relate to the sacrament of Confirmation, with which the anointing of kings is inextricably bound. Significantly, in apostolic initiation rites, this very act of *chrisma* formed the central act of a trinitarian scheme which began with Baptism and ended with the eucharistic sacrifice. I would suggest that this very scheme is reflected also in the palace.[168] The sacrament of Baptism is literally represented in three narratives on the *piano nobile*: the *Baptism of Christ* by the patron saint of the pope's titular basilica is depicted in the second room of the private apartment, and in the eastern loggia, while the *Baptism of Constantine* is depicted in the Salone di Costantino, a hall which abuts both the eastern loggia

[164] Herz, "Sixtine," *Storia dell'arte*, 241-262. It may still be possible to locate the Christological at center, be it in terms of coronations of popes, or their statues in emulation of Christ; the papal at left, entailing the embodiment of Christian charity, the passing of spiritual duties and creation of saints; and the imperial at right, corresponding to the pope's inherently regal powers given him by Christ, and entailing the justice of temporal rule, the defense of the Faith, and the peace which the pope brings to his terrestrial domain. According to this reading, the Christological components of the tombs of Pius V and Sixtus V respectively are the *Coronation of Pius V*, the statue of Pius V giving the benediction, the *Coronation of Sixtus V*, and statue of Sixtus V in prayer; the papal components, the *Battle of Lepanto*, *Pius V presenting the Papal Standards to Marcantonio Colonna*, the *Canonization of San Diego of Alcala* and *Charity*; and the imperial, *Pius V presenting the Baton of Command to Conte Sforza di Sta. Fiore*, *Conte Sforza di Sta. Fiore Victorious Over the Huguenots*, *Justice* and *Peace between King Sigismond of Poland and Emperor Rudolph II of Austria*.

[165] Massimo, *Notizie*, 42-58. Since Sixtus V was still a cardinal when he commissioned this cycle, the papal component of the Old Testament scenes when read typologically and symbolically could possibly have referred to Pius V, although this seems unlikely. Perhaps the cardinal was preparing for that fated day, revealed long ago to his parents, when he would become pope! In any case, he was most certainly alluding to his coat-of-arms in the lions which Massimo noted in many of the narratives. See note 115, above.

[166] Massimo, *Notizie*, 124-136. Even the Scala Santa, the only structure of Sixtine Rome imbued with a purely religious programme, since devoid of secular subject matter and explicit representations of, or references to the life and actions of Sixtus V, is protected by a stairway to either side, resulting in a another tripartite organizational principle. The vaults flanking the Scala Santa are frescoed with three sets of narratives, one series lining the seam of the vault and the remaining two flanking it on the coves, while the central vault above the holy stairs contains four sets of narratives, two at center vault, and two on the coves. See the diagram in Scavizzi, "Scala Santa-II," 334-335. While the subjects of the narratives informing the three vaults are taken from the Scriptures, those on the flanking vaults are taken from the Old Testament, in contradistinction to those on the central vault which are taken exclusively from the New Testament and the life of Christ. The Christological element is thus firmly, and very appropriately situated at center and agrees, therefore, with the essential place held by Christ in all secular Sixtine ensembles, as well as the secularizing component of the Sixtine Chapel. The flanking vaults are somewhat more

and private apartment. The symbolism of the cross, which is both baptismal and eucharistic, is found on the opposite sector of the palace in the Sala degli Obelischi, with the converted obelisks; in the western loggia extension, with the *Stigmatization of Saint Francis*; and in the Salone degli Imperatori, with the emperors whose coinage featured the cross. Like a point-counterpoint, baptismal and eucharistic symbolism complementing the idea of investiture runs throughout the *piano nobile*, and finds a regal synthesis within the most important narratives of the cycle, the Investiture scenes in the Salone dei Papi, as I shall explain in Chapter III below. It also finds a parallel, I would suggest, in the three personifications occupying the first landing of the grand staircase as it winds its way to the *piano nobile*, and that merited representation also in the Vatican Library (figs. 10-12). Whereas each of Rocca's four elements is included in the programme of the library, in the palace *Earth* is conspicuously absent from the company of *Air, Water* and *Fire*. Of course, the architectural given allows for only three of the four elements, but, as will become exceedingly clear in the following chapters, little if anything in the Lateran Palace programme was left to chance, so that the exclusion of *Earth*, rather than *Air* or *Water* or *Fire* must have been done for a reason. I would suggest that this lowest of the elements could well have been understood in at least one of the significations of these personifications. The element of water suggests Baptism. The net balanced on the wrists of the personification in this sense recalls the net of the apostles, the fishermen of souls, especially that of Peter, who is remembered in the Salone dei Papi for having learned the proper method of throwing out his net of conversion.[169] Her jugs of water in turn suggest the means by which the actual rite is enacted, and her bare breasts, the purity of the soul of the initiate. The element of fire suggests Pentecost, the formation of the Church as represented in the Salone degli Apostoli. Her burning hearts may well allude to Christian charity and to the replacement of the burnt offerings of the Old Testament by the Eucharist of the New, itself a potent symbol of fire, as of the *sol iustitiae*.[170] The element of air, finally, is a traditional analogue to Elijah's investiture to Elisha in the Sala d'Elia (hence the birds of flight?), and accordingly to the keys which Christ gave to Peter and which he triumphantly holds in the Salone dei Papi as testimony to his sovereignty on earth (the missing element?), and the reverberation of his acts in heaven (fig. 54).[171]

The eucharistic symbolism that pervades the programme of the palace is intimately connected to the victory of the Church as most clearly manifested by the cross-topped obelisks converted to the faith by Sixtus V, and by the landscapes populating the antichapel and logge containing Christian buildings and pagan ruins as well as such "disguised" eucharistic symbols as bread and wine.[172] In the palace, this victory is of essentially two types. On the one hand, it is a celebrative coup for Catholicism which is literally trumpeted throughout the decorative cycle and commemorated in those Sixtine devices proclaiming the victory of the "lion of the tribe of Judah," the triumph of the "glorious religion" and justice. On the other hand, it is a victory which has not yet been completely realized, hence the mottoes of those Sixtine devices which speak of vigilance, intimidation and the excise of the guilty - that is, the Protestant faction and the Turk, the heretic and infidel; for the Jews are ultimately to be converted and

problematic, if only because they often contain narratives concerning the same biblical personages, but I would not discount the possibility of a typological reading of these scenes which would result in another tripartite scheme of Christ flanked by pope and emperor per vault, nor would I discount the possibility that Sixtus V holds a significant place in the programme, despite the conspicuous absense of his Good Works and devices. First, the artists decorated the frames with the ubiquitous elements of the Sixtine heraldry, and were clearly allowed to do so by the pope, who kept a close watch on the evolution of all his commissions. Secondly, the pope's portrait is identifiable in at least one of the narrative scenes, a narrative which significantly concerns Moses: Paris Nogari's *Moses showing his People the Fruits of the Promised Land* bears a striking resemblance to Sixtus V and his stance, derived from the "Adlocutio Augusti," in this sense serves to reiterate Moses's - and Sixtus V's - temporal dominion. The Nogari fresco is reproduced in Giuseppe Scavizzi, "Gli affreschi della Scala Santa - II," *Bollettino d'arte* XLV (1960): 327, fig. 5. Erwin Panofsky, *Problems in Titian: mostly iconographic* (New York, 1969), 76-77, discusses the "Adlocutio Augusti." Thirdly, Moses, who is one of the personages represented on both flanking vaults, was traditionally invested with the tripartite power of lawgiver, priest and king, so that, depending upon the context, like the aforementioned example, one of his roles could be emphasized over the others. As far as I know, the Scala Santa has not been treated comprehensively from the point of view of content. Such a study would require monographic scale, and is outside the bounds of the present study.

[167] On Nebuchadnezzar's dream and the interpretations of the stone, or the "rock" of the Church, see Joseph Ward Swain, "The Theory of the Four Monarchies. Opposition History under the Roman Empire," *Classical Philology* XXXV, 1 (January 1940): 1-21. Also consult Aikin, "Capitoline," 19-25, who treats 16th century views in general, and Sixtus V's in particular, and suggests that "The four bronze lions supporting the Vatican obelisk and the four lions in the Moses Fountain - devices of Sixtus's arms - may have been intended to relate Sixtus to Christ himself, the lion of Judah."

[168] Discussed in Jean Danielou, *Bible et Liturgie*, 1951; reprint ed., *The Bible and the Liturgy*, trans. (London, 1964), 114-140, esp. 127. Also consult Bernice F. Davidson, *Raphael's Bible. A Study of the Vatican Logge*, CAA of America (University Park & London, 1985), 81, who draws this analogy with regard to the scenes from the life of David in Raphael's *logge*.

[169] See Chapter III, 112, below.

[170] Ripa, *Iconologia*, I, 75, 154, respectively describes the fire of charity as "il fuoco Christo N. S. in quelle parole: *Ignem veni mittere in terram, & quid volo, nisi ut ardeat?*"; and the heart

66

hence included within the fold (thus Sixtus V's exceedingly unusual lenience towards the Hebrews during his pontificate?). This defensive quality has much in common, of course, with the Camera pro Secretis Conciliis by which Callistus II had celebrated the victory of the Investiture Struggle by stomping on his foes, in the tradition of the psychomachia.[173] Although Sixtus V did not preserve this room, perhaps owing to its extremely poor condition, it nonetheless seems to have left its mark on the programme of the new Lateran Palace. One of the most defensive of the rooms on the *piano nobile* is the Sala di Daniele, the last of the Old Testament rooms. Here, amidst narratives of Daniel's demonstration and subsequent destruction of the the falsehood of the pagan faith, are Sixtine devices that refer, in one sense, to the pope's vigilance and ultimate victory, and personifications like *Defensio*, who wields the thunderbolt of excommunication, and another, with comparable meaning, raising the *malleus haereticorum*, the hammer by which heretics are subdued.[174] These formidable women find immediate counterparts in the Vatican Library, along with cousins inhabiting *grotteschi* who burn heretical books; and, among the most forceful at the Villa Montalto, the angel who smote the first-born Egyptians.[175] In the adjacent Sala d'Elia, as at the corners of the *piano nobile* in the Salone di Costantino and Sala degli Obelischi, more defensive women subdue demons at their feet, the direct ancestors of the popes in Callistus II's council room, and the analogues in the Sixtine complex to Saint Sylvester I who is enthroned in the Salone dei Papi with the dragon at his feet (fig. 56).

The ancient treasure of the Sancta Sanctorum is also important for the programme of the Lateran Palace since it contained some of the most celebrated relics of Catholicism - relics relating in a fundamental way to Sixtus V's traditional vision of the papacy as an institution descending to Old Testament times. Among its most valued relics, the heads of Saints Peter and Paul, which ultimately found a home in the basilica, are, of course, central to the very fabric of Sixtine Rome since the triumphal columns of the apostles are at the very heart of the Sixtine street system. At the Lateran Palace they are imbued with traditional symbolism as the founders of Rome; the Christian successors to the twins Romulus and Remus;[176] the respective converters of Jew and Gentile; and the bequeathers of this legacy to Sixtus V, who guides the united Church of Christ on earth as at once the *novus Petrus* and *novus Paulus*. Of course, the Princes of the Apostles would undoubtedly have held a central place in the programme, relics or no, and, with the possible exception of the Sixtine devices containing images of the seven-branched candelabrum brought back to Rome by Titus, ultimately to become the charge of the popes, this holds true for the majority of the relics of the Sancta Sanctorum, including the relics of the True Cross, of Aaron, and especially of Moses who was, after all, the builder of the Ark of the Covenant, the type of the papal chapel. Still, their presence in the Sancta Sanctorum could only have underscored their vital importance for Sixtus V, his pontificate, and his place in the history of the world.

At the Lateran Palace Moses figures prominently, even though he is physically *vis-à-vis* symbolically present in only five of the seventeen rooms, and in one secondary *grisaille* narrative in the eastern loggia on the *piano nobile*. He is represented in the main hall in both the feigned tapestry of the *Ac-*

with the lit candle of the Catholic faith as "l'illuminatione della mente nata per la Fede, che discaccia le tenebre dell'infedeltà, & dell'ignoranza, dicendo S. Agostino sopra S. Giovanni al cap. 9: *Caecitas est infidelitas, & illuminatio fides.*"

[171] Réau, *Iconographie*, II, I, 357.

[172] On these traditions, consult Erwin Panofsky, *Early Netherlandish Painting: Its Origins and Character* (New York, Hagerstown, San Francisco, London, 1971), esp. 135. Also consult E. H. Gombrich, "The Renaissance Theory of Art and the Rise of Landscape," *Norm and Form. Studies in the art of the Renaissance*, third ed. (London and New York, 1978), 116; and A. R. Turner, *The Vision of Landscape in Renaissance Italy* (Princeton, New Jersey, 1966).

[173] For the psychomachia tradition, consult Adolph Katzenellenbogen, *Allegories of the Virtues and Vices in Mediaeval Art from Early Christian Times to the Thirteenth Century* (1939; New York, 1964).

[174] The thunderbolt is a well known symbol of excommunication. See Quednau, *Sala di Costantino*, 301-314, on the thunderbolt-wielding "Fulminatio" in the Sala di Costantino. On the hammer as a weapon against heretics, see Rudolph Arbesmann, "The 'Malleus' Metaphor in Medieval Characterization," *Traditio* III (1945): 389-392. Ripa, *Iconologia*, II, 76-77, explains the hammer as a symbol of necessity, a meaning which is inherent in the "*malleus* metaphor."

[175] DEFENSIO flanks the *Prohibition of Adulterers* in the Salone Sistino. For the Villa Montalto, see Massimo, *Notizie*, 47.

qua Felice and the verse of the *Abundance*; in the Sala d'Elia, he appears in the *Transfiguration* with Elijah, as I have noted above in another context; with the apostles and Christ in the Salone degli Apostoli; with other Old Testament personages in the Salone di Costantino; in the fourth room of the private apartment, in the company of other Old Testament prophets and Christian saints; and in the eastern loggia, in the context of the lives of Christ and Saint John the Baptist. It is in the Salone degli Apostoli that the priestly, judicial, and kingly facets of what is ultimately the pope's rule may be explained most authoritatively, since actually based on the words of Sixtus V himself. Here, opposite the feigned tapestry representing the formation of the Roman Catholic Church, *The Holy Spirit descending on the Apostles at Pentecost*, Moses is depicted gathering the seventy elders who would assist him in the governing of the Hebrew nation (fig. 25). But the typology does not end with this fundamental equation, for it was precisely this action of Moses' which Sixtus V emulated when he created his Sacred College of Cardinals. As the pope himself states in his bull *Postquam verus* of 3 December 1586: "Ac, ut veteris synagogae figura sanctae et Apostolicae Ecclesiae veritati respondeat, sequi cupientes mandatum Domini factum ad Moysen, de congregandis septuaginta viris de senibus Israèl, quos nosset senes populi sustentarent, et non ipse solus gravaretur, super quos ad ostium tabernaculi ductos, loquente Domino, Spiritus requievit ...".[177]

What is more, Sixtus V introduces his bull with a comparison of the cardinals to the apostles: "Postquam verus ille atque aeternus Pastor et Episcopus animarum Christus Dominus ad gubernandam universalem Eclesiam, quam suo pretioso Sanguine acquisivit, apostolorum principi B. Petro coelestis simul ac terrenae tradidit plenitudinem potestatis, eique suas in terris vices commisit, sicut in cathedra ipsius Petri successor et verus Christi vicarius, Romanus Pontifex, divina praeordinatione, eiusdem supremae apostolicae dignitatis fastigium et locum in terris tenet, ita etiam sacrosanctae Romanae Ecclesiae cardinales repraesentantes personas sanctorum apostolorum..." .[178]

Sixtus V thus explicitly confirms his assimilation to Moses in the Salone degli Apostoli, as in the Salone dei Papi and all remaining rooms of the Lateran Palace; in Mercati's time-line; and, indeed, in the mythology of his life. He also confirms his assimilation to Moses in the remaining Sixtine ensembles with Mosaic content. In the Salone Sistino of the Vatican Library, Moses initiates a chronology that continues to the pontificate of Sixtus V: the first library of a series of ten is a representation of *Moses entrusting the tablets of the Law to the Levites*, while the last is, of course, the library built and decorated by Sixtus V. In this programme Moses is also included in the group of the twenty-six principal creators of language, as the discoverer of ancient Hebrew letters, so that an implicit link is forged between the "thick-tongued" Levite and the extremely eloquent Sixtus V.[179] He is given pride of place in the fountain of the Acqua Felice, which is also represented as a Good Work of Sixtus V's at the Lateran Palace, Vatican Library and Villa Montalto, so that the kind of conflation noted with regard to both the Leonine *triclinium* and Lateran Palace cycle is implicitly at work here as well, with Sixtus V at once Aaron and Moses and, by implication, Joshua. Moses is central to the programme of the Villa Montalto, with some twelve narratives

[176] Innocent III had drawn the analogy between Peter and Paul and Romulus and Remus in his *Sermones de Sanctis*, Sermo 22, quoted in part and discussed in Leo Steinberg, *Michelangelo's last paintings. The Conversion of St. Paul and the Crucifixion of St. Peter in the Cappella Paolina*, Vatican Palace (New York, 1975), 29.

[177] *Bullarum Romanorum*, VIII, 811.

[178] *Bullarum Romanorum*, VIII, 808. The significance of Moses' choice of seventy elders for Sixtus V's choice of seventy cardinals has often been isolated by commentators on the bull, as has his analogy of the cardinals to the apostles, but, to my knowledge, neither have been applied to the frescoes in the Salone degli Apostoli. In the context of the College of Cardinals, see Pietro Andrea Galli, *Notizie Intorno alla vera Origine, Patria, e Nascita del Sommo Pontefice Sisto V ...* (1752; Montalto, 1754), 179; and von Pastor, *History*, XXI, 227-229.

[179] Fontana, *Della trasportatione*, 85r, 89r.

describing his life, the largest number allotted any single figure in the scheme.[180] Scenes from his life are second only to those of Christ at the Scala Santa, the only "purely" religious programme commissioned by Sixtus V, and one which decorates the structure providing access to the Sancta Sanctorum and its rod of Moses and Tablets of the Law. Finally, the bull *Postquam verus* reinforces the method which I have been describing as so vital to a reading of the Lateran Palace programme, as of all cycles of Sixtine Rome, by which a typological reading of biblical occurrences and, for that matter, of historical, biblical and mythological personages, is complemented on another symbolical level by allusion to contemporary events. Hence, when one is told visually to read the "stone of help" in the Sala di Samuele as an obelisk (or *vice versa*), one is also being given the fundamental method by which the remaining scenes in this, as in all Old Testament rooms, as well as the remaining narratives and personages of the *piano nobile*, ought to be read. Likewise, when, in a panegyric on the Lateran Palace, Vincenzo Robardo compares the lion who guards the entrance to the palace to the dragon who guards the golden apples of the Hesperides, he not only indicates the importance of the western entrance, but, more importantly for the present context, he also analogizes a Christian lion to a pagan counterpart, hence divulging the key method required to understand the meaning of the Lateran Palace programme, the mythology of Sixtus V's life story, and, indeed, the iconology of Sixtine Rome.[181] Much as Boniface VIII had compared himself to Sylvester I and Constantine in his Benediction Loggia, and included his family's coat-of-arms to reinforce his omnipresence, in the Lateran Palace programme, as in the Sixtine replacement of Boniface's *pulpitum*, Sixtus V is symbolically everywhere to be found, taking on the personae of biblical, Franciscan, and pagan personages, and subsuming in his person the powers of both the emperor and Christian princes of his own day.

Ultimately, a number of interrelated historical points of reference may be localized in order to characterize the nature of the Lateran Palace programme, namely the heritage of the papal residence; the popes whom Felice Peretti honoured when he chose the name Sixtus V; the Medici, who were so instrumental in his election to the *cathedra Petri*; and Saint Francis, the founder of his Order. From early on in its history the ancient residence at the Lateran had vied for predominance with the Vatican, the site of Peter's martyrdom, and this duality would be carried into the programmes of Renaissance popes, especially Sixtus IV, Julius II, Leo X and Clement VII, that is, of Franciscan and Medicean popes who deferred to the Patriarchium in their programmes for the Sistine Chapel (the Vatican counterpart to the Sancta Sanctorum), the Stanze and the Sala dei Pontefici.[182] Sixtus V would continue this legacy in the Lateran Palace cycle by deferring to both the ancient residence, as I have tried to indicate in the foregoing, and the Vatican Palace, especially to the artistic programmes executed for his namesake Sixtus IV and his "heraldic" namesake Leo X, including the logge of Raphael, since they provided extremely important complements to the literary testimony of the pope's venerable ancestry. Although Pius V was not a great patron of the arts, he did commission Vasari in 1571 to execute three frescoes of contemporaneous history in the Sala Regia, begun by Paul III and completed ultimately by Gregory XIII. As a monument dedicated to the pope's authority in the temporal

[180] Second place was given to Abraham and the Emperor Constantine, each with ten scenes from their lives, in Massimo, *Notizie*, 46-47, 54-55.

[181] See note 45, above.

[182] Leopold D. Ettlinger, *The Sistine Chapel before Michelangelo: Religious Imagery and Papal Primacy* (Oxford, 1965), 118, for the influence of the Patriarchium Lateranense, and 86 ff, for Moses and Aaron, who play significant roles in Sixtus IV's cycle (as they do in Sixtus V's). Significantly, both the Sistine Chapel and triconch *triclinium* contain messages which are divided formally into tripartite schemes. And recently, John Shearman, "The Chapel of Sixtus IV," in *The Sistine Chapel. The Art, the History and the Restoration* (New York, 1986), 34 ff, who discusses the Constantinian influence as well as the significance of the Patriarchium Lateranense for the chapel and programme of Sixtus IV and Julius II, especially the Sancta Sanctorum. For the influence of the ancient residence on the Sala di Costantino and Sala dei Pontefici, consult Quednau, *Sala di Costantino*, 157-159, 165-172.

and spiritual realms, that is, to the visual translation of the Doctrine of the Two Swords, this glorious testimony to the supremacy of the Roman Catholic Reform would also play an important role in the formulation of the Lateran Palace programme.[183] Pius V was also the author of two particularly significant events which, in a sense, presaged and united the papal-Franciscan and papal-Medicean components of Sixtine Rome. In 1569 he crowned Duke Cosimo I de'Medici Grand Duke of Tuscany and, a year later, made Fra Felice a cardinal.[184] In his extreme wisdom, then, Pius V was instrumental in attaining the willing subservience of the secular arm, in furthering the rise of the "wonder child," and in providing the Medici with the power and authority that was so vital to Cardinal Montalto's accession to the papacy. The Lateran Palace cycle accordingly contains a *summa* of Church history, not just the heritage of apostolic times, and of the Medieval era, but also of the Renaissance and Roman Catholic Reform eras, including the vast wealth of ancient doctrine which had been synthesized with Christian doctrine.

Another historical confluence, and one which encapsulates the papal-imperial, papal-Franciscan, and papal-Dominican facets of the Lateran Palace cycle, is found in the actions of Innocent III, the pope who was instrumental in the formulation of the Doctrine of the Two Swords, and who approved the Rule of Saint Francis.[185] His momentous dream of Saints Francis and Dominic not only spawned the Franciscan Order to which Sixtus IV, Julius II, and Sixtus V belonged, as well, ultimately, as the Dominican Order of Pius V, but it was also inextricably bound to the history of the papal residence at the Lateran, and to the absolute authority exercised on earth by the popes.

Ultimately, the Christological element of the cycle, in its many manifestations as the Sun, the Eucharist, the Cross, and the Old Testament types of the Saviour, is contained in the persons of Saint Francis and his most loyal follower, Pope Sixtus V. As an *alter Christus*, the life of Saint Francis was analogized to that of the Saviour by his biographers, notable amongst them being Saint Bonaventure, whom Sixtus V raised to a Doctor of the Church.[186] Accordingly, the life of Saint Francis represented in the western loggia extension of the palace is a signpost of the method used throughout the programme whereby Francis is analogized to Christ in his many manifestations. So, too, the tripartite theme that is so prevalent in the Lateran Palace programme finds parallels in the trinitarian methodology of Bonaventure, while the emphases on the Cross and Saint Michael, as presaged in the Oratories of the Patriarchium Lateranense, were likewise as much a part of the papal heritage as of Sixtus V's Franciscan ancestry.[187] The manifest use of opposites - of good and bad, virtue and vice, pagan and Christian - as conveyed most forcefully in the symbolism of triumph, both hard won and defensive, finds a parallel in traditional Franciscan preaching practices in general, and in the sermons of Fra Felice Peretti in particular.[188] Finally, the emphasis on the landscape in the programme of the Lateran Palace is as much a summation of the Franciscan way of life, as of the Franciscan love of nature.

Given the well known fact that Sixtus V, like his spiritual mentor, was an avid nature lover, so much so, in fact, that he planted his own shrubs at the Villa Montalto, then it is appropriate that the landscape be given a place of honour in the scheme of the new papal residence, and entirely possible,

[183] These scenes concerned the auspicious Battle of Lepanto. See Philipp P. Fehl, "Vasari's 'Extirpation of the Huguenots': The Challenge of Pity and Fear," *Gazette des Beaux-Arts* LXXXIV (November-December 1974): 263; and Herwarth Röttgen, "Zeitgeschichtliche Bildprogramme der Katholischen Restauration unter Gregor XIII, 1572-1585," *Münchner Jahrbuch der Bildenden Kunst* XXVI (1975): 96. On the Sala Regia, also consult Bernice Davidson, "The Decoration of the Sala Regia under Pope Paul III," *Art Bulletin* LVIII, 3 (September 1976): 395-423.

[184] Ostrow, "Sistine," 120, note 62, notes that Fra Felice was present at the Grand Ducal ceremony.

[185] Schiffmann, *Roma Felix*, 182-183, has noted this historical confluence.

[186] I am here drawing on the excellent study by John V. Fleming, *From Bonaventure to Bellini. An Essay in Franciscan Exegesis*, Princeton Essays on the Arts, 14 (Princeton, New Jersey, 1982). For the lives of St. Francis, consult Habig, *St. Francis*.

[187] Magnuson, *Rome*, I, 24-25, has recently noted the connection between the cross and Saint Francis.

[188] See note 193, below, for a specific example of the friar's preaching methods.

moreover, that the idea was actually his own.[189] Indeed, the connecting link between the major players in the unfolding of history in the Lateran Palace cycle, namely Moses, Samuel, Solomon, Saint John the Baptist, Christ and the Virgin, Peter and Paul, Constantine, Francis and Sixtus V, is ultimately the landscape format that actually received its most prominent treatment during the pontificate of Sixtus V's hated predecessor Gregory XIII.[190] At the Lateran Palace, the landscape hosts Old and New Testament narratives, as the Sixtine artists acknowledged when they submitted their bills to the pope; it contains penitent saints and their prototypes, Francis' *Stigmatization*, and the majority of the Good Works of Sixtus V; it "decorates" the Salone di Costantino at the corners of the long walls; it contains pagan ruins and Christian monuments in the Anticappella; and it lines the logge of the *piano nobile*, as well as the ground floor landing of the grand staircase.

The landscape traditions employed in the programme, many of which will be explored in the following chapters, find their ultimate conclusion in the Sala della Gloria with the representations of the Four Seasons, though ironically they are personified, and situated not within pastoral surrounds, but within *grotteschi*. From the time of Galen and Hippocrates, through the Christian era, the Four Seasons had been associated with the Four Ages of Man, the Cardinal Humors and the Four Elements.[191] Of course, they were also associated with the Four Ages of the World, from whence they initially appeared, beginning with eternal Spring or the Golden Age, and progressing through the Silver Age, at which time the Four Seasons were born, to the more degenerate Ages of Brass and Iron.[192] Given the combination of the Four Seasons represented on the "earthly," synchronic sphere of the vault of the Sala della Gloria, and the *Glory* in the "heavenly," diachronic sphere, then the eternal glory of Sixtus V and of the Church may also be interpreted as the best of all possible ages, the Golden Age. Sixtus V was well versed with the most famous of poems on the subject, Virgil's *Fourth Eclogue*, and with its Christian interpretation as a Sibylline prediction of Christ's birth since he not only included representations of four Sibyls at the entrance to his Chapel of the Praesepio at Santa Maria Maggiore and in the Sala degli Scrittori at the Vatican Library, but he also referred to the Emperor Augustus' profound veneration of the Son of God, and his "refus[al] to be called Lord himself" on the base of the obelisk of Santa Maria Maggiore.[193] But whereas the Golden Age gave way to lesser ages for the pagan, it had always existed for the pious. As I shall demonstrate in the following pages, the Golden Age, which flourished from this *renovatio* in the first century B.C. by an emperor who believed in Christ, and whose reign was both peaceful and religiously inspired, would not only be restored in the fourth century by the Emperor Constantine, but had also, in fact, been willed by Divine Providence since the beginning of time to flourish with the advent of Saint Francis and, again, for one last and truly glorious time, with the pontificate of Sixtus V. At the Lateran Palace, the *Liber Naturae* and *Liber Scripturae* are in perfect accord, and the *respublica Christiana* made ready by Sixtus V for its translation to the Heavenly City at the end of time.

[189] Fagiolo, "La Roma di Sisto V," *Psicon* , 35-36; David R. Coffin, *The Villa in the Life of Renaissance Rome* (Princeton, New Jersey, 1979), 368. It is interesting to note that Sixtus V had very much in common with Julius III in that they were both nature lovers. Bernice F. Davidson, "The Landscapes of the Vatican Logge from the Reign of Pope Julius III," *Art Bulletin* LXV, 4 (December 1983), 593, has noted that Julius III was the instigator of the vogue for landscape painting at mid-century in Rome. As Coffin, *Villa*, 368-369, and *idem, Gardens and Gardening in Papal Rome* (Princeton, New Jersey, 1991), 142-145, explains, Sixtus V was responsible for a new conception of landscape gardening. For further information on Sixtus V's villa, see Cesare D'Onofrio, "Una grande scomparsa: Villa Montalto," *Capitolium* (1970): 59-63. For an excellent discussion of the view towards nature and landscape painting at the turn of the seventeenth century, see Glenn T. Scott, *Man and Nature: A View of the 17th Century*, exh. cat. (Hamilton, Ontario, 1980).

[190] On Gregory XIII's landscapes, see Chapter IV, 169, note 105 below.

[191] Samuel C. Chew, *The Pilgrimage of Life* (New Haven and London, 1962), 156-157, 365, note 6.

[192] Yates, *Astraea*, 29-30.

[193] Titi, *Descrizione*, 253, notes the locations of the sibyls at the Sixtine Chapel; and Hess, "Some Notes," *KSRB*, I, 169, those in the Vatican Library. Iversen, *Obelisks*, 53, translates the inscriptions on the base of the obelisk, written by Silvio Antoniano.

When preaching in Naples in 1554, Fra Felice provided an apt précis of the Golden Age in a Christian context, in *Predica*, n.p. ("Prima Parte"), as follows: "... ma cadut'el meschino Adamo nel abisso del peccato, mancato el stato de l'innocenza, passato il felice regno di Saturno, successe el stato di miseria, cominciò dominar el scelerato Gioue, sotto il cui crudel Imperio, la tirannia, e la impieta regnaua ..." Compare *idem, Predicata nella Inclita Città di Perugia*, n.p.: "... s'armò Giove contra Saturno, il ferro contra l'oro, l'iniquità contra la giustizia, la carne contra la raggione, Adamo contra dio [sic]...," in which the Franciscan use of opposites is also employed.

CHAPTER II

GOLDEN AGE AND THE GOOD WORKS OF SIXTUS V: CLASSICAL AND CHRISTIAN TYPOLOGY IN THE ART OF A ROMAN CATHOLIC REFORM POPE

One visual constant in each of the decorative ensembles commissioned for secular buildings by Pope Sixtus V is the representation *en masse* of the pope's Good Works. Most of the representations of Good Works are topographical, documenting the renovations made by Sixtus V to Rome and its environs, and, in some cases, including the complexion of Rome before the pope's improvements. The topographical Good Works are punctuated by *imprese* in the form of history painting utilizing the lion as the pope's persona together with the pears and mountains of his *stemma*.[1] The *Abundance created by Sixtus V* and the *Extirpation of the Bandits* are present in the Salone dei Papi of the Lateran Palace, the Salone Sistino of the Vatican Library, and once adorned the *gran sala* of the Palazzo delle Terme of the Villa Montalto (figs. 26-28; 29-31); the *Treasure at Castel Sant'Angelo* and the *League of Christian Princes* are present in the Salone dei Papi of the Lateran Palace and the first room of the Libreria Segreta of the Vatican Library (figs. 32-33; 35 and 37). The importance of the *imprese* featuring the Sixtine lion as protagonist is attested to by their repeated use as pendants in the decorative programmes, by their representation together in the main hall of the single most important monument commissioned by Sixtus V, the Salone dei Papi of the Lateran Palace, and by the fact that three of the four *imprese* are present in two of the portraits of Sixtus V surrounded by his Good Works engraved during his pontificate (figs. 39-40).[2]

Despite such strategic locations, and the fact that the *imprese* are well known amongst scholars of Sixtine Rome, they have never been considered collectively, nor have they been explained in more than a cursory manner - and this primarily by sixteenth century commentators. In his treatise *Della trasportatione dell'obelisco Vaticano*, Domenico Fontana usually describes the allegorical Good Works at the Vatican and Lateran monuments in some detail, yet he disregards the *imprese* at the Villa Montalto.[3] Furthermore, he offers no interpretation of the *imprese*, suggesting that they were readily understandable on at least one level, if not to the average viewer, then to the immediate circle of the pope. Mutio Pansa, who deals exclusively with the *imprese* at the Vatican Library, does not go much beyond a visual description, while Angelo Rocca treats the meaning of the same *imprese* in a very general way and does not usually concern himself with the allegories represented in the other Sixtine commissions, particularly the Villa Montalto, which he also ignores.[4] Later commentators on the monuments decorated by Sixtus V generally follow Fontana's lead, often copying him directly, or merely listing the titles of the allegories at the Vatican Library and Lateran Palace.[5] It was not until the nineteenth century that the allegorical Good Works at the Villa Montalto were at last documented in pithy

[1] The *impresa* of the *Prohibition of Adulterers* is not considered in this chapter since it is present only at the Vatican (Salone Sistino and stairway vault adjacent to the Sistine Chapel).

[2] A third portrait of Sixtus V, printed in 1589, shows two of the four *imprese* (*Abundance* and *Extirpation*). It is reproduced in P. Gustavo Parisciani, *Fra Felice Peretti Sisto V. IV centenario del pontificato 1585-1590* (Ancona, 24 April 1585), 48. I should like to thank Marcello Fagiolo and the organizers of the VI Corso Internazionale d'Alta Cultura for generously having given me a copy of Parisciani's pamphlet.

[3] Fontana, *Della trasportatione*, 83v-84, 92v and 61-61v.

[4] Pansa, *Libraria*, 97-98, 105-107, 115; Rocca, *Biblioteca*, 8-10, 12-13, 236-237, 242-246.

[5] See, for example, Mola, *Breve Racconto*, 64-65, who describes the *imprese* in the Salone dei Papi of the Lateran Palace following Fontana; Biondo, *Il Restauramento*, 14-15, who gives the titles of the *imprese* in the Salone dei Papi; Dumesnil, *Histoire*, 396, 397, 426, 427, 429, who describes the *imprese* in the Salone Sistino of the Vatican Library and in the Salone dei Papi, and accompanies each with its respective verse; Clark, *Care of Books*, 330, who briefly describes the *imprese* in the Salone Sistino and reprints the verses; Orbaan, *Sixtine*, 95, 124, who briefly explains each of the allegories utilizing the lion as Sixtus V at the Vatican Library; von Pastor, *Sisto V*, 36, who mentions three of the four allegories at both the Vatican and Lateran; Tulli, "'Sala del Concilio,'" *Per l'arte sacra*, 46, 50, who briefly describes the *imprese* at the Lateran and publishes the accompanying verses; Giovanni Bezzi, ed., "IV Centenario della nascita di Sisto V (1521-1921)," *Rassegna italiana*, fasc. V (13 March 1922): 64, and fasc. VII (13 May 1922), 90, 93, who publishes reproductions of three of the four allegories in the Vatican Library; G. Poli, *Sisto V* (Rome, 1922), 54, 62, 102, who describes three of the allegories in the Vatican Library in his discussion of contemporary events; Hess, "Some Notes, *KSRB*, I, 173, who attributes the *Abundance* in the Vatican Library to Paul Bril, but does not explain the meaning; Renato Canestrari, *Sisto V* (Turin, Milan, Genoa, Parma, Rome, Catania, 1954), between 104-105, who publishes one of the *imprese* at the Vati-

descriptions by Vittorio Massimo, the new owner of the villa.[6] It will be the purpose of this chapter, therefore, to examine the corpus of allegorical Good Works in which the lion appears as Sixtus V, and to explain the meaning of the *imprese* as fully as possible. It will be shown that the *imprese*, filled as they are with the customary erudite wit, and replete with a syncretic mixture of pagan-humanistic and Christian-theological symbols, contain *in nuce* the mystical world view of Sixtus V. This popular Renaissance art form will be shown to have provided the framework, from the perspective of Sixtus V's Franciscan heritage, for the succinct exposition of the pope's linkage with antiquity together with his office as Christ's vicar. Since the *imprese* are comprised of elements of the pope's *stemma*, the Christological and Franciscan meanings will be shown to overlay and dominate the pagan meaning, much in the same way as the cross placed above the obelisk or the apostle above the column denote a Christianity at once upheld by and triumphant over paganism.[7] It is, finally, no coincidence that the very form of the *imprese*, and the promise of salvation contained therein, emulate Early Christian art being rediscovered at this time by the Roman Catholic Reform Church eager to return to the practices of the primitive Church.[8] Indeed, as I shall attempt to show, the *imprese*, although referring to specific historical facts and/or events, transcend them by propounding a millenarian, apocalyptic view of history in which classical motifs and ideas of the Golden Age are subjected to and subsumed by a Christian and particularly Franciscan theology of history.

Like all good *imprese*, the allegorical images invented by Cesare Nebbia, very likely on the basis of ideas provided by the pope, are accompanied by mottoes or verses.[9] The verses accompanying the Good Works in the Vatican Library and Villa Montalto, composed by Guglielmo Bianco, are in the form of distychs.[10] Those in the Salone Sistino and Libreria Segreta are situated above the depictions, and those once in the *gran sala*, situated beneath. The verses in the Salone dei Papi, also penned by Guglielmo Bianco, are written in extended verse, and are more elaborate than the verses in the Vatican Library and Villa Montalto.[11] These verses are situated beneath the representations of the Good Works.[12] The commentaries accompanying the allegorical Good Works in the Libreria Segreta and Villa Montalto describe the narratives above. Those in the Salone Sistino of the library and in the Lateran Palace are generally more allusive, in keeping with the proper format of the *impresa*. They often refer to personages drawn from both the Classical and Judeo-Christian traditions, who are then related to Sixtus V. The Classical figures are those which were traditionally used for comparison with the emperor, especially Octavianus Augustus. The means used to describe Sixtus V in the verses are taken from *topoi* traditionally associated with the Golden Age myth, but like the images, the verses turn ancient and humanistic traditions upon themselves so that Sixtus V, in a pattern clearly derived from traditional rhetoric, is hyperbolically seen to triumph over all classical personages, both mythical and real.[13]

can Library; Schiavo, *Lateran*, n.p., who lists the *imprese* in the Salone dei Papi; and Gamrath, *Roma*, 106, who partially treats the *impresa* of the *League* in the Lateran Palace.

[6] Massimo, *Notizie*, 129-131.

[7] For the symbolism of Sixtus V's depaganized obelisks and columns, see Iversen, *Obelisks*, 19-72; and Cesare D'Onofrio, *Gli obelischi di Roma* (Rome, 1967), 69 ff., 154-178; and Chapter IV below.

[8] Compare the view of Paolo Aresi, *Delle Imprese Sacre con utili e dilettevoli discorsi accompagnate libro primo ...* (Verona, 1615), 33.

[9] Baglione, *Vite*, I, 159, states that "Giovanni inventava li soggetti delle storie, che dipinger si deveano, e Cesare ne faceva i disegni si, che amendue a gara in quel servigio impiegavansi e ciò durò, mentre Sisto V. sopravisse." Compare Rocca, *Biblioteca*, 272. See note 35, below, for an indication of Sixtus V's role in the inventions.

[10] Rocca, *Biblioteca*, 272, for the Vatican Library, and Massimo, *Notizie*, 129, for the Villa Montalto. Silvio Antoniano and Pietro Galesino composed the inscriptions beneath the history paintings of councils, libraries, and inventors of the alphabet in the Vatican Library, in Rocca, *Biblioteca*, 1, 272.

[11] Rocca, *Biblioteca*, 234, 254, 263, 264-265. But see Giuseppe Castiglione, *Silvii Antoniani S.R.E. Cardinalis Vita ...* (Rome, 1610), 9.

[12] There are additional inscriptions above the Good Works in the Salone dei Papi thus forming the well-known triad of the Renaissance emblem: *superscriptio*, *imago* and *subscriptio*. Although the *superscriptio* is situated on this lower register of the hall, visually united with the Good Works of Sixtus V, the messages contained therein relate to the representations of popes seated on the spiritual tier above. A vertical relationship between the lower and upper registers of the Salone dei Papi is thus insinuated. I treat this relationship in Chapter III, 127 ff, below.

[13] The literature on the Golden Age is vast. Good introductions which consider the antique sources and heritage may be found in Gustavo Costa, *La leggenda dei secoli d'oro nella letteratura italiana* (Bari, 1972); A. Bartlett Giamatti, *The Earthly Paradise and the Renaissance Epic* (Princeton, New Jersey, 1966); Harry Levin, *The Myth of the Golden Age in the Renaissance* (Bloomington and London, 1969); and James Hutton, *Themes of Peace in Renaissance Poetry*, ed. Rita Guerlac (Ithaca and London, 1984). Some useful studies on the antique origins and development of the Golden Age myth are the following: H. C. Baldry, "Who Invented the Golden Age?," *Classical Quarterly* n.s. II (1952): 83-92; Arthur O. Lovejoy and George Boas, *Primitivism and Related Ideas in Antiquity* (1935; New York, 1973); and Harold Mattingly, "Virgil's Fourth Eclogue," *Journal of the Warburg and Courtauld Institutes* X (1947):

1. *ABUNDANCE CREATED BY SIXTUS V* AND GOLDEN AGE SYMBOLISM

The *Abundance created by Sixtus V* refers to the measures taken by the pope to secure good quality foodstuffs in the face of a series of bad harvests and to regulate prices so that everyone could afford staples like bread, corn and olive oil. Sixtus V had been concerned with the problem of food shortage since the beginning of his pontificate, when he sent monies to the Marches for grain, for example, but he took his first big step in 1587, when he formed the *Congregazione dell' Abbondanza*. Thereafter, a grain storage was set up in Rome and incentives were given to increase agriculture in the Campagna, Civitavecchia and in other parts of the papal states. By 1589 Sixtus V managed to bring the price of bread down so that it was affordable by most everyone, even though in the process it had cost him some 800,000 *scudi*.[14] It is this regulation of the price of bread which is lauded in the verse beneath the *Abundance* in the Villa Montalto:

QVANTVM ANNONA VRBIS DECREVIT PRINCIPE SIXTO
PRINCIPIS HOC TANTVM NOMINE CREVIT HONOS[15]

The *impresa* of the *Abundance* shows a lion shaking a pear tree while sheep gather round to eat the fallen fruit (figs. 26-28).[16] The lion with human facial features is, of course, Sixtus V. As king of the beasts and traditional symbol of emperors and kings, the lion invests Sixtus V with the mantle of secular kingship.[17] By shaking the tree to feed the sheep, rather than instinctively hunting them, the scene evokes the Golden Age, when peace was enjoyed throughout the animal kingdom.[18] Moreover, the beneficence of the kingly lion towards his flock echoes the beneficence of kings and emperors, both ancient and modern, who were often characterized as pastors caring for their subjects in Golden Age settings.[19] The tree is reminiscent of the acorn-yielding oak tree of the Golden Age.[20] Finally, the pose of the lion who shakes the tree is one used traditionally to evoke Golden Age prosperity.[21]

The lion also represents Christ's vicar in his earthly capacity as *rex*, as well as suggesting associations with Christ as the lion of the Resurrection and the lion of Judah of Revelation, while the sheep clearly signify the Christian flock.[22] Therefore the lion who feeds the sheep is the Christian pastor-king taking care of the faithful according to Christ's charge to Peter and his successors to feed his sheep [John XXI: 15-17]. Together, the lion and the sheep are shown living in harmony during the Messianic Peace of the Christian Golden Age in fulfillment of Isaiah's prophecy [XI: 6-9]. The tree is replete with Christian and Franciscan associations. The wood of the tree signifies Christ on the Cross and the promise of Redemption to the faithful, and it echoes the tree of life of the terrestrial and celestial paradises, as well as its equivalent, the Franciscan tree of life.[23] Finally, the tree yields Peretti pears, symbolical of Christ as well as the Virgin Mary, the Christian acorns of the Sixtine Golden Age.[24] The *impresa* thus tells of the providential pontificate of Sixtus V which abounds with peace and prosperity and sets the stage for the Parousia and the deliverance of the faithful.

The verse above the *Abundance* in the Salone Sistino at the Vatican utilizes the *topos* of the Golden Age of Saturn, and

14-19. On the Early Christian and Medieval manifestations of the theme, see Ella Bourne, "The Messianic Prophecy in Virgil's Fourth Eclogue," *Classical Journal* XI (1915-1916): 390-400; George Boas, *Essays on Primitivism and Related Ideas in the Middle Ages* (1948; New York, 1966); Pierre Courcelle, "Les exégèses chrétiennes de la quatrième églogue," *Revue des Études Anciennes* LIX (1957): 294-319; Gerhart B. Ladner, *The Idea of Reform: its impact on Christian thought and action in the Age of the Fathers* (New York, Evanston and London, 1967); and Howard Rolin Patch, *The Other World According to Descriptions in Medieval Literature* (1950; New York, 1970). For the use of the Golden Age theme by the Renaissance and Counter-Reformation papacy, see Charles L. Stinger, *The Renaissance in Rome* (Bloomington, 1985), 292-319, 330, who also gives a comprehensive bibliography on the issue; and Marcello Fagiolo and Maria Luisa Madonna, "La Casina di Pio IV in Vaticano. Pirro Ligorio e l'architettura come geroglifico," *Storia dell'arte* 15/16 (1972): 260-264. For a discussion of some of the *topoi* associated with the Golden Age myth in imperial Rome, see Eugenio Manni, "La leggenda dell'età dell'oro nella politica dei cesari," *Atene e Roma* IV (1938): 108-120. See also Martin Percival Charlesworth, "Providentia and Aeternitas," *Harvard Theological Review* XXIX (April 1936): 107-132; idem, "The Virtues of a Roman Emperor: propaganda and the creation of belief," *Proceedings of the British Academy* XXIII (1937): 105-133; and Susan Saward, *The Golden Age of Marie de'Medici* (Ann Arbor, 1982). References to Golden Age symbolism and related *topoi* utilized by Renaissance (and proto-Renaissance) rulers, both secular and papal, will be given below.

14 von Pastor, *History*, XXI, 99-101.

15 Massimo, *Notizie*, 130.

16 Fontana, *Della trasportatione*, 84, describes the *impresa* of the *Abundance* at the Vatican Library as follows: " ... vn'impresa d'vn Leone, che scuote vn pero ad alcune pecorelle, che di quelle si pascono ..." Rocca, *Biblioteca*, 12-13, describes the same *impresa* as "Vbertatis hoc Emblema est. Romam enim SIXTVS V. initio sui Pontificatus, annonae caritate laborantem reperit: hinc idem SIXTVS ei prudentissime succurrit, & coempto frumento, & in Vrbem asportato, effecit, vt in summa inopia, summa esset copia. Nec eo contentus, vt non solum Vrbi, verum etiam Italiae vniversae magna ex parte succurreret, ac tempus in posterum prouideret. ... Hoc emblema venustatem habet, alludens ad gentilitia SIXTI V. stemmata, que Leone pyrum tenente constant. Quare Auctor Inscriptionis, vt fru / menti affluentiam, SIXTI V. Pontificis Maximi prouidentia, et pietate, omni ex parte laudanda, Italiae, et Romae praesertim subministratam decantet, hunc in modum inquit: / INSCRIPTIO EMBLEMATIS ... / Neminem latet, regnante Saturno, magnam frumenti in Latio fuisse vbertatem, agrosq. mirum

refs to the cornucopia, symbol of terrestrial abundance, thereby reinforcing the message of the *impresa* below:

TEMPORIBVS SIXTI REDEVNT SATVRNIA REGNA,
ET PLENO CORNV COPIA FVNDIT OPES

The verse accompanying the *Abundance* in the Lateran Palace complements the *impresa* in a somewhat more allusive manner than the explanatory verse at the Vatican and derives ultimately from Exodus XVI:

VESANA HEBRAEAE COMPRESSIT MVRMVRA GENTIS
SVPPEDITANS PLENA DVX ALIMENTA MANV,
SIC QVERVLAE PLEBI SIXTVS FRVMENTA MINISTRANS
COMPRESSIT MOSES MVRMVRA PRISSA NOVVS

This comparison of Sixtus V to Moses follows both secular- and religio-political traditions. Since Moses was a type of Christ, it would be a logical step for the ruler to adopt the stance of Moses, especially since Eusebius of Caesaria had sanctioned the analogy in connection with Constantine the Great.[25] Although the secular World Rulers preferred to adopt the metaphor of their Christ-like rule in explaining their providential mission to bring about the millenium, the Moses analogy was not unknown in the courts of Europe and found particular currency among the Medici.[26]

Of course, Moses also figures prominently in Christian tradition. As *typus Christi* and as Christ's first vicar *ante litteram* the Moses analogy was harnessed by the medieval papacy to prove that their temporal jurisdiction had been preordained by God since earliest times.[27] This tradition was revived during the Renaissance by Sixtus IV, Sixtus V's namesake, and proliferated in papal propaganda throughout the sixteenth century.[28]

In Franciscan tradition Moses was considered an important type of Saint Francis of Assisi, while the history of the Order was likened to the Exodus and final achievement of the Promised Land.[29] This meaning was certainly not lost on either Sixtus IV, Julius II, or Sixtus V, all Franciscan popes who saw themselves as both heirs of Moses and harbingers of the Golden Age.[30]

The implicit reference to manna in the verse beneath the *Abundance* thus places Sixtus V firmly within these Golden Age traditions featuring Moses as protagonist, while the grain which Sixtus V brought to Rome and the papal states takes on connotations of the Eucharist [John VI: 32] and of Holy Communion [1 Corinthians X: 1-4]. In keeping with the Roman Catholic Reform spirit, the verse utilizes Old Testament typology to point the way to the salvation which will be achieved for all Christians under Sixtine rule.[31] But the Sixtine lion, now understood as an *alter Moyses*, is also an emperor, secular king, and pontiff acting in his capacity of *rex*, and his actions conform to a traditional *sub-topos* of Golden Age prosperity, namely the emperor (or ruler) as provider.[32] By utilizing antique and humanistic secular traditions of a provider in the Golden Age with Medieval and Roman Catholic Reform papal traditions based on the biblical promise of salvation, the *Abundance* at the Lateran Palace points to the antique heritage of the pope as the successor to both Moses and the Roman emperor, proves the lineage and continuity of the pope's status as absolute ruler in the temporal and spiritual spheres, and shows

in modum excultos, cum ipse Agriculturam inuenisse dicatur. Quare Inscriptionis Auctor tamquam probatissimorum Poetarum omnium familiarissimus, mutuato sibi in priori versu Vergilij hemistichio, aurei saeculi felicitatem ab eodem Poeta inibi decantatam, nunc etiam vigere aperte demonstrat, & versu altero alludere sibi visum est, ni fallor, ad illud Horatij: *Aurea fruges / Italiae pleno diffudit Copia cornu.* Quibus ex verbis Poeta Cornucopiae Herculi datum innuere videtur. Copia autem apud Poetas pro Dea habita fuit, sicut etiam ab eodem Horatio expressius dictum est in Carmine saeculari, vbi eam appellat beatam inquiens: *Apparetq. beata pleno Copia cornu.* Nos autem cum affatim omnia inesse significare volumus, Cornucopiae dicimus, & per cornu fructibus, & floribus, frumentiq. spicis plenum abundantiam repraesentamus." Compare Pansa, *Libraria*, 97-98: "... si vede dipinto vn'albero copioso di frutti in spatiosa campagna, sotto del quale stanno molti agnelli a pascere, & vn Leone appoggiato al tronco di esso fa segno di scuoterlo, e di farne cadere i frutti; accioche si satiino, e paschino gli agnelli che vi sono di sotto. Il che ci rappresenta l'Abondanza, che egli indusse nel tempo del suo Pontificato, e massime nel principio, quando fu vna penuria vniuersale in Italia, & Europa tutta ..." Fontana, *Della trasportatione*, 61v, describes the *Abundance* at the Lateran Palace as " ... un Leone, che scuote un'arbore di pere, e ne fa cadere i frutti, de'quali le pecorelle, che vi stanno atorno si pascono ..." Massimo, *Notizie*, 130, describes the *Abundance* in the Villa Montalto as " ... un leone, che scuote un albero di pere, raccolte da pecorelle, allusivo all'arme Peretta ..."

17 See Thomas DaCosta Kaufmann, "Empire Triumphant: Notes on an Imperial Allegory by Adriaen de Vries," *Studies in the History of Art* VIII (1978): 72-73, note 22; and Robert Folz, *The Concept of Empire in Western Europe from the Fifth to the Fourteenth Century* (1953), trans. S. A. Ogilvie (London, 1969), 116. The lion was also used by the Netherlands, Bohemia, Britain, Hapsburg Spain and Austria, Venice, and Tuscany, to name the more well known examples.

18 See, for example, Ovid, *Metamorphoses*, XV, 96-103; and Virgil, *Eclogue IV*, 21-22. See also Levin, *Myth*, 17-18.

19 Manni, "La leggenda," *Atene*, 117-119, Saward, *Golden Age*, 130, and Hutton, *Themes of Peace*, 272-274, discuss the association of abundance with the Golden Age in imperial Rome. In art, this idea is manifested on the *Ara Pacis*, 13-9 B.C., for example. The *locus classicus* for the idea of the kingly pastor is Plato's *Politicus*, 271D-271E in *Plato*, trans. Harold N. Fowler, Loeb Classical Library (London; New York, 1925), III, 56-59. See also Costa, *La leggenda*, x-xi.

20 See, for example, Ovid, *Metamorphoses*, XV, 142; and Virgil, *Eclogue IV*, 30. One of the most well known Renaissance allusions to the oak in connection with the Golden Age is that

used by Pope Julius II. See Nancy Rash-Fabbri, "A Note on the Stanza della Segnatura," *Gazette des Beaux-Arts* XCIV, 1329 (1979): 102; and Loren Partridge and Randolph Starn, *A Renaissance Likeness: art and culture in Raphael's Julius II* (Berkeley, Los Angeles, London, 1980), 56.

[21] Levin, *Myth*, 198; and for a related pose, see Janet Cox-Rearick, *Dynasty and Destiny in Medici Art: Pontormo, Leo X, and the two Cosimos* (Princeton, New Jersey, 1984), 139. The lion who successfully shakes the tree for fruits is diametrically opposed to Nanni di Banco's bear of the Porta della Mandorla, 1414-1421, for example, who unsuccessfully shakes the tree for acorns and signifies vice. I wish to thank Liana Cheney for this reference to the Porta della Mandorla.

[22] Although the "Lion of Judah" of Revelation V: 5-6 is represented as a lamb, the association should not be discounted on this basis. Furthermore, it is important to keep in mind John Shearman's observation that "the idea [of equating a pope to Christ], among popes, is no more novel than it is blasphemous" in *Raphael's Cartoons*, 76. Also consult Bonaventure, *Collations in Hexameron*, XIV, 27 in *The Works of Bonaventure: Cardinal, Seraphic Doctor and Saint*, trans. José de Vinck, 5 vols. (Paterson, New Jersey, 1970), V, 213, who states, albeit erroneously, that "Christ is pointed to ... as a triumphant lion in Mark"; and Felici, *Stationi di Roma*, n.p., who states "Il Leone Rè degli altri Animali, non ci significa Christo Rè in tanti, et tanti luochi?"

[23] For Christ as the Tree of Life, see Bonaventure, *Lignum Vitae*; and Bonaventure, *Collationes*, XIV, 18. It is interesting to note that Taddeo Gaddi's Bonaventurian *Tree of Life* in the refectory of Santa Croce, c. 1360, shows Saint Francis in a variation on the traditional Golden Age pose also adopted by the Sixtine lion. Taddeo's fresco is reproduced in Andrew Ladis, *Taddeo Gaddi: critical reappraisal and catalogue raisonné* (Columbia and London, 1982), 7. Also consult Susan J. Delaney, "The Iconography of Giovanni Bellini's Sacred Allegory," *Art Bulletin* LIX, 3 (September 1977): 331-335, for the charitable associations connected with the tree, and note the pose of the youth who reaches up to pick the fruit from the tree in the Bellini allegory.

[24] For the pear as a symbol of Christ and the Virgin, as well as a symbol of virtue; and for the pear tree as a symbol of the Virgin, and its fruit, her son, see Mirella Levi D'Ancona, *The Garden of the Renaissance. Botanical Symbolism in Italian Painting*, Arte e Archeologia Studi e Documenti 10 (Florence, 1977), 296-298.

[25] Eusbius, *Ecclesiastical History*, IX, ix 3-11, trans. J. E. L. Oulton, 2 vols., Loeb Classical Library (1932; Cambridge, Mass; London, 1980), II, 360-365. See also the discussion of this analogy in Janet Cox-Rearick, "Bronzino's *Crossing of the Red Sea and Moses Appointing Joshua*: Prolegomena to the Chapel of Eleonora di Toledo," *Art Bulletin* LXIX, 1 (March 1987): 55.

[26] By the sixteenth century it was a commonplace for secular rulers to be compared to Christ, following what Yates, *Astraea*, 1-28, has termed the medieval "idea of empire." Emperor Frederick II, for example, was seen as a second Moses, as was his aid, Piero della Vigna. See Ernst Kantorowicz, *Frederick the Second 1194-1250* (1931), trans. E. O. Lorimer (New York, 1957), 609, 524 respectively. For the viscount of Flanders' (later Charles V) entry into Bruges in 1515, in which Louis of Nevers was compared to Moses, see Jean Jacquot, "Panorama des fêtes et ceremonies du Règne," *Les Fêtes de la Renaissance II: les fêtes et cérémonies au temps de Charles Quint*, ed. Jean Jacquot (1960; Paris, 1975), 413-418. For the comparison between Moses and Cosimo I de'Medici, Grand Duke of Tuscany, see Cox-Rearick, "Bronzino's," *Art Bulletin*, 45-67 and Paul William Richelson, *Studies in the Personal Imagery of Cosimo I de'Medici, Duke of Florence* (New York and London, 1978), 110 ff. For a later use of the analogy at the Hapsburg court in Spain, see Barbara von Barghahn, *Philip IV and the 'Golden House' of the Buen Retiro: in the tradition of Caesar*, 2 vols. (New York and London, 1986), I, 208.

[27] See J. A. Watt, "The Theory of Papal Monarchy in the Thirteenth Century: the contribution of the Canonists," *Traditio* XX (1964): 179-317, and especially 216 ff, with reference to Pope Innocent III and his Roman Catholic Reform follower, Robert Bellarmine.

[28] Stinger, *Renaissance*, 209-218, 330-331; and Ettlinger, *Sistine*.

[29] See Cox-Rearick, "Bronzino's," *Art Bulletin*, 65 and note 104.

[30] For Sixtus IV, see Ettlinger, *Sistine*, 185 ff. For Julius II, see Stinger, *Renaissance*, 58-59, 218. I have treated the biographical and artistic comparisons between Sixtus V and Moses in the Introduction and Chapter I above. For panegyrics penned during his pontificate, see, for example, Guglielmo Bianco, *Epigrammata ... in Obeliscum Mirae magnitudinis ... à SIXTO V. PONT. MAX. translatum, & superimposita Cruce Christianae Religioni dedicatum* (Rome, 1586), 5: "Aenea serpentis Moses simulachra sacerdos / Extulit aegrotis ut medicina foret. / Nunc alter Moses Obelisci in uertice Sixtus / Erigit aegrotis aenea signa Crucis. / Vos o'Romani sustollite ad aethera vultus, / A Cruce nam nobis uestra petenda salus."; and Bernardino Rocco, *Roma Restaurata. Alla Santità di N.S. Sisto Quinto* (Verona, 1589), n.p.: "ALMO PASTOR, ch'à guisa di quel vero / Diletto a DIO, MOSE, ministro e duce: / Di questo ampio deserto apre il sentiero / Mentre a promessi campi vi conduce. ..." Compare Catervo Foglietta, "Lettera ad un amico di ragguaglio delle Chiese di Roma, et opere fatte da Sisto V sommo Pontefice con riflessioni morali MDLxxxvii," [dated 10 May 1587], B. A. V. Ottoboni Lat. 568, 60v: "Roma, Città della Croce così disegnata da Sisto V ... uscire da un Monte percorso dalla barchetta da Mosè; per darei ad intendere chè essendo lui Vicario di Dio, Pastore, et Governatore di tutto il Christianismo, à guisa di Mosè giorno, et notte pensa al benè, et alla salute di tutti ..." In a more scholarly vein, compare Pompeo Ugonio, *Historia delle Stationi di Roma che si celebrano la Quadragesima* (Rome, 1588), 91: "Hora, dunque, non altrimenti che Mosè de'i vasi d'oro, & d'argento tolti à gli Egittij, si seruì per il culto del vero Dio, così questo nuouo Mosè [Sixtus V], il quale con la Verga della giustitia, hà quasi in vn mar rosso, sommersi i perturbatori della quiete publica; che come quello da dura selce à spegner la fede del popolo Hebreo, fece nel deserto scaturire abondante ruscello, cosi hà con nuoua acqua Felice tirata per le viscere de sassosi monti, & per longo ordine d'archi irrigati i colli deserti della città di Roma: questo nuouo Mosè, dico, ha spogliato l'Egitto di cosi altiera Mole, & ritolta à i pagani Imperatori, l'ha trasferita in honor di quello ch'è Re de' i Re, & Imperator de gli Imperatori. Vedesi adesso nella sua cima, d'oro risplendere il vessillo trionfale della Croce posato sopra gl'aurei Monti, & la radiante stella, felicissime insegne di questo gran Duce del popolo di Dio."

[31] Compare the message conveyed by the Moses scenes in the Casino of Pius IV, for example, in Graham Smith, *The Casino of Pius IV* (Princeton, New Jersey, 1977), 89-94.

[32] Hesiod, *Works and Days*, 126 in *Hesiod*, trans. Hugh G. Evelyn-White, Loeb Classical Library (London; New York, 1914), 10-11. See also Manni, "La leggenda," *Atene*, 117-119; and Saward, *Golden Age*, 146. For the use of the *topos* of liberality and fecundity by Renaissance rulers, see, for example, Yates, *Astraea*, 67-68, 77-78, 217-218, for Queen Elizabeth I of England as springtime, bringing with her an abundance of fruits and flowers, and as the "fruitful virgin"; idem, 138, for King Charles IX of France as the harbinger of abundance; idem, 210-211 for King Henry IV of France; Thomas DaCosta Kaufmann, *Variations on the Imperial Theme in the Age of Maximilian II and Rudolph II* (New York and London, 1978), 76 ff. and especially 99-102, for Emperor Rudolph II as Vertumnus; W. Chandler Kirwin, "Vasari's Tondo of 'Cosimo I with his Architects, Engineer and Sculptors' in the Palazzo Vecchio: typology and re-identification of portraits," *Mitteilungen des Kunsthistorischen Institutes in Florenz* XV (1971): 105-122, for Cosimo I de'Medici, Grand Duke of Tuscany as provider; Roy Strong, *Art and Power: Renaissance Festivals 1450-1650* (1973; Berkeley and Los Angeles, 1984), 151-152, for Ferdinand de'Medici, Grand Duke of Tuscany. For a later use of the liberality theme, see Roy Strong, *Britannia Triumphans: Inigo Jones, Rubens and Whitehall Palace* (Great Britain, 1980), 47-48, for King James I of England.

that salvation may be achieved by a munificent pope whose rule allows humanity to avail itself, on the quest for redemption, of the fruit of Christ's sacrifice for mankind.

2. *EXTIRPATION OF THE BANDITS*

When Sixtus V came to power Rome and the papal provinces were beset by bandits. The situation was so grave that travel between cities was perilous at best, and the cities and towns themselves were infested with subversives. Indeed, the situation has been likened to the Terror of 1793 by Dumesnil, and, by all accounts, this characterization cannot be far off the mark.[33] Sixtus V was not one to take such threats to the well-being of the Christian commonwealth lightly. On 10 May 1585 he dispatched a letter to King Philip II of Spain asking for his assistance in extirpating the bandits, and this was followed by similar exhortations to the dukes of the provinces and the leaders of the Italian republics. Papal bulls and constitutions were published and their mandates enforced with such severity and thoroughness that an *Avviso* of 18 September 1585 from Rome reported that more heads were seen on the Ponte Sant'Angelo in that year than watermelons in Banchi.[34] By autumn 1587 Sixtus V could proudly proclaim that the bandits had been neutralized and that Rome and the papal states were at last enjoying peace and quiet. The *Extirpation of the Bandits*, represented in each of the secular decorative programmes of Sixtus V and in the portraits, is a tribute to this achievement. The verse accompanying the narrative in the Villa Montalto echoes the pope's sentiments:

PASCITE SECVRAE PECVDES IN MONTIBVS ALTIS
DVM LEO GRASSANTES IMPETIT VNGVE LVPOS

The *impresa* of the *Extirpation of the Bandits* shows a lion standing atop a mountain, holding a thunderbolt in his right forepaw in order to ward off wolves from the flock of sheep below (figs. 29-31).[35] The thunderbolt refers in one sense to the classical attribute of Jupiter and of Iustitia, his daughter. By wielding the thunderbolt the Sixtine lion is therefore associated with these ancient dispensers of justice, and joins the rank of the emperor Augustus and his successors, including the representatives of the Valois, Hapsburg, Medici and Farnese dynasties, who were commonly likened to the supreme pagan god.[36] In addition to this symbolical assimilation of Sixtus V to Jupiter-Augustus, the actions of the lion likewise emulate those of the pagan god and emperor. Since the lion banishes the wolves, representing thieves and plunderers, according to a classical convention,[37] so that the sheep may graze peacefully, it is clear that he is dispensing *poena*, or punitive justice, that particular type of justice which characterized Hesiod's Golden Age and Horace's Rome of Augustus.[38] Standing atop a mountain, the Sixtine lion thus becomes a zoomorphic Jupiter-Augustus on Olympus, the very embodiment of justice, overseeing this pastoral paradise in which sheep flourish unharmed by beasts.

The *impresa* also contains, as in the case of the *Abundance*, Christian symbolism and Franciscan allusions which overlay and dominate the pagan symbolism. In the predominant reading, the Sixtine lion prances atop the high

[33] Dumesnil, *Histoire*, 57. On the problem and its solution, see von Pastor, *History*, XXI, 76-88; and von Hübner, *Life and Times*, I, 260-296.

[34] Quoted in Orbaan, *Sixtine*, 119.

[35] Fontana, *Della trasportatione*, 83v, describes the *impresa* in the Vatican as follows: " ... vn Leone in cima a vn Monte, che minaccia con vn fulgure a molte fiere rapaci ..." Rocca, *Biblioteca*, 8-10, explains this *impresa* as follows: "Emblema, quod Bibliothecam ingredientium oculis primo ad introitus laeuam sese offert, liberationem Italiae complectitur: quae cum antea nefariorum, perditorumq. hominum, praedonum scilicet atque exulum incursionibus esset exposita, multisq. calamititabus premeretur, SIXTO V. seden / te ab omni infestatione liberatur, ac magna quiete perfruitur, exulibus ac praedonibus vndequaque expulsis. / *Liberationis symbolum* / Oves triplicem montem circumstantes inspiciuntur, in cuius fastigio positus cernitur leo, qui ignita fulmina deorsum torquens, Lupos omnes pascenti pecori aduersantes terrore, ac metu concussos in fugam hinc inde conijcit. Quibus populi, Lupis praedones, Montibus qui supra reliquam terram se extollunt Ecclesia, Leone SIXTVS Pontifex, Fulmine Auctoritas eius & potestas repraesentantur: & ad eiusdem Pontificis insignia allusio esse potest, in quibus Montes Patriam significantes pinguntur, necnon & Leo, qui dominatum, & magnanimitatem, itemq. fortitudinem, vigilantiam, & custodiam significat. Hinc in aedificiorum, praecipue vero in Fanorum valuis, sacrarumq. Ædium vestibulis Leones marmorei siue aenei tamquam diuinorum custodes, vt est passim cernere, statui solent. / Leo enim dum vigilat, oculos clausos, cum vero dormit reseratos habere fertur: immo nonnulli putarunt, sed falso quidem, Leonem semper somni esse expertem, quippe qui magnos cum habeat oculos palpebrasq. perexiguas, oculos penitus obtegere non potest, hinc splendor ab eius pupilla emicans insomnem ipsum repraesentat. Huic autem Emblemati, liberationisq. Symbolo, SIXTI V. cum Alcide collatio aptissime quadrat, si amborum insignia Leonem habentia, fortitudo, resq. gestae perpendantur. Idcirco Inscriptionis Auctor haec secum, vt opinor, cogitans, SIXTVM cum Alcide confert, & hunc in modum ait: / INSCRIPTIO EMBLEMATIS ... / Haec Inscriptio praesefert, maiora SIXTVM praestitisse, quam Herculem, ab Alcaeo, auo paterno, Alcidem, / Auctore Herodoto, dictum: vel ab Ἀλχη, quod est robur. Hercules enim montem Aventinum, Caco Vulcani filio, praedone infami, teste Virgilio, extremamq. Calabriae & Italiae oram latrone Lacinio, a quo Promontorium Lacinium vocitatum est, dumtaxat liberauit, vt apud eundem Virgilium videre licet. Sed SIXTVS V. vniuersam Italiam a praedonum, & exulum incursionibus liberauit, ac tranquillam reddidit. Hanc liberationem Simon Cecchinus vtriusque signat. Refer. distichis ingeniose factis feliciter prosequutus est." Compare Pansa, *Libraria*, 105: " ... si

mountain, in keeping with a characteristic of the lion, and raises his tail in order to hide his spoor and confound the devil.[39] With his thunderbolt, symbol of excommunication, he then vanquishes the wolves, biblical symbols of heretic and infidel alike, and distant relatives of the Franciscan wolf of Gubbio.[40] As Christ's vicar he therefore dispenses *poena* in order to uphold God's law,[41] and is supported in this act by the mountain which points to Christ himself, Mount Golgotha, Mount Alverna, Mount Sion, Mount Sinai, and any number of biblical mountains.[42] With the defeat of the heretical wolves, the Christian sheep are united and prosper during these peaceful times of plenty, and the millenium is ushered in during the reign of the Sixtine lion who foreshadows the Second Coming of Christ, and indeed, who becomes another lion of Judah atop Mount Sion. The first Golden Age, heralded by the birth of Christ during the reign of Augustus, has therefore returned under the auspices of Divine Providence and the beneficent rule of Pope Sixtus V.

The verse beneath the *Extirpation of the Bandits* in the Salone Sistino compares Sixtus V to Hercules using what Curtius has termed the "outdoing *topos*":[43]

ALCIDES PARTEM ITALIAE PRAEDONE REDEMIT, SED TOTAM SIXTVS, DIC MIHI MAIOR VTER?

As Rocca explains, the robber referred to in the verse is the legendary Cacus, son of Vulcan and Medusa. According to Ovid and Virgil, this three-headed monster who lived in a cave on the Aventine spent his time terrorizing the shepherds of the neighbouring Tiber valley by stealing their flocks.[44] Hercules met up with Cacus, who naturally stole some of the heroes' cattle, on his return from his tenth labour at Gades. In a typically "virtuoso" display, Hercules overcame the monster, thereby regaining his flock and rendering the countryside of the future Rome safe for its inhabitants. Bianco's choice of this exploit is thus particularly appropriate since it refers to the only Herculean labour which took place in Italy, and specifically on one of the seven hills of the Eternal City.[45]

Before Sixtus V, popes, princes and prelates, emperors and kings, had been compared to this great paragon of virtue and purveyor of justice in order to raise their statuses to superhuman proportions. The Hercules analogy was particularly popular amongst the Valois, Hapsburg, Medici and Farnese clans, and it appeared not infrequently in Tudor glorifications.[46] In Medici propaganda the story of Hercules and Cacus figured as a political allegory of triumph over adversity, and it was most likely this symbolism which provided inspiration for Sixtus V and Bianco.[47] Of course the Germanic, Hispanic, and Gallic uses of the Hercules myth were certainly not lost on the pope and his poet.

The Medici had also favoured a convergence of the Hercules myth with that of the emperor Augustus, a melding most clearly seen in Antoine Caron's *Augustus and the Sibyl* (c. 1571-1573) which includes King Charles IX in the guise of the Roman emperor and an allusion to the pillars of Hercules in the Salomonic columns.[48] Like the *impresa* of the Emperor Charles V, the columns with the motto 'PLVS VLTRA," to which the Caron columns allude, the conflation of Hercules and Augustus by Renaissance rulers derived ultimately from the writings of such Augustan authors as Virgil and Horace,

vede vn Quadro di pittura, oue sono tre Monti, a pie de quali stanno molti animali sicuri a pascere, e riposarsi, & vn Leone con vn fulmine in mano sopra di essi minaccioso si vede, onde i Lupi, gli Orsi, e gli altri animali seditiosi, e rapaci sono vccisi, e discacciati. Il che ci rappresenta il grandissimo Zelo, ch'egli hebbe dalla pace, e ben viuere vniuersale, castigando seueramente i banditi, i quali furono da lui al tutto esterminati, e scacciati dallo stato Ecclesiastico ..." Fontana, *Della trasportatione*, 61v, describes the Lateran *impresa* as follows: " ... in mezo a vna Campagna vn Monte, sopra il quale sta vn Leone, e intorno al monte sono molte pecorelle, che si pascono, & per la campagna molti Lupi posti in fuga dal Leone, che li minaccia con vn fulgore in mano ..." Massimo, *Notizie*, 130, states simply that the *Extirpation* in the Villa Montalto is "rappresentata dal Leone di Sisto V, che difende un gregge ..."

An indication of Sixtus V's possible invention of this (and all?) *imprese* is provided by Pistolesi, *Sixtus Quintus*, 43: " ... the idea of the lion seated [or standing?] on three mountains we believe to be his [the pope's] since in the first months of his pontificate he wrote to the Montaltese with affectionate ambiguity that he was seated on the chair of Peter like a vigilant shepherd on a high mountain '*more vigilis Pastoris in Monte Alto collocati*.'" He seems to have been influenced by the *impresa* of his despised predecessor Gregory XIII, showing the dragon taking care of sheep while inimical lions flee the scene (!), in Principio Fabricio, *Delle Allusioni, Imprese, et Emblemi ... Sopra la vita, opere, et attioni di Gregorio XIII ... Libri VI*, 1st ed. 1585 (Rome, 1588), 331, Emblem CCXXII.

[36] For Emperor Augustus as Jupiter, see Ovid, *Metamorphoses*, XV, 858-860; and Horace, *Carminum Liber*, III, v, 1-4 in *Horace: the Odes and Epodes*, trans. C.E. Bennett, Loeb Classical Library (1914; rev. 1927; Cambridge, Mass; London, 1978), 194, 195. For the representation in art of the emperor as king of the gods, see, for example, the Julio-Claudian *Gemma Augustea*, Vienna, Kunsthistorischen Museum. For King Charles VIII of France, see Robert W. Scheller, "Imperial Themes in art and literature of the early French Renaissance: the period of Charles VIII," *Simiolus* XII (1981-1982): 5-7; for a later example of Valois-Angoulême use of the analogy, see Seznec, *Survival*, 33-36; and for Bourbon assimilation to Jupiter see Saward, *Golden Age*, 179-181. For the Emperors Charles V and Rudolph II, see Barbara von Barghahn, *Age of Gold, Age of Iron: Renaissance Spain and Symbols of Monarchy: The Imperial Legacy of Charles V and Philip II - Royal Castles, Palace-Monasteries, Princely Houses*, 2 vols., (Lanham, New York, London, 1985), I, 129-132, who quotes Marie C. Tanner, "Titian: the 'Poësie' for Philip II," diss., New York U, 1976, and who also discusses the Portuguese use of the Jupiter analogy at the court of King John III; Jacquot, "Panorama," Les *Fêtes*, II, 429 ff.; and

who compared the just Octavianus to Hercules, and his efforts to safeguard the empire to the hero's exploits.[49] When considering the verse beneath the *Extirpation* in conjunction with its *impresa*, it becomes clear that Bianco is also employing this type of syncretism, but with an important difference. As the new Christian Jupiter-Augustus and *Dominus mundi*, Sixtus V is better than Hercules and all temporal rulers with pretensions to grandeur, including Hercules Germanicus, the Emperor Rudolph II, and especially Hercules Hispanicus, King Philip II, and Hercules Gallicus, King Henry III, whose adoptions of imperial traditions Sixtus V has taken for himself. Indeed, Sixtus V is the absolute monarch who, with inimitable super-Herculean and super-Augustan virtue, is capable of meting out justice and bringing back the Golden Age.

Rather than referring to a specific *exemplum virtutis* the verse beneath the *Extirpation* in the Lateran Palace employs the *topos* of the sovereign pastor:

DVM SIBI COMMISSVM SIXTVS TVTATVR OVILE
PRAEDONES MIRA PERCVLIT ARTE LVPOS.
PAXQ. PVDORQ. VIGENT VNA: NAM TEMPORE EODEM
PERCVLIT ILLE LVPOS, PERCVLIT ILLE LVPAS

The idea of the sovereign pastor derives ultimately from Plato's *Politicus* where it is used in connection with the Golden Age.[50] The idea emerges in the Bible, notably in the Old Testament prophecies of Isaiah XL: 11 and Ezekiel XXXIV: 23 and in the New Testament wherein Christ tells Peter "PASCE OVES MEAS" [John XXI: 15-17], and it was accordingly adopted by the papacy. In the thirteenth century, it entered the "idea of empire" of the self-proclaimed *alter Christus*, Emperor Frederick II.[51] Subsequent World Rulers were thus given free reign to appropriate for themselves what had become a traditional papal prerogative. During the Renaissance the *topos* enjoyed great popularity with the Valois, Valois-Angoulême and Bourbon dynasties, the Hapsbourgs and Tudors, and it was not unknown to the Medici.[52] Moreover the sovereign pastor was often described or represented in a Golden Age setting safeguarding the sheep of the realm. When Bianco adopted the commonplace he was surely aware of both the imperial and regal appropriations of the pope's function as Christ's vicar, and the ancient and modern consolidations of the *topos* with that of the Golden Age. Thus, in giving to the pope his rightful place as pastor of the flock, Bianco also implicitly underlined Sixtus V's inherent superiority over all temporal princes.

The verse also enunciates the pope's God-given right to take vengeance on heretical forces, thereby reinforcing the symbolism of Jupiter's -and Sixtus V's- thunderbolt represented in the *impresa* above. The homonymic play of *lupos/lupas*, identifying the wolves with prostitutes, is another instance of a Sixtine adoption of a commonplace among both ancient pagan and Christian authors, and a commonplace still used during the Renaissance.[53] It is also a reference to the actual events taking place in Sixtine Rome. At the same time as Sixtus V began his crusade against the bandits, in May 1585, he began to enforce strict penalties on prostitutes comparable to those given the bandits. In 1585, 1588, and again in 1589, he issued special edicts to put a halt to prostitution altogether.[54] The *Extirpation* in the Salone dei Papi therefore shows Sixtus V extirpating the bandits who had ravaged Rome and the papal states

Kaufmann, *Imperial*, 118. The Medici dynasty utilized the Jupiter analogy in secular and religio-political contexts. For the Medici use of the analogy in the secular sphere, prevalent since the time of Cosimo il Vecchio, (Cox-Rearick, *Dynasty*, 216), see, for example, Hildegarde Utz, "The *Labours of Hercules* and Other Works by Vincenzo de'Rossi," *Art Bulletin* LIII, 3 (September 1971): 359-360, and in the papal context, see Cox-Rearick, *Dynasty*, 13, 17, 125-126, 130, 153, 169 ff. For the Farnese assimilation to Jupiter, see Stinger, *Renaissance*, 260; and Bernice F. Davidson, "Pope Paul III's Additions to Raphael's Logge: His *Imprese* in the Logge," *Art Bulletin* LXI, 3 (September 1979): 399-400.

[37] Giovanni Pietro Valeriano Bolzani, *Hieroglyphica* (1556), XI, iv, trans. I. De Montlyart (1615; New York and London, 1976), 130.

[38] Hesiod, *Works and Days*, 248-265; Horace, *Carminum Liber*, I, xii, 57-60. See the discussion of this concept in Saward, *Golden Age*, 180-181.

[39] *The Book of Beasts being a translation from a Latin Bestiary of the Twelfth Century*, T. H. White, ed. (1954; New York, 1984), 7-8.

[40] For the Franciscan wolf of Gubbio, see Edward A. Armstrong, *Saint Francis: Nature Mystic: The derivation and significance of the nature stories in the Franciscan legend* (Berkeley, Los Angeles, London, 1973), 199-217.

[41] The Christian concept of *poena* is discussed by Saward, *Golden Age*, 146-148; and Chodorow, *Christian Political Theory*, 224-246. Compare the warning issued on a coin in 1590 by King Henry IV of France with the quotation from Psalm II, treated in Corrado Vivanti, "Henry IV, the Gallic Hercules," *Journal of the Warburg and Courtauld Institutes* XXX (1967): 191.

[42] For Christ as a mountain, see Isaiah II and Andrea de'Monte, "Sanctissimo Patri atque Optimo Principi Domino nr̄o Domino Julio, divina providenza Papae Terzo ... ," B.A.V., Vat. Lat. 3561. This panegyric, written for Pope Julius III, seems appropriate for Pope Sixtus V as well. See Alessandro Nova, "Bartolommeo Ammannati e Prospero Fontana a Palazzo Firenze. Architettura e emblemi per Giulio III Del Monte," *Ricerche di Storia dell'arte* XX (1983): 65, who discusses this "lungo e tedioso poema"! Catani, *La Pompa Funerale*, 59, identifies the mountain in the *impresa* of Providence on Sixtus V's catafalque as Mount Sinai: "questo monte ci mostraua, che si come da lui vscirono quelle leggi, le quali prouiderno al tutto, così l'alto monte del purgato pensiero di Sisto, illuminato dal raggio della diuina gratia, con le sue leggi incorrotte prouide al tutto, & egli ... quasi nuouo Sina apportante celesti precetti." For the tradition which situates paradise on a mountain, see Patch, *Other World*, 151-155. Of course, this tradition was followed in the apse mosaic of Leo III's triconch *triclinium*.

[43] Curtius, *European Literature*, 162-165.

and the prostitutes who had been infesting the cities, thus rendering the Christian commonwealth safe and secure in preparation for the millenium.

3. *TREASURE AT CASTEL SANT'ANGELO*

When Sixtus V came to power, the papal coffers were, for all intents and purposes, bare. Recognizing the value of a healthy store of *scudi* in case of infringements on the papal states and allied lands, and in case of natural disasters, like famine, Sixtus V set about to rectify the situation. Being frugal himself, he saw no reason why the administration of the Holy See should not follow suit and, accordingly, cut expenditures. This, coupled with the sale of offices at inflated rates, state loans, and increased taxation, enabled the pope to see the vast sum of 5 1/2 million *scudi* deposited in the chests of Castel Sant'Angelo by the end of his five year pontificate. Not surprisingly, Sixtus V was particularly proud of his economic policy; he minted coins to commemorate the treasure, and bragged about it to the Christian Princes whenever the opportunity arose. The Roman populace, on the other hand, had to endure the resultant shortage of *scudi* and virtual halt in trade and production. Although recognizing the benefits brought to Rome by the pope's great building exploits, made possible by the treasure, by 1589 the Romans were prophesying a terrible end for Sixtus V![55]

There are a number of types of *imprese* describing the treasure amassed by Sixtus V, all variations on a theme. In the Vatican Library, the *impresa* shows a lion holding a pear branch and standing on a chest with an angel descending to place the tiara on his head. Guarding the chest are animals holding keys, signifying the Cardinals charged to care for the treasure, and an angel, sword and key in hand (fig. 33).[56] This *impresa* is echoed in the portrait of Sixtus V in Pinadello's book on popes whose surname was "The Fifth" (fig. 34). The *impresa* of the *Treasure* in the Lateran Palace is without the guardians. Here, it is the lion, seated on the chest with his mouth open, who guards the treasure, evoking the passage, often celebrated in the devices of the pope, from Amos III: 8: "The lion shall roar, who will not fear?," while the angel who descends to crown the lion holds a temporal crown rather than the papal tiara (fig. 32).[57] This *impresa* is closest to that represented in the anonymous portrait of Sixtus V (fig. 40), although there is no angel descending in the anonymous portrait, a papal tiara floats above the lion's head, the lion is standing, and a dove holding a key hovers nearby. Still another variation on the theme is given pride of place on the frontispiece to Pinadello's book (fig. 39), showing a lion positioned frontally (rather than in profile), standing atop the chest, and four lions flanking the treasure in place of the various species depicted at the Vatican and in Pinadello's own portrait of the pope. In their zeal to protect the pope's bounty, the lions have apparently broken free of the chains which once bound them to the chest. Finally, the *impresa* commemorating the treasure on the coinage of Sixtus V shows a lion seated comfortably upon the chest, resting his forepaw on the triple mountains and supporting the Sixtine star, with the motto "VIGILAT SACRI THESAVRI CVSTOS" (fig. 1).[58]

In each of the *imprese* the sovereign lion sits or stands tri-

[44] Ovid, *Fasti*, I, 543-578 in *Ovid's Fasti*, trans. Sir James George Frazer, Loeb Classical Library (London; New York, 1931), 40-43; Virgil, *Aeneid*, VIII, 190-267.

[45] Martin Weinberger, *Michelangelo the Sculptor*, 2 vols. (London; New York, 1967), I, 244, has noted the appropriateness of this myth for Roman propaganda.

[46] For the Valois, Valois-Angoulême, and Bourbon uses of the Hercules analogy, see Vivanti, "Henry," *JWCI*, 176-997; Antoniette Huon, "Le thème du Prince dans les entrées Parisiennes au XVIe siècle," *Les Fêtes de la Renaissance*, I, ed. Jean Jacquot (1956; Paris, 1973), 21-30; Margaret M. McGowan, "Les Jésuites à Avignon: les fêtes au service de la propaganda politique et religieuse," *Les Fêtes de la Renaissance*, III, ed. Jean Jacquot and Elie Konigson (1972; Paris, 1975), 153-171; Yates, *Astraea*, 208-214; and Saward, *Golden Age*, 103-106. For the Hapsburg identification with Hercules, see Guido Bruck, "Hapsburger als 'Herculier'," *Jahrbuch der Kunsthistorischen Sammlungen, Wien* n.s. L (1953): 191-198; William C. McDonald, "Maximilian I of Habsburg and the Veneration of Hercules: on the revival of myth and the German Renaissance," *Journal of Medieval and Renaissance Studies* VI (1976): 139-154, who also discusses King Henry VIII of England's use of the myth to the detriment of Emperor Maximilian I - a manner akin to Sixtus V's usage; Jonathan Brown and J.H. Elliott, *A Palace for a King: the Buen Retiro and the court of Philip IV* (1980; New Haven and London, 1986), 156-161; and von Barghahn, *Philip IV*, I, 230-235. For the Medici-Hercules analogy, see Shearman, *Raphael's Cartoons*, 89; Weinberger, *Michelangelo*, I, 243-246; Richelson, *Studies*, 79-106; Utz, "Labors," *Art Bulletin*, 356-360; Kurt W. Forster, "Metaphors of Rule: political ideology and history in the portraits of Cosimo I de'Medici," *Mitteilungen des Kunsthistorischen Institutes in Florenz* XV (1971): 72-85; and Leopold D. Ettlinger, "Hercules Florentinus," *Mitteilungen des Kunsthistorischen Institutes in Florenz* XVI (1972): 119-142. For the Farnese-Hercules analogy, see Coffin, *Villa*, 281-302; Loren Partridge, "The *Sala d'Ercole* in the Villa Farnese at Caprarola, Part I," *Art Bulletin* LIII, 4 (December 1971): 467-486; and *idem*, "The *Sala d'Ercole* in the Villa Farnese at Caprarola, Part II," *Art Bulletin* LIV, 1 (March 1972): 50-62.

[47] See Weinberger, *Michelangelo*, I, 243-246, for the Bandinelli group commissioned by Clement VII; Forster, "Metaphors," *Mitteilungen*, 80; and Utz, "Labors," *Art Bulletin*, 347-355, for the Vincenzo de'Rossi group commissioned by Cosimo I. For the influence of Medicean art on Sixtine art, see Herz, "Sixtine," *Storia dell'arte*, 243 ff, and especially 246, note 39.

[48] Reproduced and discussed in Yates, *Astraea*, 222-224. Also consult Victor E. Graham and W. McAllister Johnson, *The Paris Entries of Charles IX*

umphantly upon the treasure and is rewarded for his feat in the form of an angel who bestows a crown on his head, or in the form of the dove of the Holy Spirit. Praise of the pope's beneficence to the Church is combined with vigilance either in the form of the roaring lion or the zoomorphic protectors, aided in some instances by a messenger of God, probably the Archangel Michael for reasons which I have indicated above, and which will become clear in the following chapters. This combination of beneficence and justice is enunciated in the verse beneath the *Treasure* in the Vatican Library:

QVAE FVIT PARCO CONGESTA PECVNIA SIXTO,
TVRCAE ERIT EXITIVM, PRAESIDIVMQ. PETRI

The antique component contained within the *imprese* of the *Treasure* is not as readily grasped as that of the *Abundance* and *Extirpation*. According to the ancients, gold had no place in the Golden Age since man had no need for possessions in a pastoral existence. In fact, according to Ovid, gold was not discovered until the Iron Age, the age of man's most severe degradation and, as Kamen has shown, this state of affairs was well known during the Renaissance.[59] Since the *Treasure* is clearly a politically-oriented device, like its pendant the *League*, however, it presupposes a civilized as opposed to a pastoral ambient and a leader who has the wherewithal to look after the *patria*.[60] Virgil lauds Emperor Augustus as just such a ruler in his *Georgics*: Augustus is not only victorious in war, but he also rules over a land "rich with gold."[61] Although Virgil does not mention a treasure *per se*, this praise of the ruler who protects and defends, and of the Eternal City of Rome, the original locale of Saturn's Golden Age, may have provided inspiration for the *impresa* of the *Treasure*, especially since the Treasury at Castel Sant'Angelo recalls the Treasury of Augustan Rome appropriately housed in the Temple of Saturn, while Virgil's Rome under the *Pax Augusti* evokes associations with the Heavenly City paved in gold and its fortifications bejewelled [Revelation XXI: 10-27].[62]

The Christian and Christological import of the *Treasure* is more readily grasped especially owing to those representations in which other animals accompany the Sixtine lion. These animals, who stand attentively around the chest, suggest associations with Noah's ark, while the unicorn, whose favorite abode is the earthly paradise, as well as the dove in the *impresa* of the anonymous portrait, specify the precise time represented, namely the aftermath of the Deluge, a period of spiritual restoration foreshadowing the millenium.[63] Such visual associations are confirmed by the very etymology of the Latin word for treasure (*arca*, meaning treasure, ark, and sepulchre), and by the venerable tradition which conflates *arca* and *ara*, altar, so that the Sixtine lion becomes another Noah standing in the ark, another Christ of the Resurrection standing upright in his tomb, an *alter Christus*, Saint Francis in emulation of the Resurrected Christ, and, one might add, another mystical lamb-cum-lion of Judah upon the altar.[64] Indeed, as Rocca so perceptively noted, the *Treasure* is a eucharistic symbol *par excellence*.[65] The *imprese* thus come full circle, from the allusions to the pagan Golden Age of the *Pax Augusti*, through the Old Testament types of Christ and the millenium, to Saint Francis and the final realization of the earthly reflection of the heavenly city in the Church Militant of the Franciscan Sixtus V, second

and Elisabeth of Austria 1571 with an analysis of Simon Bouquet's Bref et sommaire recueil (Toronto and Buffalo, 1974), 65-75, for the *impresa* of King Charles IX.

[49] Virgil, *Aeneid*, VI, 791-807; Horace, *Carminum Liber*, III, xiv, 1-4. See the discussion of this analogy in Saward, *Golden Age*, 103-106. For the *impresa* of Emperor Charles V, see Earl Rosenthal, "*Plus Ultra, Non Plus Ultra*, and the Columnar Device of Emperor Charles V," *Journal of the Warburg and Courtauld Institutes* XXXIV (1971): 204-228. Also consult Chapter IV, ff, below for a specific Sixtine application.

[50] See note 19 above.

[51] This idea is implicit in Frederick II's Christ-like *persona*. See note 26 above. For a recent treatment of works of art which convey Frederick II's "idea of empire," see Jill Meredith, "The Revival of the Augustan Age in the Court of Emperor Frederick II," *Artistic Strategy and the Rhetoric of Power: political uses of art from antiquity to the present*, ed. David Castriota (Carbondale and Edwardsville, 1986), 39-46.

[52] For the Valois ruler Charles VIII as "pasteur souverain," see Scheller, "Imperial," *Simiolus*, 5-17. For the Valois-Angoulême analogy under Catherine de'Medici and the Bourbon analogy under Marie de'Medici, both hailing from the Florentine Medici family, as well as under Henry of Navarre, see Levin, *Myth*, 70, and Saward, *Golden Age*, 144, respectively. For the Hapsburg and Tudor use of the *topos*, see Yates, *Astraea*, 26, 60-61, respectively.

[53] Valeriano, *Hieroglyphica*, XI, v.

[54] von Pastor, *History*, XXI, 90-95.

[55] von Pastor, *History*, XXI, 114-126; von Hübner, *Life and Times*, I, 323-337. Also consult Antonio Martini, "Sisto V e l'Erario di Castel Sant'Angelo," *Studia Sixtina. Nel IV Centenario del Pontificato di Sisto V (1585-1590)*, Academia Sistina (Rome, 1987), 77-108. I wish to thank Oreste Ferrari for drawing this volume to my attention.

[56] Fontana, *Della trasportatione*, 92v, does not describe the *Treasure* in the Vatican Library. Rocca, *Biblioteca*, 244-246, discusses the *Treasure* as follows: "Ad alteram eiusdem partis Camerae fenestram supra coronam aerarium Pontificium repraesentatur per arcam quandam seris occlusam, & Leonem / desuper iacentem, atque Ecclesiae claues gestantem, necnon per Angelum tenentem in sublimi Tiaram Pontificiam, quam Regnum Mundi appellant, hinc inde imaginibus, vel symbolis humi consistentibus, quae Christianos Principes Ecclesiae Sanctae Romanae, Catholicae scilicet fidei operam laturos, vt superius dictum est, repraesentant: Angelo item ad partem alteram clauem, & ensem gestante. Infra vero Inscriptio in hanc legitur verborum formam: .. / Duo in omnibus humanis actibus potissimum inspici debent, modus scilicet agendi, & finis actae rei: quae quidem in praeclarissi-

ma Sixti actione erudite obseruat Blancus: priore siquidem versu modum colligendae pecuniae, posteriore vsum, & finem collectae venuste comprehendit: sicut enim Princeps, qui ad pecuniae collectionem animum adijcit non tyrannica vi, aut alijs modis illegitimis, sed honesta & legitima via, qualis est parsimonia, quae a sapientibus olim magnum vectigal dicta est, conficere debet, ita Sixtus, qui omnia recte peragit, incredibili parsimonia intra paucos dies tantam pecuniae vim, quantam nullus autem Pontificum, confecit. Quod priore, vt diximus, versu denotat Blancus, dum eum parcum appellat epitetho non ocioso, quasi dicat, Sixtum V. ex parsimonia sua pecuniam congessisse: idq. clarius expressit Inscriptionis Auctor in eucharistico suo Carmine dicens: / In tua congestos retulisti aeraria nummos. / Quos esserre potest non nisi causa gravis: / Nec tibi thesauros vis vlla tyrannica fecit. / Sola manus tantas parca parauit opes. / Vsus autem collectae pecuniae, vt etiam tradidimus, accurate considerari debet, vt non ad fouendam auaritiam malorum omium radicem, non ad prodigalitatem, non ad voluptates, & mollities, aliosve execrandos vsus, sed ad necessarios, honestos, & laudatos comparetur. Vsus autem publicae pecuniae (quod in suo ea de re Diplomate praesensit Sixtus V.) est praesidium & ornamentum Reipublicae: exitium, & interitus / hostium, quando pecunia a veteribus belli neruus appellatur. Vsum igitur explicat Blancus dum ait: / Turca erit exitium, praesidiumq. Petri, / Hoc est, Romanae, & Apostolicae sedis. Huc spectat eiusdem Blanci locus in Eucharistico suo dicens: Turca rues: tantos Arx aelia seruat in vsus: / Quae summus Princeps accumulauit opes: / Quosq. sibi belli neruos confecit abunde. / Vertet thesauros in caput ille tuum / Infelix tu Turca rues hoc nomine, Felix, / Quòd tu felici sub Duce Turca rues. / Et vt locum Blanci obiter illustrem, sciendum hanc ingentem pecuniam a Sixto V. collectam repositam esse in mole Aelij Hadriani, quam hodie Castellum S. Angeli dicimus, ob eamq. causam Arcem aeliam is appellat ab Aelio Hadriano Imp. qui eam extruxit. Hanc item rem Blancus decantauit Epigrammate alio, quod in aula Sancti Ioannis in Laterano legitur hisce verbis: ... / Qui autem plura ad id spectantia & scitu digna noscere cupit, ad dictum Diploma, seu ad alteram huius generis Inscriptionem superius declaratam confugiat." Compare Pansa, Libraria, 115: "Si vede ... l'Erario di S. Chiesa, doue egli per benefitio publico, cumulo dal principio del suo Pontificato, gran quantità de denari, per seruirsene poi al bisogno, & all'occasione contra Heretici, & infedeli, de quali fu egli sempre capitalissimo inimico ..." Orbaan, Sixtine, 124, states that the animals are "the Cardinals who held the keys to those millions." Consult Bullarum Romanorum, VIII, 693-700, for Sixtus V's bull that explains the ways in which the treasure is to be used, and the six officials given keys to the treasure.

[57] Fontana, Della trasportatione, 61, describes the impresa as follows: "E so-

pra vn'altra finestra dentro ad vn'altro quadro si rappresenta in pittura il Tesoro radunato da Nostro Signore dentro ad vno scrinio, intorno al quale si veggono dipinti gli animali, che sono nell'armi di ciascheduno di quelli, che ne tengono le chiaui ..." Rocca, Biblioteca, 246, incorporates the inscription beneath the Treasure in the Lateran Palace into the discussion of the Treasure in the Vatican Library (see note 56 above). In his somewhat garbled description, Fontana mentions the presence of animals holding keys. Since he does not describe the impresa at the library, it may well be that Fontana remembered the Vatican version of the impresa and assumed that the same configuration was used in both monuments, since this is the case with the remaining three imprese illustrating the pope's Good Works. There is also a possibility that after three restorations to the Lateran Palace, each executed due to the ruinous state of the frescoes, some elements were overlooked and others altered, although the stance of the lion is certainly that of the original.

[58] The impresa on the Sixtine numismatics found its way into Jacob Typot, Symbola Divina et Humana Pontificum Imperatorum Regum, 3 vols. (1601-1603), Instrumentaria Artium 7 (Graz, 1972), I, # XXXI, 36-37. The motto itself, with a slight alteration ("sani" instead of "sacri") was remembered by Carlo Padiglione, I motti delle Famiglie Italiane (1910; Bologna, 1972), 79, as a "Peretti motto."

[59] Ovid, Metamorphoses, I, 141-143; Henry Kamen, "Golden age, iron age: a conflict of concepts in the Renaissance," Journal of Medieval and Renaissance Studies IV (1974): 143-155.

[60] Compare the glorification of a treasure in the Festa di Agone of 1536, and of a league of Christian princes in the Carnival of 1539, in Vincenzo Forcella, Tornei e giostre, ingressi trionfali e feste carnevalesche in Roma sotto Paolo III (1885; Bologna, n.d.), 24, 77. I should thank Philip Sohm for suggesting that this impresa is a political device designed in part to justify the pope's financial policy.

[61] Virgil, Georgics, II, 148-176.

[62] For descriptions of the Heavenly City see Boas, Primitivism, 158-160. For the concept of Eternal Rome, which is integral to the return of the Golden Age, see, for example, Stinger, Renaissance, 292ff.; Kenneth J. Pratt, "Rome as Eternal," Journal of the History of Ideas XXVI (1965): 25-44; Theodor E. Mommsen, "St. Augustine and the Christian Idea of Progress," Journal of the History of Ideas XII (1951): 346-374; and Loren Partridge, "Divinity and Dynasty at Caprarola: Perfect History in the Room of the Farnese Deeds," Art Bulletin LX, 3 (December 1978): 525-528. Bonaventure characterizes the Augustan peace as the seventh time of "intermediate repose" in his Lignum Vitae, I, 4, and Collationes, XVI, 12, 16.

[63] For the unicorn, see Andrea Bacci, L'Alicorno; discorso ... nel quale si tratta della natura dell'Alicorno & delle sue virtù eccellentissime ... (1573; Florence, 1582); and Liliane Châtelet-Lange, "The Grotto of the Unicorn and the Garden of the Villa di Castello," trans. Renate Franciscond, Art Bulletin L, 1 (March 1968): 55-56. For the chiliastic import of the Deluge see Ladner, Idea of Reform, 73 ff.

[64] For the arca-ara comparison, and the representations of Noah and Christ, see Anthony K. Cassell, Dante's Fearful Art of Justice (Toronto, Buffalo, London, 1984), 23-24; for the post-Tridentine stipulation that the tomb be depicted closed rather than open, see Mâle, L'art religieux, 292-294; and for Saint Francis in emulation of the Resurrected Christ, see E. James Mundy, "Franciscus alter Christus: The Intercessory Function of a Late Quattrocento Panel," Record of the Art Museum, Princeton University XXXVI (1977): 7-8. This impresa has much in common in this context with Agostino Carracci's 1586 engraving of the Cordons of Saint Francis, as well as the later 1588 version by Julius Goltzius representing a variation on the Carracci design. See Diane DeGrazia Bohlin, Prints and Related Drawings by the Carracci Family. A Catalogue Raisonné, exh. cat. (Bloomington and London; Washington, 1979), 242-243, n. 141; and the revised Italian version, idem, Le Stampe dei Carracci con i disegni, le incisioni, le copie e i dipinti connessi. Catalogo critico. 2nd rev. ed. (Bologna, 1984), 148-149. Also consult Simonetta Prosperi Valenti Rodinò, "La diffusione dell'iconografia Francescana attraverso l'incisione," L'immagine di San Francesco nella Controriforma, Comitato Nazionale per le Manifestazioni Culturali per l'VIII Centenario della Nascita di San Francesco di Assisi, Ministero per i Beni Culturali e Ambientali, Istituto Nazionale per la Grafica, exh. cat., Calcografia, 9 December 1982-13 February 1983 (Rome, 1982),163-164, 172-173, n. 99. I wish to thank Padre Servus Gieben for kindly having dated the Goltzius print, and Joaneath Spicer for generously having provided me with the appropriate sections from DeGrazia Bohlin's Italian edition.

[65] See note 56 above. In keeping with the tendency of theologians to relate the Epiphany and the Eucharist, like the Alpha and Omega, the Treasure may also be read as the manger-altar of Christ, and the animals as stand-ins for those present at the Nativity and Adoration of the Magi. See Ursula Nilgen, "The Epiphany and the Eucharist: On the interpretation of Eucharistic Motifs in Medieval Epiphany Scenes," Art Bulletin XLIX, 4 (December 1967): 311-316. Further, the ark-altar of the Treasure may contain allusions to the Virgin, whom Sixtus V profoundly venerated, in her role as the "ark of flesh" and "altar of heaven" and thus, to the legend of the Aracoeli and the almost comparable vision of St. Francis in the Porziuncola. See the inscriptions on the base of the obelisk of Santa Maria

Augustus, vicar of Christ and vigilant guardian against that scourge of the earth, the treacherous Turk.

The verse beneath the "tapestry" of the *Treasure* at the Lateran Palace praises Sixtus V for having accumulated vast amounts of gold (some three million gold *scudi* by April 1588) and downgrades Plato, who was "foolish" enough to have banned gold from his ideal city. The verse, of course, refers to Plato's *Republic*, and specifically to a passage in Book III where Socrates explains the policy to Glaucon:[66]

AVRVM LEGE SVA PLATO QVONDAM EIECIT AB VRBE
LEGE SVA ID SIXTVS CONDIT IN ARCE PATER,
SCILICET AVRVM ESSE EXCIDIVM PLATO CENSVIT VRBIS,
VRBIS PRAESIDIVM SIXTVS ID ESSE PROBAT

That Sixtus V should be elevated above Plato would have been no surprise to learned scholars of Sixtine Rome. Shortly after the Council of Trent, Plato had entered the 'bad books' of the University of Rome and, although Marc Antoine Muret, the renowned French orator and teacher of moral philosophy, jurisprudence and rhetoric, had insisted on teaching Plato's *Republic* together with the more acceptable *De officiis* of Cicero, by 1574 he was evidently persuaded to drop Plato from his curriculum and to direct his energies to Cicero. This sentiment continued into the pontificate of Sixtus V and beyond, for when Francesco Patrizi took it upon himself to reinstate Plato in 1592, he was soon reprimanded and dismissed by Clement VIII.[67]

Indeed, it was not Plato who was the model for the pope's financial policy. As Sixtus V himself explains in his bull of 21 April 1586, his models were the Old Testament leaders who had amassed small fortunes and stored them in the Temple to protect and embellish the synagogue.[68] Like his Old Testament predecessors, Sixtus V stores his treasure in the Ark of the Covenant and prepares for the final battle to be waged and won against the Turk so that the end of time on earth will be realized and paradise regained by the faithful.

4. *LEAGUE OF CHRISTIAN PRINCES*

The political reality at the time of Sixtus V was anything but peaceful and harmonious, as the *League of Christian Princes* would have one believe. While the "Sonderling in der Kaiserburg," Emperor Rudolph II, did not pose any great threats to the See of Saint Peter during the pontificate of Sixtus V, his cousin, King Philip II of Spain, was a power to be reckoned with.[69] On the one hand, Sixtus V realized that he needed the aid of the king in order to carry out some of his reforms and to safeguard the realm, but on the other hand, Philip II was so powerful that Spanish domination of even the papal states was a very real danger.[70] To compound the problem, while walking a tightrope with Philip II, Sixtus V was faced with the possibility of a wholesale French conversion to Protestantism, and although his excommunication of Henry of Navarre and Henry of Condé in 1585 was lauded by Leaguers and Philip II, it did more to cement Protestant solidarity than to further the Catholic cause.[71] The following year the Protestants, including envoys of King Henry of Navarre, King Frederick II of Denmark, the Electors of the German States and

Maggiore, transcribed and translated in Iversen, *Obelisks*, 53, notes 1-4, and Margherita Guarducci, "Ara Caeli," *Atti della Pontificia Accademia Romana di Archeologia (Serie III). Rendiconti* XXI-II-XXIV (1947-1949): 277-290, for the Aracoeli myth. On the vision of St. Francis, and the treasure chest used by Sixtus V to house indulgences, see Mâle, *L'art religieux*, 478-480.

[66] Plato, *Republic*, III, 416E-417A in *Republic*, trans. Paul Shorey, Loeb Classical Library (1930; revised 1937; Cambridge, Mass; London, 1943), 310-313.

[67] McGinness, "Rhetoric," 97-98. On Muret, see Charles Dejob, *Marc-Antoine Muret: un professeur français en Italie dans la seconde moitié du XVIe siècle* (1881; Geneva, 1970). I am grateful to Glenn Scott for having suggested that I look into Muret and for providing possible sources.

[68] von Pastor, *History*, XXI, 122-123.

[69] Rudolph II's tendency to procrastinate angered Sixtus V, since the pope had hoped that the emperor would properly act as his fighting arm. See von Pastor, *History*, XXII, 72 ff; and von Hübner, *Life and Times*, I, 418-431.

[70] von Pastor, *History*, XXI, 262-273, 340-374; von Hübner, *Life and Times*, II, 19-37; J. Lynch, "Philip II and the Papacy," *Transactions of the Royal Historical Society* 5th ser., II (1961): 23-42.

[71] von Pastor, *History*, XXI, 273-290; von Hübner, *Life and Times*, II, 145-195; Le Comte Henri de l'Épinois, *La ligue et les papes* (Paris; Brussels; Geneva, 1886); Segretain, *Sixte-Quint et Henri IV*, 92 ff.

[72] Frances A. Yates, *The Rosicrucian Enlightenment* (1972; London and New York, 1986), 34-35.

[73] von Pastor, *History*, XXII, 155-175; von Hübner, *Life and Times*, I, 432 ff. This feat of Sixtus V's is celebrated in a relief on the pope's tomb. See Herz, "Sixtine," *Storia dell'arte*, 252, 257.

[74] von Pastor, *History*, XXII, 37-70; XXI, 291-339; von Hübner, *Life and Times*, II, 196-295.

[75] Fontana, *Della trasportatione*, 92v, 61, describes the *imprese* in the Vatican Library and Lateran Palace respectively as " ... un Leone, dentro vna vnna, il quale tira à se con catanelle procedenteli dalla lingua molti animali per l'orecchie, i quali denotano li Principi Christiani ..." and " ... vn mare, nel quale è vna barchetta entroui vn Leone, sopra il quale vn'Angelo tiene il regno, & su'l lido sono diuersi animali, che rappresentano li Principi Christiani ..." Since Fontana does not mention an angel descending to place the crown on the lion's head in the Vatican Library *impresa* of the *League*, and since there is an angel doing precisely this in the *Treasure*, it may well be that Fontana conflated the images in his memory. This would certainly account for the discrepancies between Fontana's descriptions of the *Treasure* and the *League*, and their present states. Rocca, *Biblioteca*, 236-237, discusses the *League* in the Vatican Library as fol-

Queen Elizabeth I of England, held a clandestine meeting at Lunenburg in order to form a Protestant counterpart to the Catholic League.[72] The year 1586 also saw the death of Sixtus V's ally, King Stephen Bathory of Poland, and the ensuing struggle between the Hapsburg Archduke Maximilian and Sigismund of Sweden, both of whom were proclaimed King of Poland on 22 August 1587. War naturally broke out between the two contenders and it was not until 1589 that peace was attained due in large part to Sixtus V, who finally favoured Sigismund.[73] Also during 1588, the year that the decorations of both the Vatican Library and Lateran Palace were begun, the Spanish Armada was defeated by Queen Elizabeth I of England, and King Henry III of France ordered the execution of the Duke and Cardinal of Guise - the latter's death being viewed as a most heinous crime by Sixtus V.[74] Within the Italian peninsula itself, the Catholic Princes were irrevocably divided according to their allegiance to either France or Spain, with Venice, Ferrara, and Tuscany favouring the French, and Savoy, Parma, and Urbino favouring the Spanish (along with Sicily, Naples, and Milan, then under Spanish dominion). Of course, the fickleness of politics did not preclude the occasional alliance of opposing sides, as in the case of Venice and the Hapsburgs against the Turk.

The *impresa* of the *League* shows a lion standing in a boat, holding a key in his right forepaw, and in his left, a chain-link extending to the ears of eight animals of different species standing on the shore, all with olive branches in their mouths and crowns floating above their heads (figs. 35, 37).[75] The anthropomorphic lion who has united the animals demonstrates the ability of man to communicate with animals in the Golden Age.[76] Since the animals are not free to roam, however, the Golden Age represented here is not the pastoral paradise enjoyed by the sheep of the *Abundance* and *Extirpation*. Rather, it is a more particularly political Golden Age in which the lion exerts a certain control over his princely subjects. Like representations of Christ in majesty surrounded by the Tetramorphs of Ezekiel's vision, and Christ, the lion of Judah of Revelation, surrounded by symbols of the Evangelists, images which are evoked in this *impresa*, the Sixtine lion is characterized here as the absolute sovereign.[77]

The menagerie united by Sixtus V is comprised of animals both imaginary and real, each bearing a crown and accordingly standing for a Christian prince. Rocca, the only early commentator to have discussed the identity of the "princes," states that the *League* contains Princes of the Christian Commonwealth, namely the emperor, kings and dukes. Yet he does not name the kings and dukes of the *League*, and discusses King Sigismund of Poland and King Henry III of France in the context of the politics of 1589-90. Moreover, Rocca does not connect the rulers with their respective animals since such identification must have been common knowledge at the time.[78] Gamrath, who has recenlty considered this *impresa*, limits himself to an identification of three of the animals without, however, providing corroborating evidence.[79] As a result, the various species represented have never been fully identified, much less related to their princely counterparts. My own provisional attempt yields the following (figs. 36, 38): to the left of the lion is a capricorn (?), horse (King Philip II of Spain), winged-lion (the Venetain Doge Pascal Cicogna), and imperial eagle (Emperor Rudolph

lows: "Ad eandem camerae dextram supra fenestrae secundae coronam Christianorum Principum concordia a pictore repraesentatur per varias animalium species, adumbrata. Leo enim intra Nauim, seu Cymbam stare conspicitur supra mare, hinc inde ad littus varijs animalibus consistentibus. / Nauis, siue Cymba Ecclesiam, Leo Sixtum Quintum repraesentat: & est ad ipsius stemmata gentilitia allusio manifesta. / Variae illae animaliu species hinc inde consistentes non nisi Christianae Reipublicae Principes, Imperatores scilicet, Reges, ac Duces, eorundemq. insignia, siue commentitia quaedam ad / aliquid innuendum praeseferunt. Quod quidem Emblema curam Sixti V. non modicam indicat pro Christianorum Principum pace ineunda, & concordia conseruanda, sicut ex duabus praesertim Legationibus Ponoliae, & Galliae late patet. Qua in re praestanda idem Pontifex mirificam prudentiam, ac sapientiam cunctis in rebus conficiundis declaratam patefecit: selectissimos enim Patres ad legationes tanti ponderis obeundas, delegatosq. Praesules Viros ingenio, solertia, eruditione, atque vsu rerum praestantes elegit. Nam pro Regni Poloniae pace ac tranquillitate, Sigismundo III. Rege, Hippolytum Aldobrandinum Florentinum, S. R. E. Cardinalem, & summum Poenitentiarium, Legatum a latere in Sarmatiam misit: Praesules autem fuerunt Laurentius Blanchettus Bononiensis, Rotae auditor. Ioannes Tolosanus Collensis, vtriusque signaturae referendarius. Andreas Grandius Romanus, signaturae iustitiae referendarius. Michael Mercatus Miniatensis Protonotarius Apostolicus, & Sanctissimi D. N. Sixti V. familiaris. / Ad totius Christianae Reipublicae tranquillitatem, fidei Catholicae, ac nobilissimi Regni Franciae conseruationem, Henrico III. Rege interfecto, Henricum Cardinalem Caetenum Romanum, & S. R. E. Camerarium, Legatum in Galliam misit: cuius Praesules alijq. viri sunt hi: Camillus Caetanus Patriarcha Alexandrinus, & Legati frater. Dominicus Grimaldus Genuensis, Archiepiscopus Auenionensis. Alexander Canisianus Florentinus, Archiepiscopus Aquae sextiensis. Philippus Sega Bononiensis, Episcopus Placentinus. Marcus Antonius Mocenicus Episcopus Cenetensis, F. Franciscus Panicarola Mediolanensis, Episcopus Astensis. Laurentius Blanchettus Bononiensis, Rotae auditor. Ioan. Antonius Caracciolus Neapolitanus, & Guillelmus Blancus Albiensis, Natione Gallus, Protonotarij Apostolici, & intimi Sanctissimi D. N. Sixti V. Cubicularij Hieronymus Comes de Porcìa Protonotarius Apostolicus. Robertus Bellarminus ex Societate Iesu Theologus insignis. Inscriptio ad vnionem pertinens haec est: / INSCRIPTIO EMBLEMATIS ..." Compare Pansa, *Libraria*, 106-107: "Vedesi ... la Lega, ch'egli hebbe sempre in animo di fare, con diuersi Prencipi Christiani, in estermino di gli heretici, e-spetialmente contra Elisabetha, pretensa Reina d'Inghilterra, la fucina de gli errori, l'Hidra delle sette teste, che ha

II), apparently comprising the Spanish allies united in their crusading ideal to overcome the infidel Turk; and to the right of the lion, a white eagle (King Stephen Bathory of Poland), unicorn (King Henry III of France), black eagle (Duke Carlo Emmanuele of Savoy ?), and weasel (?), apparently forming the French allies united in their quest to overcome the heretical Protestant.[80]

The only animal who does not have a crown is the lion, although this omission is not to suggest that his powers are any less than those of the princes joined by the chain-link. In fact, this use of the chain is full of allusions and serves in part to explain the nature of the Sixtine lion's prowess. In Aristophanes' *Eirene*, Hermes (Mercury) tells the Greek envoy Trygaeus that Peace has been taken hostage by War. Under Trygaeus' leadership and the counsel of Hermes, the Greeks set out to rescue Peace from the pit into which she has been thrown by War, and achieve this end by using spades, crowbars and ropes to pull her out. James Hutton has shown how the ropes used to rescue Peace were transformed into golden chains by the French writer Guillaume Des Autels and used allegorically to commemorate the Peace of Cateau-Cambrésis in 1559. In Des Autels' version, Mercury ties the ends of six chains to the sky-bound car of Peace, and gives the free ends to the six men instrumental in bringing about the peace pact, who then pull Peace back down to earth.[81] It is this very idea which is conveyed in visual form by the *League*, so that the Sixtine lion becomes a second Mercury, the harbinger and embodiment of Peace. While it is unclear whether the *League* derives from Aristophanes by way of Des Autels, or by some other source closer to home, to which I shall shortly turn, the Sixtine version modifies the particulars of the myth in order to fit the occasion. The car thus becomes a boat, the six diplomats become eight, and Peace and Mercury are conflated in the person of Sixtus V. But more importantly, the chain-link is held by the Sixtine lion, rather than being tied to the boat, and it is attached to the ears of the princes, thus rendering it virtually impossible for them to pull the boat without undergoing excruciating physical pain! Despite this political alteration, the Sixtine *impresa* has much in common with the popular Renaissance illustrations of the eloquent Mercury, as exemplified in Albrecht Dürer's version and, later, as codified by Andrea Alciato.

Emblem CLXXXI of Alciato's *Emblemata* represents Hercules wearing the skin of the Nemean lion, holding a club and bow, with a chain extending from his mouth to the pierced ears of captives. Alciato explains the image as symbolical of the persuasive powers of Hercules in his capacity as law-giver, who, by his eloquence, which surpasses even that of Mercury, rather than by his strength, is able to unite even the most discordant of rulers.[82] The boat in which the lion stands and the key held in his right forepaw, while not present in Alciato's emblem, also contribute to the Herculean meaning of the scene. The boat in this context must surely refer to the ruler as navigator, another Golden Age commonplace, while the key belongs to Hercules in his capacity of supreme lawgiver and ruler.[83] Whether the Sixtine image was devised on the basis of Alciato, of its popular adoption by the Valois, of Lucian, its ultimate source, or of other Renaissance handbooks,[84] or of the Aristophanes-Des Autels' connection, it is clear that the message is the same: the Sixtine lion, symbolical of the second Mercury-Hercules, has reconciled the political imbroglio of

86

hauuto ardire cosi sfacciatamente alzar le corna contra Dio, con-/tra la Chiesa santa, & il Romano Pontefice ..." In the Vatican version, the capricon is in the water, rather than on the shore.

[76] For man conversing with animals during the Golden Age, see Plato, *Politicus*, 272B; and the discussions in Levin, *Myth*, 81; and Hutton, *Themes of Peace*, 220 ff.

[77] Although there are eight animals, instead of the traditional four surrounding Christ, it is interesting to note that the number eight signifies Christ, the Resurrection, eternity, perfection, salvation and the day of judgement, in Mundy, "Franciscus," *Record*, 13.

[78] See note 75, above.

[79] Gamrath, *Roma*, 106.

[80] Typot, *Symbola*, I, #XXXI, 70-71, for Philip II as a horse; and #XXXIX, 58-59, for Rudolph II. For a reference to the "Polish eagle," see Rudolph Wittkower, "Eagle and Serpent," (1938-1939), *Allegory and the Migration of Symbols* (1977; Great Britain, 1987), 196, note 270; and for King Stephen Bathory's successor, King Sigismund of Poland as an eagle, see Typot, *Symbola*, I, #XII, 124-125. The winged lion is a well known symbol of the Venetian Republic, witness the façade of the Doge's Palace. Consult Typot, *Symbola*, III, frontispiece for the winged lion of a later Doge (Marino Grimano), and a representation of the Doge's crown. For the unicorn of France consult Rüdiger Robert Beer, *Einhorn. Fabelwelt und Wirklichkeit* (Munich, 1972), 118-119. But see Gamrath, *Roma*, 106. Typot, *Symbola*, III, 31-32, illustrates and discusses Duke Carlo Emmanuele of Savoy as a hatching bird, as does Jacopo Gelli, *Divisi Motti e Imprese di famiglie e personaggi italiani* (1910; Milan, 1928), #1205, 333, who specifies that this bird is an eagle. However, Gelli, *Divisi*, #1352, 380, also discusses an *impresa* of the Duke as the centaur sagittarius. Gelli, *Divisi*, #196, 60, specifies that Francesco de'Medici's animal is a weasel, however, the crown hovering above his head in the Sixtine *imprese* does not correspond to the Tuscan ducal crown. I must therefore amend my earlier identification of the weasel, in Corinne Mandel, "Golden Age and the Good Works of Sixtus V: Classical and Christian Typology in the Art of a Counter-Reformation Pope," *Storia dell'arte* 62 (January-April 1988): 45-46, and leave his identity open. The capricorn, as the birth sign of Augustus, was a favorite emblem of the Renaissance ruler who liked to regard himself as a second Augustus, Grand Duke Cosimo I de'Medici, for example. In fact, the capricorn may well stand for Grand Duke Cosimo I, in which case, the *League* could also take on connotations of the peace brought about by Sixtus V's predecessor, Pius V, with the Battle of Lepanto.

[81] Discussed in Hutton, *Themes of Peace*, 114-116, 174-178.

[82] Andrea Alciato, *The Latin Emblems: index and lists*, ed. Peter M. Daly

his time by his powers of speech, augmented by force, and ushers in the Golden Age.

When read in their Christian contexts, the components of the *League* convey apocalyptic meaning, thereby reinforcing the overall visual analogies of the *impresa* to the prophecies of Isaiah, Ezekiel and Revelation. The lion, understood as a second King Hercules, is also a second Christ, since Hercules himself is a moralized type of Christ and, one might add, an exemplar of the Church Militant. Moreover, the lion who has united the animals suggests certain associations with Saint Francis, renowned for his love of nature and abilities to converse with all living beings, and with the Word made flesh, i.e. the *Logos*.[85] The boat is an allusion to the bark of Saint Peter, first vicar of Christ and predecessor of Sixtus V. It also recalls the boat from which Saint Francis spoke to the fish on Lake Rieti.[86] Like the chest of the *Treasure*, it also evokes the ark of Noah, a type for Christ and for the Heavenly City, especially since the animals being pulled into the ark by the Sixtine lion-cum-Hercules-Christ-Francis each has an olive branch in its mouth in emulation of the dove bearing news of the end of the Deluge, itself a type for the millenium.[87] In tandem with the bark of Peter and the chain-link, which could also be understood as a rod, the keys also recall the pope's gift of the "keys of the kingdom of heaven" given to Peter and his successors by Christ [Matthew XVI: 19] as well as the rod of spiritual and temporal rulership in possession of the Lateran.[88] Since Peter is depicted in the Sixtine Chapel at Santa Maria Maggiore with two keys, however, this single key suggests rather the single keys of Revelation, namely the key of David held by the sixth angel [Revelation III:7] and the key of the bottomless pit held by the angel-king [Revelation IX: 11; XX: 1].[89] When read as the key of David, the key affirms the kingship of Sixtus V in the manner of the Matthean passage cited above, it presents Sixtus V as the vehicle by which the prophecy of Isaiah XXII: 22 is fulfilled, and it suggests analogies to the Bonaventurian interpretation of the millenium. According to Bonaventure, the key of David signifies the understanding of Scripture by one man (by implication Sixtus V) or by many. With this understanding of the Bible at last achieved by man, the way is clear for the transition from the sixth age to the seventh, the true Golden Age of Christianity in which the vision of Ezekiel is realized.[90]

Even more evocative than the reading of the key according to Revelation III: 7 is the reading according to Revelation IX and XX. In the former, the fifth angel who holds the key to the bottomless pit is given leadership of the locusts charged to torment those who have not been faithful. The locusts, who take the shape of horses, have golden crowns on their heads and "faces of men," and are analogous, therefore, to the princes under the supervision of the Sixtine lion [Revelation IX: 1-12]. Since the Sixtine lion-angel-king holds not only the key, but also the chain-link, the action of the *League* must also take place during the second appearance of the bottomless pit in Revelation, namely the time when the angel binds Satan with his chain and with his key locks the devil up for a thousand years [Revelation XX: 1-3]. The angel then transports the souls of the saints and martyrs to the first resurrection [Revelation XX: 4-6], and prepares for the fulfillment of Ezekiel's prophecy [XXXVIII: 14], namely the appearance of Gog and Magog corresponding to the second tribulation of Bonaventure's theology of history. The last great battle against

with Virginia W. Callahan, assisted by Simon Cuttler and Paola Valeri-Tomaszuk, 2 vols. (Toronto, Buffalo and London, 1985), I, n.p.

[83] For the ruler as navigator, see Plato, *Politicus*, 297A; and Saward, *Golden Age*, 160. For the key of Hercules, see Kantorowicz, *Frederick*, 453; and, with regard to Sixtus V, Gerolamo Rodolpho, *Ad Sanctiss. D. Nostrum Sixtum Quintum Pontificem Opt. Max. Io. Baptistae Evangelistae Oratio habita in almo Firmanorum Gymnasio ...* (Firmo, 1586), n.p.: "vnum ex omnibus Cardinalibus patres delegissent, qui summa autoritate, quasi claua tradita, veluti nouus Hercules orbem monstris liberares ..."

[84] For the Valois-Angoulême and Bourbon use of the image, see Vivanti, "Henry IV," *JWCI*, 184-186. The Gallic Hercules, the name by which this image of is known, is discussed in Valeriano, *Hieroglyphica*, XXXIII, xxxix; LIX, xiii; Lilio Gregorio Gyraldo, *De Deis Gentivm varia & multiplex Historia ...* (1548; New York and London, 1976), 453; and in Vincenzo Cartari, *Le imagini de i Dei de gli Antichi* (1556; New York and London, 1979), 305-307, for example. Each author credits Lucian with the invention, and Cartari connects the image with Arcadia, a Golden Age locale.

[85] For St. Francis, see Armstrong, *Saint Francis*, 42 ff; and for the *Logos* (the Word) see J. C. J. Metford, *Dictionary of Christian Lore and Legend* (London, 1983), 267. I am grateful to Elio Costa for suggesting this essential analogy to the *Logos*.

[86] See the engraving of Philip Galle, 1582 (published 1587), discussed and illustrated recently in Rodinò, "iconografia Francescana," *L'immagine*, 182, n. 115. This engraving notably includes the Dream of Innocent III, in which Francis upheld the tottering Lateran, in the left background as a foil to Francis talking to the birds at right.

[87] I am indebted to Elio Costa for having suggested this analogy. See note 63 above for Deluge-millenium symbolism, and for the unicorn living in the terrestrial paradise. Also consult Marcello Fagiolo, "Dai Palazzi ai Giardini. Il Vaticano come 'residenza laica,'" in *L'arte dei Papi. Come pontefici, architetti, pittori e scultori costruirono il Vaticano, monumento della cristianità*, ed. Maurizio Fagiolo dell'Arco (Milan, 1982), 194; *idem*, "Chiesa Celeste," *Chiese*, 46-47; and *idem* and Maria Luisa Madonna, "La Casina di Pio IV," *Storia dell'arte*, 240-244, for the traditional connections between the boat and the ark.

[88] See Chapter I, 35-36, for the *possesso*.

[89] For the meaning of the key(s) of Peter, see Carolyn Kinder Carr, "Aspects of the Iconography of Saint Peter in Medieval Art of Western Europe to the Early Thirteenth Century," diss., Case Western Reserve U, 1978, 14-17.

Satan is waged and won, and the Last Judgement arrives, at which time the bodies of the faithful are transported to the celestial paradise where they will enjoy forever the glory of God. The *impresa* of the *League* thus presents Sixtus V as the angel who holds the key of David, and as the angel with the key to the bottomless pit and the chain to bind the devil, who translates the souls of the saints and martyrs to the Heavenly City, and who prepares for both the final battle against evil, no doubt the Turk, and the translation of the faithful to the seventh age of celestial bliss.

The verse in the first room of the Libreria Segreta contains none of the typical allusions to mythological, historical or Biblical personages noted in the foregoing. Rather, it serves more to describe the *impresa*, much in the manner of the verses at the Villa Montalto:

MVTVA DISIVNCTI COEVNT IN FOEDERA REGES,
ET SIXTI AVSPICIIS PAX STABILITA VIGET

More allusive is the verse in the Lateran Palace, which not only combines the imperial and Christian connotations of the *impresa*, but also compares Sixtus V to a pagan god:

DISIVNCTAS SIXTVS DVM IVNGIT FOEDERE GENTES,
ET DICTIS MVLCET PECTORA DVRA PIIS,
IVSSA DEI AVT PERFERT, ANIMAS AVT EVOCAT ORCO,
MERCVRIVS VERVS DICIER ANNE POTEST?

In accord with the dual function traditionally attributed to Mercury, Sixtus V is here characterized as a chthonic being on earth and a celestially-inspired personage. He is capable at once of bringing peace to earth by his powers of "spoken speech," and of bringing peace to the heavens by his powers of "interior speech."[91] Horace had given to Augustus Mercury's powers as peace-bringer in his Ode to Augustus, and thereafter the notion of ruler as peace-bringer in a Golden Age found such currency amongst sovereigns that by the Renaissance it had become a commonplace.[92] Popular too was the antique pairing of Mercury and Hercules as imperial exemplars of knowledge and fortitude.[93] As usual, however, Sixtus V and his iconographer alter the traditions they draw upon in order to assert the supremacy of the Catholic cause. While complementing the lion in the *impresa*, understood as a second Mercury and Hercules Pacificator, with the reference to Mercury Pacificator, Sixtus V is shown to be "super Mercurialissimo," as it were. Indeed, he is the Christian Mercury, Saint Michael.[94] Like the statue of Mercury depicted on the ceiling of the Sala di Costantino in the Vatican, likely smashed by Sixtus V and replaced with an image of the crucified Christ (fig. 24),[95] at the Lateran Palace Sixtus V-Saint Michael surpasses all peace-bringers, save Christ, and Saint Francis, the founder of his Order and, one might add, the Angel of the Sixth Seal. Sixtus V's intercessory function as vicar of Christ is thus given full meaning: having received both the key of David and concomitant knowledge of Scriptures, and the key to the bottomless pit, whereby he may confound the devil and imprison him for a thousand years, Sixtus V is able to transport the souls of saints and martyrs to the Heavenly City by his powers of "interior speech," and to rally the Christian princes to his side in anticipation of the final battle against the devil by his powers

[90] Bonaventure, *Collationes*, XVI, 29-30. See also Joseph Ratzinger, *The Theology of History in Saint Bonaventure* (Chicago, 1971), 22-55.

[91] See Saward, *Golden Age*, 42.

[92] Horace, *Carminum Liber*, I, ii, 25-44. Saward, *Golden Age*, 167, notes that this is the first text to equate Augustus and Mercury [notably in a Golden Age setting]. Since peace was one of the precepts of the Golden Age, the ruler who brings back this blissful time is always presented as "Peace-Bringer." For the Hapsburg equation of King Philip II to Mercury, see for example C. A. Marsden, "Entrées et fêtes Espagnoles au XVIe siècle," *Les Fêtes* III, 158-160; and for the Medici analogy see Cox-Rearick, *Dynasty*, 141, note 87, for Pope Leo X; and Thomas Puttfarken, "Golden Age and Justice in Sixteenth-Century Florentine Political Thought and Imagery: observations on three pictures by Jacopo Zucchi," *Journal of the Warburg and Courtauld Institutes* XLIII (1980): 141, for Cosimo I de'Medici, Grand Duke of Tuscany.

[93] Saward, *Golden Age*, 106.

[94] For the assimilation of Mercury to St. Michael, and the Franciscan component, see my Introduction, 30, and note 47.

[95] See J. A. F. Orbaan, "La Roma di Sisto V negli avvisi," *Archivio della R. Società romana di storia patria* XXXIII (1910): 284; and Tilmann Buddensieg, "Gregory the Great, The Destroyer of Pagan Idols: the history of medieval legend concerning the decline of ancient art and literature," *Journal of the Warburg and Courtauld Institutes* XXVIII (1965): 62-63.

[96] In this context, it should also be noted that Carolyn H. Wood, "Visual Panegyric in Guercino's Casino Ludovisi Frescoes," *Storia dell'arte* 58 (September-December 1986): 228, studies both visual and literary panegyric created for Gregory XIV (Ludovisi, 1621-23), and concludes that "Guercino's frescoes introduce a new stage in the evolution of the visual panegyric. ... The Ludovisi stemma is both the medium and the message." It will by now be clear that the watershed ought to be pushed back to the pontificate of Sixtus V.

[97] Tasso, *Rime*, quoted and discussed in Costa, *La leggenda*, 105-106. Compare the sentiments of Bianco, *Epigrammata*, 23, who also sees a return of the "aurea secla" during Sixtus V's pontificate.

[98] Giovanni Francesco Bordino, *De Rebus Praeclare Gestis A Sisto V. Pon. Max. ...* (Rome, 1588), 33, 23: "Nunc Pius, en Pastor, Rexque illam fertur ad aram, / Excubet vt Pastor, munera Rexque ferat, / Pastoris Regisque insigni hoc sacra sepulchro / Pastor Rex Sixtus condidit ossa Pij ...," "Sic reduces Astraeae, & relligionis honores / Exultans, Sixto Principe, Roma videt."

[99] Sigismundo Floriano, *Sixti V. Pontificatus Maximus* in Bordino, *De Rebus*, 62-63: "terrasque Astraea reuisit

of "spoken speech." With this last battle waged and won, Sixtus V is given divine sanction to open the doors to the seventh age of heavenly bliss.

5. GOLDEN AGE IN PANEGYRICS AND THE SIXTINE 'MASTER PLAN' FOR ROME

The many panegyrics written for Sixtus V, like the *imprese* and their mottoes, employ the Golden Age *topos* time and again to extol the beneficence brought to Rome and the Christian commonwealth by the pope, very often using some of the same *sub-topoi* of the mottoes. The virtual neglect of the panegyrics as hermeneutic tools to an understanding of Sixtine art must be considered a significant lacuna in modern scholarship, since the extraordinary number of connections between Sixtus V and the Golden Age makes it absolutely clear that the *topos* was a leitmotif of papal propaganda from the very beginning of his pontificate.[96] No less a poet than Torquato Tasso speaks of a Golden Age under Sixtus V in which man no longer needs to work the land, animals live in harmony, and justice rules.[97] Giovanni Francesco Bordino extols Sixtus V and his mentor, Pius V, as shepherd-kings and he witnesses the return of both Astraea and religion under the Sixtine rule.[98] So, too, Sigismondo Floriano sees the return of Astraea, "bringing law and justice, and faith without blemish," during Sixtus V's pontificate and looks forward to the near future, when Sixtus V will achieve "unanimous peace for all of Europe and one faith."[99] For his part, Giovanni Pinadello compares Sixtus V to Octavianus Augustus, since both rulers brought peace instead of war and adorned the city of Rome with glorious buildings and public works.[100] In a similar vein, Silvio Antoniano asserts the idea of empire, calling Sixtus V "ruler of the World," and the "closest on earth to the supreme God."[101]

A number of panegyrics refer to specific building enterprises and expressly laud Sixtus V as architect of the new Golden Age. Vincenzo Robardo, to whom I have already referred, compares the Sixtine lion who guards the entrance to the Lateran Palace to the serpent who guards the golden apples of the Hesperides (fig. 13), thus evoking the Golden Age which flourished at the time of Hercules.[102] In his poem on the Praesepio in the Sixtine Chapel at Santa Maria Maggiore, Bordino speaks of peace amongst animals, the golden peace achieved by the pope, and tacitly compares Sixtus V to Mercury, since the pope conquers "the dreadful foe who holds sway on earth and in hell."[103] Pompeo Ugonio, who speaks for the *patria*, "feels weighted down with the load of his Good Works," and in addition to noting the abundance, extirpation of the bandits, the treasure and peace achieved amongst men, he mentions the streets, buildings, fountains, and palaces built by the pope, as well as the obelisks raised by "the greatest prince who has brought back a certain new splendour of a golden age."[104] Antoniano likewise extolls "the kingly buildings, the obelisks, the temples, the columns and the waters which great-hearted Sixtus has conducted on aerial arches" and he sings of the "restored happy ages to Italy."[105] Indeed, the *topos* was so prevalent at the time of Sixtus V that Catervo Foglietta, writing a letter to a friend, could make an imaginary sketch of Paradise on earth outlined by justice, coloured with religion, and led by the architect Sixtus V, who forms the *modello* for the Eternal City

/ Ius aequumque ferens, & sine labe fidem," "Hanc [labes] etiam SIXTVS conatur tollere, concors / Europae vt toti pax sit, & una fides." Compare the return of Astraea discussed in Cosimo Gaci, *Dialogo ... d'intorno all'eccellenza della Poesia. Si parla poi delle valorose operationi di Sisto V. P.O.M. et in particolare del transportamento dell'Obelisco del Vaticano ...* (Rome, 1586), 84, 85; and Mutio Pansa, *Delle Glorie di Sisto Quinto Rime ...* (Rome, 1588), 56, 58.

[100] Pinadello, *Invicti Quinarii*, 28v, 31r-31v: " ... vt Octauij Augusti tempora, quibus Iani fores clausae sunt, silente bello redijsse nostra aetate videantur ... ," "Quum vero maximis negotijs distentus / pro republica Christiana ad Vrbem exornandam Octaviani Augusti exemplo se transtulisset ..." Compare Rocco, *Roma Restaurata*, n.p., who compares Sixtus V to Augustus; Gregorio Piccha, *Oratio Ad Sixtum V. Pont. Opt. Max. Pro dignitate nuper in Evangelistam Palloctum collata* (Rome, 1588), n.p., who praises the Augustan Peace, Age of Saturn, and pontificate of Sixtus V in the same breath in his preface; and Annibale Scoti, *Sixti V. Pont. Max. Cubicularii Intimi. In P. Cornelii Taciti Annales, et Historias Commentarii ...* (Rome, 1589), 14, who compares Sixtus V's building works and Maecenas' advice to Augustus to beautify the city of Rome.

[101] Silvio Antoniano, *Ad Ioannem Franciscum Bordinum*, in Bordino, *De Rebus*, 60-61: "SIXTE ... arbiter orbis," "In terris summo proximus ipse Deo es." Aikin, "Capitoline"; and McGinness, "Rhetoric," 388, may be considered as modern exceptions since they deal with the issue of the Golden Age to some degree.

[102] Robardo, *Gesta Quinquennalia*, 7v, quoted in Chapter I, 40, note 45, above. See also the numerous panegyrics which compare Sixtus V himself to Hercules, for example Bianco, *Epigrammata*, 21; Pansa, *Delle Glorie*, 55; and Rocco, *Roma Restaurata*, n.p. See also note 83 above.

[103] Bordino, *De Rebus*, 13, 16: "Mitescunt tigres, nec laedunt vnguibus vrsi / Informes quemquam, setigeriuesues. / Non vltra magnos metuunt armenta leones, / Non vltra insequitur torua leaena lupum. / Quin lupus ipse vorax agnos innoxius inter / Iam manet, & iuncti bosque leoque cubant. / Panditur interea coelum, iamque omnis ab alto / Caelicolum terras turba beata petit."

[104] Pompeo Ugonio, *De lingua latina oratio* (Rome, 1586), 17-18. See Chapter III, 97, for the full quotation. Compare the characterization of the Franciscan Golden Age in *Legend of the Three Companions*, Prologue: "Thus did he [Francis] bring the world to *a kind of season of spring* [emphasis mine]." This prologue also compares Francis' work to "abundant fruit" and the Orders he founded to "various fruit-bearing trees." - apparent analogues to the *Abundance created by Sixtus V.*

under the inspiration of Christ and God the Father, the first architects of Paradise in heaven and on earth.[106]

As one might expect from such apparently unbounded praise of Sixtine Rome, Golden Age symbolism is not confined solely to the *imprese* of the secular monuments and portraits of Sixtus V. To be sure, it also enters the overall meaning of the secular programmes and the portraits as well as the religious commissions of Sixtus V, namely the Sixtine Chapel at Santa Maria Maggiore (to which the Bordino praise quoted above refers), and the Scala Santa at the Lateran. In fact, and as the panegyrics quite clearly state, Golden Age symbolism informs the Sixtine 'master plan' for the city of Rome. Thus, while the Golden Age theme was by no means an innovation of Sixtus V and his circle - indeed, it had become a stock element in the propaganda of the papal and secular courts of Renaissance Europe - never before had Golden Age symbolism been used in such an all-encompassing manner to cover every aspect of the arts, including architecture and urban design, not even under Augustus, the first secular archetype of a Golden Age on earth.

Sixtus V had envisaged and nearly completed a street system which was to link the seven main pilgrimage churches as well as the holy shrines of Rome so that the city would be readily accessible to the faithful. *Piazze* were created by the juncture of major streets and, in these spaces, columns were surmounted by the founders of the Roman Church, and obelisks were erected, depaganized, and surmounted with the Sixtine star-topped mountains and cross to act as landmarks for the pilgrim, and as constant reminders of the triumph of Christianity over paganism.[107] Inscriptions were placed on the base of each obelisk which related to the history and Christian mythology of the site.[108] On the majority of these sites, buildings were erected and embellished with frescoed decorations.[109] Allegorical representations of the pope's Good Works were strategically placed in each of the decorative ensembles in secular buildings to act as synecdochic markers of the terrestrial Golden Age being realized by the true head of Christendom, and in the religious monuments, representations of the genealogy, birth, Passion and legacy of Christ to humanity provided the *raison d'être* for the Sixtine master plan. The references to the "Lion of the Tribe of Judah" served to confirm the apocalyptic basis for Sixtus V's vision,[110] while the references to and representations of Saints Francis and Bonaventure provided clues as to the specific nature of this Franciscan pope's Golden Age.[111] Foglietta's architect of Paradise on earth was not only divinely inspired when forming his terrestrial Golden Age in emulation of that which existed at the time of Christ's birth, but he also derived inspiration from the *alter Christus*, Saint Francis, and from Saint Bonaventure, whom he made a Doctor of the Church.

In creating a unified Church Militant on earth, abounding with peace (*Abundance*) and justice (*Extirpation*), Sixtus V was providing the faithful with a foretaste of the bliss they would experience in the Heavenly City of the Church Triumphant, like the vision of the new city heralded by the sixth trumpet blast of Revelation. In short, he was preparing the way for the transition from the Bonaventurian sixth age of world history to the seventh and final age. By making provisions for the last battle against the Turk (*Treasure*), Sixtus V was preparing for the second great tribulation which must come before the final age of Bonaventure's history of theology may be achieved. Ide-

[105] Antoniano, *Ad Ioanannem*, in Bordino, *De Rebus*, 59, 60: "Regificas aedes, Obeliscos, Templa, Columnas, / Et quas aerio fornice duxit aquas / Magnanimus Sixtus ... ," "Nam tuus immanes grassantum sustulit ausus / Nutus, & Italiae felicia saecla reduxit."

[106] Foglietta, "Lettera," Ottob. Lat. 568, 24r-24v: "Ma sono uscito quasi del seminato, et non è stato gran fatto, poichè à fare un poco dischizzo del bene del Paradiso in questo mondo, hò sempre creduto che si possa lineare con la giustitia, et colorire in bella forma con la Religione; nelle quali sono / ascose forze potentissime et incredibili, et con poco contrasto superate le forze delli appetiti disordinati. Di questo, chè dico, n'hà fatto un modello Sisto Quinto, et di già fondatane la fabrica; la quale ogni dì comparirà con pietre più belle, et più fine, che à lui stà di volerlo; poichè l'omnipotente Dio l'hà fatto Architetto di fabrica tanto importante, et di tale, che il primo Architetto figliuol di Dio ci lasciò la vita nel fabricarla."

[107] See Sigfried Giedion, *Space, Time and Architecture: the growth of a new tradition* (1941; Cambridge, Mass, 1967), 98 ff; and recently, Magnuson, *Rome*, 16-25; Schiffmann, *Roma Felix*, 149 ff; and Simoncini, "*Roma Restaurata*," 131 ff.

[108] Discussed in Iversen, *Obelisks*, 38, 53, 63, 72. Also see Chapter IV, 141 ff, below.

[109] On the decorations of the Vatican Library, see Dupront, "Art et contre-reforme," *EFR*, 282-307; Hess, "Some Notes," *KSRB*, I, 163-179; Clark, *Care of Books*, 321-332; and recently Angela Böck, *Das Dekorationsprogramm des Lesesaals der Vatikanischen Bibliothek*, Schriften aus dem Institut für Kunstgeschichte der Universität München, Munich, 1988. I should like to thank Angela Böck for generously having given me a copy of her book. The decorations of the Sixtine Chapel at Santa Maria Maggiore have been discussed by Klaus Schwager, "Zur Bautätigkeit Sixtus V, an S. Maria Maggiore in Rom," *Miscellanea Bibliothecae Hertzianae zu Ehren von Leo Bruhns, Franz Graf Wolff Metternich, Ludwig Schudt* (Munich, 1961), 324-354; Hans Ost, "Die Capella Sistina in Santa Maria Maggiore," *Kunst als Bedeutungsträger: Gedenkschrift für Gunter Bandmann* (Berlin, 1978), 279-304; Herz, "Sixtine," *Storia dell'arte*, 241-262; and Ostrow, "Sistine." For the decorations of the Scala Santa, see Scavizzi, "Scala Santa - I," *Bollettino d'arte*, 111-122; and *idem*, "Scala Santa - II," *Bollettino d'arte*, 325-335. The only intersection in which an obelisk was erected unaccompanied by a Sixtine building and decorating campaign is at the Piazza del Popolo.

[110] See Chapter I, 53, for this motto in Sixtine secular cycles. It is also found on the eastern face of the obelisk of Saint Peter's, where it is used as an incantation to exorcise "adversaries." See Iversen, *Obelisks*, 38-39; and Ernst Kantorowicz, *Laudes Regiae: A study in liturgical acclamations and medieval ruler worship* (Berkeley and Los Ange-

ally, he was to have been aided by the emperor, who corresponded to Bonaventure's second Charlemagne and whose zeal for Catholicism should have paved the Sixtine road which would lead all Protestants back to the true faith and end disputes amongst the faithful (*League*). In this best of all possible worlds the visions of Isaiah and Ezekiel would be realized and the translation from the earthly paradise to the Heavenly City at last achieved, thanks to Pope Sixtus V, the one chosen to receive full understanding of the Scripture and to open the door to the celestial paradise.

But alas, political reality and the Sixtine ideal were worlds apart. The artists who rendered the portraits of the pope accordingly excluded the *League of Christian Princes* from their roster of Good Works. So, too, panegyrists like Floriano could do no more than express hope for a speedy resolution to the problems of the age. The pope himself, who did much to rectify the Protestant problem in France, also must have realized that he would not live to see solidarity amongst the Catholic Princes, much less a united Europe and triumphant battle against the treacherous Turk. Indeed, by 1590 the *banditi* had returned and Europe experienced one of the worst droughts in memory. While the art, architecture, and city planning of Sixtus V both propounded and embodied his ideal Golden Age on earth - an age as harmonious as the times were tumultuous - they also had a more realistic purpose: they were vehicles by which the faithful might achieve justification. The Good Works of Sixtus V, from their allegorical and topographical reflections in fresco to their most monumental manifestations in the obelisks, columns and street plan of the city of Rome, ultimately remain as Sixtus V's lasting and grandiloquent prayer for his own salvation and for the salvation of his flock. If not in life, then at least in death the pope and his followers could enjoy the fruits of paradise.

110, below, in which an analogy is made between Francis and Sixtus V. See Fontana, *Della trasportatione*, 88, for the Vatican; and Massimo, *Notizie*, 45, for the Villa Montalto. Beneath the first representation of the *Second Council of Lyon* in the Vatican Library is an inscription explaining how Saint Bonaventure helped the Church, in Fontana, *Della trasportatione*, 88. In the first room of the Libreria Segreta is the *Proclamation of Saint Bonaventure as a Doctor of the Church*, commemorating Sixtus V's act at SS. Apostoli and in the same room, to the right of the *Treasure*, is a depiction of Saint Bonaventure with an inscription relating how Bonaventure was allowed to work on behalf of Saint Francis, thanks to Saint Thomas, in *idem*, 92r, 93v. The Lateran Palace also contains four scenes from the life of Saint Francis in the western loggia extension, which I discuss in Chapter IV, 172 ff, below. At the Sixtine Chapel in Santa Maria Maggiore the sculpture of Saint Francis by Flaminio Vacca is placed to the left of the sculpted tomb of Sixtus, in *idem*, 43v-44r; F. Gerardi, *La patriarcale basilica liberiana descritta ed illustrata con incisioni a contorno* (Rome, 1839), 98, note 222, 100, note 228, 102, note 232, 104, note 234; Herz, "Sixtine," *Storia dell'arte*, 253-254, note 88; and Ostrow, "Sistine," 260 ff. "Proof" that Sixtus V's millenarism was not Joachimist (even though Bonaventure was influenced by his contemporary) is provided in the inscription beneath the *Fourth Lateran Council* in the library which states that "INNOCENTIO III. PONT. FEDERICO II. IMP. ABBATIS IOACHIM ERRORES DAMNANTVR ...," in Fontana, *Della trasportatione*, 88v.

les, 1958), 1-22. For a discussion of the use of this messianic motto during the pontificate of the "other" sixteenth century Leo, namely Pope Leo X, consult Shearman, *Raphael's Cartoons*, 16-17, 77, 82. As if to compensate for the omission of the lion of Judah in the Salone Sistino, the Alpha and Omega are depicted three times, all in connection with the image of Christ flanked by Pope Sylvester and Emperor Constantine. In this image, Christ holds a book inscribed with the letters alpha and omega and the inscription "EGO SVM PRINCIPIVM, ET FINIS." Above Christ's head the letters alpha and omega are represented again. See Fontana, *Della trasportatione*, 91. Similarly, at the Sixtine Chapel at Santa Maria Maggiore, the representations of Christ's ancestors and nativity together with the actual *presepio* denote the alpha, and the *Sanctissimum* situated above the crib together with the repre-

sentations of God the Father, the Holy Spirit and the Angels adoring Christ denote the omega. Finally, at the Scala Santa, the Old Testament and New Testament analogues to baptism and the Eucharist also suggest the Alpha and Omega, while the representation of the *Terrestrial Paradise* is a visual reminder of what lies ahead for the pious during the Sixtine pontificate. *Terrestrial Paradise* is reproduced in Cempanari, Amodei, *Scala Santa*, 76, fig. 10.

[111] In the Salone Sistino of the Vatican Library, to the right of the representation of the *Fourth Lateran Council*, is a representation of *Saint Francis appearing in a vision to Pope Innocent III* and an explanatory inscription beneath. This dream was also represented at the Villa Montalto and is referred to in an inscription in the Salone dei Papi, to which I have referred above and discuss in greater detail in Chapter III,

I. *The Pope gives the Benediction (probable portrait of Sixtus V)*, S. Giovanni in Laterano, Loggia delle Benedizioni.
Il pontefice benedicente (probabile ritratto di Sisto V). S. Giovanni in Laterano, Loggia delle Benedizioni.

IIa.   *Papal Benediction before the Patriarchium Lateranense*, Biblioteca Vaticana, Galleria.
       Benedizione papale dall'antico Patriarchium. Biblioteca Vaticana, Galleria.

IIb.   View of the New Lateran coplex, Biblioteca Vaticana, Salone Sistino.
       Veduta del nuovo complesso lateranense. Biblioteca Vaticana, Salone Sistino.

III.   Lateran Palace, detail of the vault of the grand staircase.
Palazzo Lateranense, particolare della volta dello scalone.

IV.   Lateran Palace, detail of the vault of the eastern loggia on the piano nobile.
Palazzo Lateranense, particolare della volta della loggia est al primo piano.

V.   Lateran Palace, vault of the Cappella Papale.
     Palazzo Lateranense, volta della cappella pontificia.

PASCE·
OVES·MEAS

STRVCTA·DOMVS·DVCTI·FONTES·VIA·APERTA·CABALLI
TRANSPOSITI·ATQVE·VNO·EST·AREA·STRATA·LOCO
O·FELIX·NIMIRVM·VIA·EQVI·DOMVS·AREA·FONTES
DVM·VIVENT·VATIS·CARMINA·SIXTE·TVI

VI.   *The Quirinal and the via Pia*, Lateran Palace, Salone dei Papi.
       Il Quirinale e la via Pia. Palazzo Lateranense, Salone dei Papi.

VII.   *Christ's Investiture to Peter ("Tu es Petrus")*, Lateran Palace, Salone dei Papi.
        Tu es Petrus. Palazzo Lateranense, Salone dei Papi.

VIII. *Sixtus V receives the medals found in 1587 and document listing them*, Lateran Palace, Salone degli Imperatori.
Sisto V riceve le medaglie trovate nel 1587. Palazzo Lateranense, Salone degli Imperatori.

IMPP·CHRISTIANI
SVBMISSIS·FASCIBVS
SACROSANCTAM·ROMANAM·ECCLESIAM
SVPPLICES·VENERANTVR
ET·COLVNT

S·
P·

IX. *The Church adored by Emperors*, Lateran Palace, Salone degli Imperatori.
  Omaggio degli imperatori cristiani alla Chiesa. Palazzo Lateranense, Salone degli Imperatori.

X.   Lateran Palace, vault of the Sala di Samuele.
      Palazzo Lateranense, volta della Sala di Samuele.

XI.   Lateran Palace, vault of the Sala di Davide.
        Palazzo Lateranense, volta della Sala di Davide.

XII. Lateran Palace, vault of the Sala di Salomone.
Palazzo Lateranense, volta della Sala di Salomone.

XIII.   Lateran Palace, vault of the Sala di Elia.
        Palazzo Lateranense, volta della Sala di Elia.

XIVa. *Moses gathers the seventy elders of Israel*, Lateran Palace, Salone degli Apostoli.
Mosè raduna i settanta anziani. Palazzo Lateranense, Sala degli Apostoli.

XIVb. *The Holy Spirit descends on the Apostles on Pentecost*, Lateran Palace, Salone degli Apostoli.
Pentecoste. Palazzo Lateranense, Sala degli Apostoli.

XV. *Donation of Constantine* (detail), Lateran Palace, Salone di Costantino.
Donazione di Costantino (part.). Palazzo Lateranense, Sala di Costantino.

XVI. *Saint Sylvester baptizes Constantine* (detail), Lateran Palace, Salone di Costantino.
San Silvestro battezza Costantino (part.). Palazzo Lateranense, Sala di Costantino.

CHAPTER III

THE SALONE DEI PAPI OF THE LATERAN PALACE: PAPAL PRIMACY AND CHILIASTIC PREPARATIONS IN THE GOOD WORKS OF CHRIST'S VICARS

Sixtus V's penchant for having the achievements of his pontificate written down for posterity was equalled only by his desire to see them immortalized in works of art.[1] If his frescoed programme at the Scala Santa was not the appropriate forum for self-aggrandizement, then the tombs of himself and his mentor, Pius V, in their burial chapel at Santa Maria Maggiore, at least offered a traditionally acceptable vehicle for the celebration of their pontificates and persons in a religious context. But it was in the secular cycles that the pope allowed himself the luxury of ordering a veritable storehouse of representations of Good Works, some thirty-four in all, featuring the profoundly personal stamp of his *imprese*. The Vatican Library was given the distinction of displaying thirty-two Good Works, the greatest number in any Sixtine cycle, distributed among three rooms; next came the Lateran Palace, with seventeen frescoed Good Works in two rooms; and, finally, the Villa Montalto with fourteen representations of the pope's achievements, all in a single room.

Although the Good Works are represented in a variety of combinations, they can ultimately be categorized in two ways. First, there are rooms that are given over to the specific commemoration of the pope's achievements, namely the second room of the Libreria Segreta of the Vatican Library, the main room of the Palazzo delle Terme of the Villa Montalto, and the Sala degli Obelischi of the Lateran Palace. The second, and more comprehensive, manner presents the Good Works in tandem with historical narratives and personages that relate specifically to the function and history of the site. In the first room of the Libreria Segreta the Good Works are collocated with Doctors of the Church, and in the Salone Sistino, with councils and libraries which, together with the inventors of alphabets, form the main thrust of the programme. In the Salone dei Papi, conversely, the Good Works are situated beneath the apostolic popes and biblical narratives, in proximity to the viewer, and are as essential to the meaning of the programme as the history paintings.

While each programme was designed as a homogeneous unit to convey a pointed message concerning Pope Sixtus V and his pontificate, some are more comprehensive than others and use the Good Works to greater effect. By far the more substantial are those in which Sixtus V's achievements are integrated with history painting and historical personages and, of these, the programme of the Salone dei Papi incorporates the pope's works in the most forceful, coherent, and elaborate manner; without them even a general sense of the cycle's meaning cannot be grasped.

The Salone dei Papi is the largest, most extensively and

[1] See the discussion and excerpts from the numerous biographies of Sixtus V in von Pastor, *History*, XXI, 407-418.

lavishly decorated hall of the Lateran Palace (fig. 41). Begun from the foundations in June 1585, it was constructed by April 1588 and frescoed and gilded by April 1589.[2] Thereafter, the Salone was to be used for consistories and councils,[3] like the Sala del Concilio of the Patriarchium Lateranense, which it replaced.[4] As the main hall of the Lateran Palace, one would logically expect it to be of central importance in the monumental programme of the *piano nobile* and in the understanding of its patron's view of his own pontificate. To be sure, its contents have been described more often and in greater detail than any other room of the palace, yet no consistent effort has ever been made to decipher their meaning.[5] The study of the Salone dei Papi will thus afford the opportunity to explain the significance of the most important cycle of Sixtine Rome, to determine the role played by the pope's Good Works in the most qualitatively comprehensive programme he commissioned, and consequently to shed light on the over-all meaning of the fresco cycle of the Lateran Palace.

Before delving into the particulars of the Salone dei Papi it will be necessary to describe the layout of the hall. In so doing, I shall generally follow the order given by the first, and most authoritative source to have written on the Salone: Domenico Fontana, the architect of the palace (refer hereafter to figs. 42-45).[6]

The frescoed decoration of the Salone dei Papi is in *quadratura*, with eleven "Composite-Sixtine" columns of precious marble on each of the long walls, four on each of the short walls, and a pilaster of the same order at each corner. The columns on the long walls are arranged in pairs to flank each of the five openings (with the exception of the eleventh column), while on the short walls, they create the semblance of a triumphal arch. In this way, the *quadratura* echoes the layout of the ancient Sala del Concilio conceptually, if not in detail.[7] The columns support the trabeation and attic where canopied niches each house one of the nineteen representations of seated popes (A-S), and on the main walls, "framed paintings" and accompanying inscriptions describe the Institution of the Primacy (A[1]-B[1]). Beneath each pope is an inscription describing his works, and beneath twelve of the nineteen inscriptions there are *grisaille* paintings in the form of medallions complementing the works described in the inscriptions (a-s). Above the main entrance to the room there is an inscription describing how Sixtus V rebuilt the Lateran complex, as Saint Francis of Assisi had once supported it on his shoulders (X). Also on the lower register are eleven Good Works of Sixtus V depicted as feigned tapestries (1-11), alternating with the Good Works of Sixtus V's predecessors. Beneath each of these Good Works are verses referring to the representations above. The Good Works are situated directly above the openings formed by windows on the western wall, and the niches and main door on the eastern, while on the south and north walls they take center stage.

Although Sixtus V is represented only by his temporal works on the lower tier, his presence is felt emphatically throughout the Salone dei Papi. In whole or in part, the Sixtine *stemma* finds its way into virtually every part of the decoration of the hall, from the "Composite-Sixtine" columns and coffered ceiling to the pelmets of the baldachins and the window embrasures. The profusion of these elements is incremented above the architrave so that the upper tier becomes

[2] Consult Lauer, *Palais*, 614-616, for some of the bills for the wall and ceiling decorations; and Fontana's notebook, ASR, Camerale I, Fabbriche 1527, 20.

Tod A. Marder, "Sixtus V and the Quirinal," *Journal of the Society of Architectural Historians*, XXXVII (1978): 283, note 2, reasons that the Salone dei Papi was completed by 20 April 1588 based on the *avviso* of this date which states that the pope had ordered two rooms adjoining the Benediction Loggia (i.e., the Sala degli Obelischi and Salone dei Papi) to be prepared for an overnight stay. The *avviso* does not imply that the frescoes had been painted by this time, but rather, it indicates that the rooms at the southern end of the complex had been built and were in an adequate state to warrant preparations for a brief stay. The *avviso* in question is published in von Pastor, *History*, XXI, 389. The inscription on the window embrasures of the West wall indicates that the Salone was completed in the fourth year of Sixtus V's pontificate: "SIXTVS V PONT. MAX. ANNO IIII." Since Felice Peretti became Pope Sixtus V on 24 April 1585, I understand the fourth year of his pontificate to begin on 24 April 1588 and to end on 23 April 1589. Since I have found no evidence to secure a dating for 1588, I have opted for a more liberal dating of the frescoes which also takes into account the date of the final bill.

[3] Biondi, *il Restauramento*, 14; von Pastor, *History*, XXII, 276. The only celebration held in the palace during Sixtus V's pontificate was the consistory of 30 May 1589 in honour of the diplomatic victory of Cardinal Ippolito Aldobrandini in Poland. However, this celebration took place primarily in the Salone degli Imperatori, adjacent to the Salone dei Papi, no doubt because Aldobrandini's mission regarded the choice of a temporal ruler from both Protestant and Catholic candidates, and the Salone degli Imperatori commemorates emperors who payed homage to Christianity and acted in their proper capacity as the pope's fighting arm. For the proceedings of the consistory, see Paolo Alaleone "Diaria 1585-1590," B.A.V. Vat. Lat. 12293, 415-416v. I wish to thank W. Chandler Kirwin for having suggested that I look into the diaries of the masters of ceremonies. See Orbaan, "Roma di Sisto V," *Società romana di storia patria*, 309, for the *avviso* of 31 May 1589. Also consult Schiavo, *Restauri e Nuove opere*, frontispiece, for an illustration of the medal struck in commemoration of the event; and Pansa, *Libraria*, 86.

Although Sixtus V's immediate successors used the Salone dei Papi when they took possession of the Lateran, the hall was not used for the celebration of any kind until this century, and the momentous signing of the Lateran Pact on 11 February 1929. See, for example, Paulo Alaleone, "Diarium Caeremoniarum, et Actorum Summorum Pontificum Tomus III, Ab anno Domini 1591 ad anno 1594," B. V. MS. I 66, 140-145, for Innocent IX's *possesso*.

more sumptuous and palpable than the lower tier echoing the progressive plasticity of the representations from flat "tapestries" and "medallions" to feigned panels and popes enthroned beneath a coffered Sixtine ceiling. Such decoration not only suggests that the Salone dei Papi is divided into a temporal and spiritual realm, but, more importantly given the pope's symbolical and pervasive presence in each realm, it also clearly establishes Sixtus V's rightful place among the early popes. The inescapable impression given, therefore, is that Sixtus V, the last in a long line of Christ's vicars, is the one who restores the Church to its original nature. He is the one who has providentially inherited the early vision of the Church, and, in this "return" to the beginning, a great historical cycle is closed. Finally, the "Sixtine *quadratura*," which "supports" the attic, and which forms the very structure of the hall, reinforces visually the Franciscan theme commemorated above the main door. Indeed, as I shall attempt to show, the Salone dei Papi is predicated both visually and contextually on Pope Sixtus V's dual vicarship to Christ and to Saint Francis in his role as *alter Christus*, and on his mission to realize the Heavenly Jerusalem during his pontificate. In both form and meaning, the Salone dei Papi is an elaborate manifesto of the past and future history of the Catholic Church and of its ultimate goal, to be realized by its providential leader, Pope Sixtus V. It is due to the manifest presence of Sixtus V throughout the Salone, and to the proximity of his Good Works to the visitor in the hall that I shall depart from the order first given by Fontana and begin my analysis with the lower register and the Good Works of Sixtus V.

1. TEMPORAL TIER: THE GOOD WORKS OF POPE SIXTUS V

In his description of the Good Works of Sixtus V in the Salone dei Papi, Domenico Fontana briefly identifies by title and location eleven Good Works, and furnishes the accompanying verses.[8] At best, Fontana offers no more than a summary interpretation of the illustrations, and does not attempt to discuss the verses, or, consequently, to suggest how image relates to text. Subsequent writers on the Salone dei Papi, from Mola through Schiavo, largely follow Fontana's documentary approach, sometimes altering his titles slightly, sometimes neglecting to state the location of each Good Work, and sometimes choosing to omit the verses altogether.[9] With the exception of Ludwig von Pastor, to whom I shall return, all writers also follow the order given by Fontana. It will be the purpose of this section to examine both the form and content of the Good Works and to reveal how image and text combine to convey a unified message concerning the character of Pope Sixtus V, of his pontificate, and of his station as Franciscan vicar of Christ.

With the notable exception of the *Vatican Library* (fig. 48), the feigned tapestries contain the Good Works of Sixtus V within a landscape format, all seen from above to reveal panoramic vistas (figs. 46, 47, 32, 35, 49-51, 29, 26, 52). The idea of containing Sixtus V's Good Works in tapestry formats recalls the lowest tier of Nicholas III's Sancta Sanctorum, the frescoes illustrating the life of Saint Francis at San Francesco in Assisi, and, closer to home, the Sistine Chapel of Sixtus IV

[4] The Salone dei Papi was built on the general vicinity of the site once occupied by Pope Leo III's Sala del Concilio. See my figs. 3 and 65-66. Its dimensions, 24.60 x 13.40 m., though the largest of any hall of the Lateran Palace, are moderate compared to those of the Sala del Concilio of the Patriarchium Lateranense, which measured 68 x 15.37 m. I have used Schiavo, *Lateran*, n.p., for the dimensions of the Salone dei Papi, and Richard Krautheimer, "Die Decanneacubita in Konstantinopel: Ein kleiner Beitrag zur Frage Rom und Byzanz," *Tortulae. Studien zu Altchristlichen und Byzantinischen Monumenten*, intro Walter Nikolaus Schumacher, Römische Quartalschrift für Christliche Altertumskunde und Kirchengeschichte n. 30 Supplementheft (Rome, Freiburg, Vienna, 1966), 197, for the Sala del Concilio.

[5] Fontana, *Della trasportatione*, 59-61v; Mola, *Breve Racconto*, 64-65; Biondi, *il Restauramento*, 14-15; Dumesnil, *Histoire de Sixte-Quint*, 423-430; Tulli, "La 'Sala del Concilio,'" *Per l'arte sacra*, 30-55; von Pastor, *History*, XXII, 275-276; *Palazzo del Laterano*, 18; and Schiavo, *Lateran*, n.p.

[6] Fontana, *Della trasportatione*, 59v; 59v-61v, gives two descriptions of the Salone: the first is by way of introduction to the list of individual scenes and inscriptions, which is the second (consult Appendix IV, below). Since his order is slightly different in each, I have synthesized the two descriptions in what follows.

[7] The Sala del Concilio, according to the most reliable sources, was built on a basilican plan (hence, "Basilica Leonina"), with main southern apse, five side chapels (or *accubita*) along each side of the nave and a tripartite opening leading to an anteroom and Benediction Loggia of Boniface VIII. The room had two levels, each pierced with windows. See the descriptions in Panvinio, "Basilica et Patriarchio Lateranensi," in Lauer, *Palais*, 483-484; and Ugonio in *idem*, 577; and consult the sketch by Ugonio in his "Schedario," Barb. Lat. 2160, 157v (my fig. 66). Also see Duchesne, *Liber Pontificalis*, II, 11. Raspono, *Basilica et Patriarchio Lateranensi*, 325-328, and fig. between pages 385-387, gives the hall ten apses on each of the lateral walls, probably as a result of a misreading of Panvinio. The fresco above the *Third Council of Lyons* in the Vatican Library depicts the Sala del Concilio with six apses instead of five. See my fig. 2.

[8] Fontana, *Della trasportatione*, 60v-61v.

[9] Mola, *Breve Racconto*, 64-65; Biondi, *il Restauramento*, 14-15; von Pastor, *History*, XXII, 275-276; *Palazzo del Laterano*, 18; and Schiavo, *Lateran*, n.p. do not include the verses in their descriptions vis-à-vis Dumesnil, *Histoire de Sixte-Quint*, 425-430; and Tulli,"'Sala del Concilio,'" *Per l'arte sacra*, 42-50. Von Pastor and Schiavo depart from the order given by Fontana and do not give the location of each Good Work. The guidebook, *Palazzo del Laterano*,

(and the real tapestries finally executed under Leo X).[10] The landscape tapestry format, as Bernice Davidson has shown, was in vogue from the middle of the sixteenth century when actual verdure tapestries woven in Flanders were sent to Rome and subsequently emulated in such programmes as the Vatican Logge of Daniele da Volterra (1550), the Salotto of the Villa d'Este at Tivoli (1565-72) and the Vatican Galleria delle Carte Geografiche (1580-83).[11] The idea of enframing the landscapes with an illusionistic architecture had an older and more illustrious heritage, derived ultimately from the antique illusionism of the Augustan painter Ludius and his followers. This format was resuscitated during the fifteenth century by Pinturicchio and Pope Innocent VIII for the Vatican Belvedere (1487), and then proliferated through the sixteenth century in villa and palace decoration alike.[12] While Peruzzi's Salone delle Prospettive in the Villa Farnesina (1515-17) is now the most famous example of landscape and architectural illusionism, Sixtus V and his artists probably would have been more aware of the genre through Innocent VIII's Vatican Belvedere, and especially through the main room of the papal hunting lodge at La Magliana (c. 1512), a monument in fact restored by Sixtus V.[13]

In addition to their "updated" antique form, the Good Works of Sixtus V in landscape formats also defer to antiquity in their content. The four "tapestries" containing the *imprese* of the pope have an antique component by their very nature (*Treasure at Castel Sant'Angelo* (fig. 32), *League of Christian Princes* (fig. 35), *Extirpation of the Bandits* (fig. 29) and *Abundance created by Sixtus V* (fig. 26)). The remaining six "tapestries" containing topographical views of the building exploits of Pope Sixtus V, namely the *Acqua Felice* (fig. 46), *Port of Terracina and Pontine Marsh* (fig. 47), *Harbour of Civitavecchia* (fig. 49), *Monte Cavallo* (fig. 50), *City of Montalto* (fig. 51) and *Holy House of Loreto* (fig. 52), have their ultimate source again in the works of the Augustan painter Ludius, who, as Pliny the elder relates, "introduced a delightful style of decorating walls with representations of villas, harbours, landscape gardens, sacred groves, woods, hills, fishponds, straits, streams and shores, any scene in short which took the fancy."[14] Jorgen Schulz has shown how Pinturicchio and Innocent VIII emulated antique content in the landscapes with landholdings of the Belvedere, while Sven Sandström has suggested that the landscapes were further imbued with historical and thus political meaning.[15] By the sixteenth century, the imperial connotations of landscapes containing the building pursuits and/or landholdings of the patron were fully understood and exploited, particularly by popes intent on demonstrating their vast temporal holdings.[16]

The allusions to imperial and particularly Augustan Rome in the landscapes are continued in many of the verses beneath the "tapestries" in order to emphasize the pope's jurisdiction over the temporal realm formerly ruled by emperors. Like an emperor, Sixtus V brings peace, provides for and safeguards his subjects, and erects magnificent buildings, harbours and aqueducts.[17] To show the continuity of Sixtus V's rule with that of past rulers, descending into biblical times, the verses draw upon *topoi* emanating from the ancient Roman empire to glorify the pope. The *topoi* are taken from a storehouse of commonplaces traditionally associated with the Golden Age thus enforcing further the Augustan analogy of the landscapes. Not content to merely equate the pope to the emperor, however,

concerned primarily with the antiquities of the Museo Lateranense Cristiano (now housed at the Vatican), gives only a brief indication of the contents of the hall.

[10] Shearman in *Sistine Chapel*, 41.

[11] Bernice F. Davidson, "The Landscapes of the Vatican Logge from the Reign of Pope Julius III," *Art Bulletin* LXV, 4 (December 1983): 599.

[12] J. Schulz, "Pinturicchio and the Revival of Antiquity," *Journal of the Warburg and Courtauld Institutes* XXV (1962): 35-55; and recently, Simona Olivetti, "La *Historia Naturalis* (XXXV, 116-117) di Plinio il Vecchio, fonte per la decorazione della Loggia del Belvedere di Innocenzo VIII," *Storia dell'arte* LIX (January-April 1987): 5-10. For the sixteenth century use of this format see A. Richard Turner, *The Vision of Landscape in Renaissance Italy* (Princeton, New Jersey, 1966), 198; Diocletio Redig de Campos, *I Palazzi Vaticani* (Bologna, 1967), 77; David R. Coffin, "Some Aspects of the Villa Lante at Bagnaia," *Arte in Europa: Scritti di Storia dell'arte in onore di Edoardo Arslan*, 2 vols. (Milan, 1966), I, 571-574.

[13] von Pastor, *History*, XXII, 290; Lidia Bianchi, *La villa papale della Magliana* (Rome, 1942), 64-66; and Schulz, "Pinturicchio," *JWCI*, 43 and note 23.

[14] Pliny the Elder, *Historia naturalis*, XXXV, 116-117, quoted in Schulz, "Pinturicchio," *JWCI*, 39-40.

[15] Schulz, "Pinturicchio," *JWCI*, 38-42; Sven Sandström, "The Programme for the Decoration of the Belvedere of Innocent VIII," *Konsthistorisk Tidskrift* XXIX (1960): 39.

[16] See Coffin, "Villa Lante," *Arte in Europa*, 572 ff; and recently Richard L. Kagan, "Philip II and the Art of the Cityscape," *Art and History: Images and their Meaning*, ed. Robert I. Rothberg, Theodore K. Rabb (Cambridge, New York, New Rochelle, Melbourne, Sydney, 1988), 115-135, esp. 131 ff. It is entirely possible that the idea for the politically charged Sixtine landscapes (*vis-à-vis* the contemplative Franciscan ones) came from Sixtus V himself, who would have seen Philip II's landscapes when in Spain on a diplomatic mission for Pius V.

Guglielmo Bianco, the author of the verses, sometimes introduces pagan gods traditionally associated with the emperor and, one might add, with Sixtus V's princely contemporaries, only to show how their powers have been eclipsed by those of Pope Sixtus V. Finally, there is a preponderance of *equivoque* in the verses, often used to bolster Sixtus V at the expense of his pagan antetypes, or, in a simpler vein, to add to the beholder's delectation and edification. But above all, the play on words recalls the serious pun put forth by Christ at Caesaria Philippi [Matthew XVI: 18] actually represented on the south wall of the Salone (figs. 42.A¹; 63). It was surely with this momentous event in mind that Bianco emulated the word of God, providing a Christian component based on biblical precedent for these imperial-sounding verses.

The choice of Sixtine works represented in the "tapestries" corresponds to some of the greatest feats accomplished by the pope. In 1586, for example, Pompeo Ugonio praised Sixtus V's improvements to Rome as though he were speaking of the very works represented on the lower register: "Sentit se onere beneficiorum opprimi, sicariorum metu liberata [*Extirpation*], pacis luce perfusa [*League*], aucta vijs, ornata aedificijs [*Monte Cavallo*], irrigata fontibus [*Acqua Felice*], obeliscorum molibus in coelum ipsum inserta, frugum vbertate recreata [*Abundance*], locupletata aerario [*Treasure*], munita legibus, exculta literis [*Library*], sacris amplificata [*Lateran*]: quacumque sese ipsa circunspicit ... Optimi Principis, in nouam quandam aurei saeculi speciem restituta".[18] The conspicuous absense of the "massive obelisks," and of the columns surmounted with effigies of the apostles Peter and Paul in the Salone is more than compensated for in the adjacent room in the Lateran Palace, which is devoted exclusively to these great works: the Sala degli Obelischi. The Good Works bestowed by Sixtus V on cities outside of Rome are omitted by Ugonio, since this was not within the context of his sermon. As I shall show, Ugonio's list is not only carefully and thoughtfully ordered, but also agrees with the order given in the Salone dei Papi.

The first Good Work mentioned by Fontana is the *Acqua Felice*, situated on the south wall. Since the south wall is, in fact, the principal wall of the Salone dei Papi, following the orientation of the Sala del Concilio, I shall follow the order given by Fontana in my discussion of the form and meaning of the Good Works.[19] Having done this, I shall then depart from Fontana in order to determine the underlying symmetry of the Good Works of Sixtus V on the lower register, and, in so doing, shall add to Fontana's roster a twelfth Good Work of Sixtus V, following the observation of Armando Schiavo.

The "tapestry" of the *Acqua Felice* shows a view of the Quirinal, with the terminal Moses Fountain of the aqueduct to the left foreground, the rotunda of San Bernardo delle Terme nestled amidst other buildings to the right foreground, and, in the distance, the aqueduct winding through the sprawling farmland irrigated with the new water brought to Rome (figs. 42.1, 41 and 46).[20] The only people visible in the fresco are situated in the foreground, and are shown either reaping the benefits of the Acqua Felice, or gazing in apparent awe at this feat of the pope. The artist has reproduced the sculptural programme of the triumphal Moses Fountain down to the last detail. The viewer may recognize Prospero Bresciano's statue of Moses, rod in hand, beneath the central arch, the reliefs with

[17] Charlesworth, "Providentia and Aeternitas," *Harvard Theological Review*, 114-115, 124-127. Also consult *idem*, "Virtues," *Proceedings of the British Academy*, 105-133.

[18] Ugonio, *De Lingua Latina Oratio*, 17-18.

[19] See note 7, above.

[20] Much has been written on the Acqua Felice. See, for example, Fontana, *Della trasportatione*, 54-56; Pansa, *Libraria*, 80-85; Guglielmo Bianco, *Aquae Felices Ad S. D. N. Sixtum V. Pont. Opt. Max.* (Rome, 1587); Rocca, *Biblioteca*, 24-27; von Pastor, *History*, XXII, 208-218; Aikin, "Capitoline," 60-67; Marder, "Quirinal," *JSAH*, 286-288; Gamrath, *Roma*, 59-62.

Old Testament narratives from the lives of Aaron and Joshua situated beneath shell niches in the left and right arches,[21] the four lions, two Egyptian and two Medieval, spouting water from their mouths, and, at the summit, the *stemma* of the pope supported by angels, the obelisks and the mandatory cross on the Montalto mountains. The artist has also faithfully reproduced the inscription on the actual monument which explains how Sixtus V brought water to Rome from the streams near Palestrina a distance of twenty-two miles from the springs and of twenty miles from the reservoir in just three years, between 1585-1587.[22]

The verse beneath the "tapestry" furthers the praise of the pope, eschewing the documentary approach of the triumphant inscription on the Moses Fountain in favour of hyperbole:

SICCA VELVT NILO STAGNANTE AEGYPTVS INVNDAT
DVM SOL SIDEREI SIGNA LEONIS HABET
SIC QVOQ[VE] MAGNANIMO TERRAS MODERANTE LEONE
ARIDA FELICI ROMA REDVNDAT AQVA

The idea of the ruler who brings fertility to dry land had an illustrious heritage in what Gerhardt Ladner has termed the "dry-and-green tales" originally formulated to praise the "saviour-rulers" Alexander the Great and Octavianus Augustus.[23] According to Suetonius, for example, when Augustus donned the purple, a mighty oak tree near death on the Island of Capri was miraculously restored, thus heralding the Golden Age which would characterize the emperor's reign.[24] Ladner has shown how the idea of the dry-and-green tree was conveyed in the Bible, readily adapted to Christian lore, and proliferated in religious art as in the art and panegyric of such rulers as Emperor Frederick II and Duke Cosimo I de'Medici.[25] While there is no mention of a tree *per se* in the verse beneath the *Acqua Felice*, Bianco seems to have equated the fertility of the land made possible by the aqueduct to the idea of Golden Age *renovatio*, and consequently to the "dry-and-green" *topos*, which he then altered to suit the occasion.

The double reference to the word "Leo" is a witty play on words based on the lion of the Sixtine *stemma*, which stands for Sixtus V himself. In the first instance, "Leo" is used in connection with the flooding of the Nile, which occurred from late July to early August. As such, "starry Leo" must be the astrological Sun sign that rules the month of July and is responsible for the fertility of Egypt, much as the Egyptian lions on the Moses Fountain are in part responsible for the fertility of Rome.[26] In the second instance, the "great-hearted Leo," who is compared to "starry Leo" and who "governs the land," is a clear allusion to Pope Sixtus V, who has likewise commanded nature and brought water to Rome, much as his Medieval lions on the Moses Fountain provide for the city.[27]

That the Sixtine lion should be given an added astrological meaning is not a complete surprise, since the zodiac had long played an important role in the lives of emperors, kings and popes.[28] Moreover, as Jonathan Riess has recently shown, the intimate relationship between Good Works and astrology, that is, between virtuous deeds carried out on earth prompting an equally fortuitous configuration of the heavens, leading to salvation, was part of a tradition which was at least as old as the thirteenth century.[29] For his own part, Felice Peretti had been well versed in astrology long before he became pope, and,

[21] Giovanni Battista della Porta executed the relief of the left niche representing *Aaron showing the thirsty people to the water which had sprung up miraculously in the desert* and Flaminio Vacca and Pietro Paolo Olivieri executed the relief of *Joshua selecting the Soldiers to Fight the Amalekites* in the right niche (also called *Gideon choosing his soldiers by watching the way they drank the water*). See Aikin, "Capitoline," 60 ff.; Marder, "Moses Fountain," forthcoming in *Sisto V*; and Fehl, "Hermeticism," *Artibus*, 156-159, whom I follow in the above identifications, *pace* the rod.

[22] The Moses Fountain was dedicated on 15 June 1587. The inscription is as follows: "SIXTVS V. PONT. MAX. PICENVS / AQVAM EX AGRO COLVMNAE / VIA PRAENEST. SINISTRORSVM / MVLTAR. COLLECTIONE VENARVM / DVCTV SINVOSO. A RECEPTACVLO / MIL XX. A CAPITE XXII. ADDVXIT / FELICEMQ. DE NOMINE ANTE PONT. DIXIT. / COEPIT PONT. AN. I. ABSOLVIT III."

[23] Gerhart B. Ladner, "Vegetation Symbolism and the Concept of Renaissance," *De Artibus Opuscula XL. Essays in honour of Erwin Panofsky*, ed. Millard Meiss, 2 vols. (New York, 1961), I, 311-312. I wish to thank Giuseppe Scavizzi for suggesting that this verse refers to a *topos* of water bringing fertility.

[24] Suetonius, *Divus Augustus*, XCII, 2, cited in Ladner, "Vegetation," *De Artibus*, 312, note 40.

[25] Ladner, "Vegetation," *De Artibus*, 303-322, and especially 304-305, 311-312, note 39. Also consult Davidson, "Paul III's Additions," *Art Bulletin*, 403.

[26] For a discussion of the flooding of the Nile when the Sun is in Leo, see Michele Mercati, *Consideratione ... sopra gli Avvertimenti del Sig. Latino Latini. Intorno ad alcune cose scritte nel libro de gli Obelischi di Roma. ...* (Rome, 1590), 138.

[27] Compare the poems on the lions of the Acqua Felice in Bianco, *Aquae Felices*, n.p.

[28] Ernst Cassirer, *The Individual and the Cosmos in Renaissance Philosophy*, trans. with intro by Mario Domandi (Oxford, 1963), 99-107.

[29] Jonathan B. Riess, *Political Ideals in Medieval Italian Art. The Frescoes in the Palazzo dei Priori, Perugia*, Studies in the Fine Arts: Iconography, No. 1 (Ann Arbor, Michigan, 1981), 65-75.

although he would inveigh against judicial astrology in 1586, astrological allusions still figured in the panegyrics written for Sixtus V, and in a device of the pope, published in 1589 by Giovanni Pinadello (fig. 53).[30] In fact, the device is closely related to the verse beneath the *Acqua Felice*. It shows the Sixtine lion standing on his hind legs as if to reach out to the zodiacal Leo in the sky above with the accompanying motto "ARDE-SCITQVE TVENDO." Thus, the pope's emulation of "starry Leo" in the verse accompanying the *Acqua Felice* is complemented by the device in terms of the stance of Leo-Sixtus, echoing that of the astrological Leo, while the solar qualities of the astrological lion, and consequently of Sixtus V, are emphasized by the felicitous turn of phrase.

The "tapestry" of the *Port of Terracina and the Pontine Marsh* is situated on the southernmost end of the west wall above a window, like each of the Good Works on this wall (figs. 43.2 and 47). It shows a view of the port of Terracina, bustling with activity following Sixtus V's improvements, the marsh, dried-up between 1586-1589 and signified by a stretch of land crossed by zig-zag fields, and, in the distance, the buildings of Terracina and surrounding hillsides.[31] In the middle ground, to the left of the dried-up marsh, is a temple surmounted by a figure holding a scepter or rod and flanked by crosses on the lateral pediments. Before the Christianized temple, to the viewer's right, is a nude figure, reclining on the dried-up marsh, resting her right arm on a wheel, and depicted larger than life. A third sculpture is visible near the port enclosure and Pisco Montano, standing with arms extended, and acting as a beacon to sailors.

The accompanying verse presents Sixtus V as far outshining Apollo:

CYNTHIVS VT SIXTVM VIDIT SICCARE PALVDES
PALLENTI TALES MISIT AB ORE SONOS
SOL SVVS EST TERRIS QVID EGO MEA LVMINA FVNDAM
NAM MIHI NEC LICVIT QVOD TIBI SIXTE LICET

In relating how Sixtus V has powers greater than Apollo, who traditionally holds the Sun, the verse alludes to a well known imperial tradition, derived from Hellenistic Sun worship, in which the emperor was called "*Sol Iustitiae*," and equated with Apollo.[32] From this ruler of the Golden Age, Octavianus Augustus derived many of his powers, including his ability to drive out all evil from the empire (mostly barbarians and other subversive forces) thus rendering it safe for its inhabitants. Indeed, Augustus' veneration of Apollo was so great that during his own time he was regarded as Apollo's son, both mytho-historically, by the union of his mother Atia and the serpent-Apollo, and metaphorically, as the promised Apolline child of Virgil's *Fourth Eclogue*.[33] Such imperial assimilation to the Sun-god became common throughout the history of the empire, reaching its apogee during the reign of Constantine, the *Sol Invictus Imperator*.[34] After his conversion to Christianity, Constantine relinquished the title and identified Christ as Virgil's messianic child, giving him, in addition, the emperor's qualities, so that he became the new *Sol Iustitiae*, an epithet for which Constantine would have found patristic, artistic, and biblical justification as well [Malachias IV: 2].[35] Once Christ became a new Apollo, it would not take a great leap of the imagination to give the pope these very same powers, and dur-

[30] By 1564 Felice Peretti owned some 36 books on astrology, tallied in von Pastor, *History*, XXI, 36; and listed in G. Cugnoni, "Documenti Chigiani concernenti Felice Peretti, Sisto V come privato e come pontefice," *Archivio della Società romana di storia patria* V (1882): 1-32, and especially 210-304. At the same time, Sixtus V did publish a bull against astrology. The ramifications of this contradiction are treated in Corinne Mandel, "'Starry Leo,' the Sun, and the Astrological Foundations of Sixtine Rome" *Revue d'art canadienne/Canadian Art Review (RACAR)* XVII, 1 (1990): 17-39.

[31] On Sixtus V's restorations to Terracina and the Pontine Marsh see Rocca, *Biblioteca*, 233-234; Pansa, *Libraria*, 106; and von Pastor, *History*, XXI, 102-103.

[32] Ernst H. Kantorowicz, "Oriens Augusti," *Dumbarton Oaks Papers* XVII (1963): 131, who traces the *topos* back to the ancient Near East. Also consult Jean Gagé, *Apollon Romain: Essai sur le culte d'Apollon et le développement du "vitus Græcus" à Rome des origines à Auguste* (Paris, 1955).

[33] Suetonius, *Divus Augustus*, XCIV, 4 ; Virgil, *Eclogue IV*, 8-9. Also consult Gagé, *Apollon*, 570-571; Manni, "leggenda," *Atene e Roma*, 115-116; and Saward, *Golden Age*, 28, 33. Compare the mythology of Sixtus V's life, discussed in the Introduction, 26 ff.

[34] See Gaston H. Halsberghe, *The Cult of Sol Invictus* (Leiden, 1972); and Kantorowicz, "Oriens," *Dumbarton Oaks*, 119-135.

[35] Kantorowicz, "Oriens," *Dumbarton Oaks*, 135-149, and especially 140. Also consult Marcello Fagiolo, "Theodoricus-Christus-Sol. Nuove ipotesi sul mausoleo," *Arheoloski Vestnik. Acta Archaeologica* XXIII (1972): 83-156, for a later application of solar imagery.

ing the Investiture Struggle the popes adopted the analogy, seeing themselves as the Sun and the emperor as the lesser light, the Moon. So appealing was the comparison that the jurists entered the pope-as-Sun analogy into the books of Canon Law.[36]

This tradition received new impetus during the Renaissance at which time kings joined popes and emperors in adopting the epithet. The French king Charles VIII (1483-1498), for example, seems to have resuscitated a Medieval trend, which would culminate with Louis XIV in the Baroque period, of likening himself to Constantine and taking the encomium *Sol Invictus* for himself (much as the Emperors Maximilian I and Charles V would rightfully do later, as the Frankish successors to Charlemagne).[37] At the papal courts, the assimilation of Christ's vicar to Apollo was made at least as early as Nicholas V's pontificate (Parentucelli, 1447-55), and continued to hold sway through the pontificates of such Golden Age rulers as Popes Julius II and Leo X, Paul III and Gregory XIII.[38] Thus, the equation pope-Sun, with its long and illustrious heritage, must have seemed eminently appropriate to Sixtus V in its allegorical and historical implications. Like the ancient emperors of Rome, Sixtus V had driven evil from his *respublica*, symbolized by the draining of the swamps which rid the area of malaria and rendered it fit for agricultural production. Unlike the ancient emperors and even the great Apollo, who had unsuccessfully attempted to drain the swamps, and who may well be represented in the fresco beside the Pisco Montano as the beacon to sailors,[39] Sixtus V not only accomplished the feat, but did it in a relatively short span of time, thus proving by example that the Christian Sun was more powerful than the pagan Sun.

I have discussed the *Treasure at Castel Sant'Angelo* in the previous chapter, together with the other *imprese* in the Salone, but, for reasons of clarity, shall indicate briefly my interpretation of the *imprese* and their verses as they appear in the decorative scheme. The *Treasure*, situated beside *Terracina* on the west wall, commemorates the enormous amount of *scudi* deposited by Sixtus V in the chests of Castel Sant'Angelo in order to protect and defend the *respublica Christiana* (figs. 43.3 and 32). The *impresa* of the *Treasure* shows a lion seated atop a chest being crowned by an angel. As an *impresa*, the image contains both pagan antique and Christian meaning, and, as a Sixtine *impresa*, the Christian component necessarily includes Franciscan content. In its pagan sense, the *Treasure* may well refer to the abundance of gold during the civilized Golden Age of Augustus and his successors, including Sixtus V. In its Christian-Franciscan sense, the *Treasure* is a symbol for the ark of Noah, the high altar, the tomb of the Resurrected Christ, and the *alter Christus*, Saint Francis, all of which point to the Second Coming of Christ and the realization of the millenium during the pontificate of Sixtus V. The verse accompanying the *Treasure* chastizes Plato, who was foolish enough to have banned gold from his ideal city, and lauds Sixtus V, who hordes it, as did his Old Testament precursors, in order to enrich and protect the Christian commonwealth.[40]

Situated in the center of the west wall, the "tapestry" of the *Vatican Library* shows the Salone Sistino in the process of being decorated (figs. 43.4 and 48).[41] Most of the narratives, historical figures and personifications have been completed on the vault, walls, and pilasters, and await embellishment with

[36] Ernst H. Kantorowicz, "On Transformations of Apolline Ethics," *Charites: Studien zur Altertumwissenschaft*, ed K. Schauenburg (Bonn, 1957), 269-270; idem, *The King's Two Bodies. A Study in Medieval Political Theology* (Princeton, New Jersey, 1957), 97-143.

[37] Scheller, "Imperial," *Simiolus*, 17; Ernst H. Kantorowicz, "Kingship under the Impact of Scientific Jurisprudence," *Selected Studies* (Locust Valley, New York, 1965), 165; idem, "Oriens," *Dumbarton Oaks*, 162-177. Also see Barbara Russano Hanning, "Glorious Apollo: Poetic and Political Themes in the First Opera," *Renaissance Quarterly* XXXII (1980): 485-513; and Fagiolo, "Dai Palazzi ai Giardini," in *L'arte dei papi*, 207.

[38] Schröter, "Hügel Apollons," *Römische Quartalschrift*, 208-240; Cox-Rearick, *Dynasty*, 184, 198, 204-205; Stinger, *Renaissance*, 274, 384, note 39; and McGinness, "Rhetoric," 336 ff.

[39] The Pisco Montano is a rock which looks remarkably like a lighthouse in the Sixtine fresco. If this was intended, then there was precedent for such a transformation. See Jacks, "Meta," *Architectura*, 160-161, who also discusses the analogy between the Pisco Montano, the meta and the obelisk, including those raised by Sixtus V. This has implications for the fundamental meaning of the Sixtine obelisks as well as my identification of the statue as Apollo. See Chapter IV, 137 ff, below, as well as my forthcoming "Simbolismo ermetico," *Sisto V*, for this symbolism.

[40] See Appendix I, 216, n. 60, for the verse.

[41] On the construction and decoration of the Vatican Library see Fontana, *Della trasportatione*, 82-98; Pansa, *Libraria*; Rocca, *Biblioteca*; von Pastor, *History*, XXII, 291-299; and, recently, Böck, *Dekorationsprogramm*.

grotteschi, and additional personifications, *vis-à-vis* the more traditional method of painting from ceiling downwards.

The verse beneath the *Vatican Library* alludes to three Good Works of Sixtus V: the treasure amassed at Castel Sant'Angelo, the papal fleet and, of course, the library.[42] It also praises Sixtus V's preparedness for times of war and peace, and his patronage of the arts:

NON SAT ERAT SIXTO CLASSEM, NVMMOSQ[VE] PARARE,
EXTRVCTA EST ETIAM BIBLIOTHECA SIBI,
SCILICET VT PACIS BELLORVM, ET TEMPORA CVRET,
ATQVE VTRVMQVE OBEAT MARTIS, ET ARTIS OPVS

The duty of a ruler to care for his people in times of peace as in times of war was made binding in the *proemium* of Justinian's *Institutes* (compiled between 527/28-534), in which Plato's philosopher-king is implicitly held up as a model for all rulers to follow: "It is expedient that the Imperial Majesty not only be distinguished by arms, but also be protected by laws, so that government may be justly administered in time of both war and peace ... ."[43] Ernst Kantorowicz has shown how this formula continued to hold sway in the Renaissance, especially in emblem books, and how, during the sixteenth century, the *impresa* was modified somewhat, so that peace, symbolized by a law book, became "letters," and finally "arts."[44] Of course, this sixteenth century alteration of the *topos* had antique sanction, particularly in connection with the emperor as ruler of the Golden Age. In numismatics, as in panegyric, such exemplary gods as Mars and Apollo, or Hercules and Mercury, were often paired and compared to the emperor in order to assert his proficiency in both the martial and liberal arts. Through war, the emperor would extend the empire, achieve peace, and bestow upon his subjects the benefits of learning and the arts, essential ingredients for the civilized Golden Age of Virgil's *Fourth Eclogue*.[45]

The verse beneath the *Vatican Library* "tapestry" thus combines the practical duties of the terrestrial ruler with the ideal characteristics of the Golden Age king in order to describe Sixtus V's Good Work. The phrase "for times of peace and war," which refers to the traditional duties of the emperor as codified by Justinian, is used in a general sense to characterize the pope's duties in his position of *rex*. Conversely, the phrase "war and art" is used to characterize the form and purpose of the Vatican Library in particular as a place of great artistry and scholarship (art), indicative of the flourishing of the arts during the Golden Age, and as a repository of Christian tracts which may be used in the written war against the Protestants and their *Ecclesiastica Historia* (war). Thus, having constructed the library, prepared a papal fleet to combat Turkish pirate ships, and deposited millions of gold *scudi* at Castel Sant'Angelo, Sixtus V has proven himself to be both the perfect Golden Age ruler, and a most worthy successor to Peter, "Prince of the Apostles."

The next "tapestry" in the progression represents the *League of Christian Princes*, a Good Work not actually achieved by Sixtus V (figs. 43.5 and 35). It shows a lion standing in a boat holding a key and a chain-link extending to the ears of eight crowned animals standing on the shore. In its ancient, pagan context, the *impresa* shows Sixtus V as peacemaker following the lead of Mercury-Hercules, who achieved peace by means of "eloquent" chains. The key held by Sixtus V signifies

[42] On the papal fleet see Pansa, *Libraria*, 46; Rocca, *Biblioteca*, 38-40; and von Pastor, *History*, XXI, 97-99.

[43] Justinian, *Institutes*, proemium quoted in Kantorowicz, "Kingship," *Selected Studies*, 160. Compare the inscription beneath the figure of *Lex Civilis* that once adorned the long courtyard façade of the Vatican Library, cited in Fontana, *Della trasportatione*, 96.

[44] Kantorowicz, "Kingship," *Selected Studies*, 160; Schiller, "Imperial," *Simiolus*, 16; Saward, *Golden Age*, 144. For seventeenth century versions of the *topos*, see George Withers in Robert J. Clements, *Picta Poesis: Literary and Humanistic Theory in Renaissance Emblem Books* (Rome, 1960), 74; and Cervantes' *Don Quixote* in Levin, *Myth*, 146.

[45] Virgil, *Eclogue IV*, 26-30; Saward, *Golden Age*, 15, 106-107.

that he is a regal peacekeeper and successor to Hercules in his capacity of law giver. In its Christian and Franciscan sense, the *impresa* presents Sixtus V as Christ's rightful vicar in possession of the key(s) given to Peter; as the Angel-King of Apocalypse, who has the key to the bottomless pit and the chain to lock up the devil; as an *alter Franciscus*, endowed with the ability to converse with animals and to render inimical species friendly; and as a modern day manifestation of the *Logos*, whose spoken powers must also be complemented by the use of force. The verse beneath the *League* presents Sixtus V as the true Christian Mercury, Saint Michael, whose peaceful activities surpass those of the pagan god, since inspired by the true faith.[46]

The *Harbour of Civitavecchia* "tapestry" is the last in the sequence of Good Works on the west wall (figs. 43.6 and 49). It contains a representation of the harbour of Rome after Sixtus V enlarged and refurbished it as a military port in 1587, and includes the aqueduct constructed by the pope in order to bring fresh drinking water to the community.[47]

The verse accompanying the "tapestry" suggests that Sixtus V's power extends to nature and the elements, which he may control at will:

VNDAE SVNT LIQVIDAE, SOLIDVM SED MARMOR HABETVR
MARMOR VI TRAHITVR, SPONTE SED VNDA FLVIT
QVID MIRVM EST IGITVR DVCAT SI FORNICE RIVOS
QVANDO ETIAM SIXTVS MARMORA VASTA TRAHITI

In a general sense, the references to Sixtus V's facility in moving marble for construction of the harbour recall the famous statement of Suetonius that Octavianus Augustus had transformed a Rome made of brick into a Rome made of marble by the end of his reign.[48] Similarly, the references to Sixtus V's facility in directing "streams on arches" conjures reminiscences of the great aqueducts built by the caesars, also referred to as "streams on arches" in antiquity, and draws attention to the great aqueduct of Civitavecchia represented in the feigned tapestry above.

That Sixtus V has manifest powers to counter the laws of nature, and to use them to his own advantage and to the advantage of his subjects, suggests a more pointed allusion to the powers of Orpheus, who could make wild beasts, rocks, even the hardest of oaks bend and follow him.[49] This notion of a god capable of moving mountains was naturally transferred to earthly rulers during the Empire, and by the Renaissance the *topos* was commonly associated with the Golden Age.[50] Like the *topoi* considered so far, this *topos* of a pagan ruler able to influence the elements was syncretized with Christian lore and applied to Christian rulers, a task made easy since Christ himself had, from apostolic times, been compared to Orpheus.[51] By the pontificate of Sixtus IV, our pope's namesake, Christ's vicar was considered to have eclipsed Orpheus' powers and to have been able to move anything he so desired, since imbued with divine wisdom derived from the true God.[52] Thus, when Bianco asks "what wonder is it" that Sixtus V may command the most imposing of elements, it is likely a veiled reference to the pope's inherent superiority over his pagan model, a reference that would be entirely in keeping with the rhetorical method adopted throughout the verses in the Salone dei Papi and in the panegyric of Sixtine Rome.[53]

The "tapestry" of *Monte Cavallo*, situated on the north wall, shows the Quirinal with the Dioscuri, newly restored,

[46] See Appendix I, 216, n. 62, for the verse.

[47] On the harbour of Civitavecchia see Fontana, *Della trasportatione*, 103v-104; Pansa, *Libraria*, 115-116; Rocca, *Biblioteca*, 242-243; and von Pastor, *History*, XXI, 105.

[48] Suetonius, *Divus Augustus*, XXVII, 3. For an application of this statement to a "modern" secular ruler, see Richelson, *Studies*, 45; and for its application to the papacy, Stinger, *Renaissance*, 247, 385, notes 41-42.

[49] Ovid, *Metamorphoses*, X, 86- XI, 66.

[50] Karla Langedijk, "Baccio Bandinelli's Orpheus: A Political Message," *Mitteilungen des Kunsthistorischen Institutes in Florenz* XX (1972): 37-51.

[51] For Early Christian literary and artistic sources see *Paulys Real-Encyclopädie der Classischen Altertumswissenschaft. Neue Bearbeitung*, ed. Georg Wissowa, Wilhelm Kroll, 24 vols. (Stuttgart, 1939), XVIII, 1314-1315. For Orpheus-Christ in the *Ovide Moralisé*, see the discussion in Langedijk, "Orpheus," *Mitteilungen*, 40.

[52] Stinger, *Renaissance*, 384, note 39.

[53] For a comparison between Sixtus V and Orpheus, consult Pietro Paolo de Valle, *Ad S. D. N. Sixtum Quintum Pont. Max. S. P. Q. R. Oratio Ex Tempore Habita, ... Apud Almae Urbis Celebre Templum Sanctae Mariae de Aracœli* (Rome, 1590).

moved by Sixtus V to this location in 1589, and awaiting the fountain which was to have been placed between them, and a view down the Via Pia, past the Fontana Felice and through the Porta Pia, to the fields of newly irrigated Rome (figs. 44.7 and 50; also refer hereafter to fig. 41).[54]

The accompanying verse praises the renovations made by Sixtus V to the Quirinal:

STRVCTA DOMVS, DVCTI FONTES, VIA APERTA, CABALLI
TRANSPOSITI, ATQ[VE] VNO EST AREA STRATA LOCO,
O FELIX NIMIRVM VIA, EQVI, DOMVS, AREA, FONTES,
DVM VIVENT VATIS CARMINA, SIXTE, TVI

The building referred to in the verse is most likely the Quirinal Palace, begun by Pope Gregory XIII and largely completed by Sixtus V. The fountains, of course, refer to the terminal Moses Fountain and the subsidiary fountains of the Acqua Felice, including the Quattro Fontane (1587), just barely visible in the fresco.[55] The roadway refers to the dominant thoroughfare of the *Monte Cavallo* "tapestry," namely the Via Pia, which Sixtus V realigned and restored. The horses are the Dioscuri of Phidias and Praxiteles, believed to have been moved from Alexandria and erected in the center of the Baths of Constantine by the emperor, and representing Alexander and Bucephalus, or alternately, Castor and Pollux, the "twin stars" charged to protect the city of Rome.[56] The region refers to the grading of the Piazza delle Terme, as well as the newly built and restored streets on the Quirinal hill. Finally, the reference to the "songs of your poet, Sixtus," evokes the god Pan, poet of Arcadia, and, even more, suggests that Sixtus V is to be aligned with Virgil, who had himself challenged Pan to a singing contest in the messianic *Fourth Eclogue*.[57] The phrase also alludes to the many songs composed by biblical leaders, from Moses onwards, to give thanksgiving to God for victories and blessings, to pray for the newly wedded or the deceased. But above all, and given the context of the *imprese*, it suggests the songs sung on the last days, particularly "the canticle of Moses, the servant of God, and the canticle of the Lamb," sung by the angels in honour of God [Revelation XV: 3]. As both the new emperor Augustus, and the new poet-author of the Golden Age and of the millenium, Sixtus V thus makes doubly sure that Rome, the center of the universal Church, is ready to receive Christ on his Second Coming.

The "tapestry" of the *City of Montalto* at the northernmost end of the east wall is situated above a niche, like the accompanying "tapestries" of this wall. It shows an apparently idealized view of the town where Felice Peretti was schooled after Sixtus V made it a city and episcopal see, and enriched it with walls (figs. 45.8 and 51).[58]

The verse beneath the fresco points up the reciprocal benefits bestowed on the future pope by the town, and on the town by the pope, by playing on a well - known phrase in which the ruler is called father of his country:

CVM TE SIXTE OLIM SVB LVMINIS EDIDIT ORAS
PATRIA DICTA FVIT TVNC VERA PARENS.
SED MODO DVM FIRMIS CIRCVNDAS MOENIBVS ILLAM,
QVIS PATRIAE VERVM TE NEGET ESSE PATREM?

The phrase *"pater patriae"* was first said of Cicero. It was soon given to Augustus by the Senate, the Equestrian Order, and the

[54] On Sixtus V's building and restoration works on the Quirinal, see Fontana, *Della trasportatione*, 100-101v; von Pastor, *History*, XXII, 301-302; and Marder, "Quirinal," *JSAH*, 283-294.

[55] The subsidiary fountains of the Acqua Felice are listed in Bezzi, ed, "IV Centenario," *Rassegna italiana*, 75.

[56] See the discussion of the Dioscuri in Pansa, *Libraria*, 108-113; and Rocca, *Biblioteca*, 254-263. Also consult Augusto Donini, "I cavalli di Monte Cavallo a Roma su una medaglia di Sisto V," *Numismatica* I (1960): 64-73; Aikin, "Capitoline," 121-122; and Marcello Fagiolo and Maria Luisa Madonna, "La Roma di Pio IV II: Il sistema dei centri direzionali e la rifondazione della città," *Arte Illustrata* VI, 54 (August 1973): 202-203. It is worth mentioning at this point that the Medicean *stemma* held by the personification in the lunette of *Monte Cavallo* in the Libreria Segreta of the Vatican Library, reproduced as fig. 12 in *idem*, in all likelihood refers to the providential Medicean support that was instrumental in Cardinal Montalto's accession to the papacy, rather than to Pope Pius IV.

[57] Virgil, *Eclogue IV*, 56-59.

[58] On the city of Montalto see Fontana, *Della trasportatione*, 103v; Pansa, *Libraria*, 113; Rocca, *Biblioteca*, 264-265; von Pastor, *History*, XXI, 111; Marco Kuveiller, "Lettere inedite sull'ampliamento di Loreto e di Montalto Marche," *Storia della città* 12-13 (1979): 171-172; and Parisciani, *Sisto V*, especially 139-157.

Roman people, and thereafter became a common Golden Age encomium of the emperor.[59] During the Medieval period a variation of the phrase was used to describe the pope, who became the common father of the Christian commonwealth.[60] The antique form of praise was used again in the Renaissance when, in 1465, the Florentine Signoria gave the title posthumously to Cosimo de'Medici il Vecchio, creator of the Florentine Golden Age.[61] The phrase was soon adopted by popes, emperors, and kings, and saw continued popularity through the pontificate of Sixtus V, when it was commonplace to hear of "Sixtus V, *pater patriae*."[62]

The first "fatherland" referred to in the verse is not Rome, the seat of the papacy, as one might expect, but Montalto, the town in the Marches where Felice Peretti was schooled. By referring to Montalto as the "fatherland," the provincial town-*cum*-city is raised to the status of Rome, the center of universal empire in antiquity and, in the Medieval period, the center of universal Ecclesia as reflected on earth. As the town of Felice Peretti's upbringing and formation in the Franciscan seminary, it must have seemed entirely fitting to Bianco, and to Sixtus V, to characterize Montalto as both the father and the fatherland of the future pope. Moreover, the reference to the "regions of light" under which Sixtus V was reared must surely refer not only to Saint Lucy, the patron saint of light, on whose feast day, 13 December, Felice Peretti was born, but also to the Virgin, the "*stella maris*," for whom Sixtus V held a great devotion, as well as to Saint Francis himself, the *alter Christus* and earth's Sun. The second "fatherland" also refers to Montalto and carries with it the allusions to Rome noted in the foregoing. The "strong walls" built by Sixtus V to protect the fatherland complete the Roman allusions by implicitly comparing the pope to the emperor, who likewise built fortifications to safeguard his subjects. It also conjures reminiscences of the Heavenly City, surrounded with walls. Finally, the assertion that Sixtus V is the "real father of the fatherland" not only points to the beneficence which he bestowed upon Montalto, but also surely implies the pope's right as Christ's vicar to rule the temporal sphere.

The "tapestry" of the *Extirpation of the Bandits* follows the *City of Montalto* in the progression of the east wall (figs. 45.9 and 29). It commemorates Sixtus V's expulsion of bandits and prostitutes in allegorical form, showing the lion atop a mountain, brandishing his thunderbolt at subversive wolves in order to shelter his flock of sheep. In this *impresa* Sixtus V is presented as a second Jupiter, exercising *poena* in order to maintain peace and harmony within his dominion, and as a second lion of the tribe of Judah, caring for the faithful and fulminating against heretic and infidel alike. The accompanying verse carries on the analogy by equating Sixtus V to a sovereign pastor, who maintains peace by neutralizing his enemies.[63]

The next "tapestry" on the east wall is the *Abundance created by Sixtus V*, a Good Work which utilizes an *impresa* in order to illustrate the renewed food supply brought to Rome by the pope (figs. 45.10 and 26). Of all the *imprese*, the *Abundance* most readily suggests the Golden Age theme since the pose of the lion shaking the tree is one traditionally used to evoke Golden Age prosperity. In its context in the Salone dei Papi attention is drawn to this Good Work, as though in recognition that the viewer would immediately grasp its meaning, by the feigned curtain pulled taught beneath the "ta-

[59] Manni, "leggenda," *Atene e Roma*, 115-116.

[60] Michael Wilks, *The Problem of Sovereignty in the Middle Ages: The Papal Monarchy with Augustinus Triumphus and the Publicists*, Cambridge Studies in Medieval Life and Thought, new series, v. 9, (Cambridge, 1963), 36.

[61] E. H. Gombrich, "Renaissance and Golden Age," *Norm and Form: Studies in the art of the Renaissance* (1966; London & New York, 1978), 32-34.

[62] Consult Cox-Rearick, *Dynasty*, 34-35. For Sixtus V as father of the fatherland, or variations thereof, see, for example, Ugonio, *De Lingua Latina Oratio*, 18: "Patria patrem semper appellent"; Gregorio Piccha, *Oratio Ad Sixtum V. Pont. Opt. Max. Pro dignitate nuper in Evangelistam Palloctum collata* (Rome, 1588), n.p.: "Patris patriae"; Nicholaus Munster in ... *Carmina A Variis Auctoribus in Obeliscum Conscripta* (Rome, 1586), 31: "Parens Urbis, & Oribs"; and Maurizio Bressio, *Ad Summum Pontificem Oratoris Oratio, Ad Sixtum V. Pont. Opt. Max. Romae in aula Regum habita 11 die Septemb. MDLXXXVI ...* (Rome, n.d.), n.p.: "Sixte humani parens generis."

[63] See Appendix I, 217, n. 66, for the verse.

pestry" to fit snugly between the flanking "columns," in contradistinction to those beneath the accompanying "tapestries" on the east wall that hang down to one side to fill the gap between the "tapestries" and their ill-fitting, flanking "columns." In sum, it is as though the *quadratura* of the east wall was designed first and foremost to accommodate the *Abundance* (and hence to balance the southernmost window of the west wall facing it), a priority which then resulted in the skewing of the remaining "columns" in relation to the "tapestries" which they flank. The accompanying verse provides the Old Testament prefiguration of Christian abundance in the person of Moses, who fed his "grumbling" people manna in the desert, and glorifies Sixtus V as a new and improved Moses, satisfying his subjects with eucharistic sustenance.[64] Although manifestly different from the other verses accompanying Good Works of Sixtus V, since pointed reference is made to a biblical ruler, rather than insinuating the connection to the imperial rule of Augustan Rome, the verse does, nonetheless, conform to the norm when read according to the passage in the Book of Wisdom XVI: 20 ff. In this Book, written for and ostensibly by a king, the rule of Moses in the desert is held up as an example for all subsequent rulers, particularly his actions towards his people in procuring for them the life-sustaining manna. At the same time, this passage from the Book of Wisdom, as interpreted by Early Christian commentators, provides the reason why Sixtus V's power is superior to that of Moses, since the manna fed to the Israelites in the desert was melted by the Sun of Christ, and replaced by the true Christian food [Wisdom XVI: 27 ff].[65]

The last "tapestry" in the series represents the *Holy House of Loreto*, home of the Virgin's sanctuary since the thirteenth century (figs. 45.11 and 52). The Duomo of Loreto is given a prominent place in the rear foreground, silhouetted against the sky, while around it is the fortified wall strengthened by the pope in 1587 to protect the city.[66] On the foreground ridge there is a farmer and his animals, and, beneath the plateau, a shepherd and his flock, vignettes suggesting the pastoral nature of the Virgin's abode, both past and present.

The accompanying verse continues the imagery of the fortified and peaceful city, commemorating the wall built by Sixtus V around the city of Loreto, and utilizes the <u>topos</u> of the farmer caring for his flock:

FOETAM VRBEM POPVLIS PICENO IN LITTORE SIXTVS
MOENIBVS INCINXIT, PONTIFICEMQ[VE] DEDIT,
SIC TENEROS SEPTIS INCLVDIT VILLICVS AGNOS
CVSTODEMQ[VE] ILLIS DONAT HABERE SVVM

The notion of the ruler as farmer or shepherd caring for his flock is also enunciated in the verse beneath the *Extirpation* in the Salone. There, as here, the *topos* is used to emphasize the pope's beneficence toward the faithful and his ruthlessness against the infidel and heretic in his capacity of "sovereign pastor." The verse of the *Holy House* also evokes the imperial nature of Sixtus V's building works in a manner not unlike that used in the verse beneath the "tapestry" of the other walled city, the *City of Montalto*. In similar fashion, it too evokes the Heavenly Jerusalem. Lastly, the references to the "decaying city" of Loreto, and to the improvements affected by the pope, evoke Golden Age restoration and reclamation.

[64] See Appendix I, 217-218, n. 67, for the verse.

[65] Franz Joseph Dölger, *Sol Salutis: Gebet und Gesang im Christlichen Altertum mit Besonderen Rücksicht auf die Ostung in Gebet und Liturgie* (Munster, Westfal, 1925), 119 ff.

[66] On the work done on the city of Loreto by Sixtus V see Fontana, *Della trasportatione*, 103v; Pansa, *Libraria*, 108; Rocca, *Biblioteca*, 253-254; von Pastor, *History*, XXI, 112-113; Francesco Paolo Fiore, "La 'Citta' Felice' di Loreto," *Ricerche di Storia dell'arte* IV (1977): 37-55; and Kuveiller, "Lettere," *Storia della città*, 171-172. See Kathleen Weil-Garris, *The Santa Casa di Loreto. Problems in Cinquecento Sculpture*, 2 vols. (New York & London, 1977), I, fig. 1, for a view of Loreto and its fortifications in 1540.

It has been shown how the Good Works of Sixtus V form a homogeneous unit when viewed collectively, since all are represented as feigned tapestries, and the majority have landscape settings. It has also been shown how the landscape format evokes imperial, and particularly Augustan, dreams of the Golden Age, and how such Golden Age allusions are confirmed in the accompanying verses, which draw on a host of *topoi* traditionally used in connection with the larger theme of the Golden Age. In this context, it remains to determine the specific Golden Age myth from which the unknown iconographer derived his initial inspiration and which led him and/or Bianco to the particular selection of Golden Age *sub-topoi* - a selection which sometimes repeats *topoi* (i.e., "sovereign pastor," master of the elements), rather than draw upon the myriad *sub-topoi* remaining. The answer, I believe, is to be found in Virgil's *Fourth Eclogue*, and particularly in the well known and oft' quoted phrase "tuus iam regnat Apollo."[67]

To begin with the verse beneath the *Acqua Felice*, the references to the Sun and to Leo, the astrological Sun sign, ultimately point to Phoebus Apollo, who is the Sun.[68] This connection is borne out by the adjacent verse of *Terracina*, which explicitly speaks of Apollo as the Sun. The verse of the *Treasure* lauds Sixtus V's stockpiling of gold and, as such, invites a comparison to Apollo, and Augustus-Apollo, who ruled a civilized Golden Age "rich with gold," while the foolhardy Plato was the mythological son of Apollo.[69] The verse beneath the *Vatican Library* refers to peace, art and war, insinuating a connection between Apollo as a martial exemplar, and, more importantly, as Apollo Musagetes, inventor of the liberal arts and patron god of libraries.[70] In this context, the reference to Mercury as peace-maker in the *League* would have reminded an erudite viewer that Mercury derived this power from Apollo, who gave Mercury his caduceus. Furthermore, Apollo himself was called God of the sky, of the earth, and of the underworld in antiquity, powers that accord well with the verse of the *League*, and he was sometimes represented aloft in a boat, in the manner of the Sixtine lion. Even the chain-link itself was equated to the strength of the Sun in antique lore.[71] Sixtus V's facility with nature in the verse of the *Harbour of Civitavecchia*, which I have equated to Orpheus' powers, would, by further association, allude to Apollo, the sometime father and teacher of Orpheus and original commander of Nature.[72] In the verse accompanying *Monte Cavallo*, Sixtus V and Virgil himself owe their very art to Apollo, the god and inventor of poetry.[73] The *pater patriae* of the *City of Montalto* also refers to Apollo, in this case, Pater Apollo.[74] The verse of the *Extirpation*, equating Sixtus V to a sovereign pastor, is also an allusion to Apollo Nomius, the god of shepherds and prototype of the kingly shepherd ruling the civilized Golden Age, while the thunderbolt held by the Sixtine lion belongs equally to Jupiter and Apollo.[75] The verse beneath the *Abundance*, equating Sixtus V to Moses as providers of eucharistic food for their people may also be related to Apollo as provider for his flock. More importantly, the fact that Moses descended with the tablets of the law from Mount Sinai with his face emitting rays of light "from the conversation of the Lord" [Exodus XXXIV: 29], suggests that Moses, like Apollo, and Christ, is the *Sol Iustitiae*. And finally, the reference to the chief priest and farmer of the *Holy House* applies equally to Pastor Apollo and Apollo Nomius.

106

[67] Virgil, *Eclogue IV*, 10. This phrase was appropriated for Sixtus V in Francesco Suares, *Ad Sanctiss. et Beatissimum Patrum Sixtum Quinctum Pontificem Maximum Panegyricus Primus* (Rome, 1587), 11: "REGNAT NVNC SIXTVS PONTIFEX"; and Galesino, "Vita," 120.

[68] On Phoebus Apollo see Valeriano, *Hieroglyphica*, I, esp. xix; Gyraldo, *De Deis Gentium*, 306, 335; and Cartari, *Imagini*, 56-99, and especially 71, for Apollo as a lion. Also consult Origen, *Contra Celsum*, IV: 48, trans, intro & notes Henry Chadwick (Cambridge, 1953), 223, for Apollo as the Sun.

[69] Virgil, *Georgics*, II, 148-176. For gold as the Sun and hence Apollo, see Valeriano, *Hieroglyphica*, LIX, xxiv. For Plato as Apollo's son, see Origen, *Contra Celsum*, I: 37; VI, 8. Compare Tertullian, *Apology*, XLVI: 6 in *Apologetical Works and Minucius Felix Octavius*, trans. Rudolph Arbesmann, Sister Emily Joseph Daly, Edwin A. Quain, The Fathers of the Church. A New Translation (New York, 1950), 112, who exclaims "O foolish Apollo!"

[70] On Apollo Musagetes see Gyraldo, *De Deis Gentium*, 324, 342, 484; Cartari, *Imagini*, 61-62; and Valeriano, *Hieroglyphica*, XLVII, xxvi.

[71] Cartari, *Imagini*, 62-63; *idem*, 66-67, and Gyraldo, *De Deis Gentium*, 309, for Sol-Apollo in a boat, like the Sixtine lion in the *impresa*; Mercati, *Gli Obelischi*, 128, for the boat as a symbol of Sol-Apollo; Gyraldo, *De Deis Gentium*, 450, and Valeriano, *Hieroglyphica*, III, x, for Sol-Hercules; and *idem*, LX, xiv, for the chain-link and the Sun. For Mercury as the Sun, see *idem*, XXIX, ii; and Arnobius, *Adversus Nationes Libri VII*, IV, 17; VI, 12, in Halsberghe, *Cult*, 11. Ultimately, the solar allusions of the Good Works could well, and in my view should, be read as referring to Mercury and the *Logos*.

[72] Gyraldo, *De Deis Gentium*, 177; Cartari, *Imagini*, 71. Compare Valeriano, *Hieroglyphica*, XXIII, vii and viii, for the musical connection.

[73] Valeriano, *Hieroglyphica*, L, xiii and xvi; Cartari, *Imagini*, 61-62.

[74] Gyraldo, *De Deis Gentium*, 312. Also consult Schröter, "Hügel Apollons," *Römische Quartalschrift*, 210, 220 ff.

[75] Gyraldo, *De Deis Gentium*, 313; Cartari, *Imagini*, 76-77; and for the thunderbolt of Jupiter-Apollo, *idem*, 56. Also consult Tertullian, *Apology*, XIV: 4; and Minucius Felix, *Octavius*, XXIII: 5. For Apollo displacing Jupiter, see Lactantius, *The Divine Institutes*, VII, trans. William Fletcher, *Ante-Nicene Christian Library. Translations of the Writings of the Fathers down to A.D. 325: The Works of Lactantius*, ed. Alexander Roberts, James Donaldson, 2 vols. (Edinburgh, 1871), I, 19.

The underlying allusions to Apollo, which may well have been culled from one or more popular Renaissance source-book(s), such as those by Gyraldi, Cartari, and Valeriano, and/or the writings of the Fathers of the Church, thus serve to underscore the Virgilian assertion that Apollo ruled the civilized Golden Age of Augustus, the age in which Christ chose to manifest himself on earth. On the one hand, by assimilating Sixtus V to Apollo, it is clear that the pope has become the new ruler of the Golden Age in emulation of the pagan god and emperor. On the other hand, by clearly asserting Sixtus V's patent superiority over Apollo in the *Terracina* verse, it is equally clear that the Sixtine Golden Age is the only genuine one, since informed by belief in the true Sun, namely Christ and the Church, the "starry" Virgin. On another level, it may well be a tacit commentary on King Philip II-Apollo of Spain, and his pretensions to world rulership which, by the late 1580's, had reached almost unbearable proportions for the pope.[76] But, more importantly, it asserts in visual form a favourite *topos* of the preachers and panegyricists of Sixtine Rome, who glorified Sixtus V as the Sun, sometimes even equating him to Apollo.[77] No clearer testimony to the pope's assimilation to Sol-Apollo-Christ could be found to secure the reading in the Salone dei Papi.

In addition to the pagan component of the imperial verses in the form of Apollo, solar ruler of the Golden Age, the atypical verse of the *Abundance* and the formal preference given to the rendering of the "tapestry" and its flanking columns suggests that there is a second Hebrew component over which Sixtus V emerges victorious on the lower register of the Salone dei Papi. Just as the verse of *Terracina*, the second "tapestry" in the series, reinforces the fact that Apollo is the "starry Leo" of the *Acqua Felice*, and confirms the allusions to Apollo in the remaining Good Works, the verse of the *Abundance*, the second to last "tapestry" in the series, reinforces the importance of the Moses Fountain painstakingly represented in the *Acqua Felice*, and confirms the allusions to Moses in the remaining Good Works. In short, the first "tapestry" in the series contains the clues which allow the viewer to unravel the many layers contained within the remaining "tapestries" and their verses. Lest one question the propriety of the reading of the *Acqua Felice*, or the order in which the layers ought to be unravelled, the second verse in the progression verifies the parameters for the ancient, pagan reading, while near the end of the series the *Abundance* provides the second reading according to the Old Testament and the life of Moses.

To begin with the *Acqua Felice*, then, the figure of Moses holding the rod in the Moses Fountain clearly points to the water struck by Moses from the rock shortly following his second descent from Mount Sinai during the Exodus from Egypt [Exodus XVII: 1-7; Numbers XX: 1-13], and serves to assimilate Moses to "great-hearted Leo" who brings water to the modern-day Romans.[78] In this sense, the statue atop the temple in the *Terracina* fresco may well allude to Moses as well as to Apollo, while the draining of the swamps has certain affinities to the parting of the Red Sea, since in each case the waters were moved by means of divine light [Exodus XIV: 19-31]. The *impresa* of the *Treasure* signifies the Ark of the Covenant that Moses built according to God's specifications, and in which he stored the treasures of the synagogue, much as Pope Sixtus V stores gold in his treasure chest. The *Library* also points to the

[76] For King Philip II as Apollo see von Barghahn, *Age of Gold*, I, 117 ff.

[77] For Sixtus V as Phoebus Apollo, or better than Phoebus Apollo see, for example, Bianco, *Epigrammata*, 14: " ... En ut Mons Altus septem supere minet Vrbis / Collibus? hunc posthac vos habitare decet. / Vos ille hospitio excipiet, vos ille fouebit, / Et praerit vestris alter Apollo choris. / Nec vos Parnassum montem liquisse pigebit: / Nam fuit iste biceps, ast erit ille triceps;" *idem* in ... *Carmina*, 24: "Quem Phoebo Aegyptus, quem Augustis Roma dicauit; / Tu lapidem hunc subdis, Maxime Sixte Cruci: / Felix ergo lapis, sed tu filicior esto, / Quo duce sternentur subdita cuncta cruci;" and in the same collection, compare Hermann Ardenrald, 33; and Giovanni Iannuccio, 36; Piccha, *Oratio Pro dignitate*, 1: "Aegyptus Phoebo tum, Caesar, Caesaris Vrne / Nunc Sixtus Christo Memphica dona sacrat;" Bordino, *De Rebus*, 63: " ... Nunc obelo Sixtus Phoebo quem barbara quondam / Sacrarat demens, stultaque relligio ...;" compare *idem*, 19. For Sixtus V as light and as the Sun consult Alessandro Gratiano, *Oratio de Spiritu Sancto Ad Sixtum Quintum Pontificem Maximum Habita in Basilica Sancti Pietri ...* (Rome, 1585), n.p.: "In nova populi Christiani exultatione de oblata tibi Pontificia dignitate, est quod & ego tibi gratuler, PATER Beatissime, ... Divinae beneficentiae opus, quòd nec magnorum virorum ingenia voluit latere in angulis, nec honorum virtutes includi in augustijs, sed quasi lucernam super Candelabro, ut luceret omnibus, qui in domo sunt, Te Ducem & Pastorem populorum constituit..."; and Don Sancho De Sandoval, *Sermon De La Sanctissima Trinidad Que Hizo Ala Sanctidad De Nuestro muy Sancto Padre Sisto V. Pont. Max ...*, trans. Señoras Donna Gostanza de Sandoval & Donna Leonor Godinez (Rome, n.d.), n.p.: "De la misma manera, que si ponemos los ojos de hito en hito a mirar el sol ... Por lo qual, con mucha razon el gran Señor, que habita en medio de la / luz inaccessible ..."

[78] There may be an implicit comparison between the forty days in which the Nile floods and the forty days which Moses (and Christ) spent in the desert. See note 26 above regarding the duration of the flood. Also consult Chapter II, 78-79, note 30, for a contemporaneous commentary on Moses, Sixtus V, the Acqua Felice and the desert.

tabernacle, and in particular to the tablets of the law that Moses placed in the Ark of the Covenant [3 Kings VIII: 9; Hebrews IX: 4]. In a similar vein, the *League* evokes the rods of the twelve tribes of Israel and especially the flowering rod of Aaron, placed beside the tablets of the law in the Ark of the Covenant, as well as the rod used by Moses to part the Red Sea [Numbers XVII: 1-11; Hebrews IX: 4]. The *Harbour of Civitavecchia*, like *Terracina*, presents Sixtus V as a master of the elements, especially of water, and suggests Moses' parting of the Red Sea and his transformation of water into solid walls and his rendering the sea-bed dry [Exodus XIV: 29]. The prominent thoroughfare of *Monte Cavallo* also suggests the crossing of the Red Sea, as well as a later and comparable passage led by Moses' successor Joshua across the Jordan and into the Promised Land [Joshua III: 6-17], signified by the *Porta Pia*, and reinforced by the Dioscuri, the "calvary of Salvation" [Hebrews III: 8].[79] The *City of Montalto* likewise suggests Moses and Joshua as the "fathers" of the Promised Land fortified with walls. The *impresa* of the *Extirpation*, with the lion brandishing a thunderbolt in his uplifted forearm, suggests Moses' victory over the Amelikites through raised arms [Exodus XVII: 8-13], and even more the brazen serpent, which Moses "lifted up" in the desert [Numbers XXI: 4-9]. As its verse explains, the *Abundance* refers to the manna that Moses fed to his people in the desert. Finally, the *Holy House*, like the *City of Montalto*, suggests the Promised Land and Moses' transferral of his power to Joshua, the "chief priest," shepherd, and "guardian" of the Israelites [Numbers XXVII: 14-23; Deuteronomy XXXI: 7-8, 14-15, 23; XXXIV: 9].

By distinctly glorifying Sixtus V to the detriment of his pagan models, the verses accompanying the Good Works are clear indicators that a Christian component must dominate the already overwhelming Golden Age symbolism of Sixtus V-Apollo-Augustus. Similarly, the inclusion of the atypical verse insinuating Sixtus V's superiority over Moses, the Old Testament lawgiver, king, and priest, and prototype of Christ's vicar, reinforces the Christian reading by virtue of its singularity. The underlying allusions to the Exodus in each of the Good Works, and the centrality of light in the deliverance of the Israelites, actually point to conversion by the true light, Pope Sixtus V, aided by the Virgin and Saint Lucy, much as Saint Paul himself had been converted from Judaism to Christianity by the light to then embark upon his vocation as converter of the pagans.[80] So, too, the *imprese*, with their triumphant superimposition of the Christian over the pagan and the Judaic, and as synecdochic markers of Sixtine Rome, dictate that both the Virgilian idea of the Golden Age and the Exodus-conversion symbolism informing the Good Works of Sixtus V must yield to a more dominant and universal Christian, and particularly Franciscan, interpretation. As I shall now show, the very form and arrangement of the Good Works, in tandem with their content, furnish the viewer with additional clues towards a more definitive Christian reading of the Sixtine Golden Age. It is the twelfth Good Work, a work excluded from Fontana's roster, which effectively completes and seals such a reading.

The feigned tapestries which on first consideration form a homogeneous unit, complementing the underlying theme of the Golden Age of Sixtus V-Apollo-Augustus-Moses-Paul, on second consideration reveal distinctions between the types of representations depicted within the borders, and modifications

[79] Compare Pompeo Ugonio, *De Sanctissima Cruce in Vertice Obelisci Vaticani ...* (Rome, 1587), n.p.: "Ceu Castor, aut Pollux per vndas / Dirige ..."

[80] On the Exodus and light as signs of conversion to Christianity see Charles S. Singleton, *Journey to Beatrice* (1958; Cambridge, 1967), 39-56; and *idem*, "In Exitu Israel de Aegypto," in *Dante. A Collection of Critical Essays*, ed. John Freccero, Twentieth Century Views (Englewood Cliffs, New Jersey, 1965), 102-121. Also consult Pompeo Ugonio, *Oratio de Laudibus Literarum, Habita in Templo Sancti Eustachij, in die festo Sancti Lucae, Anno 1587 ...* (Rome, 1588), conclusion, for a reference to the Sun and light of conversion.

in the scale of the "tapestries" themselves. Such departures from the norm, together with the distinct coloration of the feigned columns flanking the "tapestries," serve to impart to the alert viewer the underlying symmetry of the lower register. Of the ten "tapestries" with landscape formats, four contain the everpresent *imprese* of the pope. That these *imprese* should be read as pendants is amply attested to by their similar placements in other Sixtine decorative schemes, and in the engraved portraits of the pope. This reading is further enforced by the "columns," painted as if to represent Green Serpentine marble, and flanking the allegories in the Salone dei Papi (refer hereafter to fig. 41).[81] The allegories form pendants both along the west and east walls (*Treasure* and *League* (fig. 43.3,5); *Extirpation* and *Abundance* (fig. 45.9,10)) and across space (*Treasure* and *Abundance* (figs. 43.3 and 45.10); *League* and *Extirpation* (figs. 43.5 and 45.9)), and collectively convey the chiliastic ideas of the earth's prosperity, and the pacification of the world in preparation for the millenium.[82] Of the remaining six "tapestries" with landscape formats, four are adjacent to the allegories, flanked by feigned columns simulating Yellow Numidian marble, and form a comparable group of pendants, both along the west and east walls (*Terracina* and *Civitavecchia* (fig. 43.2,6); *Montalto* and *Holy House* (fig. 45.8,11)) and across space (*Terracina* and *Holy House* (figs. 43.2 and 45.11); *Civitavecchia* and *Montalto* (figs. 43.6; and 45.8)). Collectively, they convey the millenial imagery of reclaimed and restored lands and buldings. The two remaining "tapestries" with landscape formats, namely the *Acqua Felice* and *Monte Cavallo*, are the largest "tapestries" of the hall;[83] are also flanked by feigned Yellow Numidian columns; and are situated on the longitudinal axis of the Salone dei Papi. At the south-eastern and south-western corners, feigned Portasanta pilasters separate the feigned Yellow Numidian columns of the *Acqua Felice* from the feigned Green Serpentine columns of the intentional voids, while at the north-eastern and north-western corners, feigned Portasanta pilasters separate the simulated Yellow Numidian columns of the smaller "tapestries" from those of *Monte Cavallo*. The *Acqua Felice* and *Monte Cavallo* thus form spatial pendants, especially since the one is a close-up view of part of the prospect offered by the other (figs. 42.1 and 44.7). Together, they continue the overlying theme of the feigned landscape tapestries, namely the reclamation and restoration of land and buildings, a theme traditionally associated with the coming millenium. Although Ludwig von Pastor listed the Good Works of Sixtus V without offering an analysis of their meaning, he must surely have understood the underlying order, since his list corresponds almost precisely to the order offered here.[84]

According to Fontana, there remains but one Good Work of Sixtus V on the lower register: the *Vatican Library* - a work which departs most radically from the typical landscape format of the Good Works, and which is atypically flanked by simulated Portasanta marble columns. Given the manifest use of pendants and pendant groups throughout the lower register, and the unusual coloration of the flanking "columns," it is only sensible that the *Vatican* also have a foil, particularly since it is positioned on the main transversal axis of the Salone (fig. 43.4). In fact there is an element which is positioned opposite the *Vatican*, which is situated on the same horizontal plane as the "tapestries," and which, like the *Library*, is flanked by allegories and "columns" of Portasanta marble, albeit in abbreviat-

[81] I have used Schiavo, *Lateran*, n.p. for the nomenclature of the various types of feigned marble in the Salone.

[82] For this and the following references to the millenium, consult Ladner, *Idea of Reform*, especially 63-82, as well as the *Bible*, particularly Deuteronomy VIII: 7-13, Psalms LXXI, CIII and Revelation.

[83] Noted by von Pastor, *History*, XXII, 276. See note 84, below.

[84] von Pastor, *History*, XXII, 275-276: "Another series of frescoes in this hall, also explained by inscriptions, represent the works of Sixtus V.; the extirpation of the / bandits, his [Sixtus V's] care for the provisioning of Rome and the safety of the Papal States, the treasure laid up in the Castle of St. Angelo as well as the Vatican Library are represented, the harbours of Terracina and Civitavecchia, the cities of Loreto and Montalto, the Acqua Felice and the fountain in the Piazza S. Susanna, and the Quirinal Palace with the view towards the Porta Pia. These last two frescoes are larger than the others."

ed form. I am referring to the *Lateran*, the collective Good Work of Saint Francis and Pope Sixtus V inscribed above the main entrance to the hall, and unaccompanied by an illustration, unless one considers the *quadratura* of the Salone dei Papi as its descriptive, microcosmic counterpart (fig. 45.X):[85]

NVTANTES HVMERIS LATERANAS SVSTINET AEDES
FRANCISCVS FIDEI FIRMA COLVMNA SACRAE
FRANCISCO SIXTVS TENERIS ADDICTVS AB ANNIS
RESTITVIT LAPSAS AMPLIFICATQ[VE] MAGIS
AN MINOR EST VIRTVS QVAM SVSTENTARE LABANTES
RVRSVS COLLAPSAS AEDIFICARE DOMOS

The first couplet makes reference to Innocent III's dream, made the more famous by the fresco in the upper Church of Assisi, in which the pope saw Saint Francis holding up the "tottering Lateran Church" and, in amended Sixtine lore, the entire Lateran complex. As a result of this dream, Pope Innocent III gave verbal sanction to the Rule of Saint Francis - an act commemorated in fresco in the loggia just outside the Salone dei Papi - thus making official the mendicant Order of the Friars Minor, an order whose members were to preach the coming of the kingdom of heaven in emulation of their founder, the "Herald of the Great King."[86] The second couplet, in turn, reminds the viewer of Sixtus V's Franciscan heritage, and euphemistically alludes to his destruction of the Patriarchium Lateranense and construction of the new Lateran Palace, as well as his work at the Scala Santa and Benediction Loggia of San Giovanni in Laterano. Like his spiritual mentor, then, Sixtus V supports the "tottering Lateran" and, in keeping with Saint Francis' own restorations to churches, he "magnifie[s] them further." The final couplet reverts to the rhetoric of the verses beneath the feigned tapestries, glorifying Sixtus V's super-human powers to uphold and maintain the Lateran complex, no matter the deterrants. Unlike the majority of the "tapestry" verses, however, there are no allusions to pagan antiquity in the *Lateran* so that the true nature of Sixtus V's powers may be understood, namely his faith in Christ and in Saint Francis, the *alter Christus* and, one must add, the *alter Moyses*, that has shown him the way to the kingdom of heaven. It is this renewal of faith, signified by that "sturdy column," Saint Francis, and by a most loyal follower, Pope Sixtus V, together with the concomitant renewal of culture conveyed in the pendant *Vatican*, which are the most significant signposts of the approaching millenium. Sixtus V's Franciscan heritage and vocation as kingly builder therefore inform the transversal east-west axis of the Salone, and, by proxy of the *quadratura*, the longitudinal and subordinate axes of the topographical and allegorical Good Works. Two by two, the Good Works of Sixtus V announce the millenium, like Christ's apostles and Francis' preachers and, in the final analysis, given the pride of place allotted the *Lateran* above the main entrance to the Salone dei Papi, the Christian and Franciscan elements overlay, eclipse and, indeed, convert the pagan and the Judaic.[87]

2. SPIRITUAL AND TEMPORAL TIERS: THE APOSTOLIC POPES AND THEIR GOOD WORKS

Ranged along the upper tier of the Salone dei Papi are representations of nineteen popes, chosen from the first thirty-

[85] Although Schiavo, *Lateran*, n.p. excludes the *Lateran* from his description of Good Works, in his caption for the illustration of the Salone dei Papi he seems to realize that it is in fact a part of the series. The description is as follows: "In particular the Hall of the Popes ... documents some of his more important and significant works; in the zone above the lower windows all round the room, works of Sixtus V are reproduced: the aqueduct and "mostra" of the Felice waters, the port and reclamation at Terracina, the treasure collected in Castel Sant'Angelo, the Hall of the Vatican Library, the League of Christian Princes, the port and aqueduct at Civitavecchia, the Quirinal, the city of Montalto, the extirpation of the bandits, Abundance, the city of Loreto." Contrast the caption: "In the zone above the lower windows, all around the room are reproduced the works of Sixtus V. His [Sixtus V's] greatest work, that is the Lateran Palace, is recalled on the central door by an inscription that, alluding to the Giotto paintings, says that St. Francis, stalwart column of the faith, supports the falling structures of the Lateran; and alluding to the Patriarchate, recalls that Sixtus V had reconstructed rather than restored the buildings without however deriving any less glory from it."

[86] Consult Francesco Suares, *Ad Sanctiss. Et Beatissimum Patrum Sixtum Quinctum ... Panegyricus Primus* (Rome, 1587), 32, for a discussion of St. Francis, Sixtus V and the Lateran.

[87] Even the columns themselves are likely not without meaning, for the three colours allotted to them, white, green, and red, evoke the three theological virtues of charity, faith and hope. According to this reading, the red columns of the main walls, which enframe the *Acqua Felice* and *Monte Cavallo* are given over to charity; the white columns of the east-west axis with the *Lateran* and *Vatican* signify faith, as actually set forth in the *Lateran*, and symbolically in the feigned white pilasters, or cornerstones of the *Salone*; and the green columns of the allegorical Good Works connote hope - the hope of Sixtus V's that his actions on earth will bring him the fruits of justification in heaven. Since the three theological virtues are most often accompanied by the four cardinal virtues, it is tempting to carry this reading further, and assign to those remarkably meaningful inventions, the allegorical Good Works, the virtues of justice, prudence, temperance and fortitude. It is extremely difficult to pin down exact correspondences, since each allegory is suggestive of more than one virtue. On the basis of the prevalent ideas of each Good Work, I would provisionally assign justice to the *Abundance*; prudence to the *League*; temperance to the *Treasure*; and fortitude to the *Extirpation*.

four, from Peter through Sylvester. Since the popes are represented in succession, Fontana and all others to have listed the popes on the upper tier have naturally followed the chronological order set out in the hall.[88] The popes are seated beneath baldachins and enclosures comprised of elements taken from the *stemma* of Sixtus V. Each enclosure has an egg-and-dart frieze at its summit so that the structure appears to hold up the ceiling of the Salone, itself comprised of coffers decorated with elements of the ubiquitous heraldry of Sixtus V. At the northern corners of the Salone illusionistic putti open curtains to reveal the Sixtine lion amidst a cartouche, while on the southern end, the putti apparently conceal the lion behind the curtains.

The idea of presenting a great quorum of popes, one beside the next, defers to the ancient and venerable tradition of *viri illustres*, a tradition still flourishing in the sixteenth century, and looks to the illustrious popes represented in the Sistine Chapel clerestory, commissioned by Pope Sixtus IV, and modelled on the popes of the Oratory of Saint Nicholas at the Patriarchium Lateranense, commissioned by Callistus II.[89] The presentation of popes seated beneath baldachins most clearly evokes the popes in the Sala di Costantino in the Vatican Palace, while looking back to those in the Camera pro Secretis Consiliis at the Patriarchium Lateranense, the audience hall commissioned by Pope Callistus II in celebration of the papacy's victory over both the Investiture Struggle and the antipopes.[90]

Each of the popes is given a portrait likeness that loosely reflects the *verae effigies* of Onofrio Panvinio's *Le vite de tutti i Pontefici* as well as those of Giovanangelo Egitto's and Antonio Ciccarelli's *Le vite de' Pontefici*, engraved by Giovambattista De Cavallieri, but in accord with the Mannerist aesthetic, the portraits are more idealized and less archaizing than the *verae effigies* copied from the medallion portraits of the popes in the Early Christian basilicas of Rome.[91] In keeping with this desire for historical accuracy and truth, the information in Peter's inscription is taken from the Bible. The remaining popes' works are taken ultimately from the *Liber Pontificalis*, the official history of the popes.[92] Not only does Peter's *titulus* set a precedent which implies that the works of his successors are derived from the Scriptures, but the many letters written by the apostolic popes provide the biblical justification for their actions.[93] Further evidence for deciphering the meaning of the achievements of the early popes is to be found in the *Canons and Decrees of the Council of Trent* and the *Catechism of the Council of Trent*, both based on apostolic precedent and well known to the learned Roman Catholic Reform viewer.[94] Beneath twelve of the nineteen inscriptions on the architrave are feigned medallions containing illustrations of the Good Works of the popes seated above. With the notable exception of Peter's "medallion," the *grisaille* illustrations correspond to the acts of the popes commemorated in the *tituli*.

The first pope represented in the series is Saint Peter, situated to the right of the "framed painting" on the south wall (figs. 42.A and 54). Peter wears his traditional blue shirt, and his bare feet, signifying his humility, rest on a pillow. In his left hand, Peter holds the "keys of the kindgom of heaven" given to him by Christ, as well as the Bible, and with his right hand, he points towards the adjacent "panel," acknowledging, as I shall later explain, the source of his authority and posses-

[88] Fontana, *Delle trasportatione*, 59v-60v, lists each pope in succession but in his introductory description curiously reports that there are sixteen popes represented on the upper register; Mola, *Breve Racconto*, 64, copies Fontana's statement that there are sixteen popes represented; Biondi, *il Restauramento*, 14, lists each pope; Dumesnil, *Histoire de Sixte-Quint*, 425, also follows Fontana in his report of the "seize papes"; Tulli, "Sala del Concilio," *Per l'arte sacra*, 34-36, copies Fontana faithfully; von Pastor, *History*, XXII, 275, states that there are nineteen popes; Schiavo, *Lateran*, n.p. states that "... the seated figures of nineteen Popes are placed in niches. These were chosen from the first thirty-three [sic] beginning from St. Peter..."

[89] Much has been written on the tradition of *viri illustres*. See, for example, Theodor E. Mommsen, "Petrarch and the Decoration of the Sala Virorum Illustrium in Padua," *Art Bulletin* XXXIV (1952): 94-96; Nicolai Rubenstein, "Political Ideas in Sienese Art: The Frescoes by Ambrogio Lorenzetti and Taddeo di Bartolo in the Palazzo Pubblico," *Journal of the Warburg and Courtauld Institutes* XXI (1958): 194-195; Teresa Hankey, "Salutati's Epigrams for the Palazzo Vecchio at Florence," *Journal of the Warburg and Courtauld Institutes* XXII (1959): 363-365; and recently, Christiane Joost-Gaugier's series of articles, including: "The History of a Visual Theme as Culture and the Experience of an Urban Center: 'Uomini Famosi' in Brescia (I)," *Antichità Viva* XXII, 4 (1983): 7-17; and *idem* "... (II)," XXIII, 1 (1984): 5-14. I wish to thank Philip Sohm for the references to Joost-Gaugier's articles. As far as I know, the popes on the clerestory of the Sistine Chapel have been treated only in a general manner. See, for example, Johannes Wilde, "The Decoration of the Sistine Chapel," *Proceedings of the British Academy* XLIV (1958): 70. The identity of each of the popes has recently been listed with accompanying *tituli* by Franco Bernabei in *Sistine Chapel*, 79-87. On the Oratory of Saint Nicholas see Chapter I, 36, note 20, above.

[90] The similarity to the popes in the Sala di Costantino has been observed by Ursula Reinhardt, "La Tapisserie Feinte: un genre de décoration du Maniérisme Romain au XVIᵉ siècle," *Gazette des Beaux-Arts* LXXXIV (1974): 291. On the audience hall of Callistus II, see Chapter II, 36, note 21, above.

[91] Onofrio Panvinio, *Le Vite de tutti i Pontefici da S. Pietro in Qua, Ridotte in epitome da Tomaso Costo Napoletano ...* (Venice, 1592), 4, 6, 12-29, 43; Antonio Ciccarelli, Giovanangelo Egitto, *Le Vite de'Pontefici ...* (Rome, 1588), 1-2, 8-23, 34.

[92] A number of slightly different versions of the *Book of the Popes* existed for our sixteenth century iconographer to draw upon. I have used the edition of Duchesne, *Liber Pontificalis*, as well as *Platinae De Vitis*; Panvinio, *Vite*; Ciccarelli, Egitto, *Vite*; Baronio, *Annales*; and Pompeo Ugonio, "Vitae Romano-

sions. The inscription memorializes Peter's station as Christ's first vicar, and makes reference to the Acts of the Apostles XV: 1-31 and Galatians II: 1-10: "S. PETRVS / PRIMVS IESV CHRISTI VICARIVS / PRIMVM HIEROSOLYMIS CONC[ILIVM] / CELEBRAVIT".

According to Cesare Baronio, author of the *Annales Ecclesiastici* and the accepted authority on Church history for the Roman Catholic Reformers of the late sixteenth century, the first Council of Jerusalem was held in 51 and was attended by the apostles Peter, James, John, Paul and Barnabas, as well as the presbyters.[95] It was convened in order to resolve a dispute between the apostles Paul and Barnabas, and the Jewish Christians of Antioch, who were demanding that pagan converts to Christianity also observe the Jewish Law. As Christ's chosen vicar, Peter naturally took charge of the council and decided against the Jewish Christians, since, as Peter reasoned, salvation was made possible to anyone who received the Holy Ghost through his or her conversion to Christianity, and therefore precluded the Mosaic law. The "medallion" corresponding to the *titulus* is also situated on the lower register, within a cartouche resting on a feigned doorway contrived to balance the real doorway on the north wall and thus to provide a sense of symmetry to the hall (figs. 42.a and 55). The *grisaille* narrative of the "medallion" represents Christ in a boat with Peter and two other fishermen, James and John. On the floor of the boat are numerous fish and a broken net. Therefore the event portrayed does not correspond to the event described in the inscription above. Rather, it represents a conflated image of the miraculous draught of fishes [Luke V: 1-11], in which Christ first chooses Peter to follow in his footsteps as both preacher of, and converter to, the faith and (future) governor of the Church. By following Christ's admonition to let down the nets, Peter learns by example how to preach the faith in Christ and to convert new followers to Christianity.[96] When seen in conjunction, then, the "medallion" narrative and its *titulus* represent an early and seminal calling of Peter to be Christ's vicar, and the realization of Christ's teachings after his Ascension in the first Council of Jerusalem in which Peter determined the proper procedures for converting pagans to Christianity by recalling Christ's teaching.

Saint Linus I is represented adjacent to Saint Peter on the west wall (fig. 43.B). He wears the traditional cope and shoes, and adopts a stance of prayer, with arms crossed and head inclined upwards. His work is not illustrated, but is commemorated in the inscription below: "S. LINVS I / PP. II / SANCIVIT VT MVLIER / NON NISI VELATO CAPITE / ECCLESIAM INGREDETVR".

Just as Peter was inspired by Christ's model in making his decision at the Council of Jerusalem, Linus' act, as documented in the *Liber Pontificalis*, was also based upon biblical precedent, namely the dictates of the other apostolic founder of the Roman Church, Saint Paul.[97] The law enforced by Linus, decreeing that a woman must cover her head inside the church, derives from Paul's admonition in I Corinthians XI: 3-16.[98]

Next in the succession of popes on the west wall is Saint Sixtus I, the eighth Bishop of Rome after Saint Peter (fig. 43.C). Like Linus, Sixtus I is also seen in an attitude of prayer, with hands touching and head inclined upwards. He wears shoes and a more ornate cope with embroidered images of the apostles on the orphrey. To his right, a putto holds up a papal

rum Pontificum a B. Petro Apostolo ad Stephanum VI. cum originalibus observationibus et collationibus Pompei Ugonii," B.A.V. Barb. Lat. 2603, 1-400.

[93] During the sixteenth century it was possible to buy an edition of Clement of Rome containing the letters and decrees of the early popes, as evidenced in Pope Sixtus V's list of books in his private library, in Cugnoni, "Documenti Chigiani," *Società romana di storia patria*, 211, 232, 249, 255, 260, 262. Since I did not have the edition of Clement of Rome at my disposal, I resorted to the decretals of Gratian which also contain the epistles. Sixtus V knew the legal ramifications of the letters, having written a book on Gratian while in retirement during the pontificate of Gregory XIII.

[94] *Canons and Decrees*; *The Catechism of the Council of Trent, Published by Command of Pope Pius the Fifth*, trans. J. Donovan (1566; Dublin, 1829).

[95] Baronio, *Annales*, I, 337.

[96] On Luke V: 1-11, see Shearman, *Raphael's Cartoons*, 58, 62-64. Also consult Smith, *Casino*, 95-96.

[97] Duchesne, *Liber Pontificalis*, I, 121; Platina, *De Vitis*, 11; Panvinio, *Vite*, 6; Ciccarelli, *Egitto*, *Vite*, lv; Baronio, *Annales*, II, 4: 43; and Ugonio, "Vitae," 20v.

[98] Noted in Duchesne, *Liber Pontificalis*, I, 121, note 1.

tiara - an anachronism which signifies the pope's jurisdiction over the spiritual and temporal realms. The *titulus* accompanying Saint Sixtus I commemorates the pope's ruling regarding liturgical practice drawn from the cry of the seraphim in Isaiah VI: 3 and echoed in Revelation IV: 8:[99] "S. SIXTVS I / PP. VIII / DECREVIT VT IN MISSA / CANTARETVR / SANCTVS".

Unlike the *grisaille* "medallion" accompanying Saint Peter, that beneath the *titulus* of Saint Sixtus I is smaller, since confined between two closely spaced feigned columns and consequently compressed into an oval format (fig. 43.c). Also unlike the feigned medallion of Saint Peter, that of Sixtus I actually illustrates the decree described above. It shows a priest holding the eucharistic wafer above the chalice, accompanied by three deacons and a kneeling supplicant, all, apparently, singing the *Sanctus*.

Saint Telesphorus I follows Sixtus I on the west wall and agrees with the historical succession, being the ninth vicar of Christ (fig. 43.D). He wears a cope and shoes, holds the prayer book in his left hand, together with at least one of the "keys of the kingdom of heaven," and, with his right hand, gestures upwards. To his left, a putto holds up the papal tiara. The *titulus* accompanying Telesphorus describes the liturgical decrees instituted by the pope:[100] "S. TELESPHORVS I / PP. IX / INSTITVIT / VT IN DIE NATIVITAT[IS] DOM[INI] / TRES MISSAE CELEBRARENTVR / ET GLORIA IN EXC[ELSIS] CANTARETVR".

The feigned medallon illustrating Telesphorus' Good Work shows a priest officiating at an altar, and a kneeling supplicant (fig. 43.d), signifying both the masses, respectively celebrated in remembrance of Christ's birth, the shepherds' revelation, and his death on the cross, and the *Gloria*.[101] As Telesphorus himself explained, the *Gloria* was sung by the nine choirs of angels in heaven at the Nativity of Christ [Luke II: 14] the same night that the shepherds were told of Christ's coming by the angel. In imitation of this night, then, and in expectation of the second coming, Telesphorus reasoned that the *Gloria* should be sung.[102]

Saint Hyginus I is the next pope in line on the west wall, and is identified as the tenth vicar of Christ (fig. 43.E). Unlike his predecessors, Hyginus actually wears the papal tiara. He is garbed in a cope with images of Peter and Paul as well as the remaining ten apostles on the orphrey, wears shoes, and is apparently contemplating the decree which he is in the process of writing. The inscription explains the nature of the decree:[103] "S. HVGINVS I / PP. X / COMPATREM ET COMMATREM / IN BAPTISMO ADHIBENDOS / DECREVIT".

As both the dictates of the Council of Trent on Baptism and the *Catechism* explain, this practice had apostolic and, indeed, biblical precedent in the testimony of Peter, who explained the necessity of teaching the youth the meaning of the faith [I Peter II: 2].[104] The oval "medallion" shows the baptism of a child, using a great festooned urn, and around the urn a number of witnesses, two of whom must represent the godparents of the new Christian (fig. 43.e).

Saint Pius I, the eleventh pope in succession, is the last vicar of Christ represented on the west wall (fig. 43.F). Like Hyginus, Pius I also wears the tiara, cope and shoes, and holds a book. In this case, Pius has finished writing his decree and displays the appropriate pages to the spectator. Beneath Pius the inscription relates the pope's ruling on the proper day on

[99] Duchesne, *Liber Pontificalis*, I, 128; Platina, *De Vitis*, 18; Panvinio, *Vite*, 12; Ciccarelli, Egitto, *Vite*, 7v; and Baronio, *Annales*, II, 12: 250. Ugonio, "Vitae," 24, uses shorthand references in this section of his manuscript and I am unable to decipher them.

[100] Duchesne, *Liber Pontificalis*, I, 129; Platina, *De Vitis*, 18-19; Panvinio, *Vite*, 13; Ciccarelli, Egitto, *Vite*, 8v; and Baronio, *Annales*, II, 2: 285; and Ugonio, "Vitae," 24, 25.

[101] The significance of the three masses is explained in Platina, *De Vitis*, 18-19.

[102] Letter of Telesphorus to a certain Peter in *Corpus Juris Canonici Academicum, Emendatum & Notis P. Lancellotti Illustratum* ..., 2 vols. (Venice, 1782), I, "De Consecratione," D. I, C. XLVIII, 1158.

[103] Duchesne, *Liber Pontificalis*, I, 131, does not include this decree, even in the many variants of manuscripts listed, nor does Baronio, *Annales*, II, 286 ff; or, as far as I can tell, Ugonio, "Vitae," 24v, 25. Contrast Platina, *De Vitis*, 19; Panvinio, *Vite*, 14; and Ciccarelli, Egitto, *Vite*, 9v, who do include the decree as one of Hyginus' works.

[104] *Canons and Decrees*, 186; *Catechism*, 169.

which to celebrate Easter, a ruling derived from 1 Corinthians XVI: 2, Acts XX: 7 and echoed in Revelation I:10:[105] "S. PIVS I / PP. XI / SANCIVIT / VT PASCHA DIE DOMINICA / CELEBRARETVR". The "medallion" beneath shows Pius, still wearing his tiara and seated at a table (fig. 43.f). Before him stands Saint Michael, messenger of god and protector of Christ's vicar and of Rome, who wears a winged hat and carries a sword.[106] He is apparently giving Pius inspiration to dictate his decretal to the scribe seated to the pope's left.

The immediate successor of Saint Pius I is represented on the north wall, namely Saint Anicetus I (fig. 44.G). He too wears the papal tiara, cope and shoes, looks toward the feigned panel painting to his left, and extends his right arm, with fingers together, as if he once held something in his hand. Anicetus' *titulus* explains the pope's ruling on the consecration of archbishops and bishops, a ruling typically based upon biblical precedent:[107] "S. ANICETVS I / PP. XII / INSTITVIT VT ARCHIEPISCOPVS / AB OMNIBVS SVFFRAGANEIS / ET EPISCOPVS A TRIBVS EPISCOP[I] / CONSECRARETVR". This ruling is based upon the precedent of Peter, who was ordained by Christ in the presence of the apostles [John XXI: 17] and follows the model of Peter, James and John, who ordained Saint Jacob the Just, the first archbishop of Jerusalem.[108] As Anicetus himself explains, since the archbishop rules the see, he should be ordained by all members whom he will rule. The ordination of a bishop should follow suit, but if not possible, then at least three of his peers must be present in order to ordain a fellow bishop, and only with the consent of the archbishop.[109]

Unlike the circular "medallion" beneath Saint Peter, situated opposite on the South wall, the "medallion" accompanying Anicetus illustrates the pope's act as described in the inscription. The feigned medallion shows a future archbishop and bishop kneeling before a quorum of mitred bishops, one of whom, probably Anicetus himself, is seated and in the act of consecrating (fig. 44.g).

Flanking the feigned panel on the north wall to the right is Saint Soterus I, the thirteenth vicar of Christ and successor to Anicetus (fig. 44.H). Soterus I wears the papal tiara, cope with orphrey, adorned with Greek crosses, and shoes. He looks down, in the direction of the "panel painting" and Saint Anicetus I, and points to a passage in a book. The contents of the passage are explained in the *titulus* beneath:[110] "S. SOTERVS I / PP. XIII / DECREVIT / VASA SACRATAE DEO VIRGINES / SACRA VASA NON TANGERENT". Soterus instituted this law as a reaction to what he himself termed the "utterly reprehensible and blameworthy" practice of contemporary holy women, who were not only handling the holy vessels and consecrated cloths, but were also carrying incense around the altars.[111] The reason for forbidding such acts was obvious to Soterus, and, as far as he was concerned, to all in their "right minds," so that reference to the *locus classicus*, surely Leviticus XII: 4, was deemed unnecessary. The circular "medallion," positioned above a feigned doorway, shows two nuns, standing to either side of a bishop in possession of a sacred vessel, extending their arms as if about to touch the vessel (fig. 44.h). Of course, the bishop holds the vessel close to his chest with both hands, ensuring that the nuns are unsuccessful in their attempt, since only those "consecrated to religion" may touch holy objects [Exodus XXIX: 37].

114

[105] Duchesne, *Liber Pontificalis*, I, 132; Platina, *De Vitis*, 21; Panvinio, *Vite*, 15; Ciccarelli, *Egitto*, *Vite*, 10v; Baronio, *Annales*, II, I: 293-294; and Ugonio, "Vitae," 25v. On Christ's resurrection on Sunday, and hence the decision to celebrate Easter on this day (confirmed by the Council of Nicea), see Hans Leitzmann, *The Beginnings of the Christian Church*, trans. Bertram Lee Woolf, International Library of Christian Knowledge (New York: Charles Scribner's Sons, 1937), 85-88.

[106] Since the angel carries a sword and wears a winged hat, I have identified him as St. Michael. It is probably not coincidental that it is Pius I who accompanies St. Michael, given the relationship between Pius V and the archangel, noted in my Introduction, 30-31, note 47.

[107] Duchesne, *Liber Pontificalis*, I, 134, does not mention this Good Work, nor does Baronio, *Annales*, II, 323 ff, or Ugonio, "Vitae," 25. Panvinio, *Vite*, 16, alludes to this decree, and it is mentioned by Platina, *De Vitis*, 22; and Ciccarelli, *Egitto*, *Vite*, 11v.

[108] For the ordination of Jacob the Just see *Corpus Juris Canonici*, D. LXVI, C. II, 221.

[109] Letter of Anicetus to Bishops of Galliae in *Corpus Juris Canonici*, D. LXVI, C. I, 221.

[110] Duchesne, *Liber Pontificalis*, I, 135 and note 3; Platina, *De Vitis*, 22; Baronio, *Annales*, II, 51: 397; and Ugonio, "Vitae," 25v. Contrast Ciccarelli, *Egitto*, *Vite*, who do not include this act of Soterus' in their discussion; and Panvinio, *Vite*, 17, who refers to monks, *vis-à-vis* nuns.

[111] Second epistle of Soterus to all Bishops of Italy in *Corpus Juris Canonici*, D. XXIII, C. XXV, 77-78.

Saint Eleuterius I is the first pope in the chronology situated on the east wall (figs. 45.I and 58). He wears the papal tiara, cope and shoes, holds a book under his right arm, and with his left hand, adopts the benediction stance. He is situated above the *City of Montalto*, and is consequently unaccompanied by an illustrative "medallion." The *titulus* explains the missionary activity carried out under the auspices of the pope:[112] "S. ELEVTERIVS I / PP. XIIII / BRITANIAM INSVLAM / LVCII REGIS ROGATV / PER FVGACIVM ET DAMIANVM / LEGATOS FIDEI / SACRIS INSTITVIT'. In pointing to the apostolic origins of Catholic Britain, the *titulus* serves two fundamental purposes. First, by explaining that King Lucius was baptized with his subjects by papal envoys, the pope is accordingly memorialized for carrying on a duty explained by Christ [Matthew XXVIII: 18-20] and realized by Peter when he threw out his nets [Luke V: 1-11]. Secondly, such a history is contrary to the contemporaneous British view that had Joseph of Arimathea bring Christianity to the Island direct from Jerusalem.[113] The implication is that, despite the uninformed view of the British, the pope nevertheless held sway over the entire *respublica Christiana*. In this sense, it is entirely appropriate that Eleuterius I is the first pope in the progression who is explicitly related to Sixtus V since, in addition to his Sixtine enclosure and sustaining architecture, he is accompanied by a "tapestry" illustrating a Good Work of the Peretti pope in lieu of a "medallion" of his own (fig. 45.8). In fact, the way in which Eleuterius' *titulus* is positioned above the *City of Montalto* suggests the form of the emblem. In this way, Eleuterius' decree is borrowed by Sixtus V to serve as the *superscriptio* of the *imago* and *subscriptio* of his Good Work. When viewed in tandem, then, the work of Eleuterius becomes an exemplary precedent for Sixtus V, who ardently wished to bring Queen Elizabeth I of England and her subjects back to the flock,[114] while Sixtus V's own achievement at Montalto proves by example that he is the true father of the fatherland, a fatherland which should, on the basis of Eleuterius' conversion of England, also include the island of Britain.

Beside Pope Eleuterius on the east wall is his successor, Pope Victor I (fig. 45.J). Like his predecessor, Victor I wears the papal tiara, cope and shoes, holds an open book in his left hand, and gestures with his right. The *titulus* and accompanying "medallion" (fig. 45.j) describe Victor's decree on Baptism:[115] "S. VICTOR I / PP. XV / SANCIVIT / VT NECESSITATE VRGENTE / QVISQVE SIVE IN FLVMINE / SIVE IN FONTE SIVE IN MARI / BAPTISM SVSCIPERE POSSIT". As Victor himself explains, any body of water is appropriate for quick baptism in the case of a penitent near death, because it is the water, not the source, which is the vehicle for baptism. Similarly, Victor allowed anyone, even infidels and heretics, to affect baptism in "urgent" cases, since the Holy Spirit descended upon the baptized no matter the character of the baptist.[116]

Saint Zepherinus I is the next pope who is explicitly associated with Sixtus V. He is represented in the act of prayer, looking downwards in humility, and wearing the papal tiara and cope (figs. 45.K and 59). Zepherinus' decree concerning the liturgy, emulating Christ and the apostles at the Last Supper [Luke XXII: 11], is described in the *titulus* below:[117] "S. ZEPHERINVS I / PP. XVI / DECREVIT / VT REM DIVINAM / FACIENTI EPISCOPO / SACERDOTES OMNES / ASTARENT".

[112] Duchesne, *Liber Pontificalis*, I, 136; Platina, *De Vitis*, 23 ; Panvinio, *Vite*, 18; Ciccarelli, *Egitto, Vite*, 13v; Baronio, *Annales*, II, 3: 413, 415; and Ugonio, "Vitae," 25v, 26.

[113] Strong, *Britannia Triumphans*, 24.

[114] von Pastor, *History*, XXII, 33-36. Also consult Gregorio Piccha, *Oratio Ad Sixtum V. Pont. Max. Aliosq. Christianos Principes, et Respubl. Pro Britannico bello indicendo* (Rome, 1588), n.p., who treats Eleuterius and King Luke in his sermon propounding a war against Britain.

[115] Duchesne, *Liber Pontificalis*, I, 137; Platina, *De Vitis*, 24; Panvinio, *Vite*, 19; Baronio, *Annales*, II, 1: 479; and Ugonio, "Vitae," 27v, 28. Ciccarelli, Egitto, *Vite*, 14v, do not include this act in their discussion.

[116] Letter of Victor to Peter, in his first decretal in *Corpus Juris Canonici*, "De Consecratione," D. II, C. XXII, 1202-1203.

[117] Duchesne, *Liber Pontificalis*, I, 139; Platina, *De Vitis*, 25; Panvinio, *Vite*, 20; ; Ciccarelli, Egitto, *Vite*, 15v; Ugonio, "Vitae," 28v, 29. Baronio, *Annales*, II, 480 ff, does not mention this decree.

The *Extirpation* takes the place of the "medallion" that usually accompanies the apostolic popes. In this way Zepherinus' ruling is clearly related to Sixtus V's feat in ridding the *respublica Christiana* of heretics and infidels (fig. 45.9). By association, the lion wielding the thunderbolt in the *impresa* of the *Extirpation*, understood as Pope Sixtus V dispensing *poena*, becomes the officiating bishop of Zepherinus' decree; the sheep huddled around the mountainside become the priests assisting at the mass to exorcise the devil made incarnate in the wolves; and the triple mountain itself, symbolical of Montalto and Catholic Britain, becomes analogous to the altar, so that the feckless wolves become at once bandits, prostitutes and Protestants! Just as Sixtus V exorcised the obelisks and columns before surmounting them with their respective sphragis and effigies of the apostles, his method of exorcising the bandits and prostitutes (and Protestants) is shown to derive from liturgical practice, in emulation of the decree of his predecessor and of its source, the work of Christ himself.[118]

Beside Saint Zepherinus is Saint Callistus I (fig. 45.L), who wears the papal tiara, cope and shoes, looks upward towards the coffered heaven, and holds a book in his left hand, while with his right he adopts the benediction stance. Callistus is memorialized for a number of Good Works in the accompanying *titulus*:[119] "S. CALISTVS I / PP. XVII / INSTITVIT / IEIVNIVM QVATVOR TEMPOR / ECCLES S. M. TRANSTYBERIM / ET IN VIA APP[IA] COEMETERIVM / AEDIFICAVIT".

The accompanying "medallion" shows Callistus receiving the plans for Santa Maria in Trastevere from his architect who kneels before the pope and points to his ground plan (fig. 45.l). The pope is accompanied by church officials, and behind them is a walled structure, apparently signifying the cemetery of Callistus. The fast which he instituted at four seasons realizes the prophecy of Zacharias VIII: 19, refers to Psalm IV: 8, and may be alluded to in the remaining figures of the medallion.[120]

Saint Urbanus I is given pride of place above the main entrance to the Salone dei Papi (figs. 45.M and 60). He rests his arm on an open book balanced on his legs, and rests his right sandalled foot on a pillow, in emulation of Peter, likewise resting on a pillow. A putto to Urbanus' right holds up his papal tiara. The *titulus* beneath the pope commemorates his decree concerning liturgical vessels:[121] "S. VRBANVS I / PP. XVIII / VASA SACRA / EX ARGENTO AVRO CONFICI / ADHIBERIQVE / AD DEI CVLTVM / DECREVIT".

Since Urbanus I is situated directly above the main door of the Salone, he is accompanied by neither a "medallion" nor a "tapestry" illustrating a Good Work of Sixtus V. In their stead, and instead of the emblem format, is the *Lateran*, the combined Good Work of Sixtus V and Saint Francis (fig. 45.X). The decree of Urbanus I emulates the practice of Moses and his successors, who used only the most precious materials for the tabernacle [Exodus XXV-XXVII; compare1 Kings VI: 14-31], and recalls the silver and gold vessels offered by the princes of Israel at the dedication of the tabernacle [Numbers VII].[122] It thus serves as an appropriate justification for the grandiose and costly restorations made to the Lateran district by Sixtus V while evoking the Ark of the Covenant which is so central to both the *Library* and the allegories of the *Treasure* and *League* facing it. Like Saint Francis, the founder of his Order, Sixtus V restores sacred buildings and, with biblical prece-

[118] The exorcism for obelisks is printed in Pietro Galesino, *Ordo Dedicationis Obelisci Quem S. D. N. Sixtus V. Pont. Max.* ... (Rome, 1586), 27-30. On the particulars, see Chapter IV, 143, below.

[119] Duchesne, *Liber Pontificalis*, I, 141; Platina, *De Vitis*, 26; Panvinio, *Vite*, 21, mentions the fast; Ciccarelli, *Egitto, Vite*, 16v; Baronio, *Annales*, II, 6, 7: 545-547; and Ugonio, "Vitae," 28v, 29.

[120] Noted by Duchesne, *Liber Pontificalis*, I, 141, note 4. Ugonio, "Vitae," 28v, refers to the prophets in general as the source for this decree. Platina, *De Vitis*, 26, points to both the prophets and Psalm IV.

[121] Duchesne, *Liber Pontificalis*, I, 143, variant; Baronio, *Annales*, II,1: 581; Ugonio, "Vitae," 31. Neither Platina, *De Vitis*, 27-28, Panvinio, *Vite*, 22, nor Ciccarelli, *Egitto, Vite*, 17v, mention this decree.

[122] Compare Pietro Bianco in ... *Carmina*, 24: "Per te, Sixte, Crucis nunc Obeliscus honos / Transtulit vt Moses Aegypti argentea vasa / In Domini obsequium praecipiente Deo;" and Leon de Alava, *Concio Habita Coram Sixto V. P.O.M. Dominica Pentecostes* ... (Rome, 1589), n.p., who speaks of golden vessels in the context of the Eucharist: "postquam praeciosissima sacramenta, (velut vasa gratiae aurea) tam ad agni immaculati hostium, quam ad peccatorum expiationem necessaria, excellentiae suae auctoritate condiderat."

dent on his side, endows them with sumptuousness and imperial splendour so that he may fashion on earth a reflection of the Heavenly City, a new Ark of the Covenant constructed of gold [Revelation XXI: 18].

Saint Urbanus I is followed by Saint Pontianus I, the nineteenth vicar of Christ (fig. 45.N). Like Urbanus, Pontianus I is uncrowned, but is accompanied by a putto holding his tiara. Donned in traditional vestments and shoes, the pope is in prayer, looking up with fingers touching. Pontianus I's *titulus* describes the devout faith of the martyr-pope:[123] "S. PONTIA-NVS I / PP. XIX / IN SARDINIA OB PERPETVAM / FIDEI TVENDAE CONSTANTIAM / RELEGATVS OBIIT ET ROMAM / FABIANO PONT[IFEX] CVRANTE DELATVS / IN COEME-TERIO CALISTI SEPELITVR".

The illustrative "medallion" shows a group of figures, backs turned to the spectator, who apparently carry the pope in a funeral procession (fig. 45.n).

Saint Antherus I responds to Zepherinus I on the east wall in that they both flank the extended emblem of the *Lateran* (figs. 45.O and 61; also refer hereafter to fig. 41). Antherus I wears the tiara, cope and shoes, and rests his foot on a pillow. He looks out towards the viewer, and rests an open book on his lap, pointing to a passage with his right hand, and gesturing with his left. Antherus' *titulus* commemorates his interest in documenting Church history, in emulation of the apostles, who wrote the gospels:[124] "S. ANTHERVS I / PP. XX / SANCIVIT / VT SANCTOR[VM] MARTYRVM ACTA / A NOTARIIS CON-SCRIBERENTVR".

Antherus' decree is utilized as the superscript of the emblem describing the *Abundance* (fig. 45.10). As such, the eucharistic pears, shaken from the tree of Christ and the Church by the Sixtine lion in order to feed the faithful sheep, become the holy martyrs, the "fruits of the faith." In turn, the Sixtine lion, who feeds the faithful with the knowledge of the martyrs' sacrifices, suggests Sixtus V's publication of the Roman Martyrology, revising and correcting the work begun during Gregory XIII's pontificate.[125]

Saint Fabianus I, the twenty-first vicar of Christ, is situated adjacent to Antherus I (fig. 45.P). Fabianus I wears the papal tiara, cope and shoes, rests his right foot on a pillow, holds a book in his left hand, and gestures upwards with his right. The inscription describes his continued interest in the acts of the holy martyrs, and in the city of Rome:[126] "S. FABIANVS I / PP. XXI / INSTITVIT / SEPTEM REGIONES IN VRBE / TOTIDEMQVE DIACONOS / QVI NOTARIIS PRAEESSENT / VT SANCTOR MARTYRVM / RES GESTAS / CONQVI-RERENT".

The feigned medallion shows an enthroned Fabianus I appointing seven deacons kneeling before him, in keeping with the dictates of Christ as enacted in Acts VI: 5-6 (fig. 45.p). The scribes charged to document the history and Good Works of the martyrs are shown in the background.

The last extended emblem of the east wall incorporates Saint Cornelius I (figs. 45.Q and 62). He wears the papal tiara, cope and shoes, and places his feet on a rest supported by a pillow. Cornelius holds an open book, and points to his decretal with his left hand, while gesturing with his right. A putto to his left holds up another book, no doubt the Bible, towards the coffered heaven of the Salone. The *titulus* documents his veneration of the Apostles Peter and Paul:[127] "S. CORNELIVS I /

[123] Duchesne, *Liber Pontificalis*, I, 145; Baronio, *Annales*, II, 6: 600; Platina, *De Vitis*, 29; Panvinio, *Vite*, 23; Ciccarelli, Egitto, *Vite*, 18v; Ugonio, "Vitae," 31, 32.

[124] Duchesne, *Liber Pontificalis*, I, 147; Platina, *De Vitis*, 30; Panvinio, *Vite*, 24; Ciccarelli, Egitto, *Vite*, 19v; and Ugonio, "Vitae," 31. Baronio, *Annales*, II, 2: 601, does not ascribe this work to Antherus.

[125] On the Roman Martyrology and its revision by Baronio in 1586 and 1589 see Benedetto Cignitti, "Cesare Baronio Cultore dei Martiri," *A Cesare Baronio: Scritti vari* (Sora, 1963), 299-306; and Sergio Mottironi, "Cesare Baronio agiografo," *idem*, 307-313.

[126] Duchesne, *Liber Pontificalis*, I, 148 and variant; Platina, *De Vitis*, 30; Panvinio, *Vite*, 25; Baronio, *Annales*, II, 2: 601; and Ugonio, "Vitae," 31v, 32. Compare Ciccarelli, Egitto, *Vite*, 20v, who mention the seven deacons, but not the seven regions.

[127] Duchesne, *Liber Pontificalis*, I, 150; Baronio, *Annales*, II, 3: 534. Platina, *De Vitis*, 32 states that the apostles were buried in different locales according to their places of martyrdom, Peter in the Temple of Apollo, and Paul in the Via Ostiensis, as does Panvinio, *Vite*, 27; Ugonio, "Vitae," 32v, 33; and *idem*, *Historia delle Stationi di Roma Che si celebrano la Quadragesima ...* (Rome, 1588), 87v-88, 90 and 228. Ciccarelli, Egitto, *Vite*, 21v, omit Peter and Paul and mention Lucina only with regard to Cornelius' burial.

PP. XXII / CORPORA SS [SANCTISSIMVM] APOSTOLORVM / PETRI ET PAVLI E CATACVMBIS / LVCINAE MATRON[AE] SANCTISS[IMAE] ROGATV / AD BASILICAM B. PETRO DICATAM / TRANSTVLIT".

Rather than illustrate Cornelius I's work in a "medallion," his inscription is incorporated into the emblem of the *Holy House of Loreto* (fig. 45.11). In this sense, the basilica of Saint Peter, an anachronism to be sure, is explicitly equated to the basilica dedicated to the Virgin at Loreto, while the shrine housing the tomb of the apostles is compared to the shrine enclosing the Virgin's house. Since the Virgin's house was miraculously transported to Loreto in the thirteenth century by angels, not by Sixtus V, then the extended emblem should refer to a translation affected or planned by the pope which is comparable to both the miraculous translation of the Holy House and the translation by Cornelius I of the bodies of Peter and Paul. The most apparent analogy is Sixtus V's translation of the crib of Christ to his burial chapel in Santa Maria Maggiore, another basilica dedicated to the Virgin.[128] A second analogy is provided by a Good Work never realized by Sixtus V: the purchase from the Turks of the most sacrosanct tomb of Catholicism, the Holy Sepulchre, and its translation to the Eternal City.[129] A third possibility is that the translation alluded to in the emblem is the regular visit of Church officials to the graves of Peter and Paul, instituted by Sixtus V in the first year of his pontificate.[130] While it is unclear whether the analogy is to be found in one or more of the possibilities suggested here, it is clear that the *Holy House* is like its pendant, the *City of Montalto*, in contradistinction to the emblems with allegorical images, since the nexus uniting Cornelius' actions and Sixtus V's is to be found in the *subscriptio*, rather than in the *imago*.[131] When read in this manner, Sixtus V may be understood as continuing the work of Cornelius, who similarly protected the bodies of Saints Peter and Paul, and gave both the lambs and sheep a shrine for the veneration of the apostles.

Last in the roster of popes represented on the east wall is Saint Lucius I, the twenty-third vicar of Christ (fig. 45.R) and successor to Cornelius I. Lucius I wears the papal cope and shoes, rests his right foot on a pillow and balances a book with left knee and right hand, while holding his chest with his left hand. A putto seated to Lucius I's right holds his papal tiara. Like Linus, seated opposite him on the west wall, Lucius is unaccompanied by either a medallion or a Good Work of Sixtus V. He is remembered in the inscription below for having instituted a law to ensure that bishops' lives be documented:[132] "S. LVCIVS I / PP. XXIII / SANCIVIT VT PRESBYTERI DVO DIACONI TRES IN OMNI LOCO EPISCOPVM COMITARENTVR IN EIVS VITAE TESTIMONIVM". While Lucius' decree most certainly reflects a desire to preserve Church history for posterity, emulating the apostles who first wrote the gospels, it also had a basis in the scriptures. As Lucius himself explains, the bishop's activities had to be documented not so much to ensure that his acts were virtuous, since it was understood that a bishop would follow Paul's admonition in 1 Timothy III: 2 and Titus I: 6 ff, but, rather, to provide ammunition for use against evil doers who would dare question a bishop's activities [I Timothy III: 7].[133]

The last pope in the chronology represented in the Salone dei Papi is Saint Sylvester I, the thirty-fourth pope, who is also situated on the south wall as a pendant to Saint Peter (figs.

[128] It may also be significant in this context that Sixtus V translated the body of Pius V to Santa Maria Maggiore.

[129] In this regard, it is interesting to note that Gerolamo Badesio, *De Sacello Sixti V. Pont. Max. in Exquiliis ...* (Rome, 1588), 21, mentions a Lucina in his poem on the Praesepio. On Sixtus V's wish to translate the Holy Sepulchre, see my Introduction, 23, and note 4, above.

[130] On the visit *ad limina*, see my Introduction, 23, note 6, above.

[131] Each of the emblems has a common denominator in the Ark of the Covenant. However, this connection cannot be readily understood until the devices featuring the obelisks and columns have been analyzed together with related devices, especially those featuring the "triple mountain" *corpo*. See my forthcoming "Simbolismo ermetico," *Sisto V*, for an analysis of the "triple mountain" devices, and the Ark of the Covenant.

[132] Duchesne, *Liber Pontificalis*, I, 153; Platina, *De Vitis*, 33; Panvinio, *Vite*, 29; Ciccarelli, *Egitto*, *Vite*, 22v; Baronio, *Annales*, III, 5: 101; and Ugonio, "Vitae," 33v.

[133] Epistle of Lucius to the Bishops of France and Spain in *Corpus Juris Canonici*, "De Consecratione," D. 1, C. LX, 1162. This is also explained in Ciccarelli, *Egitto*, *Vite*, 22v.

42.S and 56). Pope Sylvester I wears the papal tiara, cope and sandals, rests his foot on a pillow, and looks upwards, left hand over chest and right hand gesturing. A roaring dragon sits at his left foot, and at his right, a tamed, reclining wolf. The dragon refers to the *Legenda Sancti Silvestri* which, as I have indicated in Chapter I, relates how Sylvester rid Rome and the Christian commonwealth of evil by binding the dragon's mouth. This act is symbolically suggested by the subservient position of the dragon at Sylvester's feet. The wolf, a traditional symbol of evil as represented in the *Extirpation*, as well as an attribute of the god Apollo, has already been subdued and lounges peacefully at the pope's feet.[134] A putto peeks at the pope from behind his throne, while another, holding a curtain over the Sixtine lion, glances at the wolf. Sylvester's *titulus* commemorates his momentous conversion of a Roman emperor, and the first ecumenical council:[135] "S. SILVESTER I / PP. XXXIIII / CONSTANTINVM IMP[ERATOR] / BAPTIZAVIT ET / OECVMENIC[VM] / NICAENVM / CONC[ILIVM] I. CELEBRAVIT".

The circular "medallion," situated above the feigned doorway, corresponding to that beneath Peter, illustrates the pope's baptism of Emperor Constantine (figs. 42.s and 57). In lieu of the actual baptism that was likely administered by Eusebius of Nicomedia at Constantine's deathbed in 337, or even of the mythological baptism in the Lateran Baptistry, the iconographer preferred to defer to the mythology of the *Legenda Sancti Silvestri*. He evidently instructed the artist(s) to render the emperor kneeling before a baptismal font and Pope Sylvester, following his bout of leprosy (the untamed wolf) and vision of Saints Peter and Paul, a vision not incidentally represented nearby in the Benediction Loggia.[136] While the Council of Nicea referred to in the *titulus* is not represented in the "medallion," the baptism of the emperor by the pope serves to underscore the momentous decree of this Council stating that the decisions of the pope outweighed all others, including, of course, the imperial representative.[137] This victory is further underscored by the Apolline wolf at Sylvester's feet who, by association, may signify Constantine *Sol Invictus Imperator*, having been tamed, or, more precisely, cleansed and converted to the true faith. This last of the popes represented on the upper tier thus embodies the first culmination of what the earlier popes had been striving for: the triumph of Christianity on earth and the temporal reflection of the spiritual Ecclesia.

When viewed collectively, the early popes form a homogeneous unit since all are enthroned beneath baldachins and enclosures, and all are represented with idealized portraits. So, too, the contributions of the early popes, as documented on the architrave, have a common basis in the Scripture, and particularly in the books of the New Testament, from which the unique *titulus* of Peter derives, and to which the apostolic popes so often refer in their letters. The *tituli* themselves were derived ultimately from the *Liber Pontificalis*, apparently by way of Platina's *Lives*, written for Pope Sixtus IV.[138] On the authority of the extended emblems it is clear that the choice of popes to be represented was made according to the correspondence of their decretals to those of Sixtus V. In this way the Golden Age being realized by Pope Sixtus V is shown to have been presaged by the early popes whose exemplary lives and works have laid the foundation for the present age. It is also clear that the iconographer did not determine the correspon-

[134] Valeriano, *Hieroglyphica*, XI, ii. It is worth noting that the British cherished Constantine because his mother had supposedly been British, in Strong, *Britannia Triumphans*, 24.

[135] Duchesne, *Liber Pontificalis*, I, 170, 171; Platina, *De Vitis*, 44; Panvinio, *Vite*, 43; Ciccarelli, *Egitto*, *Vite*, 33v, who begin the "Second Part" with Sylvester; Baronio, *Annales*, III, 18: 613 ff; and Ugonio, "Vitae," 43-43v.

[136] Baronio, *Annales*, III, "18: 620, confirms the efficacy of the *Legenda*, or *Acts of Sylvester*: "Caeterum quod spectat ad ipsa Silvestri Acti, quaenam vera sint atque legitima, lapis lydius demonstrabit."

[137] See, for example, the discussion in Pansa, *Libraria*, 127-132.

[138] The only exception is Urbanus I's decree.

dences for the emblems on the east wall on a one-to-one basis. Rather, he mustered all the creativity required to fashion those learned puzzles from which the Cinquecento observer would derive such pleasure in the deciphering. He may well have derived inspiration from Platina's Life of Peter, which contains references to imperial works which correspond *in malo* to the *exempla* of Sixtus V.[139] The connection between the conversion of Britain by Eleuterius, for example, is not simply the Sixtine bull exhorting the Christian princes to take part in the conversion of Queen Elizabeth and her wandering subjects, but the *City of Montalto*, supposedly the archetype, in a personal way, for the Christian domain.[140] In like manner, the *Abundance* was chosen instead of the Vatican Press, formed to disseminate the essential texts of Catholicism, as an analogue to the work of Antherus.[141] While a keen observer, cognizant of the achievements of Sixtus V, could grasp the correspondence between Linus' decree and the Sixtine bull forbidding women from wearing the latest in *haute couture* while demanding that they cover their heads in public,[142] or the displeasure of Sixtus V, as of Soterus, at the nuns of Spain who were mishandling sacred objects, such clear parallels do not, on the surface, hold true for each of the works of the apostolic popes in relation to those of Sixtus V. The observer steeped in Sixtine lore would be required to penetrate the subtle and even absurd nuances in the Sixtine decrees which would then facilitate the connection, much in the manner of the emblems. But it would have been sufficient, it seems to me, that the viewer grasp the essential continuity between the early Church and that being fashioned by Sixtus V by deciphering the emblems, and by reading the messages of Peter and Sylvester I on the main wall. The emblems, as I have endeavoured to show, establish the reciprocity between the early decretals and the Sixtine bulls, while the popes on the main wall, representing the Alpha and Omega of the apostolic Church, each presided over Church Councils, making their works eminently appropriate for the main wall of the hall destined to be used for Church Councils. The significance of the works of Peter and Sylvester I for the Sixtine pontificate, moreover, would have been readily understood by a late Cinquecento observer, owing to the celebrity of the bull *Immensa aeterni dei*, whereby Sixtus V not only restructured the College of Cardinals, but also clarified the pope's role in the convocation and decisions of Church Councils by taking for himself and his successors sole authority based, like every other bull issued from his court, on the decrees of the Council of Trent.[143] In a hall destined to be used for Church Councils, the message that this continuity between the early popes and Sixtus V conveys is to the point: the apostolic authority given to Christ's vicar had not only remained constant over the centuries, but the decrees of the early popes, made the more binding in Church Councils, would be upheld by Sixtus V and his successors for all time.

As I have indicated above, the organization of the south wall, with the first and last popes in the succession housed together, effectively disrupts and negates the chronology so that the popes on the upper tier, like the Good Works of Sixtus V on the lower, must also be read in an achronological manner. Like the representations of the Good Works, there are certain formal markers in the actual rendering of the popes that confirm this thematic reading. Beginning with the main wall of the Salone, Sylvester I and Peter are contained within scal-

[139] Platina, *De Vitis*, 5-6: "Neque enim inter malos omninò, neque inter bonos principes numerari potest [Tiberius]. In homine fuit multa litteratura, & grauis eloquentia: bella per se nunquam, sed per legatos gessit, tumultus exortos prudenter suppressit [League]. / ... Auaritia omnia expilauit. Tantae libidinis fuit [Caligula], vt etiam sororibus stuprum intulerit [Extirpation]. ... De conditione temporum suorum saepè etiam questus est, quòd nullis calamitatibus publicis insignirentur, velut Tiberij tempora, quibus obtrita fuerunt ad viginti millia hominum casu theatri apud Tarracinam [Terracina]. Ita autem Virgilij & Liuij gloriae inuidit [Monte Cavallo], vt paulum abfuerit, quin eorum scripta & imagines ex omnibus bibliothecis amouerit [Library] ... seipsum verò in Deos transfert [Herod]: imagines in templo Hierosolymitano collocat [Holy House] ... Inuenta est & ingens arca variorum venenorum [Treasure] ... Claudius enim C. Caligulae patruus, quem nepos in ludibrium referuauerat, imperium accipiens, quintus ab Augusto Britanniam, quam neque ante Iulium Caesarem, neque post eum quisquam attingere ausus est, in deditionem accepit [Montalto] ... Laboratum eodem quoque tempore annonae caritate vbique est, Agabo propheta tantam calamitatem praedicente [Abundance]. Ab externo hoste securus, perfecit aquaeductum [Acqua Felice], cuius ruinas apud Lateranum à Caio inchoatum [Lateran] ... Portum quoque Ostiensem, quem adhuc cum admiratione intuemur, extruxit, ducto dextra laeuaque brachio ad coërcendos maris fluctus. Messalina uxore conuicta probri interfecta ... [Civitavecchia]."

[140] *Bullarum Romanorum*, VIII, 740-742.

[141] *Bullarum Romanorum*, VIII, 724-726.

[142] *Bullarum Romanorum*, VIII, 819-821; 821-828.

[143] *Bullarum Romanorum*, VIII, 991-992, and especially subsection "Sequitur declaratio facultatum praedictarum Congregationum" in *idem*, VIII, 997-998. Also consult the discussion of the pope's autocratic interpretation of his duty in von Pastor, *History*, XXI, 274 ff.

loped baldachins enclosed by a brown marble arch surmounted by a garlanded, cartouche-like form of brown marble and
green inlay and a frieze of egg-and-dart motif (figs. 42.S,A; and
41). These baldachins and enclosures are also found on the
north wall of the Salone (fig. 44.G,H), and therefore suggest
that Popes Sylvester and Peter, Anicetus and Soterus ought to
be read as pendants across their respective walls and across
the longitudinal axis of the hall.

The pontificates of Peter and Sylvester, as commemorated
in the inscriptions describing their works, are comparable in
that both convened councils in which the authority and decrees of Christ's vicar took precedence over that of all others.
The first council resulted in a victory over the Jews, and the
second, in a victory over the pagans. As the feigned medallions
and the *titulus* of Sylvester explain, in each case the victory
was signalled by the baptismal waters respectively administered by Peter on the instruction of Christ, and by Sylvester in
the momentous conversion of the Emperor Constantine to
Christianity. The Good Works of Anicetus and Soterus are
united in their concern for the proper administration of the
dioceses in the See of Saint Peter, specifically with the ordination of archbishops and bishops, and the lawful celebration of
the mass. In each case, the bishop's supremacy in the Church
hierarchy is stressed, together with his rightful duty to ensure
that the mass is conducted properly. Collectively, then, the
popes on the south and north walls convey the lawful exercise
of the ministry under the authority of the bishop, in particular
the administration of baptism and the celebration of the mass
as vehicles by which salvation may be achieved.

Unlike the main walls of the Salone, which are composed
and decorated in like manner, the west and east walls differ
from each other, and from the main walls, both in terms of
composition and decoration. The west wall, which contains
fewer representations of popes than the east wall due to the
windows, houses two types of baldachins and enclosures.
Reading from left to right, the first type of baldachin is formed
of hanging pelmets and is positioned within a shell-niched
arch and garlanded cartouche of white marble and yellow inlay with an egg-and-dart frieze (fig. 43.B). This is the only baldachin and enclosure of this design on the west wall, and it belongs to Pope Linus, who is unaccompanied on the lower register by either feigned medallion or tapestry. The second type is
comprised of a spherical baldachin enframed by a feigned
white marble arch surmounted by a garlanded cartouche of
white marble and yellow inlay and a frieze of egg-and-dart motif (fig. 43.C,D,E,F). This type belongs to popes whose Good
Works are illustrated in feigned medallions squeezed between
the variously coloured "columns" on the temporal tier directly
beneath, namely Popes Sixtus, Telesphorus, Hyginus and Pius.
The result of this formal imbalance is to set Linus apart from
his successors and to shift the emphasis towards the right of
the wall, so that, despite the fact that there are five popes alternating with five windows, the windows serve to frame the four
remaining popes and to set them into relief. Given the precedent of the pendant groups of popes on the south and north
walls, and, of course, the pendant groups of Good Works of
Sixtus V on the lower register, Popes Sixtus, Telesphorus, Hyginus, and Pius should also be read as pendants.

Whereas the popes on the main walls form natural pendants, as do the Good Works of Sixtus V, the popes on the west

wall may be read according to all possible combinations. Since Sixtus and Telesphorus are accompanied by putti bearing tiaras (fig. 43.C,D), while both Hyginus and Pius wear their tiaras and hold books (fig. 43.E,F), then they should be read as pairs. Common to the works of both Sixtus and Telesphorus is the mass, while Hyginus and Pius signify the spiritual renewal and promise of salvation made possible by baptism and Christ's sacrifice on the Cross. Conversely, a consideration of the coloration of the "columns" flanking the popes' "medallions" yields a second set of pendants that naturally interlocks with the first. The "medallions" of both Sixtus and Pius are flanked by simulated Yellow Numidian and Green Serpentine columns, and together signify the promise of salvation made possible by Christ's death and the partaking of his body at the mass (fig. 43.c,f). The "medallions" of Telesphorus and Hyginus are flanked by simulated Green Serpentine and Portasanta columns, and together signify birth and baptism, or rebirth (fig. 43.d,e). Hence, these popes and their Good Works collectively convey the message of the promise of salvation offered by the Church and her visible head, the pope, through baptism and the mass. Such a message is consonant with that of the south and north walls.

Having thus reconciled the west wall according to the visual given of the architecture and frescoed decorations, it becomes readily apparent that the east wall, although more populated and seemingly complex, is organized according to precisely the same principles. The orientation of the west wall towards the right, or northern end, of the Salone is echoed on the east wall. Facing Linus, the odd pope out of the west wall, is Lucius, likewise situated beneath a baldachin with hanging pelmets and unaccompanied by either feigned medallion or tapestry on the lower tier (fig. 45.R). To Lucius' left, towards the northern end of the Salone, are ten popes. Five are enclosed within spherical baldachins enframed by a feigned white marble arch surmounted by a garlanded cartouche of white marble and yellow inlay and a frieze of egg-and-dart motif, and these popes face those situated under like baldachins and enclosures on the west wall (fig. 45.P,N,L,J). Also like their foils on the west wall, these popes are accompanied by feigned medallions describing their works documented on the architrave (fig. 45.p,n,l,j). The remaining five illusionistic popes are seated beneath scalloped baldachins enframed by a tripartite opening, all in yellow marble and surmounted by white mountains of Sixtus V's heraldry that pierce through the crowning segmental pediment and egg-and-dart frieze (fig. 45.Q,O,M,K,I). These popes alternate with those seated beneath spherical baldachins and are accompanied by Good Works of Sixtus V in "tapestry" formats (fig. 45.11,10,9,8), or, in the case of the central pope, by the *Lateran* (fig. 45.X). Hence, these popes correspond to the windows on the west wall which are similarly accompanied on the lower tier by Good Works of Sixtus V. Also like the windows, these popes serve to frame those with feigned medallions. By virtue of their darker coloration and disposition, these popes also serve to set those beside them into relief.

Just as Sixtus, Telesphorus, Hyginus, and Pius formed a group of interlocking pendants, so do Victor, Callistus, Pontianus, and Fabianus (fig. 45.J,L,N,P). Victor and Callistus are paired by virtue of the fact that both wear a tiara and hold a book (fig. 45.J,L), like Hyginus and Pius situated opposite them on the west wall. Complementing the message embodied in the works of the earlier popes, that of the achievements of Victor and Callistus concerns the salvation awaiting the faithful made possible through their penance. Conversely, Pontianus and Fabianus form a pair (fig. 45.N,P). Although one is in an attitude of prayer accompanied by a putto holding his tiara, while the other wears a tiara and holds a book, their attitudes and attributes correspond to those of Sixtus and Telesphorus positioned directly opposite on the west wall. Their works convey the message that faith in Christ and in the martyrs makes possible the remission of sins and ultimate gift of salvation. In turn, a second set of pendants is formed in relation to the feigned medallions and "columns" flanking them. Victor and Fabianus, whose "medallions" are enclosed by simulated columns of Yellow Numidian and Green Serpentine marble (fig. 45.j,p), signify the promise of salvation made possible through penance and faith in the martyrs, whose sacrifice formed the basis of the early Church. The "medallions" illustrating the works of Callistus and Pontianus are flanked by simulated Green Serpentine and abbreviated Portasanta columns (fig. 45.1,n), and collectively convey the idea that through penance and belief in the martyrs eternal life may be achieved. The quartet of Victor, Callistus, Pontianus, and Fabianus thus convey the message that through baptism, the mass, and the saints, salvation is made possible.

Finally, when the west and east walls are viewed as foils, then popes Linus and Lucius are no longer alone, as it were, and, in addition to forming pendants across the space of the Salone, they reinforce the principle (fig. 43.B; fig. 45.R). Together with the north wall, their message affirms the importance of the Bishop of Rome's leadership and guidance for the Catholic Church.

When viewed in their totality, the pendant groups of the apostolic popes assert a number of interrelated themes: the authority of the bishop in the hierarchy of the Church, including Church councils attended by the emperor, and the proper administration of the ministry of Christ under the supervision of the Bishop of Rome; the centrality of the mass and of baptism in the Christian rite; and the importance of penance and the saints as vehicles by which the pious Christian may receive remission of sins and embark upon that pilgrimage that leads ultimately to salvation, and entry into the Heavenly Jerusalem. Not only are each of these themes based on the teaching of Christ as reflected and emulated in the decrees and acts of the apostolic popes, but they also represent the most fundamental doctrines of the Catholic Church which were set forth by Christ himself, in his own words. As Baronio explains, it was Christ who instituted the ministry at the Last Supper when he commanded the apostles to "Do this for a commemoration of me" [Luke XXII: 19]; Christ who admonished the apostles to "teach ye all nations; baptizing them in the name of the Father, and of the Son and of the Holy Ghost" [Matthew XXVIII: 19]; Christ who promised that "whatever you [the apostles] shall bind upon earth, shall be bound also in heaven; and whatsoever you [the apostles] shall loose upon earth, shall be loosed also in heaven [Matthew XVIII: 18]; Christ who instructed the apostles "that penance and remission of sins should be preached in his name, unto all nations" [Luke XXIV: 47]; Christ who gave to the apostles the power to absolve the sins of the faithful, when he said "Receive ye the Holy Ghost, whose sins you shall forgive, they are forgiven; and whose sins you shall retain, they shall be retained" [John XX: 22-23]; and Christ who gave to Peter and his successors absolute supremacy in the hierarchy of the Church on earth [Matthew XVI: 18-19; John XXI: 17].[144] Indeed, the one, holy, Catholic and apostolic Church is shown to have been instituted by Christ, and to have been run according to the letter of his word by the apostolic popes. Furthermore, and as the emblems attest, Sixtus V continues to uphold and oversee the administration of the sacraments to the faithful and the exercise of the ministry. But at the heart of the Church, and at the heart of the messages contained in the Good Works of Christ's vicars in the Salone dei Papi, is Christ himself and his sacrifice on the Cross for humanity. As Saint Paul taught, through the mass we may relive Christ's sacrifice "on the altar of the Cross," receive remission of sins, and await our ultimate "deliverance ... from the power of darkness and translation ... into his kindgom" [Colossians I: 13].[145] Through baptism "we die and are buried together with Christ" [Romans VI: 3-4; Colossians II: 12]; we are forgiven our sins and granted remission [Acts II: 38]; receive the grace of the Holy Spirit [Titus III: 6; Ephesians I: 14; 2 Corinthians I: 22, V: 5], and an abundance of virtues [Titus III: 5-6]; and we are endowed with the "sign" by which we are "sealed" and "united to Christ," through whom the doors of Heaven are opened.[146] Through penance, "the channel through which the blood of Christ flows into the soul," those sins which are accrued after baptism may be remitted and "washed away."[147] Through the honour of saints, the invocation of their intercession, and the veneration of their relics and tombs, we may imitate these imitators of Christ and, through our penitence, receive a foretaste of the Heavenly Jerusalem.[148] Central to each of these Pauline doctrines, in fact the vehicle through which they are realized, is the Sacrament of the Eucharist. As the *Catechism of the Council of Trent* explains: "nothing is more fertile of spiritual fruit, than the contemplation of the exalted dignity of this most august Sacrament. From it we learn how great must be the perfection of the gospel dispensation, under which we enjoy the reality of that, which under the Mosaic Law was only shadowed by types and figures".[149] As the verse of the *Abundance* in the Salone dei Papi suggests, so powerful is the eucharistic sustenance that it melted the manna fed to the Israelites under Moses' rule to make way for the reception of the true Christian manna, the shining body of Christ, the *"verus sol iustitiae."*

Just as the *impresa* of the *Abundance* is the clearest indicator of the Golden Age being realized by Pope Sixtus V on the lower register, so its atypical verse provides the most salient clues for a eucharistic interpretation of the Good Works of the apostolic popes. To complete the reading, the superscript of the emblem of the *Abundance* and its illustration in the form of Antherus reinforces what is represented visually in the Salone: the apostolic popes are both illustrious exemplars and inhabitants of the Heavenly City, living with Christ in the "Communion of Saints," which is the Church, and interceding on behalf of the faithful, especially Pope Sixtus V, the "Franciscan" column who upholds these saintly popes.[150] But above all, and as Roman Catholic Reform preachers so often taught, it is through the *imitatio Christi* that the saintly popes have achieved the bliss of the Heavenly City, and with their divine inspiration and assistance, that Sixtus V achieves the Golden Age of Christianity on earth, and awaits his final translation to

[144] Baronio, *Annales*, I, 198: 164.

[145] *Catechism*, 246-251, and especially 249.

[146] *Catechism*, 156-193, and especially 179 ff.

[147] *Catechism*, 251-294, and especially 257.

[148] *Catechism*, 354-367, and especially 356-358.

[149] *Catechism*, 225.

[150] The "Composite-Sixtine" columns upholding the Salone represent the Christian *topos* that the pope upholds the Church on earth, as do his cardinals. Scipione Ammirato, *Oratione al Beatiss. et Santiss. Padre, et Signor Nostro Sisto Quinto ...* (Florence, 1594), 29, uses the *topos* with reference to Sixtus V himself. As I have shown above, the *topos* is also used with regard to St. Francis in the verse accompanying the *Lateran*; and Sixtus V himself used it regarding his cardinals in the bull *Postquam verus*. Also consult A. V. Antonovics, "Counter-Reformation Cardinals: 1534-90," *European Studies Review* II (1972): 306-307.

join the Communion of Saints.[151]   Finally, and as the preponderance of Sixtine stars attest, so profound is Sixtus V's belief in Christ and his mother and bride, the Church, and so great is his station as Christ's vicar, that his brightness and warmth illuminate and protect the Church Militant, providing a reflection on earth of the Triumphant Church in heaven.

3. SPIRITUAL TIER: THE INSTITUTION OF THE PRIMACY SCENES

In his description of the Salone dei Papi, Domenico Fontana gives the feigned panel paintings representing the Institution of the Primacy pride of place, whereas in his list of the inscriptions, he lists the "panels" after the apostolic popes and the *Lateran*.[152] The "panel paintings" are situated in the center of the upper tiers of the south and north walls of the Salone dei Papi and are the largest elements of the hall (figs. 42.A, 41, 69, 44.B1 and 64). As feigned *quadri*, the biblical narratives are not only differentiated from all other elements of the Salone, but they also project further into the beholder's space than the feigned tapestries, *Lateran*, and feigned medallions on the lower register. Since the frames of the feigned panels are broken at the bottom, they are imbued with an even higher level of reality and, in this way, exist on the same illusionistic stage as the apostolic popes, also situated on the upper register. The formal primacy of the "panels" is echoed in their content, which provides both the divinely ordained justification for the absolute supremacy enjoyed by Christ's vicars in the temporal and spiritual realms, and the god-given laws by which the Church is to function on earth.

The first narrative in chronological order is situated on the south wall and shows Christ's investiture to Peter at Caesaria Philippi (fig. 63), recalling the *Traditio Legis* represented on the main apse of Leo III's triconch *triclinium*. It is accompanied by the biblical quotation "TV ES PETRVS ET SVPER HANC PETRAM / AEDIFICABO ECCLESIAM MEAM" [Matthew XVI: 18] so as to ensure the viewer's recognition of the event represented. The second narrative, situated on the north wall, shows the resurrected Christ appointing Peter as the guardian of the Christian people (fig. 64), with the quotation "PASCE / OVES MEAS" [John XXI: 17]. Although the two investiture scenes take place at different times and places - the one at Caesaria Philippi, the other by the sea of Tiberias - in the Salone they take place before the same buildings, seen from different angles. In this way formal continuity is established for scenes representing the key biblical passages traditionally used in tandem by the papacy to prove that Christ had given to Peter, and to Peter alone among the apostles, the duty and privilege of carrying on His mission as the head of the Christian Church.[153] Moreover, such continuity agrees with the views of the Quirinal afforded by the *Acqua Felice* and *Monte Cavallo* "tapestries," located directly beneath the Investiture scenes.

The investiture given to Peter at Caesaria Philippi took place while Christ was still alive on earth. As Matthew relates, Christ chose Peter of all the apostles to serve as the foundation of the Church on earth because only Peter had received the revelation of Christ's true nature from God the Father by way of the Holy Ghost [Matthew XI: 27]. In order that there be no

[151] See McGinness, "Rhetoric," 332 and note 139.

[152] Fontana, *Della trasportatione*, 59v, 60v.

[153] See in particular Jerome, *Contra Iovin*, book 1 in Cornelio Cornelio a Lapide, *Commentaria in Sacram Scripturam ...*, ed. Sisto Riario Sforza, 10 vols. (Naples, 1857), VIII, 253.

mistake that it was Peter who was to have been singled out from the ten remaining apostles present, Christ used a play on words in his charge, namely *Cepha/Petrus* and *Cepha/Petram*, drawing on the name which he had first given to Simon at Bethania [John I: 42].[154] Yet, Christ's investiture at Caesaria Philippi did not end with his proclamation that Peter was to be the foundation of the Church. Christ went on to promise that the Church would emerge victorious over the Devil, and to grant Peter legislative and judicial authority: "And the gates of hell shall not prevail against it. And I will give to thee the keys of the kingdom of heaven. And whatsoever thou shalt bind on earth it shall be bound also in heaven: and whatsoever thou shalt loose on earth, it shall be loosed also in heaven" [Matthew XVI: 18-19].

Although the narrative on the south wall is accompanied by an inscription containing the first part of the charge only, the visual evidence allows the beholder to grasp the fuller meaning of Christ's gift. First, the figural placement and gestures of Christ and Peter in *Christ's investiture to Peter* reflect those of Christ and Peter in traditional scenes representing the last part of the charge, such as Perugino's *Giving of the Keys* (1481) in the Sistine Chapel of the Vatican. Secondly, in *Christ appoints Peter Guardian* Peter has both keys hanging from a cord and draped over his right arm as he kneels in supplication to receive his second charge from Christ. In the earliest, apostolic sense, the keys are understood as the implements by which Christ's vicar could grant indulgences and excommunicate; by which he could cleanse and convert Jew and Gentile to the faith, and extirpate the unchaste wolves from the *respublica Christiana*.[155] They are also analogues to the Lucan passage [XXII: 38] which spawned the Doctrine of the Two Swords.

Whereas the first investiture scene took place while Christ was still manifested on earth, the second scene occurred after the Resurrection. Similarly, while the first scene concerns the power bestowed upon Christ's vicar to have his acts on earth reverberate in heaven, the second concerns the power of Christ's vicar to institute spiritual laws on earth. Consequently, it is with this second narrative, wherein Christ places Peter in his spiritual shoes as pastor of the lambs and sheep, that the Bishop of Rome received confirmation of the spiritual jurisdiction promised in Matthew XVI, and of the spiritually ordained right to minister and administer the Church of Christ on earth.[156]

In their political sense, then, and in accordance with their traditional pairing as exemplified in Baronio's statement referred to above, the Institution of the Primacy scenes are manifestos of the temporal and spiritual authority of Christ's vicars, conveying the central tenet of the *Primatus Petri*.[157] In their apostolic sense, these scenes contain within them the right of Christ's vicar to administer the Sacraments, especially those of Baptism, the Eucharist, and Penance, the means by which the convert may seek to reattain the purity of soul granted at the ceremony of conversion.[158] It is as a consequence of Christ's foundation charter, as represented on the south and north walls of the Salone, that the seated popes on the upper register are represented in various spiritual attitudes and remembered first and foremost as saints, while on the lower tier they carry on Christ's evangelical mission to preach the word, to convert, and to make binding the rules by which Christ and the Holy

[154] Ugonio, "Vitae," 19; Cornelio a Lapide, *Commentaria*, VIII, 251-252.

[155] *Catechism*, 109-110.

[156] Sixtus V revived the ancient practice of distributing "magical" waxen images of the lamb of God as part of his duty to "feed [Christ's] sheep." See the discussion of the Johannine passage in the context of these waxen images in F. Vincenzo Bonardo, *Discorso Intorno all'Origine, Antichita, et Virtu de gli Agnus Dei Di Cera Benedetti* (Rome, 1586), 27. Sixtus V owned a copy of this discourse, in Cugnoni, "Documenti Chigiani," *Società romana di storia patria*, 224.

[157] See 123 ff, note 144, above.

[158] Shearman in *Sistine Chapel*, 57-62, provides patristic sources for the relationship between the Giving of the Keys and the Purification of the Leper (in Sixtine translation, the purification of Constantine) in terms of the Sacrament of Penance. Also consult, for example, Smith, *Casino*, 95-96, who quotes a tract by Leo III in which he singles out the Sacrament of Holy Communion as being part of Christ's charge. On their connotations of the Sacrament of Orders, see the interpretation of Poussin's paintings of the Investiture scenes in Anthony Blunt, *Nicholas Poussin*, Bollingen Series XXXV - 7, 2 vols. (New York, 1967), I, 195-207; and recently in Veronique Gerard Powell, "Les Annales de Baronius et l'iconographie religieuse du XVIIe siècle," *Baronio e l'arte*, 481-487, esp. 485.

Spirit dictated the Catholic Church to be run, rules, it must be stressed, which also extend to the temporal realm of the emperor.

4. SYNTHESIS: THE MEANING OF THE SALONE DEI PAPI

Since all previous commentators on the Salone dei Papi have listed the contents, but have stopped short of interpreting them, the overall meaning of the hall has never been discussed. Furthermore, the intended manner of reading the Salone as a synthetic unit has not been explained largely because the components have either been listed according to the chronological sequence set out on the upper and lower registers, or, as in the case of von Pastor, the components of the lower register have been listed for the most part according to the intended manner, but with only the briefest justification for doing so, while the apostolic popes, their works, and the Institution of the Primacy scenes merit only a mention. In neither case has there been a consideration of how the various components might relate to one another across the boundaries. In the foregoing sections, I have shown that the principle informing the placement of the Good Works of Sixtus V, the apostolic popes and their Good Works, and the Institution of the Primacy narratives, is the pendant, which conforms to the biblical and Franciscan method of preaching "two by two." Further, I have shown that the nexus of the Salone in both form and meaning is the south wall, and that a secondary nexus is to be found in the extended emblem of the *Abundance*, which naturally functions on the vertical axis. As I shall now demonstrate, there is a second reading of the Salone which overlays and interweaves with the reading according to pendants and which, therefore, continues the method that is evidently employed in each of the component parts of the Salone.

When viewed in its entirety, the main wall is clearly composed according to a tripartite system on both the upper and lower registers (fig. 42), emulating the layout of the ancient Sala del Concilio.[159] I have shown how the upper and lower registers are related on the vertical axis in terms of Sylvester I and his "medallion," and Peter and his "medallion," and I have shown how this relationship is carried through the horizontal axes of both registers in the pendant relationship of apostolic popes and their Good Works. Since the horizontal axes pass through *Christ's Investiture to Peter* on the upper tier, and the *Acqua Felice* on the lower, then they too should relate contextually to the popes and feigned medallions respectively flanking them, as the central panel of a triptych relates to its side panels. I have shown how the *Investiture*, which illustrates and describes the first part of the charge related in Matthew XVI: 18, insinuates the final part of the charge by virtue of the figural placement and gestures of Christ and Saint Peter. While the pendant narrative on the opposite wall continues the assertion, further evidence is provided by the "side panels" of Sylvester and Peter which flank the "central panel." That the "gates of hell shall not prevail" is amply attested to by the subdued dragon beneath Sylvester's feet, while Peter holds the "keys to the kingdom of heaven" which Christ bequeathed to him at the end of the charge. Both use their powers to cleanse Gentile and Jew, and to convert them to the faith, as demonstrated especially by the once "leprous" wolf at Sylvester I's feet. As further

[159] In particular the northern end, although the main apse also suggests the tripartite scheme of a triumphal arch. See 95, note 7, above, and the reconstruction of the room by Winterfeld in Belting, "Palastaulen," *Frühmittelalterliche Studien*, 60.

testimony to the efficacy of the keys, both Sylvester and Peter celebrated councils in which the word of Christ's vicar outweighed that of all others. By means of their attributes and *tituli*, then, Sylvester and Peter provide the ancillary information needed to complete the meaning of the "central panel." Similarly, the baptismal imagery of the "medallions" complements the "tapestry" of the *Acqua Felice* while clarifying the nature and purpose of the "kindly water" that the Sun-pope has brought to Rome in emulation of Christ. Finally, the reading of the south wall cannot be complete without a consideration of the *Investiture to Peter* and the *Acqua Felice*, which should relate to each other along the vertical axis.

Unlike the inherent relationship between the flanking popes and "medallions," the union of the biblical narrative and Good Work of Sixtus V is a seemingly disparate one which demands that the viewer piece together the puzzle. Since the "panel" and its inscription and the "tapestry" and its verse are organized in the same manner as the extended emblems on the east wall, of which the *Abundance* is exemplary, then the central vertical axis of the south wall should be read in like manner, as an extended emblem, with superscript and illustration above, image and subscript. In this sense, the *Investiture to Peter* and the *Acqua Felice* convey the power of Christ's vicar to rule the temporal realm, according to the Doctrine of the Two Swords, so that "great-hearted Leo [who] governs the land" restores and refurbishes it for his subjects and, through his light, offers them the life-sustaining waters of Baptism. But above all, the emblem proves by example that, through the beneficence and faith of Sixtus V, the water that Moses struck from the rock in order to quench his peoples' thirst has been replaced by the true baptismal water tapped from the true "solar" rock, at once Christ on the Cross; Saint Peter; and the Catholic Church, joined at the cornerstone by Jew and Gentile, Peter and Paul [Ephesians II: 14], and led by her providentially chosen vicar, Pope Sixtus V.

The north wall is composed according to the same tripartite system as the south wall, and the popes and their "medallions" are related both across and down the horizontal and vertical axes of this wall (fig. 44). Since neither Anicetus nor Soterus has an attribute unique to himself, however, the triptych of the upper register, of which they are the side panels, should apparently be read according to their Good Works described in the *tituli*. As such, the concern of these Bishops of Rome to ensure that the ministry of the Church is carried out according to Christ's teaching realizes the charge of *Christ appoints Peter Guardian* in the work of Peter's successors. On the lower register, the "medallions" illustrating the works of Anicetus and Soterus, with their emphasis on the administration of the Church as predicated on Leviticus and the model of Peter, complement the Dioscuri in the "tapestry" of *Monte Cavallo* when understood as their Hebraic foils Moses and Joshua, and as their "starry" Christian counterparts Peter and Paul, the joint founders of the Church of Rome, and the twin converters of the Jews and pagans. Finally, *Christ appoints Peter Guardian* in tandem with *Monte Cavallo*, forming the extended emblem of the north wall, effectively seals the symbolism of the accompanying triptychs, with Peter and Paul and their radiant successors, the Bishops of Rome, showing the faithful that the shining body of Christ is the way to the Promised Land of the Heavenly Jerusalem.

128

With the exceptions of Linus and Lucius, who are given neither a "medallion" nor a Good Work to complement their *titulus*, and of the topographical Good Works of Sixtus V (figs. 43. 2,6 and 45.8,11), the seated popes, "medallions," and "tapestries" on the west and east walls are organized according to the tripartite system which informs the south and north walls. On the west wall, the "solarian" light bathing the Salone, owing to the windows, becomes part of the scheme. The first "extended" triptych of the west wall is therefore comprised of the luminous window flanked by Popes Sixtus and Telesphorus, and the *Treasure* flanked by the popes' feigned medallions. Together, they signify the celebration of the mass at the high altar of the *Treasure*, with the eucharistic lion atop the altar, at once the shining body of Christ and the lion of Judah of Revelation, offered to the faithful by Pope Sixtus V, the luminous successor to the apostles Peter and Paul and caretaker of the new Ark of the Covenant.

The extended triptych on the east wall, facing the "high altar" of the *Treasure* on the west, is comprised of Pope Antherus flanked by Pontianus and Fabianus, and the *Abundance* with the "medallions" of the apostolic popes. Hence, Pontianus, who died a martyr, and Fabianus, who insured that the memory of the martyrs live on, form the wings of the central expanded panel which proves, by example, that the memory of the martyrs has indeed been perpetuated to the present by Pope Sixtus V, who emulates the greatest martyrs, Peter and Paul, and who feeds the body of Christ to his flock, displacing the manna fed to the Israelites.

Returning to the west wall, the extended triptych corresponding to that of the *Treasure* is comprised of a luminous window, Popes Hyginus and Pius on the upper register, and their works and the *League* on the lower. Together, they signify the united and peaceful community of the Church on earth, in emulation of the first Christian community led by Christ and his followers, the fisherman Peter, and the Mercurial Paul [Acts XIV: 7-18], and the translation of the faithful to the Heavenly City, with the radiant Pope Sixtus V-Mercury-Hercules at the helm of the new covenant.

The extended triptych facing that of the *League* on the east wall consists of Popes Victor and Callistus adjacent to Zepherinus, and their good works flanking the *Extirpation*. Victor, who sanctioned the act of baptism in any body of water for quick conversion, and Callistus, who instituted fasting to satisfy the penitent, thus form appropriate extended side panels to the central one presenting Pope Sixtus V as a dispenser of *poena*, on the model of Zepherinus, binding and loosing in order to safeguard the Church and her penitent flock.

The remaining extended triptych of the west wall is comprised of the light of the window flanked by Popes Telesphorus and Hyginus, and the *Library* with the Good Works of the apostolic popes depicted in the adjacent medallions. Telesphorus, who dictated that three masses be held and the *Gloria* sung on Christmas, and Hyginus, who initiated the rule concerning the role of godparents at baptism, signify the community of the faithful on earth. They complement the *Library*, by which Sixtus V ensures that Christian culture be perpetuated until the final days, just as Moses had safeguarded the tablets of the Law in the tabernacle, and as Peter and Paul ensured the spread of Christianity by preaching the word of Christ.

Finally, Pope Urbanus flanked by Callistus and Pontianus on the upper tier, the *Lateran* and "medallions" on the lower, form the central extended triptych of the east wall. The pervasive imagery of death in the references to cemeteries and costly eucharistic vessels, in conjunction with Saint Francis and his follower Sixtus V, both of whom uphold the faith on earth in emulation of Christ, point to the afterlife in the Heavenly Jerusalem which awaits the faithful sheep and lambs of Sixtus V's flock, and to the eucharist as the means by which salvation may be attained.

Having determined the extended triptychs which dominate the organization of the Salone dei Papi, the manner in which the hall should ultimately be read becomes readily apparent. The main wall, collectively connoting the spiritual refreshment of the baptismal waters and the key role of Christ's vicar in the administration of the earthly Church, provides unequivocal proof that the councils to be held in the Salone dei Papi are to be overseen by the pope, who has the power to veto decisions, including those of the emperor, should the need arise. On the north wall, the pope's proper duty as pastor of the flock in conjunction with his bishops is shown to emanate from Christ's words and to encompass both converted Jew and Gentile. Linus and Lucius, who form pendants across the space of the Salone at the southernmost end of the lateral walls, reiterate the message of the north wall and hence reinforce the pendant ideas contained on the south and north walls, by virtue of their proximity to the south wall. The lacunae beneath these popes serves to shift the emphasis of both west and east walls to the northern end of the Salone. The four topographical Good Works of Sixtus V which accordingly frame the central sections of the west and east walls, in conjunction with the apostolic popes and "medallions" in proximity, exemplify the earthly paradise being fashioned by Sixtus V in emulation of the Heavenly City, and demonstrate that Sixtus V will attain salvation for the faithful, who partake of the eucharist (fig. 43. 2,c), since he is Saint Michael (fig. 43.f,6) who wipes out heresy (fig. 45.I,8,J,j) and translates the pious on the Last Days to join the saints and the Trinity in the Heavenly City (fig. 45.P,p,Q,11). Finally, the central sections of both west and east walls, which reconcile into great extended triptychs, respectively extol the renewed vigour of Catholic learning, bolstered by partaking of the eucharistic offering at mass and the peaceful unity of the flock under Sixtus V's direction, and the promise of eternal life after death for the penitent Christian who emulates the martyrs, as Sixtus V himself emulates Saints Peter, Paul and Francis, and the the greatest martyr of them all, the *Sol Iustitiae*.

The Salone dei Papi, on its many levels of meaning, is both a manifesto of Roman Catholic Reform dogma and a glorification of Pope Sixtus V as the one who has triumphed over the Caligulas and Tiberiuses of his time, and created a glorious simulacra of both the Augustan age in which Christ manifested himself on earth and the Constantinian age in which the apostolic Church triumphed under Sylvester. The emphasis on the eucharist and concomitant celebration of the mass was designed as a testimony to the vital importance of *imitatio Christi* for salvation, as clearly set forth in the papal chapel and Salone degli Apostoli of the Lateran Palace. It was also designed to counter the Protestant denial of its efficacy for salvation, and echoed the prevalent use of the theme in the Church decoration of the period.[160] Moreover, the emphatic presence of Peter, at the expense of the other apostolic founder Paul, is a re-

[160] Abromson, *Painting in Rome*, 174-175.

ply, using traditional political theology connected with the keys and swords, to the Protestant propensity to glorify Paul in an effort to cement their anti-papal position. At the same time, Paul's underlying presence in the Salone, as the Hebrew convert *par excellence* of the Sixtine Good Works, and as the doctrinal theologian of the works of the apostolic popes, serves to reinforce the importance of the twin founders of the Roman Catholic Church, as clearly set forth in the twin columns that Sixtus V exorcised and surmounted with bronze effigies of Peter and Paul, and had frescoed in each of his secular monuments, including the adjacent Sala degli Obelischi, to which I shall turn in the next chapter.[161]

The presence of the converted Constantine, the seminal character in the realization of the *Pax Christiana*, testifies to Pope Sixtus V's successful maintenance of the spirit of this jubilant era in Church history, and reinforces the political inferiority of the emperor as the fighting arm of the omnipotent pope, as clearly set forth in both the Salone di Costantino and Salone degli Imperatori. The emperor's political inferiority then serves to bolster the pope's regal aspect as successor to the prophet-priest-kings of the Old Testament, as exemplified by Samuel, David, and Solomon in the adjoining rooms. So, too, the attributes given to Sylvester serve to reinforce the conversion of Constantine and the pagans, much as the underlying conversion symbolism of the "tapestries" points to the victory over both pagans and Hebrews. Together they propagate a message perfectly consonant with the obelisks and columns with which Sixtus V re-ordered the face of Rome, and which he had memorialized in all of his secular programmes. Furthermore, they relate to the rooms of Elijah and Daniel which typify the arduous trials faced by the Church and her ultimate victory. The illustrious martyr-popes chosen for commemoration in the Salone dei Papi also serve as exemplars for the Sixtine age of conversion in terms of the penance required of the faithful for the transition from a state of sin to a state of grace. It is surely for this reason that the overwhelming theme of the pope's private apartment is the desert saint, whose suffering in this earthly wilderness leads ultimately to the achievement of paradise.

The chiliastic imagery informing both the lower and upper tiers of the Salone also reflects current sixteenth century aspirations to overcome the adversity of the heretical Protestant and Turk and await the Last Days. The representation of an ideal realization of the Heavenly City in the Salone not only emulates the imagery of the Early Christian catacombs, but also the optimism of the Roman Catholic Reformatory Church of the 1580's in particular, and of the Roman Catholic Church of the Renaissance in general, reflecting, as it does, literary and artistic treatments of the theme harking back at least as far as Pope Nicholas V. That the millenium conjured in the Salone dei Papi is a particularly Franciscan one is due, of course, to Pope Sixtus V's profound belief in Saint Francis and his Order. That it is a realization in paint of the Franciscan Golden Age is amply attested to in the writings of Saint Bonaventure, the Doctor of the Church, who characterized the Church Militant, Christ, and Francis himself, as the Sun illuminating the earth.[162] Finally, Sixtus V's own equation to the Sun is attributed, in the design of the Salone, not only to his Franciscan heritage and the *stella maris*, to whom he was greatly devoted throughout his life, but to the workings of Divine Providence

[161] The apparent colour symbolism of the "columns' which reveals the Pauline triad of theological virtues would then underscore his significance for the programme and point to the Sala di Samuele, in which these very virtues are personified. In turn, the four cardinal virtues, which apparently inform the allegorical Good Works, would likewise find specific foils in another room of the *piano nobile*, namely the Sala di Davide, located adjacent to the Sala di Samuele.

[162] von Pastor, *History*, XXI, 56, 139, relates that Sixtus V would have passages from the life and work of St. Francis read to him on Fridays and that he would often don the Franciscan habit when in his private apartments. For Bonaventure's solar symbolism, consult Ratzinger, *Theology*, 33 ff.

herself, who showed the young Felice the way to the Franciscan seminary and ultimately to the chair of Peter to follow the "duo maxima mundi lumina," Peter and Paul.[163] Indeed, this solar pope is endowed with such grace that he is able to control the seasons in the Sala della Gloria, and to be carried to the heavens through a *quadratura* opening, vividly recalling that of the Salone dei Papi, to finally join his predecessors in the Community of Saints.[164]

The profoundly personal nature of the programme of the Salone dei Papi, from the clearest testimony of the "tapestries" and stars frescoed on the architrave, to the underlying layers of solar symbolism connected ultimately with Sixtus V's providential mission to realize the translation of the faithful to the Heavenly Jerusalem of the Church Triumphant during his pontificate, is a clear indicator of the personal role which the pope must surely have played in devising the multi-faceted and multi-layered programme of the Salone dei Papi, and of the Lateran Palace as a whole. The truly impressive cohesiveness of the frescoed decoration in relation to the messages conveyed, from the *quadratura* in general to the attributes of the apostolic popes in particular, makes it abundantly clear that the group of artists who worked on the Salone did so under close supervision not only of Cesare Nebbia and Giovanni Guerra, the impresarios of all Sixtine decorative schemes, but also of an advisor in close contact with the pope, who must have overseen virtually every step of the production. The identity of the iconographer of the programme is by no means clear. To my knowledge, no mention was made of him in the documents of Sixtine Rome relative to the Lateran Palace and other decorative cycles, and the actual programme for the Salone dei Papi, and for the Lateran Palace itself, has not survived.[165] Giuseppe Castiglione, the biographer of Silvio Antoniano, the celebrated poet of Sixtine Rome, maintains that Antoniano was the iconographer of the Lateran Palace programme, but he also gives him credit for having created every other programme of Sixtine Rome, including the scheme for the Vatican Library, which we know was devised by Federico Rainaldi, and the verses accompanying the Good Works of Sixtus V, which were created by Guglielmo Bianco.[166]

On the basis of the order in which the Good Works of Sixtus V are evidently to be read, it is tempting to assign the role of iconographer to Pompeo Ugonio, whose list of the pope's Good Works, cited above, agrees wholeheartedly, and is apparently unique in its order in the literature of Sixtine Rome.[167] Since the Good Works are inextricably bound to the apostolic popes and their decrees, one cannot escape the conclusion that the same person who chose and organized the achievements of Sixtus V must also have determined the order of the popes and their particular decrees. Although the acts assigned to the popes in Platina's *De Vitis* are closer to those commemorated in the Salone dei Papi than Ugonio's in his own manuscript on their lives, the discrepancies are not so numerous as to completely discount Ugonio's possible role as iconographer. Moreover, it is significant that the one decree omitted by Platina, namely Urbanus's desire to use costly vessels for the celebration of the mass, is mentioned by Ugonio.[168] There is a third reason why Ugonio seems a prime candidate as the iconographer of the Salone dei Papi, and of the Lateran Palace programme in general, and this is his connection with the Patriarchium Lateranense. Ugonio felt a profound sense of loss at

[163] Badesio, *De Sacello*, 45.

[164] Noted in Schiavo, *Lateran*, n.p.

[165] I checked the Archivio Segreto Vaticano, Biblioteca Archivio Vaticano, Archivio di Stato di Roma, Archivio di S. Giovanni Laterano, and Archivio Capitolare di S. Maria Maggiore for the Lateran Palace programme.

[166] See Chapter II, 74, note 10. The programme for the Vatican Library is extant. It was noted in Dupront, "Art et contre-reforme," *EFR*, 301, note 1; and recently transcribed in Vittorio Frajese, *Il Popolo Fanciullo. Silvio Antoniano e il sistema disciplinare della controriforma* (Milan, 1987), 116-130. I wish to thank Father Leonard Boyle, Prefect of the Vatican Library, for kindly having provided me with a copy of Rainaldi's programme. Thanks are due also to Mario Bevilacqua for alerting me to the existence of Frajese's book.

[167] See 97, and note 18 above. Contrast other lists of the pope's Good Works compiled before, during and after the Salone dei Papi was executed, which do not correspond to the order of the Good Works in the Salone: Bressio, *Ad Sixtum V. in aula Regum*, n.p.; Agostino Buccio, *Ad Sixtum Quintum Pont. Max. Oratio In publico Consistoro habita … An. M. D. LXXXVI* (Rome, 1586), n.p.; Pietro Galesino, *Familiaris Quaedam Epistola e Roma in Hispaniam Missa. In qua quid actum sit … in translatione Obelisci breviter explicatur …* (Rome, 1586), n.p.; Lelio Pellegrino, *Oratio habita in Almo Urbis Gymnasio de Utilitate Moralis Philosophiae … Anno MDLXXXVII* (Rome, 1587), n.p.; Giovanni Battista de Aguilar, *S. D. N. Sixto Quinto Pont. Opt. Max. Concio Habita In Sanctiss. Trinitatis Die Anno Domini M. D. LXXXVII … in Ad. S. D. N. Sixtum V. Pont. Opt. Max. Conciones Tres Apud Sanctum Petrum …* (Rome, 1588), 2; Piccha, *Oratio Pro Britannico bello*, n.p.; idem, *Oratione per la Guerra Contra Turchi A Sisto Quinto Pont Massimo et A Gl'Altri Principi Christiani* (1588; Rome, 1589), n.p.

On Pompeo Ugonio see Mario Emilio Cosenza, *Biographical and Bibliographical Dictionary of the Italian Humanists and of the World of Classical Scholarship in Italy, 1300-1800*, 6 vols., 2nd ed. (Boston, 1962-1967), IV, 3508; McGinness, "Rhetoric," 31, 71-77; and, recently, Ingo Herklotz, "Historia Sacra und Mittelalterliche Kunst während der zweiten Hälfte des 16. Jahrhunderts in Rom," *Baronio e l'arte*, 39-45.

[168] It is also mentioned by Baronio who may well have played a role in the creation of the programme, possibly as a consultant. See 116, note 121, above.

Sixtus V's destruction of the ancient papal residence, as may be gleaned from his report on its condition in a manuscript in the Vatican Library.[169] To preserve the Patriarchium, if only in memory, he kept a journal of its contents, and even sketched the general layout of the principal rooms. This is not to suggest, however, that Ugonio and the pope were completely opposed to each other on the issue for Sixtus V shared Ugonio's sense of loss; as I have already indicated, he decided to demolish the venerable structure since it had fallen into such disrepair as to render the buildings functionally useless, but, at the same time, managed to save parts of the venerable structure. As I shall now demonstrate with regard to the Salone dei Papi, the Patriarchium Lateranense was kept very much alive in the decorations created for the new palace, not in terms of a simple repetition of subject matter, but in a more profound way which can only be understood once the essential themes of the Sixtine cycle have been determined.

The Salone dei Papi was constructed, oriented, and decorated according to the general "basilican" scheme of the Sala de Concilio (figs. 65-66). In addition, many of the component parts of the frescoed decoration defer to certain rooms of the ancient residence. The treatment of popes recalls precedents commissioned by Callistus II: their representation as *viri illustres*, those in the Oratory of Nicholas; and their imperial stances, seated beneath baldachins, those in the Camera pro Secretis Conciliis. The first investiture scene recalls a comparable mosaic in the triconch *triclinium* saved from destruction by Sixtus V. However, the Good Works of Sixtus V, which form the crux of the entire programme, have no apparent counterparts in the Patriarchium Lateranense, and the old council hall is of little consequence when read in terms of formal and iconographic similarities: in the main apse, the Sala del Concilio contained a representation of Christ on the mountain of Paradise with the four rivers flanked by six figures, Peter, Paul, Pope Leo III and unidentified saints; the monogram of Leo III on the "keystone" of the arch; on the side walls, the twenty-four elders in two registers; above the arch of the apse, symbols of the evangelists flanking a central "clipea" of Christ; in the side chapels (or *accubita*), unspecified scenes from the mission of the apostles; a "Mensa Christi" before the main apse; and a porphyry fountain in the center of the hall.[170] When read in symbolical terms, conversely, the old council hall is of great consequence for the Salone dei Papi. The mosaics of the mission of the apostles, represented in ten rather than twelve scenes in the apses of the Sala del Concilio, correspond in both number and location to the Good Works of Sixtus V paired on the lateral walls.[171] As Hans Belting has convincingly argued, the remaining two scenes of the mission of the "apostles" in the Sala del Concilio are implied in the mosaic of the main apse with Peter and Paul flanking Christ.[172] In the Salone dei Papi, similarly, the *Acqua Felice* and *Monte Cavallo* complete the mission to convert all nations to the faith, now taken on by Sixtus V as the providentially chosen successor to the apostles. The presence of Saint Paul as convert and converter *par excellence* in the Good Works of Sixtus V, and as theological advisor for the works of the early popes, also draws on the main apse of the Sala del Concilio, which stressed the role of Saint Paul, like its model, the apse of S. Paolo fuori le mura.[173] The distinctive role of Peter in the Investiture scenes, on the other hand, defers to the companion triconch *triclinium* of Leo III.

[169] Ugonio, "Schedario," Barb. Lat. 2160.

[170] For this and the following, I am relying primarily on the descriptions of Panvinio and Ugonio, and on the modern research of Belting, as in Chapter I, 34-35, notes 5 and 14 .

[171] Given my above analysis, it is entirely possible that in the Sala del Concilio these scenes were to be read in pairs, much as they function in the Salone degli Apostoli of the Lateran Palace.

[172] Belting," Mosaici," *Roma*, 177.

[173] Belting," Mosaici," *Roma*, 176.

The Aula Leonina, with its scenes of Christ giving the military standard (*labarum*) to Constantine and the keys to Sylvester, and Peter giving the battle-standard (*vexillum*) to Charlemagne and the *pallium* to Pope Leo III, flanking the main apse with the *Traditio Legis*, may well have served as the model, both formally and contextually, for the main wall of the Salone dei Papi. Not only did these mosaics reinforce the divinely ordained origins of the pope's power, but they also pointed to the Constantinian origins of the Patriarchium Lateranense, and confirmed the continued efficacy of the *Constitutum Constantini*. In like manner, the Baptism of Constantine and celebration of the Council of Nicea, together with Christ's bestowing his mission on Peter and Peter's celebration of the Council of Jerusalem flanking the main "apse" of the Salone dei Papi, reassert the message of their Carolingian predecessors and, in formal terms, maintain the tripartite arrangement. In this context, the derivation of the seated popes from the monuments of Callistus II serves to underline further the absolute power given by Christ to the early popes, and to confirm the providential outcome of the Investiture Struggle in which Christ's vicars emerged victorious.

The overwhelming millenial imagery of the Salone dei Papi draws on the representations of Christ atop the mountain of Paradise with the four rivers in both Leonine *triclinia*, and it looks in particular to the side walls and main apse of the Sala del Concilio with its representations of the twenty-four elders of the apocalypse overseen by Christ and the symbols of the evangelists. It could well be that the millenial imagery of the Sala del Concilio provided an impetus for the creation of the most forceful Sixtine symbols used to convey the providentiality of Sixtus V's pontificate and of his mission to pacify the world: the *imprese*.[174] The most prominent of the Good Works also seem to partake of the symbolism of the ancient council halls: the *Acqua Felice* recalls the ancient porphyry fountain of the Sala del Concilio, while *Monte Cavallo* effectively assimilates the message of both *triclinia*, with the Roman Dioscuri, Peter and Paul. Finally, the importance of *imitatio Christi* in the Salone dei Papi was presaged by the "Mensa Christi" of the Sala del Concilio, the Christian counterpart to the Mosaic tabernacle and Ark of the Covenant.[175]

The foregoing analysis, though by no means complete, was intended to show that in designing the programme for the Salone dei Papi, the Sixtine iconographer was very much concerned with maintaining the link between the ancient council halls of the Patriarchium Lateranense and their modern replacement. He achieved these ends by drawing on the essential themes of the Leonine *triclinia*, supplemented by the monuments erected to commemorate the victory of the papacy in the Investiture Struggle, and then re-formed these themes to mesh with the pontificate of his patron, Pope Sixtus V. While there were a number of antiquarians involved in the study of the Patriarchium Lateranense during the early years of the Sixtine pontificate, not the least of whom was Fulvio Orsini, only one of these scholars could have created the programme for the new papal residence. Given the considerable number of coincidences that tie Ugonio to the Salone dei Papi, namely his list of the pope's Good Works in the sermon of 1586; his authorship of manuscripts on the early popes and Patriarchium Lateranense; and his emphasis on *imitatio Christi* in sermons, the likelihood is quite strong that Ugonio was the scholar in

[174] As I have noted in Chapter II, 74, above, the *imprese* look to Early Christian art in general. The similarity between the lion of the *Extirpation* and Christ on the mount of Paradise, and the animals surrounding the lion of the *League* and the tetramorphs flanking Christ, cannot be completely fortuitous.

[175] It seems to me that the Salone dei Papi may well have been conceived following the Sixtine reconstruction of the Temple of Solomon as well. The lack of a 1:3 ratio in the dimensions of the hall (24.60 x 13.40 m) need not necessarily preclude such a conclusion. Given the evident emphasis on the Ark of the Covenant in the Good Works, it is entirely possible that the analogy was devised by the iconographer following the construction of the hall. For an illustration and brief discussion of the Sixtine reconstruction of the Temple of Solomon, consult Marcello Fagiolo, ed., *Architettura e Massoneria* (Florence, 1988), 4. Also consult *idem*, "Dai Palazzi ai Giardini," in *L'arte dei papi*, 199-200, for traditional conflations of the Temple and Palace of Solomon.

question.[176] If one considers the method of distributing responsibility for the programme of the Vatican Library, in which the iconographer Federico Rainaldi was assisted by Silvio Antoniano, Pietro Galesino, and Guglielmo Bianco, then it seems that a similar situation was probably in operation at the Lateran. Hence, it is possible that Pompeo Ugonio determined the overall theme of the Church Councils (likely on the instruction of Sixtus V); used Platina's *De Vitis* and his own knowledge of the early popes in conjunction with the Sixtine bulls for his choice of Investiture scenes, *tituli*, and Good Works of Sixtus V; and then charged Bianco with the task of writing the verses for the Good Works, and possibly Antoniano for the inscriptions accompanying the "history paintings."[177] Whoever the iconographer of the programme was, he was not only highly schooled in the Christian and humanistic traditions, but he was able to take a rather bland and factual history of the papacy, assimilate it to the history of the Lateran district and of Pope Sixtus V, and transform them into what must be acknowledged as the crowning artistic achievement of the Roman Catholic Reform, a cycle so coherent and forceful that one can hardly escape concluding that Pope Sixtus V would achieve his agenda, since the Good Works of his pontificate really do recreate the Golden Ages of Christ and Augustus, Sylvester and Constantine. Indeed, through the masterful syncretization of ancient, medieval, and modern learning, and the wedding of form and content, the cycle of the Salone dei Papi is a magisterial testimony to the absolute and unchanging authority of the papacy in its continuous quest to care for Christ's flock, and of the Franciscan Pope Sixtus V, providentially chosen to steer the bark of Peter into a safe harbour.

[176] This latter is noted in McGinness, "Rhetoric," 332 and note 139. Ugonio also "divulged" Sixtus V's fated birth and pontificate in a sermon of 1587, for which see my "'Starry Leo,'" *RACAR*, 20.

[177] Antoniano also composed inscriptions for the histories in the Vatican Library, in collaboration with Galesino. See Chapter II, 74, note 10. Given my premise, there is a possibility that Ugonio also instructed the artists of the pope's engraved portraits on an appropriate order for Good Works.

CHAPTER IV

VICIT LEO DE TRIBV IVDA: CONVERSION AND TRIUMPH IN THE LATERAN PALACE PROGRAMME

The obelisks and columns that Sixtus V consecrated as everlasting monuments of Catholic supremacy are among the most highly regarded and often praised feats of the pope. During his pontificate treatises were written on the origins, meaning and history of the obelisks; on the engineering miracles of Domenico Fontana, charged by Sixtus V to raise the obelisks, sometimes from piecemeal fragments; and scores of panegyrics were devoted to the extraordinary conversion of both obelisks and columns. The monoliths also figure prominently in the secular artistic commissions of the pope. In the Salone Sistino of the Vatican Library and in the ex-Palazzo delle Terme of the Villa Montalto, the Trajanic and Antonine columns with effigies of Peter and Paul, as well as the obelisks raised at San Pietro in Vaticano and Santa Maria Maggiore, San Giovanni in Laterano and Santa Maria del Popolo, are included among the Good Works of Sixtus V, while the second room of the Libreria Segreta of the Library features the apparatus employed by Fontana in the raising of the obelisk at San Pietro. But it is in the Lateran Palace that the obelisks and columns receive their most comprehensive treatment. Not only are they given a room dedicated exclusively to the commemoration and glorification of their conversion, the Sala degli Obelischi, but the obelisks and columns, in combination or separately, are also meaningful components of the Old Testament rooms of Samuel and Solomon and of the Salone di Costantino, and they are not unimportant in the last room of the private apartment of the pope. Moreover, as I have explained in Chapter I, they punctuate the so-called *parerga* of the *piano terreno* and grand staircase, and are found as well in the logge of the *piano nobile*. While the essential meaning of the converted obelisks and columns as trophies commemorating the triumph of Christianity over paganism is well known, the proliferation of obelisks and columns in their various formats in the Lateran Palace offers the opportunity to expand upon this essential meaning and to determine in a far more comprehensive way the significance of these Good Works for both the programme and Pope Sixtus V. It will be the purpose of this chapter, therefore, to explore the significance of the Christianized obelisks and columns in their conservative nuances, and, in the process, to consider the messages of the rooms, halls and logge which host these Good Works in their various manifestations.

1. SIXTUS V'S GOOD WORKS AS "PANEL PAINTINGS": THE SALA DEGLI OBELISCHI

Given the celebrity of the obelisks and columns both during the pontificate of Sixtus V and in the modern literature on

Sixtine Rome it is somewhat surprising that the Sala degli Obelischi has been virtually ignored. I have explained the historiography in Chapter I, but shall provide an outline here for clarity's sake.¹ In his treatise on the transportation of the obelisks, Fontana curiously excludes the one room of the Lateran Palace dedicated to these famous monoliths! Mola in the seventeenth century and Biondi in the early nineteenth also omit this room from their descriptions, with the result that it was not until the late nineteenth century, when Bertolotti published documents concerning the palace, that the Sala degli Obelischi first entered the literature, and three of the four obelisks identified as those erected at San Pietro in Vaticano, San Giovanni in Laterano, and Santa Maria Maggiore. At the beginning of this century, Lauer published further documents on the palace containing a passing reference to the room, but not its contents, and the Lateran Museums guidebook identified the fourth of the obelisks as that erected at Santa Maria del Popolo, as well as the columns. It was not until the 1960's that the Sala degli Obelischi was at last considered critically, first by Giuseppe Scavizzi, who attributed some of the frescoes to Andrea Lilio and identified three of the sixteen personifications in the process, and then by Schiavo, who finally reproduced the vault and listed its general contents, without, however, identifying the personifications or considering its meaning. It was not until 1985 that René Schiffmann amended the contents listed in the 1950 guidebook, and accepted by Schiavo, and properly identified the obelisk of Santa Croce in Gerusalemme *vis-à-vis* the obelisk of Santa Maria del Popolo.

The historiography of the Sala degli Obelischi naturally leads one to question why, beginning with the architect of the palace, the room had been excluded from lists of the palace's contents until very recently. The answer, I believe, is twofold, and concerns the location of the room in relation to the layout of the *piano nobile*, and its function. Situated at the southernmost end of the western wing, the Sala degli Obelischi is adjacent to the main hall, but accessible only through the western loggia extension of the palace, or the Benediction Loggia which connects the palace to San Giovanni in Laterano (fig. 6). Given its inaccessability from the Salone dei Papi, and hence the remaining public rooms of the *piano nobile* which are all connected from this point, and its manifest function as a kind of forecourt, or "narthex" leading to the Benediction Loggia, the room was likely a private one, designed to be used by the pope before giving his benediction "urbi et orbi" and on his return to the palace. The decorations of the room, particularly the central *stemma* supported by angels, are oriented primarily for a visitor coming from the western loggia extension of the palace, and hence confirm the main function of the room as a forecourt. While it is possible that Fontana, and following him Mola and Biondi, considered the Sala degli Obelischi, like the loggia, to be part of the cathedral, rather than the palace, owing to its inaccessability, it is far more likely that, as a private room, to which only the pope and those closest to him were privy, the Sala degli Obelischi was omitted from the list of the palace's contents, like the four rooms of the pope's private apartment, and the Sala della Gloria.

On entering the Sala degli Obelischi from the western loggia extension of the palace, one's attention is immediately drawn to the monumental doorway at the western end leading to the Benediction Loggia, surmounted by a segmental pediment broken to house the *stemma* of Sixtus V overlapping the frescoed decoration of the vault (refer hereafter to fig. 67). Placed centrally above this doorway is a feigned panel painting, surmounted by a feigned pediment, representing *Saint Peter on the Column of Trajan*. To each side of the "panel" is a personification who likewise rests on the cove, and who is accompanied by a fellow personification situated respectively on the subsidiary southern and northern sides. Between the women is a festooned altar supporting crossed keys and a baldachin, located on the seams of the vault. The pairs of personifications and the altar between them are enclosed within a cartouche-like structure traversing the angles of the vault. Each cartouche in turn supports a feigned hexagonal frame housing a third personification seated on clouds, and positioned on the seam of the vault, at the level of the top of the "panel painting" and its illusionistic pediment. The triads of personifications flanking the *Column of Trajan with Saint Peter* are in turn flanked by the feigned panels of the *Obelisk of San Giovanni* and the *Obelisk of San Pietro*, situated respectively on the southern and northern coves and surmounted by a feigned segmental pediment. When viewed as a unit, then, the two "panels" representing obelisks may be read as the side panels of a triptych, with the representation of the column forming the central panel and the personifications, the hinges, while the entire structure is held together by the lion of Sixtus V stepping on a "Peretti" branch and accompanied by a ribbon with an inscription taken from the Bible. Above this "lion in profile" device rests a diminutive personification seated within a spindly triumphal arch of *grotteschi* on which rests the base of the central frame of the vault. Within this frame is a baldachin, so indicated by the pelmets at the summit and the curtains hanging in the background. Before the baldachin is the *stemma* of Pope Sixtus V, with an unusually ferocious lion, crowned by the papal tiara and keys and supported by two angels who appear to be lifting it from the space of the room to deposit it in the baldachin, indicated by the foot of the angel to the right, which overlaps the enclosing frame.

At this point the decorations cease to accommodate one who has entered the room from the palace so that one must reorient one's stance in order to view the remaining components of the vault. Following the main axis, from the *stemma* at center vault to the easternmost cove, and hence turning one's stance 180°, one finds precisely the same configuration of diminutive personification within a triumphal arch, the "lion in profile" device with *anima* taken from the Bible, and the triptych representing the *Obelisks of Santa Maria Maggiore and Santa Croce in Gerusalemme* and the *Antonine Column with Saint Paul* "hinged" by triads of personifications within architectonic surrounds. Finally, the reading of the vault is completed by turning one's stance to view the subordinate long axes of the vault, where *grotteschi* in the form of triumphal arches comprised of three baldachins each house a personification, and are flanked by the feigned panel paintings of obelisks and surmounted by the central *stemma* positioned sideways from these viewpoints.

Even without identifying the personifications - the most problematic components of the cycle - the disposition of elements on the vault enables the viewer to readily grasp its general thematic organization. First, it is clear that the most important elements of the room relate to Pope Sixtus V: his Good

Works are the main elements of the cove and his *stemma* occupies the central position of the vault. The focal points of the room are not, as the name of the room would suggest, the obelisks depaganized and sanctified to Christianity by Sixtus V, but rather the columns of Trajan and Marcus Aurelius with bronze gilt statues of the founders of the Catholic Church, Saints Peter and Paul. The obelisks, which function as the side panels of a triptych from the perspective of the main axis of the room, are therefore intended to be read as such, that is, to provide further information for the cogent reading of each of the central panels. The columns and obelisks, as Good Works of Sixtus V, belong primarily to the temporal realm as opposed to the *stemma* held by angels in center vault, which is part of the spiritual realm. Sixtus V is therefore represented in both realms, erecting monuments to the glory of God on earth, and being apotheosized as a result.

Once the clues provided by the main components of the vault are understood, the place of the remaining elements in the hierarchy is grasped just as readily. The personifications housed within cartouches, as well as those within triumphal *grotteschi*, are situated on the same horizontal plane as the Good Works of Sixtus V, and all have their feet placed firmly on the ground (or on an attribute resting on the cove), so that they are understood as belonging to the temporal sphere. Further, the altars within the cartouches are temporal objects, the keys in this context refer to the pope's power to bind and loose on earth (and to have such power reverberate in heaven), and the baldachins, by virtue of their containment within the cartouche and attachment to the altar and keys, function as symbols of the temporal dominion of the pope. In like manner, the baldachins of the *grotteschi* should also refer to the temporal sphere. The personifications contained within hexagonal frames, conversely, all rest on clouds, and therefore signify the spiritual realm. Since they are situated on the same plane as the triumphant apostles on columns and crosses on star-topped *monti* on obelisks, then they serve to reinforce the transition from the temporal to the spiritual components of the pope's Good Works. The lions at the apexes of the triptychs on the main axis of the vault are seen before a blue ground, so that they too are represented in the heavenly realm. The diminutive personifications within triumphal *grotteschi* also belong to this realm, since they are situated near the center of the vault, uniting the Sixtine *stemma* and devices. In keeping with the traditional method of organizing the subject matter to be represented on the vault, then, the iconographer assigned to the central area those elements signifying the abstract and otherworldly, while the coves, situated closest to the spectator, are given over to the concrete and temporal.[2]

For his part, Giovanni Guerra, who executed the design of the vault, surely chose the ancona format to house the Good Works of Sixtus V because it provided a clear indication of the transition from the purely temporal aspect of the obelisks and columns, enclosed precisely within the main boundaries of the frame, to the spiritual component of the Christian symbols surmounting them, emphasized by the actual ancona framing them at the apex. To ensure that the viewer grasp the message of the pope's glorification on earth and in heaven, virtually every part of the fictive architecture, from the frames of the panels to the *grotteschi*, are comprised of the mountains, pears and stars which accompany the lion of Sixtus V's heraldry. Fi-

[2] See, for example, the vaults of the Palazzo della Signoria commissioned by Duke Cosimo I de'Medici and those of the Palazzo Farnese, Caprarola. Also compare the vaults on the *piano nobile* of the Palazzo Laterano. The only exception to the rule in the Lateran Palace is the vault of the Sala di Samuele, which I treat below.

140

nally, the putti lounging on "panels" supporting cartouches, and playing amidst the *grotteschi* of the temporal sphere at once presage and confirm the angelic nature of the pope whose fame is literally trumpeted by the *genii* populating the *grotteschi* of the spiritual realm surrounding his symbolical apotheosis at center vault.

From this general reading, it is abundantly clear that the converted columns and obelisks are the means by which Sixtus V is received by angels in heaven in the Sala degli Obelischi, to join the saintly popes in the Salone dei Papi who are likewise seated beneath baldachins in the heavenly realm. And just as the apostolic popes continue to intercede on behalf of the pious through their decretals, made the more binding by their affirmation in the Sixtine bulls, so the monuments converted by Sixtus V stand in perpetuity as testaments to his continued piety, devotion and beneficence.[3] The use of pendants in the Sala degli Obelischi, and their reconciliation into triads, also conforms to the system used in the Salone dei Papi, as in all Sixtine cycles, and suggests, therefore, a reading based on the "trinitarian" method. Whereas the Good Works of the Salone dei Papi are accompanied by explanatory - and self-congratulatory - verses, those in the Sala degli Obelischi stand alone in magisterial silence, an indication that the room was intended for the private edification and enjoyment of the pope. The "full" overlying signification of the columns and obelisks is brought out only by considering the messages of the personifications, *grotteschi* and Sixtine devices. Since the personifications are, by definition, conveyers of abstract meaning, and the *grotteschi* and devices, open to a number of different interpretations, like the Sixtine *imprese*, then the viewer is expected to come to the room equipped at very least with a fundamental knowledge of the meaning of the Sixtine obelisks and columns. Most any contemporary of Sixtine Rome who was given access to the palace (and to this room) would have been well informed of the rites by which the pope converted the Egyptian and Roman monuments so that the overlying institutional meaning could be gleaned by a learned viewer. In turn, the formal organization of the vault would then provide the viewer with the method by which the remaining vaults of the *piano nobile* are to be interpreted, and, at the same time, reinforce and reiterate the method required to read the Salone dei Papi.

A. THE PETRINE TRIPTYCH

The column of Trajan was dedicated to the glory of Saint Peter on 28 November 1587. It was crowned with a bronze gilt statue of the Prince of the Apostles holding the Bible and the keys of the kingdom, sculpted by Tommaso della Porta and Leonardo Sormani da Sarzana, replacing the statue of Trajan which once stood at its apex. Before the statue of Peter was actually raised to the summit of the column, a solemn mass was held in the church of Santa Maria di Loreto, followed by a procession to an altar erected near the column and the statue, with clerics carrying the liturgical instruments: thurible, incense boat, vase with holy water, aspergillum, cross and candelabra. A second service ensued in which the statue was sprinkled with holy water and blessed, the column exorcised, first with holy water, and then, following the actual erection of Peter's image, with hysop, the most powerful of herbs, to ensure

[3] Fontana, *Della trasportatione*, 4-4v, interprets these Good Works as signifying the pope's "piety and devotion."

that the pagan demons were expunged, and, finally, with the sign of the cross. The column was then sprinkled with oil, sanctified to the Prince of the Apostles in the name of Christ the Lord, and censed. At the close of the service, a public indulgence of twenty-five years was conceded by the pope.[4]

Although the service held before the Trajanic Column is not included in the representation of this Good Work in the Salone degli Obelischi (nor is it included in those at the Library and Villa), it was as essential to the meaning of the Christianized column as the actual effigy of Saint Peter (figs. 67.A; 68). The masters of ceremonies took great pains to document the service, which was printed in a pamphlet dedicated to this Good Work, and the panegyrics written for the occasion are replete with references to the solemn ceremony.[5] One may suspect, therefore, that the service would also be conjured in the cycle dedicated first and foremost to the pendant columns converted to the glory of the apostles, especially since this is the method used in the Salone Sistino of the Vatican Library and in the *gran sala* of the Palazzo delle Terme of the Villa Montalto. There, as here, the personifications are the means by which such essential meaning is conveyed.

To the left of the "panel" of the *Column of Trajan with Peter* is a woman gesturing to the dove of the Holy Ghost with her right hand, holding a globe in her left hand, and directing her glance towards a monster on which she rests her left foot (figs. 67.I; 75). The monster, or Leviathan, under foot derives from the psychomachia tradition, as forcefully harnessed by Callistus II in the Camera pro Secretis Conciliis, and points to both the exorcism of the column and of all heretics.[6] The globe, in turn, suggests world dominion.[7] The dove, a traditional symbol of peace as amply illustrated in the anonymous version of the *Treasure* (fig. 40), is also evocative in this context of the spirit which descended on the apostles at Pentecost, and hence the formation of the Catholic Church, as well as the continued care which the Holy Ghost bestows on the faithful while on earth. Together, the attributes and gestures of this figure, whom I shall call *Knowledge of the True God*, symbolize the grace bestowed on converts to the true faith.[8] To the right of the column is a woman holding a burning candle aloft with her right hand, and a cross in her left (fig. 67.K; 76). These attributes recall the actual rite used to exorcise the column, and, as Scavizzi first noted, combine to signify *Faith*.[9] Together, *Knowledge of the True God* and *Faith* show that the true faith is spreading throughout the world, subsuming evil, and converting heretic and infidel under the aegis of the Holy Spirit.[10] By conjuring images of the solemn mass held before the column, converted by Sixtus V and dedicated to the first head of the Catholic Church, moreover, they clarify the meaning of the Sixtine Good Work as a glorious marker of this global victory, and point to Saint Peter himself who is remembered in the adjacent Salone dei Papi for having learned from Christ's example the proper procedure for preaching the faith and winning converts.

The "panels" forming the wings of the triptych on the western end of the vault represent the obelisks before San Giovanni in Laterano and San Pietro in Vaticano, the two most important cathedrals in all of Christendom (figs. 67.C, D; 70-71). As the dual seats of Christ's vicar, they are eminently appropriate foils for the column dedicated to Saint Peter. The Obelisk of San Giovanni was the greatest of the five obelisks

[4] The details are reported in Alaleone, "Diaria," 309-310v; Mucantio, "Diarium 1585-1590," B.A.V. Vat. Lat. 12315, 324-328v; and Pietro Galesino, *Dedicatio Columnae Cochlidis Traiani Caes. Augusti Ad honorem Sancti Petri ...* (Rome, 1587), 38-40. Also consult von Pastor, *History*, XXII, 240-242, who cites Mark XVI: 17, as the biblical source for the exorcism; and D'Onofrio, *Obelischi*, 178-183.

[5] For the masters of ceremony and pamphlet, see note 4 above. For references to the exorcism, see, for example, D. Emanuele Constantino, *Ad Sanctissimum D. N. Sixtum V. Pont. Opt. Max. ... Carmen* (Rome, 1588), esp. 7-8; Pansa, *Delle Glorie*, 43; idem, *Discorso Sopra la Grandezza dell'Opere di Papa Sisto V* (Rome, 1588), 109-110; Bordino, *De Rebus*, 25-27; Bordino in ... *Carmina*, 62; Ugonio, *Historia delle Stationi*, 70v, 89v; Rocca, *Biblioteca*, 13-16, 281-282; and Pansa, *Libraria*, 92-97.

[6] See Chapter I, 36.

[7] Erwin Panofsky, "'Good Government' or Fortune? The Iconography of a Newly-Discovered Composition by Rubens," *Gazette des Beaux-Arts* LXVIII, 1175 (December 1966): 309-310, 311, outlines the meanings of the globe. Compare the personification of *World Dominion*, discussed in Partridge, "Divinity," *Art Bulletin*, 499. Also consult Guy de Tervarent, *Attributs et Symboles dans l'Art Profane 1450-1600. Dictionnaire d'un langage perdu* (Geneva, 1958), 199-202, 361-362.

[8] There is a comparable personification flanking the *Obelisk of S. Maria del Popolo* in the Salone Sistino identified as COGNITIO VERI DEI.

[9] Scavizzi, "Sugli inizi," *Paragone*, fig. 33b. Also consult Ripa, *Iconologia*, I, 153-154, for the burning candle of faith.

[10] Compare the representation of the *Column of Trajan* in the Salone Sistino of the Vatican Library flanked by SVBLIMATIO and MVTATIO, in Fontana, *Della trasportatione*, 84; and that in the Palazzo delle Terme of the Villa Montalto, flanked by DISTINTIO and IVSTITIA, in Massimo, *Notizie*, 130. While neither author describes the personifications, those in the Salone Sistino are still extant and may be examined and verified; most of those once in the Villa Montalto have recently been found by Marcello Fagiolo in a private collection, and will be published by Mario Bevilacqua in *Sisto V*, proceedings of the VI Corso Internazionale d'Alta Cultura.

made by the Pharaoh Ramesses. It was erected in Thebes, and dedicated, like all obelisks, to the Sun. During the fifth century it was transported to Rome by Constantius II, and erected on the *spina* of the Circus Maximus.[11] The obelisk of San Pietro was one of two obelisks made by Nephercheres and raised in Heliopolis. It was transported to Rome by Caius Caligula and incorporated into the Circus of Nero. It was here that Peter suffered martyrdom.[12]

Like the columns, the obelisks also underwent a conversion and consecration substantially comparable to that described above for the Trajanic column. On the first Friday after the erection of the obelisks, a solemn mass of the Holy Cross was held at the church before the obelisk, after which there was a procession led by the bishop to the obelisk. The cross was blessed, and the obelisk exorcised with holy water and hysop, and blessed with the sign of the *sphragis* on each of its faces. Orations were then given in honour of Christ the Lord and the Holy Cross, and if the cross had not been raised to the summit of the obelisk prior to the service, then it was put in place at this point completing the pope's own idea of surmounting the obelisks with the cross.[13] The service concluded by the granting of a public indulgence of fifteen years to those present.[14] Whereas the Trajanic column was dedicated to the person of Saint Peter, then, the obelisks were monumental hieroglyphics dedicated to the symbol of Christianity, itself supported by the symbols of its present head, so that the ancient hieroglyphics adorning the obelisk and the monolith itself were subsumed by and forced to support the Christian hieroglyphics of Christ and Sixtus V. Form, function and meaning were thus in perfect accord.[15]

Significantly, Sixtine sources explain that the meaning of the cross placed above the obelisk was actually synonymous with the meaning of the obelisk itself.[16] The obelisk, dedicated to the Sun in antiquity and understood as such in Sixtine Rome, was therefore surmounted by the Christian Sun, the cross of the "solarian" eucharist, as of Christ himself.[17] Since the Sun was also a symbol of justice in antiquity, then the obelisk was accordingly surmounted by the cross of the *Sol Iustitiae*.[18] Lest we forget that the intermediary between the obelisk and the cross was Pope Sixtus V, as manifested by the triple mountains and star of his heraldry, and that, in the case of the Vatican obelisk, lions are located at the base of the monolith, then the implication is that these elements of Sixtus V's heraldry convey a meaning which is consonant with that of the obelisk and cross. Sixtine authorities also explain that the converted obelisks are synonymous with the converted columns![19] The cross is therefore synonymous with the apostles Peter and Paul (no doubt conflated in the person of Sixtus V, Christ's vicar), the column, the obelisk, and the Sixtine heraldry, just as the *Abundance* is essentially synonymous with the *Extirpation*, and the *Treasure* with the *League*.[20] Ultimately, then, the converted column in the Sala degli Obelischi which forms the central wing of the triptych points towards the very same meaning as its wings, featuring obelisks and the personifications forming its hinges.

Whereas the antique inscription on the base of the Trajanic column was unaccompanied by a modern one, the bases of the obelisks were adorned with Sixtine inscriptions which contributed to their meaning.[21] To the base of the obelisk of San Giovanni, which already contained verses inscribed in the age

[11] Mercati, *Gli Obelischi*, 317-323.

[12] Mercati, *Gli Obelischi*, 307-311.

[13] That this idea was the pope's is stated in Foglietta, "Lettera," Ottob. Lat. 568, cited in von Pastor, *History*, XXII, 247, note 2.

[14] The masters of ceremonies provide detailed descriptions of the service held before the obelisk of S. Pietro, but they are quite sketchy when they report those of the remaining three obelisks, since the services were comparable. For the service held before St. Peter's, see Alaleone, "Diaria," 248-249v; and Mucantio, "Diarium," 272-276. For a general description of the consecrations of the obelisks, see Mercati, *Gli Obelischi*, 305-306; and Fontana, *Della trasportatione*, 33. Also consult D'Onofrio, *Obelischi*, 99-103; Iversen, *Obelisks*, 38-39; Fagiolo, "La Roma di Sisto V," *Psicon*, 27-30; and *idem*, "Chiesa Celeste," *Chiese*, 47-49, esp. 48. The crosses on the obelisks of S. Giovanni in Laterano and S. Maria Maggiore were placed in position before the ceremonies.

[15] Aikin, "Capitoline," 131. Mercati, *Gli Obelischi*, 309, outlines the hieroglyphic meaning of the Sixtine lion, mountains and star on the obelisk of S. Pietro, as follows: "E misteriosamente ancora, come lettere ieroglifiche notano il merito della Santissima Croce, per lo quale non solamente è degna di esser innalzata sopra gli obelischi, ma ancora sopra gli monti e sopra alle cose più eminenti della terra, e, se fosse possibile anco agli uomini, sopra alle stelle nel Cielo. ... La figura del leone è contenuta anco nell'arme di Nostro Signore, e qui sotto agli obelischi dimostra la ferocità e la superbia dei gentili sottomessa al giogo della nostra santa religione." Also consult Fagiolo, "Roma," *Psicon*, 30-40; *idem* and Madonna, *Roma 1300-1875*, 198-199; and Fagiolo, "Die Psycho-Ikonologie," *Das architektonische Urteil*, 148-162.

[16] Ugonio, *Sanctissima Cruce*, 60r, cited and discussed in Jacks, "Meta," *Architectura*, 165; and noted in Magnuson, *Rome*, 25.

[17] Mercati, *Gli Obelischi*, 349. Also consult Marcello Fagiolo, "Archetipologia della piazza di S. Pietro," in *Immagini del Barocco. Bernini e la cultura del Seicento*, Atti del Convegno Bernini e il barocco europeo (Rome, 1982), 125-128; and, recently, Jacks, "Meta," *Architectura*, 164-165.

[18] M. Filippo Pigafetta, *Discorso ... d'intorno all'historia della aguglia, et alla ragione del muoverla* (Rome, 1586), n.p., points to two particular meanings of the Sun in antiquity, namely divinity and justice. He equates the latter in particular to Sixtus V.

[19] Mercati, *Gli Obelischi*, dedication, noted in Aikin, "Capitoline," 58. Also consult Marcello Fagiolo, "La Basilica Vaticana come tempio-mausoleo 'inter duas metas': Le idee e i progetti di Alberti, Filarete, Bramante, Peruzzi, Sangallo, Michelangelo," in *Antonio da Sangallo il Giovane - La vita e l'opera*, Atti del XXII Congresso di Storia

of Constantius II, were added references to the baptism of Constantine; to the emperor's "propagation," "protection," and defense of Christianity; and to Sixtus V's own dedication of the now de-paganized monument to the "invincible cross" of Christianity.[22] Those on the base of the obelisk of San Pietro mention the dedication inscribed by Tiberius; refer to the Vatican as the "threshhold of the Apostles;" and memorialize the magical formula used to exorcise the obelisk by telling of Christ, the victorious King/Emperor defending Christians from evil, of the victorious Lion of Judah (symbolically reinforced by the lions at the corners of the obelisk), and of the "invincible Cross."[23] Although it would have been difficult to decipher the inscriptions from the ground were they actually represented in the Sala degli Obelischi, there are indications that the artists provided the appearance of inscriptions in their representations of the obelisks.

To the right of the *Obelisk of San Giovanni in Laterano* is a woman with an open book in her right hand and her foot resting on a terrestrial globe (figs. 67.H; 75). The open book must surely represent the Bible or a liturgical tome and hence reflect the masses held at the consecration of the obelisk, and the globe under foot, the extent of Christianity's dominion.[24] Together, the woman's attributes symbolize a Catholic *World Dominion*, the brotherhood of Christians throughout the world.[25] In conjunction with the first patriarchal church and Cathedral of Rome, the baptistry, made the more famous by Constantine's albeit spurious conversion there, and its Christianized monolith, all represented in the "panel," the message concerns the central role of the pope in achieving and maintaining the sovereignty of the Catholic faith on earth, a sovereignty which includes the temporal domain of the emperor.

The personification to the left of the *Obelisk of San Pietro in Vaticano* rests her left foot on a square base and displays the Bible opened to the first lines of the Gospel of Saint John: "IN PRINCIPIO ERAT VERBVM ET VERBVM ERAT APVD DEVM ET DEVS ERAT VERBVM. HOC ERAT IN PRINCIPIO APVD DEV[M]" (figs. 67.L; 76). The square base, which carried a number of meanings during the Renaissance, has connotations in this context of *firmitas*, *virtù*, and the four corners of the world, and it must also surely relate to San Pietro itself as the church built on the foundation stone of Peter.[26] The Biblical passage underscores the centrality of the *Logos*, the Word made flesh in Christ, and emphasizes that Christ was born "before all ages." Signifying the *Law of Grace* or *Truth*, this personification attests to the firm foundations of Christianity which, contrary to the Hebrew view evoked by the biblical quotation (i.e., Genesis), extend through the Old Dispensation, where they were manifested through figures and types undetected by the Hebrews, to the very formation of the world.[27] Together with the Christianized obelisk, a continuity is established which runs from "the beginning" through the Egyptian and Roman empires to the time of Sixtus V. The pope accordingly continues to uphold the faith and to serve as its foundation stone, as Peter's rightful successor.

The personifications which serve to modify the "hieroglyphic" message of the column and obelisks on the western end of the vault also complement each other within their architectonic frames and, together with the "celestial" personifications and the "lion in profile" device, propound a message which serves to unify the Petrine triptych. *World Dominion*

dell'Architettura, 19-21 February 1986 (Rome, 1988), 204-205, who explains the traditional connection between Peter as the stone and the obelisk, and Peter and Paul as the *metae* of Rome, with the Church as the cosmic circus; and, recently, Flaminia Cosmelli, "L'elefante, l'albero e l'obelisco," *Storia dell'arte* 66 (May-August 1989): 115, for the traditional comparison between the obelisk and column.

[20] The *imprese* hold such meaning especially when read according to the hermetic tradition, in my "'Starry Leo,'" *RACAR*, 17-39. Consult my forthcoming "Simbolismo ermetico," *Sisto V*, for the ramifications of such "Sixtine" symbolism on the meaning of the obelisks and columns.

[21] See Pansa, *Libraria*, 93, for the antique inscription. The statue of St. Peter was accompanied by a straightforward inscription documenting the event: "SIXTVS V. PONT. MAX. / B. PETRO APOST. PONT. A. IIII."

[22] The inscriptions are transcribed, translated and discussed in Iversen, *Obelisks*, 38-41.

[23] Iversen, *Obelisks*, 63-64.

[24] The globe may also have connotations of eternity. See de Tervarent, *Attributs*, fig. 42.

[25] Compare the personification discussed in Partridge, "Divinity," *Art Bulletin*, 498.
    The representation of the Obelisk of S. Giovanni in Laterano in the Salone Sistino is flanked by SANATIO and PVRGATIO, in Fontana, *Della trasportatione*, 84r. At the Villa Montalto, if I have understood the description in Massimo, *Notizie*, 131, this Good Work was flanked by TENTATIO and INTREPIDITAS.

[26] Catani, *Pompa Funerale*, 32, characterizes the pedestals on which the personifications of Sixtus V's catafalque stand as signifiers of the "salda fermezza della cattolica fede"; Valeriano, *Hieroglyphica*, XXXIX, xlii; LX, xxii, respectively, identifies the cube as the Supreme Divinity and the Earth. For other meanings of the square base, consult Bowen, "Mercury," *JWCI*, 225; de Tervarent, *Attributs*, 135-136; Panofsky, "'Good Government,'" *GBA*, 311-315; and Edgar Wind, *Pagan Mysteries in the Renaissance* (1958) revised & enlarged (New York, 1968), 101-102 and note 16. Also see Gaci, *Dialogo*, 54-55, 57-58; and Michele Mercati, *Considerationi ... sopra gli Avvertimenti del Sig. Latino Latini. Intorno ad alcune cose scritte nel libro de gli Obelischi di Roma ...* (Rome, 1590), 41-45, on the significance of the four corners of the obelisk's base. Consult Maurizio Calvesi, *Il sogno di Polifilo prenestino*, ars fingendi 1 (1980; Rome, 1983), 93-94, for the significance of the square base beneath the elephant obelisk in Colonna's book, and compare the "stupendo cubo solido et fermo" beneath the obelisk on the temple with pyramid and obelisk, in *idem*, 69.

[27] Compare the personification of LEX GRATIAE once depicted on the courtyard façade of the Vatican Library

and *Knowledge of the True God*, on the south-western corner of the vault, symbolize the global extirpation of heresy and concomitant unification of Christianity on earth. The altar, crossed keys, and baldachin in turn show that this triumph has been affected under the guidance of Christ's sacrifice on the altar of the cross, and the *imitatio Christi* of his vicar on earth. The personification hovering above these temporal symbols and forming the apex of the triangle holds a censer and aspergillum (?) in her right hand and a wafer (?) in her left, possibly alluding to the holy water and hysop used to exorcise both columns and obelisks, and to the eucharistic substance partaken by the faithful initiate following the cleansing of his or her soul and celebration of the Mass (figs. 67.J; 75). As a symbol of *Devotion*, this personification is a summation of the means by which the true faith has reached the four corners of the world and triumphed over heretic and infidel alike.[28] Just as the Christian cross of the Sun is synonymous with the now converted pagan monolith of the Sun, the heavenly *Devotion* is synonymous with her temporal foils below. *Law of Grace* or *Truth*, and *Faith*, on the north-western "hinge" of the vault, together with the altar, crossed keys and baldachin, collectively symbolize the indisputable antiquity of the Christian religion which will continue for all time due to the faith of Christ's flock. Above these temporal personifications is a woman raising a statuette in her right hand and holding a cross in her left (figs. 67.M; 76). Reminiscent of the antique *Roma aeterna*, who holds a statuette and sceptre, the substitution of a cross for the sceptre converts the pagan symbol into a Christian one, here called *Eternity of the Roman Church*.[29] As represented in the Sala degli Obelischi, then, *Law of Grace* or *Truth*, and *Faith* are the means by which the Roman Catholic Church will remain the indefatigable institution that it has been from the beginning of time, since upheld by God's earthly representative. The obelisks triumphantly marking the basilicas of Christ's vicars are therefore hinged to the column of Peter's supremacy, and of the assured perpetuity of the church founded on him by triads of personifications promising the reverberation of temporal acts in heaven and, accordingly, salvation for the sheep of Sixtus V's flock. The obelisks raised by Sixtus V and the column which he appropriated for the glory of Catholicism and Christ's first earthly representative are hinged by the triumphant victory on earth over heretic and infidel, the conversion of the Hebrews by Peter and, following him, Sixtus V, and the unification of the world under the Law of Grace. The crosses on the star-topped mountains as well as Peter, Prince of the Apostles, are united by the devotion to the Roman Catholic Church which leads to salvation.

The elements which both hold the entire structure together and which point to the central *stemma* are the Sixtine lion stepping on a "Peretti" branch and accompanied by a ribbon with the paraphrase from the Proverbs of Solomon XXVIII: 1: "IVSTVS VT LEO CONFIDENS" and, above him, a woman holding a book in each hand, possibly personifying *Fame* (figs. 67.T; 79).[30] The biblical paraphrase concerns Solomon's counsel to rulers to administer their realms justly, and accordingly to expunge all subversive and wicked elements threatening the maintenance of the Law.[31] In the context of the Petrine triptych this proverb acts as its summation or motto. The simile utilizing a lion points to the *corpo* of the device which therefore symbolizes Sixtus V as the sage ruler who follows

as described in Fontana, *Della trasportatione*, 95v; and that of VERITAS, still partially extant on the façade of the Tower of the Winds, in *idem*, 96; and Hess, "Some Notes," *KSRB*, 167.

This Good Work is flanked by RELIGIO and MAGNIFICENTIA in the Salone Sistino, in Fontana, *Della trasportatione*, 83v-84; and by AVTORITAS and GRATITVDO in the Villa Montalto, in Massimo, *Notizie*, 130.

[28] Compare the personification of DEVOTIO on the façade of the Tower of the Winds, described in Fontana, *Della trasportatione*, 96; and Hess, "Some Notes," *KSRB*, 167.

[29] Compare the personification of ECCLESIA on the façade of the Tower of the Winds, described by Fontana, *Della trasportatione*, 96. For *Roma aeterna*, see Kaufmann, "Empire," *Studies in History of Art*, 72, note 21.

[30] de Tervarent, *Attributs*, 248-252, lists the various meanings signified by a book. Fame is the only personification in the list who holds a book in each hand, but this does not, of course, preclude other possible identifications.

[31] It is somewhat surprising that the preachers of Sixtine Rome do not seem to draw on the biblical passages used in the Sixtine devices. At least this is the conclusion I have drawn from those sermons consulted. On this passage, see Cornelio A Lapide, *Commentaria*, III, 648.

Solomon's admonition, and who is at once bold and just.[32] Since the Sixtine lion is a symbol of the Sun, then the cross-topped obelisks of the wings are as bold as the lion. Since the Sun is also a symbol of justice, and the bold lion compared to the just ruler, then the obelisks of San Pietro and San Giovanni are also just. Continuing the method set out by the Sixtine authorities, since the obelisks and crosses are bold and just, then so too are Peter and the Trajanic column supporting him. The "lion in profile" device therefore functions as a kind of hieroglyphic for the proper reading of the Sixtine obelisks and columns. It also extends to the personifications. The victory on earth over heretic and infidel, the message conveyed by the triad on the left or south-western hinge, relates to the opening lines of the proverb and, it must be added, to the white magical formula chanted before the obelisks during their exorcism: "Fugit impius, nemine persequente." The unification of the world under the Law of Grace, the message of the right or north-western triad, becomes the analogue to a realization of Solomon's admonition to the bold, leonine prince to uphold the Law (of Fear). In sum, Saint Peter's leadership of and devotion to the Church in the Sala degli Obelischi realizes the counsel of the wisest of all Old Testament leaders. As a follower of both Peter and Solomon, Sixtus V's own rule is celebrated as the modern counterpart and culmination of the impeachably bold and just administration of his forebears. To point up the exemplary character of Sixtus V, finally, his *Fame* is enclosed within a triumphal arch of *grotteschi* further underscoring his regal nature as the vicar of Christ, the "King and Emperor" of the Catholic faith.

B. THE PAULINE TRIPTYCH

To the eastern end of the vault, facing the Trajanic column, is a representation of the pendant column restored and rededicated by Sixtus V, the column of Marcus Aurelius, at that time believed to have belonged to Antoninus Pius (figs. 67.B; 68). It is surmounted by a bronze gilt effigy of Saint Paul holding the Bible and sword sculpted by Tommaso della Porta and Costantino de'Servi, replacing the statue of Marcus Aurelius which once crowned it.[33] The ceremony held before the column followed that held before the Trajanic column; Francesco Mucantio, one of the masters of ceremonies, indicates this briefly in his exposition of the event, while Alaleone goes into more detail. As far as I know, there were no pamphlets written to commemorate this specific conversion, probably owing to the similarity of the service and the comparable meaning of the columns with the founders of the Church.[34] Unlike its foil, however, the base of the Antonine column was embellished with Sixtine inscriptions which speak of its original dedication by Antoninus Pius and its restoration by Sixtus V; of the expiation of "every impiety" from the column; and of the triumph of the true faith of Christ.[35]

To the left of the column is a woman holding a wheel and resting her right foot on a cube (figs. 67.O; 77). Owing to the instability of its rotations, the wheel is usually associated with *Fortuna*.[36] In this instance, however, the woman is stopping the wheel from turning and hence controlling the fickleness of fate. The cube on which she rests her foot further designates the stability of this personification *vis-à-vis* the pagan *Fortune*,

146

[32] In this context it is instructive to note that Ripa, *Iconologia*, II, 196-197, identifies the symbol of Peter on the Trajanic column, and Paul on the Antonine, as "Sublimità della Gloria."

[33] On the Antonine column, see Alaleone, "Diaria," 363-366; Mucantio, "Diarium," 467v-468; as well as D'Onofrio, *Obelischi*, 183-187; and Giangiacomo Martines, "Silla Longhi e il restauro della Colonna Antonina," *Roma e l'Antico nell'arte e nella cultura del Cinquecento*, ed. Marcello Fagiolo, Biblioteca Internazionale di Cultura 17 (Rome, 1985), 179-209.

[34] Mucantio, "Diarium,"467v-468, refers the reader to his description of the ceremony for the Trajanic column; Alaleone, "Diaria,"363-363v, goes into some detail in his description of the ceremony. Pansa, *Discorso*, 110, states that the column "verra similmente adornata d'vna Imagine di S. Paolo." Also consult Bordino, *De Rebus*, 59-60; Rocca, *Biblioteca*, 35-36; and Pansa, *Libraria*, 66-70.

[35] The Sixtine inscriptions added to the base are in Fontana, *Della trasportatione*, 99v-100; Rocca, *Biblioteca*, 283-284; and Pansa, *Libraria*, 66; to name only a few of many sources, as follows: on the western face: "M. AVRELIVS IMP. / ARMENIS, PARTHIS, / GERMANISQ. BELLO / MAXIMO DEVICTIS, / TRIVMPHALEM HANC / COLVMNAM, REBVS / GESTIS INSIGNEM / IMP. ANTONINO PIO / PATRI DEDICAVIT"; on the northern face: "SIXTVS V. PONT. MAX. / COLVMNAM HANC / COCHLIDEM IMP. / ANTONINO DICATAM, / MISERE LACERAM, / RVINOSAMQ. PRIMAE / ROMAE RESTITVIT. / A. M. DXXXIX PONT. IV."; on the eastern face: "SIXTVS V. PONT. MAX. / COLVMNAM HANC / AB OMNI IMPIETATE / EXPVRGATAM / S. PAVLO APOSTOLO / AENEA EIVS STATVA / INAVRATA IN SVMMO / VERTICE POSITA D.D. / A. M.D.LXXXIX. PONT. IV."; and on the southern face: "TRIVMPHALIS, / ET SACRA NVNC SVM, / CHRISTI VERE PIVM / DISCIPVLVM FERENS, / QVI PER CRVCIS / PRAEDICATIONEM / DE ROMANIS, / BARBARISQ. / TRIVMPHAVIT." The inscription beneath the statue of St. Paul, which is repeated on all four sides, is as follows: 'SIXTVS V. S. PAVLO APOST. / PONT. A. IIII.'

[36] Scavizzi, "Sugli inizi," *Paragone*, fig. 34b, identifies this personification as *Fortuna*. See Valeriano, *Hieroglyphica*, XXXIX, xviii, for the antique *Fortuna*; Panofsky, "'Good Government'," *GBA*, 310; and de Tervarent, *Attributs*, 325-326, for the wheel of fortune.

who usually sits or stands on an unstable globe, and certainly never on so stable a base as a cube. *Fortune* does have a Christian foil who has a wheel as an attribute, and whose meaning is diametrically opposed to that of her pagan forerunner, namely *Theology*.[37] But *Theology*, like *Fortune*, is also associated with a globe. The Sixtine personification would therefore seem to take on connotations of *Theology*, but the force she exerts on the wheel suggests a more pointed meaning, one which may be related to a third use of the wheel in the vocabulary of the Renaissance hieroglyphic, namely as an attribute of *Obedience*. As once represented on the long courtyard façade of the Vatican Library, *Obedience* held both a wheel and a yoke, symbols which, in the context of *Law of Fear* once situated above, signified the blind obedience of the Hebrews to their wrathful god.[38] Although there is no yoke represented in the Sala degli Obelischi, there are certain affinities between the chassis enabling the woman to steady the wheel, and the yoke once held by *Obedience*, but by virtue of the fact that the woman herself is unconstrained, her obedience would appear to result from her belief in the New Dispensation, not the Old. In sum, the personification flanking the *Antonine Column with Paul* may be called *Christian Obedience*, since she seems to exemplify the stability which comes from faith in God, and obedience to the spirit, not the letter, of Christ's laws. Flanking the column to the right is a woman holding a chalice covered with a pall, the eucharistic utensil recalling the sacred mass held before the consecration and conversion of the pagan monument, and apparently symbolizing *Oblation* (figs. 67.Q; 78).[39] Together, *Christian Obedience* and *Oblation* convey the necessity of obedience to the law of Christ, and of partaking of his sacrifice on the cross as a means to achieving a community among God's children.[40] In other words, these personifications are a summation of the essential doctrine of Saint Paul, and serve therefore as apt complements to the trophy which Sixtus V set up on the Antonine Column as his contribution to the carrying out of God's work on earth.

The "outer panels" of the eastern triptych represent the obelisk raised, exorcised, and dedicated to the cross before the Marian church of Santa Maria Maggiore, as well as that intended for Santa Croce in Gerusalemme, but never realized (figs. 67.E, F; 72-73).[41] The obelisk of Santa Maria Maggiore was made and erected by the Pharaoh Smarres. It was transported from Egypt to Rome by the Emperor Augustus and raised before his mausoleum.[42] The obelisk intended for Santa Croce in Gerusalemme was made and erected by the Pharaoh Semnesertes. Like that of Smarres, it was transported to Rome by Augustus, but raised in the Circus Maximus.[43] The Sixtine inscriptions on the base of the obelisk of Santa Maria Maggiore speak of its former dedication to the deceased Augustus, and they allude to a number of myths concerning the emperor and the prediction of the birth of Christ as related in Virgil's *Fourth Eclogue*. The inscriptions conjure the apparition of both the Tiburtine Sibyl and Virgin to Augustus relating Christ's coming; Augustus' erection of an altar on the site dedicated to "the first born son of God;" the emperor's refusal to be called *Dominus* after the birth of Christ; and his secret conversion to Christianity on his death bed.[44] The obelisk at Santa Croce in Gerusalemme was not raised, and its base, as far as I am aware, accordingly unadorned with Sixtine inscriptions. Still, one could imagine that the inscriptions might have made

[37] For Theology holding a globe, see Ripa, *Iconologia*, II, 207.

[38] See Fontana, *Della trasportatione*, 95v.

[39] There is a comparable personification flanking the *Obelisk of S. Maria Maggiore* in the Salone Sistino identified as OBLATIO.

[40] The personifications of ELECTIO SACRA and VERA GLORIA flank the representation of this Good Work at the Salone Sistino, in Fontana, *Della trasportatione*, 84-84v; IVSTIFICATIO and VOLVNTAS DEI once flanked the Antonine Column at the Palazzo delle Terme, in Massimo, *Notizie*, 130.

[41] In addition to the obelisk planned for S. Croce in Gerusalemme, others were planned for the Piazza Navona, Piazza SS. Apostoli, Terme di Diocleziano, and the remaining basilicas of Rome. See the plans in Fagiolo, "La Roma di Sisto V," *Psicon*, 37; and Schiffmann, *Roma felix*, foldout.

[42] Mercati, *Gli Obelischi*, 313-316.

[43] Mercati, *Gli Obelischi*, 209-213.

[44] Iversen, *Obelisks*, 53-54.

reference to the Emperor Augustus, and to the "invincible cross" (at once the cross and the church of the cross), in keeping with the typical method employed by Silvio Antoniano in composing inscriptions for the other bases. In any case, as pendants to the column dedicated to Saint Paul, the obelisks of Santa Maria Maggiore and that intended for Santa Croce in Gerusalemme seem to point to the apostle as the converter of the gentiles, and to Augustus as the "typological" exemplar of the imperial convert. As the recipient of the vision of the Aracoeli, Augustus is understood as the pagan chosen to receive Christ on earth during his Golden Age, and to transfer the obelisks to Rome. The cross is then understood as a symbol of the emperor's secret conversion to Christianity, and of the providential conversion of Augustus' appropriated obelisks by Sixtus V. Given the choice of the church of Santa Croce in Gerusalemme, finally, there is an implicit connection between Jerusalem, the Holy City, and Rome, the Eternal City, made the more resplendant by Sixtus V.[45]

To the right of the *Obelisk of Santa Maria Maggiore*, is a woman embracing a sheathed sword tied at the hilt, and resting her left foot on a cube (figs. 67.N; 77).[46] As traditionally associated with such virtues as *Fortitude* and *Justice*, the sword is invariably unsheathed and held in an attitude which complements the meaning, that is, ready for action.[47] In this instance the woman embraces the sword with arms across her chest, effectively suggesting her modest and peaceful nature. By virtue of the fact that the sword is sheathed and tied by a rope falling around the covered blade (or possibly encircled by a serpent?), she would seem to evoke a traditional symbol of temperance.[48] On the basis of a comparable representation in the Salone Sistino of the Vatican Library, however, she is best called *Gratitude*, an identification which agrees with the "virtuous" and "steadfast" base on which she rests her foot.[49] In relation to the *Obelisk of Santa Maria Maggiore*, *Gratitude* would seem to point to the Augustan mythology of the site, particularly the emperor's humility before the "first born son of God," to the *Pax Augusti*, and to the veneration of the Madonna and Child by the faithful.

To the left of the *Obelisk of Santa Croce in Gerusalemme*, is a woman dressed in the liturgical vestments of a celebrant, holding her hands together in prayer (figs. 67.R; 78). Recalling the traditional symbol of *Hope*, altered by the vestments to a more pointedly liturgical *Prayer*, this personification recalls the mass held before the conversion and consecration of the obelisk (c.f. fig. 93). Together with the *Obelisk of Santa Croce in Gerusalemme*, these symbols suggest Augustus' veneration of Christ, and the hope of salvation, made possible by Christ's sacrifice on the cross.

When viewed as units, the messages of the personifications uniting the column and obelisks conform to the system manifest on the western end. *Gratitude* and *Christian Obedience* are surmounted by a woman holding a pyramid with statues at its sides and summit, evoking the *meta Romuli* (once near Santa Maria Traspontina) and especially, in the context of the Pauline triptych, the *meta Remi* (pyramid of Caius Cestius), as well as the Renaissance hieroglyphic for fire, and signifying *Magnificence* (figs. 67.P; 77).[50] Conversely, *Oblation* and *Prayer*, the duo to the right of the column, are crowned by a woman holding a round temple, evoking the Tempietto, site of Peter's execution, and symbolizing *Religion* (figs. 67.S; 78).[51] The

[45] There are probably connotations of a specifically "Sixtine" Rome: the cross of S. Croce in Gerusalemme is joined to the star of S. Maria Maggiore by the Via Felice, the thoroughfare connecting the basilicas. Since S. Maria Maggiore "rests" on the Esquiline, Quirinal, and Viminal hills, then the cross on the star on the mountains may be read both in plan and in elevation. I am here drawing on Marcello Fagiolo's magisterial interpretation of the Sixtine street plan, in "Die Psycho-Ikonologie," *Das architektonische Urteil*, esp. 159.

[46] At the Salone Sistino, this Good Work is flanked by OBLATIO and DEVOTIO, in Fontana, *Della trasportatione*, 84; and in the Villa, by ELECTIO and GRATIA, in Massimo, *Notizie*, 130.

[47] Scavizzi, "Sugli inizi," *Paragone*, fig. 34a, identifies this personification as *Fortitudo*.

[48] Valeriano, *Hieroglyphica*, XXVIII, vi, for "modest temperance."

[49] At the library GRATITVDO is located beside the *Translation of Pius V*, in Fontana, *Della trasportatione*, 84.

[50] Compare the personification of MAGNIFICENTIA flanking the *Obelisk of S. Pietro* in the Salone Sistino of the Vatican Library. Also compare the personification called *Gloria de'Prencipi* in Ripa, *Iconologia*, I, 189-190. Valeriano, *Hieroglyphica*, LX, xix, xx, xxi, identifies the pyramid as symbolical of nature, man's soul and fire.

[51] Compare the personification of RELIGIO represented on the façade of the Tower of the Winds in Fontana, *Della trasportatione*, 95v.

obelisks and column are therefore united by Pope Sixtus V who administers to his flock on earth and prepares them for their pilgrimage to the Heavenly Jerusalem. The cross and star-topped mountains together with Saint Paul are united by the magnificence of the true religion propagated by the apostle and Sixtus V. And the whole structure is united by the Sixtine lion holding a pear branch and accompanied by a ribbon with the paraphrase from Amos III: 8: "SI RVGIET QVIS NON TIMEBIT" together with a personification enclosed within a triumphal arch, holding a sceptre in her right hand and a globe in her left, symbolizing *Providence* (figs. 67.U; 80).[52] Like the apex of the Petrine triptych, this biblical paraphrase in tandem with *Providence* sum up the message of the Pauline triptych which they visually cohere. Unlike Peter's "lion in profile" device, however, the analogy to the "proper" syncretistic reading of the cross and obelisk, apostle and column is not as clearly manifested. The "roaring" entity is, of course, the Sixtine lion who is accordingly represented in a grimacing, ferocious attitude, and whose actions are a realization of Amos' prophecy.[53] The north-eastern triad of personifications, stating the importance of gratitude and obedience to the faith for an efficacious rule, suggests the offensive means by which punishment may be avoided and the lion's roar diverted. Stated in another way, the faithful have little to fear from the lion's roar in comparison to the heretic and infidel. The south-eastern foil, connoting the necessity of oblation and prayer, points to the attainment of the ultimate gift of salvation through the Pauline "faith-works" formula, aptly enunciated by the magnificence of the Catholic Church during the Sixtine pontificate. They also suggest the second part of the biblical passage : "Dominus Deus locutus est, quis non prophetabit?," particularly when viewed in conjunction with the figure of *Providence*. In this sense, the Sixtine pontificate may be understood as the preordained culmination of world history, with the pope accordingly making preparations for the last battle to be waged before the second coming. The offensive stance of the Pauline lion and his biblical paraphrase also serve as propitious complements to both the Petrine lion, who is actually roaring, and to the Petrine ruler, whose adversaries have been neutralized through distributive justice. The triptychs, like the apostles to whom they are dedicated, are thus paired and united through fame and providence to Pope Sixtus V, who is raised to heaven at center vault (figs. 67.g; 74). Together, *Fame* and *Providence* provide the justification for his apotheosis: chosen by Divine Providence and guided by it, the pope has become duly famous for his Good Works, which have not only changed the face of Rome, making it accessible to the pilgrim, but which also point towards the Heavenly Jerusalem, the ultimate gift to be bestowed on the faithful through his aid.

C. THE *GROTTESCHI* AND SYNTHESIS

On the subordinate sides of the vault, the Sixtine obelisks, which functioned as modifiers of and ultimately synonymous with the co-founders of the Roman Catholic Church surmounting columns on the main coves, likewise serve the secondary function of enframing the grotesque decoration at center (figs. 67.V,W; 81-82). In keeping with the late Cinque-

[52] Compare the personification of PROVIDENTIA on the façade of the Archive of the Vatican Library in Fontana, *Della trasportatione*, 96v.

[53] Cornelio A Lapide, *Commentaria*, VII, 234-235, expounds upon the ramifications of the lion's roar.

cento acceptance and use of *grotteschi* in secular cycles, the components of the triumphal arches are meaningful complements to the "panels" and personifications forming the essential matrix of the vault, while the single personification housed by each arch seems to similarly reinforce the Petrine and Pauline divisions of the vault.[54] Aside from the pears, mountains, stars and lions which populate the *grotteschi* and form the very fabric of the baldachin-comprised triumphal arch, the putti sporting pear branches, and the angels trumpeting the fame of Pope Sixtus V, there are a number of added features which visually cohere the subordinate axes to the primary one.

First, the baldachins are carried on Salomonic columns which not only remind the viewer of the ancient cochleate columns converted to the glory of the apostles, but which are also suggestive of the paraphrase from the Book of Proverbs, purportedly written by the wise monarch Solomon to whom Sixtus V is actually equated in one of the Old Testament rooms of the Lateran Palace, to which I shall later turn. The architrave is also suggestive of the feigned frames enclosing the Good Works of Sixtus V commemorated in the room since it is comprised of alternating segmental and canonical pediments, like a microcosmic counterpart to the macrocosm of the room. Such "decoration" also underscores the triptych-like arrangement of the western and eastern sides of the vault, both in terms of the decoration of the subordinate baldachins of the triumphal arch, and of the tripartite arrangement of the arch itself. The oil lamps, placed in and around the triumphal arch and held aloft by angels above the central baldachin, are replete with the symbolism of light and of the Sun, and therefore relate to the obelisks, formerly dedicated to pagan Sun gods but now converted by the Sun-pope Sixtus V and dedicated to the cross of the *Sol Iustitiae*, as well, according to the Sixtine method, as to the columns and to the apostles. The single star and *monti* of Sixtus V present beneath the cross of the obelisks and at the apex of the central baldachin, flanked by victories trumpeting the fame of the pope, carry on the solar symbolism of the obelisks and of the pope himself, as set forth in the Salone dei Papi, as in the Sala degli Obelischi, and connote as well the "stella veramente," the Virgin Mary.[55] The fundamental message of each triumphal arch is brought out, finally, by the personification housed by the *grotteschi*, each of which seems to convey a meaning which relates to either the Petrine or Pauline triptych.

The personification to the left of the *stemma*, on the northern side of the cove, depicted as a woman kneeling on a *prieu-dieu* with hands together in prayer, has certain affinities to the personification to the left of the *Obelisk of Santa Croce in Gerusalemme*, which I have identified as *Prayer*, but given her lack of pontifical vestments, may be identified as *Devotion* (figs. 67.V; 81). As one of the fundamental messages of the Pauline triptych, *Devotion* could accordingly be understood as a hieroglyphic of the eastern cove. Her foil at the southern end of the vault, who holds a double-edged sword in her right hand held towards the ground, and a winged covered chalice (?) raised aloft in her left, may be called *Justice*, since her sword recalls the two-edged sword of Revelation I: 16, and her coverered chalice, a possible allusion to the vials of plagues which are opened before the Last Judgement (figs. 67.W; 82). As the Salomonic *anima* of the Petrine triptych reveals, justice is inextricably bound with the message of the

[54] Philippe Morel, "Il funzionamento simbolico e la critica delle grottesche nella seconda metà del Cinquecento," *Roma e l'Antico*, 149-178, esp. 176-178. Also consult Davidson, *Raphael's Bible*, 61-63.

[55] See Gaci, *Dialogo*, 59, who discusses the symbolism of the star on the obelisk.

western cove. Flanked, as each personification is, by obelisks formerly associated with both the Petrine and Pauline triptychs, finally, they take on connotations of the charges of both Peter and Paul, especially since the obelisks and columns are actually synonymous. As the triptychs make abundantly clear, the Petrine and Pauline are consolidated in the person of Sixtus V, who therefore inhabits the central panel of the final triptych, whose wings are the *grotteschi*, as he is carried to heaven in all his glory.

The overall message of the Sala degli Obelischi is, in one sense, a straightforward one: the pope, as Christ's rightful representative, has jurisdiction over both the temporal administration of the *respublica Christiana*, which he endeavours to enlarge through the conversion of souls, and the spiritual welfare of its members, which he maintains by ensuring that no adverse forces be allowed to impinge on its integrity. This message is conveyed over and over again in the decoration of the vault, from the tripartite schemata of its parts, stating the role of Christ's vicar in the temporal and spiritual realms, and its efficacy in heaven, to the columns and obelisks themselves, which contain in microcosm the essential themes expounded in the room. As signs of conversion the columns and obelisks also enunciate the pope's power to subsume all earlier empires, from the Egyptian through the Roman, and to impress on them the sign of Catholicism and his own symbols as the leader of the Church on earth. The pope therefore fulfills the duties of both founders of the Church, Saints Peter and Paul, following the example of Christ and his Old Testament types. He also complies with the wishes of both Augustus, according to the mythology documented on the base of the obelisk of Santa Maria Maggiore, and Constantine, the first Christian emperor, who gave to the pope jurisdiction of his realm in the West. In this sense, it is not surprising that the Benediction Loggia contains representations of scenes from the story of Constantine's conversion and its aftermath, most notably his vision of the Cross, of Saints Peter and Paul, and of his historical Donation; it affirms the pope's right to protect the earthly Church as set out in the Sala degli Obelischi, and emphasizes the central role of Saints Peter and Paul in affecting the conversion. Moreover, the emphasis on the liturgical aspects of conversion, aspects which were inextricably bound to the meaning of the columns and obelisks, recalls the Petrine and Pauline methods of conversion as set out in the Salone dei Papi, and reinforces the pope's legacy as heir to Peter and hence to his primacy, so clearly stated in the main hall. The emphasis on the Princes of the Apostles, Christ, the Cross and conversion, as well, to a somewhat lesser degree, as the Virgin, are all particularly Franciscan ideals. It was surely for this reason that the life of Saint Francis in the western loggia extension, to which I shall eventually turn, was accompanied by representations of Sixtine obelisks and columns in device format. Finally, the "superposition symbolism" of the columns and obelisks, as Roger Aikin has termed the crowning of pagan obelisks and columns with Christian symbols, finds analogues in the triads of personifications, as in the overall organization of the vault.[56] Taken to its ultimate methodological reading, as outlined above, this symbolism clearly reveals that the pope's authority on earth has been preordained in heaven so that that which is below, on earth, is like that which is above, in the *Civitas Dei*.

[56] Aikin, "Capitoline," 131.

2. SIXTUS V'S GOOD WORKS AND BIBLICAL TYPOLOGY: THE SALA DI SAMUELE

In the Sala di Samuele, the first of the Old Testament rooms of the Lateran Palace programme, there is a representation of an obelisk in the process of being raised (fig. 87). This obelisk is being raised not in Sixtine Rome, but between Masphath and Sen by the prophet-king-judge-priest Samuel. In this context, the obelisk is not an obelisk at all, but rather a symbol of the "stone of help" [I Kings VII: 12]. This use of the Sixtine apparatus and obelisk to signify the "stone of help" is a clear indicator that the pope is being equated to Samuel so that Samuel's feat becomes the type of Sixtus V's. By implication, all other works of Samuel in the room become types for Sixtus V's Good Works, as do the works of David, Solomon, Elijah, and Daniel, as represented in the remaining Old Testament rooms of the *piano nobile*. While the Good Works proper of the pope are represented *en masse* only in the Salone dei Papi and Sala degli Obelischi, the "stone of help" makes it absolutely clear that Sixtus V's Good Works pervade at least seven of the thirteen state, or public, rooms of the *piano nobile*, located on the western and part of the northern arms of the palace. By virtue of the fact that they are prefigured in the Good Works of Old Testament prophets, the providential nature of Sixtus V's achievements is further underscored. That Samuel is the first of the Old Testament leaders to be assimilated to Sixtus V, moreover, serves to reinforce the significant place of Moses as a type for Sixtus V, since Samuel, like Saint Francis, was traditionally considered an *alter Moyses* and, in the narrative, actually holds the rod whose relic ultimately became the charge of the popes. The use of the obelisk as a stand-in for the "stone of help" further underscores the Egyptian component of the cycle, since these great monoliths were first raised by those "invincible" rulers of land and sea, the Pharaohs, who flourished during Mosaic times.[57]

The "stone of help" is referred to four times in the First Book of Kings. In chapter four, the Israelites camp beside the "stone of help" before their battle against the Philistines in which they are defeated because they did not at first bring the Ark of the Covenant with them. Even after it is transferred, their faith was still lacking. The second mention of the "stone of help" occurs in the following chapter, when the Philistines remove the Ark from the stone and carry it to the Temple of Dagon in Azotus, where its power destroys the statue of the pagan god. It is mentioned for a third time in chapter six, at which time the Philistines rid themselves of the Ark, the Levites of Bethsames gain its possession, and, together with its gold vessels, place the Ark on the "great stone." Since the men of Bethsames actually see the Ark of the Covenant, they and their people are slaughtered. Consequently, the few survivors also wish to rid themselves of the Ark. In chapter seven, the Ark is transferred to Cariathiarim and there, on the counsel of Samuel, the people turn once again to the faith, eschewing their pagan idols. This "conversion" accomplished, Samuel orders his people to go to Masphath, where the liturgy is carried out, and the people pay penance for their sins. As Samuel is making an offering of a lamb to God, a battle between the Israelites and Philistines ensues. Upon the victory of the former, Samuel erects the "stone of help" between Masphath and Sen as a monument of thanksgiving for God's assistance.

[57] Another Sixtine obelisk being raised, and represented as a Good Work of Sixtus V's, is located in the Libreria Segreta of the Vatican Library. A study of the image and accompanying text sheds light on the Egyptian and hermetic significance of the obelisks and columns. See my forthcoming "Simbolismo ermetico," *Sisto V*, for a treatment of such significance.

It will be evident that these biblical passages contain many ingredients of the Sixtine recipe for erecting, converting and consecrating the obelisks to the faith. The "stone of help," if understood as a single stone, undergoes travels comparable to the Egyptian obelisks and, like them, is subjected to the exigencies of various pagan dominions. The Ark of the Covenant, which plays an essential role in the saga, and which is placed above the "stone of help," is the sign of Judaism and, accordingly, the type for the cross, the sign of Catholicism, likewise placed above the Sixtine "stone of help." The Ark also acts as God's device to expunge the evil, pagan forces in Azotus, much as the cross which Sixtus V placed above the obelisk serves to rid the monument of "adversaries" when the magical formula is chanted and, it should be added, as the Sixtine lion of Amos' prophecy directs his roar at the houses of Azotus [III: 9].[58] Finally, the penitence of the Israelites in tandem with the liturgical rites carried out under Samuel's authority are apt similes for the papal plenitude of power enunciated on the spiritual tier of the Salone dei Papi; for the global conversion to Christianity signified by the Petrine triptych in the Sala degli Obelischi; and for the actual rite carried out under the pope's authority to expunge the demons from the obelisks and rededicate the monoliths to the true faith.[59]

The accompanying scenes in the Sala di Samuele continue the ideas enunciated by the "stone of help" and the Ark, which is not actually represented, but understood by proxy of the biblical passage to be forthcoming in the narrative and, given the Sixtine method, to be synonymous with the "stone of help" and therefore signified by it. In particular, they would seem to refer to the early "conversion" of Felice Peretti. The first scene in the chronology represents *Samuel being taken to the Temple to take a Vow* [I Kings I: 24-28], a likely analogue to the youthful Felice Peretti taking his vows in the convent of San Francesco in Montalto at thirteen years of age (figs. 84.A; 85). Conspicuous in this landscape is a palm tree, a biblical symbol of justice; in Franciscan exegesis, a symbol of Saint Francis, as well as the light; and an antique analogue to the obelisk![60] The palm tree therefore evokes the solarian nature of the "stone-of-help"-obelisk, the Ark-cross, Christ, Peter, Paul, Francis and Sixtus V. The second narrative in the chronology represents *Samuel hearing a Miraculous Voice in the Temple*, probably for the fourth and last time [I Kings III: 1-14]. It in all likelihood relates to an extremely personal vision of Sixtus V's, or perhaps to the story of his father's dream that his son would become pope (figs. 84.B; 86). Again, the scene contains a towering palm tree and the light is shown to emit from God the Father himself. Together with the position and gesture of Samuel, it recalls, even more than the previous landscape-narrative, the conversion of Paul. The following scene, as I have explained, assimilates the "stone of help" to the raising of obelisks and hence relates to the later life of Felice Peretti (figs. 84.C; 87). The final narrative, representing *Samuel anointing Saul* [I Kings X: 1], may well refer to Pius V who created Cardinal Felice Peretti da Montalto in 1570, or equally to his accession to the See of Peter in 1585 (figs. 84.D; 88).

In addition to the connections between the life and acts of the biblical leader and the pope, all of which point to the theme of conversion likewise enunciated in the Good Works of Sixtus V in the main hall and Sala degli Obelischi, the vault of the Sala di Samuele is organized in a manner not at all unlike

[58] The houses of Azotus are symbolical of the Philistines and, accordingly, of heretic and infidel. See Cornelio A Lapide, *Commentaria*, VII, 235, who cites, among others, St. Jerome.

[59] S. Bonaventure, *Opera Omnia Sixti V, Pontificis Maximi Jussu Diligentissime Emendata* ..., ed. A. C. Peltier, 15 vols. (Paris, 1867), IX, 420, characterizes the Ark of the Covenant in the context of both the "stone of help" and the Psalms, as the "gratia Salvatoris, quae servatur per obedientiam, allevatur per inobedientiam, recuperatur per poenitentiam. ..."

[60] Cosmelli, "L'elefante," *Storia dell'arte*, 115.

that of the Sala degli Obelischi. In each case, the *stemma* of the pope is held by putti at center vault and enclosed within a baldachin (figs. 84.E; 89; 74). The Sala di Samuele also contains a cloth of honour on which the putti kneel and the coat-of-arms rests, no doubt as a means of accentuating the regal aspect of the pope, while the keys reinforce the efficacy of the pope's actions on earth, as in heaven, and the cross bathed in light, the solarian nature of Christ and his present Franciscan vicar. The tripartite arrangement of the earthly section of the vault in the Sala degli Obelischi is also utilized in the Sala di Samuele, but in the place of the obelisks which form the symbols for the side panels, there are personifications. Moreover, there is a conflation of the temporal and spiritual realms on the cove of the vault, from the personifications of the "side panels," who float on clouds, to the personifications of the "hinges," who are seated beneath baldachins recalling those flanking and surmounting the altars in the Sala degli Obelischi, but here enveloped within an otherworldly golden field and flanked by verdant interwoven garlands, from the perspective of the main, north-south axis, and in a similar manner, but without the "hinges" on the subsidiary axis. In this way, Sixtus V's rise to the papacy and his actions thereafter are revealed as the workings of Divine Providence and hence raised to a spiritual level. As was the case in the Sala degli Obelischi, finally, the personifications in the corners, here raised to a spiritual level, modify their foils hovering on clouds and enclosed within quasi hexagonal frames.

The northern triptych is made up of *Charity* and *Faith* flanking *Samuel in the Temple* and "hinged" by personifications (figs. 84.G, H, B; 91-92, 85).[61] The left, or north-western, hinge is occupied by a woman holding a censer in her left hand and a paten with three loaves of bread in her right (figs. 84.J; 94). If the loaves are read according to John VI: 1-13, in which Christ multiplies the loaves to feed the faithful, then the personification may well signify *Good Work*, or *Compassion*, especially since such meaning was given to comparable personifications in the Salone Sistino.[62] The right, or north-eastern, hinge contains a woman holding the tablets of the Law close to her left side, and, in her upraised right hand, a Bible with the first word of the Apostolic Creed, "CREDO," referring to Peter's contribution to the hymn (figs. 84.K; 95). She would therefore seem to signify *Belief*, or a variation on *Knowledge of the True God*. As a unit, the triptych reveals that Sixtus V's call to the faith, as presaged by Samuel's, Moses' and, it must be added, Paul's, was predicated on the Pauline "works-faith" formula, his Good Works being symbolized by the virtually synonymous personifications of *Charity* and *Good Work*, or *Compassion*, and his faith, by *Faith* and *Belief*.

The southern triptych features *Samuel anoints Saul*, *Hope* and *Religion* "hinged" by a woman holding a sword in the manner of *Gratitude* in the Sala degli Obelischi, and a woman with a veiled head, holding a book on which rests the diminutive symbols of the four evangelists (lion, ox, man and eagle), hence symbolizing the *Gospels*, or a variant of *Law of Grace* (figs. 84.I, F, D, L, M; 93, 90, 88, 96, 97). Once again, the meaning conveyed by the diverse pairs of personifications is comparable, with *Hope* corresponding to *Gratitude*, and *Law of Grace*, to *Religion*. With its emphasis on holy investiture this triptych reiterates and expands upon Sixtus V's station as Peter's successor as conveyed in both the Sala degli Obelischi and Salone

[61] The four personifications hovering on clouds were first identified, it will be recalled, by Biondi, *il Restauramento*, 17.

[62] In the library, OPERATIO BONA is adjacent to the *Hospital of Sto. Spirito*, and MISERATIO, the *Acqua Felice*, in Fontana, *Della trasportatione*, 84v, 85.

dei Papi. It also points up the essential ingredients of the pope's earthly rule as one predicated on religion and the hope of salvation, like that begun by Samuel when he handed down the royal creed to Saul and later, as represented in the following room, to David.[63]

On the subordinate west-east axis of the vault, the Theological Virtues and *Religion* serve as the "side panels" of the biblical narratives. Like the personifications in the Sala degli Obelischi (and those in the Salone Sistino of the Vatican Library and Palazzo delle Terme of the Villa Montalto), they assert the fundamental significance of Sixtus V's works. On the western cove, *Samuel being taken to the Temple to take a Vow*, a very likely analogue to Sixtus V's vow of Franciscanism, is flanked by *Religion* and *Charity*, two of the cardinal attributes of the pope, as of Saint Francis himself (figs. 84.A, F, G; 85, 90, 91). On the eastern cove, Samuel-Sixtus V's erection of the "stone of help"-*cum*-obelisk is flanked by *Faith* and *Hope*, the faith in Christ and the new Ark of the Covenant, and the longed-for desire to be translated to the Heavenly City, to which the vertical thrust of the stone itself is directed (figs. 84.C, H, I; 87, 92, 93).

The Sala di Samuele in both form and content is a variation on the Sala degli Obelischi. In its formal aspects, the essential tripartite layout of the Sala degli Obelischi is echoed on the cove, while the central section of each vault is comparable. Contextually, the Sala di Samuele conveys a message which both draws on and complements that of the Sala degli Obelischi. First, the Petrine and Pauline emphasis of the triptychs on the main axis is a constant in each room, and reinforces the underlying presence of Paul in the Good Works of Sixtus V in the Salone dei Papi, while maintaining the explicit emphasis on Peter in the Investiture scenes. The narratives from the life of Samuel-Sixtus V-Moses-Christ-Francis on the main north-south axis form the counterparts to the columns with the Church founders. The obelisks which functioned as symbolical modifiers of the columns in the Sala degli Obelischi are replaced here by personifications which by their very nature serve a symbolical function. That three of the four main personifications symbolize faith, hope, and charity points to Saint Paul, the "author" of the Theological Virtues [I Corinthians XII: 13] and therefore suggests a continuity between the Good Works of Sixtus V in the Salone dei Papi through which Saint Paul's conversion is symbolized, and those typologically depicted in the Sala di Samuele. The biblical narratives on the east-west axis, on the other hand, may be read as the counterparts to the personifications housed within *grotteschi* on the subordinate axis of the Sala degli Obelischi, with the Petrine emphasis in the raising of the stone, itself synonymous with Peter, the rock, and the Pauline, in the vow to convert to the true faith and to execute Good Works.[64] Ultimately, the Petrine and Pauline, as manifested also in the personifications flanking the main north-south triptychs, are united in the person of Sixtus V at center vault, as the conspicuous "solarian" palm trees of justice in the Pauline narratives on the northern and western coves suggest, since, as the lesson of the Sala degli Obelischi taught, they belong to Peter's domain (hence the palm tree in Samuel's unction). The emphasis placed on the symbols of the Christian liturgy, as held by the personifications at the corners of the vault (*Good Work, Belief, Gratitude* and *Law of Grace*), finally, conveys the utter necessity of enacting God's liturgy in

[63] See Chapter I, 60, and note 147, above.

[64] Fagiolo, "Dai Palazzi ai Giardini," *L'arte dei Papi*, 204, uses the analogy of Peter and the rock to discuss the dome of S. Pietro in Vaticano. According to the reading of the Sala di Samuele offered here, the obelisk of S. Pietro would then complement the meaning of the basilica itself.

155

the manner of Moses in the Egyptian desert, of Samuel at Maspath, and of Sixtus V at Rome.

3. SIXTUS V'S GOOD WORKS AS DEVICES: THE SINGLE OBELISKS AND COLUMNS

A. THE SALONE DI COSTANTINO

As represented in the Sala di Samuele, the Egyptian component yields two significant avenues of interpretation, the one concerning Sixtus V's Franciscan heritage, to which I shall turn later, and the other, the *translatio imperii*. Appropriately, the nexus of the idea of the *translatio imperii*, from Egypt through imperial Rome to the Rome of Sixtus V, is contained in the Salone di Costantino, the hall dedicated to that Roman Emperor who quite naturally holds a significant place in the Lateran Palace programme, given his seminal role in the papacy's ownership of the Lateran District, and, indeed, in its triumphant rulership of the West (fig. 6). Much as Sixtus V had earlier embellished the Sala di Costantino at the Vatican with early versions of the "single obelisk" and "single column" devices, so in the Salone di Costantino the connection is made, first and foremost, by means of Sixtine obelisks.[65]

On the main west and east walls, Sixtine devices with "single obelisk" *corpi* and diverse *anime* contained within elaborate cartouches adorn the feigned piers of the exedra which illusionistically support the coffered ceiling (figs. 98.I, J; 99.K, L; 102-105). There are four devices, corresponding to the four corners of the hall. Given that Sixtus V had four obelisks frescoed in the Sala degli Obelischi, a correlation is implicit. The device on the east wall with the *anima* "DE PETRA SALVS" would seem to confirm this correlation, since the play on the word "Petra" applies equally, as one is reminded in the Salone dei Papi, to the rock and Saint Peter, and hence to the obelisk of San Pietro in Vaticano (fig. 105). However, this is the only instance, as far as I am able to determine, in which the analogy is so clearly presented. The remaining devices allow for the kind of conflated readings which are fundamental to understanding the obelisks and columns, the Sala degli Obelischi, and, as I have tried to demonstrate, the Sala di Samuele as well. That the Petrine reading of the devices is achieved most readily suggests that Sylvester, the vicar celebrated in the room, is quite naturally to be given tacit precedence over Constantine, the secular figure honoured in the room. The pendant device on this wall contains the verse taken from Luke XIX: 38 "GLORIA IN EXCELSIS [DEO]" (fig. 104). It would not, at this point in the analysis, appear to point to a specific obelisk, unless the original dedication of the pope's titular basilica to Christ is intended.[66] The *anime* on the main western wall, when likewise considered outside the context of the hall, would not appear to suggest specific obelisks, but then their sources, which have eluded this author, might well elucidate their significance. The one, "GLORIA DEI CORVSCAT," emphasizes the solar symbolism of the Christianized obelisk and, in one sense, may point to Saint Paul, the apostle converted by God's glory. In this way it could then conjure the obelisk of Santa Croce in Gerusalemme or the obelisk of Santa Maria Maggiore, both "shining" monoliths (fig. 102). The other, with the motto "IN VIRTVTE TVA ET IN IVSTITIA," recalling the verse used by Sixtus V's "heraldic" namesake, Leo X, points up

[65] For the devices and their verses, consult Quednau, *Sala di Costantino*, 920-921. The reader may also consult the illustrations of the narratives in the Sala di Costantino in Quednau's book, although they are not optimal.

[66] The same device is represented in the eastern loggia extension and in that context is first and foremost associated with St. Peter and then, according to the Sixtine method, with Saint Paul and the Virgin. I treat this loggia following the Salone di Costantino below.

the meaning of both the obelisk and the Sun, to which it is consecrated, as symbols of justice (fig. 103).[67] Since the ideas of justice and boldness or virtue are associated in the Sala degli Obelischi, then the obelisk also refers to Christ's first vicar. Since these same ideas are ultimately given also to Paul, then it might be possible to relate this device to the obelisk of Santa Croce in Gerusalemme, or to that of Santa Maria Maggiore.

When considered within their context in the Salone di Costantino, the Sixtine devices take on more pointed meaning. Adjacent to each of the device-bearing piers are personifications, seated within the *quadratura*, and flanked by curtains adorned with gems, Sixtine emblems, and hanging bells, evocative of the garment traditionally worn by Aaron (fig. 111). Each woman rests her foot on a square base of two steps signifying firmness, *virtù* and the four corners of the world, as well as the foundation stone or, in Sixtine translation, the converted obelisk-Ark of the Covenant, and Petrine and Pauline columns on which the Church rests.

The personifications flanking the devices on the western wall of the Salone relate clearly to the conversion of obelisks (and columns), and to the Constantinian history of the Lateran. One woman, to the left of the "virtuous and just" device, holds a book and round temple, and is garbed in pontifical vestments, including the traditional representations of Peter and Paul embroidered on her cope (figs. 98.F; 102). As a symbol of *Religion*, echoing that in the Pauline triptych of the Sala degli Obelischi (compare fig. 78), this personification suggests the service held in the churches before obelisks and columns; Constantine's vision of Saints Peter and Paul, which ultimately prompted his baptism and construction of churches; the Church herself, that is, Mary; as well as the Tempietto and Peter's crucifixion. Her companion, who may be called *Devotion* on the basis of a comparable personification in the Salone Sistino of the Vatican Library, is seated beside the "luminous" obelisk device, holding incense boat and thurible, thus recalling the rite enacted following the actual exorcism of the daemons from the monument (figs. 98.E; 103).[68]

The narrative flanked by the personifications and "single obelisk" devices represents *Constantine's Vision of the Cross* before his victorious battle with Maxentius (figs. 98.A; 106). Like the *Vision* in the Sala di Costantino at the Vatican, Constantine stands on a square podium, symbolical of his steadfastness and *virtù*. Together with his troops carrying spears, the *fasces*, and *labarum*, he beholds the cross before the Sun encircled by angels. Whereas the Vatican version includes the Greek inscription "EN TOYTRI NIKA," the Sixtine version is closer to mythological "fact," and omits the words which Constantine would hear later that night in a dream. As a vision, the Constantinian narrative evokes numerous mythological and biblical parallels, including Augustus' vision of the Aracoeli and "secret" conversion to Christianity, Saint Paul's vision of the Heavenly City, Samuel's vision as represented in the Sala di Samuele, and Moses' numerous visions, especially of God in the Burning Bush, as depicted in the eastern loggia and fourth room of the private apartment.[69] In this way, the predominantly spiritual import of the scene is reinforced and analogized to other like occurances in the history of the Church. But as the "single obelisk" devices suggest, Constantine's vision is equated first and foremost to the cross, the star and *monti* which Sixtus

[67] Cox-Rearick, *Dynasty*, 184: "VIRTVTE TVA LVX MEA IN TE."

[68] DEVOTIO flanks the representation of the *Obelisk of S. Maria Maggiore* in the Library, in Fontana, *Della trasportatione*, 84.

[69] Coleman, *Constantine*, 139, points to the parallel between Constantine's vision and Paul's.

157

V placed at the summit of the obelisks, and to the flight of Maxentius, like the flight of evil daemons.

The device with the words from Luke on the eastern wall is accompanied by a personification which is a variation on *Knowledge of the True God* represented in the Sala degli Obelischi (figs. 99.G; 104; compare fig. 75). This variation, holding cross and orb, looking heavenward, and accompanied by a monster at her feet, not only suggests conversion and world-wide triumph of the faith, but also the actual exorcism to which the obelisks (and columns) were subjected owing to the cross, which played so essential a role in the service. Her foil, seated beside the Petrine device, holds a branch of pears, an attribute which not only symbolizes Christ and the Virgin, but also suggests the sweetness of the Sixtine rule, and the virtue of the converter of obelisks and columns (figs. 99.H; 105).[70]

The narrative holding the central place on the wall, within a feigned panel painting inset before the "exedra," is the *Baptism of Constantine*. This subject is of signal importance for the papacy, the Lateran district and, indeed, the triumph of Christianity in the temporal realm. It is also a subject which complements the spiritual vision of the emperor on the facing wall (figs. 99.B; 107). Like the *Baptism* at the Vatican, and quite unlike that in the Salone dei Papi, the scene takes place within the Baptistry built by Constantine. Whereas Sylvester I wears the tiara with three crowns of Boniface VIII and is clean shaven in the earlier version, the Sixtine rendition is closer to mythological "reality," with the pope, like his successor Sixtus V (whose *stemma* is conspicuously present within the split pediment of the Baptistry entrance), wearing the mitre as a symbol of his spiritual authority. Constantine himself adopts a variation on the pose of his Vatican precursor, and a figure holds up his imperial crown, looking remarkably like that worn by Rudolph II in the *League* (figs. 36 and 38). In tandem with the personifications and devices, the *Baptism* is quite naturally equated to the conversion of obelisks. Given the liturgical allusions contained within *Knowledge of the True God* and the Christological and Marian flavour of her foil, as well as her collocation with the Petrine device, the eastern wall becomes a kind of analogue to the Petrine triptych of the Sala degli Obelischi, an analogue made the more firm on the basis of the Constantinian origins of both San Pietro in Vaticano and San Giovanni in Laterano, basilicas which the emperor built following his vision of Saints Peter and Paul and subsequent baptism by Pope Sylvester I.

If, as I have suggested, the main walls have affinities to the Sala degli Obelischi and its emphasis on the Petrine and the Pauline, as well as the Roman empire, then the lateral walls of the Salone di Costantino have affinities to the Sala di Samuele, particularly as it expands upon the Egyptian "origins" of the Sixtine rule, as implicit in the Sala degli Obelischi. In the Salone di Costantino, the Egypto-imperial component is represented by Moses and his brother Aaron. Rays of light emanate from Moses' head, and he holds the rod by which he parted the Red Sea and struck water from the rock, as well as the tablets of the law which he gave to the Hebrews (figs. 100.N; 110).[71] Aaron, the high priest of the Old Covenant, faces Moses on the opposite wall (figs. 101.O; 111). He is garbed in his traditional vestments, including the precious "cosmological" gems on his breastplate, the bells on his gown, and a two-pointed "mitre," while in his hands Aaron holds the golden censer which he alone was authorized to light within the Holy

[70] For pear symbolism, consult Chapter II, 77, note 24, above. The pear is also used as an attribute for a personification at the SS. Apostoli, for example, but there the figure holds a veil over her head so as to indicate in one sense her modest nature, in Erina Russo, "Storia e formazione delle famiglie Francescane," in *L'immagine*, 24, fig. 3.

[71] Moses was first identified, it will be recalled, in Schiavo, *Lateran*, n.p.

of Holies, and by which the prayers of the faithful could reach God.[72] The connection between Moses and Aaron as brothers and types for Christ and his vicar is, of course, a straightforward one. However, in the Salone di Costantino Moses is actually flanked by a considerably more youthful and bearded man, with a gem-studded band on his head and a psaltery in his hands (figs. 100.M; 112).[73] This figure should accordingly represent David, the author of the Psalms.[74]

The narrative flanked by Moses and David represents the spurious *Donation of Constantine* (figs. 100.C; 108). This depiction differs significantly from its precursor in the Sala di Costantino at the Vatican in that there is no statuette of Roma included in Constantine's legacy to Sylvester.[75] Whereas the emperor kneels before the pope in the basilica of San Pietro in the earlier version, moreover, in the Sixtine rendition Constantine places the document on the high altar, on which sits a crucifix flanked by Saints Peter and Paul, as well as a lit candle, symbol of the faith.[76] Sylvester I sits enthroned beneath his baldachin and watches Constantine place his Donation on the facing altar of what appears to be a somewhat fanciful rendition of the interior of San Pietro. The document, as a symbol of Constantine's relinquishing of his temporal powers to the pope, is accordingly presented to Christ and the twin founders of Christian Rome, as if to reinforce the fact, as embodied in the person of Moses, that the pope, like Christ and his Old Testament types, has always exercised the powers which the ruler of the secular sphere was now willingly confirming. In tandem with *David*, the harmony at last brought to Rome and the *respublica Christiana* through Constantine's earthly act reflects the prophecies of the Psalms, in which the king-musician and root of the tree of Jesse foretold the ultimate triumph of Christ.[77] The microcosm is accordingly brought into harmony with the macrocosm of God's divine plan.

On the north wall, Aaron is accompanied by a crowned and bearded man, apparently of a comparable age to David, who rests his left hand on an object possibly made of stone with a slightly rounded top (a stele, perhaps?), and who rests his right hand on his breast (figs. 101.P; 113). As I have already intimated, the Salone di Costantino should be read in the manner of the Salone dei Papi, that is, both along the walls and across space (a method which is echoed in the vaulted rooms as well). Given that Moses and Aaron face each other across the north-south axis of the Salone, then the crowned figure who faces David would logically relate to David as Moses relates to Aaron. This figure may be identified as Solomon, the son of David who is given a room unto himself in the Lateran Palace programme, adjacent to that of his father (see Appendix V). Just as Moses and Aaron prefigure Christ and his vicar, the lion of Judah and his son Solomon are Christ's direct ancestors. Moreover, the choice of Moses, Aaron, David and Solomon in tandem with earthly rulers, in this case Constantine and Sixtus V, had numerous precedents, especially in the iconography adopted by the Byzantine emperors.[78] Given Constantine's rulership of the East after his present of the West to the papacy, the implications of this "Eastern" grouping in a hall which ultimately glorifies the papacy, is exquisitely orchestrated, and recalls the method by which Sixtus V's Carolingian predecessors had annexed traditional Eastern imperial form and content in the decorations of the Patriarchium Lateranense.

[72] A treatise on Aaron's cosmological gems was written by Sixtus V's physician: Andrea Bacci, *Le XII. pietre pretiose, le quali per ordine di Dio nella santa legge, adornavano i vestimenti del sommo sacerdote* (Rome, 1587).

[73] See Emanuel Winternitz, *Musical Instruments and Their Symbolism in Western Art. Studies in Musical Iconology* (1967; New Haven and London, 1979), 97,133, for the psaltery.

[74] Compare the representation of Kind David in the Vatican Logge, in Davidson, *Raphael's Bible*, 65 and fig. 94. Also consult Appendix V, 258, below.

David, as the musician who soothed Saul's soul by expulsing daemons, is represented in the Sala di Davide. Here, however, he accomplishes this feat by means of a harp. Since David does not wear a crown in the Salone di Costantino, the implication is that he is to be understood first and foremost in another capacity.

[75] In this context, see the discussion in Chappell, Kirwin, "Petrine Triumph," *Storia dell'arte*, 124-125.

It is interesting to note that Joachim of Fiore saw a parallel between David and Constantine, in De Lubac, *Exégèse*, II, I, 451. I make this observation notwithstanding the fact that Sixtus V professed his official opposition to Joachim of Fiore in the Vatican Library, on which consult Chapter II, 91, note 111, above.

[76] For the symbolism of the candle, see note 9, above. There is another document already on the altar, but I have been unable to determine its precise significance.

[77] Réau, *Iconographie*, II, I, 282; Davidson, *Raphael's Bible*, 81, isolates Psalm CX in this regard.

[78] Discussed in Riess, *Political Ideals*, 30-31, with regard to Moses, David and Solomon.

The feigned panel painting which Aaron and Solomon flank represents Constantine performing the *officium stratoris* for Sylvester. In this narrative, Constantine, Sylvester and their entourage wend their way to the site on which Christ gave his double charge to Peter in the Salone dei Papi, hence reinforcing the superiority of the pope in the temporal realm (figs. 101.D; 109; compare figs. 63-64). Whereas the *Vision*, *Baptism*, and *Donation* all have foils in the Vatican Sala di Costantino, this last narrative in the series finds a parallel not at the Vatican, but at the nearby Oratory of the SS. Quattro Coronati, the thirteenth century fresco cycle which was inspired by the *Constitutum Constantini*.[79] There, as in the palace, Sylvester wears the single-crowned tiara given to him by Constantine. Constantine holds the reins of the horse and walks ahead of the mounted pope who, in both frescoes, raises his right hand in an authoritative gesture. Whereas Constantine is crowned with a bejewelled headpiece at the SS. Quattro Coronati, at the Lateran Palace he wears the laurel crown of the Roman emperor. Sylvester himself is unshaded by the parasol which the thirteenth century artist included in the scene. In tandem with the Old Testament personages who flank it, this display by the secular leader of his subservience to the spiritual leader recalls that Aaron had likewise enjoyed supreme powers as high priest, and that Solomon, due to his wisdom and grace, had merited this very same treatment from the secular arm, most notably by the Queen of Sheba, who actually visits him in the Sala di Salomone (fig. 159).

The triads at the center of the long walls are extended by means of landscapes and a seascape which have been attributed to Paul Bril and characterized as containing "genre" scenes.[80] In other words, they have been characterized as fillers with a meaning which is at best ancillary to that conveyed by the main players in the hall. The seascape located adjacent to Moses clearly belies this characterization. It contains a view of Rome in the background, with obelisk, domed church and Roman ruins, a sea battle in which a gallion with *fleurs-de-lis* and lion banners makes its way to shore, while others flounder amidst the waves (figs. 100.R; 114). The combination of Moses and a sea battle evokes his defeat of the Egyptians in the Red Sea. Given the manifest importance of Constantine in this hall, it recalls a similar incident (or at least that was how it was viewed by the emperor's contemporaries), in which Maxentius and his troops were defeated at the Milvian Bridge.[81] Since neither of these battles involved ships (a fact which does not lessen or negate the aforementioned analogies, in my view), then the seascape should also refer to another battle, or battles. One possibility is the battle which Constantine's son Crispus won over the emperor's brother-in-law Licinius, an event of extreme importance for Constantine's unquestioned authority in the temporal realm, and one which could have been intended as an *exemplum in malo* of the brotherly relationship exemplified by Moses and Aaron.[82] Another possibility, which in no way excludes the former, is suggested by the flags on the mother ship in the foreground. The *fleurs-de-lis* in particular serve to cement a post-Constantinian battle, and demonstrate first and foremost a French or Florentine connection. A great battle was waged during the pontificate of Sixtus V, that between Philip II of Spain and Queen Elizabeth of England, but the battle was waged by the Spanish, not the French and, in any case, Philip II's armada, which

[79] The *Vision* at the SS. Quattro Coronati is depicted as Sylvester showing Constantine the portraits of Saints Peter and Paul to confirm the identity of the two figures of his vision; the *Baptism* is one of immersion and does not take place in the Lateran Baptistry (its foil is located in the Salone dei Papi, in the medallion of St. Sylvester); and the *Donation* is represented as Constantine giving Sylvester the tiara.

[80] See Chapter I, 44-45, notes 68-69.

[81] Consult Chapter II, 77-78, notes 25-26, for Eusebius and the use of this *topos* by sixteenth century rulers.

[82] For the sea battle between Crispus and Licinius, and Pietro da Cortona's 1635 rendition of the subject, consult David Dubon, *Tapestries from the Samuel H. Kress Collection at the Philadelphia Museum of Art. The History of Constantine the Great designed by Peter Paul Rubens and Pietro da Cortona* (Great Britain, 1964), 36, and 121, n. 11.

went into battle with the pecuniary support of Sixtus V, was crushed by Sir Francis Drake.[83] Another battle must therefore have been intended, and, of the many battles waged during the sixteenth century, none was dearer to Sixtus V's heart than the Battle of Lepanto, won under the aegis of Pius V, and commemorated by Sixtus V on his mentor's tomb monument at Santa Maria Maggiore.[84] Not only is the seascape full of meaning, then, but it also partakes of the method employed over and over again in the Lateran Palace programme, whereby events are accreted, one upon the next in a single image, in order to convey the repetetive nature of God's divine plan. To complete the scheme, the contemporary Sixtine element is provided by the obelisk in the distant city which, given the devices on the main walls, is likely to be understood as having been surmounted by Sixtus V with his providential *monti* and star as well as the cross. In tandem with the Christian buildings and pagan ruins, the message is one of conversion and triumph and the ultimate translation from the Exodus of this life to the Promised Land.[85]

The interpretation of the landscapes is more problematic than that of the seascape owing to the manifest absense of events which might be analogized to specific occurrences. With the exception of that adjacent to Solomon, the landscapes, like the seascape, contain Christian buildings and pagan ruins, but the focal point in each is a great tree which either grows at or near the center of the composition, like the tree of Paradise, or which spreads its wind-blown boughs to enframe the composition (figs. 100.Q; 114; 101.S, T; 115; 117). As the emblem of the *Abundance* in the Salone dei Papi makes clear, the trees are analogues to the cross on which Christ was crucified; and as the analysis of the Sala di Samuele suggests, the trees are also analogues to the obelisk. In the context of the Salone di Costantino, the trees may accordingly be interpreted as counterparts to the *Vision* on the main wall, and especially to the cross, star and *monti*-topped obelisks. The landscapes, then, are intimately related to the "single obelisk" devices on the main walls.

Each landscape also contains interludes which are unique. That to the left of *David* contains a fisherman and husbandsmen with their asses, and, in the foreground, a woman hanging out her laundry beside a water wheel, a likely allusion to the purificatory rites involved in the *Baptism of Constantine*; to the exorcism of obelisks and columns; and to the drowning of the "Egyptians" in the pendant seascape (fig. 116). The landscape situated opposite this scene on the north wall, adjacent to *Solomon*, evidently does not partake of the triumphant architectural symbolism (fig. 117). In its place, the scene contains rural homes which seem to point to the contemplative life enjoyed in the country. Two figures walk through this peaceful scape, and another, at the right background, is engaged in some type of outdoor activity, but the main action takes place in the foreground, where a hunting dog accompanies his master as he shoots geese.[86] The most unusual component of this Golden Age surround is a giant chicken or rooster, located at left foreground, who has been passed, just moments before, by the couple perambulating the woods.[87] The pendant landscape on this wall contains hunters and their dogs, as well as fishermen and the architectural symbolism of triumph, made the more evident by the church at the apex of the hill and the cross located further down the mountainside (fig. 115).[88]

[83] The battle took place in 1588, after the programme was evidently written. It is possible that either later alterations to the programme were allowed, or events which occurred after it was written, readily syncretized with the exisiting iconography.

[84] I wish to thank Giuseppe Scavizzi for suggesting this analogy to the Battle of Lepanto.

If the *League of Christian Princes* contains an underlying allusion to the Battle of Lepanto, then it would be reinforced by this reference. See Chapter II, 86, note 80, for the suggestion. Further, I dare suggest that the four allegories in the Salone dei Papi may well contain yet further allusions to the four Old Testament personages represented in the Salone di Costantino, not just to Moses, who I have shown to be symbolically present in each. The Ark of the Covenant of the *League* would still relate first and foremost to Moses; the thunderbolt-wielding lion of the *Extirpation* would refer to Aaron as the victor over the sons of Corah who had pretended to exercise his powers; the *Treasure* would refer to David, since, as the angel of the Vatican version suggests, it was David who was first shown the precise locale on which the Temple was to be built; and the *Abundance*, finally, would refer to Solomon, since the scene is one of peacefulness, the very meaning of this king's name. As I shall suggest below, these four Old Testament personages also figure in the scenes from the life of St. Francis in the western loggia extension, together with Constantine, a figure whose underlying presence in the Good Works of Sixtus V in the Salone dei Papi, together with the Emperor Augustus, has been discussed already in Chapter III.

[85] See Chapter I, 66-67, and note 172.

[86] The landscapes containing fishermen and hunters evoke traditional villa decoration, discussed in Chapter III above, as well as the chivalric tradition, adopted by the Renaissance papacy, of partaking in these activities, notwithstanding that they were banned by Canon Law. However, given the battle taking place in the seascape, such activities do not seem to be the (or a) common denominator. They may, of course, contribute on one level to the meaning of the landscapes. On the papal love of the hunt (the villa at La Magliana was used for this purpose and was, it will be recalled, restored by Sixtus V), and the traditions which inspired and forbade it, see Partner, *Rome*, 156.

[87] This bird could possibly signify Peter's denial, in which case the message would involve penitence. For the symbolism of the chicken and rooster, see Gregorio Penco, "Il simbolismo animalesco nella letteratura monastica," *Studia Monastica. Barcelona* VI (1984): 14, 16; Valeriano, *Hieroglyphica*, XXIV, xvii - xxviii, who notably explains in xx that the rooster is a symbol of Apollo; and Cartari, *Imagini*, 329, who equates the rooster's vigilance to that of Mercury.

Like the "single obelisk" devices framing the main walls, the message of the Salone di Costantino is essentially one of conversion to and triumph of the faith, achieved by the powers of the Church and its cornerstone, at once Christ and the Virgin, Peter and Paul, Sylvester I and Sixtus V. On its most basic, literal level, the hall glorifies the Roman Emperor to whom God manifested the light of truth so that he could carry out the providential plan. With Constantine's momentous conversion, the persecutions of Christians were put to a halt and peace was enjoyed throughout the empire; with the Donation, the empire and *caput mundi* were translated to the Bishop of Rome so that the way was left clear for him to shepherd his flock in both the temporal and spiritual realms. In other words, it expands upon the message of Saint Sylvester I and the main wall of the Salone dei Papi. On another level, the Salone di Costantino, like the Salone dei Papi, is a glorification of the Church and her vicar. While the assimilation of Constantine to Moses was a commonplace, begun by his admirers following his extirpation of Maxentius, and hence an understandable component of the hall ostensibly dedicated to him, Moses was also a precursor of Christ and of the pope. The emperor's duties and powers had always, therefore, been subsumed by those of Christ and his vicar, and Constantine's Donation redundant, though nonetheless welcome to the *respublica Christiana*. It would seem to be on this account that Peter and Paul, as implicitly present on the main walls, are joined by Solomon and David, Aaron and Moses, rulers to whom Constantine's successors had erroneously likened themselves in their endeavour to take for themselves the prerogative always enjoyed by the pope. As the landscapes and seascape tacitly suggest, this power had been preordained from the very beginning. And as the landscapes, "single obelisk" devices, and personifications make clear, this power belongs to Sixtus V, the pope destined to convert the world, and to usher in the Golden Age of Christianity.

B. THE EASTERN LOGGIA

Just as the "single obelisk" devices act as liasons between the Sala degli Obelischi, Sala di Samuele, and Salone di Costantino, to draw forth the idea of the *translatio imperii* from Egypt through pagan and triumphant Christian Rome, they are strategically placed in the eastern loggia, located adjacent to the Salone di Costantino and accessible from it, together with "single column" devices and other equally potent Sixtine hieroglyphics, to bring out the Christological and Marian, Petrine and Pauline import of the obelisks and columns, and its ramifications for the papacy and its care of Christ's flock (fig. 6). In this loggia, containing some of the more traditional Christian iconography of the programme, the narratives begin with the pronouncements of the births of both John the Baptist and Christ, and end with their providential meeting in the prime of their lives, with John's baptism of Christ and the appearance of the Holy Ghost to seal the magnitude of the "conversion," the anointing of the messiah. To ensure that each scene is properly identified by the viewer, the feigned panel paintings are surmounted by inscriptions taken from the biblical passages given visual description. Beneath each narrative is a feigned cartouche containing scenes in *grisaille*. These cartouche scenes provide the Old Testament typologies of the

[88] There is also an animal on the mountain which looks like a deer. It likely has symbolical meaning, possibly the ability to understand celestial mysteries, or God's divine plan. See Penco, "simbolismo animalesco," *Studia Monastica*, 15; and Valeriano, *Hieroglyphica*, VII, xix, who also provides additional possibilities.

events unfolding before the viewer's eyes, and are the most problematic components of the vault, since difficult to identify with certainty. It is clear, in any case, that their overall function is to underscore the providentiality of the coming of both Saint John the Baptist and Christ, and to emphasize the Alpha and Omega: the Sacrament of Baptism, which will be sanctified by the sacrifice of Christ on the cross, and the Sacrament of the Eucharist, the symbolism of which pervades the programme of the Lateran Palace. The western loggia, which physically responds to the eastern, completes the unfolding of history back in time, to the very beginning and the Creation of the Sun and the Plants, that is, of Christ and the *Liber Naturae*, which are likewise celebrated throughout the cycle. It also points forward, past the central point of history represented in the eastern loggia, through a second providentially ordained nodal point in the birth and stigmatization of Saint Francis in the western loggia extension, to the end of time and the Heavenly City to which the Sixtine obelisks and columns point.[89]

The Sixtine devices featuring single obelisks and columns are located on the seam of the eastern vault in the heavenly realm. They are accompanied by lion devices, and by a device unique to the Lateran Palace programme, featuring a papal tiara, orphrey, and cross behind a solarian golden field. This device is located in the third bay, but it is not at center vault, as one might expect. At center are two "single column" devices, and the remainder branch out from this point, according to the bilateral symmetry of the western loggia vaults and, in their lack of one-to-one correspondences between types of devices, according to the second arm of the main stairway which ascends to the *piano nobile*.[90] A reading according to the Sixtine devices, specifically the columns and obelisks, the focus of this chapter, must of necessity be an achronological one, much in the manner by which the Salone dei Papi, and all ensembles considered thus far, are ultimately to be understood.

In keeping with the "trinitarian" method pervading the programme, each device is flanked by two feigned panel paintings, themselves flanked by a *grisaille* narrative so as to form an extended triptych. The first "single obelisk" device, located at the southernmost end of the loggia, has the *anima* taken from Luke XIX: 38 "GLORIA DEO IN EXCELSIS," echoing that on the east wall of the Salone di Costantino. It is flanked by the *Annunciation to Zacharias* and the *Marriage of the Virgin*. In the first scene (fig. 119), the high priest Zacharias is in the Holy of Holies, with his lit censer, as an angel appears to tell him that his elderly, barren wife will give birth to a child, whom he is instructed to name John. In the second scene, Joseph and the Virgin stand before the high priest, and Joseph holds the rod which flowered as a sign that he was the chosen suitor, while the rejected and dejected suitors either throw their ineffectual rods to the ground or crack them in two (fig. 120). Common to each of these scenes is Aaron, the high priest whose successor is Zacharias, and whose flowering rod, which gave to him and the Levites sole authority to officiate in the most hallowed precinct of the Jewish faith, the type for Joseph's. In tandem with the Old Testament *grisailles* respectively representing the *Sacrifice of Manoah*, with Samson's future father and mother before the altar, and a scene of divine unction, possibly representing Solomon's son Jeroboam before Rehoboam, these Aaronic narratives and the "single obelisk" device would seem to suggest thanksgiving for this preor-

[89] Davidson, *Raphael's Bible*, 87, interprets the Vatican Logge scenes in these terms and makes the connection to the liturgy for Holy Saturday, which is as pertinent there as it is in the Lateran Palace programme.

Significantly, the western loggia (*vis-à-vis* the western loggia extension), which ends with narratives concerning Abraham, Sara and Isaac, responds on the diagonal with the beginning of the eastern loggia featuring scenes from the lives of Simeon, Mary and Elizabeth and in this way corresponds to the Joachimite view of world history which compares Abraham, Sara and Isaac with Simeon, Mary and Elizabeth, in De Lubac, *Exégèse*, II, I, 451.

[90] The columnar devices at center vault are flanked in turn by a lion device in the sixth vault and a tiara device in the fourth; an obelisk in the seventh responding to a lion in the second; and a lion in the ninth corresponding to the obelisk in the first. See Appendix I, 198 ff, for a complete listing of the *corpi* and *anime* in their placement in the scheme.

dained "repetition" of historical events which would culminate in Christ's birth by the Virgin, another flowering rod (hence the Lucan *anima*, sung by the angels at the Nativity); his divine unction by John the Baptist; and his ultimate sacrifice on the cross. The foil of this device is found at the northern end of the loggia, in conjunction with *Christ among the Doctors* and *John the Baptist preaching in Judea* (figs. 121 and 122). Its *anima*, "IN HOC SIGNO," is full of allusions, and relates as much to Constantine's dream following the *Vision*, depicted in the adjacent Salone di Costantino, as to the Gospel of Luke, in which Christ is often referred to as a "sign." As one of the more lucid triads, the message concerns the conversion of souls to the true faith; the superiority of the New Dispensation over the Old; and the penance which is so vital to attaining salvation.

The "single obelisk" devices are complemented by two "single column" devices which may be conclusively identified as the Antonine and the Trajanic because their *anime* set forth their identities: the one, which is flanked by the *Adoration of the Shepherds* and the *Circumcision* belongs to Saint Paul "D. VAS ELECT[IONIS] S P," the chosen vessel, and the other, collocated with the *Adoration of the Magi* and *Presentation in the Temple*, belongs to Saint Peter, the "S P PAS[TOR] OVIVM" of John X: 7-10; 16.[91] The *Adoration of the Shepherds* shows Mary, with a halo around her head, kneeling in prayer before her child as Joseph, the ox and ass of the Old and New Dispensations, the midwife (?), and the shepherds, look on from about the ramshackle shed (fig. 123). One of the shepherds kneels in the foreground. At his side lies the lamb, with feet tied, brought as a gift to the newly born sacrificial lamb of God resting comfortably on the bed which will one day be the altar.[92] His companions likewise bring gifts, and although extremely difficult to read, appear to be the traditional musical instruments, including the bagpipe which Joseph now seems to hold. In the background, through the shed, one can glimpse a burst of light and figures in distant fields, suggesting the previous announcement to the shepherds of Christ's birth. Just as the *Adoration* features the shepherds who were understood as members of the Old Dispensation, the *Circumcision* continues to stress that Christ was born into a family of the Jewish faith (fig. 124). The scene is set within the synagogue, according to traditional practice, and the priest, accompanied by an acolyte, onlookers and Joseph, is in the process of circumcizing the child, held in Mary's arms. As a particularly potent symbol of the blood which Christ first shed, the circumcision was traditionally regarded as a type for his ultimate sacrifice on the cross. It was also, as a Jewish ceremony, intended to bind the boy with the Old Covenant, a testimony to the Hebraic origins and genealogy of Jesus. In tandem with the *Adoration of the Shepherds* and the Old Testament *grisailles*, the connection between the Antonine Column with Paul is not, as one might at first suspect, his mission as converter to the Gentiles. Rather, as the *anima* of the device reveals, the nexus is Paul's calling as the chosen Hebraic vessel, the greatest of the Jewish converts to Christianity in the history of the Church.

The Magi who adore Christ in the narrative flanking the Trajanic column with Peter were traditionally regarded as Gentile *vis-à-vis* the Hebrew shepherds (fig. 125).[93] The scene is set before the shed of the previous adoration scene, now upheld by a more pristine, classicizing pier. The ox and ass are present, as are Joseph and the train of the magi who look on as

[91] Compare the Giulio of Sixtus V struck during the first year of his pontificate with the inscription referring to both Peter and Paul: "PASTOR OV VAS ELECT," in *Corpus Nummorum Italicorum Primo Tentativo di un Catalogo Generale delle Monete Medievali e Moderne Coniate in Italia o da Italiani in altri paesi* (Milan, 1936), XVI, 88, n. 64.

[92] Davidson, *Raphael's Bible*, 85, notes that in the representation of this event in the Vatican Logge, "the child ... is seated upon a linen cloth draped over a block of stone: table, altar and cornerstone of the Church." The same may be said for the Sixtine rendition.

[93] Davidson, *Raphael's Bible*, 86.

Mary holds an erect and seated child, on whom shines a radiant burst of light. Christ holds the gold given to him by the magus, extends his right hand in a gesture of benediction, and watches as the magus, with hat on the ground, kneels and kisses his foot in deference. The other two magi stand by, with their gifts of frankincense and myrrh, ready to be received by this royal child. The pendant scene of the *Presentation in the Temple* features a haloed Virgin Mary presenting the child to the high priest. Joseph is at her side, extending his arm with the five shekel payment, it is understood, and nearby a maidservant balances a basket on her head, presumably containing the doves of Mary's purification, and another object in her hand (fig. 126). Anna is also present behind the high priest, and auxiliary figures view the proceedings. As a traditional analogue to the slaying of the first-born in Egypt, the *Presentation* would seem to point to a kind of exorcism of heretical forces (the Egyptian children), who were subjected to God's unrelenting punishment. With the traditional addition of Mary's ritual cleansing after childbirth, it would also suggest the purity of the Roman Catholic Church, which has been and continues to be free of blemish. With the "single column" device featuring Saint Peter as Pastor of the Sheep above the Trajanic column, the triad reveals that Christ's vicar exercises jurisdiction over the temporal realm in keeping with the obeisance first given to Christ by the Gentile rulers, including, it is understood, the Roman and Holy Roman emperors. It reveals too that the flock under his guidance, like the flock of the *Extirpation*, is unspotted and safeguarded from forces which endeavour, but ultimately fail, to undermine and destroy Christ's convenant on earth.

The devices featuring single obelisks and columns are accordingly positioned within narrative scenes in order to draw forth the essential meaning of the papacy; of the missions of Peter and Paul as the apostolic founders of the Roman Catholic Church and the direct ancestors of Sixtus V; and of the function of the secular arm in relation to papal authority. The "single obelisk" device which is collocated with the *Annunciation to Zacharias* and the *Marriage of the Virgin*, and which points up Sixtus V's essential role as a *novus Aaron*, conveys a meaning which is complementary to the "single column" device belonging to Peter, and flanked by the *Adoration of the Magi* and the *Presentation in the Temple*. The message of the "single obelisk" triptych concerns the pope's spiritual authority which derives from both his Aaronic ancestry and the spiritual key given to Peter in the Salone dei Papi. The message of the "single column" triptych, conversely, centers on the kingly authority of Christ's vicar, and his ability to judge, with the aid of his temporal key, which of his sheep are chaste, and which are blemished; to grant absolution and to excommunicate. In other words, the extended Petrine triptychs of the eastern loggia revolve around the dual powers with which Christ's vicar is invested in the main hall of the Lateran Palace, and show, by example, that the authority to bind and to loose, to unify Jew and Gentile in one flock, and to enforce the Sacrament of Penance on those unchaste souls within the fold who desire salvation, had been preordained by God from earliest times. The "single obelisk" device which is collocated with *Christ among the Doctors* and *John the Baptist preaching in Judea*, and which points up Sixtus V's mission to convert the world to the true faith, likewise complements the meaning conveyed by the "single column" device belonging to Paul, and flanked by the *Adoration of the Shepherds* and *Circumcision*, whereby Paul receives his revelation from God to become the *vas electionis*. The mission to convert is accordingly complemented by the momentous conversion of the apostle, and the investiture to Peter is complemented by the investiture to Paul. Together, the Petrine and Pauline triptychs emphasize their common duty: the apostles are to preach the Word and to convert; Peter is to throw out his net to the Jews, and Paul, through his eloquence, is to reveal the light to the Gentiles. Ultimately, their complementary duties, like the complementary obelisks and columns, become one, and the Petrine and Pauline triptychs syncretized and united in Christ and the Virgin, His mother, bride and Catholic Church.[94] As author of the converted obelisks and columns, the Egyptian and Roman empires, finally, Sixtus V completes the work of his predecessors, and his pontificate becomes the culmination and fulfillment of their charges.

4. SIXTUS V'S GOOD WORKS AS ATTRIBUTES AND DEVICES: THE COLUMNS AND OBELISKS

The obelisks and columns are represented together as both the attributes of a personification and the *corpo* of devices (figs. 18, 19, 128, 137, 151-152). The combination of obelisks and columns in each case is always constant: the two columns surmounted by the apostles Peter and Paul flank a solitary cross, star and *monti*-topped Sixtine obelisk. While this image is clearly an original creation, made expressly for Sixtus V - perhaps on his own suggestion, like the crowning of the obelisks with crosses, or, in all likelihood, the lion atop the *monti* of the *Extirpation* - it is not without precedent. In particular, it recalls one of the most well known and celebrated devices of the Cinquecento: the columnar device of the Emperor Charles V, a device which was also used by the Medici Pope Leo X, a pope and a family with which Sixtus V and the art he commissioned have much in common.[95] Like the imperial and Medicean *corpi*, which regularly featured two columns, each surmounted by a crown, with a third crown between them, the Sixtine image evokes the Columns of Hercules located at the Straits of Gibralter, signifying the end of the Roman empire and of the known world. As markers of the extent of the Roman empire, soon to be bypassed as the Herculean ruler travels beyond them, the two columns assert a message concerning the pope's authority in the temporal realm of the emperor. In this sense, the columns flanking the Good Works of Sixtus V and of his predecessors in the Salone dei Papi are intimately related to the Sixtine hieroglyphics, particularly given the Herculean allusions contained within the allegorical Good Works. Also on a contemporaneous note, the allusions to the Battle of Lepanto in the Salone di Costantino seascape, (as, in all likelihood, in the *League*) together with the "obelisk and column" devices, conjure reminiscences of Marcantonio Colonna, the great naval commander who crushed the Ottoman fleet, and who was commemorated on Pius V's tomb at Santa Maria Maggiore.[96] Surmounted, as they are, by the twin founders of the Roman Catholic Church, the columns also suggest that Christianity is to be extended beyond the known boundaries of the world, to encompass the globe in preparation for the Sec-

[94] It may well be that the implicit connection to the East in the Salone di Costantino is present also in the eastern loggia. According to Joachim of Fiore, the second age is divided between East and West, with St. John the Evangelist and the Virgin Mary standing for the former, and St. Peter and St. John the Baptist the latter, in De Lubac, *Exégèse*, II, I, 449-450.

[95] For this and the following, I am drawing on the research of Rosenthal, "*Plus Ultra*," JWCI, 204-228; *idem*, "The Invention of the Columnar Device of Emperor Charles V at the Court of Burgundy in Flanders in 1516," *Journal of the Warburg and Courtauld Institutes* XXXVI (1973), 198-230; and *idem*, "*Plus Oultre*: The Idea Imperial of Charles V in his Columnar Device on the Alhambra," *Hortus Imaginum*, ed. Robert Enggass, Marilyn Stokstad, University of Kansas Publications Humanistic Studies, 45 (Lawrence, Kansas, 1974), 85-93. Leo X's use of the imperial device, and its relevance to the iconography of the art commissioned by Cosimo de'Medici are discussed in Richelson, *Studies*, 84 and 98, note 14.

Significantly, Sixtus V's hated predecessor Gregory XIII was given a columnar device encircled by the Boncompagni dragon in Fabricio, *Delle Allusioni*, VI, 312, in which one column signifies Prudence, and the other Fortitude. Fabricio dedicated the reprint edition to Sixtus V!

Sixtus V had planned to erect two columns, taken from the Patriarchium Lateranense, at the Campidoglio, together with the bronze globe which had surmounted the Vatican obelisk. Aiken, "Capitoline," 137-140, discusses the symbolism of the columns by drawing on the imperial device.

[96] Herz, "Sistine," *Storia dell'arte*, 258, for Pius V's tomb. The columns also suggest Nicholas IV (Colonna).

166

ond Coming, a meaning which was likewise contained in the imperial and Medicean device, despite their "omission" of Peter and Paul. In this sense, temporal and spiritual are united. Since the meaning of the columns and obelisks are one and the same, the Sixtine image states in two ways the very same message which was expounded in the temporal and spiritual tiers of the Salone dei Papi, as in the Sala degli Obelischi, Sala di Samuele, Salone di Costantino, eastern loggia and, indeed, all rooms and halls of the *piano nobile*.

The double columns of the Sixtine image, and of its imperial and papal precedent, also suggest numerous biblical events in which columns or pillars figure prominently. For example, they evoke the Temple of Jerusalem, built by King Solomon and upheld by the spiralling columns named after him.[97] The Temple of Jerusalem accordingly acts as the type for the cochleate columns which once supported the emperors Trajan and Marcus Aurelius, but which now support Peter and Paul. No wonder, given this interpretation, that the "obelisk and column" device is included in the decorations of the room dedicated to King Solomon on the *piano nobile*. The columns also evoke the nativity of Christ, in which Mary held on to the column (or pillar) to aid her in childbirth, as well as the flagellation of Christ, and, in this sense, are consonant with the use of paired "single column" devices in the eastern loggia with its emphasis on Christ's early life. They also recall that Paul himself had likened Peter, James, and John to pillars in his Epistle to the Galatians [II: 9]. It was as pillars that these converters of the circumcised went about their mission, just as Paul himself, as the converter to the Gentiles, went about his. The columns also recall the gates and posts at Gaza, which Samson tore from the ground, as well as the columns of the Temple of Dagon, which the hero likewise dislocated in order to quell his captors and, in the process, bring about his own death [Judges, XVI: 1-3; XVI: 4-31]. That Samson was at once a prefiguration of Christ, as the typology of the eastern loggia acknowledges, and a prefiguration of Saint Francis, helps further to explain the presence of Sixtine columns in the eastern loggia, as in the western loggia extension with its scenes from the life of Saint Francis, not to mention the *Lateran* of the Salone dei Papi.[98] At the same time, such a typology sheds light on the more global significance of the repeated citations in the Lateran Palace of Samson's famous riddle. The double columns also evoke the columnar legs of the angel who brought Saint John the Evangelist the message of God and commanded him to eat it [Revelation X: 1-11]. This angel, who was enveloped in a cloud and whose legs were "like pillars of fire," stood with one leg on land and one on sea (like an Egyptian pharaoh), as testimony to the world dominion to be enjoyed at the end of time by Christ and his earthly vicar, the solarian Sixtus V, a time to which Saint John would now be made privy. And finally, to complete the list of the more evocative meanings by which the columns could be interpreted, they suggest the two pillars, the one made of cloud and the other of fire, by which Francis and the Franciscans, and before them, Moses and the Israelites, were directed on their Exodus from Egypt, through the Red Sea to the Promised Land [Exodus XIV: 19-31].[99]

Much as the Herculean analogy of the double columns is borne out in the Good Works of Sixtus V in the Salone dei Papi, one or more of these aforementioned analogies, and most

97 Noted in Aiken, "Capitoline," 251, note 52.

98 For Francis as an *alter Samson*, see Habig, *St. Francis*, 856.

99 Noted in Aiken, "Capitoline," 251, note 52.

certainly others, are drawn forth depending upon the specific locale in which Sixtus V and his iconographer chose to place the obelisk and column hieroglyphic. As an attribute, the image is found twice in the palace and in both cases, the personification who holds it is accompanied by another holding the "Peretti" scale of justice. By extreme good fortune, the personification on the *piano terreno* was still accompanied, between 1963-1966 when photographic documentation of the palace was carried out, by part of the inscription which once clearly revealed her identity (figs. 5 and 18). While the modern iconographer might imagine that her name was a relatively lengthy one, encompassing the ideas of triumph and especially conversion, as well as the name of or allusion to Sixtus V, the first part of her name, "RELIGIO," and the relatively small space remaining for further characters, indicate that she was originally called by a somewhat general, all-encompassing name, in keeping with the Sixtine method employed in the palace, as in the Vatican Library and Villa Montalto, possibly "RELIGIO SACRA." The scale which her "anonymous" foil holds is an attribute which was given in classical antiquity to Mercury in his role as psychopomp and weigher of souls, as well as to his Christian counterpart, Saint Michael, since he was invested with these very same powers.[100] As the *League of Christian Princes* makes clear, it had very recently been given to yet a third providentially ordained dispenser of justice, that paragon of virtue and man of many manifestations, Pope Sixtus V. The pear which undoubtedly once maintained the equilibrium of the scale and the considerably heavier regal crown and keys that it balances on the ground floor, and which is still extant on the *piano nobile* (fig. 129), accordingly asserts the extremely personal nature of this personification, so that in one fundamental sense, *Sacred Religion* and this woman, whom I shall call *Justice*, or a more pointed *Sixtine Justice*, are distinctly Sixtine "virtues." The grimacing lions accompanying the personifications on the ground floor serve to underscore their autobiographical flavour. The pedestals on which they rest their bare feet surely serve to underscore the conviction of this just and virtuous architect of Christ's work on earth and the sacredness of the city of Rome and the *respublica Christiana* (for one removes ones shoes on holy ground). When viewed together, as was clearly the intention, in one sense *Sacred Religion* and *Sixtine Justice* reveal that Sixtus V, the vigilant lion of Judah, not only spreads the faith far and wide, beyond the pillars of Hercules, but he also exercises the powers invested in him by the two keys in his possession (and on his Mercurial scale) to bind and to loose; to mete out the heretic and infidel, and to create peace on earth. These hieroglyphic symbols accordingly present Pope Sixtus V in his now familiar guise as a *novus Hercules-Mercurius*, an identification reinforced by the obelisk itself, now understood on the basis of the Mercurial columns and scale as an analogue to the most ancient manifestation of Mercury as a stone, placed at the junctions of three roads, like the obelisks in the *piazze* of the main basilicas of Sixtine Rome.[101] As the *anime senza corpi* of the adjacent vault on the *piano terreno* reveal, it is in his Mercurial guise, and the Christian and Franciscan counterparts, that Sixtus V "protects his own," and "strikes down those who threaten" the well being of the *respublica Christiana* (TVTANDOS SVOS; DEPELENDOS NOXIOS).[102]

[100] Guarino, "Iconografia," *L'Angelo e la Città*, 84-86.

[101] Bowen, "Mercury," *JWCI*, 222-224.

[102] I would suggest that, far from fortuitous, the decision to place the personifications of *Providence* and *Felicity*, respectively holding the small temple and censer, sceptre and armillary sphere, while resting bare feet on a pedestal on the *piano nobile* (illustrated in part in my "'Starry Leo,'" *RACAR*, fig. 14), directly above *Sacred Religion* and *Sixtine Justice*, was calculated to reinforce and reiterate in different "words" their essential messages (fig. 18). *Sacred Religion*, holding hieroglyphics of the Ark of the Covenant, conversion and triumph, is located directly beneath the personification of *Providence*. The Sixtine *stemma*, crowned with papal tiara, orphrey, and keys, is a constant on both floors. And finally, *Sixtine Justice* responds to *Felicity* holding regal sceptre and the armillary sphere, traditional symbols of kingly powers and universal rule or glory, made the more providential by means of the "starry Leo," so that the justice which Sixtus V dispenses in the temporal and spiritual realms is shown to have been preordained in the stars. On the ramifications of this analysis, see my forthcoming "Simbolismo ermetico," *Sisto V*.

A. THE FOURTH ROOM OF THE PRIVATE APARTMENT

In the fourth room of the private apartment, *Sacred Religion* and *Sixtine Justice* are joined by Old Testament prophets, Saint John the Baptist, and hermit saints in landscapes on the coves (figs. 6; 130-135); a rondel with Sixtus V's name and year of his pontificate and the cryptic verse from Judges, "DE FORTI EGRESSA EST DVLCEDO," at center vault (fig. 136);[103] as well as the typical Sixtine "decorations" comprised of elements from his heraldry interspersed among angels and *genii* - in short, the kind of decoration which characterizes Christian and specifically Sixtine *grotteschi*. Since the verse from Judges was spoken by Samson, then the double columns held by *Sacred Religion* take on connotations of Samson's leonine strength, and the pear which balances the regal crown and keys, the sweetness and virtue of the lion, at once Sixtus V and the *Logos*. The inscription of Sixtus V's name and year of his pontificate together with the already autobiographical attributes held by the personifications, serve to reinforce the equation of Sixtus V and Samson, an equation underscored by his station as Christ's Franciscan vicar.[104]

Reminiscent of the landscapes commissioned by Gregory XIII, especially those on the vault of the Gallery of Geographic Maps (1580-83), as well as the landscapes created for Julius III and Pius IV, popes whom Sixtus V had served early on in his career, the landscapes with saints penitent derive ultimately from a tradition illustrating monks in landscapes in which the setting itself was a metaphor of the ascetic way of life.[105] As Michelle Métraux has shown, this tradition had infiltrated Rome by the late fifteenth century, when Antonio da Viterbo painted the Capella dei Ponziani at Santa Cecilia (c. 1480), and reached its first real culmination with Polidoro da Caravaggio's San Silvestro al Quirinale frescoes (1525), in which the landscape at last became the dominant focus.[106] These representations are also consistent with Baronio's tenets that the saints should be included in the history of the Church, and are of a specific type: hermit saints and their prototypes who searched for Christ in the desert.[107]

The figures inhabiting the landscape lunettes were first identified in the 1950 guidebook to the Lateran Museums, as follows: a nineteenth century landscape, which is no longer inhabited, facing Saint John the Baptist (figs. 127.A, B; 130 and 131); Elijah and the Angel opposite God speaking to Abel (figs. 127.C, D; 132 and 133); and Onuphrius facing Mary of Egypt (figs. 127.E, F; 134 and 135). While it is entirely possible that Saint John the Baptist was originally paired with Christ (or the *alter Christus*, Saint Francis) on the east wall, given their intimate relationship in the Bible as on the vault of the eastern loggia, and given the pairing across the space of the lateral coves of Old Testament prophets and Christian hermit saints, the nineteenth century alteration of the fresco, and the lack of written evidence on the room, make a positive identification impossible. The identification of the kneeling figure as Abel is no less problematic (fig. 133). On the one hand, the identification is reasonable when considering that Abel's sacrifice of his first-born lamb was acceptable to God *vis-à-vis* Cain's corn, prompting Christ to place him first in the line of Old Testament martyrs [Matthew XXIII: 35]. However, the incident depicted is described not in the biblical account of Abel's life [Genesis IV: 1-8], but rather in that of

[103] This octagonal design is repeated almost exactly in the Libreria Segreta of the Vatican Library. It differs from that described here only in that the Sixtine lion replaces the inscription stating the patron of the programme and year of execution.

Although contemporaneous sermons and panegyrics do not, curiously enough, seem to address the biblical passages singled out in the Lateran Palace cycle, this verse from Judges XIV is discussed in Bonardo, *Agnus Dei*, 23. See note 113, below, for another exception, notably by the same author.

[104] Samson figures prominently in the programme of the Scala Santa. There, as here, Sixtus V is implicitly being equated to Samson, as he is likewise equated to Moses.

[105] The sources are sparse on the landscapes executed in the Tower of the Winds (c. 1572-82) and Gallery of Geographic Maps under Gregory XIII. There is some discussion of them in R. Buscaroli, *La Pittura di Paesaggio in Italia* (Bologna, 1935), 64-65; Vaes, "Matthieu Bril," *BIHBR*, 283-331; P. I. Stein, "La Sala della Meridiana nella Torre dei Venti in Vaticano," *L'Illustrazione Vaticana* 9 (16-31 May 1938): 403-410; John W. Stein, "The Meridian Room in the Vatican Tower of the Winds," *Specola Astronomica Vaticana. Miscellanea Astronomica*, 97-98 (1950): 33-55; Fabrizio Mancinelli and Juan Casanovas, *La Torre dei Venti in Vaticano* (Vatican City, 1980); and recently, in Nicola M. Courtright, "Gregory XIII's Tower of the Winds in the Vatican," diss., New York U, 1990 (a dissertation unavailable to the author until just before the manuscript went to press). On the Gallery, also see Claudio Strinati, "Roma nell'anno 1600: studio di pittura," *Ricerche di Storia dell'arte* 10 (1980): 18-20; and, recently, Iris Cheney, "The Galleria delle Carte Geografiche at the Vatican and the Roman Church's View of the History of Christianity," *Renaissance Papers* (1989): 21-37. I should like to thank Iris Cheney for very kindly sending me this paper. As it arrived virtually as this book was going to press, I could not harness some of her valuable and complementary ideas. For the landscapes commissioned by Julius III in the Vatican Logge (c. 1550), see Bernice F. Davidson, "The Landscapes of the Vatican Logge from the Reign of Pope Julius III," *Art Bulletin* LXV, 4 (December 1983): 587-602; and for those in the Room of Cleopatra (c. 1550), Norman W. Canedy, "The Decoration of the Stanza della Cleopatra," *Essays to Wittkower*, I, 110-118; Smith, *Casino*, 98 ff, discusses and illustrates the landscapes ordered by Pius IV for his Casino (1561-63).

[106] Michelle Métraux, "The Iconography of San Martino ai Monti in Rome," diss., Boston U, 1979, 127-136. I wish to thank Michelle Métraux for graciously having put her dissertation at my disposal. On Polidoro's landscapes at S. Silvestro al Quirinale, see A. Richard Turner, "Two Landscapes in Renaissance Rome," *Art Bulletin* XLIII (1961): 275-87.

Moses, the youthful shepherd to whom God appeared in a burning bush, beckoning him back to Egypt as the deliverer of the Israelites [Exodus III: 1-10]. Accordingly, I would identify the figures in the southern lunette landscapes as *Elijah and the Angel* [1 Kings XIX: 45] and *Moses and the Burning Bush* (figs. 132 and 133).

In its Christian meaning, Moses' vision of God in the burning bush which "was not consumed" by fire was traditionally viewed as a type for the purity of Mary and of the Church, as tacitly reinforced in the eastern loggia, where a *grisaille* narrative representing this very scene is set beneath the *Annunciation* [Luke I: 30]. As pastor of the Israelite flock, moreover, Moses is again presented as the prefigurement of both Christ and his vicar. The angel who appeared to Elijah while he rested beneath a juniper tree, exhausted from his flight from Mount Carmel and the heretical Queen Jezabel, also brought him food, the type for the spiritual refreshment gained by partaking in the Eucharist. Together, these scenes seem to convey the idea of the Church's purity and the Eucharist. Since both Moses and Elijah spent forty days in the wilderness following the events depicted in the lunettes, then they would seem also to be presented as types for the forty days which Christ spent in the desert, and accordingly as symbolical of penance and victory over the devil. In tandem with *Sacred Religion*, whom they flank (fig. 128), the message apparently concerns the deliverance of the Christian flock through belief in the Church and the Eucharistic sacrifice, analogues to the converted obelisks and columns as the pillars of cloud and of fire by which Moses led his people out of Egypt through the Red Sea of Baptism towards the Promised Land, as well as the penitence which is a requisite of salvation following baptism.

The figures on the northern wall, apparently *Onuphrius* and *Mary of Egypt* (figs. 134-135), are both hermit saints who lived in the Egyptian desert during the fourth century. Though usually dressed in ragged clothing or in her long hair, like the Magdalen of Provençale myth, Mary is here dressed in a robe, belted at the waist, recalling the Franciscan habit. At her side a rock supports a crucifix - yet another analogy to the Sixtine obelisks and columns. Whereas Mary looks up to heaven, with arms outstretched, Onuphrius, the one-time prince turned hermit, looks down to the earth, with arms crossed in prayer. He wears a hair shirt, and rests his knee on a rock. Beside him is a book, no doubt the Bible, as well as a crucifix lying on the ground before it. In tandem with the personification whom I have called *Sixtine Justice*, *Mary* and *Onuphrius* convey the idea that through penance and living a life in emulation of Christ (as of Moses and Elijah) in the desert, salvation and the crown of justice will be attained. By enduring the torments of the wilderness, moreover, they fight the devil, as had Christ when he descended to Limbo, as had Mercury "before" him, and, as the scales of *Sixtine Justice* make clear, as does Sixtus V himself.[108]

The rocks, which are conspicuously present in these "hermit landscapes," recall that Christ made Peter the foundation stone of the Church and that, as both the spiritual tier of the Salone dei Papi and the "single obelisk and column" devices of the eastern loggia demonstrate, Peter's spiritual sword gave him powers enabling him to bind and to loose, to separate the chaste from the blemished, and to give remission of sins. The

[107] Discussed in Pullapilly, *Baronius*, 145.

[108] For this and the following interpretation of the hermit saints and the wilderness I am drawing on the research of George H. Williams, *Wilderness and Paradise in Christian Thought. The Biblical Experience of the Desert in the History of Christianity and the Paradise Theme in the Theological Idea of the University*, The Menno Simons Lectures (New York, 1962), esp. 22 ff; 28 ff.

[109] Jezabel (or Queen Elizabeth I of England), who is actually depicted in

rocks also evoke the "stone of help" in the Sala di Samuele, especially given their collocation with crucifixes. According to the Sixtine method, then, the triad of *Onuphrius*, *Sixtine Justice* and *Mary of Egypt* should relate to the obelisk and column-bearing *Sacred Religion* and, accordingly, to her pendants, *Elijah and the Angel* and *Moses and the Burning Bush*. As a harlot "converted" by her vision of the Virgin, Mary of Egypt's message is not at all unlike the burning bush in which God showed himself to Moses; as a former prince, who forsook his earthly luxuries to enter the wilderness of paradise, and who was brought a loaf of bread each day by a raven to sustain him, Onuphrius' message is consonant with Elijah's, both as a statement of kingly (or princely) submission to Christ's vicar and a glorification of the Eucharist.[109] The prophets and saints when viewed on the diagonal accordingly convey like meaning, and when viewed across the space of the room, as clearly intended, *Elijah* and *Mary*, *Moses* and *Onuphrius*, convey complementary messages which agree with those conveyed by their pendant collocation of *Elijah* and *Moses*, *Mary* and *Onuphrius*. Although the pendant to *Saint John the Baptist* is no longer extant, the messages of the baptist, which center on the translation from the Old Dispensation (symbolized by the antique ruins in the landscape, as by John himself) to the New, death and rebirth in Baptism (hence his attribute of the lamb of God), and penitence, are consonant with those propagated by the prophets and saints in their various combinations, as with those contained in the Investiture scenes in the Salone dei Papi - the thesis of the Salone and, indeed, of the Lateran Palace programme.

Ultimately, the *locus classicus* uniting the diverse histories of Old Testament prophets and Christian saints in the fourth room of the private apartment is the Exodus from Egypt - from the first, in which Moses led his people across the Red Sea, through those of Saint Francis and the Franciscan Order, and of Pope Sixtus V, the sweet "lion of Judah" who will translate the Church Militant to the Church Triumphant in the last stage of world history. That Egypt holds a significant place in this room is demonstrated by the obelisk held by *Sacred Religion* and by the Egyptian desert to which Moses and Elijah, Mary and Onuphrius, and John the Baptist, fled. The Egyptian component is revealed as a particularly Sixtine one, given that Moses and Elijah are understood to be on Mount Horeb, the same mountain on which Moses received the Tablets of the Law, and the quintessential type for the Sixtine mountains of Montalto; that both Mary of Egypt and Onuphrius were buried by lions, the predecessors of the Sixtine lion;[110] and that the weighty pear of *Sixtine Justice*'s scale has been picked from the pear branches of the pope's heraldry. The verse from Judges at center vault recalls the Sixtine pears in its sweetness, and contains the leonine aspect of Sixtus V's persona. Although the star is present only in the *grotteschi*, finally, I would suggest that it is implicit on the main wall, with the landscape containing Saint John the Baptist, for, as Bonaventure explained in his Preface to the *Legenda Maior*: "By the glorious splendour of his life and teaching *Francis shone like the day-star* amid the clouds and by the brilliance which radiated from him he guided those who live in d a r k - ness in the shadow of death, to the light. [...] *Like St. John the Baptist, he was appointed by God to prepare a way in the desert* – that is, by the complete renunciation involved in perfect

the Sala d'Elia, is in this instance an *exemplum in malo* of the secular arm's reception of the *Logos*.

[110] Metford, *Dictionary*, 170, 185.

poverty – and preach repentance by word and example [emphasis mine]".[111]

[111] Bonaventure, *Legenda Maior*, 631.
[112] See Chapter III, 124, note 150, for this *topos*.

B. THE WESTERN LOGGIA EXTENSION

The implicit analogy between the Sixtine pontificate as an Egyptian and specifically Franciscan Exodus to the Promised Land in the fourth room of the private apartment is confirmed and expanded upon on the vault of the western loggia extension, containing lunettes with scenes from the life of Saint Francis. Again, the connection is made by means of obelisks and columns, this time in the form of devices (fig. 6). The message of the Sala di Samuele, in which the Old Testament prophet erects the "stone of help," as Moses had constructed the Ark of the Covenant, to bring the converted and penitential Israelites across the Red Sea to a state of grace and understanding of the True God, and of the Salone di Costantino, in which the obelisks and crosses lead Constantine, the *novus Moyses*, to the conversion of the empire to the true faith, are given a specifically Franciscan pertinence in the western loggia extension. This is reinforced not only by means of the Sixtine devices in tandem with *grotteschi* and narrative scenes depicted in lunettes, to which I shall shortly turn, but also by the very placement of the loggia before the Sala degli Obelischi and Benediction Loggia with scenes from the life of Constantine. In other words, the architectural given provided a natural triptych, so that Francis in the western loggia extension and Constantine in the Benediction Loggia flank the Sala degli Obelischi, and the columns and obelisks converted by Sixtus V. Yet another connection is made by virtue of the fact that the scenes from Francis' life were situated in the loggia located adjacent to the main door of the Salone dei Papi, featuring the *Lateran*. Indeed, I would suggest that, in addition to drawing on a *topos* which was not incidentally used by Sixtus V himself in his bull *Postquam verus*, this uncanonical Good Work referring to Saint Francis as a "sturdy column of faith" serves to analogize column to obelisk; Francis to Moses-Samuel-Elijah-John the Baptist-Constantine (to name only a few!); and the Lateran, which the saint upholds, to the cross and apostolic founders of the Church, respectively supported by Sixtine obelisks and columns.[112] It can not be coincidental that the iconographer chose to join scenes from the life of Saint Francis in the lunettes by two "obelisk and column" devices in the adjoining seam of the vault, nor can it be coincidental that these scenes are located precisely between the Salone dei Papi and its laudatory inscription, and the Sala degli Obelischi, the room dedicated to those Egyptian and Roman monuments which Sixtus V-Moses-Samuel-Elijah-John the Baptist-Constantine-Francis converted to the true faith. In this sense, it was an entirely logical decision to join the scenes from the life of that "sturdy column" with Sixtine devices comprised of the hieroglyphics for Christ, his vicar, and the "other" sturdy supports, the obelisks and columns. It is entirely possible, moreover, that this connection was worked out by Fontana and the iconographer in the early planning stages of the new Lateran Palace.

The *anime* which are collocated with the column and obelisk *corpo* of the devices concern the triumph of the faith "RELIGIO MIRANDA TRIVNPHAT [sic]," and the glory of God "GLORIA DEI EXALTAT" (fig. 137). These devices are complemented by a quorum of four "lion in profile" devices within rondels at the center of the southernmost vault, whose *anime* have unfortunately disappeared with time. They are flanked on the lateral coves by two others, taken from Psalm XLIV: 8: "DILEXISTI IVSTITIAM" (fig. 142), and "VNXIT TE DEVS" (fig. 141), representing the beginning and end of the passage quoted in the "disembodied" device inscribed above the lunette personifications at the juncture of the southern and eastern logge "DILEXISTI IVSTITIAM ET ODISTI INIQVITATEM" (fig. 118).[113] A connection between the life of Saint Francis, of Christ, and of John the Baptist, as implied in the fourth room of the private apartment, is accordingly confirmed on the evidence of the devices of the eastern loggia and western loggia extension.

The first narrative in the chronology contained within the lunettes of the western loggia extension concerns the *Birth of Saint Francis*, as Scavizzi first noted (fig. 138).[114] The scene quite naturally takes place indoors and features, at the center of the composition, Francis' mother Pica in labour and about to give birth. The midwife is seated before Pica, assisting in the birth, and the maidservant carries an amphora of water on her head and a platter with sheets in her hand. Two companions hold Pica, another friend looks on from a doorway beside the bed (itself upheld by "sturdy columns"), while yet another is in prayer before an icon of the Virgin and Child hanging on the wall. The composition has much in common with that representing the birth of Saint John the Baptist in the eastern loggia, and in this way serves to confirm that Pica was "like another Elizabeth."[115] To the left of the birthing scene a conspicuous column, supported on an equally sturdy square base of constancy and *virtù*, forms the segue to the next scene in this continuous narrative which shows the same maidservant, with platter and sheets still in her hand, attending to the pilgrim who came to beg at the Bernardone household on the day of Francis' baptism (when he was named John). The maidservant gives the beggar a coin. We are reminded in this way that the pilgrim's wishes to see the child were granted by Pica, and that he "took the baby into his arms with great devotion and joy, as Simeon had once taken the infant Jesus, and said 'Today two children have been born in this city; this one will be among the best of mankind, and the other among the worst.'"[116] A curtain separates the third part of the narrative from the central birth, and shows the maidservant washing the young John, with Pica, his father Pietro, and another. Pietro is seated in a chair, with arms closed in prayer, and he looks up, apparently alluding to his wish that the boy be called Francis, rather than John, in honour of the country of France from which he had recently returned. This subsidiary scene may therefore reinforce the analogy between Francis and John the Baptist, as its pendant reinforces that between Francis and Christ, by drawing on the parallel decisions to give each child a different name than that first intended.[117] In this first of the scenes from the life of Saint Francis, then, the parallels between his life and those of Christ and John the Baptist, as indicated by the repetition of like Sixtine devices in the eastern loggia and western loggia extension, are reinforced by means of both form and content, in keeping with the extremely lucid method consistently employed in the Lateran Palace cycle.

The second narrative in the chronology of Francis' life is located adjacent to the *Birth of Francis* ..., on the eastern cove,

[113] Psalm XLIV: 8 is as follows: "Dilexisti iustitiam, et odisti iniquitatem; / Propterea unxit te Deus, Deus tuus, / Oleo laetitiae, prae consortibus tuis." See Bonaventure, *Opera Omnia*, IX, 212-213. Also consult Bonardo, *Agnus Dei*, 25, for a discussion of this Psalm.

[114] See Chapter I, 46, note 74.

[115] *Legend of the Three Companions*, I, 2.

[116] *Legend of the Three Companions*, I, 2.

[117] John's father Zacharias had originally wished his son to take his name, but the child was finally named John according to the wishes of Elizabeth and the angel who had first visited Zacharias to bring him news of his wife's imminent motherhood, and ultimately of John himself [Luke I: 11-13; 59-63].

but, according to the organization of the vault springing from the first narrative, the viewer is directed across space, to the scene of *Francis receives official sanction to create the Order of the Friars Minor from Pope Honorius III* (fig. 139). This narrative presents Francis kneeling before the clean-shaven pope on both knees, with hands appropriately crossed in humility. Francis is accompanied by his companions, prelates look on, and, in the foreground, auxiliary figures with backs to the spectator likewise view the proceedings. The action takes place in the middle ground, like so many Mannerist compositions, and shows the pope, seated beneath his baldachin, being handed the bull by which he has legalized the Order of the Friars Minor.

Significantly, there are a number of formally comparable scenes in the Lateran Palace cycle. In the Benediction Loggia and Salone di Costantino, *Francis before Honorius III* finds a parallel in scenes also concerning a legal action, specifically Constantine's Donation (figs. 146 and 108).[118] As scenes concerning the climax of events in the institutional histories of both the Franciscan Order and Roman Catholic Church, the one demonstrating recognition of the Order and its leader by the pope, the other, of the Church's temporal sovereignty by the emperor, the narratives accordingly demonstrate the remarkable contrasting parallels of sacred history, in keeping with the method apparently used to compare the naming of Saint John the Baptist and the naming of Saint Francis in the first narrative of the western loggia extension.[119] In a similar vein, the scene of *Solomon and the Queen of Sheba* (fig. 159) reflects *Francis before Honorius III*, both formally, with Francis and the Queen of Sheba corresponding to the pope and Solomon, and iconographically, when read according to what I have termed contrasting parallels. Always one to bring a point home, in the one portrait of Sixtus V in the palace, showing him receiving the document listing the imperial medals excavated from the Lateran site as well as the actual medals, he is represented in the manner and stance of the emperor who traditionally accepts plans and/or models from his architect (fig. 147).[120] In this variation on the theme, whereby Sixtus V receives a document in lieu of a building project,[121] the wise Solomon and his temple, the Donation of Constantine, and the bull of Honorius III, are recalled, and this momentous event effectively analogized to those which preceded it.[122]

The vault uniting the two narratives is decorated with Sixtine *grotteschi* featuring putti with wreaths beside flaming urns, and angels crowning seated figures with yet more wreaths; reclining figures, one with a book and the other with a cornucopia; and figures seated beneath baldachins within triumphal arches, comprised of interlace comparable to that on the angles of the Sala di Samuele (fig. 140; compare figs. 84, 90-93). At center vault, four putti raise aloft a wreath inscribed with a single Sixtine - and Franciscan - star. The *Birth of Francis...* is accordingly surmounted by a personification of *Abundance*, signifying the innumerable gifts which he would bestow on mankind, and his *Formation of the Order of Friars Minor*, a personification who signifies the *World Dominion* of Catholicism, made possible by the dissemination of the faith and the conversion of souls by the Franciscans.[123]

The southernmost vault of the loggia contains one narrative scene from the life of Saint Francis, located on the eastern cove beside the *Birth of Francis...* which it follows in the

[118] With the exception of the narrative in the Salone di Costantino, in which the emperor places the document on the altar located opposite Sylvester, rather than beside the pope, as in the Benediction Loggia version, the compositions are comparable.

[119] By "contrasting parallels," I am referring to the use of opposites in the second, in which Francis receives the legal document affirming his Order from the pope, while Constantine gives his legal document to the pope, thereby relinquishing his sovereignty. Significantly, Bonaventure compared Francis and Constantine: "God revealed the sign of the cross... to members of Christ's mystical body: to Emperor Constantine I and to St. Francis. ... As he chose to imprint the sign of victory on Constantine, so he chose to imprint the sign of penance on St. Francis". In Eric Doyle, *The Discipline and the Master: St. Bonaventure's Sermons on St. Francis of Assisi* (Chicago, 1983), 87.

[120] von Pastor, *History*, XXII, 72; Lanciani, *Storia*, IV, 139. For this imperial tradition, I am drawing on the excellent discussion in Herz, "Sixtine," *Storia dell'arte*, 248 ff. There is no question in my mind that the pope and/or his iconographer told the artists to represent the narratives in the loggia, Salone di Costantino, Sala di Salomone and Salone degli Imperatori in a comparable manner, according to specific tradition(s).

[121] Compare the variation on the theme in the Sala dei Fasti Farnesiani at the Farnese Palace in Caprarola representing *Julius III giving Ottavio Farnese jurisdiction over Parma*, illustrated in G. Labrot, *Le Palais Farnèse de Caprarola. Essai de Lecture* (Paris, 1979), plate 27.

[122] Sixtus V is explicitly compared to Popes Sylvester and Honorius III (and Innocent III) as well as to the Emperor Constantine in this scene. Since Francis did not, of course, attain the Chair of St. Peter, he is not as clearly related to the pope. Yet, as another Moses-Christ, the analogy must, I think, be understood, much as the humble Sixtus V at S. Maria Maggiore emulates Christ as another Francis. On this latter analogy, see Ostrow, "Sistine," 253 ff, esp. 259-260.

[123] Recall the characterization of Francis and the Franciscans in the the *Legend of the Three Companions*, cited in part in Chapter II, 89, note 104.

chronology (fig. 141). The scene concerns his meeting with Pope Innocent III, and the pope's verbal approval of the Rule following his dreams of the friar upholding the Lateran and of the palm tree. The stance of Francis, as he accepts the habit by which the Franciscan Order and its emulation of Christ on the cross was to be signified, is remarkably like that of *Samuel anoints David* in the Sala di Davide (fig. 148).[124] Both are on bent knee, with right arm inclined (and, in the case of Francis, joined in prayer), and head bent. The unction of David takes place before two "sturdy" columns supporting the roof of the temple, much as Francis' donning of his habit is flanked by the "obelisk and column" device. Moreover, there is a palm tree in the distant landscape, visible through the balcony, which functions as both an analogue to Francis, as Innocent III himself divulged, and, as the Sixtine iconographer seems to tell the viewer in the Sala di Samuele, to the obelisk, and hence to Francis as both "sturdy column" and obelisk "of holy faith."[125] Even the shepherd's staff held by David has metamorphosed from the traditional rounded crook, manifested in the adjacent narrative of *David hearing of Goliath's braggadoccio*, into one which is squared, as if to evoke the sign of the Tau, the sign of Saint Francis.[126] The stance of Francis, kneeling in humility before a bearded Innocent III, is also remarkably like that of Constantine in the the scenes of his baptism represented in the Benediction Loggia and Salone di Costantino (figs. 149 and 107). Both the Franciscan and Constantinian narratives are organized in comparable manners, with onlookers acting as typical Mannerist *"festaiuoli"* figures, framing the sides of the compositions.[127] At the center of each narrative, an aid to the pope provides a robe either to Francis or to Constantine, and, although the purpose of the garment differs considerably, the visual similarities are striking. As the initiation of what would ultimately become a legalized order, Francis' receipt of Innocent III's approval is evidently presented as an analogue to Constantine's baptism by Sylvester. As if to tacitly confirm the analogy, the onlooker sitting on the steps of the temple in the divine unction of David is accompanied by an ox or bull, an animal which not only suggests the Old Dispensation, but which also recalls the bull of the *Legenda Sancti Silvestri* which the rabbis had killed by whispering in its ear the name of their God, and which Pope Sylvester I then resuscitated by likewise whispering Christ's name. It was this act, following Sylvester's proof against the rabbis of the Trinity and Incarnation, which spurred Constantine's mother Helena to convert then and there to Christianity, and which was instrumental in Constantine's ultimate conversion commemorated in the Salone di Costantino, Benediction Loggia and Salone dei Papi.[128]

If the Old Testament scene tacitly underscores the analogies drawn between Francis, David, and Constantine, then the device located directly above Francis donning his habit in the western loggia extension effectively seals the equation (fig. 141). Although not a "Sixtine" device *per se*, since devoid of elements of the pope's heraldry, the *corpo* is comprised of crossed keys held together with a cord, raised aloft by putti, and surmounted by a crown. The two keys joined by the cord are the keys of the kingdom of heaven given to Peter and his successors by Christ. The cord holding them together, like that on the vault of the Sala degli Obelischi and Sala di Samuele (figs. 89, 74), is an admittedly functional one. Nevertheless, it may also connote the Franciscan Order, especially in relation

[124] Bonaventure, *Legenda Maior*, 632, states that "his [Francis'] own habit ... was shaped like a cross."

[125] See my description of Innocent's dream in Chapter I, 37, above.

[126] Fleming, *From Bonaventure to Bellini*, 99 ff.

[127] On the *festaiuolo*, consult Michael Baxandall, *Painting and Experience in Fifteenth Century Italy. A Primer in the Social History of Pictorial Style* (1972; Oxford, New York, 1988), 71 ff.

[128] Coleman, *Constantine*, 163-164, discusses this part of the *Legenda Sancti Silvestri*.

to the cord which all Franciscans tie around their waist, as Francis himself is about to demonstrate in the narrative below.[129] The crown which the putti support above the keys is emphatically not a papal tiara but rather the crown worn by earthly kings, like David in the Sala di Davide, Solomon in the Sala di Salomone, and indeed Constantine in the Salone di Costantino and Benediction Loggia. Together, the keys, rope and crown make unmistakable reference to the *League* (fig. 35). The *anima* enspiriting the device, "VNXIT TE DEVS," taken from the words of David, finally, is explicit testimony (for a change!) to the kingly powers invested in Francis as leader of his Order.[130] Moreover, it substantiates the visual allusions which bind Francis with David and Constantine.

The western lunette which responds to this scene from Francis' life in the eastern one contains a segmental pediment broken by a sculpted cartouche with the *stemma* of Sixtus V complete with the expected crossed keys, orphrey, and papal tiara, as well as ropes hanging conspicuously to the sides of the heraldic lion (fig. 142). A luscious array of sculpted fruit, including grapes and, as one might well imagine, pears, falls from behind the cartouche. The area remaining in the lunette above the door is frescoed with elements from the *stemma* within a fan design, like that located on the lunette above the door of the Salone dei Papi, and like those on the landing of the grand staircase leading to the *terzo piano*. In one sense, the *stemma* reiterates, in a kind of hieroglyphic manner, the message of the personifications in the *grotteschi* of the adjacent vault with the *Birth of Francis* ... and *Francis before Honorius III*, to which it responds (hence the "abundant" fruit and rope of Francis; the triple-crowned papal tiara and keys). It is also surmounted by a non-Sixtine device which complements that located across the space of the vault. Comprised of two putti holding a wreath inscribed with the opening lines of the verse inscribed in its pendant "DILEXISTI IVSTITIAM," this device apparently confirms the Davidian allusions conveyed through the composition and placement of Francis in the facing lunette narrative. Moreover, when seen from below, as it was unquestionably intended to be viewed, the wreath held by the angels is illusionistically being placed above the tiara, and complements Francis' and, by proxy of the *stemma*, Sixtus V's, "unction" (fig. 143) To reinforce the fact, or hope, that Sixtus V is being crowned in recognition of his justice, the *grotteschi* of the vault feature female figures placing wreaths on the heads of flamboyant lions holding pears, with star-and triple mountain-studded sashes tied across their bellies, while putti descend from above playing trumpets of fame or immortality, and holding palm branches of Salomonic wisdom, martyrdom, or victory - analogues to the personifications in the southern lunette of the eastern and southern logge, flanking a comparable Sixtine *stemma* and surmounted by the first two lines of the verse from Psalm XVII: 17 (fig. 118).[131] This allusion is further substantiated and strengthened by the octagon at center vault, featuring four rondels with "lion in profile" devices, the *anime* of which are regrettably no longer extant (fig. 144).[132] Nevertheless, as Sixtine lions of the tribe of Judah, the reference to King David is unmistakable. Sixtus V's Davidian heritage, like Saint Francis', is thus reinforced, while the surrounding *grotteschi*, the *stemma*, and the evidence of the eastern loggia, make it absolutely clear that the pope is emulating both Christ, like

129 The rope was so significant that Sixtus V sanctioned the formation of a confraternity dedicated to it. See Chapter II, 83, note 64, above, on this confraternity.

130 Compare Bonardo, *Agnus Dei*, 25: "La Chresima significa l'oglio pretiosissimo della gratia, de cui Christo fù vnto da Dio, come ben'disse Dauid, Vnxit te Deus, Deus tuus, oleo laetitiae; & douendo egli gouernare, insegnare, santificare la Chiesa sua, fù vnto per nostro Rè, nostro Profeta, & nostro Sacerdote."

131 III Kings VI for the Salomonic palm branches; and Ripa, *Iconologia*, II, 293; 227; 246, for the trumpets and palm branches, respectively.

132 It would be tempting to assign to each of these devices verses which correspond to those on the vault of the western loggia extension directly beneath. Unfortunately, only one motto is extant below. See Appendix I, 191. 208-210.

the martyrs glorified in the fourth room of the private apartment, and the founder of his Order.

In keeping with the method employed in the fourth room of the private apartment (and all rooms of this ensemble), the lunettes on the eastern and western coves of the western loggia extension flank a central component which is specifically Sixtine, in this case, an "obelisk and column" device (fig. 137). That on the eastern cove contains the *anima* "GLORIAM DEI EXALTAT." The *Birth of Francis* ... is accordingly equated to the now chaste columns converted by Sixtus V as trophies to the martyrs and to God's glory. As a marker of Francis' Aaronic ancestry (by means of his relationship to John the Baptist), moreover, the narrative draws forth the spiritual meaning inherent in the columns and obelisks, as well as the future mission of the child to carry out Good Works and to convert the world to the true faith. The flanking narrative commemorating Francis' donning of his habit-*cum*-divine unction draws forth the regal and sacerdotal facets of the friars dual powers, as the Davidian analogy in tandem with the obelisks and columns makes clear.

On the western cove, the Sixtine *stemma* and *Francis before Honorius III* flank an "obelisk and column" device with the verse "RELIGIO MIRANDA TRIVNPHAT."[133] As the Franciscan narrative demonstrates, the religion which is triumphing is at once Christianity and the Order of the Friars Minor formed by the *alter Christus* and, one might add, the *alter Salomone*. Francis is accordingly analogized to the apostles Peter and Paul above the columns, saints to whom the Franciscan was greatly devoted, as well as to the cross above the obelisk, another object of great devotion for the Franciscans. The simile, enunciated in the Salone dei Papi, is yet again borne out by example. Finally, the Sixtine *stemma*, complete with the rope of Francis, serves to reiterate the means by which Catholicism triumphs, and further reinforces the simile of the main hall, whereby the man who raised the columns and obelisks is like the founder of his Order.

The last narrative from the life of Saint Francis is located beside *Francis before Honorius III* and opposite the grand staircase. It represents the momentous conversion and assimilation of the saint to Christ, the *Stigmatization* - an event which occurred while Francis was undergoing a forty day fast in honour of Saint Michael the Archangel (fig. 145). In deference to tradition, Francis himself kneels before his vision of the Man Crucified, with arms outstretched. Five lines emanate from the crucifix to leave on Francis' palms and feet the marks of the nails which had punctured Christ's earthly body, and on his right side, the gash left by the centurion's lance. Significantly, the Sixtine narrative departs from Bonaventure's description of the event in its inclusion of Brother Leo as the witness to the event, and in the apparent exclusion of the seraph with the six flaming wings in favour of a lone crucified Christ (the seraph holds the Man Crucified between his wings in Bonaventure's description). The inclusion of Brother Leo was not, of course, unique. It had been used early on, in the cycle of the Upper Church of San Francesco in Assisi, and, in the sixteenth century, had been used again by Titian and his followers on the basis of Brother Leo's own testimony.[134] For Sixtus V, the parallel between Francis' companion and his own heraldic persona must have been too inviting to omit, so that the pope himself may be understood as witnessing the event, much as the viewer stand-

[133] Whereas the image of the imperial device actually served as the object of the prepositional phrase of the *anima*, as Rosenthal, "*Plus Ultra*," *JWCI*, 217-218, has shown, a characteristic which accounted for the praise bestowed upon the invention by humanist emblematists, the Sixtine devices would not appear to be quite as organic. The biblical paraphrases which form the mottoes of Sixtus V's devices allude certainly to the image, but they can stand on their own, since grammatically complete. Nonetheless, their meaning is clarified by the image and it is possible to read the *corpo* as a prepositional phrase for the motto, in a manner exactly opposite to the imperial device. "The glorious religion triumphs" is described by the *corpo* and may be read as follows: 'The marvellous honour triumphs through the superimposition of the Princes of the Apostles and the cross over pagan column and obelisk by Sixtus V.' Likewise, "The glory of God is exalted" may be completed 'by Sixtus V who has triumphed over pagan, heretic and infidel alike, through the counsel of Saints Peter and Paul and the veneration of the cross.' The two mottoes therefore convey complementary messages which are underscored by images common to both.

[134] Pamela Askew, "The Angelic Consolation of St. Francis of Assisi in Post-Tridentine Italian Painting," *Journal of the Warburg and Courtauld Institutes* XXXII (1969): 282-294. Also consult Rodinò, "iconografia Francescana," *L'immagine*, 159-160.

ing in the loggia is made privy to it. Whereas the presence of Brother Leo was sanctioned by tradition, the exclusion of the winged seraph is most unusual. It is possible, of course, that originally the crucified Christ was enveloped by the seraph (there are two horn-like rays of light emanating from his head which could well have been part of the angel's wings), and that it has since been lost through restorations to the cycle, but the present evidence indicates that only a burst of light envelops him. Accordingly, the assimilation of Francis to the luminous Christ on the cross is conveyed by reducing the narrative to its bare essentials, and, as a result, the analogy to the columns and obelisks raised by Sixtus V, brought to the fore.

Interestingly enough, my analysis of the Saint Francis cycle yields associations to the very same biblical figures who were given a special place in the Salone di Costantino: the *Birth of Francis* ... recalls Aaron, the ancestor of Saint John the Baptist, as of Saint Francis; the *Stigmatization* conjures Moses, the one chosen by God to learn the secrets of the universe during the Exodus; *Francis before Innocent III*, King David, the lion of the tribe of Judah and the root of the tree from which Christ would issue; and *Francis before Honorius III*, King Solomon, revered by earthly rulers near and far for the supreme wisdom and grace which God had bestowed on him. In this way the assimilation of Francis to Constantine, as manifested in the like form and content of the scenes from their lives, as in the tripartite arrangement of the western loggia extension, Sala degli Obelischi and Benediction Loggia, is tacitly confirmed, and the march of world history, shown to have culminated once with the saint and, as the Sixtine *stemma* and devices featuring his obelisks and columns make clear, again during the pontificate of Sixtus V.

C. THE SALA DI SALOMONE

The allusions to Solomon in the scene of *Francis and Honorius III* and the assimilation of Francis, and by implication Solomon, to the Sixtine obelisks and columns, are substantiated in the room dedicated to the wisest of Old Testament kings by the significant use of the very same devices adorning the western loggia extension: the north-western cove of the Sala di Salomone contains the "obelisk and column" device with the motto "RELIGIO MIRANDA TRIVMPHAT," and the south-eastern cove, "GLORIAM DEI EXALTAT" (figs. 150.E, G; 151-152). Moreover, without exception, each of the narratives from Solomon's life contains conspicuous columns which are incorporated matter-of-factly into the scenes, much as they infiltrate the scenes representing Saint Francis' life. Located at the intersection of the western and northern arms, the Sala di Salomone accordingly acts as the mid-point between the Sala degli Obelischi and Salone di Costantino, that is, the room and hall at the corners of the *piano nobile*, whose messages are conveyed with the aid of Sixtine obelisks and columns. Given the fundamental relationship between the Sala di Salomone and the western loggia extension in terms of Sixtine devices, and the relationship between this outermost point in the inner area of the *piano nobile*, and the eastern loggia and private apartment (not to mention additional rooms of the outer area of the plan), then the implication is that the outer rooms and halls of the programme extol messages which are comparable, as do the inner logge and the private apartment. The Sixtine "obelisk and column" devices, in other words, are strategically placed signposts which enable the viewer to piece together the fundamentally diachronic view of history being extolled in the palace. In terms of the plan of the *piano nobile*, Solomon is honoured as a kind of watershed in this history, as if to confirm his position as the last in the greatest of Old Testament figures in the Salone di Costantino, as in the western loggia extension.

Within the Sala di Salomone, the "obelisk and column" devices are located at opposite junctures of the vault so that they function, quite literally, as cornerstones, and take on all of the connotations which this implies. They are given foils at the south-western and north-eastern corners in the form of the "blind triple mountain" device which populates the ground floor logge and grand staircase (figs. 150.H, I; 153-154; compare fig. 14), but which is relatively sparse on the *piano nobile*, being present only in this room and in the Sala della Gloria. The devices are flanked in turn by narratives of Solomon's life so that the typical Sixtine system of pairing narratives and then reconciling them into triads is again enforced.

As I have noted in passing above, the columnar device of the Emperor Charles V and Pope Leo X, which is evoked by the personification of *Sacred Religion* and especially by the "obelisk and column" device of Sixtus V, often featured a crown enclosed within the columns, with the columns themselves each surmounted by a crown. Of course, the Sixtine device substitutes a converted obelisk for the central crown, and the Princes of the Apostles for those surmounting the columns, but as the organization of the devices in the Sala di Salomone seems to suggest, the three prodigal crowns, traditional attributes of Solomon, have returned to encircle the star-topped triple Montalto mountains. In another sense, the three crowns may be understood as those which, owing to Boniface VIII, adorn the papal tiara and signify, in one sense, that the pope is a prince, judge and priest.[135] In lieu of the papal tiara, then, the ideator of the device chose the triple mountains of Montalto. The crowns also recall the *impresa* of the *Treasure*, in which the Sixtine lion is crowned with a regal crown rather than the tiara of the Vatican version (fig. 32). In the Salone dei Papi, the crown takes on connotations of the laurel wreath which crowned Peace in commemoration of Augustus' victory at Action. The abundant laurel wreaths in the Sixtine *grotteschi*, that which Constantine wears as he performs the *officium stratoris*, and that which crowns the Sixtine *stemma* in the western loggia extension, may accordingly be read as counterparts to the crowns of the Sixtine device. Finally, the crowns evoke the three crowns adopted by King Henry III of France for his device (likewise inspired by the columnar device?), and referring to the world-wide peace which would result from his mystical monarchy, in opposition to the war-like monarchy of Spain which crushed foes by force.[136] That the Sixtine monarchy is fundamentally peaceful is amply reinforced by the placement of this device in the room dedicated to the Old Testament king whose name means "peacemaker," and who was regularly associated with the cherub and palm, owing to his decoration of the Temple of Jerusalem [III Kings VI]. That the Sixtine monarchy is also a particularly Franciscan one, finally, is conveyed by both the rope, which keeps the keys bound together, and the abundant fruit, which hangs from the cartouche, recalling the peace of the Golden Age of the *Abundance*, and the

[135] Shearman in *Sistine Chapel*, 55.

[136] Vivanti, "Henry IV," *JWCI*, 188 and plate 21c.

179

fruitful and abundant rulership of Saint Francis in the western loggia extension.

The *anime* inspiriting the "triple mountain" *corpi* in the Sala di Salomone emphasize the triads of crowns and mountains, and accordingly draw on the Francisco-Sixtine view of world history. That on the north-eastern angle, "TERNA HAEC TRIPLICI" (figs. 150.H; 153), conjures the nine orders of the celestial hierarchy, the nine gifts of the Holy Spirit [Galatians V: 22-24], with which Sixtus V has been endowed, as well as a host of threesomes.[137] That on the south-west angle, "SCIENTIAE BONITATIS DISCIPLINAE," is taken from Psalm CXVIII: 66, corresponding to the ninth letter of the Hebrew alphabet, and concerns David's request that God teach him these three virtues in order to learn God's "justifications" [Psalm CXVIII: 68, 71]. Each of the three mountains and crowns in this sense takes on a meaning of one of God's virtues, and the crowns become as well the crowns of the justified; the gift bestowed on those who, through faith and Good Works, merit God's grace and the gift of salvation.[138]

With the exception of the scene at center vault, the narratives in the Sala di Salomone were once accompanied by explanatory verses - a method which is unique to this Old Testament room.[139] The first narrative in the sequence shows *Solomon riding to Gihon where he will be anointed king* [III Kings I: 38], as a throng of onlookers watch the procession wind its way into the distance (figs. 150.A; 155). The accompanying inscription filled in the successive anointing of Solomon with oil by proclaiming that the youthful king rules the realm according to God's wishes so that good will - and works - abound amongst his subjects. As the "stone of help" in the Sala di Samuele makes clear, this scene ought to contain implicit reference(s) to a like occurrence in Sixtus V's life and pontificate - very possibly the *possesso* which proceeded from San Pietro in Vaticano to San Giovanni in Laterano at the beginning of his pontificate. The following scene is located at center vault, and was unaccompanied by an inscription (figs. 150.B; 156). Representing *God appearing to Solomon in his sleep* [III Kings III: 5-9], this otherworldly occurrence is made understandable by separating the crowned king, who sits up in his bed, from the trinitarian God the Father, with triangular nimbus, globe in hand and seated before the radiant Sun, by means of a "column" of cloud as well as playful putti floating beneath the godhead. As an occurrence in which Solomon, like Moses, Samuel, Paul, and Francis, among others, learns the divine secrets of the universe, the scene could well relate to the same incident in Sixtus V's life to which the scene of *Samuel hearing a miraculous voice in the Temple* refers.[140] The famous and often represented *Judgement of Solomon* [III Kings III: 16-28] is next in the chronology of events in the king's life and, in keeping with traditional representations, depicts the climax of the event, when the real mother begs the king to spare the child's life by giving the false mother custody (figs. 150.C; 157). Accordingly, Solomon, who is seated on an Egyptian-like throne with griffins in lieu of his traditional lions, gestures with his right hand for the soldier to lower his sword, while, with his left hand, extends the rod given to him as king of the Israelites and successor to Moses and Aaron. As a symbol of fidelity, a dog rests beside the real mother, while onlookers view the event as witnesses to Solomon's divine wisdom. One particularly theatrical analogue in the life of Sixtus V occurred on 7

[137] Padre Fra Felice Peretti, *Predica Della Purissima Concettione*, n.p., sets forth a number of threesomes, which are worth quoting in part to give the reader an idea of the truly polysemous reading to which this device could be subjected: "E perche questo nostro Eccelso Signor, amar douemo, trino in persone & vno in essentia, ha voluto mostrarsi in tutte le cose Trino. Sap. 12. Fecit omnia in numero, pondere, & mensura, Tutte le creature son'distinte in tre, Creatura spirituale: Corporale: e mista: la spirituale che è l'Angelica diuisa in tre hierarchie, la prima: la seconda, e la terza. Ciascuna hierarchia, in tre ordini, primo, secondo, e terzo, Ciascun' ordine in tre gradi: infimo, medio, sopremo: La creatura corporal come li Elementi ciascuno diuiso in tre cose. Tre cose ha il Fuogo, la luce; il calore, & il splendor: L'aria in tre regioni, infima: media, e suprema, L'acqua: in tre maniere: densa nella nuuola, gelata nel giaccio: liquida nel fonte: La terra se ben è diuisa in cinque zone, tre sono le principali, la frigida: la torrida, e la temperata: La mista in tre, uegetatiua: sensitiua: & intellettiua: ... Tre sono le scientie: rational: organice, e real .../ La rethorica tre geni, deliberatiuo, demonstratiuo, e giuditiale ... Tre sono le principali, la lana, l'agricoltura, e la militia ... E lo soldato fa tre cose, offende, defende, e guarda. L'attiua fa tre, ò gouerna l'huomo l'etica, La citta la politica, la famiglia l'ecconomica: La contemplatiua diuisa in tre, phisica, methapisica, e mathematica ... L'astrologia contempla tre cose, segni, pianete, e stelle ... La fede e de tre cose, d'articoli, di precetti, e de consigli. La speranza de tre cose, della gratia, della uenia, e dela gloria. ... Tres sunt qui testimonium dant in coelo, Pater, Verbum, & Spiritus Sanctus; Et hi tres unum sunt ..."

[138] According to Joachim of Fiore, the three ages of world history correspond to "scientia, ... sapientiae ... & plenitudine intellectus," characterizations which have much in common with the Psalm CXVIII: 66, and he compares the leadership of Saul, David and Solomon to these ages, in De Lubac, *Exégèse*, II, I, 447. It is precisely these three Old Testament prophet-kings who are celebrated in the first three Old Testament rooms of the Lateran Palace programme. Also consult Bonaventure, *Opera Omnia*, IX, 404-405, for his commentary on the Psalm.

[139] For this and the following, consult Appendix I, 227, nos. 167-171.

[140] Foglietta, "Lettera," Ottob. Lat. 568, 8v, states that in Sixtus V "ricordandosi della gratia, che Dio fece à Salomone quando constituito Rè, in caso simile la ricerco." The comparison of Sixtus V to Solomon is a *topos* in this letter, see 5r, 43r, 44v and 57r.

August 1588, and concerned an ongoing dispute between the communities of Zagardo and Corneto over which should rightfully own the reliquary of Saint Agapito. "In the guise of simulated cruelty," Pope Sixtus V-Solomon determined that the reliquary would be cut into two parts so that each community could have its way![141] The next narrative represents the *The Ark of the Covenant carried out of the City of David* [III Kings VIII: 1-4] to be deposited in the Temple of Solomon (figs. 150.D; 158), the temple built according to God's specifications, and visible in the background, looking very much like the apse of the churches in the Investiture scenes in the Salone dei Papi, and in the procession of Sylvester I to San Giovanni in the Salone di Costantino (figs. 63, 64 and 109).[142] In the foreground, the Levites are shown carrying the Ark, while others carry the vases of silver and gold, one of which is complete with lion's head. Before the Ark, King Solomon is represented officiating at the altar, ready to offer the sacrificial lamb at his feet. In the distance, another sacrifice takes place, this time of a bull. Contemporaneous import may be found in the manifold processions held during Sixtus V's pontificate, notably the procession which carried the body of Pius V to Santa Maria Maggiore.[143] Given the altar and sacrificial lamb, however, clearer analogues may be found in the processions and subsequent services held before the obelisks and columns, the Sixtine counterparts to the Ark of the Covenant, and close cousins, as it were, to the Holy Sepulchre and Sancta Sanctorum of the *Abundance* emblem (fig. 45.Q.11).[144] The series ends with another event favoured by Renaissance rulers, *Solomon and the Queen of Sheba* [III Kings X: 1-9], in which the queen, followed by her retinue, bows before the king (figs. 150.E; 159), much as the "Libyan" Queen of Sheba would later come before Sixtus V, as testimony to his "wisdom" and noble deeds (fig. 160).[145]

The deceptively simple organization of the vault dictates that the narratives be read first across space, and then according to a number of variations on the tripartite theme. For example, the devices may act like personifications flanking the narratives; or pairs of narratives on the diagonal may be read with either the "obelisk and column" or "triple mountain" device at their center. The central scene of Solomon receiving the wisdom imparted to him by God is the constant, and functions like the "lion in profile" devices and Sixtine *stemma* of the Sala degli Obelischi, as the crowning component of the triptychs below. I shall follow the method used to consider the eastern loggia vault, and focus on the triads featuring the "obelisk and column" device as central "panel" in order to draw forth the essential meaning which these Good Works of Sixtus V convey in this context.

One of the oddest components of the first narrative in the series, *Solomon rides to Gihon*, is the inclusion of an onlooker who is barely clad, holding a staff, and sitting as though on the very "frame" enclosing the scene (fig. 155). By virtue of his "modest" nudity in contrast to the remaining onlookers, notably the woman who holds onto his staff and who is clothed in the manner of a nun (or of Saint Elizabeth?), and of his proximity to the viewer *vis-à-vis* Solomon himself, who is relegated to the middle ground, this figure should hold a specific meaning (or meanings). Since the accompanying inscription emphasized the fact that Solomon is ruling, notwithstanding that he is *en route* to his divine unction, then I would suggest that the figure in the foreground may well be intended to signify Baptism

[141] *La Gazzetta de L'anno 1588*, ed. Enrico Stumpo (Florence, 1988), 100.

[142] This structure has certain affinities to that in the scene of *Samuel taken to the Temple* (fig. 85) in the Sala di Samuele. The accompanying scene of *Samuel in the Temple* (fig. 86) presents a distinctly different temple - perhaps owing to two artistic hands at work.

[143] Bordino, *De Rebus*, 32, illustrates this event in a manner which is not unlike that describing the Salomonic narrative.

[144] Gamrath, *Roma*, 131-152, discusses the processions.

[145] The references to Solomon and Sixtus IV on the triumphal arches of the *Giving of the Keys* in the Sistine Chapel may have contributed to the "imperial" idea to include him in the Lateran Palace programme, but it would not have contributed to the specific scenes chosen. See Ettlinger, *Sistine*, 91. Solomon is also represented in Raphael's Logge, and two of the scenes there are also represented at the palace: *Solomon's Judgement* and *Solomon visited by the Queen of Sheba*. While the scene of Sheba visiting Solomon clearly influenced the artist who painted this scene at the palace, the remaining scenes from Solomon's life in the Logge are not those used at the palace. Consult Davidson, *Raphael's Bible*, 82-85.

so that the analogy between the two sacraments (as well as Christ and Saint John the Baptist?) is carried on here, as throughout the Lateran Palace cycle. Its pendant, when the "obelisk and column" device is regarded as its centerpiece, or hinge, is the *Judgement of Solomon*, which contains two auxiliary soldiers at the right foreground. One holds his shield, sword, and jousting pole, while resting his foot on an overturned vase, as if in order to respond to the soldiers at the left foreground of the first scene, but in this instance holding an understandable place as the companions of the soldier-executioner of the main action (fig. 157). He also suggests the idea of baptism by means of the emptied jar. The main action centers on the great wisdom which God imparted to King Solomon and his ability to dispense justice. As the griffin on his throne tacitly suggests, Solomon's powers are at once spiritual and earthly, so that the pope's power to bind and to loose, to separate the chaste from the unblemished, is recalled.[146] When the traditional meaning of the *Judgement* as a prefiguration for the Last Judgement is recalled, finally, it becomes clear that the soldiers are the aides of Michael who will lead the battle against evil during the last days.[147] Together, the symbolism of Solomon's divine unction (and baptism) and the justice dispensed by the king on earth, as in heaven, draw forth the essential meaning of the Sixtine obelisks and columns as symbols of conversion and victory, and in this way complement the *anima* proclaiming the triumph of Catholicism (fig. 151).

Whereas *Solomon rides to Gihon* is given subsidiary information which ultimately helps to shed light on at least one level of meaning, the *quadro* devoted to *Solomon and the Queen of Sheba* is primarily focused on the queen's visit (fig. 159). Hence, in one corner, a youth lifts a magnificent vase as a foil to the soldier resting his feet on one in the adjacent narrative, but, in this case, the vase is understood as one of the gifts which the queen gave to Solomon, and the youth, her servant. The two men who watch Solomon welcome the queen are likewise understood to belong to the king's court and, as far as I can determine, the same holds true for the seated youth (since he is on a red carpet, he may well represent Solomon's son Rehoboam). As a narrative concerning the homage paid to Solomon by a fellow temporal ruler who has learned of his vast wealth of "knowledge and wisdom and goodness," it evokes the homage paid to earthly rulers in accord with the Doctrine of the Two Swords, and the power which Christ bestowed on Peter and his successors when he handed him the keys. The pendant *Carrying of the Ark of the Covenant*, including the sacrifices overseen by Solomon in his role as high priest, on one level signifies the power of the spiritual sword and accordingly complements the temporal sword of *Solomon and the Queen of Sheba* (fig. 158). Much as the "subsidiary" figures in *Solomon rides to Gihon* provide additional clues as to the manner in which the scene is to be read, the *Carrying of the Ark* contains onlookers who are somewhat out of place in the context of the narrative, notwithstanding that their presence in the composition is so well orchestrated that they seem on first notice to belong. Before the Levites who follow the Ark in procession is a scantly-clad youth, holding a pole and resting his foot on a "virtuous" cube, accompanied by a youthful woman who is fully dressed. This youth is comparable, formally and iconographically, to the youth in *Solomon rides to Gihon*. In the context of the *Carrying of the Ark* this figure, together with the

146 Consult the description in Ripa, *Iconologia*, II, 69. Since the griffin was also an attribute of Apollo, then its appearance on Solomon's throne was likely intended as an analogue to the usual lion. See Valeriano, *Hieroglyphica*, XXIII, xxiv, for the griffin as a symbol of Apollo. Also consult Smith, *Casino*, 87, for Apollo's griffins in the context of Pius IV's Casino.

147 Réau, *Iconographie*, II, I, 289.

Ark-*cum*-cross, the ox or bull of the Old Dispensation, and the ram about to be sacrificed, suggests the translation from the Old Covenant to the New, and the spiritual refreshment which comes from death in Christ and rebirth: Baptism. The shepherds, who watch the proceedings from the other side of the composition, evoke the adoration of the shepherds, with the Ark and lamb standing for the cross, star and *monti*-topped obelisk, as well as Christ. In this sense, the *anima* "GLORIA DEI EXALTAT" recalls the Lucan verse which was sung shortly before the arrival of the shepherds at Christ's Nativity (fig. 152). When one then recalls that the visit of the Queen of Sheba was most commonly regarded as a prefiguration not only of Christ and the Church, but also of the adoration of the magi,[148] then the reading of this triad, and of the vault itself is seemingly elucidated: Christ is adored by both Jew and Gentile, who, under the aegis of Peter and Paul and their present successor, will be converted to the true faith. At the Last Judgement their souls will be weighed, and Pope Sixtus V, as an *alter Salomone*, will receive justification for his faith and Good Works - the gift of the threefold crown of justice.

[148] Réau, *Iconographie*, II, I, 294.

5. CONCLUSION

The obelisks and columns are positioned ever so strategically in the corners of the *piano nobile*, both inner and outer, along the eastern loggia, as well as in the first of the Old Testament rooms and last of the rooms of the private apartment, to act as markers demonstrating that like ideas consonant with those expounded in the main hall are being promulgated. They are also given pride of place at the center of the arms of the grand staircase as it ascends to the third floor (fig. 19). If the visitor to the *piano nobile* had not already grasped their significance, then one's "pilgrimage" might prompt a return to the main floor and a reconsideration of the meaning just taken from it. At the same time, these Sixtine hieroglyphics point to the Heavenly Jerusalem to which their real counterparts in the *piazze* of Sixtine Rome aspire, so that the ascent to the *terzo piano* might be understood as a voyage by which the viewer, especially Sixtus V himself, is taken yet steps further to the salvation which faith and Good Works, it is hoped, will bring. Since it is highly unlikely that a visitor to the palace would have been taken to the third floor, then these devices would, in all probability, have been intended for the private edification of the pope and his entourage, as confirmation of the conversion of the world during Sixtus V's tenure on earth, and of the translation of the Church Militant to the Church Triumphant.

183

APPENDIX I

LIST OF FRESCOES BY LOCATION

This appendix is intended as a reference tool for readers who may wish to obtain information on any given room or hall, loggia, entrance vestibule or stairway of the Lateran Palace. It indicates in point form the subjects of all narratives represented including biblical references when applicable, the presence of historical and biblical personages and personifications (some of which are identified for the first time) and devices (with the possible sources of *anime*), and provides a synopsis of the "*parerga*," without, however, describing each element in detail. The reader should agree that the following is quite detailed as it is! The subjects are listed in a progression from "1" onwards for the state and private rooms of the *piano nobile*. There are far too many elements in the logge and staircase to make listing each and every one in succession a feasable or valuable undertaking for the purposes of this study. The Roman numerals refer to the numbers placed beneath the lunettes in the logge in the nineteenth century, and are used here for convenience to conform to the illustrations taken before restorations were begun and the numbers subsequently removed. The reader is referred to the 1950 guidebook *Palazzo del Laterano* for confirmation of the numerology. The letters refer to my schematic diagrams of the rooms and halls of the *piano nobile*. Those narratives, personages, devices and personifications which are illustrated are not described. Conversely, those which are unillustrated are described with the exception of the smaller personifications. Finally, all inscriptions and verses are documented in this appendix for reasons of clarity. Those inscriptions and verses which are no longer extant are so indicated, and the relative material taken from Fontana, *Della trasportatione* and/or the photographic documentation of the palace, as of 1964, housed in the Photographic Archives of the Vatican. Translations of the Latin inscriptions in Fontana's treatise were graciously done by Terence Tunberg, whom I should like to thank for his invaluable assistance.

1. THE *PIANO TERRENO*

A. THE WESTERN ENTRANCE VESTIBULE

Abbreviated west lunette (since above the window)	"Lion in profile" device within a cartouche is upheld by two putti, and contains the *anima* from Psalm CXX: 4: NON DORMIT NEQ. DORMITABIT HE WILL NOT BE DROWSY, NOR SHALL HE SLEEP fig. 13

The band enclosing this lunette, and the arch at the eastern end, contain elements from the pope's heraldry in geometrical surrounds.

Westernmost vault	A rondel encloses a fan design at center, and is surrounded on the north-south axis by the star-topped *monti*, putti with papal tiara or baldachin, angels with trumpets, and arabesques, all within geometrical surrounds. On the west-east axis, the central rondel is flanked by inscriptions, also within geometrical surrounds, as follows: "SIXTVS V. P. M." and " AN. PONT IIII."
Center vault	The Sixtine *stemma* is enclosed within another rondel. It is flanked, on the west-east axis, by the above-mentioned elements, with the addition of another inscription: "SIXTVS V. P. M," while on the north-south axis, there are female figures with outstretched arms who crown the lions flanking them, as well as angel faces, personifications, arabesques and assorted *grotteschi*.
Easternmost vault	A rondel encloses a fan design at center, and is surrounded on the north-south axis by the star-topped *monti*, putti with papal tiara or baldachin, angels with trumpets, and arabesques, all within geometrical surrounds. On the west-east axis, the central rondel is flanked by the above-mentioned elements, with the addition of another inscription: " AN. PONT IIII."

B. THE WESTERN LOGGIA

West lunette	A woman, seated beneath a baldachin, holds wreathes within an *all'antica* surround of *grotteschi* comprised of flaming urns and putti
vault	geometrical surrounds containing the inscription "SIXTVS. V. PONT. MAX. ANNO. III[I]," with lions and angels on the coves

West lunette	A woman, seated beneath a baldachin, holds wreathes within an *all'antica* surround of *grotteschi* comprised of flaming urns and putti
East lunette	loggia arch
vault	geometrical surrounds containing triple mountains, crowns, pear branches and star at center, with lions and angels on the coves

West lunette	A woman, seated beneath a baldachin, holds wreathes within an *all'antica* surround of *grotteschi* comprised of flaming urns and putti
East lunette	loggia arch
vault	geometrical surrounds containing lions and angels on the coves, and a "lion in profile" device at center, with the *anima* taken from Psalm CXX: 4:
	NON DORMIT NEQ. DORMITABIT
	HE WILL NOT BE DROWSY, NOR SHALL HE SLEEP

West lunette	A woman, seated beneath a baldachin, holds wreathes within an *all'antica* surround of *grotteschi* comprised of flaming urns and putti
East lunette	loggia arch
vault	geometrical surrounds containing triple mountains, crowns, pear branches and star at center, with lions and angels on the coves

West lunette	A woman, seated beneath a baldachin, holds wreathes within an *all'antica* surround of *grotteschi* comprised of flaming urns and putti
East lunette	loggia arch
vault	geometrical surrounds containing the Sixtine *stemma* crossed by keys and crowned by papal tiara, with the inscription "SIXTVS. V. P. M. AN. PONT. IIII," with lions and angels on the coves

West lunette	A woman, seated beneath a baldachin, holds wreathes within an *all'antica* surround of *grotteschi* comprised of flaming urns and putti
East lunette	loggia arch
vault	geometrical surrounds containing triple mountains, crowns, pear branches and star at center, with lions and angels on the coves

West lunette	A woman, seated beneath a baldachin, held wreathes within an *all'antica* surround of *grotteschi* comprised of flaming urns and putti
	This lunette fresco is no longer extant.
East lunette	loggia arch
vault	geometrical surrounds containing lions and angels on the coves, and a "lion in profile" device at center, with the *anima* taken from Amos III: 8:
	SI RVGIET QVIS NON TIMEBIT
	IF HE ROARS, WHO WILL NOT FEAR?

West lunette	A woman, seated beneath a baldachin, held wreathes within an *all'antica* surround of *grotteschi* comprised of flaming urns and putti
	This lunette fresco is no longer extant.
East lunette	loggia arch
vault	geometrical surrounds containing triple mountains, crowns, pear branches and star at center, with lions and angels on the coves

The juncture between the northern and western *logge* contains a Sixtine rondel enclosing lions, mountains, pear branches and a star at center, with a geometrical foliate design containing the following verses, the latter of which are taken from Judges XIV: 14:

186

TVTANDOS SVOS

PROTECTING ONE'S OWN

DEPEL[L]ENDOS NOXIOS

STRIKING DOWN THOSE WHO THREATEN

EGRES[S]A DVLCEDO

SWEETNESS HAS EMERGED

EXIVIT CIBVS

MEAT HAS COME FORTH

North lunette	Personifications flank central Sixtine *stemma* fig. 18

The bands separating the vaults here, as in all remaining *logge*, are comprised of putti, trumpets and wreathes, and "triple mountain" and "lions head" devices of Sixtus V. The former contain the *anima*: CAELVM AEQVORA TERRAS [The heavens, the sea, the earth]; the latter, either DE COMEDENTI EXI-VIT CIBVS [Out of the eater came forth meat] taken from Judges XIV: 14, or DE FORTI EGRESSA EST DVLCEDO [Out of the strong came forth sweetness], also from Judges XIV: 14.

C. THE EASTERN LOGGIA

East lunette	Two putti hold up the papal keys which cross a baldachin (or parasol) adorned, as always, with elements from the Sixtine heraldry
West lunette	loggia arch
vault	geometrical surrounds containing triple mountains, crowns, pear branches and star at center, with lions and angels on the coves
East lunette	A woman, seated beneath a baldachin, holds wreathes within an *all'antica* surround of *grotteschi* comprised of flaming urns and putti
West lunette	loggia arch
vault	geometrical surrounds containing lions and angels on the coves, and a "lion in profile" device at center, with the *anima* possibly taken from Psalm XV: 11: DVLCIA A DEXTRIS SWEETNESS AT THE RIGHT
East lunette	A woman, seated beneath a baldachin, holds wreathes within an *all'antica* surround of *grotteschi* comprised of flaming urns and putti
West lunette	loggia arch
vault	geometrical surrounds containing triple mountains, crowns, pear branches and star at center, with lions and angels on the coves
East lunette West lunette	Arch providing access to eastern entrance vestibule loggia arch
vault	geometrical surrounds containing the Sixtine *stemma* crossed by keys and crowned by papal tiara, with the inscription "SIXTVS. V. P. M. AN. PONT. IIII," with lions and angels on the coves
East lunette	Two women, seen from their waists up, hold a plaque, surmounted by a "Borrominian" angel's head and the inscription "SIXTVS. V. PONT. MAX."
West lunette	loggia arch
vault	geometrical surrounds containing triple mountains, crowns, pear branches and star at center, with lions and angels on the coves
East lunette	A woman, seated beneath a baldachin, held wreathes within an *all'antica* surround of *grotteschi* comprised of flaming urns and putti This lunette fresco is no longer extant.

West lunette	loggia arch
vault	geometrical surrounds containing lions and angels on the coves, and a "lion in profile" device at center, with the *anima* possibly taken from Psalm CXXVI: 1:
	CVSTOS VIGILI
	VIGILANT CVSTODIAN
East lunette	Two male personifications, no longer extant.
West lunette	loggia arch
vault	geometrical surrounds containing triple mountains, crowns, pear branches and star at center, with lions and angels on the coves

The juncture between the northern and eastern *logge* contains a Sixtine rondel enclosing lions, mountains, pear branches and a star at center, with a geometrical foliate design containing the following verses, the latter of which are taken from Judges XIV: 14:

TVTANDOS SVOS

PROTECTING ONE'S OWN

DEPEL[L]ENDOS NOXIOS

STRIKING DOWN THOSE WHO THREATEN

EGRES[S]A DVLCEDO

SWEETNESS HAS EMERGED

EXIVIT CIBVS

MEAT HAS COME FORTH

North lunette	Personifications with lower torsos extant flank central Sixtine *stemma*, now in extremely poor condition.

D. THE NORTHERN LOGGIA

North lunette	A woman, seated beneath a baldachin, holds wreathes within an *all'antica* surround of *grotteschi* comprised of flaming urns and putti
South lunette	loggia arch
vault	geometrical surrounds containing triple mountains, crowns, pear branches and star at center, with lions and angels on the coves
North lunette	A woman, seated beneath a baldachin, holds wreathes within an *all'antica* surround of *grotteschi* comprised of flaming urns and putti
South lunette	loggia arch
vault	geometrical surrounds containing lions and angels on the coves, and a "lion in profile" device at center, with the *anima* taken from Psalm XXIII: 8:
	POTENS IN PRAELIO
	MIGHTY IN BATTLE
North lunette	A woman, seated beneath a baldachin, holds wreathes within an *all'antica* surround of *grotteschi* comprised of flaming urns and putti
South lunette	loggia arch
vault	geometrical surrounds containing triple mountains, crowns, pear branches and star at center, with lions and angels on the coves
North lunette	Arch providing access to northern entrance vestibule
South lunette	loggia arch
vault	geometrical surrounds containing the Sixtine *stemma* crossed by keys and crowned by papal tiara, with the inscription "SIXTVS. V. P. M. AN. PONT. IIII," with lions and angels on the coves

North lunette	A woman, seated beneath a baldachin, held wreathes within an *all'antica* surround of *grotteschi* comprised of flaming urns and putti This lunette is no longer extant.
South lunette	loggia arch
vault	geometrical surrounds containing triple mountains, crowns, pear branches and star at center, with lions and angels on the coves
North lunette	A woman, seated beneath a baldachin, held wreathes within an *all'antica* surround of *grotteschi* comprised of flaming urns and putti This lunette is no longer extant.
South lunette	loggia arch
vault	geometrical surrounds containing lions and angels on the coves, and a "lion in profile" device at center, with the *anima* possibly responding to Judges XIV: 18: REGNVM IN FORTITVDINE ET DVLCEDINE RULE IN STRENGTH AND SWEETNESS
North lunette	A woman, seated beneath a baldachin, holds wreathes within an *all'antica* surround of *grotteschi* comprised of flaming urns and putti
South lunette	loggia arch
vault	geometrical surrounds containing triple mountains, crowns, pear branches and star at center, with lions and angels on the coves

E. THE NORTHERN ENTRANCE VESTIBULE

North lunette	Two angels hold back curtains to reveal a "triple mountain" device sprouting pear branches, and the *anima*: TRISMEGISTOS.

The bands enclosing this lunette, and the arch at the southern end of the vestibule, are decorated with geometrical patterns hosting lion's heads, stars, angel faces and arabesques.

Northernmost vault	At center is a "lion in profile" device with an *anima* which is today illegible. It is flanked by two more devices, each of which is contained within a cartouche. That on the western side of the cove features a "three-branched candelabrum" device with a double *anima*, as it were, the first of which is taken from Psalm CXVIII: 66, and the second, possibly paraphrasing Ecclesiasticus XLIII: 4: SCIENTIA BONITATIS DISCIPLINA; TERNA HAEC TRIPLICI OF GOODNESS OF WISDOM OF KNOWLEDGE; THESE THREE THINGS THREEFOLD On the eastern side of the cove is a "seven-branched candelabrum" device, with an *anima* possibly paraphrasing Proverbs XXIV: 16: LVCEANT SEPTIES IVSTO THE LIGHT SHINES SEVEN TIMES FOR THE JUST MAN
Center vault	At center is the Sixtine *stemma* situated within a cartouche, flanked at top and bottom by angel's faces, and surmounted by the papal keys, scarf and tiara. To balance the "lion in profile" device located at its top, or northern end, is another like device at its bottom, or southern end. This *anima* is also illegible. Personifications are located to the west and east of the *stemma*.
Southernmost vault	At center is a "lion in profile" device with an *anima* which is today illegible. It is flanked by two more devices, each of which is contained within a cartouche. That on the western side of the cove features a "column and obelisk" device with the *anima*: RELIGIO MIRANDA TRIVMPHAT THE GLORIOUS RELIGION TRIUMPHS That on the eastern side is no longer extant.

189

13

F. THE SOUTHERN LOGGIA

South lunette	A woman, seated beneath a baldachin, holds wreathes within an *all'antica* surround of *grotteschi* comprised of flaming urns and putti
North lunette vault	loggia arch geometrical surrounds containing triple mountains, crowns and star at center, with lions and angels on the coves
South lunette	A woman, seated beneath a baldachin, holds wreathes within an *all'antica* surround of *grotteschi* comprised of flaming urns and putti
North lunette vault	loggia arch geometrical surrounds containing rampant lions with pear branches, with more lions and angels on the coves
South lunette	A woman, seated beneath a baldachin, holds wreathes within an *all'antica* surround of *grotteschi* comprised of flaming urns and putti
North lunette vault	loggia arch geometrical surrounds containing triple mountains, crowns and star at center, with lions and angels on the coves
South lunette	Two personifications flank a plaque now containing the inscription "GREGORIVS XVI RESTITVTI." The female to the left holds the "keys of the kingdom of heaven" as well as an olive (?) branch, and her foil to the right holds a cardinal's hat (clearly referring to the Cappellari coat-of-arms) and a sceptre (?)
North lunette vault	loggia arch geometrical surrounds containing the Sixtine *stemma* crossed by keys and crowned by papal tiara, with the inscription "SIXTVS. V. P. M. AN. PONT. IIII," with lions and angels on the coves
South lunette	A woman, seated beneath a baldachin, holds wreathes within an *all'antica* surround of *grotteschi* comprised of flaming urns and putti
North lunette vault	loggia arch geometrical surrounds containing triple mountains, crowns and star at center, with lions and angels on the coves
South lunette	A woman, seated beneath a baldachin, holds wreathes within an *all'antica* surround of *grotteschi* comprised of flaming urns and putti
North lunette vault	loggia arch geometrical surrounds containing rampant lions with pear branches, with more lions and angels on the coves
South lunette	A woman, seated beneath a baldachin, holds wreathes within an *all'antica* surround of *grotteschi* comprised of flaming urns and putti
North lunette vault	loggia arch geometrical surrounds containing triple mountains, crowns and star at center, with lions and angels on the coves
South lunette	A woman, seated beneath a baldachin, holds wreathes within an *all'antica* surround of *grotteschi* comprised of flaming urns and putti
North lunette vault	loggia arch geometrical surrounds containing triple mountains, crowns, pear branches and star at center, with lions and angels on the coves

The juncture between the southern and eastern *logge* contains a Sixtine rondel enclosing lions, mountains, pear branches and a star at center, with a geometrical foliate design containing the following verses taken from Judges XIV: 14:

EGRES[S]A DVLCEDO

SWEETNESS HAS EMERGED

EXIVIT CIBVS

South lunette	Personifications flank central Sixtine *stemma*

G. THE WESTERN LOGGIA EXTENSION

West lunette East lunette vault	Landscape geometrical surrounds containing triple mountains, crowns, pear branches and star at center, with lions and angels on the coves
West lunette East lunette vault	Landscape fig. 8 geometrical surrounds containing triple mountains, crowns, pear branches and star at center, with lions and angels on the coves
West lunette East lunette vault	A female figure reclines within a geometrical surround, and is accompanied by lions and angels with wreaths, likewise compartamentalized within foliate enclosures geometrical surrounds containing triple mountains, crowns, pear branches and star at center, with lions and angels on the coves
West lunette East lunette vault	A female figure reclines within a geometrical surround, and is accompanied by lions, mountains sprouting pear branches and crowned with a star and angels with wreaths, likewise compartamentalized within foliate enclosures geometrical surrounds containing angels raising the star-topped *monti* before a cloth of honour and beneath a wreath on the coves, and two "lion in profile" devices flanking a central design of *monti*, pear branches and star at the mid-point. Only one *anima* is legible, taken from Amos III: 8: SI RVGIET QVIS NON TIMEBIT IF HE ROARS, WHO WILL NOT FEAR? The other *anima* was, in all likelihood, taken from Psalm CXX: 4.

The band separating this vault from that which follows contains a Sixtine coat-of-arms supported by two angels who also hold papal keys and thereby support the scarf and tiara. The inscription beneath the *stemma* is as follows: "SIXTVS. V. PONT. MAX." Flanking this central oval are two personifications seated on clouds within feigned *quadri*.

West lunette East lunette vault	Landscape fig. 9 geometrical surrounds containing angels raising the star-topped *monti* before a cloth of honour and beneath a wreath on the coves, and two "lion in profile" devices flanking a central design of *monti*, pear branches and star at the mid-point. The *anime*, taken from Judges XIV: 14, are as follows: DE COMEDENTI EXIVIT CIBVS OUT OF THE EATER CAME FORTH MEAT DE FORTI EGRESSA EST DVLCEDO OUT OF THE STRONG CAME FORTH SWEETNESS

2. THE GRAND STAIRCASE

A. THE FIRST ARM

Westernmost vault

The *monti*, enclosed within sumptuous arabesques, flank a central "lion in profile" device with the *anima* from Judges XIV: 14:
DE FORTI EGRESSA EST DVLCEDO

OUT OF THE STRONG CAME FORTH SWEETNESS

Proceeding east

Two angels holding up a cloth of honour housing the star-topped *monti*, and encircled by *grotteschi* and geometrical designs, are flanked by the "triple mountain" device. That on the northern cove has the *anima* taken from Psalm LXVII: 17:
MONS IN QVO BENEPLACITVM EST DEO

A MOUNTAIN IN WHICH GOD IS WELL PLEASED
That on the southern cove is a curious hybrid with eyes, and has the *anima*:
CAELVM AEQVORA TERRAS

THE HEAVENS, THE SEA, THE EARTH
fig. 14

The *monti*, enclosed within sumptuous arabesques, flank a central "lion in profile" device with the *anima* from the Proverbs of Solomon XXVIII: 1:
IVSTVS VT LEO CONFIDENS

HE IS JUST AS THE LION IS BOLD

Two angels holding up the *stemma* of Sixtus V crowned with papal keys, scarf and tiara, and encircled by *grotteschi* and geometrical designs, are flanked by the "triple mountain" device. The *anime* are taken from Psalm LXXXVI:
FVNDAMENTA EIVS

THE FOUNDATIONS THEREOF

IN MONTIBVS ALTIS

IN THE HIGH MOUNTAIN

The *monti*, enclosed within sumptuous arabesques, flank a central "lion in profile" device with the *anima* from Revelation V: 5:
VINCIT LEO DE TRIBV IVDA

THE LION OF THE TRIBE OF JUDAH HAS CONQUERED

Two angels holding up the *stemma* of Sixtus V crowned with papal keys, scarf and tiara, and encircled by *grotteschi* and geometrical designs, are flanked by the "triple mountain" device, one of which contains eyes, and the expected *anima*:
CAELVM AEQVORA TERRAS

THE HEAVENS, THE SEA, THE EARTH

The other has an *anima* taken from Psalm LXVII: 17:
MONS IN QVO BENEPLACITVM DEO EST

A MOUNTAIN IN WHICH GOD IS WELL PLEASED

The *monti*, enclosed within sumptuous arabesques, flank a central "lion in profile" device with the *anima* from Judges XIV: 14:
DE COMEDENTI EXIVIT CIBVS

OUT OF THE EATER CAME FORTH MEAT

192

landing	Sixtine rondel with personifications in the four pendentives, as well as lions holding pear branches, *monti*, and star at center, and the verse taken from Psalm CXXIV: 2: MONTES IN CIRCVITV EIVS MOUNTAINS ARE ROUND ABOUT
East lunette	Personification: *Fire* PROCREATIONIS EXPERS EXPERT IN CREATION fig. 10
South lunette	Personification: *Air* INANITATIS IMPATIENS UNABLE TO BEAR EMPTY SPACE fig. 11

B. THE SECOND ARM

Bands between rondels contain *grotteschi* comprised of elements taken from the Sixtine heraldry.

landing	Sixtine rondel with personifications in the four pendentives, as well as lions holding pear branches, *monti*, and star at center, and the verse possibly taken from Psalm CXLVIII: 9: MONTES IN OMNES COLLES MOUNTAINS AND ALL HILLS
North lunette	Personification: *Water* PROCREATIONVM ORIGO ORIGIN OF CREATION fig. 12
Easternmost vault	Lion heads, enclosed within sumptuous arabesques, flank a central "triple mountain" device with the *anima* from Psalm LXXXVI: FVNDAMENTA EIVS THE FOUNDATIONS THEREOF
Proceeding west	Two angels holding up a cloth of honour housing the star-topped *monti*, and encircled by *grotteschi* and geometrical designs, are flanked by the "lion in profile" device. That on the northern cove has an *anima* which may respond to the riddle in Judges XIV: 14: IN ORE EIVS DVLCEDO ET CIBVS IN HIS RISING SWEETNESS AND MEAT That on the southern cove is taken from Amos III: 8: SI RVGIET QVIS NON TIMEBIT IF HE ROARS, WHO WILL NOT FEAR? Lion heads, enclosed within sumptuous arabesques, flank a central "triple mountain" device with eyes, and an *anima* taken from Psalm CXVIII: 66: BONITATIS SCIENTIAM DISCIPLINAM OF GOODNESS OF WISDOM OF KNOWLEDGE Two angels holding up the *stemma* of Sixtus V crowned with papal keys, scarf and tiara, and encircled by *grotteschi* and geometrical designs, are flanked by the "lion in profile" device, with *anime* taken from Judges XIV: 14:

DE FORTI EGRESSA EST DVLCEDO

OUT OF THE STRONG CAME FORTH SWEETNESS

DE COMEDENTI EXIVIT CIBVS

OUT OF THE EATER CAME FORTH MEAT

Lion heads, enclosed within sumptuous arabesques, flank a central "triple mountain" device with eyes, and an *anima* taken from Psalm LXXXVI: 1:
IN MONTIBVS ALTIS

IN THE HIGH MOUNTAIN

Two angels holding up a cloth of honour housing the star-topped *monti*, and encircled by *grotteschi* and geometrical designs, are flanked by the "lion in profile" device, with *anime* respectively taken from the Proverbs of Solomon XXVIII: 1, and Revelation V: 5:
IVSTVS VT LEO CONFIDENS

HE IS JUST AS THE LION IS BOLD

VINCIT LEO DE TRIBV IVDA

THE LION OF THE TRIBE OF JUDAH HAS CONQUERED

Lion heads, enclosed within sumptuous arabesques, flank a central "triple mountain" device with eyes and the *anima*:
CAELVM AEQVORA TERRAS

THE HEAVENS, THE SEA, THE EARTH

landing:	Western loggia extension, *piano nobile* (see below)

C. THE THIRD ARM

Westernmost vault	Personifications within geometrical surrounds flank a central design of *monti* sprouting pear branches, crowned with a star, and supported by putti.
Proceeding east	Two angels holding up a cloth of honour housing the star-topped *monti*, and encircled by *grotteschi* and geometrical designs, are flanked by a lion on the cove.

Personifications within geometrical surrounds flank a central design of *monti* sprouting pear branches, crowned with a star, and supported by putti.

Lions on the cove flank a central "column and obelisk" device within a cartouche, upheld and crowned by angels, with an *anima* possibly taken from Psalm XCII: 4-5:
MIRABILIA TVA CREDIBILIA

THY CREDIBLE WONDERS

Personifications within geometrical surrounds flank a central design of *monti* sprouting pear branches, crowned with a star, and supported by putti.

Two angels holding up a cloth of honour housing the star-topped *monti*, and encircled by *grotteschi* and geometrical designs, are flanked by a lion on the cove.

Personifications within geometrical surrounds flank a central design of *monti* sprouting pear branches, crowned with a star, and supported by putti.

landing	Sixtine rondel with four personifications in the pendentives, as well as angels supporting *monti* before a cloth of honour, females with wreathed crowns, and, at center, crowned *monti* and lion heads encircling a star.
South lunette	fan design contains arabesques, putti, and female figures, both reclining and standing, as well as a "triple mountain" device at center, with the *anima*: IVSTVS CONSPICI I AM CONSIDERED JUST
East lunette	This is a later addition, owing to the *corpo* of six mountains flanked by *fleurs-de-lis*, and the coloration of the design which is tonally inconsistent with that of the Sixtine fresco painting, even after restorations. The *anima* cannot, with certainty, be regarded as reflecting the original, and is as follows: IN NOMINE DOMINI IN THE NAME OF THE LORD
East lunette	This is a later addition, owing to the *corpo* of six mountains flanked by *fleurs-de-lis*, and the coloration of the design which is tonally inconsistent with that of the Sixtine fresco painting, even after restorations. The *anima* cannot, with certainty, be regarded as reflecting the original, and is as follows: IN NOMINE DOMINI IN THE NAME OF THE LORD

A band between rondels contains *grotteschi* comprised of elements taken from the Sixtine heraldry, as well as the inscription: "SIXTVS V. PONT. MAX. PONTIFICI SVI ANNO IIII."

D. THE FOURTH ARM

landing	Sixtine rondel with four personifications in the pendentives, as well as angels supporting *monti* before a cloth of honour, females with wreathed crowns, and, at center, crowned *monti* and lion heads encircling a star.
NORTH lunette	fan design contains arabesques, putti, and female figures, both reclining and standing, as well as a "triple mountain" device at center, with the *anima* taken from Psalm XCVI: 11: LVX ORTA EST IVSTO LIGHT IS RISEN TO THE JUST Personifications within geometrical surrounds flank a central design of *monti* sprouting pear branches, crowned with a star, and supported by putti. Two angels holding up a cloth of honour housing the star-topped *monti*, and encircled by *grotteschi* and geometrical designs, are flanked by a lion on the cove. Personifications within geometrical surrounds flank a central design of *monti* sprouting pear branches, crowned with a star, and supported by putti. Lions on the cove flank a central "column and obelisk" device within a cartouche, upheld and crowned by angels, with an *anima* taken from Luke XIX: 38: GLORIA IN EXCELSIS DEO

GLORY TO GOD ON HIGH
fig. 19

Personifications within geometrical surrounds flank a central design of *monti* sprouting pear branches, crowned with a star, and supported by putti.

Two angels holding up a cloth of honour housing the star-topped *monti*, and encircled by *grotteschi* and geometrical designs, are flanked by a lion on the cove.

Personifications within geometrical surrounds flank a central design of *monti* sprouting pear branches, crowned with a star, and supported by putti.

to *secondo piano* ...

3. THE *PIANO NOBILE*

A. THE WESTERN LOGGIA

West lunette	Landscape #XVII
East lunette	Window
South cove	*God creates the Sun and the Plants* [Genesis I: 1-31]; flanked by a personification within a cartouche on which lounge putti with the *monti*, while the whole structure is crowned by a putto with a regal crown
East cove	*Creation of Adam* [Genesis II: 7]; flanked by a personification within a cartouche on which lounge putti with the *monti*, while the whole structure is crowned by a putto with a regal crown
North cove	*Creation of Eve* [Genesis II: 21-22]; flanked by a personification within a cartouche on which lounge putti with the *monti*, while the whole structure is crowned by a putto with a regal crown
West cove	*Adam and Eve in the Garden of Eden* [Genesis II: 25]; flanked by a personification within a cartouche on which lounge putti with the *monti*, while the whole structure is crowned by a putto with a regal crown
Center vault	two putti, seen *dal di sotto in su*, hold a plaque inscribed "S.V.P.M."
Band separating vaults	A central Sixtine lion in profile is flanked by a personification and elements of the Sixtine heraldry
West lunette	Landscape #XVIII
East lunette	Window
South cove	*God calls Adam and Eve* [Genesis III: 8-13]; flanked by a triumphal arch housing a personification being crowned with papal tiara by two angels
East cove	*Expulsion* [Genesis III: 23-24]; flanked by a triumphal arch housing a personification being crowned with papal tiara by two angels
North cove	*Adam and Eve after the Fall* (?) [Genesis III: 23 ff]; flanked by a triumphal arch housing a personification being crowned with papal tiara by two angels
West cove	*God banishes Cain* [Genesis IV: 9-15]; flanked by a triumphal arch housing a personification being crowned with papal tiara by two angels
Center vault	*quadratura* opening
West lunette	Landscape #XIX
East lunette	Window
South cove	*Building of Noah's Ark* [Genesis VI: 14-22]; flanked by an elaborate cartouche surmounted by an obelisk, supported by a putto-herm, and housing figures
East cove	*God tells Noah to enter the Ark* [Genesis VII: 11]; flanked by an elaborate cartouche surmounted by an obelisk, supported by a putto-herm, and housing figures
North cove	*Deluge* [Genesis VII: 21-22]; flanked by an elaborate cartouche surmounted by an obelisk, supported by a putto-herm, and housing figures
West cove	*Cain kills Abel* [Genesis IV: 9-15]; flanked by an elaborate cartouche surmounted by an obelisk, supported by a putto-herm, and housing figures
Center vault	an angel, seen *dal di sotto in su*, holds a wreath

196

The bands separating these and the remaining vaults are like the above-mentioned, with two or more personifications flanking either a Sixtine lion or a crown or the *monti* with pear branches. The design always has a foil, according to the bilateral symmetry of the vault.

West lunette	Landscape #XX
East lunette	Window
South cove	*The Dead after the Deluge* [Genesis VII: 21-22]; flanked by an elaborate cartouche housing the *monti* and star, flanked by two female personifications, supported by a third female below, and crowned by a baldachin and two putti with papal tiara
East cove	*Noah builds an altar unto the Lord* [Genesis VIII: 20]; flanked by an elaborate cartouche housing the *monti* and star, flanked by two female personifications, supported by a third female below, and crowned by a baldachin and two putti with papal tiara
North cove	*God blesses Noah and his sons* [Genesis IX: 1]; flanked by an elaborate cartouche housing the *monti* and star, flanked by two female personifications, supported by a third female below, and crowned by a baldachin and two putti with papal tiara
West cove	*Drunkenness of Noah* [Genesis IX: 23]; flanked by an elaborate cartouche housing the *monti* and star, flanked by two female personifications, supported by a third female below, and crowned by a baldachin and two putti with papal tiara
Center vault	fan design

West lunette	Landscape #XXI
East lunette	Window
South cove	*Tower of Babel* [Genesis XI: 2-4]; flanked by female personifications seated within triumphal arches formed by *grotteschi*, flanked by lions, supported by a fan design and the *monti*, and surmounted by a cartouche housing another Sixtine lion
East cove	*Abraham, Sarah and Lot leave Haran* [Genesis XII: 5]; flanked by female personifications seated within triumphal arches formed by *grotteschi*, flanked by lions, supported by a fan design and the *monti*, and surmounted by a cartouche housing another Sixtine lion
North cove	*Abraham in Egypt* [Genesis XII: 16]; flanked by female personifications seated within triumphal arches formed by *grotteschi*, flanked by lions, supported by a fan design and the *monti*, and surmounted by a cartouche housing another Sixtine lion
West cove	*Abraham, Sarah and Lot leave Egypt* [Genesis XIII: 1]; flanked by female personifications seated within triumphal arches formed by *grotteschi*, flanked by lions, supported by a fan design and the *monti*, and surmounted by a cartouche housing another Sixtine lion
Center vault	two putti, seen *dal di sotto in su*, bear aloft a plaque inscribed "SIXTVS V"

West lunette	Landscape #XXII fig. 20
East lunette	Window
South cove	*Abraham and Lot in the land between Beth-el and Ai* [Genesis XIII: 2-9]; flanked by an elaborate cartouche housing the *monti* and star, flanked by two female personifications, supported by a third female below, and crowned by a baldachin and two putti with papal tiara
East cove	*Abraham near the terebinths of Mamre* [Genesis XII: 14-18]; flanked by an elaborate cartouche housing the *monti* and star, flanked by two female personifications, supported by a third female below, and crowned by a baldachin and two putti with papal tiara
North cove	*Abraham fights to retrieve Lot from captivity* [Genesis XIV: 14-15]; flanked by an elaborate cartouche housing the *monti* and star, flanked by two female personifications, supported by a third female below, and crowned by a baldachin and two putti with papal tiara
West cove	*Hagar and the Angel* [Genesis XVI: 7-14]; flanked by an elaborate cartouche housing the *monti* and star, flanked by two female personifications, supported by a third female below, and crowned by a baldachin and two putti with papal tiara

Center vault	fan design
West lunette	Landscape #XXIII
East lunette	Window
South cove	*God appears to Abraham* [Genesis XVIII: 1-8]; flanked by an elaborate cartouche surmounted by an obelisk, supported by a putto-herm, and housing figures
East cove	*Lot before the angels at Sodom* [Genesis XIX: 1-2]; flanked by an elaborate cartouche surmounted by an obelisk, supported by a putto-herm, and housing figures
North cove	*God destroys Sodom and Gomorrah* [Genesis XIX: 24-25]; flanked by an elaborate cartouche surmounted by an obelisk, supported by a putto-herm, and housing figures
West cove	*Abraham sees the destruction of Sodom and Gomorrah* [Genesis XIX: 28]; flanked by an elaborate cartouche surmounted by an obelisk, supported by a putto-herm, and housing figures
Center vault	an angel, seen *dal di sotto in su*, holds a wreath
West lunette	Landscape #XXIV
East lunette	Window
South cove	*Abraham and Sarah in Gerar* (?) [Genesis XX: 14-16]; flanked by a triumphal arch housing a personification being crowned with papal tiara by two angels
East cove	*God appears to Abraham, Sarah and Isaac* [Genesis XXI: 1-7]; flanked by a triumphal arch housing a personification being crowned with papal tiara by two angels
North cove	*Abraham makes a feast on the day Isaac is weaned* [Genesis XXI: 8]; flanked by a triumphal arch housing a personification being crowned with papal tiara by two angels
West cove	*Hagar and the Angel* [Genesis XXI: 15-17]; flanked by a triumphal arch housing a personification being crowned with papal tiara by two angels
Center vault	*quadratura* opening
West lunette	Landscape #XXV
East lunette	Landscape above the entrance door to the private papal apartment
North lunette	Two personifications, *Providence* and *Felicity* flank a central Sixtine *stemma*
South cove	*Sacrifice of Isaac* [Genesis XXII: 1-19]; flanked by a personification within a cartouche on which lounge putti with the *monti*, while the whole structure is crowned by a putto with a regal crown
East cove	*Death of Abraham* [Genesis XXV: 8]; flanked by a personification within a cartouche on which lounge putti with the *monti*, while the whole structure is crowned by a putto with a regal crown
North cove	*Burial of Abraham* [Genesis XXV: 9]; flanked by a personification within a cartouche on which lounge putti with the *monti*, while the whole structure is crowned by a putto with a regal crown
West cove	*Birth of Esau and Jacob* [Genesis XXV: 25]; flanked by a personification within a cartouche on which lounge putti with the *monti*, while the whole structure is crowned by a putto with a regal crown

B. THE EASTERN LOGGIA

South lunette	*Stemma* of Sixtus V flanked by two Personifications: *Religion* and *Providential Rule* (#IX), and the inscription, taken from Psalm XLV: 8: DILEXISTI IVSTITIAM ET ODISTI INIQVITATEM THOU HAST LOVED JUSTICE, AND HATED INIQUITY
East lunette	#VIII - destroyed landscape (?)
West lunette	Window

Between the narratives throughout the vault (with the exception of the last one, which is not of the period), the coves host putti seated on clouds, directly above the landscapes, and at center vault, four putti hold a wreath, and are flanked by cartouches with the *monti*, crowns, and pear branches. Between these areas, towards center vault, angels hold wreathes and trumpet fame, while *"ignudi"* are suspended above the empty lunettes, flanking the putti on clouds.

Seam of vault	putti with a rondel and the inscription: MDL / XXXIX
East cove	*Annunciation to Zachary* [Luke: I: 13], with the inscription: EXAVDITA EST DEPRECATIO
	THY PRAYER IS HEARD Old Testament type in *grisaille*: *Sacrifice of Manue* [Judges XIII: 2- 20]
West cove	*Marriage of the Virgin* [Luke I: 27], with the inscription: VIRGO DESPONSATVR VIRO DE DOMO DAVID
	A VIRGIN ESPOUSED TO A MAN OF THE HOUSE OF DAVID Old Testament type in *grisaille*
Seam of vault	"Single obelisk" device, with the *anima* taken from Luke XIX: 38: GLORIA DEO IN EXCELSIS
	GLORY TO GOD ON HIGH
Seam of vault	putti with a rondel and the inscription: ANNO PONT. XVI IIII
East lunette	#VII - destroyed landscape (?)
West lunette	Window
East cove	*Annunciation* [Luke I: 30], with the inscription: INVENISTI GRATIAM APVD DEVM
	THOU HAST FOUND GRACE WITH GOD Old Testament type in *grisaille*: *Moses and the Burning Bush* [Exodus III: 1-10]
West cove	*Visitation* [Luke I: 45], with the inscription: BEATA QVAE CREDIDISTI
	BLESSED ART THOU THAT HAS BELIEVED Old Testament type in *grisaille*
Seam of vault	"Lion" device, with the *anima* taken from Revelation V: 5: VINCIT LEO DE TRIBV IVDA
	THE LION OF THE TRIBE OF JUDAH HAS CONQUERED
Seam of vault	putti with a rondel and the inscription: PONT MAXIMVS
East lunette	#VI - destroyed landscape (?)
West lunette	Window
East cove	*Birth of John the Baptist* [Luke I: 15], with the inscription: ERIT MAGNVS CORAM DOMINO
	HE SHALL BE GREAT BEFORE THE LORD Old Testament type in *grisaille*
West cove	*Angels announce the birth of Christ* [Luke II: 13-14], with the inscription: COGNOVIT BOS POSSESSOREM SVVM
Seam of vault	Old Testament type in *grisaille* "Papal Tiara" device, with the *anima*: A DOMINO FACTVM EST ISTVD
	THIS IS MADE FOR GOD
Seam of vault	putti with a rondel and the inscription: †/ SIXTVS / V
East lunette	#V - destroyed landscape (?)
West lunette	Window
East cove	*Adoration of the Shepherds* [Luke II: 16], with the inscription: VENERVNT FESTINANTES ET INVENERVNT
	THEY CAME WITH HASTE; AND THEY FOUND [HIM] Old Testament type in *grisaille*

West cove	*Circumcision* [Luke II: 21], with the inscription: VOCATVM EST NOMEN EIVS IESVS HIS NAME WAS CALLED JESUS Old Testament type in *grisaille*
Seam of vault	"Antonine column" device, with the *anima*: D. VAS ELECT[IONIS] SP
Seam of vault	putti with a rondel and the inscription: DIX FOLLEX (?)
East lunette	#IV - destroyed landscape (?)
West lunette	Window
East cove	*Adoration of the Magi* [paraphrase of Matthew II: 1-11], with the inscription: REGES ARABVM ET SABA DONA ADDVCVNT ARABIC AND SABAEAN KINGS BRING GIFTS Old Testament type in *grisaille*
West cove	*Presentation in the Temple* [Luke II: 30], with the inscription: VIDERVNT OCVLI MEI SALVTARE TVVM MY EYES HAVE SEEN THY SALVATION Old Testament type in *grisaille*
Seam of vault	"Trajanic column" device, with the *anima*: PAS[TOR] OVIVM
Seam of vault	putti with a rondel and the inscription: † / SIXTVS / V
East lunette	#III - destroyed landscape (?)
West lunette	Window
East cove	*Rest on the Flight* [Matthew II: 20], with the inscription: SVRGE ET VADE IN TERRAM ISRAEL ARISE, AND GO INTO THE LAND OF ISRAEL Old Testament type in *grisaille*
West cove	*Flight into Egypt* [Matthew II: 21], with the inscription: VENIT IN TERRAM ISRAEL HE CAME INTO THE LAND OF ISRAEL Old Testament type in *grisaille*
Seam of vault	"Lion" device, with the *anima* taken from the Proverbs of Solomon XXVI-II: 1: IVSTVS VT LEO CONFIDENS HE IS JUST AS THE LION IS BOLD
Seam of vault	putti with a rondel and the inscription: PONT MAXIMVS
East lunette	#II - destroyed landscape (?)
West lunette	Window
East cove	*Christ among the Doctors* [Luke III: 46-50], with the inscription: STVPEBANT AVTEM OMNES ALL THAT HEARD HIM WERE ASTONISHED Old Testament type in *grisaille*
West cove	*John the Baptist preaching in Judea* [Matthew III: 2], with the inscription: POENITENTIAM AGITE DO PENANCE Old Testament type in *grisaille*
Seam of vault	"Single obelisk" device, with the *anima*: IN HOC SIGNO IN THIS SIGN
Seam of vault	putti with a rondel and the inscription: ANNO / PONT SVI / IIII

East lunette	#I - destroyed landscape (?)
West lunette	Window
East cove	*Baptism of Christ* [Matthew III: 17], with the inscription: HIC EST FILIVS MEVS DILECTVS

THIS IS MY BELOVED SON
Old Testament type in *grisaille*

West cove	*The Holy Spirit descends after Christ's Baptism* [John I: 29, 36], with the inscription: ECCE AGNVS DEI

BEHOLD THE LAMB OF GOD
Old Testament type in *grisaille*

Seam of vault	"Lion" device, with the *anima* possibly taken from Psalm CXXVI: 1: CVSTOS VIGILI

VIGILANT CUSTODIAN

East lunette	personifications flanking a *stemma* repainted in 1969: MANSVETVDO, with an elephant, and SANCTITAS, with a dove and a halo
West lunette	personifications flanking a *stemma* repainted in 1969: PAX, with an olive branch, and IVSTITIA, with a sword
Vault	repainted *grotteschi*, following those Sixtine examples of the ground floor junctures, with the following inscription: REDINTEGRARI IVSSIT / PAVLVS VI. P. M. A. D. / MCMLXIX.
North lunette	personifications flanking a *stemma* repainted in 1969: RELIGIO, with a cross and temple and her foot on a globe, and FIDES, with a chalice, host and cloth, and a veil on her head

C. THE APPARTAMENTO PRIVATO PONTIFICIO

a. FIRST ROOM

1.		East lunette Landscape
2.		West lunette Landscape
3.		North lunette Landscape
4.		South lunette Landscape
5.		North cove "Decorative figure"
6.		North cove "Decorative figure"
7.		North cove Personification
8.		North cove Personification
9.		South cove "Decorative figure"
10.		South cove "Decorative figure"
11.		South cove

Personification

12. South cove
Personification

13. North-East angle
Personification
A standing woman with long, flowing hair holds a long rod in both hands.

14. South-West angle
Personification
A standing woman wears a turban on her head and raises her right arm.

15. North-West angle
Personification
A standing male holds an unsheathed sword in his right hand and a shield in his left.

16. South-East angle
Personification
A standing woman holds a mask under her left arm.

17. Center vault
Stemma of Sixtus V with four angels and the verse taken from
I Peter I: 25:
MANET IN ETERNVM

IT ENDURETH FOREVER

b. SECOND ROOM

18. East lunette
Landscape

19. East cove
Personification
A girl is seated. She holds a mask in her left hand and two trumpets in her right. She wears a veil and a crown on her head. One of her breasts is bare. She is flanked by *grotteschi*.

20. West lunette
Landscape

21. West cove
Personification: *Abundance* (?)
A girl is seated. She holds a bunch of flowers in her left hand and a cornucopia in her right. She is flanked by *grotteschi*.

22. North lunette
Landscape

23. North cove
"Decorative figure"

24. North cove
"Decorative figure"

25. North cove
Personification

26. North cove
Personification
A seated woman, surrounded by *grotteschi*, points to her left with her left index finger. She holds a censer in her right hand.

202

27.	North lunette Landscape
28.	North cove "Decorative figure"
29.	North cove "Decorative figure"
30.	North cove Personification
31.	North cove Personification A seated woman looks upwards. She holds a palm branch and an oak branch in her left hand, and outstretches her right hand. She is surrounded by *grotteschi*.
32.	South lunette Landscape
33.	South cove "Decorative figure"
34.	South cove "Decorative figure"
35.	South cove Personification: *Fortitude*
36.	South cove Personification: *Sixtine Fame* (?) A seated woman holds a trumpet in her right hand, and a branch with three pears in her left.
37.	South lunette Landscape
38.	South cove "Decorative figure"
39.	South cove "Decorative figure"
40.	South cove Personification
41.	South cove Personificaton: *Economics* (?) A seated woman looks downwards. She holds a compass in her left hand, and a T-square in her right.
42.	North cove Personification A seated girl holds a crown and a palm branch in her right hand, and a pear in her left.
43.	North cove Putti hold fruit.
44.	South cove Personification A seated woman holds her left hand upwards and points with her index finger. In her right hand she holds fetters.

45.	South cove Putti hold flowers and fruit.
46.	Center vault *Stemma* of Sixtus V

c. THIRD ROOM

47.	East lunette Landscape
48.	East cove Personification: *Prophecy* (?) A seated woman looks downwards. She holds her left index finger upwards and in her right hand, a palm branch and trumpet. She is flanked by *grotteschi*.
49.	West lunette Landscape
50.	West cove Personification: *Abundance* A seated girl holds a cornucopia in both hands at her left side. She is flanked by *grotteschi*.
51.	North lunette Landscape
52.	North cove "Decorative figure"
53.	North cove "Decorative figure"
54.	North cove Personification
55.	North cove Face of a putto and *grotteschi*
56.	North lunette Landscape
57.	North cove "Decorative figure"
58.	North cove "Decorative figure"
59.	North cove Personification
60.	North cove Face of a putto and *grotteschi*
61.	South lunette Landscape
62.	South cove "Decorative figure"
63.	South cove "Decorative figure"

204

64.		South cove Personification
65.		South cove Face of a putto and *grotteschi*
66.		South lunette Landscape
67.		South cove "Decorative figure"
68.		South cove "Decorative figure"
69.		South cove Personification
70.		South cove Face of a putto and *grotteschi*
71.		North cove Personification A helmeted woman is seated. She holds a spear in her right hand and an unidentifiable object in her left. Above her are two putti, one holding a laurel crown, and the other, a branch with three pears.
72.		South cove Personification A woman holds the scales of justice and a sword. Above her are two putti, one holding a laurel crown, and the other, a branch with three pears.
73.		Center vault *Stemma* of Sixtus V

d. FOURTH ROOM - fig. 127

74.	A	East lunette 19th Century Landscape fig. 130
75.	a	East cove Two female *genii* fly beneath a canopy. They hold up the curtain to show themselves and the three mountains encircled by two crowns and topped by a third which they hold between them.
76.	B	West lunette *Landscape with Saint John the Baptist* fig. 131
77.	b	West cove Two female *genii* fly beneath a canopy. They hold up the curtain to show themselves and the three mountains encircled by two crowns and topped by a third which they hold between them.
78.	C	South lunette *Landscape with Elijah and the Angel* fig. 132
79.	D	South lunette *Landscape with Moses and the Burning Bush* fig. 133
80.	E	North lunette *Landscape with Saint Onuphrius* fig. 134

14

81.	F	North lunette *Landscape with Mary of Egypt* fig. 135
82.	G	South cove Personification: *Sacred Religion* fig. 128
83.	H	North cove Personification: *Sixtine Justice* fig. 129
84.	I	Center vault Medallion encircled by eight putti with the inscription: SIXTVS V PONT. MAX. ANNO IIII SIXTUS V, PONTIFEX MAXIMUS, IN THE FOURTH YEAR OF HIS REIGN and another verse, taken from Judges XIV: 14: DE FORTI EGRESSA EST DVLCEDO OUT OF THE STRONG CAME FORTH SWEETNESS fig. 135
85.	J	North cove Female *genii* hold up a tassled canopy and hold the *monti*.
86.	K	North cove Female *genii* hold up a tassled canopy and hold the *monti*.
87.	L	South cove Female *genii* hold up a tassled canopy and hold the *monti*.
88.	M	South cove Female *genii* hold up a tassled canopy and hold the *monti*.

D. THE SOUTHERN LOGGIA

South lunette	Landscape #XVI
North lunette	Window
South cove	*Nabuchodonosor marshals his forces against King Arphaxad* (?) [Judith I: 5]; the narrative is flanked by a female personification seated on a throne suported by the *monti* encircled by crowns and a fan design, and surmounted by an angel's face
West cove	*Nabuchodonosor announces to Holofernes that he will wage war on the region and puts Holofernes in charge* (?) [Judith II: 5-6]; the narrative is flanked by a female personification seated on a throne supported by the *monti* encircled by crowns and a fan design, and surmounted by an angel's face
North cove	*Holofernes and his men wish to kill Achior*(?)[Judith V: 26-29]; the narrative is flanked by a female personification seated on a throne suported by the *monti* encircled by crowns and a fan design, and surmounted by an angel's face
East cove	*Holofernes speaks to Achior* (?) [Judith VI: 1-6]; the narrative is flanked by a female personification seated on a throne suported by the *monti* encircled by crowns and a fan design, and surmounted by an angel's face
Center vault	an angel, seen *dal di sotto in su* and seated on a cloud, holds an open book

As is the case on the vault of the western loggia, the bands dividing each vault are populated with personifications and the elements of Sixtus V's heraldry, according to the symmetrical disposition of elements on the vault.

South lunette	Landscape #XV
North lunette	Window
South cove	*The Israelites take Achior to the town magistrates of Bethulia* [Judith VI: 10-13]; the narrative is flanked by two female personifications supporting a cartouche with a third, surmounted by a garland, and supported by a putto within a geometrical surround
West cove	*Holofernes and his army march on Bethulia* [Judith VII: 1-3]; the narrative is flanked by two female personifications supporting a cartouche with a third, surmounted by a garland, and supported by a putto within a geometrical surround
North cove	*Holofernes seizes the springs of Bethulia* [Judith VII: 6]; the narrative is flanked by two female personifications supporting a cartouche with a third, surmounted by a garland, and supported by a putto within a geometrical surround
East cove	*The Israelites gather round Ozias beseeching him to surrender* [Judith VII: 12-25]; the narrative is flanked by two female personifications supporting a cartouche with a third, surmounted by a garland, and supported by a putto within a geometrical surround
Center vault	two putti, seen *dal di sotto in su*, carry aloft a crown and pear branches
South lunette	Landscape #XIV
North lunette	Window
South cove	*Judith summons the elders of Bethulia* (?) [Judith VIII: 9-34]; the narrative is flanked by two female personifications flanking the Sixtine *stemma* which supports an angel's face and a feigned *quadro*
West cove	*Judith puts ashes on her head and prays to God* (?) [Judith IX: 1-19]; the narrative is flanked by two female personifications flanking the Sixtine *stemma* which supports an angel's face and a feigned *quadro*
North cove	*Judith puts on her finery* (?) [Judith X: 1-4]; the narrative is flanked by two female personifications flanking the Sixtine *stemma* which supports an angel's face and a feigned *quadro*
East cove	*Judith and her maidservant (and another unidentified woman) at the Assyrian outpost* (?) [Judith X: 11-15]; the narrative is flanked by two female personifications flanking the Sixtine *stemma* which supports an angel's face and a feigned *quadro*
Center vault	an angel, seen *dal di sotto in su*, holds a pear branch
South lunette	Landscape #XIII
North lunette	Window
South cove	*One of the men from the town of Bethulia* (?) [Judith X: 6-10]; the narrative is flanked by a female personification in a *quadro* surmounting another figure within a geometrical surround and surmounted by two putti
West cove	*Judith prostrates herself before Holofernes* [Judith X: 20]; the narrative is flanked by a female personification in a *quadro* surmounting another figure within a geometrical surround and surmounted by two putti
North cove	*Judith tells Holofernes her story* [Judith XI: 4-17]; the narrative is flanked by a female personification in a *quadro* surmounting another figure within a geometrical surround and surmounted by two putti
East cove	*Holofernes' servants bring Judith and her maidservant into the tent* [Judith XII: 4]; the narrative is flanked by a female personification in a *quadro* surmounting another figure within a geometrical surround and surmounted by two putti
Center vault	two putti hold a plaque inscribed "SIXTVS V"
South lunette	Landscape #XII
North lunette	Window
South cove	*Holofernes allows Judith to go out and pray* [Judith XII: 5-6]; the narrative is flanked by two female personifications flanking the Sixtine *stemma* which supports an angel's face and a feigned *quadro*
West cove	*Judith praying to the Lord at the spring* [Judith XII: 7-8]; the narrative is flanked by two female personifications flanking the Sixtine *stemma* which supports an angel's face and a feigned *quadro*
North cove	*Vagao asks Judith to dine with Holofernes* [Judith XII: 12]; the narrative is flanked by two female personifications flanking the Sixtine *stemma* which supports an angel's face and a feigned *quadro*

East cove	*Holofernes holds a banquet for personal servants* [Judith XII: 15-20]; the narrative is flanked by two female personifications flanking the Sixtine *stemma* which supports an angel's face and a feigned *quadro*
Center vault	an angel, seen *dal di sotto in su*, holds a pear branch
South lunette	Landscape #XI
North lunette	Window
South cove	*Judith, her maidservant and Vagao at Holofernes' tent* (?) [Judith XIII: 1]; the narrative is flanked by two female personifications supporting a cartouche with a third, surmounted by a garland, and supported by a putto within a geometrical surround
West cove	*Holofernes, on his bed dead drunk, and Judith* [Judith XIII: 4-5]; the narrative is flanked by two female personifications supporting a cartouche with a third, surmounted by a garland, and supported by a putto within a geometrical surround
North cove	*Judith kills Holofernes* [Judith XIII: 6-10]; the narrative is flanked by two female personifications supporting a cartouche with a third, surmounted by a garland, and supported by a putto within a geometrical surround
East cove	*Judith gives the maidservant Holofernes' head* [Judith XIII: 11]; the narrative is flanked by two female personifications supporting a cartouche with a third, surmounted by a garland, and supported by a putto within a geometrical surround
Center vault	two putti, seen *dal di sotto in su*, carry aloft a crown and pear branches
South lunette	Landscape #X
North lunette	Window
South cove	*Judith and her maidservant having entered the city gates of Bethulia* (?) [Judith XIII: 12-18]; the narrative is flanked by a female personification seated on a throne suported by the *monti* encircled by crowns and a fan design, and surmounted by an angel's face
West cove	*Judith shows the head of Holofernes* [Judith XIII: 19-31]; the narrative is flanked by a female personification seated on a throne suported by the *monti* encircled by crowns and a fan design, and surmounted by an angel's face
North cove	*The Assyrians rip their shirts in despair over Holofernes' death* [Judith XIV: 17-18]; the narrative is flanked by a female personification seated on a throne suported by the *monti* encircled by crowns and a fan design, and surmounted by an angel's face
East cove	*The Assyrians flee by every path and are defeated by the Israelites* [Judith XV: 1-8]; the narrative is flanked by a female personification seated on a throne suported by the *monti* encircled by crowns and a fan design, and surmounted by an angel's face
Center vault	an angel, seen *dal di sotto in su* and seated on a cloud, holds an open book

E. THE WESTERN LOGGIA EXTENSION

West lunette	"SIXTVS. V. PO.M.," fan design with putti holding wreathes and *grotteschi*
East lunette	stairway arch (from, or to, *piano nobile*)
South cove	Landscape in oval "frame" flanked by two putti in a hexagonal frame, each surmounted by a personification
East cove	Landscape in oval "frame" flanked by two putti in a hexagonal frame, each surmounted by a personification
North cove	Landscape in oval "frame" flanked by two putti in a hexagonal frame, each surmounted by a personification
West cove	Landscape in oval "frame" flanked by two putti in a hexagonal frame, each surmounted by a personification [there are four hexagonal *"quadri"* in toto]
Center vault	*Monti* alternating with lion's heads encircle a star
West lunette	*Stigmatization of Saint Francis* #1 fig. 145
East lunette	stairway arch (to, or from, *terzo piano*)
South cove	Landscape in oval "frame" flanked by two putti in a hexagonal frame, each surmounted by a personification

East cove	Landscape in oval "frame" flanked by two putti in a hexagonal frame, each surmounted by a personification
North cove	Landscape in oval "frame" flanked by two putti in a hexagonal frame, each surmounted by a personification
West cove	Landscape in oval "frame" flanked by two putti in a hexagonal frame, each surmounted by a personification [there are four hexagonal "*quadri*" *in toto*]
Center vault	*Monti* alternating with lion's heads encircle a star
West lunette	*Francis receives Official Sanction to create the Order of the Friars Minor by Pope Honorius III #2* fig. 139
East lunette	*Birth of Saint Francis #VII* fig. 138
South cove	reclining figure surmounts two putti and both are flanked by *grotteschi* of putti with fiery urns
East cove	triumphal arch formed of *grotteschi* houses a personification holding a cornucopia
North cove	reclining figure surmounts two putti and both are flanked by *grotteschi* of putti with fiery urns
West cove	triumphal arch formed of *grotteschi* houses a personification fig. 140
Center vault	four putti hold a wreath encircling a star
Band separating vaults	Two narrow bands flank a central one containing Sixtine devices. These smaller bands are populated by four personifications and a central design comprised of lion's heads, *monti*, pears and a star at center. This same configuration is continued on all remaining narrow bands of the western loggia extension.
West end	"Obelisk and column" device housed within a cartouche supported by and supporting putti, with the *anima*: GLORIAM DEI EXALTAT GLORY OF GOD IS EXALTED fig. 137
East end	"Obelisk and column" device housed within a cartouche supported by and supporting putti, with the *anima*: RELIGIO MIRANDA TRIVNPHAT THE GLORIOUS RELIGION TRIUMPHS fig. 137
West lunette	Stuccoed *stemma* of Sixtus V with fan design, surmounted by two putti holding a wreath inscribed with the following verse from Psalm XLIV: 8 : DILEXISTI IVSTITIAM THOU HAST LOVED JUSTICE fig. 142-143
East lunette	*Francis is received by Pope Innocent III #V*, surmounted by two putti holding papal keys, crossed by the following verse from Psalm XLIV: VNXIT TE DEVS GOD HATH ANOINTED THEE fig. 141
South cove	"lion in profile" device within a rondel, and flanked by *grotteschi*; the *anima* is no longer extant fig. 144
East cove	"lion in profile" device within a rondel, and flanked by *grotteschi*; the *anima* is no longer extant fig. 144
North cove	"lion in profile" device within a rondel, and flanked by *grotteschi*; the *anima* is no longer extant fig. 144

West cove		"lion in profile" device within a rondel, and flanked by *grotteschi*; the *anima* is no longer extant fig. 144
Center vault		fan design
South lunette		now empty

F. THE SALA DEGLI OBELISCHI - fig. 67

1.	A	West cove *Trajanic Column with Saint Peter* fig. 68
2.	B	East cove *Antonine Column with Saint Paul* fig. 69
3.	C	South cove *Obelisk of San Giovanni in Laterano* fig. 70
4.	D	North cove *Obelisk of San Pietro in Vaticano* fig. 71
5.	E	North cove *Obelisk of Santa Maria Maggiore* fig. 72
6.	F	South cove *Obelisk of Santa Croce in Gerusalemme* fig. 73
7.	G	Center vault Two angels bearing Sixtine *stemma* surmounted by two crossed keys and papal tiara. fig. 74
8.	H	South-West angle Personification: *World Dominion* fig. 75
9.	I	South-West angle Personification: *Knowledge of the True God* fig. 75
10.	J	South-West angle Personification: *Devotion* fig. 75
11.	K	North-West angle Personification: *Faith* fig. 76
12.	L	North-West angle Personification: *Law of Grace* fig. 76 On her left knee she supports a book with the inscription from John I: 1: IN PRINCIPIO ERAT VERBVM ET VERBVM ERAT APVD DEVM ET DEVS ERAT VERBVM POGERAT IN PRINCIPIO APVD DEV IN THE BEGINNING THERE WAS THE WORD AND THE WORD WAS WITH GOD AND THE WORD WAS GOD

13.	M	North-West angle Personification: *Eternity of the Roman Catholic Church* fig. 76
14.	N	North-East angle Personification: *Gratitude* fig. 77
15.	O	North-East angle Personification: *Christian Obedience* fig. 77
16.	P	North-East angle Personification: *Magnificence* fig. 77
17.	Q	South-East angle Personification: *Oblation* fig. 78
18.	R	South-East angle Personification: *Prayer* fig. 78
19.	S	South-East angle Personification: *Religion* fig. 78
20.	T	West vault "Lion in profile" device with the *anima* from the Proverbs of Solomon XXXVIII: 1 (fig. 79): IVSTVS VT LEO CONFIDENS HE IS JUST AS THE LION IS BOLD
21.	U	East vault "Lion in profile" device with the *anima* from Amos III: 8 (fig. 80): SI RVGIET QVIS NON TIMEBIT IF HE ROARS, WHO WILL NOT FEAR?
22.	V	North cove Personification amidst *grotteschi*: *Devotion* fig. 81
23.	W	South cove Personification amidst *grotteschi*: *Justice* fig. 82

G. THE SALONE DEI PAPI - figs. 41-45

| 24. | A | South wall
Saint Peter
fig. 54
S. PETRVS PRIMVS IESV CHRISTI VICARIVS PRIMVM HIE-
ROSOLYMIS CONCILIVM CELEBRAVIT

SAINT PETER, FIRST VICAR OF CHRIST, CELEBRATED THE FIRST
COUNCIL OF JERUSALEM |
| 25. | a | South wall
Medallion of Saint Peter
fig. 55 |

26.	B	West wall *Saint Linus I* S. LINVS I. PP. II. SANCIVIT VT MVLIER NON NISI VELATO CAPITE ECCLESIAM INGREDERETVR SAINT LINUS I, THE SECOND POPE, ORDAINED THAT A WOMAN SHOULD NOT ENTER THE CHURCH EXCEPT WITH HER HEAD COVERED
27.	C	West wall *Saint Sixtus I* S. SIXTVS I. PP. VIII. DECREVIT VT IN MISSA CANTARETVR SANCTVS SAINT SIXTUS I, THE EIGHTH POPE, DECREED THAT THE *SANCTUS* SHOULD BE SUNG DURING MASS
28.	c	West wall Medallion of Saint Sixtus I
29.	D	West wall *Saint Telesphorus I* S. TELESPHORVS I. PP. IX. INSTITVIT VT IN DIE NATIVITATIS DOMINI TRES MISSAE CELEBRARENTVR ET GLORIA IN EXCELSIS CANTARETVR SAINT TELESPHORUS I, THE NINTH POPE, ESTABLISHED THAT ON THE BIRTHDAY OF OUR LORD, THREE MASSES SHOULD BE CELEBRATED AND THE *GLORIA* SUNG
30.	d	West wall Medallion of Saint Telesphorus I
31.	E	West wall *Saint Hyginus I* S. HYGINVS I. PP. X. COMPATREM ET COMMATREM IN BAPTISMO ADHIBENDOS DECREVIT SAINT HYGINUS, THE TENTH POPE, DECREED THAT ONES GODFATHER [GODMOTHER] SHOULD BE SUMMONED TO A BAPTISM
32.	e	West wall Medallion of Saint Hyginus I
33.	F	West wall *Saint Pius I* S. PIVS I. PP. XI. SANCIVIT VT PASCHA DIE DOMINICA CELEBRARETVR SAINT PIUS I, THE ELEVENTH POPE, ORDAINED THAT EASTER SHOULD BE CELEBRATED ON THE LORD'S DAY
34.	f	West wall Medallion of Saint Pius I
35.	G	North wall *Saint Anicetus I* S. ANICETVS I. PP. XII. INSTITVIT VT ARCHIEPISCOPVS AB OMNIBVS SVFFRAGANEIS ET EPISCOPVS A TRIBVS EPISCOPIS CONSECRARETVR SAINT ANICETUS I, THE TWELFTH POPE, ESTABLISHED THAT THE ARCHBISHOP SHOULD BE CONSECRATED BY ALL THE SUFFRAGENS AND A BISHOP BY THREE [OTHER] BISHOPS

36.	g	North wall Medallion of Saint Anicetus I
37.	H	North wall *Saint Soterus I* S. SOTERVS I. PP. XIII. DECREVIT VT SACRATAE DEO VIRGINES SACRA VASA NON TANGERENT SAINT SOTERUS I, THE THIRTEENTH POPE, DECREED THAT NUNS SHOULD NOT TOUCH THE SACRED VESSELS
38.	h	North wall Medallion of Saint Soterus I
39.	I	East wall *Saint Eleuterius I* fig. 58 S. ELEVTERIVS I. PP. XIIII. BRITANIAM INSVLAM LVCII REGIS ROGATV PER FVGACIVM ET DAMIANVM LEGATOS FIDEI SACRIS INSTITVIT SAINT ELEUTERIUS I, THE FOURTEENTH POPE, ESTABLISHED THE ISLAND OF BRITAIN AT THE REQUEST OF KING LUKE BY MEANS OF THE ENVOYS FUGACIUM AND DAMIANUM IN THE RITES OF THE FAITH
40.	J	East wall *Saint Victor I* S. VICTOR I. PP. XV. SANCIVIT VT NECESSITATE VRGENTE QVISQVE SIVE IN FLVMINE SIVE IN FONTE SIVE IN MARI BAPTISMVM SVSCIPERE POSSIT SAINT VICTOR I, THE FIFTEENTH POPE, SANCTIONED THAT IN URGENT NECESSITY ANYONE MIGHT UNDERTAKE BAPTISM WHETHER IN A RIVER OR A SPRING OR IN THE SEA
41.	j	East wall Medallion of Saint Victor I
42.	K	East wall *Saint Zepherinus I* fig. 59 S. ZEPHERINVS I. PP. XVI. DECREVIT VT REM DIVINAM FACIENTI EPISCOPO SACERDOTES OMNES ASTARENT SAINT ZEPHERINUS I, THE SIXTEENTH POPE, DECREED THAT WHEN A BISHOP WAS CONDUCTING A SERVICE [MASS] ALL PRIESTS SHOULD STAND BY [ASSIST]
43.	L	East wall *Saint Callistus I* S. CALISTVS I. PP. XVII. INSTITVIT IEIVNIVM QVATVOR TEMPORVM. ECCLESIAM SANCTAE MARIAE TRANSTYBERIM ET IN VIA APPIA COEMETERIVM AEDIFICAVIT SAINT CALLISTUS I, THE SEVENTEENTH POPE, ESTABLISHED A FAST AT FOUR SEASONS. HE BUILT THE CHURCH OF SANTA MARIA TRASTEVERE AND A CEMETERY IN THE APPIAN WAY
44.	l	East wall Medallion of Saint Callistus I
450.	M	East wall *Saint Urbanus I* fig. 60

213

S. VRBANVS I. PP. XVIII. VASA SACRA EX ARGENTO AVRO CONFICI
ADHIBERIQVE AD DEI CVLTVM DECREVIT

SAINT URBANUS I, THE EIGHTEENTH POPE, DECREED THAT
HOLY VESSELS SHOULD BE MADE OF SILVER AND GOLD FOR THE
WORSHIP OF GOD

| 46. | N | East wall |
| | | *Saint Pontianus I* |

S. PONTIANVS I. PP. XIX. IN SARDINIA OB PERPETVAM FIDEI
TVENDAE CONSTANTIAM RELEGATVS OBIIT. ET ROMAM FABIA-
NO PONTIFICE CVRANTE DELATVS IN COEMETERIO CALISTI SE-
PELITVR

SAINT PONTIANUS I, THE NINETEENTH POPE, DIED HAVING BEEN
EXILED TO SARDINIA ON ACCOUNT OF HIS UNDYING LOYALTY TO
THE FAITH. HIS BODY WAS CARRIED TO ROME BY POPE FABIA-
NUS AND BURIED IN THE CEMETERY OF CALLISTUS

| 47. | n | East wall |
| | | Medallion of Saint Pontianus I |

48.	O	East wall
		Saint Antherus I
		fig. 61

S. ANTHERVS I. PP. XX. SANCIVIT VT SANCTORVM MARTYRVM AC-
TA A NOTARIIS CONSCRIBERENTVR

SAINT ANTHERUS I, THE TWENTIETH POPE, ORDAINED THAT THE
ACTS OF THE HOLY MARTYRS SHOULD BE RECORDED BY
SCRIBES

| 49. | P | East wall |
| | | *Saint Fabianus I* |

S. FABIANVS I. PP. XXI. INSTITVIT SEPTEM REGIONES IN VRBE
TOTIDEMQVE DIACONOS QVI NOTARIIS PRAEESSENT VT SANC-
TORVM MARTYRVM RES GESTAS CONQVIRERENT

SAINT FABIANUS I, THE TWENTY-FIRST POPE, ESTABLISHED SEV-
EN DISTRICTS IN THE CITY AND AS MANY DEACONS TO SUPER-
VISE THE SCRIBES IN ORDER TO INVESTIGATE THE ACHIEVE-
MENTS OF THE HOLY MARTYRS

| 50. | p | East wall |
| | | Medallion of Saint Fabianus I |

51.	Q	East wall
		Saint Cornelius I
		fig. 62

S. CORNELIVS I. PP. XXII. CORPORA SANCTORVM APOSTOLORVM
PETRI ET PAVLI E CATACVMBIS LVCINAE MATRONAE SANCTISSI-
MAE ROGATV AD BASILICAM B. PETRO DICATAM TRANSTVLIT

SAINT CORNELIUS I, THE TWENTY-SECOND POPE, TRANSFERRED
THE BODIES OF THE HOLY APOSTLES PETER AND PAUL FROM
THE CATACOMBS AT THE REQUEST OF THE DEVOUT MATRON LU-
CINA TO THE BASILICA DEDICATED TO ST. TER

| 52. | R | East wall |
| | | *Saint Lucius I* |

S. LVCIVS I. PP. XXIII. SANCIVIT VT PRESBYTERI DVO DIACONI
TRES IN OMNI LOCO EPISCOPVM COMITARENTVR IN EIVS VITAE
TESTIMONIVM

SAINT LUCIUS I, THE TWENTY-THIRD POPE, ORDAINED THAT TWO PRESBYTERS AND THREE DEACONS SHOULD ACCOMPANY A BISHOP IN EVERY PLACE AS WITNESS TO HIS LIFE

53.	S	East wall *Saint Sylvester I* fig. 56 S. SILVESTER I. PP. XXXIIII. CONSTANTINVM IMPERATOREM BAP- TIZAVIT ET OECVMENICVM NICAENVM CONC. I. CELEBRAVIT SAINT SYLVESTER I, THE THIRTY-FOURTH POPE, BAPTISED THE EMPEROR CONSTANTINE, AND CELEBRATED THE FIRST OECU- MENICAL COUNCIL OF NICAEA
54.	s	East wall Medallion of Saint Sylvester I fig. 57
55.	X	East wall Inscription: NVTANTES HVMERIS LATERANAS SVSTINET AEDES FRANCISCVS FIDEI FIRMA COLVMNA SACRAE FRANCISCO SIXTVS TENERIS ADDICTVS A BANNIS RESTITVIT LAPSAS AMPLIFICATQ. MAGIS AN MINOR EST VIRTVS QVAM SVSTENTARE LABANTES RVRSVS COLLAPSAS AEDIFICARE DOMOS? FRANCISCUS BEARS THE TOTTERING LATERAN BUILDINGS ON HIS SHOULDERS: A STURDY COLUMN OF HOLY FAITH SIXTUS, BOUND TO FRANCISCUS FROM AN EARLY AGE, RESTORED THE COLLAPSING STRUCTURES AND MAGNIFIED THEM FURTHER. IS HIS VIRTUE NOT POTENT ENOUGH TO SUPPORT CRUMBLING BUILDINGS, AND IF THEY HAVE COLLAPSED, TO ERECT THEM AGAIN?
56.	A¹	South wall *Christ's Investiture to Peter* fig. 63 Beneath this fresco is the inscription, taken from Matthew XVI: 18: TV ES PETRVS ET SVPER HANC PETRAM AEDIFICABO ECCLESIAM MEAM YOU ARE PETER, AND ABOVE THIS ROCK I SHALL BUILD MY CHURCH
57.	B¹	North wall *Christ Appoints Peter Guardian of the Christian Peoples* fig. 64 Beneath this fresco is the inscription, taken from John XXI: 16,17: PASCE OVES MEAS FEED MY SHEEP
58.	1.	South wall *Acqua Felice* fig. 46 SICCA VELVT NILO STAGNANTE AEGYPTVS INVNDAT DVM SOL SIDEREI SIGNA LEONIS HABET SIC QVOQ. MAGNANIMO TERRAS MODERANTE LEONE ARIDA FELICI ROMA REDVNDAT AQVA JUST AS DRY EGYPT IS SOAKED WHEN THE NILE FLOODS WHILE THE SUN HOLDS THE SYMBOLS OF STARRY LEO,

SO ALSO WHEN GREAT HEARTED LEO GOVERNS THE LAND
PARCHED ROME ABOUNDS WITH KINDLY WATER

59.   2.

West wall
Port of Terracina and the Pontine Marsh
fig. 47
CYNTHIVS VT SIXTVM VIDIT SICCARE PALVDES
PALLENTI TALES MISIT AB ORE SONOS
SOL SVVS EST TERRIS QVID EGO MEA LVMINA FVNDAM
NAM MIHI NEC LICVIT QVOD TIBI SIXTE LICET

CYNTHIUS (APOLLO), WHEN HE SAW SIXTUS DRAIN THE SWAMPS,
UTTERED FROM PALE LIPS WORDS OF THIS SORT:
'THE EARTH HAS ITS SUN: WHY SHOULD I PUT FORTH MY RAYS?
FOR WHAT IS GRANTED TO YOU, SIXTUS, WAS NOT WITHIN MY
POWER.'

60.   3.

West wall
Treasure at Castel Sant'Angelo
fig. 32
AVRVM LEGE SVA PLATO QVONDAM EIECIT AB VRBE
LEGE SVA ID SIXTVS CONDIT IN ARCE PATER,
SCILICET AVRVM ESSE EXCIDIVM PLATO CENSVIT VRBIS,
VRBIS PRAESIDIVM SIXTVS ID ESSE PROBAT

PLATO BY HIS LAW ONCE BANISHED GOLD FROM HIS CITY
BY HIS LAW FATHER SIXTUS STORES IT IN THE CITADEL
INDEED PLATO DECLARED GOLD TO BE THE RUIN OF A CITY
SIXTUS PROVES IT TO BE THE SAFEGUARD OF HIS CITY

61.   4.

West wall
Vatican Library
fig. 48
NON SAT ERAT SIXTO CLASSEM, NVMMOSQ. PARARE,
EXTRVCTA EST ETIAM BIBLIOTHECA SIBI,
SCILICET VT PACIS BELLORVM, ET TEMPORA CVRET,
ATQ. VTRVMQ. OBEAT MARTIS, ET ARTIS OPVS

IT WAS NOT ENOUGH FOR SIXTUS TO PREPARE A FLEET AND FI-
NANCES
A LIBRARY HAS ALSO BEEN BUILT FOR HIM,
SO THAT HE MAY PROVIDE FOR TIMES OF PEACE AND WAR
AND THAT HE MIGHT PERFORM EITHER TASK - THE TASK OF
WAR AND ART

62.   5.

West wall
League of Christian Princes
fig. 35
DISIVNCTAS SIXTVS DVM IVNGIT FOEDERE GENTES,
ET DICTIS MVLCET PECTORA DVRA PIIS,
IVSSA DEI AVT PERFERT, ANIMAS AVT EVOCAT ORCO,
MERCVRIVS VERVS DICIER ANNE POTEST?

WHILE SIXTUS JOINS DIVIDED PEOPLES BY TREATY
AND SOFTENS CRUEL HEARTS WITH PIOUS WORDS,
HE EITHER CONVEYS THE COMMANDS OF GOD OR SUMMONS
SOULS FROM HADES
CAN HE BE CALLED THE TRUE MERCURY?

63.   6.

West wall
Harbour of Civitavecchia
fig. 49
VNDAE SVNT LIQVIDE, SOLIDVM SED MARMOR HABETVR,
MARMOR VI TRAHITVR, SPONTE SED VNDA FLVIT.

QVID MIRVM EST IGITVR DVCAT SI FORNICE RIVOS,
QVANDO ETIAM SIXTVS MARMORA VASTA TRAHITI?

WATERS ARE FLUID, BUT MARBLE IS CONSIDERED SOLID
MARBLE IS DRAWN BY FORCE, BUT THE FLOOD FLOWS FREELY,
WHAT WONDER IS IT THEREFORE IF SIXTUS GUIDES STREAMS
ON ARCHES
SINCE HE ALSO MOVES VAST [BLOCKS OF] MARBLE?

64.	7.	

North wall
Monte Cavallo with the new streets, palace and Dioscuri transported and restored by Sixtus V
fig. 50
STRVCTA DOMVS, DVCTI FONTES, VIA APERTA, CABALLI
TRANSPOSITI, ATQ. VNO EST AREA STRATA LOCO,
O FELIX NIMIRVM VIA, EQVI, DOMVS, AREA, FONTES,
DVM VIVENT VATIS CARMINA, SIXTE, TVI

THE BUILDING HAS BEEN ERECTED, THE FOUNTAINS CONDUCT-
ED,
THE ROADWAY OPENED, THE HORSES MOVED, AND THE REGION
LAID OUT FLAT IN ONE PLACE
O ROADWAY TOO FORTUNATE, HORSES, BUILDING, REGION,
FOUNTAINS:
WHILE THE SONGS OF YOUR POET, SIXTUS, WILL ENDURE!

65.	8.	

East wall
City of Montalto
fig. 51
CVM TE SIXTE OLIM SVB LVMINIS EDIDIT ORAS
PATRIA DICTA FVIT TVNC VERA PARENS.
SED MODO DVM FIRMIS CIRCVNDAS MOENIBVS ILLAM,
QVIS PATRIAE VERVM TE NEGET ESSE PATREM?

WHEN THE FATHERLAND ONCE BROUGHT YOU FORTH UNDER
THE REGIONS OF LIGHT, SIXTUS,
IT WAS THEN CALLED YOUR TRUE PARENT.
BUT NOW, WHEN YOU SURROUND IT WITH STRONG WALLS
WHO WOULD DENY THAT YOU ARE THE REAL FATHER OF THE
FATHERLAND?

66.	9.	

East wall
Extirpation of the Bandits
fig. 29
DVM SIBI COMMISSVM SIXTVS TVTATVR OVILE
PRAEDONES MIRA PERCVLIT ARTE LVPOS.
PAXQ. PVDORQ. VIGENT VNA: NAM TEMPORE EODEM
PERCVLIT ILLE LVPOS, PERCVLIT ILLE LVPAS.

WHILE SIXTUS GUARDED THE FLOCK ENTRUSTED TO HIM
HE SUBDUES THE SCAVENGING WOLVES WITH MARVELLOUS
SKILL
PEACE AND MODESTY THRIVE TOGETHER: FOR AT THE SAME
TIME
HE TAMES THE HE-WOLVES, AND HE TAMES THE SHE-WOLVES

67.	10.	

East wall
Abundance created by Sixtus V
fig. 26
VESANA HEBRAEAE COMPRESSIT MVRMVRA GENTIS
SVPPEDITANS PLENA DVX ALIMENTA MANV,
SIC QVERVLAE PLEBI SIXTVS FRVMENTA MINISTRANS
COMPRESSIT MOSES MVRMVRA PRISSA NOVVS

HE [MOSES] SUPPRESSES THE INSANE MUTTERINGS OF THE HE-
BREW RACE
A LEADER OFFERING SUSTENANCE WITH GENEROUS HAND
SO SIXTUS, A NEW MOSES MINISTERING FOOD TO THE COM-
PLAINING MOB,
SUPPRESSED ANCIENT GRUMBLINGS

68.   11.   East wall
Holy House of Loreto
fig. 52
FOETAM VRBEM POPVLIS PICENO IN LITTORE SIXTVS
MOENIBVS INCINXIT, PONTIFICEMQ. DEDIT,
SIC TENEROS SEPTIS INCLVDIT VILLICVS AGNOS
CVSTODEMQ. ILLIS DONAT HABERE SVVM

SIXTUS ENCLOSED THE DECAYING CITY IN THE PICENE SHORE
WITH WALLS,
AND GAVE THE PEOPLE A CHIEF PRIEST
SO THE FARMER ENCLOSES TENDER LAMBS IN HIS FOLDS
AND GRANTS THAT THEY HAVE THEIR GUARDIAN

H. THE SALONE DEGLI IMPERATORI

69.   North wall
Constantine the Great
An emperor stands beneath an arch. He holds horse's reins in both
hands and in his left hand he also holds a sword. Above his head is his
Latin name, CONSTANTINVS MAGNIVS, and, beneath his feet, the fol-
lowing inscription:
PRIMVS / IMPERATORVM / CHRISTIANAE / FIDEI / PROPAGATOR

CONSTANTINE THE GREAT, FIRST OF THE EMPERORS TO BE A
PROPAGATOR OF THE CHRISTIAN FAITH

70.   East wall
Theodosius
An emperor stands beneath an arch. Both of his hands are folded on his
chest. A sword hangs from his left side. Above his head is his Latin
name, THEODOSIVS, and, beneath his feet, the following inscription:
VNAM SE FIDEM SEQVI, / QVAM S. PETRVS AP. / ROMANIS TRADI-
DIT APVD CVNCTOS POPVLOS / PROFESSVS EST

THEODOSIUS PROCLAIMED AMONG ALL PEOPLES THAT HE FOL-
LOWED ONE FAITH THE ONE WHICH SAINT PETER THE APOSTLE
HANDED DOWN TO THE ROMANS

71.   East wall
Arcadius
An emperor stands beneath an arch. He leans his right hand on an object
and rests his left hand on his hip. Above his head is his Latin name, AR-
CADIVS, and, beneath his feet, the following inscription:
PERSIS PER CRVCEM SVPERATIS, / AVREAM MONETAM / CVM SI-
GNO CRVCIS / EXCVDI IVSSIT

ARCADIUS ORDERED GOLDEN COINAGE TO BE STRUCK WITH
THE SIGN OF THE CROSS WHEN THE PERSIANS WERE SUBDUED
BY THE CROSS

72.   East wall
Onorius
An emperor stands beneath an arch. He points to a dragon with his right
hand. A sword hangs at his left side. Above his head is his Latin name,
ONORIVS, and, beneath his feet, the following inscription:
AFRICANOS / HAERETICOS / COERCVIT
ONORIUS SUBDUED THE AFRICAN HERETICS

218

73.

East wall
Theodosius
An emperor stands beneath an arch. He holds a sword in his right hand and a bookstand in his left. Above his head is his Latin name, THEODOSIVS, and, beneath his feet, the following inscription:
EXIMIVM / CHRISTIANAE PIETATIS / IN EPHESINA / SYNODO FOVENDA / SPECIMEN PRAEBVIT

THEODOSIUS OFFERED A NOBLE EXAMPLE OF CHRISTIAN PIETY IN SPONSORING THE COUNCIL OF EPHESUS

74.

East wall
Valentinianus
An emperor stands beneath an arch. He holds a temple with both hands. Above his head is his Latin name, VALENTINIANVS, and, beneath his feet, the following inscription:
ARGENTEVM / LATERAN. ECCL. FASTIGIVM / A BARBARIS EREPTVM MAGNO SVMPTV REFECIT

VALENTINIANUS REBUILT AT GREAT EXPENSE THE SILVERED ROOF OF THE LATERAN CHURCH SNATCHED AWAY BY THE BARBARIANS

75.

South wall
Marcianus
An emperor stands beneath an arch. He holds a book stand surmounted with the cross and supporting what must certainly be the Bible. Above his head is his Latin name, MARCIANVS, and, beneath his feet, the following inscription:
OB SINGVLARE / CATH. FID. STVDIVM / A CHAL. CONC. / NOV. CONSTANTIN. / EST APPELLATVS

MARCIANUS WAS NAMED THE NEW CONSTANTINE BY THE COUNCIL OF CHALCEDON ON ACCOUNT OF HIS SPECIAL ZEAL FOR THE CATHOLIC FAITH

76.

South wall
Leo
An emperor stands beneath an arch. He holds a cathedra with both hands. A sword with a lion's head hangs at his left side. Above his head is his Latin name, LEO, and, beneath his feet, the following inscription:
A DEO ET S. LEONE PP. / ROBORATVS / IN CHALCED. CON DEFENSIONE PERSEVERAVIT

LEO STAYED STEADFAST IN HIS DEFENSE AT THE COUNCIL OF CHALCEDON STRENGTHENED BY GOD AND SAINT LEO, THE POPE

77.

West wall
Iustinus
An emperor stands beneath an arch. He holds a tablet with the representation of a kneeling figure and a standing figure. Above his head is his Latin name, IVSTINVS, and, beneath his feet, the following inscription:
AD. S. IO PP. ET MART. PEDES / XPI [CHRISTI] VICARIVM AGNOSCENS / SVMMA CVM HVMILITATE / PROCVBVIT

IUSTINUS KNELT WITH UTMOST HUMILITY AT THE FEET OF SAINT JOHN, POPE AND MARTYR, ACKNOWLEDGING THE POPE THE VICAR OF CHRIST

78.

West wall
Iustinianus
An emperor stands beneath an arch. He holds an object on a shield with a lion decorating it. Above his head is his Latin name, IVSTINIANVS, and, beneath his feet, the following inscription:

S. AGAPITO. PP. OBTEMPERANS / EGREGIVM ERGA SEDEM AP. OBEDIENTIAE / POSTERIS RELIQVIT / EXEMPLVM

IUSTINIANUS LEFT TO POSTERITY A NOBLE EXAMPLE OF OBEDIENCE TOWARDS THE APOSTOLIC SEE IN SUBMITTING TO SAINT AGAPETUS, THE POPE

79.

West wall
Tuberius
An emperor stands beneath an arch. He points to the right with his left hand. A sword hangs at his left side. Behind him is a crocodile and sheafs of wheat. Above his head is his Latin name, TVBERIVS, and, beneath his feet, the following inscription:
VRBEM ROMAM / LONGOBARDORVM OBSIDIONE / OPPRESSAM LIBERAVIT

TUBERIUS FREED THE CITY OF ROME BELEAGUERED BY THE SIEGE
OF THE LOMBARDS

80.

West wall
Mauritius
An emperor stands beneath an arch. He holds a sword in his right hand. He gives a coin (?) to an old woman with a cane on his left. Above his head is his Latin name, MAVRITIVS, and, beneath his feet, the following inscription:
CVM IMPERII GLORIA / ITA PIETATEM CONIVNXIT, / VT A S. GREGORIO PAPA / CELEBRARI MERVERIT

MAURITIUS SO JOINED PIETY WITH IMPERIAL GLORY THAT HE DESERVED TO BE HONOURED BY SAINT GREGORY, THE POPE

81.

West wall
Phocas
An emperor stands beneath an arch. He holds a book, keys and the papal tiara with both hands. A sword hangs at his left. Above his head is his Latin name, PHOCAS, and, beneath his feet, the following inscription:

SVMMAM R. ECC. POTESTATEM / A CHRISTO TRADITAM / VT OMNES VENERARENTVR / EDIXIT

PHOCAS DECREED THAT EVERYONE SHOULD VENERATE THE EXALTED POWER OF THE ROMAN CHURCH CONFERRED BY CHRIST

82.

North wall
Heraclius
An emperor stands beneath an arch. He holds a cross and a cloth in his right hand. Behind him is his imperial crown. Above his head is his Latin name, HERACLIVS, and, beneath his feet, the following inscription:
CRVCEM A PERSIS / [RECEP. IN CALVARIAE MONT. HVMERIS] / REPORTAVIT

HERACLIUS CARRIED BACK TO THE MOUNT OF CALVARY THE CROSS RECAPTURED FROM THE PERSIANS ON HIS SHOULDERS

83.

South wall
The Church adored by Emperors
IMPP. CHRISTIANI / SVBMISSIS FASCIBVS / SACROSANCTAM / ROMANAM ECCLESIAM / SVPPLICES VENERANTVR, / ET COLVNT

CHRISTIAN EMPERORS, THEIR FACES LOWERED,
VENERATE AND CHERISH THE SACRED ROMAN CHURCH AS SUPPLIANTS

84.   North wall
Sixtus V receives the medals found in 1587 and a document listing them
fig. 147
SIXTVS V. CHRISTIANOR. IMPP. NVMISMATA
CRVCIS IMAGINE INSIGNITA,
IN AVLAE LATERANEN. PARIETIS PERVETVSTI
DEMOLITIONE DIVINITVS A SE REPERTA,
REGIBVS, AC PRINCIPIBVS VIRIS
CVM PRIVILEGIIS ET INDVLGENTIIS AMPLISSIMIS ROGAVIT

SIXTUS V GAVE OUT TO KINGS AND LEADING MEN,
ALONG WITH PRIVILEGES AND MOST GENEROUS INDULGENCES
THE COINS OF CHRISTIAN EMPERORS MARKED WITH THE SIGN
OF THE CROSS, WHICH HE, BY DIVINE INSPIRATION, DISCOV-
ERED IN THE DEMOLITION OF THE VERY ANCIENT WALL OF THE
LATERAN PALACE

I. THE ANTICAPPELLA

85.   South cove
Landscape

86.   South cove
"Decorative figure"

87.   South cove
"Decorative figure"

88.   North cove
Landscape

89.   North cove
"Decorative figure"

90.   North cove
"Decorative figure"

91.   West cove
Landscape

92.   East cove
Landscape

93.   Center vault
Personification: *Sixtine Abundance* or *Prosperity*
fig. 17

94.   Beneath center vault
oval rendered in sepia with "decorative figure"
An old woman reclines.

95.   Above center vault
oval rendered in sepia with "decorative figure"
An old man reclines.

96   South-West angle
Personification
A young woman is seated within a frame. In her left hand she holds a sac, and in her right, a pole. She wears a garland of flowers on her head.

97.   North-West angle
Personification: *Agape Love* (?)
A matron is seated within a frame. Her left hand is on her heart. In her right hand she holds a heart. On her head there is a fluttering veil.

221

98.

North-East angle
Personification: *Eternity*
A matron is seated within a frame. She looks upwards. In her left hand, she holds a cornucopia, and in her right hand, a pole. Beneath her left foot is a globe.

99.

South-East angle
Personification: *Music of the Spheres* or *Prophecy* (?)
A woman is seated within a frame. She holds a woodwind instrument in her left hand. She points upwards with her right arm and right index finger.

100.

West cove
"Decorative figure"
A figure stands and holds her right hand on her hip. She holds a pole in her left hand.

101.

West cove
Personification: *Abundance* or *Peace* (?)
A woman is seated beneath a garlanded arch. In her left hand she holds a caduceus and in her right hand, a goblet. There is a garland of flowers on her head. One of her breasts is bare.

102.

West cove
"Decorative figure"
A standing figure holds a pole in her right hand. On her head she wears a helmet.

103.

West cove
"Decorative figure"
A standing figure is represented here, however, the objects which she holds are unidentifiable, due to the condition of the fresco.

104.

West cove
Personification
A woman is seated beneath a garlanded arch. She wears a crown on her head, and holds a papal tiara with both hands.

105.

West cove
"Decorative figure"
A standing figure holds a sceptre in her left hand, and her skirt with her right. On her head she wears a turban-like covering.

106.

East cove
"Decorative figure"
A standing figure points upwards with her right arm and index finger. She holds a palm branch in her left hand, and wears a jewel on her forehead.

107.

East cove
Personification
A woman is seated beneath a garlanded arch. She has a turban-like covering on her head. Her left hand is on her breast. She holds a sceptre in her right hand. Her right foot rests on a dice.

108.

East cove
"Decorative figure"
A standing figure points upwards with her right hand and index finger. She holds an object directed downwards in her left hand.

109.

East cove
"Decorative figure"
As is the case with "Q," it is extremely difficult to determine what this standing figure holds in her hand(s).

110. East cove
      Personification
      A young woman is seated beneath a garlanded arch. She wears a turban-like covering on her head. In her left hand she holds a sceptre, and in her right, an open book.

111. East cove
      "Decorative figure"
      A standing figure holds a spear in her left hand.

J. THE CAPPELLA PAPALE

112. Center vault
      Ascension [Mark XVI: 19; Luke XXIV: 6;
      Acts I: 9-11; II: 32]
      fig. 16

113. South cove
      Resurrection [John XX: 1-9]

114. North cove
      Apparition to Mary Magdalen [John XX: 14-18]

115. West cove
      Apparition to Saint Thomas [John XX: 24-29]

116. East cove
      Apparition to the Apostles

117. South-East angle
      Saint Matthew
      A man is seated in a hexagonal frame. He holds a book on his knee with his left hand, and a quill in his right. A man stands behind him to his left.

118. East cove
      Saint Gregory the Great
      A man is seated. He wears the papal tiara. In his left hand he holds a book, and with his right, he gestures upwards at a dove (the Holy Ghost), situated to his left. A number of books are placed to his right, including an open book with writing (only the first letters of each paragraph are visible, as follows: C, E, Q, O, C, A).

119. South cove
      Doctor of the Church
      A bearded man wearing a bishop's mitre is seated. He holds a closed book in his left hand, and points to the book with his right. There is an open book to his left.

120. North-West angle
      Saint Mark
      A man is seated within a hexagonal frame. He holds a book with both hands at his right side. A lion sits at his right.

121. West cove
      Doctor of the Church
      A seated man wears a bishop's mitre. He holds a closed book in his left hand, and points to the book with his right. At his left there are a number of books, including one opened on which the first letters of each paragraph are legible: E, C and F.

122. North cove
      Saint Thomas
      A bearded man is seated. In his left hand he holds a round temple (a church). In his right hand he holds an object from which there emit rays

into the temple door. At his right there is an open book in which the first letters of each paragraph are visible: C, F, A and C.

123.   North-East angle
Saint Luke
A man is seated within a hexagonal frame. He holds a closed book in both hands, and at his right there is an ox.

124.   North cove
Doctors of the Church
Two men are seated. Both are bearded and both wear a bishop's mitre. The man seated in the foreground holds an orb in his right hand, and in his left, a closed book.

125.   East cove
Doctors of the Church
Two men are seated, both are bearded, and both wear bishop's mitres. The man in the foreground looks down as he writes in a book. The man in the background holds a closed book in his right hand, and looks at the man engaged in writing.

126.   South-West angle
Saint John the Evangelist
A man is seated within a hexagonal frame. He points to a passage written on a tablet at his left, while looking towards the eagle at his right.

127.   South cove
Doctor of the Church
A man with a gray beard is seated. He reads a book avidly. At his left is an open book.

128.   West cove
Doctor of the Church
A bearded man wearing a bishop's mitre is seated. He holds an open book with both hands. At his right there are a number of books, including an open book whose letters, unfortunately, are not legible.

K. THE SALA DI SAMUELE - fig. 84

129.   A   North cove
Samuel being taken to the Temple to Take a Vow
[I Kings I: 24-28]
fig. 85

130.   B   East cove
Samuel hears a Miraculous Voice in the Temple [I Kings III]
fig. 86

131.   C   South cove
Samuel erects the "Stone of Help" [I Kings VII: 12]
fig. 87

132.   D   West cove
Samuel anoints Saul [I Kings X: 1-8]
fig. 88

133.   E   Center vault
Stemma of Sixtus V
fig. 89

134.   F   West cove
Personification: *Religion*
fig. 90

135.	G	West cove Personification: *Charity* fig. 91
136.	H	East cove Personificaton: *Faith* fig. 92
137.	I	East cove Personificaton: *Hope* fig. 93
138.	J	South-West angle Personification: *Good Work* fig. 94
139.	K	North-East angle Personificaton: *Belief* fig. 95 This young woman holds an open book with the word "CREDO," I BELIEVE.
140.	L	North-West angle Personificaton: *Gratitude* fig. 96
141.	M	South-East angle Personification: *Law of Grace* fig. 97

L. THE SALA DI DAVIDE

142.		West cove *Samuel anoints David* [I Kings XVI: 13] fig. 148
143.		South cove *David plays the harp for Saul* [I Kings XVI: 23]
144.		North cove *David hears of Goliath's bravura* [I Kings XVII: 23]
145.		Center vault *David has killed Goliath and is about to decapitate him with his own sword* [I Kings XVII: 49-51]
146.		East cove *David enters Jerusalem with Goliath's head* [I Kings XVII: 54]
147.		West cove Personification: *Justice* A seated woman holds a balance in her left hand and a sword in her right.
148.		North cove Personification: *Fortitude* A seated woman holds a column with both hands. There is a jewel on her forehead. To her left there is a lion.
149.		South cove Personification: *Prudence* A seated woman looks into a mirror held in her right hand.
150.		West cove Personificaton: *Temperance*

A seated woman supports herself with her left arm. She holds a bridle in her right hand.

151. North cove
Personification: *Harmony* (?)
A seated woman holds *fasces* in both hands. There is a jewel on her forehead, and a face on her collar.

152. East cove
Personification: *Truth*
A seated woman holds her right hand on her waist. She holds a torch in her left hand. At her left, behind the torch, is a mask.

153. East cove
Personification: *Devotion*
A seated woman holds a thurible in her left hand, and an incense boat in her right.

154. South cove
Personification: *Religion* (?)
A seated woman holds a mirror outwards with her right hand. She holds a round temple and a pole in her left hand.

155. North-West angle
Genius of Sixtus V
A male figure is dressed in a toga-like garment. He holds a curtain up with his right hand. He holds a laurel wreath with his left hand.

156. North-West angle
Genius of Sixtus V
A male figure is dressed in a toga-like garment. He holds a curtain up with his right hand. He holds a laurel wreath with his left hand.

157. South-West angle
Genius of Sixtus V
A male figure is dressed in a toga-like garment. He holds a curtain up with his right hand. He holds a laurel wreath with his left hand.

158. South-West angle
Genius of Sixtus V
A male figure is dressed in a toga-like garment. He holds a curtain up with his right hand. He holds a laurel wreath with his left hand.

159. North-East angle
Genius of Sixtus V
A male figure is dressed in a toga-like garment. He holds a curtain up with his right hand. He holds a laurel wreath with his left hand.

160. North-East angle
Genius of Sixtus V
A male figure is dressed in a toga-like garment. He holds a curtain up with his right hand. He holds a laurel wreath with his left hand.

161. South-East angle
Genius of Sixtus V
A male figure is dressed in a toga-like garment. He holds a curtain up with his right hand. He holds a laurel wreath with his left hand.

162. South-East angle
Genius of Sixtus V
A male figure is dressed in a toga-like garment. He holds a curtain up with his right hand. He holds a laurel wreath with his left hand.

163. North-West angle
Stemma of Sixtus V crowned by crossed keys and papal tiara.

164.
South-West angle
Stemma of Sixtus V crowned by crossed keys and papal tiara.

165.
North-East angle
Stemma of Sixtus V crowned by crossed keys and papal tiara.

166.
South-East angle
Stemma of Sixtus V crowned by crossed keys and papal tiara.

M. THE SALA DI SALOMONE - fig. 150

167.　A
West cove
Solomon rides to Gihon where he will be anointed King
[III Kings I: 38]
fig. 155
The following inscription is no longer extant:
NON AFFECTATO, SED BONIS OMNIBVS VIRIS LAETITIA
GESTIENTIBVS A VIVENTE PATRE REGNO SIBI TRADITO
ADOLESCENS POTITVR SALOMON.

THE YOUTHFUL SOLOMON RULES THE REALM ENTRUSTED TO
HIM BY THE LIVING FATHER, WHILE ALL GOOD MEN ARE CAR-
RIED AWAY, NOT FALSELY, BUT WITH TRUE DELIGHT.

168.　B
Center vault
God appears to Solomon in his sleep [III Kings III: 5-9]
fig. 156

169.　C
North cove
Judgement of Solomon [III Kings III: 16-28]
fig. 157
The following inscription is no longer extant:
IN FICTAE CRVDELITATIS SPECIE SALOMONIS IVDICIO
QVEM DEVS EXPETITA REPLEVERAT SAPIENTIA
VERA, ET PIA ELVCET IVSTITIA.

IN THE GUISE OF SIMULATED CRUELTY, TRUE AND PIOUS JUS-
TICE SHINES FORTH BY THE JUDGEMENT OF SOLOMON, WHOM
GOD HAD FILLED WITH SOUGHT-FOR WISDOM.

170.　D
South cove
Carrying of the Ark of the Covenant of the Lord out of the City of David [III
Kings VIII: 1-4]
fig. 158
The following inscription is no longer extant:
INTER CANTANTES CHOROS, SACRAS POMPAS, ET MVLTIPLICATA
SACRIFICIA SALOMON IN TEMPLVM A SE MAGNIFICE POSITVM,
ET EXORNATVM ARCAM DOMINI INFERENDAM PROCVRAT.

AMONG THE SINGING CHOIRS, AND THE SACRED PROCESSIONS,
SOLOMON OVERSEES BOTH THE NUMEROUS SACRIFICES AND
THE BEARING OF THE LORD'S TABERNACLE INTO THE TEMPLE
THE TEMPLE MAGNIFICENTLY SITED AND ADORNED BY HIM.

171.　E
East cove
Solomon and the Queen of Sheba [III Kings X: 1-9]
fig. 159
The following inscription is no longer extant:
SALOMONIS SAPIENTIAM, ET FACTA PRAECLARA RVMORE
AC FAMA MVLTO MAIORA SABA EXPERITVR REGINA.

THE SABEAN QUEEN ESSAYS THE WISDOM OF SOLOMON AND
HIS NOBLE DEEDS, GREATLY AUGMENTED BY RUMOUR AND
FAME.

172.	F	North-West angle "Column and obelisk" device, with the *anima*: RELIGIO MIRANDA TRIVMPHAT THE GLORIOUS RELIGION TRIUMPHS fig. 151
173.	G	South-East angle "Column and obelisk" device, with the *anima*: GLORIAM [DEI EX]ALTAT GLORY OF GOD IS EXALTED fig. 152
174.	H	South-West angle "Triple mountain" device, with the *anima* from Psalm CXVIII: 66: SCIENTIAE BONTATIS DISCIPLINAE OF GOODNESS OF WISDOM OF KNOWLEDGE fig. 153
175.	I	North-East angle "Triple mountain" device, with the *anima*: TERNA HAEC TRIPLICI THESE THREE THINGS IN THREEFOLD fig. 154

N. THE SALA D'ELIA

176.		East cove *Elijah reprehends King Acab for his Idolatry* [III Kings XVII: 1]
177.		North cove *Elijah's God lights the offering on Mount Carmel* [III Kings XVIII: 30-38]
178.		South cove *The rain that comes after Elijah's God has lit the offering and King Ahab embarking for Jezreel* [III Kings XVIII: 44-45]
179.		West cove *The Ascension of Elijah* [IV Kings II: 11] fig. 22
180.		Center vault *Elijah and Moses appear in the Transfiguration of Christ* [Matthew XVII: 1-6; Mark IX: 4; Luke IX: 30-31]
181.		East cove Personification: *Chastity* (?) A seated woman looks downward, and holds a sieve in her right hand.
182.		East cove Personification A seated woman holds a sceptre in her left hand, and points upward with her right index finger.
183.		East cove Personification A seated woman holds a veil off her face with her left hand. She rests her right hand on a closed, upright book, and holds an apple. She looks downwards.

184.   East cove
                        Personification: *Triumph of Christianity*
                        A seated woman looks downward at a creature with fangs. In her left
                        hand she holds a cross, and in her right, an orb.

185.   West cove
                        Personification: *Peace* (?)
                        A seated woman looks to her left hand in which she holds olive (?)
                        branches.

186.   West cove
                        Personification: *World Dominion* (?)
                        A seated woman holds a globe in her left hand, and gestures upwards
                        with her right.

187.   West cove
                        Personification: *Extirpation of Heresy* (?)
                        A seated woman has a veil tied on her head. She holds closed books un-
                        der her right arm, and gestures towards burning books at her right side
                        with her left hand. She looks downwards.

188.   West cove
                        Personification: *Charity*
                        A seated woman holds two small boys; one in her lap, and the other at
                        her side.

O. THE SALA DI DANIELE

189.   North cove
                        *A servant puts ashes on the floor of the Temple at Daniel's request and on
                        the witness of King Cyrus of Persia* [Daniel XIV: 13]

190.   East cove
                        *Daniel shows King Cyrus the footprints of the priests, their wives and chil-
                        dren who had entered the Temple clandestinely and eaten the food set out
                        for the idol Baal* [Daniel XIV: 18-19]

191.   South cove
                        *Daniel feeds the "Divine" Serpent cakes of pitch, fat and hair so as
                        to demonstrate that the serpent is not a living god* [Daniel XIV: 26]
                        fig. 23

192.   Center vault
                        Daniel in the lion's den and Habakuk and the Angel bringing Food [Daniel
                        XIV: 35-37]
                        fig. 15

193.   West cove
                        Daniel's Accusors are cast into the Lion's Den and are devoured
                        [Daniel XIV: 41]

194.   North-West angle
                        Personification
                        A young woman is seated. She has a jewel on her forehead and looks to
                        her left. With both hands she holds an ornate vase with two doves kiss-
                        ing on its rim. A crow and a dove stand at her right foot.

195   North-West angle
                        Personification
                        A woman, rendered in sepia, is seated. She looks forlornly downwards.
                        In her right hand she holds a sceptre which she balances on her knee.
                        She holds a globe in her left hand.

196.   North-East angle
Personification
A young woman is seated. She looks at a peacock and a hare to her left. In her left hand she holds a pitcher upside down so that water spills forth, revealing eight insects. She holds an object of red, brown, and yellow coloration that looks like a thunderbolt in black and white reproduction, in her upstretched right hand.

197.   North-East angle
Personification: *Magnificence*
A matronly woman, rendered in sepia, is seated. With both hands she holds a pyramid flanked by two figures and one at its summit. She looks to her right.

198.   South-East angle
Personification: *Extirpation of Heresy*
A woman is seated. She has a jewel on her forehead. In her right hand, which is upraised, she holds a hammer. In her left hand she holds a scroll. Her right foot rests on a mask. Her left foot rests on a bundle of arrows. To her right is a yellow and green striped flag, a trumpet, and other objects of battle. Beneath her left thigh is an animal of indeterminate species.

199.   South-East angle
Personification
An older woman, rendered in sepia, is seated. She looks forlorn and has a veil on her head. She holds a sceptre in her right hand, and keys (?) in her left.

200.   South-West angle
Personification
A seated woman wears a plumed helmet and carries an unsheathed sword in her right hand. In her left hand she holds a shield at her back, to reveal weapons. A wolf kills a deer at her side.

201.   South-West angle
Personification: *Eternity* (?)
A seated woman, rendered in sepia, has a veil on her head. She looks upwards. In her left hand she holds a serpent, and in her right, a ring (?), or possibly ouroborus (?).

202.   North cove
Personification: *Truth*
A woman lifts a veil from her head with her left hand. With her right hand she holds a torch which burns two masks situated at her right side. One of her breasts is bare. Beneath this personification is her name in Latin: VERITAS [TRUTH].

203.   North cove
"Lion in profile" device with the *anima* taken from Psalm CXX: 4:
NON DORMITABIT NEQVE DORMIET

HE WILL NOT BE DROWSY, NOR SHALL HE SLEEP

204.   North cove
Personification: *Vanity*
A standing young woman wears a plumed hat, and holds a mirror in her right hand. Beneath her is her Latin name: VANITAS [VANITY].

205.   North cove
"Lion in profile" device with the *anima* taken from Judges XIV: 14:
EXIVIT CIBVS

MEAT CAME FORTH

230

206.
East cove
Personification: *Wickedness*
A standing woman holds a shield in her left hand, and a lance in her right. Beneath her is the inscription: PERFIDIA [WICKEDNESS].

207.
East cove
"Lion in profile" device with the *anima* taken from Amos III: 8:
SI RVGIET QVIS NON TIMEBIT

IF HE ROARS, WHO WILL NOT FEAR?

208.
East cove
Personification: *Fraud*
A standing woman wears a mask and has serpentine hair. She is dressed in a cuirass and skirt, and holds a lance in her right hand. Her feet are those of an animal. Beneath her feet is her Latin name: FRAVS [FRAUS].

209.
East cove
"Lion in profile" device with the *anima* taken from Psalm CXX: 4:
NON DORMITABIT NEQVE DORMIET

HE WILL NOT BE DROWSY, NOR SHALL HE SLEEP

210.
South cove
Personification: *Robbery*
A standing young woman shows one of her breasts. She holds a balance in her right hand, and with her left, holds her dress. Beneath her feet is her Latin name: RAPINA [ROBBERY].

211.
South cove
"Lion in profile" device with the *anima* taken from Judges XIV: 14:
EXIVIT CIBVS

MEAT CAME FORTH

212.
South cove
Personification: *Rigor*
A standing young woman looks downwards. One of her breasts is bare. With her right hand above her head she holds an object (a weapon?) comprised of a pole attached with three ropes and balls at the ends. She holds her skirt with her left hand. Beneath her feet is her Latin name: RIGOR [RIGOR].

213.
South cove
"Lion in profile" device with the *anima* taken from Revelation V: 5:
VINCIT LEO DE TRIBV IVDA

THE LION OF THE TRIBE OF JUDAH HAS CONQUERED

214.
West cove
Personification: *Corruption*
A standing young woman looks upwards. She holds shackles with both hands. Beneath her feet is her Latin name: INPORTVNITAS [CORRUP-TION].

215.
West cove
"Lion in profile" device with the *anima* taken from Amos III: 8:
SI RVGIET QVIS NON TIMEBIT

IF HE ROARS, WHO WILL NOT FEAR?

216.
West cove
Personification: *Goodness*
A standing old woman wears a veil on her head. She looks downwards,

and cares for a young girl who stands at her left side. Beneath her feet is her Latin name: BONITAS [GOODNESS].

217.   West cove
                         "Lion in profile" device with the *anima* taken from Revelation V: 5:
                         VINCIT LEO DE TRIBV IVDA

                         THE LION OF THE TRIBE OF JUDAH HAS CONQUERED

P. THE SALA DELLA GLORIA

218.   A   East cove
                         Personification: *Spring*

219.   B   South cove
                         Personification: *Summer*

220.   C   West cove
                         Personification: *Autumn*

221.   D   North cove
                         Personification: *Winter*

222.   E   Center vault
                         Glory of Sixtus V

223.   F   South-West angle
                         "Three-branched candelabrum" device with the *anima* taken from Psalm
                         CXVIII: 66:
                         SCIENTIAE BONITATIS DISCIPLINA

                         OF GOODNESS OF WISDOM OF KNOWLEDGE

224.   G   South-West angle
                         Personification

225.   H   South-West angle
                         Personification

226.   I   North-East angle
                         "Seven-branched candelabrum" device with the *anima* possibly inspired
                         by Proverbs XXIV: 16:
                         LVCEANT SEPTIES IVSTO

                         THE LIGHT SHINES SEVEN TIMES FOR THE JUST

227.   J   North-East angle
                         Personification

228.   K   North-East angle
                         Personification

229.   L   South-East angle
                         "Triple mountain" device with the *anima* adapted from Psalm
                         XCVI: 11:
                         LVX ORTA EST IVSTO ΤΡΥ[Σ]ΜΕΓΙΣΤΟΣ

                         THE LIGHT, THRICE GREAT ONE, IS RISEN TO THE JUST

230.   M   South-East angle
                         Personification:

231.   N   South-East angle
                         Personification

232

232.	O	North-West angle "Triple mountain" device with the *anima* adapted from Psalm XCVI: 11: LVX ORTA EST IVSTO ΤΡΥ[Σ]ΜΕΓΙΣΤΟΣ THE LIGHT, THRICE GREAT ONE, IS RISEN TO THE JUST
233.	P	North-West angle Personification
234.	Q	North-West angle Personification

Q. THE SALONE DEGLI APOSTOLI

235.		South wall *Moses gathers the Seventy Elders of Israel* [Exodus XIX: 25-26] fig. 25 MOYSES / VIROS LXX DE SENIBVS ISRAEL, / QVI SECVM POPVLVM REGERENT, / DEI IVSSV CONGREGAT MOSES GATHERS, BY THE COMMAND OF GOD, SEVENTY MEN FROM THE ELDERS OF ISRAEL SO THEY MIGHT GOVERN THE PEOPLE WITH HIM
236.		North wall *The Holy Spirit descends on the Apostles on Pentecost* [Matthew XXVIII: 9; Acts I: 8] APOSTOLI, ET DISCIPVLI / SACRO DIE PENTECOSTES / VIRTVTEM DE CAELO / SVPERVENIENTIS SPIRITVS / S. ACCIPIVNT THE APOSTLES AND DISCIPLES ON THE SACRED DAY OF PENTE- COST RECEIVE THE FORCE OF THE HOLY SPIRIT COMING FROM HEAVEN
237.		East wall *Christ summons the Fishermen and Paupers* [Matthew XXVIII: 19] The following inscription is no longer extant: CHRISTVS SALVATOR PISCATORES, ET PAVPERES AD HOMINVM PISCATIONEM VOCAT CHRIST THE SAVIOUR SUMMONS THE FISHERMEN AND THE PAU- PERS TO THE FISHING OF MEN
238.		South wall *Christ summons Matthew* [Matthew IX: 9] The following inscription is no longer extant: MATTHAEVS PVBLICANVS A TELONII INFAMIA AD APOSTOLATVS GLORIAM VOCATVR MATTHEW THE TAX COLLECTOR IS SUMMONED FROM THE IN- FAMY OF THE CUSTOM-HOUSE TO THE GLORY OF THE APOSTO- LATE
239.		East wall *Christ with his Seventy-two Disciples* [Luke X: 1-2] The following inscription is no longer extant: DOMINVS DESIGNATIS ALIIS LXXII DISCIPVLIS, OPERARIOS IN MESSEM MITTIT THE LORD, WITH SEVENTY-TWO OTHERS DESIGNATED AS DISCI- PLES, SENDS DAY-LABOURERS TO THE HARVEST

240.		North wall

240.

North wall
Two by two the Apostles carry out the preaching and driving out of the Devil
[Luke X: 1-2]
The following inscription is no longer extant:
DOMINVS DISCIPVLOS AD POENITENTIAM PRAEDICANDAM, ET
DAEMONIA SVBIICIENDA BINOS MITTIT

THE LORD SENDS TWO DISCIPLES TO PREACH PENITENCE
AND SUBDUE DEMONS

241.

West wall
Christ appears to the Disciples [Mark XVI: 14]
The following inscription is no longer extant:
CHRISTVS A MORTVIS RESVRGENS, DISCIPVLIS RECVMBENTIBVS
APPARET, ET CORDIS DVRITIAM EXPROBRAT

CHRIST, RISING FROM THE DEAD, APPEARS TO THE RECUMBENT
DISCIPLES AND REPROACHES THEIR HARDNESS OF HEART

242.

North wall
Christ announces peace and breathes the Holy Spirit on the Disciples [John
XX: 19-22; Luke XXIV: 36]
The following inscription is no longer extant:
CHRISTVS DISCIPVLIS REDIVIVVS PACEM ANNVNTIAT, ET
SPIRITVM SANCTVM SACRO AFFLATV INSPIRAT

THE RISEN CHRIST ANNOUNCES PEACE TO THE DISCIPLES AND
WITH SACRED BREATH BREATHES UPON THEM THE HOLY SPIRIT

243.

West wall
Matthias takes the place of the traitor Judas [Acts I: 22-26]
The following inscription is no longer extant:
S. MATTHIAS B. PETRI MONITV IN IVDAE IMPII LOCVM DIVINO
IVDICIO SVFFICITVR

WITH THE ADVICE OF SAINT PETER, SAINT MATTHIAS, BY DIVINE
JUDGEMENT, IS ADOPTED INTO THE PLACE OF THE IMPIOUS JEW

244.

South wall
The Apostles divide the Provinces [Luke XXIV: 47]
The following inscription is no longer extant:
APOSTOLI DOMINI SPIRITV S. ACCEPTO AD PRAEDICANDVM IN
OMNES GENTES EVANGELIVM, PROVINCIAS PARTIVNTVR

HAVING RECEIVED THE HOLY SPIRIT THE APOSTLES OF THE
LORD DIVIDED UP THE PROVINCES FOR THE PURPOSE OF
PREACHING THE GOSPEL TO ALL NATIONS

245.

East wall
Stemma of Sixtus V held by two angels
Beneath this *stemma* was an inscription which is now illegible and, un-
fortunately, undocumented by earlier sources.

246.

West wall
Stemma of Sixtus V held by two angels
Beneath this *stemma* was an inscription which is now illegible and, un-
fortunately, undocumented by earlier sources.

R. THE SALONE DI COSTANTINO - figs. 98-101

247.   A   West wall
Constantine's Vision of the Cross
fig. 106
CONSTANTINVS IMP.
BELLVM CONTRA MAXENTIVM PARANS,

234

VICTRICIS CRVCIS SIGNVM
IN CAELO VIDET

EMPEROR CONSTANTINE, PREPARING WAR AGAINST MAXEN-
TIUS, SEES THE SIGN OF THE VICTORIOUS CROSS IN HEAVEN

248. B East wall
Constantine is baptised by Sylvester
fig. 107
FL. CONSTANTINVS PRIMVS ROM. IMP.
CHRISTIANA FIDE PVBLICE SVSCEPTA,
A S. SILVESTRO PAPA
BAPTIZATVR

FLAVIUS CONSTANTINE, FIRST TO BE ROMAN EMPEROR WITH
THE CHRISTIAN FAITH ADOPTED PUBLICLY, IS BAPTISED BY
SAINT SYLVESTER, THE POPE

249. C South wall
Donation of Constantine
fig. 108
FL. CONSTANTINVS MAX. IMP.
AD PIETATEM TESTIFICANDAM
ROMANAM ECCLESIAM
DONIS AMPLISSIMIS CVMVLAT

FLAVIUS CONSTANTINE MAXIMUS, EMPEROR, ADORNS THE RO-
MAN CHURCH WITH GENEROUS GIFTS TO DEMONSTRATE HIS
PIETY

250. D North wall
Constantine acts as strator for Pope Sylvester I
fig. 109
IMP. FL. CONSTANTINVS MAX.
CHRISTVM D. IN EIVS VICARIO AGNOSCENS
S. SILVESTRVM EQVO INSIDENTEM
DEDVCIT

EMPEROR FLAVIUS CONSTANTINE MAXIMUS, RECOGNISING
CHRIST THE LORD IN HIS VICAR, MOVES TO HELP DOWN SAINT
SYLVESTER SITTING ON HIS HORSE

251. E West wall
"Single obelisk" device (fig. 102) with the *anima*:
GLORIA DEI CORVSCAT

THE GLORY OF GOD SHINES

252. F West wall
Personification: *Religion*
fig. 102

253. G West wall
Personification: *Devotion*
fig. 103

254. H West wall
"Single obelisk" device (fig. 103) with the *anima*:
IN VIRTVTE TVA ET IN IVSTITIA

IN YOU VIRTUE AND IN YOUR JUSTICE

255. I East wall
"Single obelisk" device with the *anima* taken from Luke XIX: 38
(fig. 104):

GLORIA IN EXCELSIS

GLORY TO GOD ON HIGH

256.	J	East wall Personification: *Knowledge of the True God* fig. 104
257.	K	East wall Personification: *Sixtine Rule* (?) fig. 105
258.	L	East wall "Single obelisk" device (fig. 105) with the *anima*: DE PETRA SALVS

IN PETER [THE ROCK] THERE IS SALVATION

259.	M	South wall *Moses* fig. 110
260.	N	North wall *Aaron* fig. 111
261.	O	South wall *Solomon* fig. 112
262.	P	North wall *David* fig. 113
263.	Q	South wall Seascape fig. 114
264.	R	North wall Landscape fig. 115
265.	S	South wall Landscape fig. 116
266.	T	North wall Landscape fig. 117

APPENDIX II

THE DEVICES OF THE LATERAN PALACE FRESCO CYCLE

This appendix lists and provides sources for the devices of Sixtus V in the Lateran Palace. It is organized according to location(s) and the two components of the device, *corpo* and *anima*. Beneath each *anima* I have listed the English translation, the Biblical passage from which the majority of *anime* are culled, and, in these cases, the original Biblical passage from the Latin Vulgate edition of the Bible, and the English Vulgate translation.

CORPO AND LOCATION

lion in profile with pear branch:
western loggia, *piano terreno*
western loggia extension, *piano terreno*
staircase to *piano nobile*
Obelisk Room
Room of Daniel (2 times)

lion in profile with pear branch:
western loggia, *piano terreno*
western entrance vestibule
Room of Daniel (2 times)

lion in profile with pear branch;
lion seen frontally:
eastern loggia, *piano terreno*
eastern loggia, *piano nobile*

lion in profile with pear branch:
eastern loggia, *piano terreno*

lion in profile with pear branch:
northern loggia, *piano terreno*

lion in profile with pear branch:
northern loggia, *piano terreno*

three mountains, sometimes with three eyes,
three crowns, keys and star:

ANIMA

SI RVGIET QVIS NON TIMEBIT
"If he roars, who will not fear?"
Amos III: 8
["Leo rugiet, quis non timebit?"]
["The lion shall roar, who will not fear?"]

NON DORMIT NEQ.[VE] DORMITABIT
"He will not be drowsy, nor shall he sleep"
Psalm CXX: 4
["Ecce non dormitabit neque dormiet"]
["Behold he shall neither slumber nor sleep..."]

CVSTOS VIGILI
"Vigilant custodian"
Psalm CXXVI: 1 ?
["Nisi Dominus custodierit civitatem, / Frustra vigilat qui custodit eam."]
["Unless the Lord keep the city, he watcheth in vain that keepeth it."]

DVLCIA A DEXTRIS
"Sweetness at the right"
Psalm XV: 11 ?
["Delectationes in dextera tua usque in finem."]
["at thy right hand are delights even to the end."]

POTENS IN PRAELIO
"Mighty in battle"
Psalm XXIII: 8
["Dominus potens in praelio."]
["the Lord mighty in battle."]

REGNVM IN FORTITVDINE ET DVLCEDINE
"Rule in strength and sweetness"
a response to the riddle of Judges XIV: 18 ?
["Quid dulcius melle, / Et quid fortius leone?"]
["What is sweeter than honey? and what is stronger than a lion?"]

throughout *piano terreno*
also on staircase to *piano nobile*

CAELVM AEQVORA TERRAS
"The heavens, the sea, the earth"

lion's head;
lion in profile with pear branch:
bands at junctures of logge on *piano terreno*
western loggia extension, *piano terreno*
staircase to *piano nobile*

DE COMEDENTI EXIVIT CIBVS
"Out of the eater came forth meat"
Judges XIV: 14
["De comedente exivit cibus"]
["Out of the eater came forth meat"]

lion's head;
lion in profile with pear branch;
within Sixtine rondel senza corpo:
bands at junctures of logge on *piano terreno*
western loggia extension, *piano terreno*
staircase to *piano nobile*
fourth room of private apartment

DE FORTI EGRESSA EST DVLCEDO
"Out of the strong came forth sweetness"
Judges XIV: 14
["Et de forti egressa est dulcedo."]
["And out of the strong came forth sweetness."]

within Sixtine rondel senza corpo:
north-east and north-west junctures
south-east juncture

EGRESSA DVLCEDO
"Sweetness came forth"
Judges XIV: 14

within Sixtine rondel senza corpo;
lion in profile with pear branch:
north-east and north-west junctures
south-east juncture
Room of Daniel

EXIVIT CIBVS
"Meat came forth"
Judges XIV: 14

within Sixtine rondel senza corpo:
north-east and north-west junctures

TVTANDOS SVOS
"Protecting one's own"

within Sixtine rondel senza corpo:
north-east and north-west junctures

DEPEL[L]ENDOS NOXIOS
"Striking down those who threaten"

lion in profile with pear branch:
western loggia extension, *piano terreno*
staircase to *piano nobile*
eastern loggia, *piano nobile*
Obelisk Room

IVSTVS VT LEO CONFIDENS
"He is just as the lion is bold"
Proverbs of Solomon XXVIII: 1
["Iustus autem, quasi leo confidens ..."]
"But the just, bold as a lion, shall be without
dread."]

three mountains, three crowns,
pear branches and star:
northern entrance vestibule

TRISMEGISTOS
"Thrice Great One"

three-branched candelabrum with circle,
triangle and square;
three mountains, three crowns, keys and star;
three-branched candelabrum with three books:
northern entrance vestibule
staircase to *piano nobile*
Room of Solomon
Room of the Glory

SCIENTIA BONITATIS DISCIPLINA
[SCIENTIAM BONITATIS DISCIPLINAM]
[SCIENTIAE BONITATIS DISCIPLINAE]
"Of goodness of wisdom of knowledge"
Psalm CXVIII: 66
["Bonitatem, et disciplinam, et scientiam
doce me"]

238

["Teach me goodness and discipline and knowledge"]

three-branched candelabrum with three books;
three mountains, three crowns, keys and star:
northern entrance vestibule
Room of Solomon

TERNA HAEC TRIPLICI
"These three things threefold"
Ecclesiasticus XLIII: 4 ?
["Tripliciter sol exurens montes"]
["The sun three times as much, burneth the mountains"]

seven-branched candelabrum with
seven open books:
northern entrance vestibule
Room of the Glory

LVCEANT SEPTIES IVSTO
"The lights will shine seven times for the just man"
Proverbs XXIV: 16 ?
["Septies enim cadet justus, et resurget."]
["For a just man shall fall seven times and shall rise again."]
compare Isaiah II: 2

Trajanic and Antonine columns
flanking an obelisk:
northern entrance vestibule
western loggia extension, *piano nobile*
Room of Solomon

RELIGIO MIRANDA TRIVMPHAT
"The glorious religion triumphs"

within Sixtine rondel senza corpo:
northern entrance vestibule

DVLCEDO
"Sweetness"

within Sixtine rondel senza corpo:
northern entrance vestibule

FRAGRANTIA
"Fragrance"

lion in profile with pear branch:
staircase to *piano nobile*
eastern loggia, *piano nobile*
Room of Daniel (2 times)

VINCIT LEO DE TRIBV IVDA
"The lion of the Tribe of Judah has conquered"Revelation V: 5
["... ecce vicit leo de tribu Iuda, ..."]
["...behold the lion of the tribe of Juda, ... hath prevailed [to open the book, and to loose the seven seals thereof."]]

three mountains, three crowns,
keys and star:
staircase to *piano nobile*

MONS IN QVO BENEPLACITVM EST DEO
"A mountain in which God is well pleased"
Psalm LXVII: 17
["Mons in quo beneplacitum est Deo habitare in eo"]
["A mountain in which God is well pleased to dwell"]

three mountains, three crowns,
keys and star:
staircase to *piano nobile*

FVNDAMENTA EIVS
"The foundations thereof"
Psalm LXXXVI: 1

three mountains, three crowns,
keys and star:
staircase to *piano nobile*

IN MONTIBVS ALTIS
"In the high mountains"

239

Psalm LXXXVI: 1
["Fundamenta eius in montibus sanctis"]
["The foundations thereof are in the holy mountains"]

three mountains, three crowns, keys and star:
staircase to *piano nobile*

IN ORTI EIVS DVLCEDO ET CIBVS
"In his rising sweetness and meat"
c.f. Judges XIV: 14

within Sixtine rondel:
staircase to *piano nobile*

MONTES IN CIRCVITV EIVS
"Mountains are round about it"
Psalm CXXIV: 2
["Montes in circuitu eius"]
["Mountains are round about it"]

within Sixtine rondel:
staircase to *piano nobile*

MONTES IN OMNES COLLES
"Mountains and all hills"
Psalm CXLVIII: 9 ?
["Montes, et omnes colles"]
["Mountains and all hills"]
c.f. Isaiah XL: 4
["Et omnis mons et collis humiliabitur"]

Air:
staircase to *piano nobile*

INANITATIS IMPATIENS
"Unable to bear empty space"

Water:
staircase to *piano nobile*

PROCREATIONVM ORIGO
"Origin of creation"

Fire:
staircase to *piano nobile*, by proxy of Vatican Library

PROCREATIONIS EXPERS
"Expert in creation"

Trajanic and Antonine columns flanking an obelisk:
staircase to *terzo piano*

MIRABILIA TVA CREDIBILIA
"Thy credible wonders"
Psalm XCII: 4-5
["Mirabilis in altis Dominus. / Testimonia tua credibilia facta sunt nimis."]
["Wonderful is the Lord on high. / Thy testimonies are become exceedingly credible."]

Trajanic and Antonine columns flanking an obelisk;
single obelisk:
staircase to *terzo piano*
eastern loggia, *piano nobile*
Hall of Constantine

GLORIA IN EXCELSIS DEO
"Glory to God on high"
Luke XIX: 38
["... pax in caelo, et gloria in excelsis"]
["... peace in heaven, and glory on high!"]
compare Luke II: 14

Trajanic and Antonine columns flanking an obelisk;
single obelisk:

western loggia estension, *piano nobile*
Room of Solomon

GLORIA[M] DEI EXALTAT
"Glory of God is exalted"

three mountains, three crowns,
keys and star:
staircase to *terzo piano*

IVSTVS CONSPICI
I am considered just

three mountains, three crowns,
keys and star:
staircase to *terzo piano*

LVX ORTA EST IVSTO
[compare LVX ORTA EST EIS]
"Light is risen to the just"
Psalm XCVI: 11
["Lux orta est iusto"]
["Light is risen to the just"]

three mountains, three crowns,
keys and star:
Room of the Glory

LVX ORTA EST IVSTO ΤΡΥ[Σ]ΜΕΓΙΣΤΟΣ
"The light, thrice great one, is risen to the just"
Psalm XCVI: 11 (with addition)

two putti with wreath:
western loggia extension, *piano nobile*

DILEXISTI IVSTITIAM
"Thou hast loved justice"
Psalm XLIV: 8

two putti with crosses keys
and regal crown:
western loggia extension, *piano nobile*

VNXIT TE DEVS
"God hath anointed thee"
Psalm XLIV: 8
["Dilexisti iustitiam, et odisti iniquitatem; /
Propterea unxit te Deus, Deus tuus ..."]
["Thou hast loved justice, and hated iniquity:
therefore God, thy God, hath anointed thee
with the oil of gladness"]

DILEXISTI IVSTITIAM ET ODISTI
INIQVITATEM
"Thou hast loved justice, and hated iniquity"
Psalm XLIV: 8

inscription:
juncture of south-eastern logge, *piano nobile*

Antonine Column with Paul:
eastern loggia, *piano nobile*

VAS ELECTIONIS
[Saint Paul]

Trajanic Column with Peter:
eastern loggia, *piano nobile*

PASTOR OVILE
John X: 7-10; 16
["Ego sum ostium ovile ovium"]
["I am shepherd of the sheep"]

tiara, scarf and cross:
eastern loggia, *piano nobile*

A DOMINO FACTVM EST ISTVD
"This is made for God"

single (Lateran) obelisk:
eastern loggia, *piano nobile*

IN HOC SIGNO
"In this sign"
c.f. Constantine's vision
Luke's references to Christ

*lion seen frontally with pear branch
and keys and wearing a tiara:*
first room of private apartment

MANET IN ETERNVM
"It endureth forever"
1 Peter I: 25
["Verbum autem Domini manet in aeternum"]
["But the word of the Lord endureth forever"]

single obelisk:
Hall of Constantine

IN VIRTVTE TVA ET IN IVSTITIA
"In your virtue and in your justice"

single obelisk:
Hall of Constantine

DE PETRA SALVS
"From the rock [in Peter] is salvation"

single obelisk:
Hall of Constantine

GLORIA DEI CORVSCAT
"The glory of God shines"

APPENDIX III

THE ORDER OF THE ROOMS

This appendix has been compiled due to confusion in the literature as to the order in which the *piano nobile* should be presented. It contains a comparative listing of the rooms and halls described, and the order in which they are presented by Fontana, *Della trasportatione*; Mola, *Breve Racconto*; Biondi, *il Restauramento*; and Schiavo, *Lateran*. It does not include the 1950 guidebook, *Palazzo del Laterano*, since the order in this work follows the organization of the Musei Lateranensi, which is quite unrelated to those presented in the aforementioned works, and in my own.

Fontana:

"La sala maggiore"
"La sala de gli Imperatori"
"La sala di Samuele"
"La Cappella"
"[Anti] cappella"
"La sala di Davit"
"La sala di Salomone"
"La sala d'Elia"
"La sala di Daniele"
"La sala di Costantino"
"La sala delle vocationi degli Apostoli"

Mola:

"La sala p.le [pontificale]"
"La stanza di Imperatori"
"La camera di samuello"
"La stanza de David"
"La stanza de Salomone"
"La stanza d'Elia"
"La sala di Costantino"
"La sala d'Apostoli"

Biondi:

"L'aula massima, o de'pontefici"
"L'aula dagl'imperatori"
"La stanza di Samuele"
"La Cappella"
"La retrostanza"
"La stanza David"
"La stanza di Salomone"
"La stanza d'Elia"
"La stanza di Daniele"
"La stanza sesto [delle quattro stagioni]"
"L'aula dagli apostoli"
"L'aula da Costantino"

Schiavo:

"Obelisk Hall"
"Hall of the Conciliation"
"Hall of the Emperors"
"Hall of Samuel"
"Hall of David"
"Hall of Solomon"
"Hall of Elijah"
"Hall of Daniel"
"Hall of the Seasons"
"Hall of the Apostles"
"Hall of Costantine"
"Private Pontifical Apartment"

APPENDIX IV

THE CONTENTS OF THE ROOMS

This Appendix has been compiled due to confusion in the literature as to the contents of the rooms and halls of the *piano nobile*, and the order in which the vaults and walls are to be read. It comprises a comparative listing of the narrative scenes, personifications, historical figures, *parerga, imprese* and *stemmi*, as ordered and described in Fontana, *Della trasportatione*; Mola, *Breve Racconto*; Biondi, *il Restauramento*; *Palazzo del Laterano*; and Schiavo, *Lateran*. It also contains the pithy descriptions given to the ground floor in those sources listed above. Since I have organized the first and second appendices according to the natural progression from ground floor to *piano nobile*, this appendix accordingly begins with the *piano terreno* and grand staircase.

PIANO TERRENO AND GRAND STAIRCASE

Fontana:

"... le stanze a terreno, e le loggie sono tutte in volta, ... e tutte le loggie, e le scale sono dipinte a grotteschi, e paesi con varie imprese ..."

Mola:

"Le stanze del p.o et 2.o piano tutte in volta, ... finalm.te die questo Palazzo si e descritto solo le cose ple, che troppo sarebbe nararlo tutte minutam.te ..."

Biondi:

"Non parlerò delle dipinture a grotteschi, a paesi, a fogliami, che sparse di monti, di stelle, di leoni, di fame alate e di belle imprese con motti che si riferiscono a Sisto, adornano le volte non solo del primo e secondo loggiato, ma sì pure delle magnifiche scale."

Schiavo:

"The ornamentation is like that of the loggias in the courtyard of St. Damasus and the Sistine Library. The general design is essentially decorative, even in the case of the largest paintings. Most of the pictures on the piano nobile are figurative; on the ground floor there are geometric panels. ... The scenes painted in the lunettes and the many panels provide a rich assortment of landscapes. The works accomplished by Sixtus V during the short but active period that he was Pope are illustrated, while his heraldic emblems, achievements with mottoes, the obelisks raised by him and the celebrative columns he restored appear as a constant theme of the figurative compositions. ... Th[e] great stairway has several flights and has highly decorated vaults."

PIANO NOBILE

SALA DEGLI OBELISCHI:

Palazzo del Laterano:

"Sala XV ... Nella volta stemma di Sisto V e affreschi riproducenti opere dal suo pontificato cioè le due colonne Traiana e Antonina sulle quali il papa fece porre le statue in bronzo degli Apostoli Pietro e Paolo; poi gli obelischi fatti erigere nelle piazze di San Giovanni, San Pietro, Santa Maria Maggiore e Santa Maria del Popolo."

Schiavo:

"The room which establishes direct communication between the Sistine Benediction Loggia and the piano nobile of the palace is called the Obelisk Hall, because the four monoliths that Sixtus V had placed at St. Peter's, St. Mary Major, St. John Lateran and S. Maria del Popolo, are reproduced here. Reproduced too are the triumphal columns of Trajan and Marcus Aurelius. ... The coat of arms, the heraldic lions of Sixtus V and various allegorical figures complete the decoration of the vault."

SALONE DEI PAPI:

Fontana:

"La sala maggiore è dipinta tutta da alto a basso con le sotto scritte istorie, prima quando CHRISTO diede le chaiui a San Pietro, l'altra, quando gli diede auttorità di poter legare, e sciorre, vi sono ancora molte imprese fatte da Nostro Signore poste dentro a paesi, e prospettiue bellissime diuerse con molti altri adornamenti: di più a torno a torno v'è il ritratto de'sottoscritti sedici Pontefici in Pontificale sotto a Baldachini, e ciascheduno ha vna inscrittione sotto, come segue, nelle quali inscrittioni sono notati alcuni decreti più importanti fatti da essi, il primo è.
S. PETRVS. Sotto questo è scritto ... (See my Appendix I for the Latin inscriptions given by Fontana for this and the remaining frescoes).

S. LINVS I. PP. II.
S. SIXTVS I. PP. VIII.
S. TELESPHORVS I. PP. IX.
S. HYGINVS I. PP. X.
S. PIVS I. PP. XI.
S. ANICETVS I. PP. XII.
S. SOTERVS I. PP. XIII.
S. ELEVTERIVS I. PP. XIIII.
S. VICTOR I. PP. XV.
S. ZEPHERINVS I. PP. XVI.
S. CALISTVS I. PP. XVII.
S. VRBANVS I. PP. XVIII.
S. PONTIANVS I. PP. XIX.
S. ANTHERVS I. PP. XX.
S. FABIANVS I. PP. XXI.
S. CORNELIVS I. PP. XXII.
S. LVCIVS I. PP. XXIII.
S. SILVESTER I. PP. XXXIIII.

E più dalla banda di dentro sopra la porta della medesima sala si leggono li seguenti versi ...

E in testa alla medesima sala alla banda dritta di chi entra in vn quadro si vede dipinto CHRISTO Nostro Signore, con San Pietro ...

E all'incontro dalla banda sinistra sotto vn'altro quadro, dou'è dipinto l'istoria Evangelica, quando CHRISTO interrogò gli Apostoli dicendo. QVEM DICVNT HOMINES ESSE FILIVM HOMINIS? si leggono le sottoscritte parole ...

Et sotto questo quadro in prospettiua si vede il capo dell'acqua Felice dipinta al naturale, sotto la qual pittura si leggono i seguenti versi ...

E sopra vna finestra della medesima sala dentro vn quadro si vede dipinto il porto di Terracina, & le paludi fatte seccare da Nostro Signore, e sotto vi sono li seguenti versi ...

E sopra vn'altra finestra dentro ad vn'altro quadro si rappresenta in pittura il Tesoro radunato da Nostro Signore dentro ad vno scrinio, intorno al quale si veggono dipinto gli animali, che sono nell'armi di ciascheduno di quelli, che ne tengono le chiaui, e sotto si legge ...

E sopra la finestra seguente in vn'altro quadro si vede dipinto la prospettiua della parte di dentro della libreria Vaticana fabricata da Nostro Signore, e sotto questa pittura stanno li seguenti versi ...

E sopra vn'altra finestra si rappresenta la Lega de Principi Christiani in pittura in questo modo, si vede vn mare, nel quale è vna barchetta entroui vn Leone, sopra il quale vn'Angelo tiene il regno, & su'l lido sono diuersi animali, che rappresentano li Principi Christiani, e sotto vi si leggono i seguenti versi ...

E seguitando sopra l'altra finestra si vede in pittura il Porto di Ciuita Vecchia, e l'aqua condottaui da Nostro Signore, e sotto vi stanno questi versi ...

E sotto il quadro, dou'è scritto PASCE OVES MEAS si vede dipinto la strada nuoua, & il Palazzo fabricatoui da Nostro Signore in Prospettiua, & li caualli trasportati, e ristorati a Monte Cauallo, sotto la qual pittura sono scritti i seguenti quattro versi ...

E sopra vn'altra finestra pur nella medesima Sala si vede dipinto la Città di Montalto, sotto la qual si legge ...

E sopra vn'altra finestra si rappresenta in pittura l'estirpatione de'fuor'vsciti in questo modo, si vede

in mezo a vna Campagna vn Monte, sopra il quale sta vn Leone, e intorno al monte sono molte pecorelle, che si pascono, & per la campagna molti Lupi posti in fuga dal Leone, che li minaccia con vn fulgore in mano, & sotto vi si legge ...

E sopra vn'altra finestra si rappresenta l'abbondanza fatta da Nostro Signore sotto questa pittura, che si vede vn Leone, che scuote vn'arbore di pere, e ne fa cadere i frutti, de'quali le pecorelle, che vi stanno atorno si pascono, e sotto vi sono scritti li seguenti versi ...

E sopra l'vltima finestra si vede dipinto in prospettiua la Santa Casa di Loreto, con la Città nuoua fattaui da Nostro Signore, sotto la quale sono posti le seguenti verse ...”

Mola:

“La sala p.le e pinta tutta da alto a basso con le seg.ti istorie P.a quando N. S. diede le Chiavi à S. Pietro Quando li diede lautorità di legare et sciogliere con altre imprese fatte dal'd.o Pontefice, con prospettiva, et bellissimi paesi
Vi sono i retratti de sedici pontefici, cioè Lino 2.o, Telesforo nono. Iginio X.o, Aiceto XIII., Sotero XIII, Eleuterio p.o., Antero p.o, fabiano p.o, Cornelio p.o, Lucio p.o, Silvestro p.o, Vittorio, Leferino p.o, Calisto p.o, Urbano p.o, et Pontiano p.o, et oltre le sud.i, vi e anco dipinto quando N. S. disse a i Discepoli suoi,
Gl'huomini cosa dicono di me.
Vi e hanco dipinto lorigine delacqua felice, et il porto de Teracina, con le paludi potine fatte da esso serbare.
Dunaltra parte il Tesoro da esso ord.o in Castel'Sant'Angelo con la libraria Vaticana.
Sop.a una finestra la lega de Prencipi Christ.ni cioè un mare con barchette, entrovi un Leone s.a il quale un Angelo tiene il Reg.o, et sop.a il lido diversi Animali che rapresentano li Principi Christiani
S.a laltra finestra il Porto de Civitavechia con lacqua da esso condottavi.
Et sotto vi è pasce oves meas, la strada nova et il Palazzo da esso fabbricato, con i Cavalli di fidia e prasitele trasportati sula piazza de m.te Cavallo, et da esso fatti restaurare.
In un'altra parte la Città de monti Alto et s.a una finestra, le stirpat.e delli fuor uscisti come s.a
Vi è efigiato una Campag.a con un monte nel'mezzo, et s.a di esso un leone, intorno il m.te pecorelle che pascono, e p la Campagna molti lupi posti in fuga dal'leone che li minaccia ass.e con un falcone.
E sop.a unaltra finestra si rapresenta labondanza fatta da esso Pontefice in questo modo cioè, un leone che scose un albero de Pera che cadeno, et pecorelle che le pascono.
In unaltra parte la Santa Casa de Loreto con la nova Città da esso eretta.”

Biondi:

“Nella edificazione dell'aula massima, o de'pontefici, ebbe in animo il gran Sisto che dovesse in certo modo rivivere l'antica aula massima del patriarchio: perciò volle data alla nuova aula la stessa comunicazione colla basilica, e la stessa posizione verso occidente che già ebbe l'antica, con tale e sì grandiosa ampiezza, che come quella era stata, così questa pur fosse atta ai concistori e ai concilii. E perchè la dipintura corrispondesse al nome dell'aula, vi fece nell'alto dipingere sotto baldacchini XIX santi pontefici, con tale ai piedi uno scritto che alcun lor fatto accennasse. E dopo s. Pietro, che celebrò il primo concilio in Gerusalemme; e dopo s. Lino, che fu secondo nel reggimento della Chiesa; altri XVI pontefici vi furono per ordine ritratti dall'ottavo al vigesimoterzo: e sono: Sisto, Telesforo, Igino, Pio, Aniceto, Sotero, Eleuterio, Vittore, Zeferino, Calisto, Urbano, Ponziano, Antero, Fabiano, Cornelio, Lucio, tutti primi di questi nomi: e chiuse la serie colla immagine del santo Silvestro, che battezzò Costantino, e celebrò il primo de'concilii niceni. Sotto queste immagini sono, dove sì dove no, alcuni piccoli dipinti a chiaroscuro, che si riferiscono ai pontefici sotto i quali sono posti, ed hanno forma di medaglioni. In altri luoghi le dipinture dimostrano, e i sottoposti versi rammentano le grandi cose da Sisto in breve tempo operate. Imperciocchè in capo della sala alla mano sinistra di chi entra, sotto un quadro dove è Gesu coi discepoli, vedesi rappresentata l'acqua felice da quel magnanimo pontefice per XXII miglia condotta in Roma: poi sopra le cinque finestre, che guardano sulla piazza ove innalzasi l'obelisco, sono a vedere le seguenti imprese: sulla prima finestra il porto di Terracina, e le paludi pontine ridonate all'agricoltura: sulla seconda il tesoro nel forte S. Angelo ragunato a presidio della città: sulla terza la magnifica biblioteca edificata nel Vaticano, e arricchita di una immensa preziosità di manoscritti: sulla quarta i discordanti principi in cristiana lega riuniti: e sulla quinta l'antico porto traiano restaurato in Civitavecchia, e la acque salubri ivi condotte. Quindi appiè della sala, sotto la dipintura ov'è il Signore che dà a pascere all'apostolo s. Pietro le sue pecorelle, viene ricordata agli spettatori la lunga, retta, e maestosa strada aperta sul Quirinale, e al mezzo di essa la bella fonte presso le terme, e in fine la grande piazza, ed ivi i traslocati cavalli, e il palazzo da Paolo III incominciato, e da Sisto quasi a fine condotto. Finalmente nell'altro lato, dalla parte ove si entra, al di sopra di quattro nicchie sono figurate le seguenti cose: sulla prima nicchia la città di Montalto, patria del pontefice, circondata di forti mura: sulla seconda la sicurezza e tranquillità renduta ai popoli, mercè della estirpazione de'forusciti: sulla terza l'abbondanza ad essi popoli procacciata colla istituzione de'monti frumentarii: e sulla quarta la città di Loreto fabbricata, cinta di mura, e a vescovile seggio innalzata. All'ultimo sulla gran porta d'ingresso è rammentata la riedificazione del patriarchio lateranense."

Palazzo del Laterano:

"Sala XIV. detta del Concilio e dei Papi. E'un salone rettangolare di m. 34 per 14, alto m.17 con soffitto dorato a cassettoni e fregi del tempo di Sisto V, come gli affreschi nelle pareti che rappresentano i primi papi di ciascun nome da S. Pietro a S. Silvestro; in oltre sono illustrate le opere edilizie compiute sotto il pontificato di Sisto V ...; ivi vennero firmati i Patti Lateranensi l'll febbraio 1929."

Schiavo:

"In particular the Hall of the Popes (after: Hall of the Conciliation) documents some of his [Sixtus V's] more important and significant works; in the zone above the lower windows all round the room, works of Sixtus V are reproduced: the aqueduct and "mostra" of the Felice waters, the port and reclamation at Terracina, the treasure collected in Castel Sant'Angelo, the Hall of the Vatican Library, the League of Christian Princes, the port and aqueduct at Civitavecchia, the Quirinal, the city of Montalto, the extirpation of the bandits, Abundance, the city of Loreto. At this point one should note that ths is the only room of the Palace with architectural decoration which, therefore, brings to mind the Mappamondo Room of Palazzo Venezia: Corinthian columns painted in imitation of Portasanta, Yellow Numidian and Green Serpentine marble, stand on a stylobate and sustain the trabeation with high attic where the seated figures of nineteen Popes are placed in niches. These were chosen from the first thirty-three beginning from St. Peter, and are surmounted by canopies. The latter, even in the time of Sixtus V, were added for greater decorative splendour perhaps or as indispensable attributes, being placed so low that they could not have risen from their seats. There is a more limited architectural decoration on the vault of the Hall of the Seasons or of Glory, which in the centre has the central view and perspective of a temple. At the center of the two minor sides in big pictures: Christ commits the flock to Peter, and Our Lord founds the church with Peter. Corresponding to the 19 figures of the Popes there are explanations relative to their work, some decorated with monochrome medallions. In the zone above the lower windows, all around the room are reproduced works of Sixtus V. His greatest work, that is the Lateran Palace, is recalled on the central door by an inscription that, alluding to the Giotto paintings, says that St. Francis, stalwart column of the faith, supports the falling structures of the Lateran; and alluding to the Patriarchate, recalls that Sixtus V had reconstructed rather than restored the buildings without however deriving any less glory from it."

SALONE DEGLI IMPERATORI

Fontana:

"La sala contigua ha li fregi grandi, e vi sono dipinto li sottoscritti quatordici Imperatori, le medaglie de' quali si sono trouate nelle ruine delle fabriche antiche in detto luogo, & quiui

sono stati dipinti per memoria delle cose notabili, c'hanno fatto per la Chiesa, come si conosce dalle inscrittioni poste sotto a ciascuno, come segue, il primo.
CONSTANTINVS MAGNVS.
THEODOSIVS.
ARCADIVS.
HONORIVS.
THEODOSIVS.
VALENTINIANVS.
MARCIANVS
LEO
IVSTINVS.
IVSTINIANVS
TYBERIVS.
MAVRITIVS.
PHOCAS.
HERACLIVS.
Di più nella sudetta sala degli Imperatori si veggono due quadri, in vno de'quali è dipinta la Chiesa sotto figura d'vna femina con piuiale, in vna mano tiene il regno, & nell'altra vn tempio, & gli Imperatori, che l'adorano come dinota la seguente inscrittione postoui sotto ...
E nell'altro quadro, ch'è nel mezo dell'altra facciata dirimpetto al primo, si vede Nostro Signore con alcuni Cardinali, che priuilegia le medaglie trouate nel fabricare questo palazzo, e sotto si leggono le seguenti parole ...”

Mola:

“Nella stanza acanto vi sono lefigge di 14 Imp.ri cavati dale medagle antiche trovate nelle ruvine di questo loco, con linscritioni delle cose più notabili fatti da essi in favore de S.ta Chiesa.
Il P.o è Costantino Magno, Teodosio, Valentiniano, Marciano, Arcadio, Honorio, laltro Teodosio, Marciano, Leone, Justino, Justiniano, Tiberio, Mauritio, Foca, et Eraclio, con le sue decchiarationi sotto.
Vi sono hanco due quadri, in uno la Chiesa sotto in figura di femine con Piviale, in una mano il'Regno, è nellaltra un Tempio, con limper.e che ladorano
Nellaltra stanza il Pontefice con alcuni Cardinali che privileggia le d.e medagle trovate.”

Biondi:

“La seguente aula s'ebbe nome dagl'imperatori; perciocchè essendo avvenuto che fra le ruine dell'antico patriarchio, mentre il nuovo palazzo riedificavasi, fossero trovate quattordici monete, tutte colla insegna della croce, come quelle che pertenevano ad augusti che la religione santissima di Cristo avevano e confessata e difesa; volle il sommo pontefice che di tal fatto, che tenea del miracoloso, rimanesse memoria nelle dipinture di questa sala: e le immagini di tutti quegl'imperatori, colla indicazione delle cose che operarono per la vera fede, vi fece ordinatamente rappresentare. E sono: Costantino il grande, che primo propagò la religione cristiana: Teodosio, che confessò innanzi a tutti i popoli sè essere seguitatore

di quella fede, che il santo apostolo Pietro ebbe data ai romani: Arcadio, il quale volle che un aureo nummo colla insegna della croce fosse improntato; perciocchè per quel segno ebbe superati i persiani: Onorio, che pose freno agli eretici di Affrica: l'altro Teodosio, che il sinodo efesino con pietà cristiana protese: Valentiniano, che il fastigio argenteo della basilica lateranense, dai barbari rapito, volle che a sue spese si rifacesse: Marciano, che per le affettuose sue cure inverso la cattolica fede si meritò che nel concilio calcedonico il nome gli fosse dato di Costantino novello: Leone, che fu sempre saldo nella difesa di quel concilio: Giustino, che umilmente prostrossi ai piedi del santo pontefice Giovanni, che poi fu martire, riconoscendo in lui il vicario di Cristo: Giustiniano, che seguendo gli ammonimenti del santo pontefice Agapito lasciò ai posteri egregio esempio di ubbidienza verso la sede apostolica: e Tiberio, che liberò Roma oppressa dall'assedio dei longobardi: e Maurizio, che dal santo papa Gregorio ebbe lode dell'aver congiunta la pietà cristiana alla gloria della milizia: e Foca, il quale decretò che tutti i popoli avessero a venerare la suprema potestà della chiesa romana: e finalmente Eraclio, che avendo ricuperata dai persiani la croce del Signore, quella sulle proprie spalle riportò alla sommità del Calvario.
Sono oltre a ciò in essa sala due dipinture ne'due lati minori. Dalla parte che si congiunge all'aula massima è una figura rappresentante la Chiesa: ha nell'una mano un tempio, nell'altra insieme colle chiavi il triregno; ad indicare le due potestà, spirituale e temporale: e gl'imperatori genuflessi l'adorano. Dall'altra parte è il pontefice Sisto V, che benedice e privilegia le monete imperiali da se trovate, per farne dono ai principi in allora regnanti.”

Palazzo del Laterano:

“Sala XIII ... Soffitto a cassettoni rifatto sotto Gregorio XVI. Fregi con le immagini degli imperatori Costantino Magno ed Eraclio, scena relativa a Sisto V ecc.”

Schiavo:

“The fresco decoration, which does not cover the entire wall surface but covers a wide frieze, represents the 14 emperors whose coins were found when foundation work was begun on the palace. One of the two major pictures illustrates this fact with the tribute paid by Sixtus V to the memory of these sovereigns, by the issue of a special document; the other, on the opposite wall, shows the Church adored by the Emperors.”

SALA DI SAMUELE

Fontana:

“Nella prima camera dopo la sala de gli Imperatori è dipinta l'istoria di Samuele, prima quando egli fu condotto per voto al Tempio, poi quando

248

in esso Tempio fu chiamato per voce miracolosa, vn'altra istoria, quando esso Samuele fa drizzare il sasso cognominato de adiutorio: l'altra quando esso Samuele onse Saul con molti altri adornamenti di figure, fogliami, cornici, e compartimenti di stucco tutto dorato."

Mola:

"Nela Camera che seg.e vi è listoria di samuello quando fu ordinato p voto al'Tempio, poi quando in d.o loco fu Chiamato con voce miracolosa, in un'altra quando esso Samuello fa drizzar il sasso d.o de Adiutorio, nellaltra quando vinse Saul', con infiniti orn.ti."

Biondi:

"La prima delle sei [the six rooms situated between the halls], quella cioè che è posta appresso alla descritta aula degl'imperatori, ha in sulla volta, e in sull'alto delle pareti dipinti i principali fatti della vita di Samuele: quando fu condotto per voto al tempio: quando, ivi stando, udì voce miracolosa che lo chiamò: quando la gran pietra detta del soccorso fece innalzare, affinchè attestasse la vittoria, col divino ajuto, riportata sui filistei: e quando unse Saulle. E vi sono oltre a ciò quattro grandi figure, rappresentanti la Fede, la Speranza, la Carità, e la Religione: ed altrettante pure negli angoli."

Palazzo del Laterano:

"Nella XII sala del tempo di Sisto V, volta con episodi della vita del re Samuele."

Schiavo:

"In the center is the coat of arms of Sixtus V with tapestry and canopy; close by are the figures of Faith, Hope, Charity and Religion; in the panel corresponding t the lower part of the coat of arms: Samuel called into the Temple by a mysterious voice; in the opposite panel: Saul anointed king by Samuel; on the two sides: Samuel led by vote to the temple, and Samuel sets up the stone; in the corners: four female figures. As a whole the decoration is distinguished in particular for its richness of colour."

ANTICAPPELLA & CAPPELLA PAPALE

Fontana:

"...a canto a questa stanza [Sala di Samuele] è la capella con vn'altra stanza, doue N. Signore può stare ad vdire messa senza essere visto, & in detta capella sono dipinti cinque misterij di Nostro Signore GIESV CHRISTO dalla Resurrettione fino all'Ascensione, quando egli apparue à diuersi."

Biondi:

"Ivi presso, in una retrostanza è la cappella: nella cui volta hanno luogo le seguenti dipinture: nel

mezzo la trasfigurazione del Signore, da capo la resurrezione, da piedi l'apparizione alla santa Maria Maddalena, a destra l'apparizione a s. Tommaso, a sinistra l'ascensione. Negli angoli sono figurati i quattro evangelisti, ed otto fra i principali dottori della Chiesa. Congiunta ad essa cappella è un'altra retrostanza (dipinta nell'alto a paesi, arabeschi e figure simboliche), ove il sommo pontefice può, senza essere veduto, rimanersi ad udire la santa Messa; e d'onde, per una segreta scala a chiocciola, può ascendere e discendere alle altre parti dell'edifizio."

SALA DI DAVIDE

Fontana:

"Nella stanza, che segue è dipinta l'istoria di Dauit, prima quando egli ascolta la brauura del Gigante Golia: l'altra quando egli amazzo detto Golia, in oltre quando egli torna vittorioso, e trionfante, quando
placa lo spirito di Saul con suoni musicali, e quando è vnto da Samuele con molti altri adornamenti di figure, stucchi, & oro."

Mola:

"Nela stanza che seg.e, vi è listoria de David'quando avolta la braura del'Gigante Golia, laltra quando lamazzò, laltra quando tornava Vittorioso, laltra quando lo spirito de Saul'con suoni musicali et quando e unto da Samuele."

Biondi:

"Vedesi nella prima stanza [after that of Samuel] David commoversi a santo sdegno per le oltraggiose voci dello smisurato Golia: poi vedesi, nel mezzo della volta, essergli sopra ed ucciderlo: indi tornar vittorioso: appresso con suoni musicali placare lo spirito di Saulle: infine ricevere la sagra unzione da Samuele. Riempie i quattro angoli di questa stanza lo stemma gentilizio di Sisto V, con ai lati due figure per angolo, le quali rappresentano otto virtù."

Palazzo del Laterano:

"Sala XI ... Nella volta episodi della vita del re David dal tempo di Sisto V."

Schiavo:

"The coat of arms of Sixtus V is repeated in the four corners and is bordered - as one can read in descriptions - 'with eight virtues characteristic of His Beatitude, and above, accompanying them, are images of his genius, which place wreaths of flowers on the ovates;' in fact other four couples of figures are seated on the cornices in the central squares, where five episodes of the life of David are illustrated: listening to the narration of the feats of Goliath, kills Goliath (centre), placates the spirit of Saul with music, is anointed by Samuel."

SALA DI SALOMONE

Fontana:

"Nella terza stanza è l'istoria di Salomone prima, quando il Padre lo misse al gouerno del Regno, come dinota l'inscrittione seguente postaui sotto ... La seconda, quando egli in visione ottenne gratia di gouernare bene. La terza, quando diede la sentenza del figlio morto, il che si dimostra nella seguente inscrittione, che vi stà sotto ... La quarta, quando la Regina Saba l'andò a visitare, la qual cosa è dinotata dall'inscrittione, che v'è sotto, che dice ... La quinta, quando egli portò in processione l'arca del Signore, come mostra la seguente inscrittione, che vi si legge sotto ... Et oltre le sopradette Istorie vi si veggono molti altri adornamenti, oro, stucchi, e pitture."

Mola:

"Nela 3.a stanza listoria de Salomone P.a quando il Padre lo mese al governo del Regno.
Laltra quando egli in visione otenne gratia di governar bene, la 3.a quando diede la sentenza del figlio morto.
la 4.a quando la Regina Saba landò à visitare la quinta quando porto in proces.e larca del Signore."

Biondi:

"Nell'altra stanza è Salomone, che giovinetto riceve dal padre il governo del popolo; che in visione ottiene grazia di ben governare; che, giudicando, scopre quale sia delle due madri la vera; che riceve la regina Saba, la quale ne maraviglia la sapienza; che fra i cori, le pompe, i sagrifizi fa portare l'arca del Signore nel tempio fatto magnificamente edificare in Gerusalemme."

Palazzo del Laterano:

"Sala X ... affreschi relativi al re Salomone del tempo di Sisto V."

Schiavo:

"In the corners, achievements and herladic emblems of Sixtus V. In the panels, episodes from the life of Solomon: his father places him at the head of the government of his country, in a vision he receives the grace to govern well (centre), gives judgement on the dead son [sic], receives the Queen of Sheba, carriers of the ark in procession."

SALA D'ELIA

Fontana:

"Nell'altra stanza, che seguita dopo questa è dipinta l'istoria d'Elia, prima, quando esso riprendeua Acab Re, e Iezabel dell'Idolatria: quando egli fece sacrificio a paragone de'falsi profeti: quando egli predisse la pioggia anuntiatagli da Nostro SIGNORE DIO ad Acab: quando salì sul carro del fuoco: quando apparue nella transfiguratione di Nostro Signore GIESV CHRISTO insieme con Moisè con varij, e diuersi adornamenti d'altre pitture, stucchi, & oro."

Mola:

"Nellaltra stanza che seg.e vi è listoria d'Elia p.a quando riprendeva Arrab'Re, et Jezabel'dallidolatria laltra quando fece sacrificio del'paragone delli Profeti falsi.
Laltra quando li predisse la pioggia anunciatoli da N.S.Iddio ad Arab'.
Vi è quando salì sul'carro del Foco, e quando aparve nella Trasfigurat.e di N.S."

Biondi:

"Succedono la quarta e la quinta stanza: nell'una delle quali le istorie di Elia, nell'altra quelle di Daniele appaiono figurate. Questi veri profeti, onde i falsi si rimasero confusi e vinti, furono posti a dimostrare come il sommo pontefice è depositario della vera Fede, trionfatrice di ogni falsa credenza. Elia è in cinque modi rappresentato: fa rimprovero d'idolatria ad Acab e a Iezabele: offre a Dio il sacrifizio, che miracolosamente è consumato dalle fiamme: predice ad Acab la pioggia: ascende sul carro del fuoco: e vedesi in sull'alto della volta apparire con Enoc nella trasfigurazione del Redentore. Questi quadri sono intramezzati da angeli, e da altre figure emblematiche."

Palazzo del Laterano:

"Sala IX ... nella volta trasfigurazione ed episodi del profeta Elia, del tempo di Sisto V."

Schiavo:

"The Transfiguration of Christ with Elijah and Moses is depicted on the central panel. In the other sections: He prophesies rain; He assists at the sacrifice; He deplores the idolation of Baal and Astarte by Ahab, the King of Israel and Queen Jezebel; He ascends in a fiery chariot."

SALA DI DANIELE

Fontana:

"Nell'altra stanza è seguente dipinta l'istoria di Daniele, quando contrasta con Nabucdonosor mostrandogli, che l'Idolo di Bel non era DIO viuente, nell'altra istoria appare, quando esso Daniele semina le ceneri per mostrare al sudetto Re le fraudi de'sacerdoti, ch'andauano per la stanza: in vn'altra istoria poi se vede, che li mostra le pedate de'detti sacerdoti, ch'erano iti a mangiar le viuande appresentate all'Idolo: in vn'altra parte, quando amazza il Drago di quei sacerdoti: in oltre quando esso Daniele fu posto nel lago de'Leoni insieme con la rappresentatione d'Abacuc profeta portato da l'Angelo per dargli da mangiare: vltimamente, quando i nimici d'esso Daniele furono gettati, e deuorati da Leoni con molti adornamenti d'oro, & altre pitture."

Biondi:

"In altrettanti modi è rappresentato Daniele: mostra a Nabucco l'idolo di Belo non essere Dio vivente, e semina le ceneri, perchè possa, mercè di esse, far chiara al re la frode dei sacerdoti: gli mostra le pedate da quelli in sulla cenere impresse per girne a cibarsi delle vivande offerte all'idolo: uccide il loro drago: posto nel lago dei leoni, che non l'offendono, vede (e ciò è nel mezzo della volta) Abacucco, che portato dall'angelo viene a recargli di che si nutra: infine vede i suoi nemici gittati in quello stesso lago, e divorati dai leoni. In ciascuno degli angoli è la figura di una virtù con arabeschi ed imprese."

Palazzo del Laterano:

"Sala VIII ... volta con scene del profeta Daniele e allegorie del tempo di Sisto V."

Schiavo:

"The subjects of the principal paintings are an occasion for repeated representation of the lion, an heraldic emblem of Sixtus V. There are also numerous isolated figures. The main subjects are: Daniel disputes with Nebuchadnezzar, showing him that the idol Baal is not the Living God; Daniel spreads the ashes to demonstrate to the king the deception of the priests; Daniel shows the priests' own footprints to prove that they themselves had eaten the offerings laid before the Idol; Daniel slays the Dragon; Daniel is cast into the lion's den by his enemies but is delivered unharmed."

SALA DELLA GLORIA

Biondi:

"Finalmente nella sesta stanza, ove imbandivasi forse la mensa, furono dipinte le quattro stagioni con intorno figure e arabeschi."

Palazzo del Laterano:

"Sala VII ... volta con simboli della gloria e delle quattro stagioni dal tempo di Sisto V (1585-89)."

Schiavo:

"The seasons are named on the scrolls at the intersections of the borders and are represented by the various fruits of the earth. At the centre is the Gloria, a winged figure supporting the monti of Sixtus V on her right and a festoon on her left,

framed in a temple, shown in central perspective from below, with architectural features similar to those of the walls of the Hall of the Conciliation."

SALONE DEI PARAMENTI

Fontana:

"L'altra sala doue sua Santità si para per scendere dentro la Chiesa in Pontificale, è con varie pitture delle vocationi degli Apostoli, & atti loro.
Prima, quando lo Spirito santo discese sopra gli Apostoli sotto la qual pittura è la seguente inscrittione ... L'altra pittura rappresenta Moise, che raduna settanta vecchi, che seco regessero il popolo, e sotto vi si legge ... Di più in vn'altro quadro si vede, quando CHRISTO Nostro Signore chiamò i poueri, e pescatori, per farli pescatori de gli huomini, come dinota la seguente inscrittione postaui sotto. ... Dopo questo si vede, quando CHRISTO chiamo Matteo all'Apostolato, come dimostra questa inscrittione, che vi è sotto ... In oltre vi si vede, quando gli Apostoli dopo riceuuto lo Spirito santo, partono fra di loro le prouince del mondo, doue hanno d'andare a predicare l'Euangelio, come dice l'inscrittione, che v'è scritta sotto ... Vi si vede anco, quando S. Mattia fu eletto, e sustituito in loco di Giuda il Traditore, e sottovi si legge la seguente inscrittione ... Di più, quando CHRISTO apparue a discepoli, e rinfacciò la loro incredulità, e ostinatione, come dice la seguente inscrittione, che vi si legge sotto ... E più, quando CHRISTO resuscitato da morte, annuntia loro la pace, & li da lo Spirito santo, come appare nelle seguenti parole, che sotto vi si leggono ... E più si vede, quando il Signore mandò i Discepoli a due a due a predicare, & a scacciare li demonij, sotto la qual pittura si legge ... Vltimamente, quando Nostro Signore GIESV CHRISTO designò altri settantadue Discepoli, e li mandò per il mondo a predicare, come dinota la seguente inscrittione, che vi si vede sotto..."

Mola:

"Nellatra sala dove sua Santita si para si rapresenta quando lo Spirits.to scese s.a l'Apostoli
In unaltra pittura si rapresenta quando Moisè adunava i 70 vechi che seco regessero il popolo
In un'altro quadro si vede quando Christo Sig.e N. chiamo i poveri pescatori p farli pescatori d'huomini
In un altro quando l'Apostoli doppo haver receuto lo Spi.to partono fra essi loro le province del'Mondo p predicarvi l'Evangelio
In un altro quando S.Mattia fu divinam.te eletto in loco de Giuda
In unaltra Istoria, rapresentasi quando Christo Sig.r N. aparve à suoi Apostoli rinfacciandoli la loro incredulità, et ostinat.e
Vien anco rapresentato quando listesso Christo resuscitato da morte annuncia la loro Pace e li da lo Spiri.S.to
Vien hanco rapresentato quando listesso N.S. mandò i Discepoli à due, a due à predicare et scacciare i Demonij

Ultimam.te si rapresenta N.S. Gesù Christo q.do elesse li 12 Discepoli, e li mando p il mondo à predicare, et sotto ad'ogni Istoria è la sua Dichiaratione."

Biondi:

"Ed eccoci giunti alle altre due aule: delle quali per ultimo farò parola, tralasciando di parlare delle stanze interne che sovrastano al cortile. La prima di esse aule, come ho già detto, ha nome dagli apostoli. Ivi nel mezzo della lunga parete a destra è rappresentato Mosè, che per comandamento di Dio congregò LXX seniori, perchè seco reggessero il popolo d'Israelle; in che furono adombrati i discepoli che sarebbero stati eletti da Gesù Cristo. Nella parte opposta, cioè nel mezzo della parete a sinistra, vedesi lo Spirito Santo discendere nel cenacolo. Tiene il mezzo delle pareti minori lo stemma del pontefice. Poi presso a ciascuno degli angoli sono due quadri. Nel fondo a destra veggonsi i poveri pescatori da Gesù chiamati a seguirlo; e vedesi Matteo che alla voce: *seguimi*, lascia il telonio. Nel corrispondente angolo a sinistra è a vedere la elezione degli altri LXXII discepoli; e come a due a due furono mandati a predicare e a discacciare i demoni. Rammentano le due pitture poste ad angolo alla sinistra di chi entra, come il Signore risorto apparve ai discepoli annunziando loro la pace; e come mostrandosi ad alcuni di essi, ch'erano seduti a mensa, fece loro rimprovero di poca fede. E finalmente nell'altro angolo a destra è rappresentata la surrogazione di Mattia nel luogo dell'infame Giuda; e lo spartirsi altresì che gli apostoli fecero delle provincie per condurvisi a spargere la luce dell'evangelo."

Palazzo del Laterano:

"Sala VI ... Nel soffitto rifatto da Gregorio XVI episodio del Vecchio e del Nuovo Testamento."

Schiavo:

"The broad frieze, though it is all fresco, gives the impression of large tapestries alternating with painted panels. The subjects of the paintings are: at the centre of the lesser sides, the coat of arms of Sixtus V; at the centre of the greater sides, Moses gathers the seventy elders, and the Pentecost; near the corners, Christ calls the Apostles, the Calling of Matthew, Christ appoints the seventy disciples, He sends them out two by two to preach the Word, the Last Supper, He appears to his disciples, the destitution of Judas, the election of Matthias in the place of Judas."

SALONE DI COSTANTINO

Fontana:

"Nell'altre stanze seguenti, che sono sei al medesimo piano sono dipinte molte cose, che si lasciano per breuità con le medesime ricchezze da pertutto di stucco, & oro, & oltre a questo dall'altra banda sono due sale grandi, vna chiamata di Constantino, doue sono le sue historie dipinte, cioè quando fu battezzato da San Siluestro Papa, come mostra l'inscrittione postaui sotto, che dice ... L'altra, quando egli preparando la guerra contra Massentio Tiranno vide nel Cielo la Croce di Nostro Signor GIESV CHRISTO, & vdì dirsi, *in hoc signo vinces*, la qual'Istoria ha sotto la seguente inscrittione ... In oltre si vede ancora, quando egli donò amplissimi doni alla Chiesa Romana, il qual'atto si rappresenta in pittura in questo modo, cioè l'Imperatore in habito imperiale con vna carta in mano, quale egli stesso presenta sopra l'altare alla presentia di San Siluestro Papa, e de'Cardinali, e sotto vi si legge la seguente inscrittione ... E dopo questa si vede, quando egli conoscendo il Vicario di CHRISTO per honorarlo maggiormente a piedi, con la mano al freno del cauallo conduce l'istesso San Siluestro à San Giouanni Laterano, sotto la qual'Istoria si legge ..."

Mola:

"Nellaltre stanze seguenti che sono seij alistesso piano son depinte molt'altra belle cose che p breuità si lasciano
Dallaltra parte nele due sale grande una chiamata de Costantino, ove sono listoria della sua Conversione, et batizzatione.
Nellaltra quando preparava la guerra contro Massentio Tiranno che vidde nel'celo la Croce di N.S. Gesu Christo et udi dirsi in hoc signo vinces. Inoltre quando donò ala Chiesa Romana amplissimi doni, il qual'atto si rapresenta in questo modo, L'Imper.re in habito imp.le con una carta in mano, quale egli stesso presenta s.a laltare ala presenza de S.Silvestro e di Cardinali.
Doppo questa si rapresenta quando il Vicario di Christo p magiorm.te onorarlo à piedi con la mano al freno del Cavallo conduce listesso S.Silvestro a S.Gio.Laterano."

Biondi:

"Finalmente nella ultima grande aula, che prende nome da Costantino, sono quattro grandi quadri intramezzati da paesi, figure, ed imprese. Di faccia all'ingresso è rappresentato il battesimo di quell'imperatore: sull'opposto lato l'apparizione ch'egli ebbe della croce: alla destra i doni onde fu generoso alla Chiesa; alla sinistra l'umile atto con che si fece ad accompagnare il santo papa Silvestro alla basilica lateranense, tenendo la mano al freno del cavallo sul quale era il pontefice."

Palazzo del Laterano:

"Si passa poi a sinistra nel grande salone V. Il soffitto a cassettoni è rifatto da Gregorio XVI (1831-46); affreschi con episodi di Costantino, le quattro virtù teologali, profite e patriarchi." Fregi con le immagini degli imperatori Costantino Magno ed Eraclio, scena relativa a Sisto V ecc."

Schiavo:

"The paintings in the broad frieze illustrate episodes from the lif of Constantine: the Defeat of Maxentius at th Milvian Bridge, the Donation to the Church, the Emperor baptized by Sylvester I, the Pope at St. John Lateran. There are also four large landscapes, four male figures (including one of Moses), and four allegorical female figures."

APPARTAMENTO PRIVATO PONTIFICIO

Palazzo del Laterano:

"I Sala ... Le pitture nella volta sono del tempo di Sisto V (1585-90) e rappresentano motivi araldici della famiglia del Pontefice e storia di Tobia e dell'arcangelo Raffaele [first room]."

"II Sala ... Affreschi nella volta del tempo di Sisto V col battesimo di Gesù Christo; Roma città sacra [second room]"

"III Sala ... Nella volta episodi della vita del profesa Elia; il corvo gli porta gli alimenti ecc. [third room]"

"IV Sala ... Affreschi nella volta con allegorie relative alla vita di Sisto V; nelle lunette San Giovanni Battista e un paesaggio del secolo XIX; poi il colloquio del Signore con Abele, Elia nel deserto, Sant'Onofrio e Santa Maria Egiziaca [fourth room]."

Schiavo:

"This apartment consists of four rooms en suite on the side of the courtyard facing south ... the ceiling is frescoed and has lunettes with landscapes."

LOGGE

Palazzo del Laterano:

"Le volte della galleria furono affrescate da vari artisti tra il 1586 e il 1589 e rappresentano i episodi tratti dal nuovo testamento (pareti I-IX) [eastern loggia] poi dal vecchio testamento la storia di Giuditta e Oloferne (pareti X-XVI) [southern loggia]; dalla creazione del mondo alla nascità di Esaù e Giacobbe (pareti XVII-XXV) [western loggia]."

"Si volge a destra [from the Salone dei Papi] e nel ripiano le volte sono affrescate con episodi della vita di San Francesco d'Assisi [western loggia extension]."

Schiavo:

"The three arms of the loggia differ in width and hence in the roof covering and consequent pictorial decoration of the vaults. On the walls there are eight pictures relating to the same number of episodes from the life of the Baptist. These were painted for the Baptistery by Andrea Sacchi, where they have been substituted by modern copies; there are also some pictures representing Jesus, the Apostles, and other saints, dating from the Farnese period [sic]. The door in the back gives direct access to the Hall of Daniel."

SCALONE PRINCIPALE

Palazzo del Laterano:

"Si ritorna nella galleria dei sarcophagi [scalone principale] la cui volta è affrescata da Paolo Brill con paesaggi ideali, stemmi del papa Sisto V, festoni figure allegoriche ecc."

APPENDIX V

DOMENICO FONTANA'S NOTEBOOK ON THE LATERAN PALACE FRESCO CYCLE

This appendix reprints sections on the Lateran Palace fresco cycle contained in A.A. Arm B. 18, Fondo di N. S. Papa Sisto V. S. Giovanni in Laterano e Loggia della Benedizione, 200ʳ ff, housed in the Archivio Segreto Vaticano (echoing the notebook in the Archivio di Stato di Roma). Specifically, it reprints *stime* concerning the frescoes of the palace proper, and excludes those treating the Benediction Loggia and corridor, or ramp-staircase, both of wich act as liasons between the palace and the basilica. This appendix is intended to complement both Appendix IV and documents reprinted in Bertolotti, *Artisti Modenesi* and Lauer, *Palais*.

La pittura nella volta della stanza innanziche si entri nella loggia della beneditione stimata come qui sotto si vede

In prima un'arme di S. Beatitudine in mezzo della volta con due figure grande di S. M. ... L'una con suoi ornamenti dentro stimiamo scudi quaranta...   40

Le quattro cantonate della volta con figure puttini cartelli ombrelle et altri ornamenti stimiamo scudi centotrenta...   130

Li sei quadri di Prospettiva fattoci dentro l'Aguglia di S. Pietro in un altro l'Aguglia di San Giovanni nell'altro l'Aguglia di Santa Maria Maggiore et nelli altri quadri le due colonne Traiana et Antonina et sopraui le statue de' Principi delli Appostoli con le medesime Prospettive, come l'altre con altri suoi ornamenti d'intorno stimiamo scudi nouantacinque...   95

Tutte le grottesche che riempiono tutta la volta assai copiose stimiamo scudi cinquanta...   50

Li due quadri nelli quali ci sono due leoni con loro ornamenti et fogliami finiti in campo rosso stimiamo scudi venti...   20

[...]

La prima stanza contigua alla seconda sala dello appartamento principale verso l'Aguglia dipinta contiene nelli quattro Paesi il suggetto delle Historie di Samuele et nella sommitade l'arme di S. Beatudine con molti abbigliamenti et in spatij delle cantoniere quattro grottesche in campo d'oro con una figura grande in ogni cantone et in quattro spatij che sono per interuallo delle Historie sopradette sono in esse quattro figure fede, speranza, carita et Religione et oltra di queste una legatura generale d'intagli finti et abbigliamenti in campo d'oro et figura coerente d'ogni cantone et insieme l'imposta indorata in diuersi membri di essa stimiamo scudi quattro cento ottanta sette...   487

La seconda stanza contigua a questa in volta dipinta contenente in cinque spatij l'Historia di Davit cominciando nel primo scontro esso David che

intende la Braueria di Golia. Di Ricontro è esso Giovanetto che con l'Armonia placa l'infermità di re Saul. Alla parte verso le finestre è il Re David unto da Samuele. Nella sommita della uolta la uittoira di Davit contro Golia et nell'altra Historia scontro alle finestre esso Re Davit trionfante nelli quattro ouati son quattro Arme di S. Beatudine accompagnate ogni uno di esse da due figure di diverso soggetto che rappresentano otto virtù peculiari di S. Beatudine et sopra per accompagnamento sono le imagini del genio di esse che porgano Corona di fiori sopra l'ouati la ligatura generale et le Rilievi di intagli dorati nelli [p...] finte sono ornamenti finti in campo dorato e nell'imposta nella medesima stanza sono di rilievo diuersi membri dorati che tutto stimiamo scudi cinquecento venticinque...   525

La terza stanza della cantonata del palazzo verso la guglia et contigua alla sopradetta nominata di Davit contiene l'Historia di Salomone con l'ordine infrascritto. In prima nella sommità della uolta un quadro tirato a grandezza proportionata all'Angolo della stanza contiene il Padre Eterno che dona al medesimo Re giouane lo spirito di sapienza conforme alla petitione di esso stimiamo scudi venticinque...   25

Nel fianco della volta in uerso mezzogiorno la constitutione del medesimo Re giouanetto nel possesso del Regno fatta dal Padre di esso vivente dandogli il trionfo stimiamo scudi...   50

Nell'altro fianco uerso ponente e tramontana un altro quadro di poco minor grandezza contiene la sententia di esso giouane Re nella distintione delle madri del uiuo te morto figliuolo stimiamo scudi quaranta...   40

Nel fianco scontro al primo et di conforme grandezza si rappresenta la Regina di Meroe alle accoglienze del savio Re curiosa di intendere presentialmente quello che per fama di esso inteso aueua stimiamo scudi quinquanta...   50

Nell'altro scontro al secondo e della medesima grandezza è dipinta la trasportatione dell'Arca del

Signore con le solennita de sacrificij stimiamo scudi quaranta...   40

Nelle quattro Cantoniere sono quattro imprese sopra gli atti et segni di N. Signore di uaria inuentione. La prima all'angolo verso la guglia et in sul canto del palazzo in mezzo di essa la Aguglia sopraui la croce et alli lati di essa le colonne Traiana et Antonina con le statue delli santissimi Apostoli con il motto Religio miranda Triumphat. La medesima risponde per il Diagonale nelle stanza della forma medesima mutate le Parole sole Gloriam Dei exaltat et nelli altri due Angoli sono li segni dei Monti coronati sopra di essi la stella et le chiaui col motto. All'angolo d'oriente Terna heac triplici et la corrispondente Bonitatis scientiae disciplinae vagliano scudi trenta cinque...   35

La Dorata di tutte gli ornamenti di detta stanza cosi nelli piani et fondi come in ogni sorte di rilieuo et altre abbigliamenti di cartelli finti di Rilievo sotto l'ornamento d'ogni Historia con campi azzurri per inscrittione Conueniente all'Historia vagliano insieme scudi cento dieci...   110

Somma tutta la sudetta stanza in sette partite scudi trecento cinquanta...   350

Somma sommata delle tre stanze infra scritte importa scudi mille trecento sessanta due...   1362

Dalla Porta segreta della chiesa fino alla testa del suo scontro Computandone tutti li sordelli et le due salite della scala sino all'entrare della prima loggia al piano Reale stimiamo scudi mille cento...   1100

Somma le tre partite scudi...   1300

Somma dello somme di tutti li lavori di Pittura et Oro fatti nel Palazzo Apostolico in San Giovanni come qui à dietro si vede a partita per patria. Stimate l'historia della loggia della beneditione da ms. Matteo Neroni tutti gli altri lauori cosi nelle stanze come all'entrata ed alle scale et suoi Ricetti si sono stimati e misurati dalla Parte do N. Signore da m.s. Giovanni Capito et per li pittori da m. Iacomo Rocchetti che in tutto sommano le dette stime scudi quattromila trecento diecidotto...   4318

Hauendo noi altre volte sotto li 15 di Gennaro 1589 saldato un contro di diuerse Pitture fatte da Cesare Nebbi et Giovanni Guerra Pittori in diverse fabriche quale ascendeua alle somma di scudi - 14658b17 et da noi fu ridotto a 12600 nel qual conto son comprese le sopra dette Pitture fatte nel nostro Palazzo Appostolico di San Giovanni Laterano et loggia della beneditione che ascendono alla somma di scudi 4318 ridotti a 3585. ... [signed by Nebbia and Guerra]

Stima delle pitture, e oro fatte nel palazzo Lateranense cioè il porticale sotto la loggia de la beneditione, e parte de le loggie da basso, e le loggie di sopra, el salone, salotto, cappella, et altre stanze sia doppo l' ultimo saldo fatto sotto l'ultimo di

Gennaro 1589 tutto stimato per la parte della R. Camera da me Girolamo Mutiano per l'ordine del Signore Cavaliere Fontana, e per la parte de Pittori da me Iacomo Rocchetti. Quali stime habbiamo uisto e ben considerato.

Quali Pitture son fatte tutte sotto condotta di ms Cesare Nebbi, e ms Giouanni Guerra Pittori, e compagni, e stimate da noi sopradetti, come sotto si uede à partita per partita.
                            [...]
Nell'andito del palazzo all'entrar de la facciata uerso tramontana nel mezzo della uolta è un'arme di N. S. e molti ornamenti, imprese, et abbigliamenti importa scudi cento uenti...   120

La loggia da basso al piano e da la banda dal detto andito cominciando da la testa de la loggia dipinta prima all'altra testa, doue in aspetto ui è l'arme di N. S. con due figure grandi figurate per l'Honore e l'Otio bono, et al sordello appreso à questa è l'arme di Santa Chiesa con due altre figure figurate per la Verità, e la Devotione, et il resto de la loggia conforme all'altra sopradetta dipinta importa scudi quattrocento cinquanta...   450

La loggia al piano reale, doue cominciandosi in capo de la scala a man dritta sino alla sua testa si son fatte in noue uolticine l'historie del testamento uecchio cominciando da la creation dell'huomo síno à la morte d'Abraam con molti adornamenti, imprese, et intagli finti, e nella testa di essa l'arme di N. S. con due figure del naturale la Providentia, e la Felicità, e nelli sordelli paesi. Da la scala in la verso la chiesa di S. Giovanni sonno cinque altre volticine con paesi, grottesche, imprese, et abbigliamenti, e nelli sordelli sette historie de la vita di S. Francesco importa scudi mille settecento uenticinque...   1725

Le due branche di scale, che uanno all'appartamento superiore del palazzo con due volticine, doue sonno imprese di N. S. figurine, grottesche, et abbigliamenti importa scudi trecento...   300

La sala grande del palazzo, doue sonno dipinti Pontefici santi cominciando da S. Pietro insino à S. Siluestro sonno numero dicinoue dentro in tabernacoli con padiglioni, alle cantonate figure per ornamenti, alle teste due historie grande, in una de le quale si rappresenta N. S. che dà le chiaui à S. Pietro, e nell'altra quando dice Pasce oues Meas. Sotto a li detti Pontefici è un'ornamento di colonnati finti de mischi con dentro ornamenti fattoci molte attioni di N. S. et historie finte di bronzo, che dentro ui sonno delli fatti di quelli Pontefici importa scudi mille e quattrocento...   1400

Nel salotto ui è un fregio dall'arco de le finestre in su doue sonno in tabernacoli quattordici Imperadori Christiani cominciando da Costantino à Eraclio con due historie, nell'una è la Santa Chiesa adorata da questi Imperadori, e nell'altra N. S. che da l'indulgentia alle medaglie d'oro trouate a S. Giovanni Laterano e l'archi de le finestre dipinte importa scudi quattrocento...   480

La cappella di detto palazzo, doue sonno cinque historie di N. S. dopo la resurrettione, nelle cantonate otto dottori di Santa Chiesa Romana e Greca, e la doratura sopra li rilievi importa scudi duecento uinti...   220

La stanza appresso alla detta cappella, doue sonno imprese di N. S. figurini, paesi, et altri abbigliamenti, et oro, importa scudi cento settanta...   170

La stanza d'Helia presso à quella di Salomone, doue sonno cinque historie del Profeta, otto figure nelle cantonate della volta, quattro Angeli, et altri abbigliamenti d'intagli finti, et oro importa scudi duecento cinquanta ...   250

La stanza di Daniel con cinque historie di esso Profeta con legature d'intagli finti, grottesche, figure grandi nelle cantonate tempietti con figurine, e molti abbigliamenti, e la doratura importa scudi cinquecento...   500

La stanza de la Gloria, doue nel mezzo della volta è una prospettiua uista di sotto in su con una figura figurata per la Gloria con abbigliamenti diuersi, figure grandi, grottesche, imprese, et intagli finti importa scudi trecento uinti...   320

[signed by Mutiano and Rocchetti; Sixtus V on 20 May 1589; and Nebbia and Guerra on 5 February 1590]

Misura et stima delle Pitture fatte ultimamente doppo l'ultimo saldo de 20 di maggio 1589 dentro al palazzo Lateranense cioè le due parti di logge di sotto che cingono il cortile et l'altre due parti di sopra al piano reale, uerso leuante et al mezzogiorno il Salone di Costantino, il salotto Apostolico contiguo à detto Salone et le cinque stanze contigue al sopradetto salone et salotto et alla stanza della gloria e'l capo scala aggiunto alla scala che ua dal porticale uecchio di San Giouanni al Salone di Costantino. Quali Pitture son fatte sotto condotta di m. Cesare Nebbi et m. Giovanni Guerra et compagni Pittori stimate per la parte di N. Signore da m. Girolamo Mutiano Pittore chiamato da monsignore della Corgna e per la parte di essi pittori da m. Iacomo Rocchetti Pittore stimate come si uede appresso et prima

In Prima le due logge al primo piano del cortile del Palazzo Lateranense ultimamente fatte che cingono il cortile una parte uerso il Saluatore et l'altra uerso la chiesa quale son stimate di ualore conformi all'altre due partite incontro alle dette scudi nouecento...   900

L'altre parti delle due logge di sopra al piano reale che si trouano salendo a detto primo piano l'una uolta uerso san Giouanni et l'altra uerso il Saluatore che finisce all'entrata della sala di Costantino contengono l'ordine seguente

In Prima nella prima loggia che uolta uerso san Giouanni sono sette cupolette entroui historie del testamento uecchio cio è quattro per ciascuna, con legature d'intagli finti abbigliamenti figure et Imprese quali son stimate scudi cento dieci l'una e tutte insieme settecento settanta...   770

Sette sordelli doue sono in ciascuno un paese et all'incontro di essi li sottoarchi sono dipinti intagli finti che stimiamo scudi...   110

Li due sott'archi grandi al principio di detta loggia l'altro al confine dell'altra loggia, entroui Imprese figure et abbigliamenti stimiamo in tutto scudi uenti l'uno e tutti insieme scudi quaranta ...   40
somma ...   910

La seconda loggia che uolta uerso il Saluatore che finisce all'entrata della sala di Constantino contiene in prima una legatura d'intagli finti che ricinge tutta la uolta, et ne peducci di essa sono Historie di N. S. Gesu Cristo et di san Gio. Battista in tutto numero sedici et sotto a dette Historie nel fine de peducci sono Historie del Testamento Vecchio, che figurano le di sopra et fra l'uno Peduccio e l'altro che s'incontra et ua a trouare la sommita della uolta sono imprese di S. Beatudine di n. otto tolte in mezzo da gli ornamenti di esse Historie, che tutto stimiamo insieme scudi quattrocento sessantacinque...   465

Le due lunette entroui cori d'Angeletti con uarij instrumenti Musicali quali stanno su le nuuole et nel mezzo della uolta à dritto fra lunetta e lunetta sono quattro Angeli in campo azurro che sostengano una ghirlanda con un motto di S. B. et fra ogni lunetta appresso l'Historie in certi spatij di campi Rossi sono Angeli che suonano Trombe et negli Angoli d'ogni lunetta appresso il Peduccio sono altre figure in diuerse attitudine che tutto stimiano scudi trecento ottantacinque....   385

Nelli otto sordelli di detta loggia sono otto paesi et allo scontro di essi sotto gli archi sono dipinti intagli finti che stimiamo scudi cento   100

Sopra la porta che ua nella sala di Constantino et uno sordello entroui l'arme di S. Beatudine con due figure grandi con uarij ornamenti et al suo scontro un altra arme conforme alla detta che tutta stimiamo scudi cinquanta...   50

Due porte finte uno allo scontro della sudetta Porta et l'altra nella risuolta con la chiocciola sgraffita in detta loggia stimiamo scudi dieci... 10
somma...   1010

Nel Salone di Constantino sono con l'infrascritto ordine le seguenti Pitture stimate

In Prima le quattro Historie di Constantino Imperatore. La prima nella testa di detta sala uerso l'altre stanze del Palazzo è la uisione che hebbe Constantino della croce uista in Aere con il suo Ornamento di detta historia...   100

257

Per li due lati di essa Historia sono due figure grandi rappresentanti uarie uirtù et nei cantoni sono due Imprese di N. Signore che in tutto stimiamo scudi quaranta...   40

Allo scontro di detta historia è l'altra quando Constantino è battizato da san Siluestro con le simili figure et ornamenti che la soprascritta al suo rincontro quale stimiamo scudi centoquaranta...   140

Nella facciata uolta uerso Santa Maria Maggiore è la processione pontificale di San Siluestro doue interuiene Constantino Imperatore che guida per freno il cauallo con il suo ornamento come l'altre con due figure grandi ai lati l'una per Mosè et l'altra per Aaron che pigliano in mezzo detta Historia quale stimiamo scudi cento trenta et le dette due figure scudi uenti che tutto insieme stimiamo scudi centocinquanta...   150

Le due Paesi grandi che pigliano in mezzo l'historia sudetta et le figure con il suo ornamento stimiamo scudi uenti in tutto...   40

Nell'altra facciata rincontro a questa è una Historia della Donatione che fece Constantino a Santa Chiesa con il suo ornamento stimiamo scudi cento dieci et le due figure figurate per l'una Davit e l'altra per Salamone scudi uenti che in tutto stimiamo scudi cento trenta...   130

Li Due paesi conformi alli sudetti che li sono a rincontro al medesimo prezzo che li di sopra... 40

Tutti gli ornamenti delle facciate dall'Historie sino in terra con le finestre doue sono ornamenti et partimenti di Pietre mischie con le Historiette finte di Bronzo et imprese di N. S. stimiamo in tutto scudi cento Diciamo...   100

Somma in tutto...   740

Nel Salotto delli Apostoli contiguo al Salone di Constantino antedetto sono Historie due come apresso

In Prima nella facciata grande uerso il cortile del palazzo è l' istoria quando Dio diede lo Spirito Santo alli Settanta Seniori per gouerno del popolo d'Israele in compagnia di Mosè et Aaron, con il suo ornamento quale stimiamo scudi centouenticinque...   125

Allo scontro di essi ui è la missione dello Spirito Santo nella Pentecoste con il suo ornamento come di rincontro, quale stimiamo scudi cento uenticinque...   125

Otto Historie delli Apostoli due per cantonata parte di esse delle elettioni loro e parte delli atti con li loro ornamenti scudi sessanta l' una che tutto insieme fanno scudi quattrocento ottanta... 480

Nelle due teste di detto salotto nel mezzo delle facciate sono due Arme di N. Signore con due fi-

gure per ciascuna arme quale stimiamo scudi uenticinque l'una in tutto...   50
somma   780

Il finimento in capo alla scala grande che principia dalla porta santa di san Giouanni che sale nel Salone di Constantino doue sono dipinte legature d'intagli finti, grottesche et Paesi Abbigliamenti et figure al naturale piccole et nel sordello della risalita è una arme di N. Signore con figure Puttini et Angeli, et al suo scontro sopra la porta un'altra arme di N. Signore con figure et Puttini che tutto insieme stimiamo scudi trecento... 300
somma   300

Le cinque stanze attaccate al sudetto Salone di Constantino et salotto che guardano uerso il cortile

Nella prima stanza uerso la scala grande sudetta la quale stanza ha ricetto doue si passa fra la sala di Constantino è la loggia contiene prima nei quattro sordeli grandi un paese per ciascuno con figure di santi et nella uolta una legatura d'intagli finti fogliami imprese et altri ornamenti et nel mezzo della uolta sono Angeli che reggono una impresa di N. Signore che tutto stimiamo scudi nouanta...   90

Nella seconda stanza a canto alla detta è una legatura di stucchi finti nelli ornamenti di sei sordelli dentroui sei Paesi et in essi una figura d'un santo et ne Peducci della uolta figure che rappresentano uirtù et nella uolta Angeli et puttini che tengano imprese di N. Signore che tutti stimiamo scudi centouenti cinque...   125

Nella terza stanza è una legatura d'intagli finti et listelli doue sono grottesche e imprese di N. Signore et uarij abbigliamenti et nel mezzo della uolta è un'arme di N. Signore et in ogni testa di detta stanza son due Paesi grandi in due sordelli et ne quattro sordelli di fianchi sono paesi piu piccoli adornati d'imprese et uarij ornamenti e ne peducci di esse uolte sono figure che rappresentano diuerse uirtu che tutto stimiamo scudi centosettanta...   170

La quarta stanza quale è dipinta conforme alla terza sopradetta è stimata scudi cento settanta...
                                       170

La quinta et ultima di forma minore dell'altre ci è una ligatura d'intagli finti et listelli doue sono Paesi grottesche et uarij ornamenti et Imprese di N. Signore quali stimiamo scudi centodieci... 110

Come si uede montano tutte le Pitture fatte ultimamente al Palazzo Lateranense dopo l'ultimo saldo scudi cinquemila trecento cinque di moneta stimata per la parte di Monsignore Ill.mo della Corgna da ms. Girolamo Mutiano Pittore, et per la parte de Pittori da ms. Jacomo Rocchetti Pittore quali si sotto scriueranno qui appresso Dico...   5305

SISTO V E IL PALAZZO LATERANENSE. RIASSUNTO

Il Palazzo Lateranense è il più importante e il meno studiato tra i principali edifici commissionati da Sisto V. Costruito tra il 1585 e il 1587 su parte del sito fino ad allora occupato dal Patriarchium, l'antica residenza pontificia, l'edificio voluto da Sisto V venne decorato con un ciclo di affreschi esteso su tre piani (eseguito in fasi successive tra il 1588 ed il 1589), di cui si vuole qui indagare, in gran parte per la prima volta, il significato.

Uno degli aspetti che più colpisce nel vasto ciclo decorativo è la presenza delle realizzazioni o Opere buone di Sisto: raffigurate in modi diversi (scene narrative, imprese), sono presenti in più punti del ciclo, così che la presenza del pontefice è sempre percepita. Il mio punto di partenza è dunque la figura del committente e le sue opere buone. Nell'introduzione si analizza il carattere e il contesto delle Opere buone di Sisto (realizzate o solo progettate), immortalate per la posterità sia ad affresco che in scultura nei principali monumenti eretti per volere pontificio. Da essi emerge come essenziale per la comprensione del ciclo lateranense la duplice natura - spirituale e temporale - del potere pontificio.

Le Opere buone di Sisto alludono sia al pontificato che all'intera biografia del papa, soprattutto nelle allegorie dell'Abbondanza, Estirpazione dei banditi, Tesoro di Castel S. Angelo, Lega dei principi cristiani. Si è quindi presa in considerazione la vita del papa a partire dalle premonizioni alla sua nascita fino alla sua assunzione alla Cattedra di Pietro, evidenziando tutta una serie di temi che informano sia il ciclo decorativo che tanta letteratura panegirica: tra questi, il ruolo del papa come successore di Mosè, tradizionale typus papae; il suo francescanesimo; il suo carattere augusteo; la sua natura solare. Mentre da un lato ognuno di questi temi in ultima istanza consente una lettura occulta della vita e dell'arte pontificie, nei capitoli successivi l'attenzione si concentra sulle tradizioni conservatrici, francescane e papali al fine di caratterizzare la valenza istituzionale dei significati del programma.

Il primo capitolo tratta dell'antica residenza pontificia, dalle favoleggiate origini come residenza imperiale donata da Costantino a papa Melchiade (o a papa Silvestro, secondo la tradizione mitico-agiografica), fino alle condizioni di disastroso abbandono in cui Sisto trovò il Patriarchium nel 1585. Come Giulio II all'inizio del secolo, così Sisto prese la drastica decisione di abbattere una struttura considerata intoccabile per la cristianità; ma al contrario di Giulio II, la decisione di Sisto coincideva con la nascita dell'archeologia cristiana come disciplina e con la grande venerazione per la Chiesa delle origini che caratterizzò l'età posttridentina. Di conseguenza, la decisione del pontefice fu controversa, anche tra gli intellettuali legati alla corte. L'effettiva ragione della decisione di Sisto viene analizzata alla luce della testimonianza di Domenico Fontana, l'architetto personale di Felice Peretti dall'epoca in cui era cardinale, e architetto del Palazzo Lateranense.

All'analisi della forma e funzione della nuova residenza pontificia segue una rassegna della storiografia del ciclo decorativo, attestante il relativo disinteresse da parte degli studiosi per numerosi anni; viene inclusa una trattazione degli artisti impegnati nella decorazione sotto la generale supervisione degli imprenditori Cesare Nebbia e Giovanni Guerra, fornendo un elenco di quelle parti del programma che sono state specificamente identificate dagli studiosi a partire dalla costruzione del palazzo e dalla Trasportatione dell'obelisco Vaticano *del Fontana fino ai nostri giorni.*

*Poiché il programma del Palazzo Lateranense è composto da tante componenti da rendere impossibile una trattazione individuale esaustiva e convincente, si è tentato di dare una panoramica dei temi fondamentali, basata su testimonianze intrinseche alla decorazione stessa. L'analisi si concentra sull'aspetto secolare, imperiale della personalità e delle Opere buone del pontefice, basandosi sul fatto che la maggior parte delle Opere buone affrescate nel palazzo, soprattutto nel salone principale (il Salone dei Papi), mostra un carattere essenzialmente secolare. Allo stesso tempo, va riconosciuto che la carica del pontefice, nonché le sue imprese, sono essenzialmente sacre. Per questa ragione viene proposta una più ampia analisi del programma, basata su testimonianze esterne, e concentrata sulle scene narrative del piano nobile. La contrapposizione cattolicesimo-protestantesimo è essenziale per la comprensione del programma; in particolare, all'*Ecclesiastica Historia *(1559-1574) vengono contrapposti gli* Annales Ecclesiastici *(1588-1607), e un gran numero di temi caratteristici della Riforma cattolica romana si enucleano come chiavi di lettura dell'intero ciclo decorativo. Tra tali temi sono i Sacramenti, l'efficacia delle immagini sacre, il culto dei santi, il primato e l'infallibilità pontifici, l'efficacia della fede. L'attenzione per il Patriarchio*

Lateranense (soprattutto per quel che concerne l'essenziale organizzazione trinitaria del ciclo decorativo del palazzo, ma anche di tutti gli altri cicli della Roma sistina), completa la discussione generale della rilevanza del programma: a mio avviso temi politici quali l'investitura, l'unzione divina e la traslazione dell'impero, nonché il Battesimo e l'Eucarestia, vennero molto plausibilmente ispirati dal trattamento che questi stessi temi avevano avuto nell'antica residenza pontificia. L'evidente importanza di san Francesco e di papa Innocenzo III per il Patriarchio Lateranense, nonché per il francescano Sisto, è ovviamente da considerare come presupposto per la comprensione della rilevante valenza francescana e politico-teologica del programma decorativo. Infine, la presenza della dimensione paesaggistica può essere letta come nesso attraverso cui componenti pagane, cristiane e specificamente francescane, secolari e sacre, vengono sincretizzate e infine unificate.

Avendo fornito una lettura delle componenti principali, nel Capitolo II la discussione si concentra su quattro delle dodici imprese del Salone dei Papi, attraverso cui illuminare gli aspetti dell'intero ciclo più specificamente sistini ed istituzionali. Più in particolare, le quattro allegorie che utilizzano elementi dello stemma pontificio vengono analizzate insieme agli affreschi di analogo soggetto della Biblioteca Vaticana e di Villa Montalto, concludendo che il Palazzo Lateranense in particolare, come la Roma sistina in generale, celebra la fine del millennio, ovvero il ritorno dell'Età dell'oro con la provvidenziale elezione di Sisto.

Il Capitolo III analizza il Salone dei Papi; dopo una introduzione generale, vengono presi in considerazione il registro inferiore temporale e le raffigurazioni delle Opere buone pontificie, la maggior parte delle quali inserite in paesaggi. Le imprese vengono analizzate dal punto di vista di imago *e* subscriptio, *con approfondimento e chiarimento delle componenti cristiane e pagane. Come per le imprese allegoriche, il registro inferiore è unificato nel segno del simbolismo solare, già prepotente nella "mitologia" del fanciullo Felice Peretti, come del resto il simbolismo mosaico e in ultima analisi paolino. Comune al simbolismo solare, mosaico e paolino è la conversione a causa della luce: questo concetto, analizzato nel capitolo seguente, si rivela predominante nel ciclo del Palazzo Lateranense. L'analisi del registro inferiore viene completata con lo studio dei finti medaglioni che accompagnano le raffigurazioni dei papi apostolici che rappresentano le loro azioni o Opere buone; viene presa in considerazione ogni singola figura di pontefice e la corrispettiva Opera buona dipinta nel medaglione e descritta dal* titulus *relativo. Nei quattro casi atipici in cui i pontefici sono collocati al di sopra delle Opere buone di Sisto V e non in corrispondenza delle proprie azioni, il metodo di analisi segue quello dell'emblema. Per concludere, i registri inferiore e superiore si dimostrano uniti formalmente e iconograficamente nella persona del committente del ciclo. L'analisi si volge quindi alla discussione delle scene dell'Istituzione del primato, cui viene data grande rilevanza nel registro superiore delle pareti principali. Leggendo il Salone dei Papi come un tutto sintetico, diviene chiara la relazione col programma della Sala del Concilio del Patriarchio Lateranense. Il capitolo si conclude con una discussione sull'autore del programma iconografico del Salone e dell'intero ciclo lateranense: Pompeo Ugonio potrebbe essere indicato come una possibilità alternativa a Silvio Antoniano, l'intellettuale tradizionalmente considerato autore dell'intero programma sulla scorta della biografia scritta dal Castiglione all'inizio del XVII secolo.*

Il Capitolo IV si apre con una discussione delle più famose tra le Opere buone di Sisto V: gli obelischi e le colonne. La Sala degli Obelischi, l'unico ambiente del palazzo in cui le Opere buone vengono rappresentate senza iscrizioni, viene analizzata formalmente ed iconograficamente. Le cerimonie svolte di fronte agli obelischi e alle colonne possono contribuire a comprendere i significati dei monoliti e delle colonne convertiti alla fede. Insieme alle personificazioni che accompagnano le raffigurazioni degli obelischi e delle colonne, gli apostoli Pietro e Paolo costituiscono un mezzo essenziale per l'interpretazione della volta della Sala degli Obelischi e più in generale di tutto il programma del Palazzo Lateranense. Analogamente al Salone dei Papi, questa Sala è incentrata sul tema dell'autorità temporale e spirituale del pontefice e sull'idea della conversione che è intimamente legata all'erezione, esorcizzazione e coronamento degli obelischi col segno della croce e coi simboli sistini, nonché delle colonne con le statue di Pietro e Paolo. Il tema della conversione va letto come essenziale complemento alla nozione di translatio imperii *che informa di sé sia la Sala degli Obelischi che il Salone dei Papi. Infine il messaggio del salone principale, riecheggiato dalla Sala degli Obelischi, viene continuato a mio avviso nei restanti ambienti, saloni e logge del palazzo, soprattutto in quelli contenenti Opere buone di Sisto V raffigurate in modo non canonico come episodi biblici, imprese e attributi di personificazioni.*

La volta della Sala di Samuele, formalmente ricollegabile alla Sala degli Obelischi, contiene una rappresentazione di Samuele che erige la "pietra del soccorso"; è significativo notare come la "pietra del soccorso" venga raffigurata come obelisco eretto secondo il modo descritto ed illustrato dal Fontana. Le molteplici implicazioni di questa analogia includono le nozioni che l'Egitto figuri in posizione preminente nel contesto della propaganda del pontificato sistino, che la creazione della "pietra del soccorso" sia in relazione con la conversione degli obelischi e colonne sistini, e che gli altri personaggi celebrati nel ciclo del palazzo, come Samuele, debbano essere comparati a Sisto V. Tali idee vengono discusse e chiarite nell'analisi che considera gli obelischi e le colonne come imprese ovvero attributi delle personificazioni nel Salone di Costantino, nella loggia est del piano nobile, nella quarta sala dell'appartamento privato, nell'estensione della loggia ovest del piano nobile, nella Sala di Salomone. In ognuno di questi casi la lettura sincretistica delle Opere buone del Salone dei Papi, della Sala degli Obelischi e della Sala di Samuele viene corroborata dall'interpretazione delle altre sale e logge del palazzo, in cui Sisto V è manifestamente presente.

Il messaggio del programma, affidato a una disposizione particolare di scene narrative, imprese, emblemi e personificazioni, è particolarmente diretto: durante il pontificato di Sisto V il mondo deve essere convertito dalla fede cattolica, e la Chiesa Militante traslata in Chiesa Trionfante.

Il testo viene completato da cinque appendici. La prima contiene una lista dei soggetti affrescati suddivisi per ambiente, proposta come una guida per chi volesse un'esatta descrizione, in vista anche di ulteriori approfondimenti, di quanto raffigurato nei vari ambienti. La seconda elenca le imprese, riportando le fonti note delle "anime". La terza fornisce una serie di elenchi, tratti dalla letteratura sul palazzo, indicanti le contrastanti opinioni circa l'ordine di percorso attraverso camere e saloni del piano nobile. La quarta ripropone le affermazioni sui contenuti e significati degli ambienti fatte dai pochi autori che hanno trattato il ciclo lateranense in modo meno episodico. La quinta ed ultima appendice riporta il testo della stima delle pitture nel libro dei conti di Domenico Fontana conservato nell'Archivio Segreto Vaticano.

SELECTED BIBLIOGRAPHY

PRIMARY SOURCES: UNPUBLISHED

Archivio Laterano (AL)

A XXXXIX
Giuseppe Maria Soresini, "Annali Laterani di Giuseppe Maria Soresini, 1674- Libro XIII [Sisto V]"
K XXX
"Liber Decretorum Capitulj Annorum 1589"

Archivio di Stato di Roma (ASR)
Camerale I
Fabbriche, reg. 1527/8
"Libro XXI a - 1589" [Lateran Palace]

Archivio della Biblioteca Vaticana (BAV)
BAV 1
Federico Rainaldi's journal

Archivio Segreto Vaticano (ASV)
S. Palazzo Apostolico. Titoli, 122.4
"Palazzo Lateranense. Fascicoli 1-4"

Biblioteca Apostolica Vaticana (BAV)
Fondo Barberiniano Latino, cod. 2160
Pompeo Ugonio, "Schedario"
Barb. lat. cod. 2603
Pompeo Ugonio, "Vitae Romanorum Pontificum a B. Petro Apostolo ad Stephanum VI. cum originalibus observationibus et collationibus Pompei Ugonii"
Barb. lat. cod. 2793
"Diaria sub Sixto V in annis D.ni 1585-1590"
Fondo Capponi cod. 57
"Memorie in tempo di Sisto V"
Fondo Chigiani, cod. S. III. 4
G. Cugnoni, "Inventario delle scritture che erano inventario 3575 nello studio del Papa Sisto V"
Fondo Ottoboniano Latino cod. 568
Catervo Foglietta, "Lettera ad un amico di ragguaglio delle Chiese di Roma, et opere fatte da Sisto V sommo Pontefice con riflessioni morali MDLxxxvii"
Fondo Vaticano Latino cod. 3561
Andrea de' Monte, "Sanctissimo Patri atque Optimo Principi Domino nrō Domino Julio, divina providenza Papae Terzo ... "
Vat. lat. cod. 5438
Pietro Galesino, "Sanctissimo Patri Sixto Quinto... ac rectori commentarium hoc de vita, rebusque ab eo in singulos annos diesq. publice et pontificie actis gestiq. distribute, ac luculente ..."
Vat. lat. cod. 9721
Vita di Papa Sisto V Principiando dalla sua Nascita fino alla di lui Morte con tutti gl'accidenti segniti nel corso del suo Pontificato"
Vat. lat. cod. 12141
"De Vita Sixti Quinti ipsius manu emendata"
Vat. lat. cod. 12142
"Memorie del Pontificato di Papa Sisto V^{to}"
Vat. lat. cod. 12293
Paulo Alaleone, "Diaria 1585-1590"
Vat. lat. cod. 12315
Francesco Mucantio, "Diarium ex scriptis F. M. sub Sixto V. à die obitus Gregorij xiii videlicèt co 24 Aprilis 1585 usque ad diem obitus eiusd. Sixti videlicèt 27 Aug.ti 1590"
Biblioteca Vallicelliana (BV)
cod. I 66

Paulo Alaleone, "Diarium Caeremoniarum, et Actorum Summorum Pontificum Tomus III, Ab anno Domini 1591 ad anno 1594"

PRIMARY SOURCES: PUBLISHED

de Aguilar, Giovanni Battista. *S. D. N. Sixto Quinto Pont. Opt. Max. Concio Habita In Sanctiss. Trinitatis Die Anno Domini M. D. LXXXVII ... in Ad. S. D. N. Sixtum V. Pont. Opt. Max. Conciones Tres Apud Sanctum Petrum* ... Rome, 1588.

de Alava, Leon. *Concio Habita Coram Sixto V. P.O.M. Dominica Pentecostes* ... Rome, 1589.

Alberti, R. P. Frate Innocentio. *Ragionamenti intorno alla giustitia di N. S. Papa Sisto Quinto* ... Urbino, 1587.

Alciato, Andrea. *The Latin Emblems: index and lists.* Ed. Peter M. Daly with Virginia W. Callahan, assisted by Simon Cuttler and Paola Valeri-Tomaszuk, 2 vols. Toronto, Buffalo and London, 1985.

Alemanno, Nicola. *De Lateranensibus parietinis ab illustriss. & Reverendiss. Domino D. Francisco Card. Barberino Restituis Dissertatio Historica.* Rome, 1625.

Ammirato, Scipione. *Oratione al Beatiss. et Santiss. Padre, et Signor Nostro Sisto Quinto* ... Florence, 1594.

Aresi, Paolo. *Delle Imprese Sacre con utili e dilettevoli discorsi accompagnate libro primo* ... Verona, 1615.

Bacci, Andrea. *L'Alicorno; discorso ... nel quale si tratta della natura dell'Alicorno & delle sue virtù eccellentissime* ... 1st ed. 1573. Florence, 1582.

__. *Le XII. pietre pretiose, le quali per ordine di Dio nella Santa Legge, adornavano i vestimenti del sommo sacerdote.* Rome, 1587.

Badesio, Gerolamo. *De Sacello Sixti V. Pont. Max. in Exquiliis* ... Rome, 1588.

Baglione, Giovanni. *Vite de pittori, scultori, architetti ed intagliatai dal Pontificato di Gregorio XIII del 1572 a tempi di Papa Urbano VIII nel 1642.* 1st ed. 1642. Ed. C. Gradara Pesci, Italica Gens Repertori di bio-bibliografia italiana N. 77, 2 vols. Bologna, 1975.

Bano, Enea *Rime Sopra la Creatione del S. S. N. Sisto PP. V.* Perugia, 1587.

Baronio, Caesare S. R. E. Card. *Annales Ecclesiastici Denuo Excusi et ad Nostra Usque Tempora Perducti.* 1st ed. 1588-1607. Reprint ed. 37 vols. Paris, Brussels, 1864-1887.

Benigno, Giulio. *Oratio De Christi Domini In Caelum Ascensu Habita Ad Sixtum V. Pont. Max. In Sacello Vaticano.* Rome, 1589.

Bianco, Guglielmo. *Aquae Felices Ad S. D. N. Sixtum V. Pont. Opt. Max.* Rome, 1587.

__. *Epigrammata ... in Obeliscum Mirae magnitudinis ... à SIXTO V. PONT. MAX. translatum, & superimposita Cruce Christianae Religioni dedicatum.* Rome, 1586.

Biblia Sacra iuxta Vulgatam Clementinam. Ed. Alberto Colunga and Laurentio Turrado. Biblioteca de Autores Cristianos, 14, 6th ed. Madrid, 1982.

Bocchio, Achille. *Symbolicarum Quaestionum, De universo genere, quas serio Ludebat, Libri Quinque.* Bologna, 1574.

Bonardo, F. Vincentio. *Discorso Intorno all'Origine, Antichita, et Virtu de gli Agnus Dei Di Cera Benedetti.* Rome, 1586.

Bonaventure. *Opera Omnia Sixti V. Pontificis Maximi Jussu Diligentissime Emendata* ... Ed. A. C. Peltier, 15 vols. Paris, 1867.

__. *The Works of Bonaventure: Cardinal, Seraphic Doctor and Saint.* Trans. José de Vinck, 5 vols. Paterson, New Jersey, 1970.

Bordino, Giovanni Francesco. *De Rebus Praeclare Gestis A Sisto V. Pon. Max.* ... Rome, 1588.

Bressio, Maurizio. *Ad Summum Pontificem Oratoris Oratio, Ad Sixtum V. Pont. Opt. Max. Romae in aula Regum habita 11 die Septemb. MDLXXXVI* ... Rome, n.d.

Buccio, Augustino. *Ad Sixtum Quintum Pont. Max. Oratio In publico Consistoro habita ... An. M. D. LXXXVI* Rome, 1586.

Bullarum Diplomatum et Privilegiorum Sanctorum Romanorum Pontificum Taurinensis Editio ... Ed. Francisco Gaude, Aloysio Bilio, 25 vols. n.p.; Naples, 1857-1872.

Canons and Decrees of the Council of Trent: original text with English translation. Trans. & Intro. H. J. Schroeder. 1st ed.1941. Rockford, Illinois, 1978.

... Carmina A Variis Auctoribus in Obeliscum Conscripta ... Rome, 1586.

Cartari, Vincenzo. *Le imagini de i Dei de gli Antichi.* 1st ed.1556. New York and London, 1979.

Castiglione, Giuseppe. *Silvii Antoniani S.R.E. Cardinalis Vita* ... Rome, 1610.

Catani, Baldo. *La Pompa Funerale fatti dall'Ill.mo & R.mo S.r Cardinale Montalto nella trasportatione dell'ossa di Papa Sisto Quinto.* Rome, 1591.

The Catechism of the Council of Trent, Published by Command of Pope Pius the Fifth. 1st ed. 1566. Trans.

J. Donovan. Dublin, 1829.

Colonna, Ascanio. *Oratio Ad Sixtum V. P. M. ...* Rome, 1773.

Conti, Natale. *Mythologiae.* 1st ed. 1551. Reprint ed. 1567. New York and London, 1976.

Corpus Juris Canonici Academicum, Emendatum & Notis P. Lancellotti Illustratum ... 2 vols. Venice, 1782.

Costantino, D. Emanuele. *Ad Sanctissimum D. N. Sixtum V. Pont. Opt. Max. ... Carmen.* Rome, 1588.

Dante Alighieri. The Divine Comedy. Trans., commentary by Charles S. Singleton, Bollingen Series LXXX, 6 vols. 1st ed. 1970-1975. Revised ed. Princeton, New Jersey, 1977.

Eusebius. *Ecclesiastical History.* Trans. J.E.L. Oulton, 2 vols. Loeb Classical Library. 1st ed. 1932. Cambridge, Mass; London, 1980.

Fabricio, Principio. *Delle Allusioni, Imprese, et Emblemi ... Sopra la vita, opere, et attioni di Gregorio XIII ... Libri VI.* 1st ed. 1585. Rome, 1588.

Felici, Pompeo. *La prima delle Cinquanta Quattro Stationi di Roma ...* Rimini, 1586.

Fontana, Domenico. *Della trasportatione dell'obelisco Vaticano et delle fabriche di Nostro Signore Papa Sisto V ...* 1st ed. 1590. Ed. Adriano Carugo, intro. Paolo Portoghesi. Milan, 1978.

Fontes Historiae Religionis Aegyptiacae. Ed. Theodorus Hopfner, Fontes Historiae Religionum Ex Auctoribus Graecis et Latinis Collectos Edidit Carolus Clemen Fasciculi II Pars I. Bonn, 1922.

Gaci, Cosimo. *Dialogo ... d'intorno all'eccellenza della Poesia. Si parla poi delle valorose operationi di Sisto V. P.O.M. et in particolare del transportamento dell'Obelisco del Vaticano ...* Rome, 1586.

Galesino, Pietro. *Dedicatio Columnae Cochlidis Traiani Caes. Augusti Ad honorem Sancti Petri ...* Rome, 1587.

__. *Familiaris Quaedam Epistola e Roma in Hispaniam Missa. In qua quid actum sit ... in translatione Obelisci breviter explicatur ...* Rome, 1586.

__. *Ordo Dedicationis Obelisci Quem S. D. N. Sixtus V. Pont. Max. ...* Rome, 1586.

Georgi, Francesco. *De Harmonia mundi totius Cantica tria.* Venice, 1525.

__. *In Scripturam Sacram Problemata ...* Venice, 1536.

Gratiano, Alessandro. *Oratio de Spiritu Sancto Ad Sixtum Quintum Pontificem Maximum Habita in Basilica Sancti Pietri ...* Rome, 1585.

Gyraldo, Lilio Gregorio. *De Deis Gentium varia & multiplex Historia ...* 1548. New York & London, 1976.

Hesiod. *Works and Days* in *Hesiod.* Trans. Hugh G. Evelyn-White, Loeb Classical Library. London; New York, 1914.

Holy Bible translated from the Vulgate. Douay Version, Old Testament 1609; New Testament 1582. Rockford, Illinois, 1971.

Horace. *Carminum Liber* in *Horace: the Odes and Epodes.* Trans. C.E. Bennett, Loeb Classical Library 1st ed. 1914. Rev. 1927. Cambridge, Mass; London, 1978.

Hyginus. *Poeticon Astronomicon* in *C. Iulii Hygini Augusti Liberti Fabularum Liber, ... eiusdem poeticon astronomicon ...* 1st ed.1535. New York & London, 1976.

Josephus, *Jewish Antiquities* in *Josephus.* Trans. H. St. J. Thackeray, Loeb Classical Library, 9 vols. Cambridge, Mass; London, 1961.

Lactantius. *The Divine Institutes.* Trans. William Fletcher, Ante-Nicene Christian Library. Translations of the Writings of the Fathers down to A.D. 325: The Works of Lactantius, ed. Alexander Roberts, James Donaldson, 2 vols. Edinburgh, Scotland, 1871.

a Lapide, Cornelio Cornelio. *Commentaria in Sacram Scripturam ...* Ed. Sisto Riario Sforza, 10 vols. Naples, 1857.

Le Liber Pontificalis. Texte, Introduction et Commentaire. Ed. L'Abbé L. Duchesne. 2 vols. 1st ed. 1886, 1892. Paris, 1955.

Macrobius. *Commentary on the Dream of Scipio.* Trans., Intro & Notes by William Harris Stahl. 1st ed. 1952. New York & London, 1966.

Matasilani Bolognese, Mario. *La Felicità del Serenissimo Cosimo Medici Granduca di Toscana ...* Florence, 1572.

Mercati, Michele. *Consideratione ... sopra gli Avvertimenti del Sig. Latino Latini. Intorno ad alcune cose scritte nel libro de gli Obelischi di Roma. ...* Rome, 1590.

__. *Gli Obelischi di Roma.* 1st ed. 1589. Ed. Gianfranco Cantelli. Bologna, 1981.

Mola, Giovanni Battista. *Breve Racconto delle miglior opere d'architettura scultura et pittura fatte in Roma et alcuni fuor di Roma.* 1st ed.1663. Ed., intro., Karl Noehles, Quellen und Schriften zur bildenden Kunst. Berlin, 1966.

Oliva, Giuseppe. *In Sanctissimi D. Nostri Sixti V. Pont. Maximi Creationem Carmen.* Cremona, 1585.

Origen. *Contra Celsum.* Trans, intro & notes Henry Chadwick. Cambridge, 1953.

Ovid. *Fasti* in *Ovid's Fasti*. Trans. Sir James George Frazer, Loeb Classical Library. London; New York, 1931.

__. *Metamorphoses*. Trans. Frank Justus Miller, 2 vols. Loeb Classical Library. 1st ed. 1916. Cambridge, Mass; London, 1958.

Pansa, Mutio. *Delle Glorie di Sisto Quinto Rime* ... Rome, 1588.

__. *Della Libraria Vaticana* ... Rome, 1590.

__. *Discorso sopra la grandezza dell'opere di Papa Sisto V*. Rome, 1588.

Panvinio, Onofrio. *Le Vite de tutti i Pontefici da S. Pietro in Qua, Ridotte in epitome da Tomaso Costo Napoletano* ... Venice, 1592.

Peregrino, Laelio. *Oratio habita in Almo Urbis Gymnasio de Utilitate Moralis Philosophiae ... Anno MDLXXXVII*. Rome, 1587.

Peretti da Montalto, Padre Fra Felice. *Predica della Purissima Concettione della Gloriosa Madre de Dio Maria Vergine*. 1st ed.1554. Naples, 1588.

__. *Predica Sopra il non men difficil che misterioso Vangelo della Settuagesima* ... Naples, 1554.

__. *Predicata nella inclita citta di Perugia il di delle Cineri ... Predica della necessita della sacra scrittura à reformare l'huomo* n.p., n.d..

__. *Prediche del R. Padre Fra Felice Peretti da Mont'alto Regente in S. Lorenzo di Napoli* ..., n.p., n.d.

Peretti da Tarentino, Giovanni Antonio. *Sixti Quinti Pont. Max. Creatio* ... Rome n.d.

Philo of Alexandria, *Questions and Answers on Exodus*. Trans. Ralph Marcus in *Philo*. Trans. F. H. Colson, G. H. Whitaker, Loeb Classical Library, 10 vols. and 2 supp. vols. Cambridge, Mass; London, 1961-1962.

Piccha, Gregorio. *Oratio Ad Sixtum V. Pont. Max. Aliosq. Christianos Principes, et Respubl. Pro Britannico bello indicendo*. Rome, 1588.

__. *Oratio Ad Sixtum V. Pont. Opt. Max. Pro dignitate nuper in Evangelistam Palloctum collata*. Rome, 1588.

__. *Oratione per la Guerra Contra Turchi A Sisto Quinto Pont Massimo et A Gl'Altri Principi Christiani*. Delivered1588. Rome, 1589.

Pigafetta, M. Filippo. *Discorso ... d'intorno all'historia della aguglia, et alla ragione del muoverla*. Rome, 1586.

Pinadello, Giovanni. *Invicti Quinarii Numeri Series Quae Summation a Superioribus Pontificibus et Maxime A Sisto Quinto* ... Rome, 1589.

Platina, Battista. *Historia B. Platinae De Vitis Pontificum Romanorum Ad. N. Iesu Christo Vsque ad Paulum II ... annotationum Onuphrii Panvinii ... & Antonii Ciccarelli* ... Cologne, 1600.

__. *Historia delle vite de'sommi pontefici*. Trans., emended by Girolamo Beroardi. Venice, 1608.

Plato. *Politicus* in *Plato*. Trans. Harold N. Fowler, Loeb Classical Library. London; New York, 1925.

__. *Republic* in *Republic*. Trans. Paul Shorey, Loeb Classical Library. 1st ed.1930. Revised 1937. Cambridge, Mass; London, 1943.

Rasponi, C. *De Basilica et Patriarchio Lateranensi Libri Quattuor, Ad Alexandrum VII Pont. Max.* Rome, 1656.

Ripa, Cesare. *Iconologia overo descrittione di diverse imagini cavate dall'antichità, e di propria inventione*. 1st ed. 1593. Reprint 1618. Ed. Piero Buscaroli, preface by Mario Praz, "La Torre d'avorio," 2 vols. Turin, 1986.

Robardo, Vincenzo. *Sixti V. Pont. Max. Gesta Quinquennalia Ac. Ill.morum et Rev.morum S.R.E. Car.lium* ... Rome, 1590.

Rocca, Angelo. *Biblioteca Apostolica Vaticana A Sixto V, Pont. Max. in splendidiorem. Commodioremq. locum translata, et a Fratre Angelo Roccha a Camerino Ordinis Eremitarum S. Augustini, ... Ad S. D. N. Gregorium XIV*. Rome, 1591.

Rocco, Bernardino. *Roma Restaurata. Alla Santità di N.S. Sisto Quinto*. Verona, 1589.

Rodolpho, Gerolamo. *Ad Sanctiss. D. Nostrum Sixtum Quintum Pontificem Opt. Max. Io. Baptistae Evangelistae Oratio habita in almo Firmanorum Gymnasio* ... Firmo, 1586.

De Rossi, Filippo, ed. *Descrizione di Roma Moderna formata nuovamente con le Autorità del Cardinal Baronio, Alfonso Ciaconio, D'Antonio Bosio, Ottavio Panciroli, E d'altri celebri Autori* ... Rome, 1597.

De Sandoval, Don Sancho. *Sermon De La Sanctissima Trinidad Que Hizo Ala Sanctidad De Nuestro muy Sancto Padre Xisto V. Pont. Max* ... Trans. Señoras Donna Gostanza de Sandoval & Donna Leonor Godinez. Rome, n.d.

Scoti, Annibale. *Sixti V. Pont. Max. Cubicularii Intimi. In P. Cornelii Taciti Annales, et Historias Commentarii* ... Rome, 1589.

Sforza, Mutio. *Oratione ... Alla Santità Di N. Sig. Sisto V. Fatta da lui nel tempo, che usu grido, ch'esso Pontefice Mass. voleva ricoverare il S. Sepolcro dal Turco per danari ... in Tre Orationi del S. Mutio Sforza* ... Venice, 1590.

266

St. Francis of Assisi: Writings and Early Biographies. English Omnibus of the Sources for the Life of St. Francis. Ed. M. A. Habig, Trans. Ralph Brown *et al.* Chicago, 1973.

Suare, Francesco. *Ad Sanctiss. Et Beatissimum Patrum Sixtum Quinctum ... Panegyricus Primus.* Rome, 1587.

__. *Ad Sanctiss. et Beatissimum Patrum Sixtum Quinctum Pontificem Maximum Panegyricus Primus.* Rome, 1587.

Suetonius. *Divus Augustus* in *Suetonius.* Trans. J. C. Rolfe, 2 vols. Loeb Classical Library. Cambridge, Mass; London, 1964.

Tertullian. *Apology* in *Apologetical Works and Minucius Felix Octavius.* Trans. Rudolph Arbesmann, Sister Emily Joseph Daly, Edwin A. Quain, The Fathers of the Church. A New Translation. New York, 1950.

Typot, Jacob. *Symbola Divina et Humana Pontificum Imperatorum Regum.* 3 vols. 1st ed. 1601-1603. Instrumentaria Artium 7. Graz, 1972.

Ugonio, Pompeo. *Historia delle Stationi di Roma Che si celebrano la Quadragesima ...* Rome, 1588.

__. *De lingua latina oratio.* Rome, 1586.

__. *Oratio De Laudibus Literarum. Habita in Templo Sancti Eustachij, in die festo Sancti Lucae, Anno 1587 ...* Rome, 1588.

__. *De Sanctissima Cruce in Vertice Obelisci Vaticani ...* Rome, 1587.

Valeriano Bolzani, Giovanni Pietro. *Hieroglyphica.* 1st ed. 1556. Trans. I De Montlyart, 1615. New York and London, 1976.

Valla, Lorenzo. *The Profession of the Religious and the principal arguments from the Falsely-Believed and Forged Donation of Constantine.* Trans., ed. Olga Zorzi Pugliese. Renaissance and Reformation Texts in Translation 1. Toronto, 1985.

de Valle, Pietro Paolo. *Ad S. D. N. Sixtum Quintum Pont. Max. S. P. Q. R. Oratio Ex Tempore Habita, ... Apud Almae Urbis Celebre Templum Sanctae Mariae de Aracœli.* Rome, 1590.

Virgil. *Eclogue IV* and *Aeneid* in *Works.* Trans. H. Rushton Fairclough, 2 vols. Loeb Classical Library. 1st ed. 1916. Revised. Cambridge, Mass; London, 1935.

SECONDARY SOURCES

Abromson, Morton C. *Painting in Rome during the Papacy of Clement VII (1592-1605): a documented study.* New York and London, 1981.

A Cesare Baronio: Scritti vari. Sora, 1963.

Amadio, G. "Come e perchè Sisto V non nacque a Montalto." *Rassegna Marchigiana* VII (1929): 250-252.

d'Amico, Fabrizio. "Su Paolo Guidotti Borghese e su una congiuntura di tardo manierismo romano." *Ricerche di Storia dell'arte* 22 (1984): 71-102.

L'Angelo e la Città. Exh. Cat. Museo Nazionale di Castel Sant'Angelo, 29 September - 29 November 1987. Rome, 1987.

Antonovics, A. V. "Counter-Reformation Cardinals: 1534-90." *European Studies Review* II (1972): 306-307.

Arbesmann, Rudolph. "The 'Malleus' Metaphor in Medieval Characterization." *Traditio* III (1945): 389-392.

Arcangeli, Luciano and Pietro Zampetti, Eds. *Andrea Lilli nella pittura delle Marche tra Cinquecento e Seicento.* Exh. Cat. Rome, 1985.

Armstrong, Edward A. *Saint Francis: Nature Mystic: the derivation and significance of the nature stories in the Franciscan legend.* Berkeley, Los Angeles, London, 1973.

Askew, Pamela. "The Angelic Consolation of St. Francis of Assisi in Post-Tridentine Italian Painting." *Journal of the Warburg and Courtauld Institutes* XXXII (1969): 280-306.

Baldry, H. C. "Who Invented the Golden Age?" *Classical Quarterly* n.s. II (1952): 83-92.

von Barghahn, Barbara. *Age of Gold, Age of Iron: Renaissance Spain and Symbols of Monarchy: The Imperial Legacy of Charles V and Philip II - Royal Castles, Palace-Monasteries, Princely Houses.* 2 vols. Lanham, New York, London, 1985.

__. *Philip IV and the 'Golden House' of the Buen Retiro: in the tradition of Caesar.* 2 vols. New York and London, 1986.

Barroero, Liliana, ed. *Guide Rionali di Roma: Rione I - Monti, Parte I.* 2nd ed. Rome, 1982.

Bartlett Giamatti, A. *The Earthly Paradise and the Renaissance Epic.* Princeton, New Jersey, 1966.

Baumgart, F. "La Caprarola di Ameto Orti." *Studj Romanzi* XXV (1935-37): 77-179.

Baxandall, Michael. *Painting and Experience in Fifteenth Century Italy. A Primer in the Social History of Pictorial Style*. 1st ed. 1972. Oxford, 1988.

Beer, Rüdiger Robert. *Einhorn. Fabelwelt und Wirklichkeit*. Munich, 1972.

Beldon Scott, John. *Images of Nepotism. The Painted Ceilings of Palazzo Barberini*. Princeton, New Jersey, 1991.

Belting, Hans. "Der Einhardsbogen." *Zeitschrift für Kunstgeschichte* XXXVI, 2/3 (1973): 93-121.

__. "I Mosaici dell'Aula Leonina come testimonianza della prima 'Renovatio' nell'arte Medievale di Roma." in *Roma e l'età Carolingia*. Atti delle giornate di studio 3-8 maggio 1976, Istituto di Storia dell'Arte dell'Università di Roma, Istituto Nazionale di Archeologia e Storia dell'Arte, ed. Rome, 1976.

__. "Die beiden Palastaulen Leos III. im Lateran und die Entstehung einer päpstlichen Programmkunst." *Frühmittelalterliche Studien* XII (1978): 55-83.

Bernabei, Franco, et al. *The Sistine Chapel. The Art, the History, and the Restoration*. New York, 1986.

Bernini, Dante. *et al, Il voltone di Pietro da Cortona in Palazzo Barberini*. Quaderni di Palazzo Venezia, 2 Rome, 1983.

Bertolotti, A. *Artisti Modenesi, Parmensi e Della Lunigiana in Roma nei secoli XV, XVI e XVII. Ricerche e studi negli archivi Romani*. 1st ed. 1882. Bologna, n.d.

Bianchi, Lidia. *La villa papale della Magliana*. Rome, 1942.

Biondi, Luigi. *Intorno il Restauramento nel Palazzo Pontificio Lateranense ...* Rome, 1835.

Blunt, Anthony. *Artistic Theory in Italy, 1450-1600*. Oxford, 1962.

__. *Nicholas Poussin*. Bollingen Series XXXV - 7, 2 vols. New York, 1967.

Boas, George. *Essays on Primitivism and Related Ideas in the Middle Ages*. 1st ed. 1948. New York, 1966.

Böck, Angela. *Das Dekorationsprogramm des Lesesaals der Vatikanischen Bibliothek*. Schriften aus dem Institut für Kunstgeschichte der Universität München. Munich, 1988.

Bon, Caterina. "Una proposta per la cronologia delle opere giovanili di Giovanni Baglione." *Paragone* XXXII, 373 (March 1981): 17-48.

Bourne, Ella. "The Messianic Prophecy in Virgil's Fourth Eclogue." *Classical Journal* XI (1915-1916): 390-400.

Bouwsma, W. J. *Venice and the Defense of Republican Liberty: Renaissance Values in the Age of the Counter Reformation*. Berkeley and Los Angeles, 1968.

Bowen, Barbara C. "Mercury at the Crossroads in Renaissance Emblems." *Journal of the Warburg and Courtauld Institutes* 48 (1985): 222-229.

Breckenridge, J. D. "Lateranus Redivivus." *Art Bulletin* LIV, 1 (March 1972): 69-76.

Brown, Jonathan and J.H. Elliott. *A Palace for a King: the Buen Retiro and the court of Philip IV*. 1980; New Haven and London, 1986.

Bruck, Guido. "Hapsburger als 'Herculier'." *Jahrbuch der Kunsthistorischen Sammlungen, Wien* n.s. L (1953): 191-198.

Buddensieg, Tilmann. "Gregory the Great, The Destroyer of Pagan Idols: the history of medieval legend concerning the decline of ancient art and literature." *Journal of the Warburg and Courtauld Institutes* XXVIII (1965): 44-69.

Burkart, Bettina. *Der Lateran Sixtus V und sein Architekt Domenico Fontana*. Bonn, 1987.

Buscaroli, R. *La Pittura di Paesaggio in Italia*. Bologna, 1935.

Cali, Maria. *Da Michelangelo all'Escorial*. Turin, 1980.

Calvesi, Maurizio. *Il sogno di Polifilo prenestino*. ars fingendi 1. 1st ed. 1980. Rome, 1983.

Canestrari, Renato. *Sisto V*. Turin, Milan, Genoa, Parma, Rome, Catania, 1954.

Cappelli, A. *Cronologia, Cronografia e Calendario Perpetuo dal principio dell'èra cristiana ai nostri giorni*. 5th ed. Milan, 1983.

Cassell, Anthony K. *Dante's Fearful Art of Justice*. Toronto, Buffalo, London, 1984.

Cassirer, Ernst. *The Individual and the Cosmos in Renaissance Philosophy*. Trans. with Intro by Mario Domandi. Oxford, 1963.

Cecchelli, Carlo. "Laterano e Vaticano." *Capitolium* V (1929): 63-78.

Cempanari, Mario, and Tito Amodei. *La Scala Santa*. Le chiese di Roma illustrate, 72. Rome, 1974.

Chandler Kirwin, W. "Vasari's Tondo of 'Cosimo I with his Architects, Engineer and Sculptors' in the Palazzo Vecchio: typology and re-identification of portraits." *Mitteilungen des Kunsthistorischen Institutes in Florenz* XV (1971): 105-122.

Chappell, Miles L. and W. Chandler Kirwin. "A Petrine Triumph: The Decoration of the Navi Piccole in San Pietro under Clement VII." *Storia dell'arte* XXI (1974):

Charlesworth, Martin Percival. "Providentia and Aeternitas." *Harvard Theological Review* XXIX (April 1936): 107-132

__. "The Virtues of a Roman Emperor: propaganda and the creation of belief." *Proceedings of the British*

Academy XXIII (1937): 105-133.

Châtelet-Lange, Liliane . "The Grotto of the Unicorn and the Garden of the Villa di Castello." Trans. by Renate Franciscond. *Art Bulletin* L, 1 (March 1968): 55-56.

Cheney, Iris. "The Galleria delle Carte Geografiche at the Vatican and the Roman Church's View of the History of Christianity." *Renaissance Papers* ( ): 21-37.

Chew, Samuel C. *The Pilgrimage of Life*. New Haven and London, 1962.

Chodorow, Stanley. *Christian Political Theory and Church Politics in the Mid-Twelfth Century: the ecclesiology of Gratian's Decretum*. Berkeley, Los Angeles, London, 1972.

Clark, J. W. *The Care of Books*. 1st ed.1901. London, 1975.

Clements, Robert J. *Picta Poesis: Literary and Humanistic Theory in Renaissance Emblem Books*. Rome, 1960.

Cochrane, Eric. *Historians and Historiography in the Italian Renaissance*. Chicago and London, 1981.

Coffin, David R. *Gardens and Gardening in Papal Rome*. Princeton, New Jersey, 1991.

__. "Some Aspects of the Villa Lante at Bagnaia." in *Arte in Europa: Scritti di Storia dell'Arte in onore di Edoardo Arslan*. 2 vols. Milan, 1966.

__. *The Villa d'Este at Tivoli*. Princeton, New Jersey, 1960.

__. *The Villa in the Life of Renaissance Rome*. Princeton, New Jersey, 1979.

Coleman, Christopher Bush. *Constantine the Great and Christianity. Three Phases: the Historical, the Legendary and the Spurious*. New York, 1914.

Combet-Farnoux, Bernard. *Mercure Romain. Le culte public de Mercure et la fonction mercantile à Rome de la République Archaïque à l'époque Augustéenne*. Bibliothèque des Écoles Françaises d'Athènes et de Rome, n. 138. Rome, 1980.

O'Connell, M. R. *The Counter Reformation 1559-1610*. New York, Evanston, San Francisco, London, 1974.

Corbo, Anna Maria. "Appunti su una fonte per la storia urbanistica e edilizia di Roma: la serie "fabbriche" del Camerale I." *Rassegna degli Archivi di Stato* XXV, 1 (January-April 1965).

Corpus Nummorum Italicorum Primo Tentativo di un Catalogo Generale delle Monete Medievali e Moderne Coniate in Italia o da Italiani in altri paesi. Milan, 1936.

Cosenza, Mario Emilio. *Biographical and Bibliographical Dictionary of the Italian Humanists and of the World of Classical Scholarship in Italy, 1300-1800*. 6 vols. 2nd ed. Boston, 1962-1967.

Cosmelli, Flaminia. "L'elefante, l'albero e l'obelisco." *Storia dell'arte* 66 (May - August 1989): 107-118.

Costa, Gustavo. *La leggenda dei secoli d'oro nella letteratura italiana*. Bari, 1972.

Courcelle, Pierre. "Les exégèses chrétiennes de la quatrième éclogue." *Revue des Études Anciennes* LIX (1957): 294-319.

Courtright, Nicola M. "Gregory XIII's Tower of the Winds in the Vatican." diss., New York U, 1990.

Cox-Rearick, Janet "Bronzino's *Crossing of the Red Sea and Moses Appointing Joshua*: Prolegomena to the Chapel of Eleonora di Toledo." *Art Bulletin* LXIX, 1 (March 1987): 45-67.

__. *Dynasty and Destiny in Medici Art: Pontormo, Leo X, and the two Cosimos*. Princeton, New Jersey, 1984.

Cuesta, Ugo. *Una papa fascista*. Milan, 1929.

Cugnoni, G. "Documenti Chigiani concernenti Felice Peretti, Sisto V come privato e come pontefice." *Archivio della Società romana di storia patria* V (1882): 1-32, 210-304, 542-589.

Curtius, Ernst Robert. *European Literature and the Latin Middle Ages*. 1st ed. 1948. Trans. Willard R. Trask, Bollingen Series XXXVI. Princeton, New Jersey, 1973.

Cushing Aikin, Roger. "The Capitoline Hill During the Reign of Sixtus V." diss., U of California, 1977.

DaCosta Kaufmann, Thomas. "Empire Triumphant: Notes on an Imperial Allegory by Adriaen de Vries." *Studies in the History of Art* VIII (1978): 63-75.

__. *Variations on the Imperial Theme in the Age of Maximilian II and Rudolph II*. New York and London, 1978.

Danielou, Jean. *The Bible and the Liturgy*. Trans. 1st ed. 1951. London, 1964.

Davidson, Bernice F. "The Decoration of the Sala Regia under Pope Paul III." *Art Bulletin* LVIII, 3(September 1976), 395-423.

__. "The Landscapes of the Vatican Logge from the Reign of Pope Julius III." *Art Bulletin* LXV, 4 (December 1983): 587-602.

__. "Pope Paul III's Additions to Raphael's Logge: His *Imprese* in the Logge." *Art Bulletin* LXI, 3 (September 1979): 385-404.

__. *Raphael's Bible. A Study of the Vatican Logge*. CAA of America. University Park and London, 1985.

Davis-Weyer, Cäcilia. *Early Medieval Art 300-1150*. Sources and Documents in the History of Art. 1st ed. 1971. Toronto, Buffalo, London, 1986.

__. "Eine patristische Apologie des Imperium Romanum und die Mosaiken derAula Leonina." in *Munuscula Discipulorum. Kunsthistorische Studien H. Kaufmann zum 70 Geburtstag.* Berlin, 1968.

__. "Karolingisches und Nicht-Karolingisches in zwei Mosaikfragmenten der Vatikanischen Bibliothek." *Zeitschrift für Kunstgeschichte* XXXVII (1974): 31-39.

Dejob, Charles. *De l'influence du Concile de Trente dur la litterature et les beaux-arts chez les peuples catholiques. Essai d'introduction a l'histoire litteraire du siècle de Louis XIV.* Paris, 1884.

__. *Marc-Antoine Muret: un professeur français en Italie dans la seconde moitié du XVIe siècle.* 1st ed.1881. Geneva, 1970.

Delaney, Susan J. "The Iconography of Giovanni Bellini's Sacred Allegory." *Art Bulletin* LIX, 3 (September 1977): 331-335.

Dempsey, Charles "*Mercurius Ver*: The Sources of Botticelli's *Primavera.*" *Journal of the Warburg and Courtauld Institutes* XXXI (1968): 251-273.

Dölger, Franz Joseph. *Sol Salutis: Gebet und Gesang im Christlichen Altertum mit Besonderen Rücksicht auf die Ostung in Gebet und Liturgie.* Munster, Westfal, 1925.

Donati, U. "Di alcune opere ignorate di Domenico Fontana a Roma." *L'Urbe* (December 1929): 15 ff.

Donini, Augusto. "I cavalli di Monte Cavallo a Roma su una medaglia di Sisto V." *Numismatica* I (1960): 64-73.

Dubon, David. *Tapestries from the Samuel H. Kress Collection at the Philadelphia Museum of Art. The History of Constantine the Great designed by Peter Paul Rubens and Pietro da Cortona.* Great Britain, 1964.

Dumesnil, M.-A.-J. *Histoire de Sixte-Quint: sa vie et son pontificat.* Paris, 1869.

Dupront, A. "Art et contre-reforme: les fresques de la bibliotheque de Sixte-Quint." *École français de Rome: archeologie et histoire* XLVIII (1931): 282-307.

de l'Épinois, Le Comte Henri. *La ligue et les papes.* Paris: Société Générale de Librairie Catholique; Brussels: Société Belge de Librairie; Geneva, 1886.

Elling, C. "Function and Form of the Roman Belvedere." *Danske Videnskabernes Selskab. Copenhagen Arkaeologisk-kunsthistorisken Meddelelsar* III, 4 (1950): 3-59.

Enggass, Robert, and Marilyn Stokstad, Eds.*Hortus Imaginum.* Lawrence, Kansas, 1974.

Epp, Sigrid. *Konstantinszyklen in Rom. Die päpstliche Interpretation der Geschichte Konstantins des Großen bis zur Gegenreformation.* Schriften aus dem Institut für Kunstgeschichte der Universität München. Munich, 1988.

Ettlinger, Leopold D. "Hercules Florentinus." *Mitteilungen des Kunsthistorischen Institutes in Florenz* XVI (1972): 119-142.

__. *The Sistine Chapel before Michelangelo: religious imagery and papal primacy.* Oxford, 1965.

Fagiolo, Marcello. "Arche-tipologia della piazza di S. Pietro," in *Immagini del Barocco. Bernini e la cultura del seicento.* Atti del Convegno Bernini e il barocco europeo. Rome, 1982.

__, Ed. *Architettura e Massoneria.* Florence, 1988.

__. "La Basilica Vaticana come tempio-mausoleo 'inter duas metas': Le idee e i progetti di Alberti, Filarete, Bramante, Peruzzi, Sangallo, Michelangelo. in *Antonio da Sangallo il Giovane - La vita e l'opera.* Atti del XXII Congresso di Storia dell'Architettura. Rome, 1988.

__. *Chiese e Cattedrali.* Italia meravigliosa. Milan, 1978.

__. "Preistoria dei prati di Castello fino all'ottocento," in *Carlo Menotti e la sua dimora. Un esempio di stile per Roma capitale.* Rome, 1988.

__. "Die Psycho-Ikonologie." *Das architektonische Urteil. Annäherungen und Interpretationen von Architektur und Kunst.* Basel, Boston, Berlin, 1989.

__. "La Roma di Sisto V, Le Matrici del policentrismo." *Psicon* 3 (1976): 25-40.

__, Ed. *Roma e l'Antico nell'arte e nella cultura del Cinquecento.* Biblioteca Internazionale di Cultura 17. Rome, 1985.

__. "Theodericus-Christus-Sol. Nuove ipotesi sul mausoleo." *Arheoloski Vestnik. Acta Archaeologica* XXIII (1972): 83-156.

__ and Maria Luisa Madonna. "La Casina di Pio IV in Vaticano. Pirro Ligorio e l'architettura come geroglifico." *Storia dell'arte* 15/16 (1972): 237-281.

__. "La Roma di Pio IV: La 'Civitas Pia,' La 'Salus Medica,' La 'Custodia Angelica,' I: Il programma." *Arte Illustrata* V, 51 (November 1972): 383-402.

__. *Roma 1300-1875. L'arte degli anni santi.* Exh. Cat. Palazzo Venezia, 20 December 1984-4 April 1985. Milan, 1985.

Fagiolo dell'Arco, Maurizio, Ed. *L'Arte dei Papi. Come pontefici, architetti, pittori e scultori costruirono il Vaticano, monumento della cristianità.* Milan, 1982.

Farmer, D. H. *The Oxford Dictionary of Saints.* Oxford: Clarendon Press, 1978.

Fea, C. "Lavori di Sisto V," *Miscellanea Filologica* II (1836): 2-23.

Fehl, Philipp P. "Hermeticism and Art: Emblem and Allegory in the Work of Bernini." *Artibus et historiae* 14, VII (1986): 156-159.

___. "Vasari's 'Extirpation of the Huguenots': The Challenge of Pity and Fear." *Gazette des Beaux-Arts* LXXXIV (November-December 1974): 217-283.

Fiore, Francesco Paolo. "La 'Citta' Felice' di Loreto." *Ricerche di Storia dell'arte* IV (1977): 37-55.

Fleming, John V. *From Bonaventure to Bellini. An Essay in Franciscan Exegesis.* Princeton Essays on the Arts. Princeton, New Jersey, 1982.

Folz, Robert. *The Concept of Empire in Western Europe from the Fifth to the Fourteenth Century.* 1st ed. 1953. Trans. S. A. Ogilvie. London, 1969.

Forcella, Vincenzo. *Tornei e giostre, ingressi trionfali e feste carnevalesche in Roma sotto Paolo III.* 1st ed. 1885. Bologna, n.d.

Forster, Kurt W. "Metaphors of Rule: political ideology and history in the portraits of Cosimo I de'Medici." *Mitteilungen des Kunsthistorischen Institutes in Florenz* XV (1971): 72-85.

Frajese, Vittorio. *Il Popolo Fanciullo. Silvio Antoniano e il sistema disciplinare della controriforma.* Milan, 1987.

Fraser, Douglas, Howard Hibbard and Milton J. Lewine, Eds. *Essays in the History of Architecture Presented to Rudolph Wittkower.* 2 vols. London, 1967.

Frugoni, Arsenio. "A pictura cepit." *Bullettino dell'istituto storico italiano* (1967): 123-136.

Gagé, Jean. *Apollon Romain: Essai sur le culte d'Apollon et le développement du "vitus Graecus" à Rome des origines à Auguste.* Paris, 1955.

Galbreath, Donald Lindsay. *Papal Heraldry.* 1st ed.1930. 2nd Rev. ed. Ed. Geoffrey Briggs. London, 1972.

Galli, Pietro Andrea . *Notizie Intorno alla vera Origina, Patria, e Nascita del Sommo Pontefice Sisto V ..* 1st ed. 1752. Montalto, 1754.

Gallis, Diana. "Concealed Wisdom: Renaissance Hieroglyphic and Lorenzo Lotto's Bergamo Intarsie." *Art Bulletin* LXII, 3 (September 1980): 363-375.

Gamrath, Helge. *Roma Sancta Renovata. Studi sull'urbanistica di Roma nella seconda metà del sec. XVI con particolare riferimento al pontificato di Sisto V (1585-1590).* Analecta Romana Instituti Danici, Suplementum XII. Rome, 1987.

Gardner, Julian. "Nicholas III's Oratory of the Sancta Sanctorum and its decorations." *Burlington Magazine* CXV, 842 (May 1973): 283-294.

Gelli, Jacopo. *Divisi Motti e Imprese di famiglie e personaggi italiani.* 1st ed. 1910. Milan, 1928.

Gerard Powell, Veronique. "Les Annales de Baronius et l'iconographie religieuse du XVIIIe siècle." in *Baronio e L'Arte.* Atti del Convegno Internazionale di Studi Sora 10-13 ottobre 1984. Ed. Romeo de Maio, Agostino Borromeo, Luigi Gulia, Georg Lutz, Aldo Mazzacane. Sora, 1985.

Gerardi, F. *La patriarcale basilica liberiana descritta ed illustrata con incisioni a contorno.* Rome, 1839.

Giedion, Sigfried. *Space, Time and Architecture: the growth of a new tradition.* 1st ed.1941. Cambridge, Mass, 1967.

Gombrich, E. H. *Norm and Form: Studies in the art of the Renaissance.* 1st ed.1966. London & New York, 1978.

___. *Symbolic Images: Studies in the Art of the Renaissance II.* 1st ed.1972. Oxford; New York, 1978.

Graham, Victor E. and W. McAllister Johnson. *The Paris Entries of Charles IX and Elisabeth of Austria 1571 with an analysis of Simon Bouquet's Bref et sommaire recueil.* Toronto and Buffalo, 1974.

Grassi Fiorentino, Silvia. "Note sull'antiquaria romana nella seconda metà del secolo XVI." in *Baronio storico e la controriforma: atti del convegno internazionale di studi Sora 6-10 ottobre 1979.* Ed. Romeo de Maio, Luigi Gulia, Aldo Mazzacane. Sora, 1982.

DeGrazia Bohlin, Diane. *Prints and Related Drawings by the Carracci Family. A Catalogue Raisonné.* Exh. Cat. Bloomington & London; Washington, D. C., 1979.

___. *Le Stampe dei Carracci con i disegni, le incisioni, le copie e i dipinti connessi. catalogo critico.* 2nd. rev. ed. Bologna, 1984.

Guarducci, Margherita. "Ara Caeli." *Atti della Pontificia Accademia Romana di Archeologia (Serie III). Rendiconti* XXIII-XXIV (1947-1949): 277-290.

Guidoni, Enrico, Angela Marino, Angela Lanconelli, "I 'Libri dei conti' di Domenico Fontana. Riepilogo generale delle spese e Libro I." *Storia della città. Rivista internazionale di storia urbane e territoriale* 40 (October - December 1986): 45-77.

Halsberghe, Gaston H. *The Cult of Sol Invictus.* Leiden, 1972.

Hankey, Teresa. "Salutati's Epigrams for the Palazzo Vecchio at Florence." *Journal of the Warburg and Courtauld Institutes* XXII (1959): 363-365.

Hanning, Barbara Russano. "Glorious Apollo: Poetic and Political Themes in the First Opera." *Renaissance Quarterly* XXXII (1980): 485-513.

Hartt, Frederick. "*Lignum Vitae in Medio Paradisi*: The Stanza d'Eliodoro and the Sistine Ceiling." *Art Bulletin* XXXII, 2-3 (June/September 1950): 135-136.

Haskell, Francis. *Patrons and Painters. Art and Society in Baroque Italy*. New York, 1963.

Herklotz, Ingo. "Die Beratungsräume Calixtus' II. im Lateranpalast und ihre Fresken. Kunst und Propaganda am Ende des Investiturstreits." *Zeitschrift für Kunstgeschichte* 52, 2 (1989): 145-214.

__. "Historia Sacra und Mittelalterliche Kunst während der zweiten Hälfte des 16. Jahrhunderts in Rom." in *Baronio e L'Arte*. Atti del Convegno Internazionale di Studi Sora 10-13 ottobre 1984. Ed. Romeo de Maio, Agostino Borromeo, Luigi Gulia, Georg Lutz, Aldo Mazzacane. Sora, 1985.

Herz, Alexandra . "The Sixtine and Pauline Tombs: documents of the Counter-Reformation." *Storia dell'arte* XLIII (September-December 1981): 241-262.

Hess, Jacob. "Some Notes on the Paintings in the Vatican Library." (1938) *Kunstgeschichtliche Studien zu Renaissance und Barock*. 2 vols. Rome, 1967.

Hibbard, Howard. *Carlo Maderno and Roman Architecture 1580-1630*. Ed. Anthony Blunt and Rudolph Wittkower, Studies in Architecture. London, 1971.

Holland, Louise Adams. *Janus and the Bridge*. Papers and Monographs of the American Academy in Rome, v. XXI. Rome, 1961.

von Hübner, Baron. *The Life and Times of Sixtus the Fifth*. Trans. Herbert E.H. Jerningham, 2 vols. London, 1872.

Hutton, James. *Themes of Peace in Renaissance Poetry*. Ed. Rita Guerlac. Ithaca and London, 1984.

L'immagine di San Francesco nella Controriforma. Comitato Nazionale per le Manifestazioni Culturi e Ambientali, Istituto Nazionale per la Grafica, Exh. Cat. Calcografia, 9 December 1982-13 February 1983. Rome, 1982.

Nel IV Centenario della nascita di Sisto V (1521-1921). *Rassegna italiana* VI (13 November1921- March 1923): 2-208.

Iversen, Eric. *Obelisks in Exile; obelisks of Rome, I*. Copenhagen, 1968.

Jacks, Philip. "A Sacred Meta for Pilgrims in the Holy Year 1575." *Architectura* 19, 2 (1989): 137-165.

__. "Baronius and the antiquities of Rome." in *Baronio e L'Arte*. Atti del Convegno Internazionale di Studi Sora 10-13 ottobre 1984. Ed. Romeo de Maio, Agostino Borromeo, Luigi Gulia, Georg Lutz, Aldo Mazzacane. Sora, 1985.

Jacquot, Jean, Ed. *Les Fêtes de la Renaissance I, II, III*. 1st ed. 1956, 1960, 1972. Paris, 1973, 1975.

Jones, Roger and Nicholas Penny. *Raphael*. New Haven and London, 1983.

Joost-Gaugier, Christiane. "The History of a Visual Theme as Culture and the Experience of an Urban Center: 'Uomini Famosi' in Brescia (I)." *Antichità Viva* XXII, 4 (1983): 7-17; (II)," XXIII, 1 (1984): 5-14.

Kagan, Richard L. "Philip II and the Art of the Cityscape." in *Art and History: Images and their Meaning*. Ed. Robert I. Rothberg, Theodore K. Rabb. Cambridge, New York, New Rochelle, Melbourne, Sydney, 1988.

Kamen, Henry. "Golden age, iron age: a conflict of concepts in the Renaissance." *Journal of Medieval and Renaissance Studies* IV (1974): 143-155.

Kantorowicz, Ernst H. *Frederick the Second 1194-1250*. 1st ed.1931. Trans. E. O. Lorimer. New York, 1957.

__. *The King's Two Bodies. A Study in Medieval Political Theology*. Princeton, New Jersey, 1957.

__. "Kingship under the Impact of Scientific Jurisprudence." in *Selected Studies*. Locust Valley, New York, 1965.

__. *Laudes Regiae: A study in liturgical acclamations and medieval ruler worship*. Berkeley and Los Angeles, 1958.

__. "On Transformations of Apolline Ethics," *Charites: Studien zur Altertumswissenschaft*. ed K. Schauenburg. Bonn, 1957.

__. "Oriens Augusti." *Dumbarton Oaks Papers* XVII (1963): 117-177.

Katzenellenbogen, Adolph. *Allegories of the Virtues and Vices in Mediaeval Art from Early Christian Times to the Thirteenth Century*. 1st ed. 1939. New York, 1964.

Kinder Carr, Carolyn. "Aspects of the Iconography of Saint Peter in Medieval Art of Western Europe to the Early Thirteenth Century." diss., Case Western Reserve U, 1978.

Klibansky, Raymond and Erwin Panofsky and Fritz Saxl. *Saturn and Melancholy. Studies in the History of Natural Philosophy Religion and Art*. London, 1964.

Krautheimer, Richard. "Die Decanneacubita in Konstantinopel: Ein kleiner Beitrag zur Frage Rom und Byzanz." in *Tortulae. Studien zu Altchristlichen und Byzantinischen Monumenten*. Intro Walter Nikolaus Schumacher, Römische Quartalschrift für Christliche Altertumskunde und Kirchengeschichte n. 30 Supplementheft, Rome, Freiburg, Vienna, 1966.

__. *Rome: Profile of a City, 312-1308*. Princeton, New Jersey, 1980.

Kuveiller, Marco. "Lettere inedite sull'ampliamento di Loreto e di Montalto Marche." *Storia della città* 12-13 (1979): 171-172.

Labrot, G. *Le Palais Farnèse de Caprarola*. Essai de Lecture. Paris, 1979.

Ladis, Andrew. *Taddeo Gaddi: critical reappraisal and catalogue raisonné*. Columbia and London, 1982.

Ladner, Gerhart B. *The Idea of Reform: its impact on Christian thought and action in the Age of the Fathers*. New York, Evanston and London, 1967.

___. "I mosaici e gli affreschi ecclesiastico-politici nell'antico Palazzo Lateranense." *Rivista di Archeologia Cristiana* XII (1935): 265-292.

___. *Die Papstbildnisse des Altertum und des Mittelalters*. 2 vols. Vatican City, 1941.

___. "Vegetation Symbolism and the Concept of Renaissance." in *De Artibus Opuscula XL. Essays in honour of Erwin Panofsky*. Ed. Millard Meiss, 2 vols. New York, 1961, I, 311-312.

Lanciani, Rodolfo. *Storia degli scavi di Roma e notizie intorno le collezioni Romana di Antichità*. 4 vols. Rome, 1913.

Langedijk, Karla. "Baccio Bandinelli's Orpheus: A Political Message." *Mitteilungen des Kunsthistorischen Institutes in Florenz* XX (1972): 37-51.

Lauer, Philippe. *Le Palais de Latran: étude historique et archéologique*. Paris 1911.

Lechner, George S. "Tommaso Campanella and Andrea Sacchi's Fresco of *Divina Sapienza* in the Palazzo Barberini." *Art Bulletin* LVIII (1976): 97-108.

Lee, Egmont. *Sixtus IV and Men of Letters*. Temi e Testi 26. Ed. Eugenio Massa. Rome, 1978.

Leitzmann, Hans. *The Beginnings of the Christian Church*. Trans. Bertram Lee Woolf, International Library of Christian Knowledge. New York, 1937.

Letarouilly, P. *Edifices de Rome Moderne ou Recueil des Palais, Maisons, Églises, Couvents et autres monuments publics et particuliers les plus remarquables*. Liège, 1849.

Levi D'Ancona, Mirella. *The Garden of the Renaissance. Botanical Symbolism in Italian Painting*. Arte e Archeologia. Studi e Documenti 10. Florence, 1977.

Levin, Harry. *The Myth of the Golden Age in the Renaissance*. Bloomington and London 1969.

Levison, Wilhelm. "Konstantinische Schenkung und Silvesterlegende." *Miscellanea Francesco Ehrle*. Scritti di storia e paleografia ... Studi e Testi 38, 2 vols. Rome, 1924.

Logan, O. M. T. "Grace and Justification: Some Italian View of the Sixteenth and Early Seventeenth Centuries." *Journal of Ecclesiastical History* XX, 1 (April 1969): 67-78.

Lovejoy, Arthur O. and George Boas. *Primitivism and Related Ideas in Antiquity*. 1st ed.1935. New York, 1973.

Loy, Nicola. *Cenni Biografici intorno a Felice Peretti indi Sisto V ...* Grottamare, 1928.

de Lubac, Henri. *Exégèse Médiévale. Les Quatre Sens de l'Ecriture*. 2 vols., 2 parts. Paris, 1959.

Lynch, J. "Philip II and the Papacy." *Transactions of the Royal Historical Society* 5th ser., II (1961): 23-42.

Madonna, Maria Luisa. "La biblioteca." in *S. Giovanni Evangelista a Parma*. Ed. B. Adorni. Parma, 1979.

___, Ed. *La Roma di Sisto V. L'Arte, L'Architettura, La Città*. Exh. Cat. Rome, 1992. Forthcoming.

___. "*Septem mundi miracula* come templi della virtù. Pirro Ligorio e l'interpretazione cinquecentesca delle Meraviglie." *Psicon* 7 (1977): 24-63.

Magnuson, Torgil *Rome in the Age of Bernini, I: From the election of Sixtus V to the death of Urban VIII*. Stockholm; New Jersey, 1982.

De Maio, Romeo, Agostino Borromeo, Luigi Gulia, Georg Lutz, Aldo Mazzacane, Eds. *Baronio e L'Arte*. Atti del Convegno Internazionale di Studi Sora 10-13 ottobre 1984. Sora, 1985.

De Maio, Romeo , Luigi Gulia, Aldo Mazzacane, Eds. *Baronio storico e la controriforma: atti del convegno internazionale di studi Sora 6-10 ottobre 1979*. Sora, 1982.

Mâle, Emile. *L'art religieux de la fin du XVIe siècle au XVII siècle: Étude sur l'iconographie après le Concile de Trente*. Paris, 1951.

___. *The Gothic Image: Religious Art in France of the Thirteenth Century*. Trans. Dora Nussey 1st ed. 1913. New York, Hagerstown, San Francisco, London, 1972.

Mancinelli, Fabrizio. "Arte medioevale e moderna." *Bollettino dei Musei e Gallerie Pontificie* I (1959-1974): 112-139.

___ and Juan Casanovas. *La Torre dei Venti in Vaticano*. Vatican City, 1980.

Mandel, Corinne. "Golden Age and the Good Works of Sixtus V: Classical and Christian Typology in the Art of a Counter-Reformation Pope", *Storia dell'arte* 62 (1988): 29-52.

___. "Problems in the Study of the Lateran Palace." in *La Roma di Sisto V. L'Arte, L'Architettura, La Città*. Ed. Maria Luisa Madonna. Exh. Cat. Rome, 1992. Forthcoming.

___. "Simbolismo ermetico negli obelischi e colonne della Roma Sistina." in *Sisto V*. Atti del VI Corso Internazionale d'Alta Cultura. Ed. Marcello Fagiolo, Maria Luisa Madonna. Forthcoming.

__. "'Starry Leo,' the Sun, and the Astrological Foundations of Sixtine Rome," *Revue d'art canadienne/Canadian Art Review (RACAR)* XVII, 1 (1990): 17-39.

Manni, Eugenio. "La leggenda dell'età dell'oro nella politica dei cesari." *Atene e Roma* IV (1938): 108-120.

Marder, Tod A. "Sixtus V and the Quirinal." *Journal of the Society of Architectural Historians* XXXVII (1978): 283-294.

__. "The Moses Fountain of Sixtus V." in *Sisto V*, VI Corso Internazionale d'Alta Cultura. Ed. Marcello Fagiolo, Maria Luisa Madonna. Forthcoming.

Martini, Antonio. "Sisto V e l'Erario di Castel Sant'Angelo." in *Studia Sixtina. Nel IV Centenario del Pontificato di Sisto V (1585-1590)*. Rome, 1987.

Massimo, Vittorio. *Notizie istoriche della Villa Massimo alle Terme diocleziane, con un'appendice di documenti*. Rome, 1836.

Mattingly, Harold. "Virgil's Fourth Eclogue." *Journal of the Warburg and Courtauld Institutes* X (1947): 14-19.

Mayer, A. *Das Leben und die Werk der Brüder Matthäus und Paul Brill*. Leipzig, 1910.

McDonald, William C. "Maximilian I of Habsburg and the Veneration of Hercules: on the revival of myth and the German Renaissance." *Journal of Medieval and Renaissance Studies* VI (1976): 139-154.

McGinness, Frederick John. "Rhetoric and Counter-Reformation Rome: Sacred Oratory and the Construction of the Catholic World View, 1563-1621." diss., U of California, Berkeley, 1982.

Mercier, Robert. *Le Retour d'Apollon ou les cycles apolliniens*. Paris, 1963.

Meredith, Jill. "The Revival of the Augustan Age in the Court of Emperor Frederick II." in *Artistic Strategy and the Rhetoric of Power: political uses of art from antiquity to the present*. Ed. David Castriota. Carbondale and Edwardsville, 1986.

Metford, J.C.J. *Dictionary of Christian Lore and Legend*. London 1983.

Métraux, Michelle. "The Iconography of San Martino ai Monti in Rome." diss., Boston U, 1979.

Mitchell, Charles. "The Lateran Fresco of Boniface VIII." *Journal of the Warburg and Courtauld Institutes* XIV (1951): 1-6.

Mommsen, Theodor E. "Petrarch and the Decoration of the Sala Virorum Illustrium in Padua." *Art Bulletin* XXXIV (1952): 94-96.

__. "St. Augustine and the Christian Idea of Progress." *Journal of the History of Ideas* XII (1951): 346-374.

Morel, Philippe. "Il funzionamento simbolico e la critica delle grottesche nella seconda metà del Cinquecento." in *Roma e l'Antico nell'arte e nella cultura del Cinquecento*. Ed. Marcello Fagiolo. Biblioteca Internazionale di Cultura 17. Rome, 1985.

Moroni, Gaetano. *Dizionario di erudizione storico-ecclesiastica da S. Pietro fino ai nostri giorni*. 109 vols. Venice, 1840-1879.

Morrogh, Andrew, Fiorella Superbi Goffredi, Piero Morselli, Eve Borsook, Eds. *Renaissance Studies in Honor of Craig Hugh Smyth*. 2 vols. Florence, 1985.

Mundy, E. James. "*Franciscus alter Christus*: The Intercessory Function of a Late Quattrocento Panel." *Record of the Art Museum, Princeton University* XXXVI (1977): 4-15.

Murray, Robert H. *The Political Consequences of the Reformation. Studies in Sixteenth-Century Political Thought*. New York, 1960.

Narducci, Enrico. *Intorno al alcune prediche stampate di Sisto Quinto. Notizie raccolte da E. N.*. Rome, 1870.

__. "Storia-Documenti storici relativi al taglio dell'istmo di Suez ed alla conquista dell' Egitto ideata da Sisto V." *Reale Accademia dei Lincei- Rendiconti* 1, Serie 4 (19 April 1885): 300-302.

Nilgen, Ursula. "The Epiphany and the Eucharist: On the interpretation of Eucharistic Motifs in Medieval Epiphany Scenes." *Art Bulletin* XLIX, 4 (December 1967): 311-316.

Nova, Alessandro. "Bartolommeo Ammannati e Prospero Fontana a Palazzo Firenze. Architettura e emblemi per Giulio III Del Monte." *Ricerche di storia dell'arte* XX (1983): 53-76.

Nuzzo, Lorenza di. "La progettazione sistina della piazza di San Giovanni in Laterano." *Storia della città* 40 (October-December 1986): 5-44.

Olivetti, Simona. "La *Historia Naturalis* (XXXV, 116-117) di Plinio il Vecchio, fonte per la decorazione della Loggia del Belvedere di Innocenzo VIII." *Storia dell'arte* LIX (January-April 1987): 5-10.

D'Onofrio, Cesare. *Gli obelischi di Roma*. Rome, 1967.

__. "Una grande scomparsa: Villa Montalto." *Capitolium* (1970): 59-63.

Orbaan, J.A.F. *Documenti sul barocco in Roma*. Rome, 1920.

__. "La Roma di Sisto V negli avvisi." *Archivio della R. Società romana di storia patria* XXXIII (1910): 277-312.

__. *Sixtine Rome*. London, 1910.

Ost, Hans. "Die Capella Sistina in Santa Maria Maggiore." *Kunst als Bedeutungsträger: Gedenkschrift für Gunter Bandmann.* Berlin, 1978.

Ostrow, Steven F. "The Sistine Chapel at S. Maria Maggiore: Sixtus V and the art of the Counter Reformation." diss., Princeton U, 1987.

Padiglione, Carlo. *I motti delle Famiglie Italiane.* 1st ed. 1910. Bologna, 1972.

Il Palazzo del Laterano e i Musei Lateranensi Cristiano-Missionario, Etnologico e Profano: testo riveduto dalla Direzione Generale dei Musei e Gallerie Pontificie. Rome, 1950.

Panofsky, Erwin. *Early Netherlandish Painting: Its Origins and Character.* New York, Hagerstown, San Francisco, London, 1971.

__. "'Good Government' or Fortune? The Iconography of a Newly-Discovered Composition by Rubens." *Gazette des Beaux-Arts* LXVIII, 1175 (December 1966): 305-326.

__. *Problems in Titian: mostly iconographic.* New York, 1969.

__. *Studies in Iconology. Humanistic Themes in the Age of the Renaissance.* New York, 1967.

Pansoni, Nicola. *Il Mercoledi di Sisto V e Gregorio XIII.* Cossignano, 1924.

Parisciani, Gustavo. *Fra Felice Peretti Sisto V. IV centenario del pontificato 1585-1590.* Ancona, 24 April 1985.

__. *Sisto V e la sua Montalto.* Ricerche francescane. Padua, 1986.

Partner, Peter. *Renaissance Rome 1500-1559. A Portrait of Society.* Berkeley, Los Angeles, London, 1976.

Partridge, Loren and Randolph Starn. *A Renaissance Likeness: art and culture in Raphael's Julius II.* Berkeley, Los Angeles, London, 1980.

Partridge, Loren. *Caprarola, Palazzo Farnese.* Milan, 1988.

__. "Divinity and Dynasty at Caprarola: Perfect History in the Room of the Farnese Deeds." *Art Bulletin* LX, 3 (September 1978): 494-530.

__. "The *Sala d'Ercole* in the Villa Farnese at Caprarola, Part I." *Art Bulletin* LIII, 4 (December 1971): 467-486.

__. "The *Sala d'Ercole* in the Villa Farnese at Caprarola, Part II." *Art Bulletin* LIV, 1 (March 1972): 50-62.

von Pastor, Ludwig. *The History of the Popes from the Close of the Middle Ages.* Trans., ed., Frederick Ignatius Antrobus, Ralph Francis Kerr, 40 vols. London; St. Louis, 1891-1954.

__. *Sisto V. Il creatore della Nuova Roma.* Rome, 1922.

Patch, Howard Rolin. *The Other World According to Descriptions in Medieval Literature.* 1st ed. 1950. New York, 1970.

Penco, Gregorio. "Il simbolismo animalesco nella letteratura monastica." *Studia Monastica.* Barcelona VI (1984):

Pericoli Ridolfini, Cecilia. "Uno stemma di Sisto V da Villa Montalto al cortile del Palazzo dei Conservatori." *Bollettino dei musei comunali di Roma* XXV-XXVII (1978-1980): 102-110.

Perry, Marilyn. "'Candor Illaesus': The 'Impresa' of Clement VII and other Medici Devices in the Vatican Stanze." *Burlington Magazine* CXIX (October 1977): 676-686.

Pistolesi, Francesco. *La Prima Biografia Autentica di Papa Sisto Quinto Scritta dell'anonimo della Biblioteca Ferraioli di Roma.* Montalto March, 1925.

__. *Sixtus Quintus. XIII Decembris MDXXI - XIII Decembris MCMXXI. Album.* Rome, 1921.

Pohle, J. "Merit." *The Catholic Encyclopedia.* Ed. Charles G. Herbermann, et al, 15 vols. New York, 1911.

Poli, G. *Sisto V.* Rome, 1922.

Pope-Hennessy, John. *An Introduction to Italian Sculpture: Italian High Renaissance and Baroque Sculpture.* London, New York, 1970.

Pratt, Kenneth J. "Rome as Eternal." *Journal of the History of Ideas* XXVI (1965): 25-44.

Pullapilly, Cyriac K. *Caesar Baronius. Counter Reformation Historian.* Notre Dame, London, 1975.

Puttfarken, Thomas. "Golden Age and Justice in Sixteenth-Century Florentine Political Thought and Imagery: observations on three pictures by Jacopo Zucchi." *Journal of the Warburg and Courtauld Institutes* XLIII (1980): 130-149.

van Puyvelde, Leo. *La Peinture Flamande a Rome.* Brussels, 1950.

Quast, Matthias, "Le piazze di Santa Maria Maggiore, Termini e del Laterano nell'ambito della progettazione sistina." in *Sisto V*, VI Corso Internazionale d'Alta Cultura. Ed. Marcello Fagiolo, Maria Luisa Madonna. Forthcoming.

Quednau, Rolf. *Die Sala di Costantino im Vatikanischen Palast. Zur Dekoration der beiden Medici-Päpste Leo X und Clemens VII.* Studien zur Kunstgeschichte, vol. 13. Hildesheim, New York, 1979.

von Ranke, Leopold. *The History of the Popes during the last four centuries.* 1st ed. 1874. Trans. Mrs.

Foster, revised G. R. Dennis, 3 vols. London 1913.

Rash-Fabbri, Nancy. "A Note on the Stanza della Segnatura." *Gazette des Beaux-Arts* XLIV, 1329 (1979): 97-104.

Ratzinger, Joseph. *The Theology of History in Saint Bonaventure*. Chicago, 1971.

Réau, Louis. *Iconographie de l'art Chrétien*. 2 vols., 2 pts. Paris, 1955.

Redig de Campos, Diocletio. *I Palazzi Vaticani*. Bologna, 1967.

Reinesio, T. *De palatio Lateranense*. Jena, 1679.

Reinhardt, Ursula. "La Tapisserie Feinte: un genre de décoration du Maniérisme Romain au XVIe siècle." *Gazette des Beaux-Arts* LXXXIV (1974): 285-296.

Renazzi, Filippo Maria. *Notizie storiche degli antichi Vicedomini del patriarchio Lateranense e dei modern prefetti del sacro palazzo apostolico ...* Rome, 1784.

Richelson, Paul William. *Studies in the Personal Imagery of Cosimo I de'Medici, Duke of Florence*. New York and London, 1978.

Riess, Jonathan B. *Political Ideals in Medieval Italian Art. The Fresoes in the Palazzo dei Priori, Perugia*. Studies in the Fine Arts: Iconography, No. 1. Ann Arbor, Michigan, 1981.

Rodinò, Simonetta Prosperi Valenti. "La diffusione dell'iconografia Francescana attraverso l'incisione." in *L'immagine di San Francesco nella Controriforma*. Comitato Nazionale per le Manifestazioni Culturi e Ambientali, Istituto Nazionale per la Grafica, Exh. Cat. Calcografia, 9 December 1982-13 February 1983. Rome, 1982.

Rosenthal, Earl. "*Plus Ultra, Non Plus Ultra*, and the Columnar Device of Emperor Charles V." *Journal of the Warburg and Courtauld Institutes* XXXIV (1971): 204-228.

__. "The Invention of the Columnar Device of Emperor Charles V at the Court of Burgundy in Flanders in 1516." *Journal of the Warburg and Courtauld Institutes* XXXVI (1973): 198-230.

Rothberg, Robert I. and Theodore K. Rabb, Eds. *Art and History: Images and their Meaning*.   Cambridge, New York, New Rochelle, Melbourne, Sydney, 1988.

Röttgen, Herwarth. "Zeitgeschichtliche Bildprogramme der Katholischen Restauration unter Gregor XIII, 1572-1585." *Münchner Jahrbuch der Bildenden Kunst* XXVI (1975): 89-122.

Rubenstein, Nicolai. "Political Ideas in Sienese Art: The Frescoes by Ambrogio Lorenzetti and Taddeo di Bartolo in the Palazzo Pubblico." *Journal of the Warburg and Courtauld Institutes* XXI (1958): 194-195.

Russo, Erina. "Storia e formazione delle famiglie Francescane." in *L'immagine di San Francesco nella Controriforma*. Comitato Nazionale per le Manifestazioni Culturi e Ambientali, Istituto Nazionale per la Grafica, Exh. Cat. Calcografia, 9 December 1982-13 February 1983. Rome, 1982.

Sandström, Sven. "The Programme for the Decoration of the Belvedere of Innocent VIII." *Konsthistorisk Tidskrift* XXIX (1960): 35-75.

Sansolini, Cecilia. *Il pensiero teologico spirituale di Sisto V nei sermoni anteriori al pontificato*. Vatican City, 1989.

Sarazani, Fabrizio. *La Roma di Sisto V "er papa tosto": Potere assoluto e grandezza irrazionale di un personaggio entrato nella fantasia popolare*. Iconographical research by Giulio Fefé. Rome, 1979.

Saward, Susan. *The Golden Age of Marie de'Medici*. Ann Arbor, Michigan, 1982.

Scavizzi, Giuseppe. *Arte e architettura sacra. Cronache e documenti sulla controversia tra riformati e cattolici (1500-1550)*. Rome, 1981.

__. "Gli affreschi della Scala Santa ed alcune aggiunte per il Tardo Manierismo Romano-I." *Bollettino d'arte* XLV (1960): 111-122.

__. "Gli affreschi della Scala Santa - II." *Bollettino d'Arte* XLV (1960): 325-335.

__. "Storia ecclesiastica e arte nel secondo Cinquecento." *Storia dell'arte* LIX (1987): 29-46.

__. "Sugli inizi del Lilio e su alcuni affreschi del Palazzo Lateranense." *Paragone* (May 1961): 44-48.

Schauenburg, K., Ed. *Charites: Studien zur Altertumswissenschaft*. Bonn, 1957.

Scheller, Robert W. "Imperial Themes in art and literature of the early French Renaissance: the period of Charles VIII." *Simiolus* XII (1981-1982): 5-69.

Schiavo, Armando. *The Lateran Palace and Baptistry*. Rome, 1969.

__. *Restauri e nuove opere nella zona extraterritoriale Lateranense (1961-1968) ...* Vatican City, 1968.

Schiffmann, René. *Roma Felix. Aspekte der städtebaulichen Gestaltung Roms unter Papst Sixtus V*. Europäische Hochschulschriften, Reihe XXVIII Kunstgeschichte, Band 36. Bern, Frankfurt am Main, New York, 1985.

Schröter, Elisabeth. "Der Vatican als Hügel Apollons und der Musen. Kunst und Panegyrik von Nikolaus V. bis Julius II." *Römische Quartalschrift für Christliche Altertumskunde und Kirchengeschichte* LXXV (1980): 208-240.

Schwager, Klaus. "Zur Bautatigkeit Sixtus V, an S. Maria Maggiore in Rom." in *Miscellanea Bibliothecae Hertzianae zu Ehren von Leo Bruhns, Franz Graf Wolff Metternich, Ludwig Schudt*. Munich, 1961.

276

Schulz, J. "Pinturicchio and the Revival of Antiquity." *Journal of the Warburg and Courtauld Institutes* XXV (1962): 35-55.

Scott, Glenn T. *Man and Nature: A View of the 17th Century*. Exh. Cat. Hamilton, Ontario, 1980.

Segretain, E. A. *Sixte-Quint et Henri IV: introduction du Protestantisme en France*. Paris, 1864.

Seznec, Jean. *The Survival of the Pagan Gods: the mythological tradition and its place in Renaissance humanism and art*. Studies of the Warburg Institute, vol. XI. 1st ed.1940. Trans. Barbara F. Sessions, Bollingen Series XXXVIII. Princeton, New Jersey, 1972.

Shearman, John. *Raphael's Cartoons in the collection of Her Majesty the Queen and the tapestries for the Sistine Chapel*. London and New York, 1972.

__. "The Vatican Stanze: Functions and Decoration." *Proceedings of the British Academy* LVII (1971): 369-425.

Simoncini, Giorgio. *"Roma Restaurata" Rinnovamento urbano al tempo di Sisto V*. L'ambiente Storico. Studi di storia urbana e del territorio 1. Florence, 1990.

Singleton, Charles S. *Journey to Beatrice*. 1st ed.1958. Cambridge, Mass, 1967.

__. "In Exitu Israel de Aegypto." in *Dante. A Collection of Critical Essays*. Ed. John Freccero, Twentieth Century Views. Englewood Cliffs, New Jersey,1965.

Smith, Graham. *The Casino of Pius IV*. Princeton, New Jersey, 1977.

__. "Review of Janet Cox-Rearick. *Dynasty and Destiny in Medici Art: Pontormo, Leo X, and the Two Cosimos*. Princeton, New Jersey, 1984." *Art Bulletin* LXIX, 2 (June 1987): 304-307.

Soresino, Giuseppe Maria. *De capitibus Sanctorum apostolorum Petri, et Pauli in Sacrosancta Lateranensi Ecclesia assernatis opusculum*. Rome, 1673.

__. *Compendio istorico cronologico Delle cose più cospicue concernenti La Scala Santa e Le SS. teste delli Gloriosi Apostoli Pietro, e Paulo ... con un sommario Delle Reliquie ...* Trans. Giuseppe Pazzaglia. 1st ed. 1673. Rome, 1674.

Spezzaferro, Luigi. "Il recupero del Rinascimento." in *Storia dell'arte italiana. II: Dal Cinquecento all'Ottocento. I: Cinquecento e Seicento*. Turin, 1981.

Stein, John W. "The Meridian Room in the Vatican Tower of the Winds." *Specola Astronomica Vaticana. Miscellanea Astronomica* III, 97-98 (1950): 33-55.

Stein, P. I. "La Sala della Meridiana nella Torre dei Venti in Vaticano." *L'Illustrazione Vaticana* 9 (16-31 May 1938): 403-410.

Steinberg, Leo. *Michelangelo's last paintings. The Conversion of St. Paul and the Crucifixion of St. Peter in the Cappella Paolina. Vatican Palace*. New York, 1975.

Stevenson, Enrico. *Topografia e monumenti di Roma nelle pitture a fresco di Sisto V della Biblioteca Vaticana. Omaggio Giubilare della biblioteca Vaticana al Sommo Pontefice Leone XIII*. Rome, 1888.

Stinger, Charles L. *The Renaissance in Rome*. Bloomington, 1985.

Strinati, Claudio. "Roma nell'anno 1600. Studio di pittura." *Ricerche di Storia dell'arte* 10 (1980): 15-48.

Strong, Roy. *Art and Power: Renaissance Festivals 1450-1650*. 1st ed.1973. Berkeley and Los Angeles, 1984.

__. *Britannia Triumphans: Inigo Jones, Rubens and Whitehall Palace*. Great Britain, 1980.

Studia Sixtina. Nel IV Centenario del Pontificato di Sisto V (1585-1590). Academia Sistina. Rome, 1987.

Stumpo, Enrico, Ed. *La Gazzetta de L'anno 1588*. Florence, 1988.

Swain, Joseph Ward. "The Theory of the Four Monarchies. Opposition History under the Roman Empire." *Classical Philology* XXXV, 1 (January 1940): 1-21.

Tempesti, P. M. Casimiro *Storia della vita e delle gesta di Sisto Quinto Sommo pontefice*. 1st ed. 1754. Revised ed., 2 vols. Rome, 1866.

de Tervarent, Guy. *Attributs et Symboles dans l'Art Profane 1450-1600. Dictionnaire d'un language perdu*. Geneva, 1958.

Thorndike, Lynn. *A History of Magic and Experimental Science during the first Thirteen Centuries of our Era*. 8 vols. New York, 1923-1958.

__. *Michael Scot*. London and Edinburgh, 1965.

Tierney, Brian. *The Crisis of Church and State 1050-1300*. Princeton, New Jersey, 1964.

Titi, F. *Descrizione della pitture, sculture ed architetture esposte al pubblico in Roma*. 1st ed. 1763. Reprint ed. Ed. Hugh Honor. n.p., n.d.

Tomaro, John Butler "The Papacy and the Implementation of the Council of Trent: 1564-1588." diss., U of North Carolina at Chapel Hill, 1974.

Touring Club Italiano, *Roma e Dintorni*. Guida D'Italia. 1st ed. 1962. Milan, 1965.

Tulli, Alberto. "La 'Sala del Concilio' nel Palazzo Laterano." *Per l'arte sacra* VII (March-April 1929): 30-55.

Turner, A. Richard. "Two Landscapes in Renaissance Rome." *Art Bulletin* XLIII (1961): 275-287.

__. *The Vision of Landscape in Renaissance Italy*. Princeton, New Jersey, 1966.

Ullmann, Walter. *The Growth of Papal Government in the Middle Ages. A Study in the ideological relation of classical to lay power*. 1st ed. 1955. London, 1970.

__. *Law and Politics in the Middle Ages. An Introduction to the Sources of Medieval Political Ideas*. Ithaca, New York, 1975.

__. "Leo I and the Theme of Papal Primacy." *Journal of Theological Studies* II (1960): 25-51.

__. *A Short History of the Papacy in the Middle Ages*. London, 1972.

Utz, Hildegarde. "The *Labours of Hercules* and Other Works by Vincenzo de'Rossi." *Art Bulletin* LIII, 3 (September 1971): 344-366.

Vaes, Maurice. "Matthieu Bril 1550-1583." *Bulletin Institut Historique Belge de Rome* VIII (1928): 283-331.

Vitzthum, Walter. "A comment on the iconography of Pietro da Cortona's Barberini Ceiling." *Burlington Magazine* (1961): 427-433.

Vivanti, Corrado. "Henry IV, the Gallic Hercules." *Journal of the Warburg and Courtauld Institutes* XXX (1967): 176-197.

Waddington, Raymond B. "The Sun at the Center: structure as meaning in Pico della Mirandola's Heptaplus." *Journal of Medieval and Renaissance Studies* 3 (1973): 69-86.

Walter, Christopher. "Papal Political Imagery in the Medieval Lateran Palace." *Cahiers archéologiques: fin de l'antiquité et moyen âge* XX (1970): 155-176.

__. "Papal Political Imagery in the Medieval Lateran Palace - II." *Cahiers archaéologiques: fin de l'antiquité et moyen âge* XXI (1971): 109-136.

Watt, J. A. "The Theory of Papal Monarchy in the Thirteenth Century: the contribution ofthe Canonists." *Traditio* XX (1964): 179-317.

Weil-Garris, Kathleen. *The Santa Casa di Loreto. Problems in Cinquecento Sculpture*. 2 vols. New York & London, 1977.

Weinberger, Martin *Michelangelo the Sculptor*. 2 vols. London: Routledge and Kegan Paul; New York, 1967.

White, John and John Shearman. "Raphael's Tapestries and their Cartoons." *Art Bulletin* (1958): 193-221, 299-323.

White, T.H., Ed. *The Book of Beasts being a translation from a Latin Bestiary of the Twelfth Century*. 1st ed. 1954. New York, 1984.

Wilde, Johannes. "The Decoration of the Sistine Chapel." *Proceedings of the British Academy* XLIV (1958): 61-81.

Wilkinson, Catherine. "The Iconography of Bernini's Tomb of Urban VIII." *L'Arte* IV (1971): 54-68.

Wilks, Michael. *The Problem of Sovereignty in the Middle Ages: The Papal Monarchy with Augustinus Triumphus and the Publicists*. Cambridge Studies in Medieval Life and Thought, new series, v. 9. Cambridge, 1963.

Williams, George H. *Wilderness and Paradise in Christian Thought. The Biblical Experience of the Desert in the History of Christianity and the Paradise Theme in the Theological Idea of the University*. The Menno Simons Lectures. New York, 1962.

Wind, Edgar. *Pagan Mysteries in the Renaissance*. 1st ed. 1958. Revised and Enlarged. New York, 1968.

Winternitz, Emanuel. *Musical Instruments and Their Symbolism in Western Art. Studies in Musical Iconology*. 1st ed. 1967. New Haven and London, 1979.

Wissowa, Georg and Wilhelm Kroll, Eds. *Paulys Real-Encyclopädie der Classischen Altertumswissenschaft. Neue Bearbeigung*. 24 vols. Stuttgart, 1939.

Witcombe, Christopher L. C. Ewart. "Sixtus V and the Scala Santa." *Journal of the Society of Architectural Historians* XLIV (December 1985): 368-379.

Wittkower, Rudolph. *Allegory and the Migration of Symbols*. 1st ed. 1977. Great Britain, 1987.

__. *Architectural Principles in the Age of Humanism*. London, 1949.

Wood, Carolyn H. "Visual Panegyric in Guercino's Casino Ludovisi Frescoes." *Storia dell'arte* 58 (September - December 1986): 223-228.

Woodruff, John, D., Ed. *The Popes: A Concise Biographical History*. New York, 1964.

Yates, Frances A. *Astraea: the imperial theme in the sixteenth century*. 1st ed. 1975. London, Boston, Melbourne and Henley, 1985.

__. *The Rosicrucian Enlightenment*. 1st ed. 1972. London and New York, 1986.

Zeri, Federico. *Pittura e Controriforma. L'arte senza tempo di Scipione Pulzone da Gaeta*. Turin, 1957.

Zucconi, A. *Sisto Quinto e Benito Mussolini. Ritorni Storici*. Rome, 1934.

Zupnick, I. L. "The Significance of the Stanza dell'Incendio. Leo X and François I." *Gazette des Beaux-Arts* (October 1970): 195-204.

ILLUSTRATIONS

1. *Portrait of Sixtus V with the Medals of his Pontificate*, in Alphonso Ciacconio, *Vitae et Res Gestae Pontificum Romanorum Et S. R. E. Cardinalium Ab initio nascentis Ecclesiae usque ad Clementem IX. P. O. M.* 4 vols. Rome, 1677, 139-140.
Ritratto di Sisto V con le medaglie del suo pontificato (da A. Ciacconio, *Vitae et Res Gestae Pontificum Romanorum...*, Roma 1677).

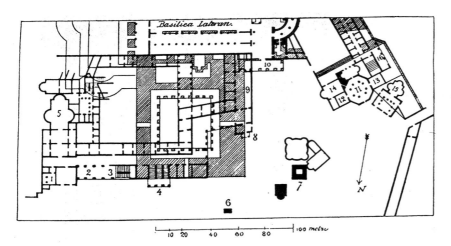

2. *Patriarchium Lateranense*, Salone Sistino, Vatican Library.
   Il Patriarchium lateranense. Biblioteca Vaticana, Salone Sistino.

3. Ground plan of the Patriarchium Lateranense, in Liliana Barroero, ed. *Guide Rionali di Roma, Rione I, Monti, Parte 1*. Rome, 1978, 14. *Piano terra del Patriarchium lateranense* (da L. Barroero, *Guide rionali di Roma. Rione I, Monti, I*, Roma 1978).

4. *Lateran Palace and Obelisk*, Salone Sistino, Vatican Library.
   Il Palazzo lateranense e l'obelisco. Biblioteca Vaticana, Salone Sistino.

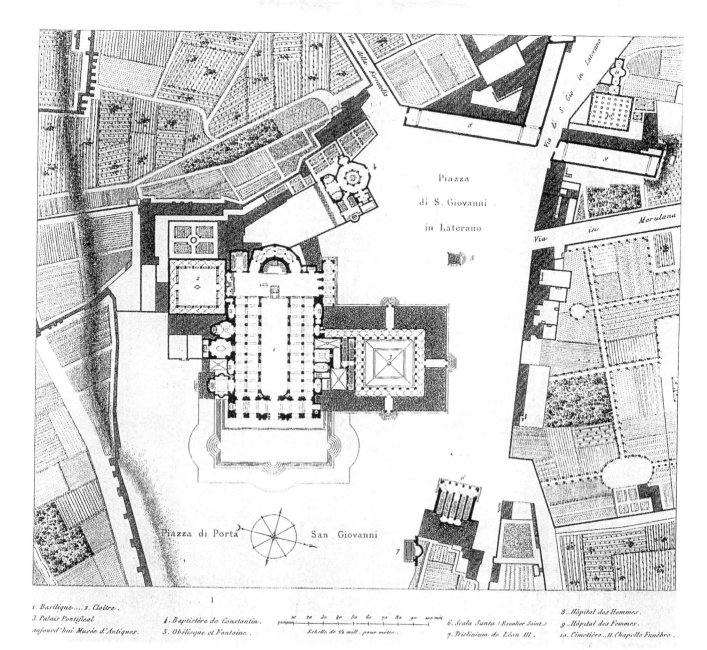

1. Basilique....2. Cloître .
3. Palais Pontifical
aujourd'hui Musée d'Antiques.
4. Baptistère de Constantin.
5. Obélisque et Fontaine .

Echelle de ½ mill . pour mètre .

6. Scala Santa (Escalier Saint.)
7. Triclinium de Léon III .

8. Hôpital des Hommes.
9. Hôpital des Femmes.
10. Cimetière .11. Chapelle Funèbre .

5. Ground plan of the *piano terreno* of the Lateran Palace and Basilica, P.M. Letarouilly.
Pianta del complesso Lateranense (da P. M. Letarouilly).

5a. Plan of the *piano terreno* of the Lateran Palace and Basilica (Touring Club Italiano, *Guida d'Italia. Roma e dintorni*, Milan 1965).
Pianta della basilica Lateranense e del piano terra del Palazzo (da Touring Club Italiano, *Guida d'Italia. Roma e dintorni*, Milano 1965).

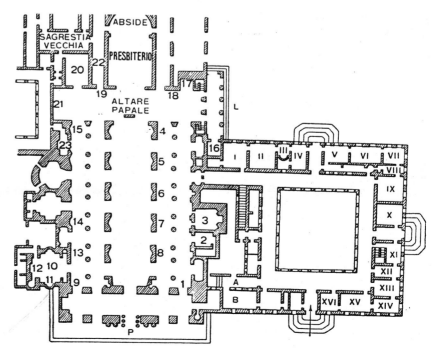

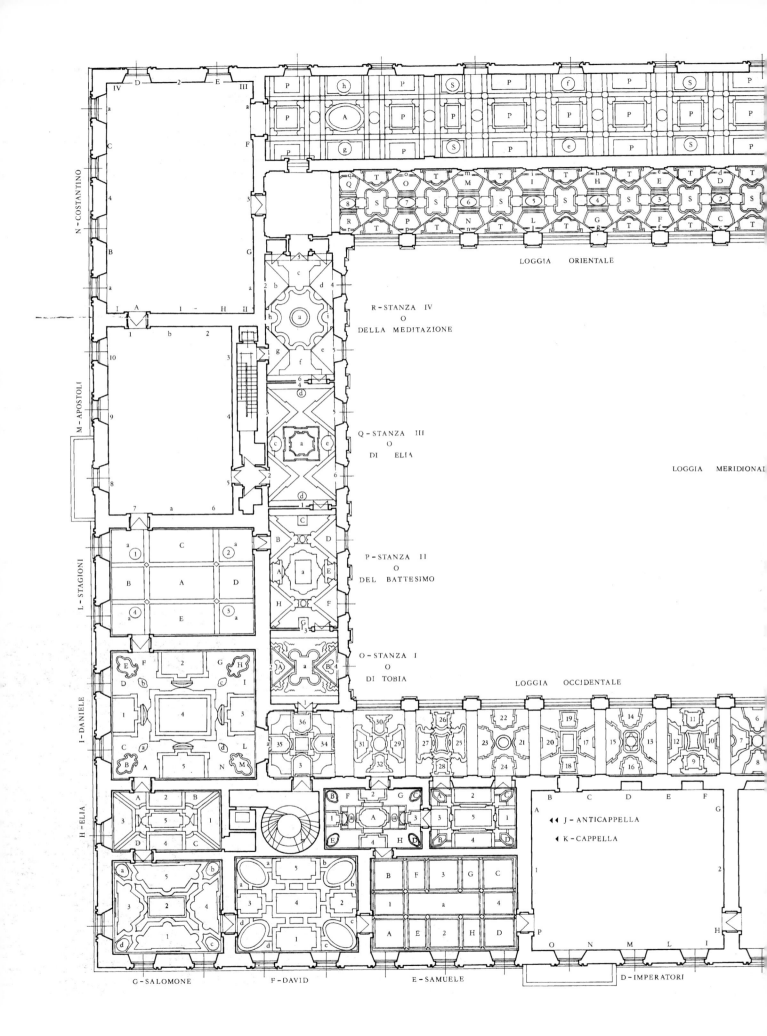

N - COSTANTINO

M - APOSTOLI

L - STAGIONI

I - DANIELE

H - ELIA

LOGGIA   ORIENTALE

R - STANZA IV
O
DELLA MEDITAZIONE

Q - STANZA III
O
DI ELIA

LOGGIA   MERIDIONAL

P - STANZA II
O
DEL BATTESIMO

O - STANZA I
O
DI TOBIA

LOGGIA   OCCIDENTALE

◀◀ J - ANTICAPPELLA

◀ K - CAPPELLA

G - SALOMONE   F - DAVID   E - SAMUELE   D - IMPERATORI

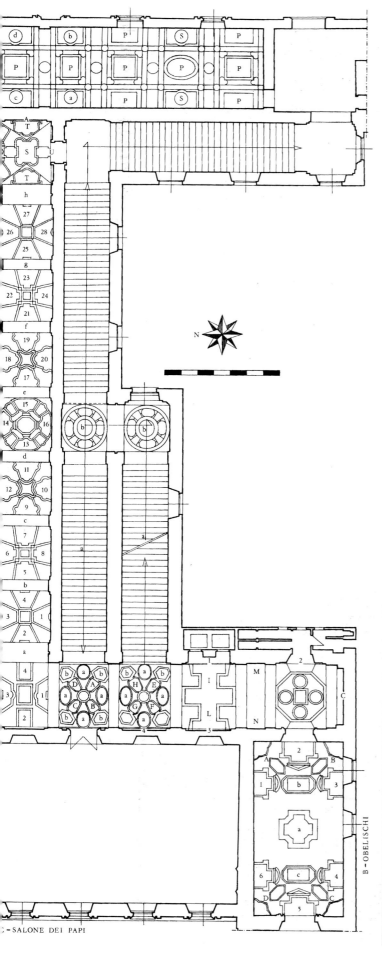

6. Ground plan of the *piano nobile* of the Lateran Palace (drawing by S. Pelle, after M. L. Madonna 1993).
Pianta del piano nobile del Palazzo Lateranense (disegno di S. Pelle, da M. L. Madonna 1993).

7. *Stemma* of Sixtus V, ex-Villa Montalto.
Stemma di Sisto V da Villa Montalto.

8. *Landscape with wine-makers and picnicers, piano terreno*, Lateran Palace.
   Paesaggio con banchetto e pigiatori di vino. Palazzo Lateranense, piano terra.

9. *Landscape with a villa (Villa Montalto?), people in fancy dress and hunters, piano terreno*, Lateran Palace.
   Paesaggio con villa (Villa Montalto?), personaggi in costume e cacciatori. Palazzo Lateranense, piano terra.

10. *Fire*, first landing of the grand staircase, Lateran Palace.
    Fuoco. Palazzo Lateranense, primo ripiano dello scalone.

11. *Air*, first landing of the grand staircase, Lateran Palace.
    Aria. Palazzo Lateranense, primo ripiano dello scalone.

12. *Water*, first landing of the grand staircase, Lateran Palace.
    Acqua. Palazzo Lateranense, primo ripiano dello scalone.

INANITATIS · IMPATIENS

PROCREATIONVM · ORIGO

13. "Lion in profile" device, western entrance vestibule, Lateran Palace.
Impresa con leone di profilo. Palazzo Lateranense, vestibolo d'entrata ovest.

14. "Triple mountain" devices, with and without eyes, first arm of grand staircase, Lateran Palace. Impresa col trimonzio con e senza occhi. Palazzo Lateranense, primo braccio dello scalone.

15. *Daniel in the Lion's Den and Habakuk and the Angel bringing Food*, vault, Sala di Daniele, *piano nobile*, Lateran Palace.
Daniele nella fossa dei leoni e Abacuc e l'angelo col cibo. Palazzo Lateranense, volta della Sala di Daniele.

16. *Ascension of Christ above the City of Montalto*, vault, Cappella Papale, *piano nobile*, Lateran Palace.
Ascensione di Cristo sulla città di Montalto. Palazzo Lateranense, volta della cappella privata.

17. *Sixtine Abundance* or *Prosperity*, vault, Anticappella, *piano nobile*, Lateran Palace.
Abbondanza o Prosperità sistina. Palazzo Lateranense, volta dell'Anticappella.

19. "Obelisk and column" device, fourth arm of grand staircase, Lateran Palace.
Impresa con obelischi e colonne. Palazzo Lateranense, quarto braccio dello scalone.

18. *Sacred Religion and Sixtine Justice*, lunette, north-west logge, *piano terreno*, Lateran Palace.
    Religione Sacra e Giustizia Sistina. Palazzo Lateranense, lunetta della loggia nord-ovest a piano terra.

20. *Landscape with Crucifixion and Hunters*, western loggia, *piano nobile*, Lateran Palace.
    Paesaggio con crocifissione e cacciatori. Palazzo Lateranense, loggia occidentale del piano nobile.

21. *Constantine the Great*, Salone degli Imperatori, *piano nobile*, Lateran Palace.
Costantino il Grande. Palazzo Lateranense, Salone degli Imperatori.

22. *Ascension of Elijah*, Sala d'Elia, *piano nobile*, Lateran Palace.
Ascensione di Elia. Palazzo Lateranense, Sala di Elia.

23. *Daniel feeds the "Divine" Serpent*, Sala di Daniele, *piano nobile*, Lateran Palace.
Daniele nutre il serpente divino. Palazzo Lateranense, Sala di Daniele.

24. *Triumph of the Faith*, Sala di Costantino, Vatican Palace.
Trionfo della Fede. Palazzi Vaticani, Sala di Costantino.

25. *Moses gathers the Seventy Elders of Israel*, Salone degli Apostoli, *piano nobile*, Lateran Palace.
Mosè raduna i Settanta anziani di Israele. Palazzo Lateranense, Salone degli Apostoli.

26. *Abundance created by Sixtus V,* Salone dei Papi, *piano nobile*, Lateran Palace.
Abbondanza sistina. Palazzo Lateranense, Salone dei Papi.

27. *Abundance created by Sixtus V*, Salone Sistino, Vatican Library.
    Abbondanza sistina. Biblioteca Vaticana, Salone Sistino.

28. *Abundance created by Sixtus V*, *gran sala*, Palazzo delle Terme, ex-Villa Montalto.
    Abbondanza sistina. Già nella Sala Grande del Palazzo alle Terme di Villa Montalto.

29. *Extirpation of the Bandits*, Salone dei Papi, *piano nobile*, Lateran Palace.
    Estirpazione dei banditi. Palazzo Lateranense, Salone dei Papi.

30. *Extirpation of the Bandits*, Salone Sistino, Vatican Library.
    Estirpazione dei banditi. Biblioteca Vaticana, Salone Sistino.

PASCITE·SECVRÆ·PECVDES·IN·MONTIBVS·ALTIS
DVM·LEO·GRASSANTES·IMPETIT·VNGVE·IVPOS

31. *Extirpation of the Bandits*, *gran sala*, Palazzo delle Terme, ex-Villa Montalto.
    Estirpazione dei banditi. Già nella Sala Grande del Palazzo alle Terme di Villa Montalto.

32. *Treasure at Castel Sant'Angelo*, Salone dei Papi, *piano nobile*, Lateran Palace.
    Tesoro di Castel S. Angelo. Palazzo Lateranense, Salone dei Papi.

33. *Treasure at Castel Sant'Angelo*, second room of the Libreria Segreta, Vatican Library.
Tesoro di Castel S. Angelo. Biblioteca Vaticana, seconda sala della Libreria Segreta.

34. *Treasure at Castel Sant'Angelo*, in Giovanni Pinadello, *Invicti Quinarii Numeri Series Quae Summatim a Superioribus Pontificibus et Maxime A Sixto Quinto ...*, Rome, 1589, frontispiece.
Tesoro di Castel S. Angelo (da G. Pinadello, *Invicti Quinarii Numeri...*, Roma 1589).

35. *League of Christian Princes*, Salone dei Papi, *piano nobile*, Lateran Palace.
Lega dei principi cristiani. Palazzo Lateranense, Salone dei Papi.

36. Detail of fig. 35.
Particolare della fig. 35.

37. *League of Christian Princes*, second room of the Libreria Segreta, Vatican Library.
Lega dei principi cristiani. Biblioteca Vaticana, seconda sala della Libreria Segreta.

38. Detail of fig. 37.
Particolare della fig. 37.

39. *Portrait of Sixtus V*, in Pinadello, *Invicti Quinarii*, 3.
Ritratto di SistoV (da Pinadello, *Invicti Quinarii*).

Civitas Lauret.

Sacellum S. Mariæ Maioris

Templum S. Hieronymi

Civitas   Montis   Alti

Obeliscus S. Iois   Obelis S. Mariæ m̃   Templum Sancti Petri   Hospitale Pontis Sixti   Obel S. Mar de Popul   Obel S. Petri

Scala Sancta

Benedictio Pontificalis ad S. Ioannem

Translatio Corporis Pij Quinti

Ærarium Romanæ Ecclesiæ

Collegium Picenorum in Bononia

Bibliotheca Vaticana

Viæ nouæ cum Palatio S. Ioannis

Canonizatio S. Didaci

SIXTO QVINTO PONT. MAX.
AVCTORI.

Fons Aquae Foelicis

Mons Capitolinus

40. Anonymous, *Portrait of Sixtus V*, published by Nicolas van Aelst, 1589.
Anonimo. *Ritratto di Sisto V*, pubblicato da N. van Aelst, 1589.

41. Salone dei Papi, *piano nobile*, Lateran Palace.
Palazzo Lateranense, Salone dei Papi.

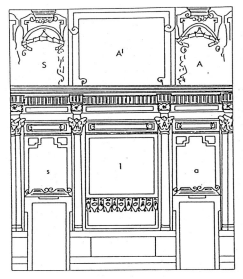

42. Schematic diagram of south wall, Salone dei Papi, *piano nobile*, Lateran Palace.
Schema della parete meridionale del Salone dei Papi.

43. Schematic diagram of west wall, Salone dei Papi, *piano nobile*, Lateran Palace.
Schema della parete occidentale del Salone dei Papi.

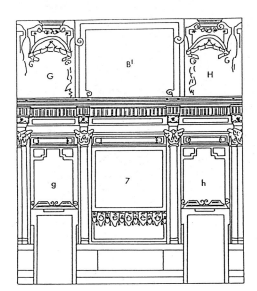

44. Schematic diagram of north wall, Salone dei Papi, *piano nobile*, Lateran Palace.
Schema della parete settentrionale del Salone dei Papi.

45. Schematic diagram of east wall, Salone dei Papi, *piano nobile*, Lateran Palace.
Schema della parete orientale del Salone dei Papi.

46. *Acqua Felice*, Salone dei Papi, *piano nobile*, Lateran Palace.
Acqua Felice. Palazzo Lateranense, Salone dei Papi.

48. *Vatican Library*, Salone dei Papi, *piano nobile*, Lateran Palace.
La Biblioteca Vaticana. Palazzo Lateranense, Salone dei Papi.

47. *Port of Terracina and Pontine Marsh*, Salone dei Papi, *piano nobile*, Lateran Palace.
Porto di Terracina e paludi pontine. Palazzo Lateranense, Salone dei Papi.

50. *Monte Cavallo*, Salone dei Papi, *piano nobile*, Lateran Palace.
Monte Cavallo. Palazzo Lateranense, Salone dei Papi.

49. *Harbour at Civitavecchia*, Salone dei Papi, *piano nobile*, Lateran Palace.
Porto di Civitavecchia. Palazzo Lateranense, Salone dei Papi.

52. *Holy House of Loreto*, Salone dei Papi, *piano nobile*, Lateran Palace.
Santuario di Loreto. Palazzo Lateranense, Salone dei Papi.

S · ELEVTERIVS · I
PP · XIIII

BRITANIAM · INSVLAM
LVC II · REGIS · RO GATV
PER · FVGACIVM · ET · DAMIANVM
LEGATOS · FIDEI
SACRIS · INSTITVIT

51. *City of Montalto*, Salone dei Papi, *piano nobile*, Lateran Palace.
Città di Montalto. Palazzo Lateranense, Salone dei Papi.

53. "Starry Leo" device, in Pinadello, *Invicti Quinarii*, 39.
Impresa col leone e le costellazioni (da Pinadello, *Invicti Quinarii*).

54. *Saint Peter*, Salone dei Papi, *piano nobile*, Lateran Palace.
San Pietro. Palazzo Lateranense, Salone dei Papi.

56. *Saint Sylvester*, Salone dei Papi, *piano nobile*, Lateran Palace.
San Silvestro. Palazzo Lateranense, Salone dei Papi.

55. *Medallion of Saint Peter*, Salone dei Papi, *piano nobile*, Lateran Palace.
Medaglione di san Pietro. Palazzo Lateranense, Salone dei Papi.

57. *Medallion of Saint Sylvester*, Salone dei Papi, *piano nobile*, Lateran Palace.
Medaglione di san Silvestro. Palazzo Lateranense, Salone dei Papi.

58. *Saint Eleuterius*, Salone dei Papi, *piano nobile*, Lateran Palace.
Sant'Eleuterio. Palazzo Lateranense, Salone dei Papi.

60. *Saint Urbanus*, Salone dei Papi, *piano nobile*, Lateran Palace.
Sant'Urbano. Palazzo Lateranense, Salone dei Papi.

59. *Saint Zepherinus*, Salone dei Papi, *piano nobile*, Lateran Palace.
San Zefirino. Palazzo Lateranense, Salone dei Papi.

61. *Saint Antherus*, Salone dei Papi, *piano nobile*, Lateran Palace.
Sant'Antero. Palazzo Lateranense, Salone dei Papi.

62. *Saint Cornelius*, Salone dei Papi, *piano nobile*, Lateran Palace.
   San Cornelio. Palazzo Lateranense, Salone dei Papi.

63. *Christ's Investiture to Peter*, Salone dei Papi, *piano nobile*, Lateran Palace.
Tu es Petrus. Palazzo Lateranense, Salone dei Papi.

64. *Christ appoints Peter Guardian of the Christian People*, Salone dei Papi, *piano nobile*, Lateran Palace.
Pasce oves meas. Palazzo Lateranense, Salone dei Papi.

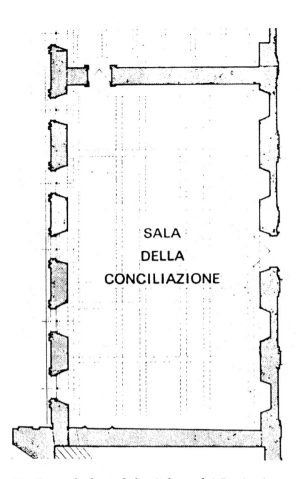

65. Ground plan of the Salone dei Papi, *piano nobile*, Lateran Palace, after Schiavo, *Lateran*, n.p.
Pianta del Salone dei Papi (da Schiavo, *Palazzo Lateranense*).

66. Ground plan of the Sala del Concilio, Patriarchium Lateranense, in Pompeo Ugonio, "Schedario," 157v. Photo: BAV MSS Barb. Lat. 2160.
Pianta della Sala del Concilio del Patriarchium Lateranense (da P. Ugonio, *Schedario*, c. 157v). Biblioteca Apostolica Vaticana.

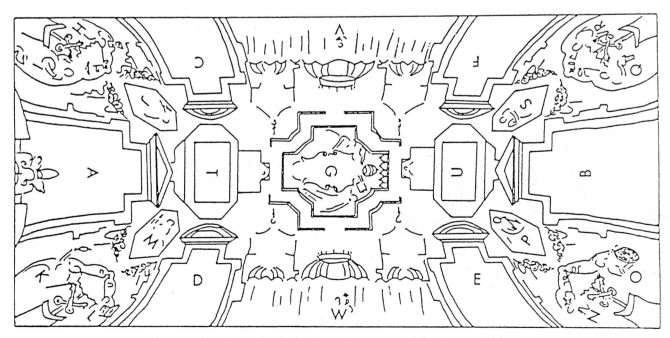

67. Schematic diagram of the vault of the Sala degli Obelischi, *piano nobile*, Lateran Palace.
Schema della volta della Sala degli Obelischi.

68. *Trajanic Column with Saint Peter*, Sala degli Obelischi, *piano nobile*, Lateran Palace.
Colonna Traiana con san Pietro. Palazzo Lateranense, Sala degli Obelischi.

69. *Antonine Column with Saint Paul*, Sala degli Obelischi, *piano nobile*, Lateran Palace.
Colonna Antonina con san Paolo. Palazzo Lateranense, Sala degli Obelischi.

70. *Obelisk of San Giovanni in Laterano*, Sala degli Obelischi, *piano nobile*, Lateran Palace.
Obelisco Lateranense. Palazzo Lateranense, Sala degli Obelischi.

71. *Obelisk of San Pietro in Vaticano*, Sala degli Obelischi, *piano nobile*, Lateran Palace.
Obelisco Vaticano. Palazzo Lateranense, Sala degli Obelischi.

72. *Obelisk of Santa Maria Maggiore*, Sala degli Obelischi, *piano nobile*, Lateran Palace.
Obelisco di S. Maria Maggiore. Palazzo Lateranense, Sala degli Obelischi.

73. *Obelisk of Santa Croce in Gerusalemme*, Sala degli Obelischi, *piano nobile*, Lateran Palace.
Obelisco di S. Croce in Gerusalemme. Palazzo Lateranense, Sala degli Obelischi.

74. *Stemma* of Sixtus V supported by angels, Sala degli Obelischi, *piano nobile*, Lateran Palace.
Stemma di Sisto V retto da angeli. Palazzo Lateranense, Sala degli Obelischi.

79. "Lion in profile" device, Sala degli Obelischi, *piano nobile*, Lateran Palace
Impresa con leone di profilo. Palazzo Lateranense, Sala degli Obelischi.

80. "Lion in profile" device, Sala degli Obelischi, *piano nobile*, Lateran Palace.
Impresa con leone di profilo. Palazzo Lateranense, Sala degli Obelischi.

75. *World Dominion*, *Knowledge of the True God*, and *Devotion*, Sala degli Obelischi, *piano nobile*, Lateran Palace.
Dominio sul mondo, Conoscenza del Vero Dio, Devozione. Palazzo Lateranense, Sala degli Obelischi.

76. *Faith*, *Law of Grace* or *Truth*, and *Eternity of the Roman Catholic Church*, Sala degli Obelischi, *piano nobile*, Lateran Palace.
Fede, Legge della Grazia o Verità, Eternità della Chiesa Cattolica Romana. Palazzo Lateranense, Sala degli Obelischi.

77. *Gratitude*, *Christian Obedience*, and *Magnificence*, Sala degli Obelischi, *piano nobile*, Lateran Palace.
Gratitudine, Obbedienza Cristiana, Magnificenza. Palazzo Lateranense, Sala degli Obelischi.

78. *Oblation*, *Prayer*, and *Religion*, Sala degli Obelischi, *piano nobile*, Lateran Palace.
Oblazione, Preghiera, Religione. Palazzo Lateranense, Sala degli Obelischi.

81. *Grotteschi* with *Devotion*, Sala degli Obelischi, *piano nobile*, Lateran Palace.
Grottesche con Devozione. Palazzo Lateranense, Sala degli Obelischi.

82. *Grotteschi* with *Justice*, Sala degli Obelischi, *piano nobile*, Lateran Palace.
Grottesche con Giustizia. Palazzo Lateranense, Sala degli Obelischi.

83. Apparatus employed to raise obelisks, in Domenico Fontana, *Della trasportatione dell'obelisco Vaticano et delle Fabriche di Nostro Signore Papa Sisto V ...* 1590. Ed. Adriano Carugo. Intro. Paolo Portoghesi, Milan 1978, 18r.
Macchina per l'erezione dell'Obelisco Vaticano (da D. Fontana, *Della Trasportatione...*).

84. Schematic diagram of the vault of the Sala di Samuele, *piano nobile*, Lateran Palace.
Schema della volta della Sala di Samuele.

85. *Samuel being taken to the Temple to Take a Vow*, Sala di Samuele, *piano nobile*, Lateran Palace.
Samuele condotto al tempio a prendere i voti. Palazzo Lateranense, Sala di Samuele.

86. *Samuel hears a Miraculous Voice in the Temple*, Sala di Samuele, *piano nobile*, Lateran Palace.
Samuele sente una voce miracolosa nel Tempio. Palazzo Lateranense, Sala di Samuele.

87. *Samuel erects the "Stone of Help,"* Sala di Samuele, *piano nobile*, Lateran Palace.
Samuele erige la "pietra del soccorso". Palazzo Lateranense, Sala di Samuele.

88. *Samuel anoints Saul*, Sala di Samuele, *piano nobile*, Lateran Palace.
   Samuele unge Saul. Palazzo Lateranense, Sala di Samuele.

89. *Genii* support the *stemma* of Sixtus V, Sala di
Samuele, *piano nobile*, Lateran Palace.
Genii reggenti lo stemma di Sisto V. Palazzo
Lateranense, Sala di Samuele.

90. *Religion*, Sala di Samuele, *piano nobile*, Lat-
eran Palace.
Religione. Palazzo Lateranense, Sala di
Samuele.

91. *Charity*, Sala di Samuele, *piano nobile*, Lateran Palace.
Carità. Palazzo Lateranense, Sala di Samuele.

92. *Faith*, Sala di Samuele, *piano nobile*, Lateran Palace.
Fede. Palazzo Lateranense, Sala di Samuele.

93. *Hope*, Sala di Samuele, *piano nobile*, Lateran Palace.
Speranza. Palazzo Lateranense, Sala di Samuele.

94. *Good Work*, Sala di Samuele, *piano nobile*, Lateran Palace.
Opera buona. Palazzo Lateranense, Sala di Samuele.

95. *Belief*, Sala di Samuele, *piano nobile*, Lateran Palace.
Credo. Palazzo Lateranense, Sala di Samuele.

96. *Gratitude*, Sala di Samuele, *piano nobile*, Lateran Palace.
Gratitudine. Palazzo Lateranense, Sala di Samuele.

97. *Law of Grace*, Sala di Samuele, *piano nobile*, Lateran Palace.
Legge della Grazia. Palazzo Lateranense, Sala di Samuele.

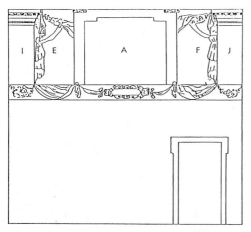

98. Schematic diagram of the west wall of the Salone di Costantino, *piano nobile*, Lateran Palace.
Schema della parete occidentale del Salone di Costantino.

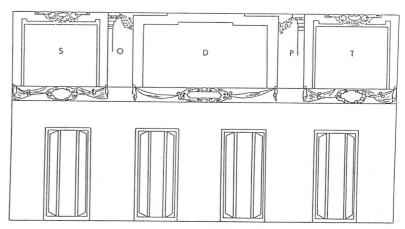

100. Schematic diagram of the north wall of the Salone di Costantino, *piano nobile*, Lateran Palace.
Schema della parete settentrionale del Salone di Costantino.

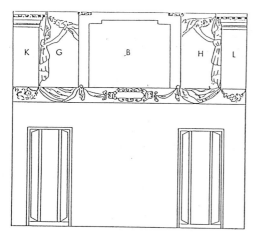

99. Schematic diagram of the east wall of the Salone di Costantino, *piano nobile*, Lateran Palace.
Schema della parete orientale del Salone di Costantino.

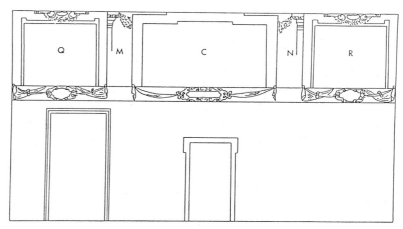

101. Schematic diagram of the south wall of the Salone di Costantino, *piano nobile*, Lateran Palace.
Schema della parete meridionale del Salone di Costantino.

102. "Single obelisk" device and *Religion*, Salone di Costantino, *piano nobile*, Lateran Palace.
Impresa con obelisco singolo e *Religione*. Palazzo Lateranense, Salone di Costantino.

103. *Devotion* and "single obelisk" device, Salone di Costantino, *piano nobile*, Lateran Palace.
Devozione e impresa con obelisco singolo. Palazzo Lateranense, Salone di Costantino.

104. "Single obelisk" device and *Knowledge of the True God*, Salone di Costantino, *piano nobile*, Lateran Palace.
Impresa con obelisco singolo e *Conoscenza del Vero Dio*. Palazzo Lateranense, Salone di Costantino.

105. Personification with pear branch and "single obelisk" device, Salone di Costantino, *piano nobile*, Lateran Palace.
Personificazione con ramo di pere e impresa con obelisco singolo. Palazzo Lateranense, Salone di Costantino.

106. *Constantine's Vision of the Cross*, Salone di Costantino, *piano nobile*, Lateran Palace.
    La visione di Costantino della Croce. Palazzo Lateranense, Salone di Costantino.

107. *Baptism of Constantine*, Salone di Costantino, *piano nobile*, Lateran Palace.
    Battesimo di Costantino. Palazzo Lateranense, Salone di Costantino.

108. *Donation of Constantine*, Salone di Costantino, *piano nobile*, Lateran Palace.
Donazione di Costantino. Palazzo Lateranense, Salone di Costantino.

109. *Constantine acts as strator for Pope Sylvester I*, Salone di Costantino, *piano nobile*, Lateran Palace.
Costantino strator di papa Silvestro. Palazzo Lateranense, Salone di Costantino.

110. *Moses*, Salone di Costantino, *piano nobile*, Lateran Palace. *Mosè*. Palazzo Lateranense, Salone di Costantino.

111. *Aaron*, Salone di Costantino, *piano nobile*, Lateran Palace. *Aronne*. Palazzo Lateranense, Salone di Costantino.

112. *David*, Salone di Costantino, *piano nobile*, Lateran Palace. *David*. Palazzo Lateranense, Salone di Costantino.

113. *Solomon*, Salone di Costantino, *piano nobile*, Lateran Palace. *Salomone*. Palazzo Lateranense, Salone di Costantino.

114. *Seascape*, Salone di Costantino, *piano nobile*, Lateran Palace. *Paesaggio marino*. Palazzo Lateranense, Salone di Costantino.

115. *Landscape*, Salone
di Costantino, *pia-
no nobile*, Lateran
Palace.
Paesaggio. Palazzo
Lateranense, Sa-
lone di Costantino.

116. *Landscape*, Salone
di Costantino, *pia-
no nobile*, Lateran
Palace.
Paesaggio. Palazzo
Lateranense, Sa-
lone di Costantino.

117. *Landscape*, Salone
di Costantino, *pia-
no nobile*, Lateran
Palace.
Paesaggio. Palazzo
Lateranense, Sa-
lone di Costantino.

118. *Martyrdom, Immor-
tality*, and *anima
senza corpo*, lunette,
juncture of eastern
and southern logge,
piano nobile, Later-
an Palace.
*Martirio, Immorta-
lità*, anima senza
corpo. Palazzo La-
teranense, volta tra
le logge est e sud
del piano nobile.

119. "Single obelisk" device, *Annunciation to Zacharias*, and *Sacrifice of Manaases*, eastern loggia, *piano nobile*, Lateran Palace.
Impresa con obelisco singolo, *Annunciazione a Zaccaria, Sacrificio di Manaases*. Palazzo Lateranense, volta della loggia est del piano nobile.

120. "Single obelisk" device, *Marriage of the Virgin*, and *Moses and the Burning Bush*, eastern loggia, *piano nobile*, Lateran Palace.
Impresa con obelisco singolo, *Sposalizio della Vergine, Mosè e il roveto ardente*. Palazzo Lateranense, volta della loggia est del piano nobile.

121. "Single obelisk" device, *Christ among the Doctors*, and Old Testament type, eastern loggia, *piano nobile*, Lateran Palace.
Impresa con obelisco singolo, *Cristo fra i Dottori, personaggio veterotestamentario*. Palazzo Lateranense, volta della loggia est del piano nobile.

122. "Single obelisk" device, *John the Baptist preaching in Judea*, and Old Testament type, eastern loggia, *piano nobile*, Lateran Palace.
Impresa con obelisco singolo, *Giovanni Battista predica in Giudea, personaggio veterotestamentario*. Palazzo Lateranense, volta della loggia est del piano nobile.

123. "Single column" device, *Adoration of the Shepherds*, and Old Testament type, eastern loggia, *piano nobile*, Lateran Palace. Photo: the author.
Impresa con colonna singola, *Adorazione dei pastori, personaggio veterotestamentario.* Palazzo Lateranense, volta della loggia est del piano nobile.

124. "Single column" device, *Circumcision*, and Old Testament type, eastern loggia, *piano nobile*, Lateran Palace.
Impresa con colonna singola, *Circoncisione, personaggio veterotestamentario.* Palazzo Lateranense, volta della loggia est del piano nobile.

125. "Single column" device, *Adoration of the Magi,* and Old Testament type, eastern loggia, *piano nobile*, Lateran Palace.
Impresa con colonna singola, *Adorazione dei Magi, personaggio veterotestamentario.* Palazzo Lateranense, volta della loggia est del piano nobile.

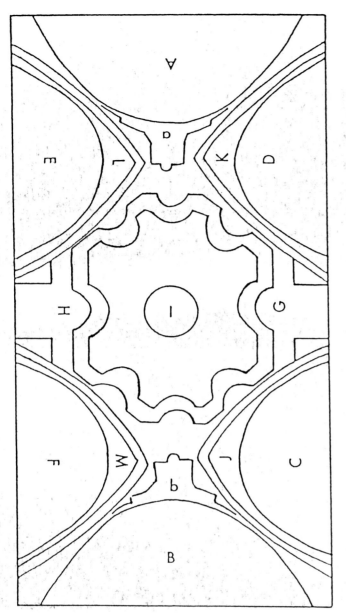

127. Schematic diagram of the vault of the fourth room of the private apartment, *piano nobile*, Lateran Palace.
Schema della volta della quarta stanza dell'appartamento privato pontificio.

128. *Sacred Religion*, fourth room of private apartment, *piano nobile*, Lateran Palace.
Religione Sacra. Palazzo Lateranense, quarta stanza dell'appartamento privato pontificio.

129. *Sixtine Justice*, fourth room of private apartment, *piano nobile*, Lateran Palace.
Giustizia Sistina. Palazzo Lateranense, quarta stanza dell'appartamento privato pontificio.

130. *Landscape*, by a nineteenth century hand, fourth room of private apartment, *piano nobile*, Lateran Palace.
Paesaggio (XIX sec.). Palazzo Lateranense, quarta stanza dell'appartamento privato pontificio.

131. *Landscape with Saint John the Baptist*, fourth room of private apartment, *piano nobile*, Lateran Palace.
Paesaggio con san Giovanni Battista. Palazzo Lateranense, quarta stanza dell'appartamento privato pontificio.

132. *Landscape with Elijah and the Angel*, fourth room of private apartment, *piano nobile*, Lateran Palace.
Paesaggio con Elia e l'Angelo. Palazzo Lateranense, quarta stanza dell'appartamento privato pontificio.

133. *Landscape with Moses and the Burning Bush*, fourth room of private apartment, *piano nobile*, Lateran Palace.
Paesaggio con Mosè e il roveto ardente. Palazzo Lateranense, quarta stanza dell'appartamento privato pontificio.

134. *Landscape with Onuphrius*, fourth room of private apartment, *piano nobile*, Lateran Palace.
Paesaggio con Onofrio. Palazzo Lateranense, quarta stanza dell'appartamento privato pontificio.

135. *Landscape with Mary of Egypt*, fourth room of private apartment, *piano nobile*, Lateran Palace.
Paesaggio con Maria d'Egitto. Palazzo Lateranense, quarta stanza dell'appartamento privato pontificio.

136. Medallion at center vault, fourth room of private apartment, *piano nobile*, Lateran Palace.
Parte centrale della volta. Palazzo Lateranense, quarta stanza dell'appartamento privato pontificio.

137. "Obelisk and column" devices, western loggia extension, *piano nobile*, Lateran Palace.
Imprese con obelisco e colonne. Palazzo Lateranense, prolungamento ovest della loggia al piano nobile.

138. *Birth of Saint Francis*, western loggia extension, *piano nobile*, Lateran Palace.
Nascita di san Francesco. Palazzo Lateranense, prolungamento ovest della loggia al piano nobile.

139. *Francis receives official sanction to create the Order of the Friars Minor from Pope Honorius III*, western loggia extension, *piano nobile*, Lateran Palace.
San Francesco ottiene la regola da papa Onorio III. Palazzo Lateranense, prolungamento ovest della loggia al piano nobile.

140. *Francis receives official sanction to create the Order of the Friars Minor from Pope Honorius III*, *grotteschi*, and *World Dominion*, western loggia extension, *piano nobile*, Lateran Palace.
San Francesco ottiene la regola da papa Onorio III, *grottesche*, *Dominio sul mondo*. Palazzo Lateranense, prolungamento ovest della loggia al piano nobile.

141. *Francis is received by Pope Innocent III*, western loggia extension, *piano nobile*, Lateran Palace.
San Francesco ricevuto da Innocenzo III. Palazzo Lateranense, prolungamento ovest della loggia al piano nobile.

142. Sixtine *stemma* and non-Sixtine device, western loggia extension, *piano nobile*, Lateran Palace.
Stemma sistino e impresa non sisitina. Palazzo Lateranense, prolungamento ovest della loggia al piano nobile.

143. Sixtine *stemma* and non-Sixtine device, seen from below, western loggia extension, *piano nobile*, Lateran Palace.
Stemma sistino e impresa non sisitina. Veduta dal basso all'alto; Palazzo Lateranense, prolungamento ovest della loggia al piano nobile.

144. "Lion in profile" devices, western loggia extension, *piano nobile*, Lateran Palace.
Imprese con leone di profilo. Palazzo Lateranense, prolungamento ovest della loggia al piano nobile.

145. *Stigmatization of Saint Francis*, western loggia extension, *piano nobile*, Lateran Palace.
Le stimmate di san Francesco. Palazzo Lateranense, prolungamento ovest della loggia al piano nobile.

146. *Donation of Constantine*, Benediction Loggia, San Giovanni in Laterano.
Donazione di Costantino. S. Giovanni in Laterano, Loggia delle Benedizioni.

147. *Sixtus V receives the medals found in 1587 and document listing them*, Salone degli Imperatori, *piano nobile*, Lateran Palace.
Sisto V riceve le medaglie trovate nel 1587. Palazzo Lateranense, Salone degli Imperatori.

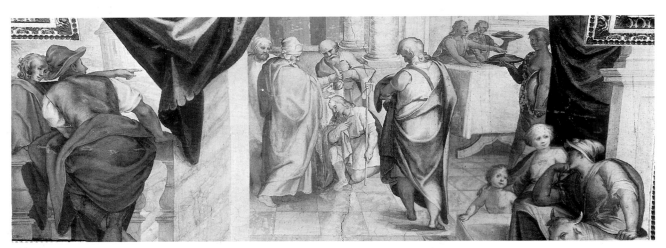

148. *Samuel anoints David*, Sala di Davide, *piano nobile*, Lateran Palace.
Samuele unge David. Palazzo Lateranense, Sala di Davide.

149. *Baptism of Constantine*, Benediction Loggia, San Giovanni in Laterano.
Battesimo di Costantino. S. Giovanni in Laterano, Loggia delle Benedizioni.

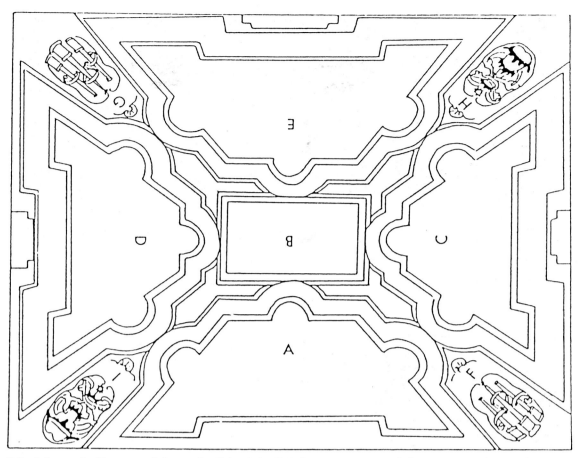

150. Schematic diagram of the vault of the Sala di Salomone, *piano nobile*, Lateran Palace.
Schema della volta della Sala di Salomone.

151. "Obelisk and column" device, Sala di Salomone, *piano nobile*, Lateran Palace.
Impresa con obelisco e colonne. Palazzo Lateranense, Sala di Salomone.

152. "Obelisk and column" device, Sala di Salomone, *piano nobile*, Lateran Palace.
Impresa con obelisco e colonne. Palazzo Lateranense, Sala di Salomone.

153. "Triple mountain" device, Sala di Salomone, *piano nobile*, Lateran Palace.
Impresa col trimonzio. Palazzo Lateranense, Sala di Salomone.

154. "Triple mountain" device, Sala di Salomone, *piano nobile*, Lateran Palace.
Impresa col trimonzio. Palazzo Lateranense, Sala di Salomone.

155. *Solomon rides to Gihon where he will be anointed king*, Sala di Salomone, *piano nobile*, Lateran Palace.
Salomone cavalca verso Gihon dove verrà unto re. Palazzo Lateranense, Sala di Salomone.

156. *God appears to Solomon in his Sleep*, Sala di Salomone, *piano nobile*, Lateran Palace.
   Dio appare in sogno a Salomone. Palazzo Lateranense, Sala di Salomone.

157. *Judgement of Solomon*, Sala di Salomone, *piano nobile*, Lateran Palace.
   Giudizio di Salomone. Palazzo Lateranense, Sala di Salomone.

158. *The Ark of the Covenant is carried out of the City of David*, Sala di Salomone, *piano nobile*, Lateran Palace.
L'arca della salvezza portata fuori dalla città di Davide. Palazzo Lateranense, Sala di Salomone.

159. *Solomon and the Queen of Sheba*, Sala di Salomone, *piano nobile*, Lateran Palace.
Salomone e la regina di Saba. Palazzo Lateranense, Sala di Salomone.

160. Sixtus V and the Libyan "Queen of Sheba," in Giovanni Francesco Bordino, *De Rebus Praeclare Gestis A Sixto V. Pon. Max.* Rome, 1588, 30.
Sisto V e la "Regina di Saba" libica (da Bordino, *De Rebus Praeclare Gestis...*).